Development Impact Fees

Development Impact Fees

*Policy Rationale, Practice,
Theory, and Issues*

Edited by
ARTHUR C. NELSON

PLANNERS PRESS
AMERICAN PLANNING ASSOCIATION
Chicago, Illinois   Washington, D.C.

This book is being published in cooperation with the
Journal of the American Planning Association, whose winter
and spring 1988 symposiums on development impact fees
formed the core of this book.

Copyright 1988 by the American Planning Association
1313 E. 60th St., Chicago, IL 60637
ISBN 0-918286-55-7
Library of Congress Catalog Card Number 88-70565

For
Knute
Lori
Monika
and
Emily

Contents

Tables

Figures

Figures

Acknowledgments

This volume would not have been possible were it not for the support and contributions made by many individuals and organizations. Foremost is Fritz Wagner and the School of Urban and Regional Studies at the University of New Orleans, who provided me with considerable support and encouragement. I owe him and his faculty a great debt. Ray Burby and Ed Kaiser, editors of the *Journal of the American Planning Association*, could almost be considered coeditors because they devoted two issues of the journal to impact fees and reviewed and edited mountains of material. I am grateful to Mardi Zeiger and Paula Stephenson for their editing. David S. Sawicki of the city planning program at the Georgia Institute of Technology provided valuable support. Sylvia Lewis of the American Planning Association choreographed all the steps needed to publish this work. The contributors, however, are the people to whom this acknowledgment is mostly directed. Without their innovation, willingness to write and rewrite, insights, and leadership, this book could not be possible. They are standing at the threshold of a new ethic in public finance, and their professional and scholarly work will no doubt shape the direction of local finance for generations to come.

Contributors

David P. Amborski is a faculty member in the School of Urban and Regional Planning at Ryerson Polytechnic Institute, Toronto, Canada.

Christine I. Andrew is an associate attorney with the law firm of Robinson and Cole, Hartford, Connecticut.

Elliot Auerhahn is development management director in the Broward County, Florida, Office of Planning.

Jeff Bachrach is an attorney with the Portland, Oregon, law firm of O'Donnell, Ramis, Elliott, and Crew.

Mark P. Barnebey is assistant county attorney for Manatee County, Florida.

Timothy Beatley is assistant professor in the Division of Urban and Environmental Planning of the School of Architecture at the University of Virginia.

Robert A. Blewett is associate professor of economics, St. Lawrence University.

Raymond J. Burby is professor in the Department of City and Regional Planning at the University of North Carolina at Chapel Hill, a faculty associate at the university's Center for Urban and Regional Studies, and former

coeditor of the *Journal of the American Planning Association.*

Charles E. Connerly is an associate professor in the Department of Urban and Regional Planning at Florida State University.

Paul B. Downing is professor of economics and policy sciences at Florida State University.

James E. Frank is associate professor of urban and regional planning at Florida State University. He also is coauthor of *Development Exactions* (Chicago: Planners Press, 1987).

Linda L. Hausrath is an urban economist and principal of Recht Hausrath & Associates, Oakland, California.

David C. Heath is assistant planning director of Orange County, Florida.

Forrest E. Huffman, Jr., is assistant professor of real estate at Temple University, Philadelphia, Pennsylvania.

Julian Conrad Juergensmeyer is professor of law and director of Growth Management Studies at the University of Florida.

Edward J. Kaiser is a professor in the Department of City and Regional Planning at the University of North Carolina at Chapel Hill, a faculty associate at the university's Center for Urban and Regional Studies, and former co-editor of the *Journal of the American Planning Association*.

W. Dennis Keating is an associate professor in the Urban Studies Department at Cleveland State University.

Glenn Kreger is on the staff of the transportation department in Montgomery County, Maryland.

Bill Lambert is the business analyst in the Office of Economic Development in Berkeley, California.

Douglass B. Lee is senior transportation planner at the U.S. Department of Transportation Systems Center, Cambridge, Massachusetts, and adjunct professor in the City Planning Program of the Georgia Institute of Technology.

Martin L. Leitner is partner with the law firm of Freilich, Leitner, Carlisle, and Shortlidge, of Kansas City, Missouri.

Jane H. Lillydahl is associate professor of economics at the University of Colorado at Boulder.

Tom MacRostie is senior planner for the city of San Jose, California.

Neil S. Mayer is director of the Office of Economic Development, Berkeley, California.

Dwight H. Merriam is a partner in the law firm of Robinson and Cole, Hartford, Connecticut, and chairman of the firm's land use group. He

also is editor of *Inclusionary Zoning Moves Downtown* (Chicago: Planners Press, 1985).

David H. Moreau is a professor in the Department of City and Regional Planning, a faculty associate of the Center for Urban and Regional Studies, and director of the Water Resources Research Institute, all of the University of North Carolina.

Terry D. Morgan has a private law practice in Austin, Texas. He is a former assistant city attorney for Austin, and now is of counsel to Freilich, Leitner, Carlisle, and Shortlidge, of Kansas City, Missouri. He also is an adjunct professor at the School of Architecture, Graduate Program in Regional and Community Studies, University of Texas at Austin.

Arthur C. Nelson is associate professor of city planning at the Georgia Institute of Technology.

James C. Nicholas is professor of urban and regional planning, affiliate professor of law, and codirector of Growth Management Studies in the College of Law at the University of Florida.

Glenn Orlin is chief of the planning and program section, Department of Transportation, Montgomery County, Maryland.

Richard Peiser is academic director of the Real Estate Development Program in the School of Urban and Regional Planning at the University of Southern California.

Douglas R. Porter is director of development policy research for the Urban Land Institute, Washington, D.C. His recent publications include *Working with the Community: A Developer's*

Guide, Growth Policy: Keeping on Target?, and *Covenants and Zoning for Research/Business Parks.*

Timothy V. Ramis is a partner in the Portland, Oregon, law firm of O'Donnell, Ramis, Elliot, and Crew.

J. Richard Recht is a principal of the firm Recht Hausrath & Associates, Urban Economists, Oakland, California.

Meg Riesett is manager, Planning Policies Group, Department of Environmental Planning, Montgomery County, Maryland.

Antero Rivasplata is principal planner in the state of California Office of Local Government Affairs.

Steven R. Schell is an attorney with the Portland, Oregon, law firm of Rapplyea, Beck, Helterline, Spencer, and Roskie.

Gary J. Schoennauer is planning director for the city of San Jose, California.

George T. Simpson is assistant director of the Engineering and Development Department of San Diego, California.

Marc T. Smith is assistant professor of real estate at the University of Florida–Gainesville.

Michael A. Stegman is professor of urban and regional planning at the University of North Carolina at Chapel Hill.

Harry A. Stewart is county attorney of Orange County, Florida.

Eric J. Strauss is professor of urban planning at the University of Kansas and of counsel to Freilich, Leitner, Carlisle, and Shortlidge, Kansas City, Missouri.

Nancy Stroud is a partner in the firm of Burke, Bosselman, and Weaver of Boca Raton, Florida, and Chicago, Illinois.

Jan Winters is county administrator of Palm Beach County, Florida, and former planning director of Loveland, Colorado.

Preface

Growth is expensive. In Florida and California, for example, the cost per dwelling of providing water, sewerage, drainage, police, fire, library, school, park, recreation, and other community facilities to new development averages more than $20,000 (California Office of Planning and Research 1982; Florida Advisory Committee on Intergovernmental Relations 1986). To pay for those services and facilities, communities increasingly look to the private sector for help. Development impact fees are one way to shift the burden of paying for new facilities onto new development. Impact fees are really the latest step in the continuing process of shifting the cost for facilities from the community at large to those who benefit. To place development impact fee policy into perspective, one need only look at the history of development exactions.

Prior to the 1920s, local governments readily extended infrastructure to undeveloped land in order to serve existing demand and to induce economic development. It was not uncommon to find speculators subdividing vast tracts considerable distances from cities in anticipation that purchasers would demand, and eventually receive, city services. That kind of behavior was one of the reasons why the U.S. Department of Commerce wrote the Standard City Planning and Zoning Enabling acts of the 1920s. Among other things, the model acts showed states how they could enable local governments to take control of service and facility extensions required for growth and development.

During the Great Depression, many local governments could finance the extension of water, sewer, and road services to the perimeter of new developments, but they could not afford to extend facilities to every house and along every street within new subdivisions. Thus, by the 1940s a new kind of partnership emerged: Local governments would extend trunk or main lines and roads to the perimeter of projects and developers would connect those services to each lot or home.

As local governments discovered that rapid new development places demands on community park and school facilities that could not be met easily through traditional means (e.g., general obligation bonds), they found ways to require either land for those facilities or fees in lieu of land. Mandatory dedications and fees in lieu of dedication, common today (Shultz and Kelley 1985), were the first tools enabled by state statute by which local governments could require new development to shoulder some of the burden it placed on off-site public facilities.

Until the environmental movement of the 1960s and 1970s, most communities believed that growth was fundamentally good. It not only brought economic prosperity, but it led to new and better community services. Challenges to the growth ethic emerged in the late 1960s, however, as environmentalists and others pointed out that unbridled growth caused pollution, congestion of streets, overuse of community services, increased crime, and generally lowered the quality of life. Furthermore, cost–revenue studies showed that in many cases growth did not pay its own way (see Burchell et al. 1978). Many citizens concluded that growth was inimical to the reasons they chose to live in their communities (see Scott, Brower, and Miner 1975).

Also beginning in the 1960s, federal, state, and local governments began reducing their commitment to finance community facilities. In fact, government capital financing has not kept pace with either inflation or population growth since about 1965 (Duncan, Morgan, and Standerfer 1985). Government capital financing was 3.4 percent of gross national product in 1965, for example, but fell steadily to 1.3 percent in 1984. While capital outlays for infrastructure increased in nominal dollars from $20.6 billion in 1965 to $50.7 billion in 1984, adjusting for inflation, outlays in constant 1972 dollars dropped from $31.3 billion to $20.5 billion over that period. The decline in per capita capital outlays for infrastructure from $161 in 1965 to less than $87 in 1984 is even more dramatic.

The falloff in government support for community facilities resulted in part from the taxpayer revolt of the 1970s, which manifested itself in electoral rejection of new general obligation bonds for capital improvements and in severe restrictions on taxation of real property (Chapman 1981). To replace these funding sources, many rapidly growing communities turned to development impact fees to finance public facilities for new development. Pioneering studies by Downing and Frank (1982) and Downing, Frank, and Lines (1985a, 1985b) revealed that impact fees were first used in fast-growing southern and western states, such as California, Colorado, Florida, Oregon, Texas, and Washington, and in growth islands within other states such as Illinois and Utah. By the mid-1980s, impact fees were used to finance an impressive variety of facilities including those for fire and police, water and sewer, drainage, school, libraries, museums, and even government offices (Frank and Rhodes 1987). Many planners consider development impact fees the latest step in the evolution of public facility finance (see Snyder and Stegman 1986; Nelson 1987).

This book discusses development impact fees in eight parts.

PART I: THE POLICY RATIONALE FOR DEVELOPMENT IMPACT FEES

In the first chapter of Part I, James E. Frank and Paul B. Downing provide a review of the rationale and extent to which development impact fees are used throughout the United States. Much of their contribution stems from a series of national surveys they conducted throughout the 1980s which showed that the number of communities assessing impact fees rises annually. What is surprising is that the number of different kinds of impact fees that are assessed is also rising. Several socio-political-economic dimensions of communities that choose to adopt development impact fees are discussed. One interesting finding is that communities adopt impact fees in order to achieve as many as five political objectives, including shifting the capital financing burden to new development, synchronizing new development with the installation of new facilities, imposing economic discipline on land development decisions by requiring development to absorb the costs of providing new services and facilities, enhancing the quality of life within communities, and mollifying the anti- or slow-growth sentiments of locally vocal interest groups.

In Chapter 2, Edward J. Kaiser, Raymond J. Burby, and David H. Moreau report results of a survey they conducted in 1986 of 145 local water and sewer utilities in nine southeastern states. They found that the use of impact fees and related policies to finance water and sewer extensions and system expansion is much more widespread than reported in previous studies. The likelihood that utilities will use impact fees varies with the *need*—expressed as higher growth rates, increases in water and sewer treated, and undercapacity problems—and *capacity to innovate*, which is reflected by the educational level of administrators, staff that is receptive to new ideas, and more and better internal planning and external coordination of water and sewer extensions with comprehensive/land use plans. Their findings suggest that improved planning within utilities and better coordination of utility policy with land use controls will improve the effectiveness and legal defensibility of impact fees and contribute to community land use objectives—not to mention generating additional revenues.

The variety of community approaches to development impact fees is reflected in Chapter 3, written by Mark P. Barnebey, Tom MacRostie, Arthur C. Nelson, Gary J. Schoennauer, George T. Simpson, and Jan Winters, who review how San Jose and San Diego, California, Loveland, Colorado, and Manatee County, Florida, design and administer their programs. Those communities were selected for review because of their diversity and their aggressiveness in finding ways to pay for growth. San Jose's system of impact charges evolved over two decades. San Diego applies a comprehensive menu of impact fees only to planned communities outside the built-up urban area. Loveland applies a comprehensive capital facility cost recovery system citywide. Manatee County recently applied an impact fee system over the entire county, but fees vary by location within the county. The chapter closes with advice for those planners and public officials who are considering impact fee programs for their communities.

The use of development charges in Canada generally and in Ontario particularly is the subject of Chapter 4, written by David P. Amborski. Development charges are equivalent to impact fees and have been assessed in some Canadian provinces since the 1950s. Focusing on Ontario, Amborski argues that despite unclear legislative basis, those charges have increased in both magnitude of assessment and the range of services for which they are collected. Judicial decisions have not provided clear interpretation on the kinds of services that are financed appropriately by development charges, or even on the method of calculating those charges. Uncertainty and appeals will likely persist until new legislation is enacted. That does not seem forthcoming, however.

PART II: PUBLIC AND PRIVATE SECTOR ATTITUDES TOWARD DEVELOPMENT IMPACT FEES

Chapters 5 and 6 introduce public and private sector attitudes toward development impact fees. In Chapter 5, Harry A. Stewart admonishes planners that impact fee deliberations begin with consensus among public officials that there simply is not enough revenue to pay for new facilities to accommodate new development. A committee is appointed to study the matter and make recommendations. The process of impact fee adoption follows three phases from there on. In the first, what he calls the "hell no, we won't pay" phase, the developers on the committee are opposed to impact fees of any sort, but eventually all on the committee come to the same conclusion that the public officials did. This leads to the second, or "let's study the problem," phase. Here, committee work can get bogged down in detail unless staff can usher the process along. At some point the "love it to death" phase begins where the development community recognizes that impact fees are a practical necessity, but only with a few "friendly amendments" that include transition rules, exemptions, and other maneuverings.

The view of the developer is expressed in Chapter 6 by Douglas R. Porter. He claims that developers may cavil at development fees in principle but accept them in practice, provided that local public officials formulate, administer, and expend fees in a reasonable manner. Most developers view fees as more desirable than case-by-case exactions and certainly preferable to halting development altogether to await public funding for infrastructure. However, in return for contributions to pay for public infrastructure, developers want more assurance that projects will be allowed to proceed as planned and that fees will be spent wisely for necessary improvements.

PART III: LEGAL DEFENSE, ISSUES, AND TRENDS

Chapter 7 opens this part with Nancy Stroud's discussion on the legal considerations of development impact fees. Although development impact fees are relative newcomers to the legal scene, precedents for them exist in subdivision dedication requirements and utility charges. An increasing number of courts, especially state courts, require that such fees meet a "rational nexus test." She describes the basis for that test, its more sophisticated forms, and some applications to particular types of fees, and also admonishes that the U.S. Supreme Court decision in *Nollan* v. *California Coastal Commission* adds a federal constitutional requirement for a close fit between the fee and the purpose it serves. The implication of that decision for planning practice is that planners need to conduct more complete background studies than they have in the past to support a legally defensible development impact fee program.

A more detailed look at the non-*Nollan* legal issues of development impact fees is offered by Julian Conrad Juergensmeyer in Chapter 8. After distinguishing between in-lieu fees, other forms of exaction, and impact fees, he reviews the constitutional challenges to impact fees. He focuses on whether impact fees are a form of land use regulation or taxation and the judicial criteria for determining the constitutionality of impact fees. Then, since no other state judicial system has evaluated the legal dimensions of impact fees so thoroughly as Florida's, Professor Juergensmeyer presents a case-by-case study of that judicial process. He also provides an outline for drafting impact fee ordinances to pass judicial scrutiny.

In Chapter 9, Terry D. Morgan identifies the shortcomings of impact fee law and future trends. He warns of impending legal challenges. He suggests that future legal challenges may focus on equity considerations concerning who in the market actually pays impact fees on housing. If impact fees can be shown to effectively exclude certain households from an area, there might be some grounds for challenging those fees. He warns of the possibility that impact fees may undermine affordable housing objectives. He also focuses on legislative trends, suggesting that many disputed issues about the equity of impact fees may be resolved not by the courts but by state and local lawmakers. One avenue of legislation may more carefully prescribe the legitimacy of assessing development for off-site improvements. Legislation also may more carefully prescribe the design of impact fee programs. In recognition of the prospective impact of impact fees on affordable housing, future legislation may require communities to consider affordable housing counterweights. A newly emerging area of legislative action may consider linkage programs.

PART IV: MODEL ENABLING ACTS AND MODEL ORDINANCES

Chapters 10 to 14 get to the heart of whether and how communities may be legally enabled to assess impact fees. The need for a standard state impact fee enabling act is expressed in Chapter 10 by Jane H. Lillydahl, Arthur C. Nelson, Timothy V. Ramis, Antero Rivasplata, and Steven R. Schell. They find that communities across the nation have received varying degrees of legislative and judicial guidance in the use of development impact fees. The types of guidance range from general, liberal legislation in California to more rigid judicial and legislative guidelines in Florida to reactive statutory authorization in Oregon to vague judicial and little statutory guidance in Colorado. Based on their review of the nature and problems of facility financing in those states, the authors argue that the use of impact fees in all states can be greatly advanced by preparation of a standard impact fee enabling act in the tradition of the familiar standard planning and zoning enabling acts of the 1920s. State legislatures could then adapt principles of such an act.

Chapter 11 presents a model act that restricts the use of impact fees more than some state courts currently allow, yet builds on public finance considerations offered in Chapter 24 and incidence issues raised in Chapter 25. It is authored by Jeff Bachrach, Julian C. Juergensmeyer, Arthur C. Nelson, James C. Nicholas, Timothy V. Ramis, and Eric J. Strauss. Provisions of that act include fee calculation, collection, reporting, expenditure, and refund. It also allows for local governments to pay the fees for projects that meet other policy objectives such as low income housing and job retention or creation.

A model development impact fee ordinance implementing that model law, with commentary, is offered by Martin L. Leitner and Eric J. Strauss in Chapter 12. That ordinance is designed for communities with either a mayor–council or commission–manager form of municipal government. With some modification, counties in any state should be able to use it, perhaps without an enabling act.

Chapter 13 is a more flexible model act that allows for the use of development impact fees for the provision of virtually any facility that is included in a capital improvements program, provided dual, rational nexus criteria are met. It also provides additional detail on fee calculation, collection, expenditure, and refund. It is written by Julian C. Juergensmeyer and James C. Nicholas.

Strauss and Leitner in Chapter 14 offer an alternative to the impact fee: excise taxes. There are several reasons why a community may not want to use impact fees. It may not want to restrict the geographic area in which impact fees must be spent, or perhaps a fund for major facilities has to be funded over a longer time period than the courts would allow under impact fee approaches. A community also might not want to risk the possibility that highly technical provisions of the impact fee ordinance might be held invalid, thereby forcing the return of all funds collected. Instead, communities may want to impose an excise tax on new development. An excise tax cuts across all those concerns and many others. It should be seriously considered as an option.

PART V: CALCULATING DEVELOPMENT IMPACT FEES

The next three chapters detail the calculation of development impact fees. In Chapter 15, James C. Nicholas and Arthur C. Nelson review how local governments may apply the rational nexus test in order to attribute facility improvement costs to growth. They also discuss how to determine whether fee payers adequately benefit from the fees they pay and how to calculate impact fees for water and sewer, road, park, and police facilities.

Since an increasing number of communities are assessing traffic impact fees, and since traffic impact fees account for the vast majority of all impact fees collected, Chapters 16 and 17 are exclusively devoted to the determination and administration of those fees. In Chapter 16, David C. Heath, Glenn Kreger, Glenn Orlin, and Meg Reisett review the traffic impact fees of Loveland, Colorado, Montgomery County, Maryland, and Orange County, Florida. These communities were selected for the cross section of communities and approaches they represent.

In Chapter 17, James E. Frank reviews the case of road impact fees in Broward County, Florida. Those fees are based on the Traffic Review Impact and Planning System (TRIPS), which is the only traffic impact fee system of its kind. In contrast to the general formula, recoupment approach used by the three communities reviewed in Chapter 16, TRIPS is a site-specific, nonrecoupment approach; TRIPS assesses a fee based on both the location of development and the routes that trips generated by those developments are likely to take. The appendix to Chapter 17 includes the details of TRIPS.

PART VI: LINKAGE FEES

A variant of traditional impact fees, the linkage fee, is considered here. That fee is based on the assumption that new downtown office development may exacerbate housing affordability in two ways. First, it may directly reduce the supply of affordable housing by demolition to clear sites for office tower development. Second, it may increase the value of real estate resulting from more intense use of urban land, principally by creating an additional housing demand by new employees attracted to the new building. This additional demand causes new housing to be built farther out, but also makes existing housing closer in more expensive. The effects of higher housing prices or rents are generally greatest for subgroups of households furthest from the price or rent level at which new housing is provided. To the leaders of some American cities, such as Boston and San Francisco, the addition of housing units at lower price or rent levels is a key consideration in mitigating those impacts of new downtown office development and concomitant employment growth. In those cities, the mitigation takes the form of a per-square-foot assessment on new downtown office construction, the proceeds of which are used by the city to provide additional lower cost housing to qualifying households. Those assessments are usually called *downtown office development–housing linkage fees* or simply *linkage fees.*

Linkage fees are really a political response to a problem that may be more properly addressed through general taxes. Cities extend infrastructure to new downtown development at a cost of millions, much of which is paid for out of taxes paid by all city residents. It is conceivable that by simply charging new downtown office development for the provision of infrastructure, enough tax revenue could be freed up to provide additional housing without charging linkage fees. The political reality of most cities, however, is that public officials know or perceive that the local electorate would not tolerate the use of their taxes for that purpose. Politicians therefore try to solve the housing affordability problem through innovative, nongeneral tax schemes, while on the other hand continuing to subsidize downtown office development through politically acceptable means. City officials also walk this political tightrope to charge linkage fees for the provision of day care centers, transit, and other services. This part discusses the legal defense, economic impact, and methodology of linkage fees principally for housing.

Part VI opens with W. Dennis Keating's discussion in Chapter 18 of linkage programs and comprehensive planning. He argues that linkage fees must be incorporated into downtown and citywide plans to be optimally effective. This would allow those plans to address social equity issues which underlie linkage programs.

Christine I. Andrew and Dwight Merriam continue in Chapter 19 with the legal defense of linkage fees. One of the principal legal considerations, among many cited in their article, is the question of whether linkage fees can be construed as a taking. Citing the recent *Nollan*

case, they conclude that this Supreme Court ruling has the potential for affecting many kinds of development exaction programs, including linkage programs. They warn linkage supporters and others attempting to draft and implement linkage ordinances that there must be sufficient evidence in the record of the necessary nexus between, say, the need for affordable housing resulting from new development and the fee charged to meet that need. Linkage fees can be a legitimate exercise of police power when that nexus is established.

In Chapter 20, Neil S. Mayer and Bill Lambert discuss Berkeley's menu of mitigation (linkage) fees including housing and child care, transportation and public art, and employment targeting. They discuss the types of analyses needed before those mitigation fees can be assessed and review the politics and practicalities involved in moving from case-by-case fee assessment to fee schedules.

Linda L. Hausrath shows in Chapter 21 how the nexus required according to Merriam and Andrew may be determined and a housing linkage fee calculated. The nexus and the fee are determined by two major tasks. The first task involves determining the additional households with office workers generated by new downtown office development and entails estimating the net addition of office space expected over time, the net addition of employees occupying that space, the net increase in office workers residing in the city, and the additional households residing in the city with office workers. The second task involves determining the additional housing required to mitigate the impact of additional households residing in the city with office workers and determining the cost of producing that housing. This entails estimating the additional housing needed to accommodate additional households of different income levels, and the subsidy required to produce housing that is affordable to those households.

In Chapter 22, Forrest E. Huffman, Jr., and Marc T. Smith offer a theory with a simulation of the economic impact of linkage fees on downtown and regional office markets. Developers of new downtown office space somehow must offset linkage fees. Their ability to pass the fee along to tenants is limited as higher rents will cause tenants to choose other locations, whether or not those locations include the downtown. Their ability to get landowners to bear the fee is limited considering the characteristics of the typical downtown land market. Developers cannot absorb the fee by taking lower profits because their profit margins are already at equilibrium considering the rate of return needed to justify the risk of development. That risk, by the way, may increase in those downtowns where linkage fees are assessed because developers may perceive city officials as more antagonistic to new development than those in other substitutable communities.

They argue that developers can raise rents to offset linkage fees only in areas enjoying monopoly advantages of location. However, even in monopoly locations, demand for downtown space at some point will level off as a result of rent increases. Firms will find alternative locations within the region; only very price insensitive firms would remain. Communities throughout the region may become inundated by additional demand for office construction—which is happening in the new suburban downtowns springing up throughout the San Francisco Bay Area and the Boston region. Smith and Huffman's simulation of the effect of linkage fees in a location that does not enjoy mo-

nopoly advantages, Philadelphia, shows that linkage fees will force marginal new development out of downtown and into the suburbs.

PART VII: ISSUES SURROUNDING DEVELOPMENT IMPACT FEES

Six chapters are devoted to addressing many of the economic, public finance, incidence, equity, ethical, and social issues that surround the use of development impact fees. In Chapter 23, Robert A. Blewett and Arthur C. Nelson review the public choice and efficiency argument for development impact fees. Impact fees can be used as a pricing instrument that guides development and allows the planning process to adjust efficiently to unforeseen changes in economic conditions. They discuss the relationship between urban spatial structure and the pricing of public services. They then outline a system of pricing that allows for efficient development and explore the natural political resistance to such a pricing scheme. Impact fees are found to be an imperfect, but practical, alternative to the preferred pricing system without the difficulties of that preferred system. Probable effects of impact fees on growth and development are explored. Impact fees may be used to aid in the planning process so as to improve development efficiency in the community.

Douglass B. Lee provides a critical evaluation of development impact fees within the framework of public finance in Chapter 24. Two fundamental questions guide his inquiry. The first is an efficiency question: Do impact fees improve, worsen, or have no effect on the total net benefits generated by scarce resources? The second is an equity question: Are impact fees fair? Through a highly structured series of arguments, Dr. Lee concludes that direct user fees, development exactions, and special improvement districts can be superior mechanisms to impact fees. User fees allocate costs rationally among users. Development exactions can tailor charges to individual project impacts. Special improvement districts can achieve the same result. One major problem with development exactions, however, is the need for astute negotiators on the public side. The problem with special districts is the general lack of skill or experience in their administration so as to achieve efficiency and equity. With only modest effort, however, special districts can achieve the benefits of impact fees without the inequities, and metered user charges can reduce the need for facilities.

In Chapter 25, Forrest E. Huffman, Jr., Arthur C. Nelson, Marc T. Smith, and Michael A. Stegman consider who bears the burden of development impact fees. They theorize how the real estate market will respond to impact fees under different market conditions and look at the effect of impact fees on residential and nonresidential real estate under different short- and long-term supply and demand conditions. They go on to examine prices that developers, home buyers and tenants, and sellers of buildable land will pay or receive. They also explore how impact fees affect the distribution of development among communities in a metropolitan area. They conclude that neither developers nor sellers of buildable land will bear the major burden of paying impact fees; rather, in the long term home buyers, renters, and nonresidential tenants will pay a major share of development impact fees.

Richard Peiser discusses an approach to calculating equity-neutral water and sewer impact fees in Chapter 26. The purpose of his contribution is to show how impact fee incidence and equity considerations may be incorporated in impact fee design. Equity-neutral impact fees should equalize the burden of paying for infrastructure facilities on all residents in a community regardless of when they move there. He determines that impact fees, if set properly, can achieve an equity-neutral result. Equity-neutral fees are highly dependent on inflation, financing, and assumptions on absorption rates. Since economies of scale must be significant for cost savings at capacity to outweigh the carrying costs during the period in which excess capacity is absorbed, it may be preferable to build smaller facilities with less excess capacity to be absorbed.

Timothy Beatley reviews in Chapter 27 the ethical issues in the use of development impact fees. He begins by examining problems of intertemporal fairness; that is, the questions of fairness that arise from treating new residents differently from existing residents. He proceeds to examine several key questions related to determining what constitutes a fair allocation of the costs associated with new growth, including who benefits from growth, who can afford to pay for growth, who generates the costs of growth, and the consideration of impact fees as forms of quid pro quo trading and their ethical implications. Other ethical issues arise concerning political representation, social exclusivity, the sense of community, and the practical problems of implementing impact fee systems. Professor Beatley argues conditions under which impact fees are most and least ethically defensible.

In Chapter 28, Charles E. Connerly discusses impact fees as social policy and argues for alternative policies. Beginning with a definition of social policy as that "through which government seeks to correct inequities, to improve the condition of the disadvantaged, and to provide assistance to the less powerful," Professor Connerly argues that impact fees are bad social policy. Following the arguments laid out by Huffman, Nelson, Smith, and Stegman, he starts with the assumption that it will be home buyers and renters who pay those fees in the long term. He goes on to propose that impact fees be replaced by property taxes as the primary source of financing community growth. This would have the effect of distributing the burden of paying for growth throughout the community instead of assessing the full burden on new development as intended by impact fee policy. He also recommends that planners seek to develop alternative sources of funding infrastructure so that the production of low income housing is not stifled by impact fees. He then argues for aggressive use of the federal Low Income Housing Tax Credit policy, perhaps spearheaded by planning officials. Finally, Professor Connerly argues that planners should lobby for more, not less, federal low income housing and infrastructure financial assistance.

PART VIII: IMPLEMENTING AND ADMINISTERING DEVELOPMENT IMPACT FEE PROGRAMS

The final two chapters consider the administration of development impact fee programs. In Chapter 29, Elliot Auerhahn draws on his decade-plus experience in implementing the impact fee system in Broward County, Florida. He observes that, although much attention has been given to the adoption of impact fee ordinances, the tasks required to implement such a system successfully have received little attention. Mr. Auerhahn sets forth five major administrative concerns. First, impact fee systems must be capable of assessing not just the usual case but the unusual case as well, such as con-gregate housing and mixed-use projects. Second, systems must include credit and waiver provisions so that projects are not over or double charged, and desirable development can proceed. Third, questions about who collects fees and how records on fee receipts and disbursements are kept must be addressed. Fourth, there must be enforcement to ensure the timely payment of appropriate fee amounts. Fifth, many kinds of data must be collected, organized, and maintained for the continuous recalculation of fees and the projects for which they are used.

In Chapter 30, J. Richard Recht admonishes that "rose bushes have thorns" in his discussion of the difficulties involved in the design and administration of impact fees. Based on his decade-plus experience in analyzing impact fee options for northern California communities, Mr. Recht reviews the policy basis for impact fees and then focuses on the practical problems in designing fee systems. While impact fee systems require careful assumptions about impacts and relationships, in reality those assumptions are difficult to hold or justify. A sampling of those assumptions includes the determination of the time horizon over which impacts and costs are calculated, how the future is forecast, the appropriate level of facility service to be financed by fees versus reasonable alternative levels of service, the treatment of opportunity costs or the amount of excess capacity that should be paid by fees or outstanding indebtedness, the situation when usage turns out not to be a good measure of benefit received, and the attribution of impact (for example, is it homes or industry that generates demand for schools?). These are only a few of the thorny issues that must be considered when designing and administering impact fees. Mr. Recht suggests a set of strategies for planners that serve as the last word in this book.

CONCLUDING THOUGHTS

Many impact fee considerations and issues remain. Many local governments have found that they must turn to development impact fees to pay for new facilities needed to serve new development. How they assess those fees can affect growth patterns, fiscal bases, and the distribution of low and moderate income households. There must be some determination of the *impact* of impact fees so that to the extent possible unintended social, economic, and development outcomes can be offset. In my view, a better linkage needs to be formed between planning practitioners and analysts. While practitioners must forge new tools such as impact fees to deal with new problems (or old problems finally receiving due attention), analysts ought to be involved in evaluating the theory, application, and effects of those tools, such as impact fees, and they ought to advise practitioners on ways to avoid undesirable outcomes. If this book accelerates the formation of such a linkage, it will have been successful.

Arthur Christian Nelson
Georgia Institute of Technology
Atlanta
April 1988

References

Burchell, Robert and David Listokin. 1978. *Fiscal Impact Handbook*. New Brunswick, N.J.: Center for Urban Policy Research.

California Office of Planning and Research. 1982. *Paying the Piper*. Sacramento, Calif.: State Capitol.

Chapman, J. I. 1981. *Proposition 13 and Land Use: A Case Study of Fiscal Limits in California*. Lexington, Mass.: Lexington Books.

Downing, Paul B. and James E. Frank. 1982. *Recreational Impact Fees*. Tallahassee: Florida State University.

——— and Elizabeth R. Lines. 1985a. *Community Experience with Fire Impact Fees: A National Survey*. Tallahassee: Florida State University.

———. 1985b. *Community Experience with Sewer Impact Fees: A National Survey*. Tallahassee: Florida State University.

Duncan, James B., Terry D. Morgan, and Norman R. Standerfer. 1986. *Simplifying and Understanding the Art and Science of Impact Fees*. Austin, Tex.: City of Austin Planning Department.

Florida Advisory Council on Intergovernmental Relations. 1986. *Impact Fees in Florida*. Tallahassee: State of Florida.

Frank, James E. and Paul B. Downing. 1986. National Experience with Impact Fees. Paper presented to the 1986 conference of the Association of Collegiate Schools of Planning (October).

———. 1987. Patterns of Impact Fee Usage. Paper presented to the 1987 conference of the American Planning Association (May).

Frank, James E. and R. M. Rhodes, eds. 1987. *Development Exactions: Issues and Impacts*. Chicago: American Planning Association.

Nelson, Arthur C. 1987. Impact Fees as an Emerging Method of Infrastructure Finance. *Florida Policy Review* 2, 2: 22–26.

Schultz, Michael M. and Richard Kelley. 1985. Subdivision Improvement Requirements and Guarantees: A Primer. *Journal of Urban and Contemporary Law* 28: 3–106.

Scott, Randall W., with David J. Brower and Dallas D. Miner, eds. 1975. *Management and Control of Growth*, three vols. Washington, D.C.: Urban Land Institute.

Snyder, Thomas P. and Michael A. Stegman. 1986. *Financing the Public Costs of Growth*. Washington, D.C.: Urban Land Institute.

The Policy Rationale for Development Impact Fees

1

Patterns of Impact Fee Use

JAMES E. FRANK
PAUL B. DOWNING

THE GENESIS OF IMPACT FEES

The history of impact fees is found in the evolution of two primary responsibilities of local governments: land use regulation and the provision of public facilities. The regulation of land development became widespread in the 1920s, a decade marked by the U.S. Supreme Court's validation of zoning in the Euclid case and the U.S. Commerce Department's publication of the model statutes for state enablement of local government planning and zoning. For the next four decades, development regulation was performed as a local government process facilitating growth. During this time the construction of facilities to serve that growth was an unquestioned civic responsibility. But beginning in the 1960s, three fundamental changes occurred: (1) a "quiet revolution" in land use regulation gave regional and state interests a role in land use policy, (2) the advent of the environmental movement shattered the nation's unswerving faith in the benefits of growth, and (3) the fiscal revolt of the 1970s and 1980s fostered local government experimentation with alternatives to the property tax. Within this framework, public sentiment frequently demanded that growth pay its way through impact fees to finance construction of facilities needed to serve a new development.

The idea of requiring new development to pay for or install the community facilities that it needs is not new. The Standard Planning Enabling Act, subsequently copied almost verbatim by most states, required as a condition precedent to the approval of development the provision of streets, water mains, sewer lines, and other utility structures (U.S. Department of Commerce, 1922). Thus, from the outset of development regulation, infrastructure *internal* to the development was required of the developer as a condition of approval (Snyder and Stegman 1986, p. 22).

What is new about impact fees is the idea that growth should pay for facilities located *outside the development site,* the need for which results from numerous developments. These are the facilities most likely to have been financed from general revenue sources in the past, and it is the public's resistance to general revenue increases that has provided a powerful stimulus to the expanding use of impact fees.

We can define impact fees as single payments required to be made by builders or developers at the time of development approval and calculated to be the proportionate share of the capital cost of providing major facilities (arterial roads, interceptor sewers, sewage treatment plants, regional parks, etc.) to that development. Attention is drawn to several important facets of this definition. First, the fact that impact fees constitute single payments, in contrast to the periodic payments of general taxes, means that the capital outlay necessary to construct facilities is available at the time that facilities become needed, thereby reducing the need for the issuance of bonds. Second, the emphasis on the amount of the fee being a proportionate share of facility costs implies that new development will not be required to pay other than its own fair share. Put another way, deficiencies in facility capacity resulting from the accumulation of demand stemming from earlier development are not appropriately funded by impact fees on new development. On the other hand, it also implies that in those circumstances where impact fees are appropriate, the *full* cost rather than some nominal fraction of the cost of needed facilities will be apportioned.

Understanding of the definition of impact fees is sharpened by contrasting them to impact taxes, with which they are sometimes confused, and mandatory land dedications, an earlier experiment in the provision of development-induced facilities from which impact fees evolved. Impact taxes, currently permitted in only California and Arizona, are an exercise of the tax power rather than the police power from which impact fees derive their authority (Snyder and Stegman 1986, p. 60; Jacobsen and Redding 1977). Because of this, there is no obligation for the amount of the impact tax to bear any relationship to the cost of facilities needed to serve the development and, further, there is no need to spend the money to construct facilities to benefit the development paying the tax. In short, impact taxes can be set at whatever levels are necessary to balance the municipal budget (short of being confiscatory) and can be spent for any legitimate municipal purpose. In contrast, the amount of an impact fee levied under the police power must bear a reasonable relationship to the cost of providing facilities to serve the development paying the fee and can only be spent to construct those facilities. So impact fees are much less flexible than impact taxes, which can be used to defray operating costs or meet other budget obligations not necessarily related to new development.

The mandatory land dedication appears earlier in the evolution of development exactions and still is employed extensively to acquire parkland, street rights-of-way, and school sites. It differs from the impact fee in that it is directed solely at the problem of providing land and makes no pretense at addressing the question of financing the construction of the facility upon the land. Further, in its pure form (without the later addition of the cash in lieu of land feature) it is effectively restricted to the provision of land located within the development site. In contrast, impact fees are directed at the full capital cost of providing facilities and, because they are a cash exaction, can address the need for facilities not necessarily located on the development site.

Impact fees are still a relatively new device, the diffusion of which will probably continue for some time. But their presence in the development regulatory process has begun to be strongly felt as some communities adopt multiple impact fees to finance the construction of virtually all types of facilities necessary to serve new development, including roads, sewers, water systems, schools, parks, drainage systems, police facilities, fire stations, solid waste disposal sites, resource recovery facilities, libraries, and emergency medical facilities. It is no longer surprising to hear of communities charging impact fees totaling several thousand dollars per dwelling unit.

THE NATIONAL EXPERIENCE WITH IMPACT FEES

We conducted three national surveys of impact fees that focused on the use of this revenue device for recreational facilities, fire facilities, and sewers (Downing and Frank 1983; Frank, Lines, and Downing 1985a; Frank, Lines, and Downing 1985b). We also conducted a follow-up survey of the sewer impact fee respondents and have participated in a national survey of development exactions generally (Purdom and Frank 1987). The following discussion summarizes some of the major dimensions of impact fee usage those surveys revealed. It also draws on several studies not done by the authors, including: an exhaustive survey of impact fee usage in Florida by the Florida Advisory Council on Intergovernmental Relations (1986), a thorough survey of development fees in the San Francisco area done by the Association of Bay Area Governments (1982), a survey of 500 builders taken by the staff of *Builder* magazine (Lemov 1986), and an examination of the use of mandatory dedications and fees for parks in California communities reported by the Construction Industry Research Board (1981) of that state.

Is the Use of Impact Fees Increasing?

The question of whether the use of impact fees is expanding has three dimensions: Are more communities now using impact fees than previously was the case? Has the dollar magnitude of impact fees risen? Are impact fees being charged for a greater range of community facilities than in the past? Apparently, the answer to each of these is *yes.*

Three surveys examined the chronological pattern of impact fee adoption. The survey of Florida communities found impact fees being charged for 11 types of facilities. Plotting the year of adoption as shown in Figure 1–1, that study concluded that, "When impact fees are carefully separated from other charges local governments impose, it is clear that their use is rapidly expanding." The follow-up survey of sewer impact fee adopters across all states also examined the year of adoption. As shown in Figure 1–2, there is a distinct clustering of adoptions in the late 1970s and an earlier clustering of adoptions by California communities in the late 1950s. There is no doubt that the number of communities using impact fees has been expanding for the past 20 years, but examination of the cumulative frequency distribution in Figure 1–3 indicates that *the rate of adoption may be slowing.* The national survey of development exactions looked at three types of regulatory requirements: mandatory land dedications, requirements to build or install facilities, and cash payments as reported by 452 cities and counties in a stratified random sample. The peak period of adoption occurred during the second half of the 1970s for cash payments for roads, schools, and parks and during the first half of the 1970s for sewer and water facilities, lending support to the notion that impact fee adoptions continue, but at a reduced pace. This slowing of adoptions is to be expected based on research into the diffusion of other types of innovation (Mahajan and Peterson 1983).

More than 80 percent of respondents to the *Builder* magazine survey said the dollar amount of individual impact fees had risen, and more than 70 percent estimated the increase to be more than 20 percent. In the Construction Industry Research Board study, 11 California com-

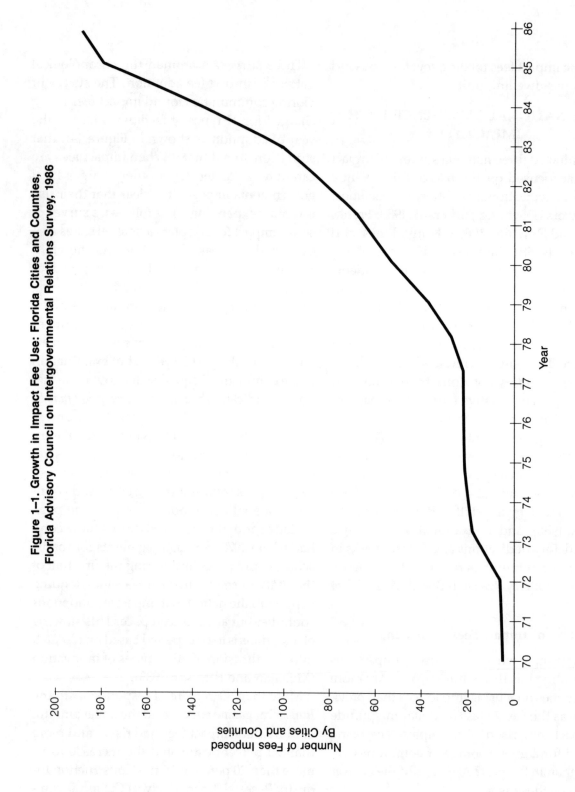

Figure 1–1. Growth in Impact Fee Use: Florida Cities and Counties,
Florida Advisory Council on Intergovernmental Relations Survey, 1986

Figure 1–2. Adoption of Sewer Impact Fees

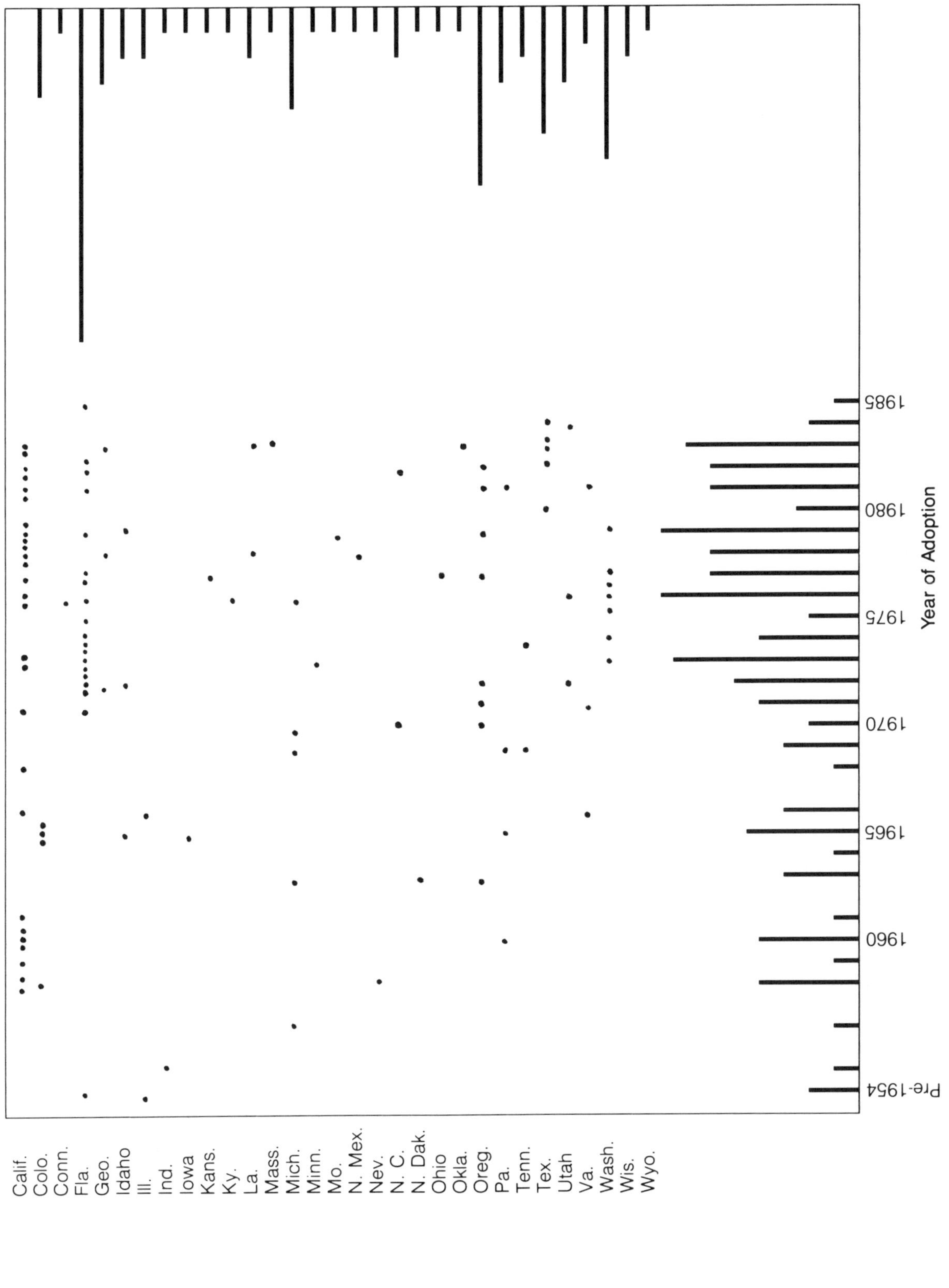

Calif.
Colo.
Conn.
Fla.
Geo.
Idaho
Ill.
Ind.
Iowa
Kans.
Ky.
La.
Mass.
Mich.
Minn.
Mo.
N. Mex.
Nev.
N. C.
N. Dak.
Ohio
Okla.
Oreg.
Pa.
Tenn.
Tex.
Utah
Va.
Wash.
Wis.
Wyo.

Year of Adoption

Pre-1954   1960   1965   1970   1975   1980   1985

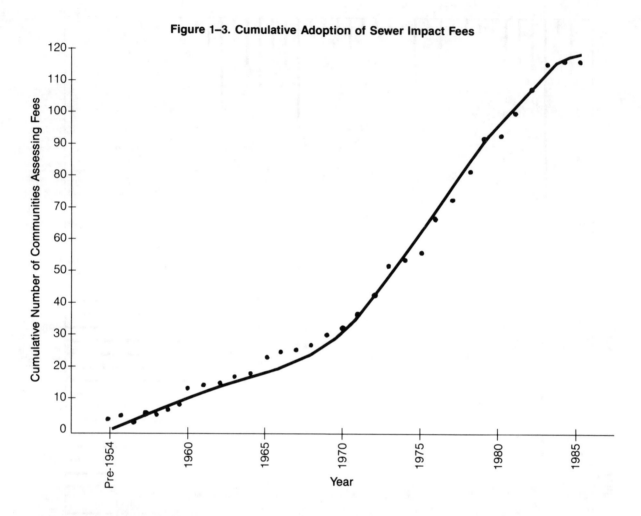

Figure 1–3. Cumulative Adoption of Sewer Impact Fees

munities charging in-lieu park fees in both 1975 and 1980 displayed an increase in average fee charged of 163 percent, compared with a 53 percent increase in the Consumer Price Index and a 116 percent increase in the price of a new home. The San Francisco Bay Area study showed that impact fees charged by all cities and counties in that region rose an average of 26 percent between 1979 and 1981, and that much of that increase was attributable to increases in dollar amounts for previously adopted fees rather than new adoptions. Of the 500 home builders responding to the *Builder* magazine survey, 67 percent said they were paying on-site impact fees for more items than they had five years earlier and *56 percent said that was the case for off-site fees as well.* The Florida ACIR survey shows communities adopting impact fees for at least 11 types of facilities. It would appear that part of the increase in impact fee use is an expansion of their application to a wider range of facilities. Hence, it seems that all three factors—more communities adopting impact fees, for more purposes, and at higher amounts—are operating to increase local community use of impact fees.

**Table 1–1. Average and Highest Fees Levied on Single-Family Detached Dwellings:
Evidence from Four Studies (figures are in dollars)**

	Downing and Frank	Construction Industry Research Board	California ABAG	Florida ACIR
Total Planning Fees	—	—	55/335	—
Total Building Fees	—	—	651/1,786	—
Park Impact Fees	383/1,800	850/22,860	802/1,650	224/375
School Impact Fees	—	—	784/1,790	—
Storm Drainage Impact Fees	—	—	164/1,520	—
Sewer Impact Fees	689/6,199	—	739/2,750	739/1,500
Water Impact Fees	—	—	572/3,497	481/1,250
Road Impact Fees	—	—	—	729/1,158
Fire Impact Fees	182/621	—	—	257/750
Police Impact Fees	—	—	—	118/250
Impact Taxes	—	—	483/1,715	—
Total Development Fees	—	—	3,527/8,568	—

Note: The number to the left of the slash is the average; the number to the right of the slash
is the highest observed value.

How Big is the Impact Fee Bite?

The most consistent data on the dollar magnitude of impact fees are available for those fees levied to construct sewer and water systems (Table 1-1). The national survey of sewer impact fees, the San Francisco area study, and the Florida ACIR report show a pattern of average sewer impact fees clustered around $700 per dwelling unit for single-family homes. The Bay Area and Florida studies show average water impact fees in the neighborhood of $525 per unit. In all cases, individual impact fees can be found that exceed the averages by several orders of magnitude, but the distributions around the central value are reasonably compact and the magnitude of the mean is consistent across studies.

A less consistent pattern is found among the studies reporting on park impact fees. The two California studies show average fees of more than $800 per dwelling unit, whereas the national and Florida surveys report average fees of less than $400. The reason why California communities apparently charge so much more than the rest of the country may lie in the fact that parkland dedications were somewhat of a cause célèbre in California in the early 1970s, as evidenced by the adoption in 1974 of an explicit statutory delegation of authority for mandatory dedication of parkland known as the Quimby Act. The preparation and distribution of a model parkland dedication ordinance by the League of California Cities that recommended the adoption of a standard of five acres of parkland per thousand persons as the basis for the dedication requirement appears to have had its intended effect, since the Quimby Act survey showed the five-acre standard to have been adopted by more communities than any other standard. This argument is made more plausible by the authors' earlier study indicating that a standard of five acres per thousand required a fee of at least $750 at prevailing park development costs (Downing and Frank 1983).

The total dollar amount of impact fees can

be substantial. The data for each type of impact fee have shocking outliers at the upper end of the distribution, such as the sewer impact fee of $6,199 found by Frank, Lines, and Downing (1985b) and the park impact fee of $22,860 uncovered in California (Downing and Frank 1983). If the exceptional fees were added together, their amount would be monstrous. Fortunately, this does not occur in practice. Rather, the observable high total impact fee bill is in the $7,000 to $10,000 range (Snyder and Stegman 1986, p. 78). In San Diego, impact fees are $9,500 per dwelling unit; in Tiburon, California, they are $8,568; in Fairfield, California, they are $8,269 (Lemov 1986).

How Prevalent Are Fiscal Impact Fees?

Using fairly careful survey procedures and getting higher than normal response rates, the three national surveys of impact fees uncovered 49 communities charging impact fees for parks, 190 doing so for sewerage systems, and 21 for fire facilities. Given that there are slightly more than 10,000 municipalities and counties in the United States, one can not argue that the current use of impact fees is widespread. But simply looking at the total number of municipalities and counties as the total pool of potential adopters presents a skewed picture because not all municipalities and counties offer sewer services, fire services, or recreational services. Furthermore, many communities are not growing and do not need to expand the physical capacity of their systems. In order to get an idea of the extent to which it understates impact fee use, the authors ran a special tabulation of the 1982 Census of Governments to identify communities "in the sewer construction business." This found that 4,257 municipalities and counties had sewer construction expenditures in ex-

cess of $1,000, and 1,298 spent more than $100,000. If the 1,298 communities constitute the pool of potential users of impact fees, then the existence of 190 adopters says that while impact fees surely are not routinely adopted, their use for sewerage is not insignificant. (Similar special tabulations have not been done for recreation and fire.)

The national survey of development exactions found that 58 percent of all cities and counties levy some kind of cash exaction, with the highest category being that of sewer lines, for which 35 percent impose a levy. That cash exactions for sewers occur more often than impact fees for sewers may be a result of the inclusion of tap-ins in the definition of a cash exaction; tap-ins are excluded from the definition of an impact fee since impact fees are defined as being charges for off-site capacity.

Patterns of Impact Fee Adoption

The three national surveys of impact fees show a consistent pattern of use across states, with California having the largest number of adopting communities, followed by Florida, Washington, Oregon, Colorado, and Texas (Table 1–2, Figure 1–2). The pattern of impact fee use being greater in growth states is understandable, given that impact fees can be levied only on new construction. But a surprising number of adopting communities showed up in nongrowth states, prompting a closer examination of those specific communities and revealing them to be growth islands in nongrowth states.

Is impact fee adoption by a large community a phenomenon? A small community one? Or is there no pattern? The national survey of sewer impact fees is the only data set providing sufficient information to illuminate this question. When sewer impact fee communities are tabulated by the population size of the community, the fees appear to be mostly a small-commu-

Table 1–2. Number of Communities Charging Impact Fees for Parks, Sewers, and Fire Facilities

State	Parks	Sewers	Fire Facilities
Ariz.	3	4	0
Calif.	20	45	8
Colo.	4	10	2
Conn.	0	2	0
Del.	0	0	0
Fla.	2	27	7
Ga.	0	5	0
Hawaii	0	0	0
Idaho	0	3	0
Ill.	0	8	2
Ind.	0	2	0
Iowa	0	2	0
Kans.	0	1	0
Ky.	0	2	0
La.	0	2	1
Md.	0	1	0
Mass.	0	2	0
Mich.	0	5	0
Minn.	0	3	0
Mo.	0	1	0
Nev.	1	1	0
N.J.	0	1	0
N. Mex.	0	2	0
N.Y.	3	1	0
N.C.	0	3	0
N.Dak.	0	1	0
Ohio	3	4	0
Okla.	0	1	0
Oreg.	2	10	0
Pa.	3	4	0
R.I.	0	0	0
Tenn.	0	1	0
Tex.	0	9	0
Utah	3	3	0
Vt.	0	1	0
Va.	0	6	0
Wash.	3	11	1
Wis.	0	5	0
Wyo.	0	4	0
TOTAL	**48**	**190**	**21**

nity tactic because communities with populations of less than 50,000 show the largest number of sewer impact fees. But this outcome is very much affected by the fact that there are many more small than large communities in the United States. When the frequency of sewer impact fees is analyzed by population size and compared to the number of communities in each population class, it is quite clear that the larger the community, the more likely it is to employ sewer impact fees (see Table 1–3). Although the absolute number of small communities using them will be greater, the likelihood of a small community employing them is less. The authors also tested whether this holds true when the size of communities "in the sewer construction business" is examined. A tabulation of the 1982 Census of Governments was done to determine how many municipalities and counties in each size class had sewer construction expenditures and therefore might be likely candidates for impact fee use. These results are also displayed in Table 1–4 and support a similar conclusion to that for communities in general. So while the *frequency* of impact fee use is greater in small communities, the *likelihood* of impact fee adoption is greater in large communities.

The Pattern of Impact Fee Magnitudes

Turning from the pattern of adoption to the pattern of the dollar magnitude of impact fees, several interesting points emerge. Our earlier discussion of the findings of four surveys of *recreational* impact fee use indicated that California communities charged higher dollar amounts than communities in other states, but examination of the pattern for *sewer* impact fees failed to show similar results (Frank, Downing, and Lines 1985b, Table 2). In fact, for sewers

Table 1–3. Sewer Impact by Community Size and as a Proportion of Total Communities and Those Communities in the Sewer Construction Business

Population Size	Frequency of Impact Fee	Municipalities and Counties	Proportion 2–3	Municipalities and Counties in Sewer Construction Business
0–5,000	2	2,921	.0007	2,287
5,991–50,000	67	5,900	.011	1,541
50,001–100,000	27	652	.041	211
100,001–500,000	29	453	.064	158
500,001–1,000,000	4	65	.062	41
1,000,001 +	7	26	.269	19

Sources: Column 2, national survey of sewer impact fees (Frank, Downing, and Lines 1985b). Column 3, 1984 *Municipal Yearbook*. Column 5, special tabulation of 1982 Census of Governments tapes done by the authors. "In the sewer construction business" defined as having spent more than $1,000 on sewer construction in the census year.

Table 1–4. Average Development Fees Levied on Single-Family Homes, San Francisco Bay Area, 1981 (per dwelling unit)

Fee Charged for	Metropolitan Zone		
	1	2	3
Planning and Building Fees	$ 700	$ 723	$ 676
Growth Impact Fees	105	908	2,526
Utilities Connections	815	1,901	2,993
Total Development Fees	$1,619	$3,532	$6,194

Note: The zones might be roughly characterized as: Zone 1 = Core; Zone 2 = Suburban; Zone 3 = Exurban.

Source: Association of Bay Area Governments 1982.

there was no discernible clustering of high fees and low fees by state. This suggests that the pattern of impact fee utilization may be different across fee types.

Further, the Bay Area survey found that "development fees tend to rise moving outward from older, more built-out core areas, to the outer, more rapidly developing areas." Apparently, the amount charged for impact fees is sensitive to the magnitude of the infrastructure investment task. Additional support for this is provided when the Bay Area data are analyzed by metropolitan zone and when total development fees are decomposed into planning and building fees (e.g., plan checking, site inspections, etc.), growth-impact fees (consisting of park impact fees, school impact fees, impact taxes, and other miscellaneous growth-related fees), and utility connection fees (including tap-in, meter connection, and capacity charges). As shown in Table 1–4, charges related to the administrative processing of permits are virtually uniform across metropolitan zones, whereas fees for infrastructure rise consistently from Zone 1 to Zone 2 to Zone 3. The implication is that the administrative costs of processing development permits may not vary among communities nearly as much as the cost of constructing facility capacity.

The magnitude of the sewer impact fee does not vary systematically with treatment plant size, service population, or miles of pipe network, all of which measure some aspect of system size. Given that treatment plant costs exhibit substantial positive economies of scale and transmission costs increase with system size, one might anticipate higher impact fees at the very large system sizes where transmission costs associated with distance from the treatment plant overtake the economies of scale available in larger treatment plants. This pattern did not appear in data and we wondered why. Further analysis revealed that only 5 out of 190 of our respondents varied the amount of the impact fee by distance. Given this, it is likely that the economies of scale available in large systems are reflected in the fee amount, but that the increased transmission costs are not reflected, except on an average cost basis.

On the other hand, a factor that *was* found to be associated with the magnitude of the fee was the number of system elements for which the impact fee was levied. Respondents were asked which system elements they charged impact fees for—treatment plants, effluent disposal facilities, transmission mains and interceptors, transmission pumping stations/lift stations, collection network pipes, or collection pumping stations/lift stations. When the number of systems charged for is tabulated against the magnitude of the fee, there is a strong positive association.

In summary, impact fee magnitudes may exhibit variations across the types of systems (sewers, schools, etc.) for which fees are levied, such that patterns of fee magnitude are unique to the type of infrastructure system for which the fees are levied. But further research on that question is needed before that assertion can be made in more than a tentative fashion. Impact fee magnitudes appear to increase with distance from the center of the urban area, reflecting a possible response to the magnitude of growth-induced need for infrastructure invest-

ment. While impact fee magnitudes do not vary systematically with service area size, they are positively correlated with the comprehensiveness of the impact fee's cost basis as reflected in the number of system components for which the fee is charged.

The Design of Impact Fees

When a community adopts an impact fee, there are many issues to be resolved about how to calculate the magnitude of the fee, such as what factors to incorporate in the computational methodology, how much flexibility to allow in setting the fee amount, and whether to allow offsets for donated land, other revenue sources, or existing facility capacity.

Communities using impact fees prefer to *not* leave the determination of the amount of the fee to negotiation. More than 80 percent of the responding communities in all three national surveys said they used either a formula or a published schedule as the means for determining the fee applicable to a particular development (see Table 1–5). They also varied the amount of the fee according to the need for facility capacity as expressed by population size, sewage flow, and building size. But when it comes to varying the fee by location in order to reflect spatial variations in the cost of providing facilities, less than 3 percent of sewer impact fees and 5 percent of fire impact fees vary by location. (Comparable results are not known for park impact fees, since this question was not asked on the park impact fee survey.) The absence of spatial variation in the impact fee is disappointing because it means that the beneficial effects of impact fees as spatial prices are forfeited and the impact fee cannot operate to discourage development at locations that are expensive to serve.

Table 1–5. Procedures for Setting Impact Fee Amounts (figures are percents)

	Parks	Sewers	Fire
Q. *Is the procedure for determining the amount of fee which a particular development must pay (choose one):*			
Negotiable	4.2	0.0	9.5
Negotiable w/guidelines	6.3	3.2	0.0
According to formula	16.7	32.1	33.3
Fixed by schedule	64.6	64.2	47.6
No answer	8.3	0.5	9.6
Q. *Can a developer pay the impact fee by making a noncash payment?*			
Yes	71.2	47.6	84.2
No	64.6	64.2	47.6
No answer	18.6	4.8	0.5
Q. *The combination of impact fees and ad valorem taxes paid by a development might constitute double payment. How is this handled?*			
By ignoring it	14.4	5.3	19.0
No ad valorem is used	0.0	70.5	0.0
By expending ad valorem solely for operation and maintenance and impact fees solely for capital outlay	57.4	10.5	61.9
Other	10.7	11.6	14.3
No answer	17.4	2.1	4.8
Q. *Courts have been concerned that impact fees not be used to fund the needs of existing neighborhoods instead of the needs of the new developments paying the fees. How does your fee avoid this problem?*			
By ignoring it	18.8	17.9	9.5
By expending fees only for sewer facilities located in developing areas and using other revenue sources to fund the needs of existing neighborhoods	37.5	45.3	52.4
By using a set of benefit districts which require that fees collected in those districts be spent only for sewer facilities located therein	8.2	8.4	4.8
Other	34.7	26.8	28.6
No Answer	0.8	1.6	4.7

Credits against the impact fee for the value of land or facilities donated by the developer are allowed in more than 70 percent of the communities charging impact fees for recreation and fire facilities, but in slightly less than 50 percent for sewer impact fees. (See Table 1–5.) The 20 percent difference may reflect the fact that land is frequently the easiest item for a developer to donate, but in the case of sewers it is the least usable item since most elements of a sewer system do not require a separate piece of land.

A particularly bothersome aspect of impact fee design arises when *ad valorem* taxes are also used to fund capital expansion of a system for which impact fees are being charged. This presents the possibility that the combination of the impact fee paid by the new development and the *ad valorem* tax payment levied on the same development after occupancy will constitute a double charge for the same facilities or that the impact fee is payment for the new development's facilities and the *ad valorem* tax is payment for someone else's facilities. (The same can be said of other revenue devices used to finance capital outlay for the targeted facilities, although we will confine our discussion to property taxes.) There is a particularly interesting court case in Utah that deals with this question. In light of that judicial dicta, a carefully designed impact fee will provide offsets against the impact fee in the amount of the present value of that portion of the new development's stream of *ad valorem* tax payments going to finance similar facilities so that all double charging is eliminated (Bosselman and Stroud 1987). The pattern of responses to survey questions about this is interesting. As shown in Table 1–5, up to 19 percent of respondents in the three national surveys admitted to ignoring the question altogether. The presumption is that their impact fees are potentially flawed on that dimension. The difference in responses across the three national surveys also is interesting. Those using sewer impact fees were least likely to ignore the double charge problem. But more than 70 percent of the sewer impact fee communities spend no *ad valorem* revenue on sewers, whereas none of the communities charging recreational or fire impact fees responded in this way. This apparently reflects the fact that user charges are the primary revenue source for sewer systems, while *ad valorem* taxes are the principal support for parks and fire protection systems.

Builders and developers fear that impact fees will be used to build facilities to serve existing rather than new development. In communities where capital outlay has been deferred over a long period of time, a buildup of accumulated

capacity deficiencies may fuel political pressure to use impact fees to solve the problem. While there is ample legal precedent to strike down such schemes, nevertheless their political attractiveness can be very compelling. When asked how they handled the problem, between 9 and 19 percent of the national survey respondents admitted to ignoring it and between 37 and 52 percent said they handled it by expending impact fees only in developing areas (see Table 1–5).

WHY ARE IMPACT FEES ADOPTED?

The impact fee is a relatively new municipal invention and our understanding of its use is quite incomplete. This chapter has summarized what little is currently known about the use of this new device by local governments across the nation, focusing entirely on the questions related to what? where? how much? and for what purpose? Remaining to be examined are those aspects dealing with why impact fees are adopted—the questions surrounding the causality of the phenomenon. In this area we are curious about the factors that set the stage for the entire movement to impact fee adoption, as well as the more specific factors that influence a particular community's decision to use impact fees. In other words, the examination of causal factors is logically done at two levels: A general level in which societywide shifts in values are important and a community level in which the specific circumstances of a particular local government become important.

BACKGROUND FACTORS CONTRIBUTING TO THE TREND OF IMPACT FEE ADOPTION

There have been three broad trends in American public life that seem to have contributed to the willingness of local governments to engage in widespread experimentation with impact fees. Two of these trends involve shifts in the fundamental attitudes and perceptions that permeate our culture (Weschler, Mushkatel, and Frank 1987, p. 34) and the third results from a gradual ripening of the judicial standards by which regulatory fees are judged to be a reasonable or unreasonable exercise of the police power (Bosselman and Stroud 1987, p. 76). The first trend was manifested during the environmental movement of the 1960s that caused American society to discard its long-held perception that growth was a uniformly beneficial phenomenon. While the substantive focus of this movement was on problems of the environment, its effect on attitudes relevant to our discussion of impact fees was also profound. Concern for the environment set the stage for the public to question whether new development, under a general tax regime, produced more in new tax revenues than it did in new service costs. After all, if new development could produce substantial environmental externalities, could this not be the case in regard to fiscal burdens as well? If new development in fact produced a net fiscal deficit, then existing development would have to make up the difference or new facility investment would have to be deferred, thereby imposing congestion costs on existing residents. The question of whether new development produces a net fiscal deficit or surplus is an unsettled one, but the important thing to observe in terms of its effect on impact fees is that the *perception* of that possibility became prevalent.

Following close behind the environmental movement was the fiscal revolt that began in the early 1970s and first demonstrated decisive strength with the overwhelming public approval of Proposition 13, the 1978 California ballot initiative placing limits on property taxes. By means of a series of tax limitation measures adopted in many states, the public demonstrated that its appetite for taxes had been exceeded. Further, by the artful use of initiative and referendum, it bypassed traditional modes of representation and participation to express its displeasure. A corollary to this movement was the shift from an emphasis on general taxation to that of user fees, reflecting the mood of the tax revolt that those who wanted government services should be charged for them and those who choose not to consume the services should enjoy a lower tax rate. This shift to user fees has progressed so rapidly that the property tax—the classical mainstay of local government finance—has recently been eclipsed by user fees and charges as a source of revenue for municipal governments in the United States.

The combination of the above two trends, the emergence of a public perception that new development may produce a fiscal deficit that must be borne by existing taxpayers and the revolt against any further local government tax increases, produced very potent political sentiment to shift fiscal burdens away from existing residents and onto new residents. But a third factor—entirely unrelated to public attitudes toward new development or fiscal matters—was operating as well. Beginning in the post-World War II suburban housing boom, local governments began to experiment with new uses of the police power as a means of trying to provide community facilities to serve new development, a need that previously had been relegated almost entirely to the power to tax and spend. Expanding on the long-standing municipal practice of requiring developments to provide on-site streets and utilities, some communities started to delve into the problem of how to require new development to provide needed facilities that might not be located on the development site and typically would be used by numerous developments. This first took the form of mandatory dedications of park and school sites, followed by cash payments in lieu of land dedications, and now impact fees. During the period 1945–1975 in which this evolution was taking place, courts in many states had the opportunity to review and judge the reasonableness of these devices in relation to constitutionally protected property rights. The pattern of the judicial review initially demonstrated a very liberal standard in which the community was able to require the development to contribute to facilities with almost no regard to whether their need stemmed from the development's occupancy. It later embraced a very strict test in which the development could be made to provide only those facilities needed for its *exclusive* use. Finally, a more balanced test was enunciated in which a development could be required to provide facilities needed by it and other developments as long as its participation was limited to a proportionate share. This is the rational nexus test which has gradually come to be embraced by virtually all state court systems as the standard of reasonableness for development exactions. The emphasis in the rational nexus test on the idea of proportional participation in shared-use facilities is the dimension that makes possible the increasing use of impact fees, since most of their applicability is to facilities needed to serve many developments. When added to the taxpayers' revolt and the public perception that new development may actually cost more than the revenue it produces, the availability of a ready-made judicial test to support impact fees charging a proportionate share becomes an important third piece in the staging of their adoption.

Community-Level Motivations in Impact Fee Adoption

Within the general trend of impact fee adoption, it is apparent that individual local governments adopt impact fees for a number of reasons that may vary in importance across communities. Five reasons can be suggested as follows:

1. To shift fiscal burdens from existing taxpayers to the occupants of new development.
2. To better synchronize the construction of facility capacity with the arrival of new development demand.
3. To subject development decisions to the discipline of a kind of pricing mechanism.
4. To enhance the community's life-style by attempting to exclude certain types of development and social groups.
5. To engage in "symbolic politics" by only nominally responding to political demands for adoption.

The desire to shift fiscal burden to the occupants of new development is politically beguiling. After all, the voters to whom the burden will be shifted are not present to oppose the measure or campaign against the elected officials responsible for adoption, and the chief beneficiaries are the existing residents whose votes at the next election are highly prized. This strategy of shifting fiscal burdens to new development can take two distinct forms: (1) new development is gouged by a political process intent on shifting as much tax burden as possible regardless of the niceties of legal and fiscal theories of fair share cost allocation, and

(2) a sincere attempt is made to achieve an equitable allocation of the cost of growth-induced facilities.

The possibility of a local government using the first form is fueled by an all-too-frequent fact of life in communities that use general revenue financing for new facility investment: Capital outlay for growth-related facilities has been routinely delayed in order to hold down tax rates in the face of resistance by existing voters. The result is the almost universal accumulation of existing capacity deficiencies in roads, drainage systems, parks, and other infrastructure categories. Take the resulting high levels of facility congestion and combine them with taxpayer resistance to rate increases. Then introduce a new revenue device, the political implications of which are all positive in the near term. The result can be a situation in which some communities will be unable to resist the temptation to adopt impact fees that will be used to overcome the backlog of existing deficiencies rather than to build capacity to serve the new developments that are paying the fee. While this temptation is somewhat tempered by the common knowledge that judicial standards such as the rational nexus test guarantee certain death for such an impact fee if taken to court, that prospect is sufficiently distant to allow some current office holders to consider it politically irrelevant. Consider our earlier statement that between 9 and 19 percent of the communities in our three national surveys of impact fees reported ignoring the question of impact fees possibly being used to remedy existing deficiencies.

The second observable form of tax shifting is that in which the community (1) adopts impact fees that are carefully designed to charge new development only its fair share allocated cost of facilities and (2) guarantees that the money will be used to construct facilities benefiting the paying developments by imposing fairly strict expenditure controls and facility programming mechanisms. When used in conjunction with a program to remedy existing capacity deficiencies with nonimpact fee monies and a scheme of credits against the impact fee for new development's contribution to that, the likely result is that development will pay only for growth-induced facilities and preexisting development will pay for accumulated deficiencies. This is essentially the standard required by the rational nexus test.

The second motivation for impact fee adoption is that of improving the degree of coordination in the location and timing of the installation of new facility capacity in relation to new development. By requiring that facilities needed to serve new development be constructed or paid for at the time of permitting, this orientation tries to avoid the chronic congestion of facilities resulting from development approvals issued without regard to the availability of facility capacity. Florida has embarked upon an approach to growth management that emphasizes this strategy. Legislation adopted in 1985 requires all municipalities and counties to cease issuing development permits when insufficient capacity is observable in any of the physical facilities covered by the community's comprehensive plan, including streets, sewers, water systems, drainage, and solid waste. This aspect of the legislation becomes operative around 1989, after communities have prepared a comprehensive plan and adopted a full set of implementing regulations (Bosselman and Stroud 1985).

The third in our list of motivations for adopting impact fees comes from those interested in them as quasi-market prices. Impact fees are seen as imposing price discipline on decisions to develop land, requiring those decisions to reflect the cost of providing services and facilities. This orientation stresses the fact that the cost of providing facilities varies across space, with some locations being more costly to serve than others. It argues that impact fees should be imposed at levels that reflect the true cost of providing facilities, thereby ensuring that land development decisions take into account those costs. With general taxation, the extra cost involved in providing facility capacity to locations that are expensive to serve is effectively externalized on the general community. With impact fees, the possibility exists to structure the magnitude of the fee to reflect spatially varying costs, thereby forcing the development decision to internalize or privatize that variation and providing a financial incentive for development to choose less costly locations. This is the same effect that is sought in peak period surcharges for water and electricity. It should be noted that impact fees will achieve this effect only if they employ marginal costing techniques rather than an average cost (Snyder and Stegman 1986, p. 30; Downing and McCaleb 1987, pp. 50-53). In our three national surveys of impact fees, the proportion of communities that allowed their fee to vary by location was below 5 percent, indicating that this is something less than standard practice.

It is probable that some communities adopt impact fees in order to promote a desired lifestyle by setting the impact fee high enough to effectively exclude low cost development and low income populations (Danielson 1976). While the phenomenon is infrequent there are observable exceptions in which a community charges thousands of dollars per dwelling unit to provide a facility that normally costs only a fraction of that amount. That these cases represent "snob fees" is not very debatable.

The final motivation for a community's adoption of impact fees is observable in the form of symbolic politics. This is when a community adopts an impact fee at a very nominal level for the purpose of satisfying a vocal political demand, but with no sincere intention of using impact fees for one of the other four reasons (Edelman 1964). One does not have to look far to discover, say, a road impact fee charging only a few hundred dollars per dwelling unit when most estimates of the real cost of off-site roads to serve new development are in the vicinity of several thousand dollars.

Empirical Evidence on Factors Associated With the Impact Fee Adoption

We are investigating the factors that seem to be statistically operative in the adoption of impact fees by communities in the United States. Using a theoretical framework similar to that described in the discussion above on factors affecting impact fee adoption, we have attempted to determine which factors are statistically significant in increasing the probability of a community's adoption of impact fees.

To do this, a random sample of municipalities "in the sewer construction business" was selected and data for a number of variables were collected for each sample municipality from the Census of Governments and the Census of Population. The statistical population from which the sample was selected was defined as all municipalities that might consider charging impact fees for sewers. This was operationalized as those municipalities with sewer capital expenditures in excess of $100,000 in the census year, hence the category "in the sewer construction business." The sample of municipalities was then divided into the categories of adopters and nonadopters, depending on whether they showed up in our national survey of sewer impact fees. Using the adopter/nonadopter distinction as a binary dependent variable, probit analysis was conducted to examine which community variables were significantly related to the probability of impact fee adoption.

The results available to date show three independent variables to be consistently related to the probability of impact fee adoption at a level of statistical significance of 5 percent or better. These are:

1. The magnitude of the municipality's population growth rate interacting with that of its SMSA.

2. The degree of fiscal stress in the community, as measured by per capita own-source revenues divided by per capita income.

3. The extent to which the judicial system of the state in which the municipality is located can be characterized as "pro-citizen" on a three-point continuum of "pro-developer," "neutral," and "pro-citizen."

These results seem to support the ideas expressed in the section above dealing with background factors contributing to impact fee adoption which emphasizes: (1) distrust of the benefits of growth, (2) the taxpayers' revolt, and (3) the development of judicial standards to judge the reasonableness of impact fees. The community-specific factors discussed above do not emerge as statistically significant in the limited testing conducted on them to date. This is to be expected if they operate such that each community adopting an impact fee does so for only one of the five reasons. But it must be emphasized that our testing is still far too incomplete to derive that conclusion with any firmness.

SUMMARY

Impact fees are a relatively recent invention, although they have roots that extend to the inception of municipal efforts to deal with the problem of providing public facilities necessitated by growth. The range of municipal facilities to which impact fees are being applied is expanding, the number of local governments employing this device is growing, and the dollar amount of specific impact fees has risen. The average amount of impact fees for specific facilities is usually less than $1,000 for a typical dwelling, but fees in individual communities are observable at levels considerably above and below the average value. For communities employing numerous impact fees, the total impact fee bill can exceed $10,000. The pattern of impact fee use across states shows that communities in growth states are the most likely to employ them, but that growth islands in nongrowth states show up as well. Within urban areas, there is some evidence of higher fees in outlying areas where growth rates are highest and levels of facility capacity are the lowest. Across urban areas, the frequency of impact fee adoption is highest in small communities, but the likelihood of adoption is highest in large communities. While explicit judicial standards have been enunciated to prescribe fairness in the levying of impact fees, it may be the case that in a minority of impact fee communities the allure of a politically feasible solution to the problem of deferred capital outlay is quite irresistible. The underlying factors that seem to operate to stimulate the trend to impact fee adoption appear to be the dawning of a "growth may not be so good" public attitude, the advent of the taxpayers' revolt, and the evolution of a workable judicial standard applicable to regulatory fees. The factors that may operate individually or in concert to convince a specific community to adopt impact fees are thought to be the shifting of fiscal burdens, the rationalization of the infrastructure investment process, the imposition of public prices, the exclusion of low income persons, and the symbolic use of impact fees.

References

Association of Bay Area Governments. 1984. *Development Fees in the San Francisco Bay Area: An Update.* Berkeley, Calif.: California Association of Bay Area Governments.

Bosselman, Fred P. and Nancy Stroud. 1985. Pariah to Paragon: Developer Exactions in Florida 1975–85. *Stetson Law Review* 14, 3: 527–63.

————. 1987. Legal Aspects of Development Exactions. In *Development Exactions,* edited by James E. Frank and Robert M. Rhodes. Chicago: Planners Press.

Construction Industry Research Board. 1981. *Quimby Act Survey, Park and Recreation Dedication and Fees, California Cities and Counties.* Los Angeles: CIRB.

Danielson, Michael N. 1977. *The Politics of Exclusion.* New York: Columbia University Press.

Downing, Paul B. and James E. Frank. 1983. Recreational Impact Fees: Characteristics and Current Usage. *National Tax Journal* 37: 477–90.

———— and Thomas S. McCaleb. 1987. The Economics of Development Exactions. In *Development Exactions,* edited by James E. Frank and Robert M. Rhodes. Chicago: Planners Press.

Edelman, Murray. 1964. *The Symbolic Uses of Politics.* Urbana, Ill.: University of Illinois Press.

Florida Advisory Council on Intergovernmental Relations. 1986. *Impact Fees in Florida.* Tallahassee: FACIR.

Frank, James E., Elizabeth R. Lines, and Paul B. Downing. 1985a. *Community Experience with Fire Impact Fees: A National Study.* Tallahassee: Policy Sciences Department, Florida State University.

————. 1985b. A National Survey of Sewer Impact Fees. *Journal of the Water Pollution Control Federation.* 57: 1055–61.

Jacobsen, F. A. and J. Redding. 1977. Impact Taxes: Making Development Pay Its Own Way. *North Carolina Law Review* 44: 407–20.

Lemov, Penelope. 1986. Passing the Buck. *Builder.* June: 72–77.

Mahajan, Vijay and Robert A. Peterson. 1983. *Models for Innovation Diffusion.* Newbury Park, Calif.: Sage Publications.

Purdom, Elizabeth D. and James E. Frank. 1987. Community Use of Exactions: Results of a National Survey. In *Development Exactions,* edited by James E. Frank and Robert M. Rhodes. Chicago: Planners Press.

Snyder, Thomas P. and Michael A. Stegman. 1986. *Paying for Growth: Using Impact Fees to Finance Infrastructure.* Washington, D.C.: Urban Land Institute.

U.S. Department of Commerce. 1922. *Standard Planning Enabling Act.* Washington, D.C. Section 14 as reproduced as an appendix to American Law Institute, 1968, *A Model Land Development Code, Tentative Draft Number I.* Washington, D.C.: American Law Institute.

Weschler, Louis F., Alvin H. Mushkatel, and James E. Frank. 1987. Politics and Administration of Development Exactions. In *Development Exactions,* edited by James E. Frank and Robert M. Rhodes.

2

Local Governments' Use of Water and Sewer Impact Fees and Related Policies: Current Practice in the Southeast

Edward J. Kaiser
Raymond J. Burby
David H. Moreau

For decades, local governments have used exactions to shift some of the burden of infrastructure for new development onto developers. The use of exactions increased in the 1970s and skyrocketed in the 1980s as additional factors such as escalating costs of infrastructure and decreasing federal aid combined to lead local governments to search for new ways to finance infrastructure (Frank and Downing 1987; Downing and Frank 1983; Frank, Lines, and Downing 1985a; and Frank, Downing, and Lines 1985b; and Snyder and Stegman 1986)

The increasing use of one type of exaction—impact fees—in particular raises a number of questions. Just how widely has that practice spread? Why do some communities use impact fees and others do not? Is land use planning related to the use of impact fees? If so, how? There has been a considerable amount of conjecture about impact fees at conferences and

in the literature, but empirical evidence in answer to those questions is scarce.

Drawing data from a survey of water and sewer extension financing practices in nine southeastern states, we show in this chapter that impact fees and related infrastructure financing practices (termed *private financing* here) are more widespread than previously thought. We also examine variation in the extent of use of such practices, first looking to the literature and theory to hypothesize in what situations we would expect to find it and then testing those hypotheses with the survey data. We find that a utility's capacity to innovate is as important an explanation of the use of impact fees as expansion pressures from growth and inadequate capacity to accommodate that growth. Finally, we examine the role of planning in easing the use of impact fees. We find that better planning within the utility is indirectly associated with the use of such financing. The extent of prior coordination between a utility's service extension policies and comprehensive or land use plans is directly related. That is an important finding, we argue, because even greater coordination between utility extension financing practices and community planning will be needed if impact fees are to be fully effective and legally defensible and also are to contribute to community land use as well as fiscal objectives.

METHODS

To document the extent of impact fee use, explain its variation from community to community, and explore its relationship to planning, we conducted a mail survey of a simple random sample of 213 water and sewer utilities serving 10,000 or more persons in the nine southeastern states of Alabama, Florida, Georgia, Kentucky, Mississippi, North Carolina, South Carolina, Tennessee, and Virginia. We obtained usable responses from 145 utilities (a 68 percent response rate), using a postcard follow-up and two follow-up letters with replacement questionnaires.[1] The sample included 91 municipal water and sewer utilities, 28 county utilities, and 26 special districts and authorities. The distribution of responses across the nine states is shown in Table 2-1; Florida had the highest number of responses with 29 and Mississippi the least with 4. A typical utility in the southeast provides both water and sewer services, has 30 employees, serves about 70,000 people, and is located in a metropolitan county where housing units increased by 50 percent between 1970 and 1980. See Table 2-2.

Because an important part of our analysis applies to a conceptual model, we use path anal-

Table 2–1. Random Sample of Utilities, by State

State	Sample Size	Type of Utility (%)		
		Municipal	County	Special District
Alabama	11	36	27	36
Florida	29	76	17	7
Georgia	18	67	33	0
Kentucky	14	57	14	29
Mississippi	4	100	0	0
N. Carolina	20	70	15	15
S. Carolina	15	53	20	27
Tennessee	17	70	0	30
Virginia	17	41	29	29
Total	145	63	19	18

ysis to report and test our findings. The paths among the variables diagrammed in a flow chart constitute a system of least squares regression equations from which parameters can be estimated for each segment of each path from independent variables through intermediate variables to the ultimate dependent variable – use of impact fees. The results are similar to regression analysis. Coefficients for path segments represent the expected change in the dependent and intermediate variables for each unit of change of the preceding variable, controlling for the effect of other variables in the model. Path coefficients reported here have been standardized to ease comparison of the paths and variables. The total effects of the independent and intermediate variables in the model are calculated as the aggregate of direct effects and indirect effects (through other variables). Normal tests of significance were calculated and are reported. To be certain about statistical significance of independent variables, the individual regression analyses were backed by logit analyses, which are more appropriate for analyzing dependent variables that are nominal

Table 2–2. Description of Random Sample Respondents: Utility and Service Area Characteristics
(means, except for % in metro area)

	Total Sample	Type of Utility		
		City	County	Other
Employees	70[a]	60	99	84
Water Service Population	72,630	57,484	122,242	75,173
Annual Growth	6.1%	5.0%	10.6%	5.8%
Sewer Service Population	71,442	44,479	137,832	116,261
Annual Growth	5.3%	4.8%	7.1%	5.5%
1980 County Population	204,700	218,400	231,000	138,100
1970–80 County Growth Rate				
Population	29%	29%	36%	24%
Housing Units	51%	51%	51%	44%
% in Metropolitan Locations	62%	59%	60%	73%

[a]Median = 30

measures—such as use versus nonuse of impact fees. The coefficients of the logit model are not appropriate for path analysis, however, and the actual results of the logit analysis are not reported although they consistently supported the regression analysis findings.

The percentages reported in the text and in tables should be within 4 percent of the population percentage at the 95 percent confidence level.

THE EXTENT OF USE OF WATER AND SEWER IMPACT FEES

The considerable attention given to impact fees at conferences and short courses and the prolific recent literature on the topic provide evidence that the use of private financing is increasing.[2] Frank and Downing (1987), for example, indicate a distinct upward swing in the use of impact fees at about 1970. The same authors found 190 communities to be using sewer impact fees in 1984 and estimated that those communities constituted about 15 percent of the 1,298 U.S. communities that spend more than $100,000 per year in sewer construc-

tion. Among the nine southeastern states we surveyed in 1986, for example, Frank, Lines, and Downing (1985a) reported that about 3 percent of the communities were using impact fees. A Florida ACIR report (1986) found that the number of all types of impact fees used in that state rose nearly tenfold from slightly more than 20 communities in 1976 to approximately 180 in 1986. Our 1986 survey provides additional evidence of a rapid increase in the use of impact fees.

We found that 35 percent of the utilities in the Southeast are using water and sewer impact fees.[3] That is a much higher proportion than reported in earlier studies, as we explain below. There is considerable variation from state to state, however, in the proportion of utilities using impact fees. In Florida, 71 percent of the utilities employ impact fees compared to 26 percent of utilities in the other eight states in the region, plus or minus a statistical confidence interval of 4 percent. Figure 2–1 illustrates utilities' impact fee adoption rates for each state in the region.

Our finding that Florida leads the region in

Figure 2–1. Proportion of Utilities That Charge Impact Fees*

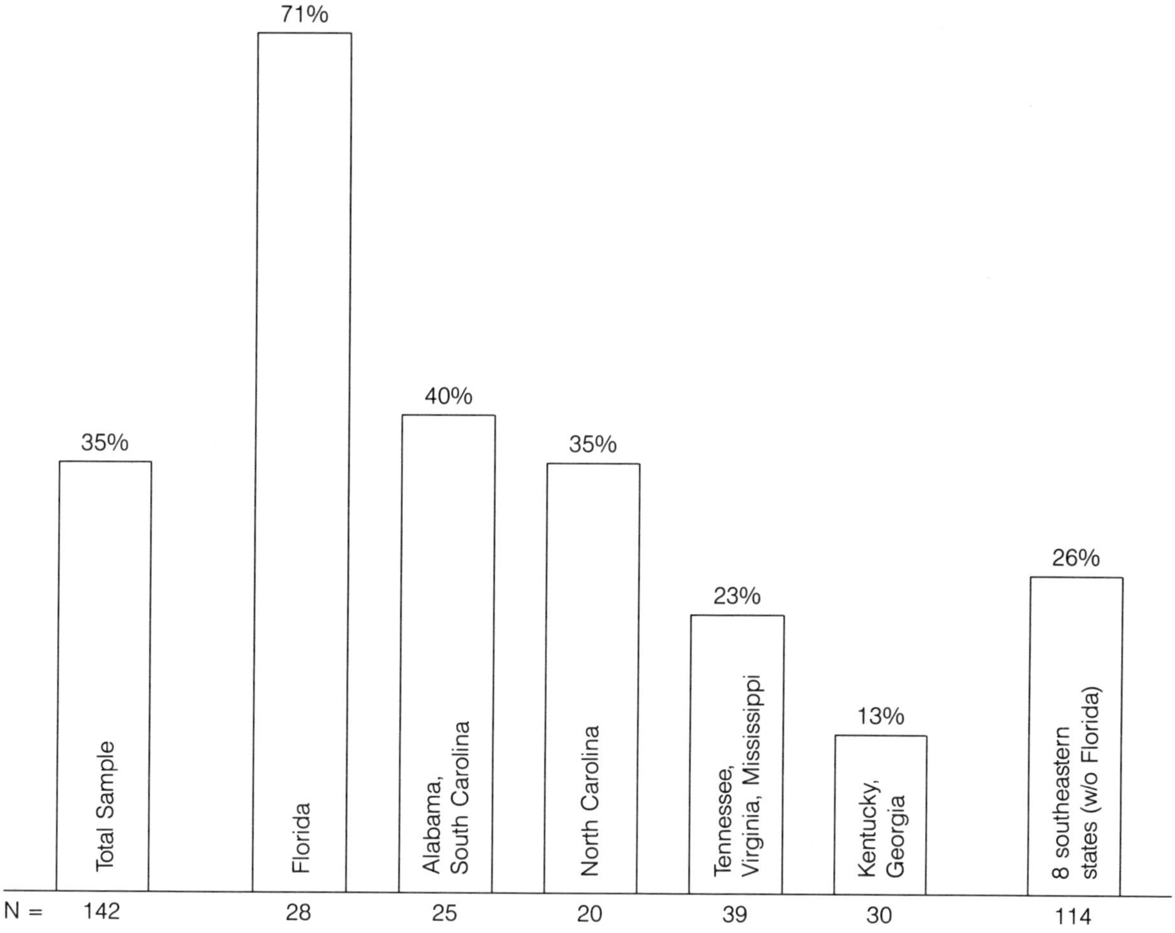

35%	71%	40%	35%	23%	13%	26%
Total Sample	Florida	Alabama, South Carolina	North Carolina	Tennessee, Virginia, Mississippi	Kentucky, Georgia	8 southeastern states (w/o Florida)

N =   142   28   25   20   39   30   114

*"Land development ordinances require developers to pay an 'impact fee' based, in part, on the costs of water or sewerage service required by their projects" was circled answer in response to question asking respondent to circle ways in which water or sewer policies are incorporated in community planning procedures employed in their service area.

Note: Figures for individual states should be interpreted with caution because of the small N's at individual state levels.

the use of impact fees is corroborated by other studies. Snyder and Stegman (1986), for example, found that California, Colorado, and then Florida were the three states in which impact fees were the most prevalent in 1985. Frank, Downing, and Lines (1985a) found Florida to be second only to California in number of communities adopting sewer impact fees, with Colorado coming in third. When Frank and Downing's figures are converted to proportions of municipalities in a state to adjust for the size of the state and the number of cities there, then the rates of adoption of impact fees in Florida, California, and Colorado, along with Washington and Oregon, were all about the same—between 12 and 13 percent—in 1984. Thus they found 12 percent adopting sewer impact fees in Florida in 1984; we found 71 percent adopting sewer or water impact fees in 1986. Even accounting for differences in type of service for which the fee is collected and the differences in survey method,[4] our more recent survey provides strong evidence that the use of impact fees for water and sewer is higher than previous literature suggests and that considerable expansion in the use of such fees is occurring during the mid-1980s.

Use of Other Private Approaches to Finance Water and Sewer Facilities

The imposition of impact fees through a land development ordinance is but one of several approaches to shift costs of public water and sewer infrastructure to the development industry. We also asked utility directors whether the utility employed "one-time charges levied on benefited parties (special assessments, tap-on fees, front-footage fees, development fees, availability charges, system development charges, etc.) to finance water or sewer system expansion or extensions that have been undertaken since 1980." Fifty-six percent of the utilities use such fees. Some utilities used both a land development ordinance-imposed impact fee and the one-time charge levied on benefited parties. But as Table 2–3 indicates, in addition to the 35 percent that used impact fees, another 31 percent did not use impact fees but did use special assessments, tap-on fees, development fees, and the like in the absence of impact fees

Table 2–3. Use of Alternatives to Impact Fee Land Development Ordinance

Policy/Practice	Proportion of Sample
Use land development ordinance requiring impact fee	35%
Do not use impact fee ordinance but do use special assessments, tap-in fees, development fees, availability charges, system development charges, and the like to finance expansions and extensions	31%
Total: Use either impact fee or other one-time charges to finance extensions	66%
Use neither	34%
	N= 131

Table 2–4. Financing Policies for Extending Water/Sewer Lines to New Development

Policy/Private	Inside Corporate/ Service Area Limits	Outside Corporate/ Service Area Limits
Use land development ordinance requiring impact fee	36%	33%
No impact fee but require developer to pay full costs	34%	51%
No impact fee but require developer to pay some of the costs	23%	16%
No impact fee and government pays all extension costs	7%	0%
	100%	100%
	N = 129	N = 118

per se.[5] Thus, only about one-third of the utilities use neither of the two approaches to private financing. In other words, two-thirds of

Figure 2–2. Paths Hypothesized to Influence Adoption of Impact Fees

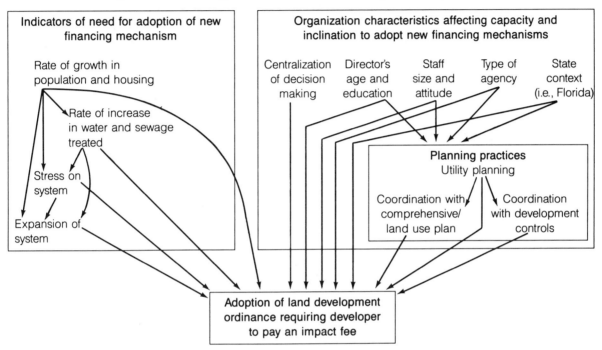

the utilities in the southeastern United States are using cash exactions in some form.

We also asked about other water and sewer extension policies that shift the costs of extensions to new development. As shown in Table 2–4, in addition to those utilities that levy impact fees, an additional 34 percent require developers to pay the full costs of extending water or sewer lines inside the utility corporate limits and 51 percent require the same outside their corporate limits. All of the remaining utilities require the developers to pay at least some of the cost outside the corporate limits, and all but 7 percent require that at least part of the cost of extending service inside the corporate limits be paid by developers. In almost all cases (more than 80 percent) the form of developers' contributions was installation of the facilities required for their projects, including, for about 50 percent of the utilities, oversized lines if needed.[6]

A CONCEPTUAL MODEL FOR EXPLAINING VARIATION IN USE OF IMPACT FEES

While the use of fees and other exactions to shift the costs of public infrastructure to developers has increased, a number of communities still rely on public rather than private financing of the extension of water and sewer services. In this section, we explore that variation and explain it conceptually and statistically. The question is: What explains why some communities adopt impact fees and others do not?

We hypothesize that explanatory factors divide into two categories—factors that indicate a need for new water and sewer financing mechanisms, and characteristics of the utility's organization and staff and its overall situation that indicate an inclination and capability to adopt new financing methods. In other words, we believe impact fees are a result of both a need for them and a capability/inclination to use them. Figure 2-2 illustrates our conception of how constellations of both types of factors act on each other and ultimately on the likelihood that utilities will adopt impact fees. Figure 2-2 constitutes a path model in the tradition of systematic comparative research on determinants of public policy because all of these factors can be expected to affect the use of impact fees simultaneously (Dye and Robey 1980).

The first group of factors in our conceptual model defines the need for policy innovation. In the case of water and sewer extension and system expansion, need is associated closely with population growth, which creates a demand for expansion of the water and sewer system. Where increased demand produces indications of inadequacy in the existing system—termed stress in our model—that should act as an additional stimulant pushing utilities to adopt impact fees.[7] Thus our conceptual model, in flow diagram format shown in Figure 2-2, hypothesizes that population growth leads to increased demand for water and wastewater treatment, stress, and expansion activities and all four factors lead to the need to improve financing sources and hence to increased likelihood of adopting impact fees.

The second group of factors defines the organizational context that eases or hinders the adoption of new policy. Evidence suggests that the size of organizations, degree of centralization of decision making, and degree of professionalism and innovativeness of agency staff and leadership may affect how an organization adapts to environmental change, needs, and resulting stress.

Larger organizations are more likely to be better able to implement policy (Van Meter and Van Horn 1975) and introduce policy innovations (Bingham 1976). Since larger organizations have more differentiated job functions, they are more likely to be exposed to new ideas as more specialized employees are brought into the organization.

Jenne (1984) found centralization of control had a positive effect on the extent to which local governments used various capital budgeting techniques. Like rigorous capital budgeting techniques, impact fees require extra effort and may not be adopted unless there is a strong directive to do so from some central authority.

Though organizations are constrained by available personnel and other factors, there is room for the preferences and leadership ability of utility directors to have an effect (Sabatier 1977). We hypothesize that the use of impact fees will increase with the director's level of education and the staff's openness to innovation. In addition, since impact fees are a relatively new concept, we expect younger utility directors will be more likely than older ones to have been exposed to new financing ideas in school and to be more receptive to them.

We also hypothesize that planning practices of the utility are relevant. Internal planning activities, such as capital improvement planning and coordination of utility extension policies with the comprehensive or land use plan and with development control procedures should lead utilities to use impact fees administered through land development ordinances as one way of shifting the costs of growth from the utility to developers.

To summarize: We view the adoption of impact fees to be determined both by indicators of need for innovative financial policy and by

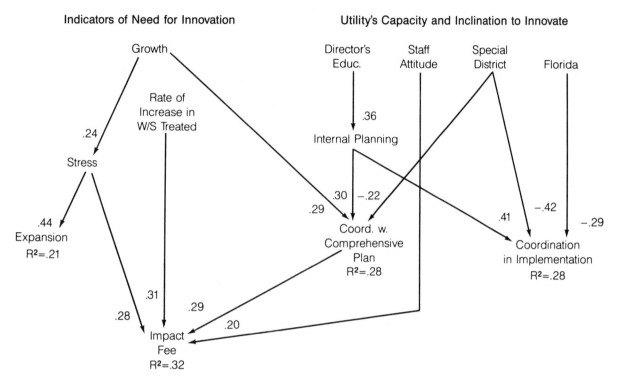

Figure 2–3. Paths Influencing Adoption of Impact Fees*

*Only path coefficients statistically significant at the .05 level are shown.

capacity of the utility agency to adopt such policy. We expect population growth to lead to increased demand for water and wastewater treatment, to stress on the water and sewer system and/or to expansion of that system, all of which would lead to the need for new funding sources. On the other hand, some organizations may be better able to adopt innovative policy—such as impact fees, to deal with the needs—than other organizations. The agencies that should be better able to adopt impact fee policy are the larger agencies, those with younger and better educated directors and staffs more receptive to new ideas, those with centralized control, those that are part of the general government (i.e., not special districts), those in Florida, and those that do more internal planning and external coordination with comprehensive plans and land use controls.

FINDINGS

The conceptual model performs reasonably well in explaining variation in the adoption of water and sewer impact fees. Multiple regression equations we developed to explain the intermediate and ultimate dependent variables are shown in Tables 2–5 and 2–6, and statistically significant relationships (at the .05 level) are shown in the path diagram provided in Figure 2–3. Except for the explanation of the rate

Table 2–5. Relative Effects of Water and Sewer Need Indicators on Each Other: Standardized Regression Coefficients*

Explanatory Factors (Need Indicators)	Intermediate Dependent Variables in Path Model		
	Increase in Water/Sewage Treated	System Stress	System Expansion
Pop./hsg growth rate	.03	.24	.10
Rate of increase in water/sewage treated	—	−.05	.09
System stress	—	—	.44
System expansion	—	—	—
Adjusted R^2	.00	.04	.21
F-ratio	.10	3.20	9.77
Significance level	NS	.05	.00

* Circled standardized coefficients are statistically significant at .05 level or better.

of increase in water or wastewater treated, every equation is statistically significant as indicated by the F-ratio. Furthermore, the equations explain from one-fifth to about one-third of the variation in use of impact fees, which is respectable for this type of research. (Jenne [1984], for example, was able to explain 17 percent of the variation in use of capital budgeting techniques among a sample of 337 cities.)

Indicators of Need

The annual rate of increase in water and sewage treated and stress on the existing system have strong direct effects on the use of impact fees. County growth in population and housing is related to impact fees only indirectly through its effect on stress. That is, a more rapid rate of growth in a county is related to increased stress, which in turn is related to increased likelihood of using impact fees. A higher county growth rate also leads to higher probability of the utility coordinating its expansions with the comprehensive plan of the community, which in turn leads to higher likelihood of using im-

pact fees. Thus, three of the four indicators of need are related, either directly or indirectly, to increased likelihood of using impact fees. The degree of utility system expansion between 1980 and 1986, however, does not seem to lead to the adoption of impact fees. That is an unexpected finding. It seems to indicate that actual expansions of the system are not as important as stress and increases in amounts of water and wastewater being treated in stimulating adoption of new financing techniques.

Utility Characteristics

The more positive the staff's attidude toward new ideas and the greater the agency's coordination of utility extensions with the comprehensive or land use plan, the more likely it is to be using impact fees. In addition, the education of the director, an indication of professionalism, has an indirect positive effect on the use of impact fees through its effect on planning within the utility. That in turn affects coordination with the comprehensive and land use plan which in turn affects impact fee adoption.

Table 2–6. Relative Effects of the Water and Sewer Need Indicators and Utility Agency Capability Indicators in Explaining Adoption of Impact Fees: Standardized Regression Coefficients*

Explanatory Factors	Intermediate Dependent Variables			Ultimate Dependent Variables
	Internal Planning	Coord. with Comprehensive Plans	Coord. with Development Controls	Adoption of Impact Fees
Need				
Population growth	.07	(.29)	.04	−.07
Rate of increase in water/sewer treated	.16	.05	−.16	(.31)
System stress	−.08	−.03	.14	(.28)
System expansion	.10	.04	−.04	−.09
Utility/Governmental Characteristics				
Type of government (special district)	.06	−(.22)	−(.42)	−.05
Number of employees	.38	.65	−.14	.16
Staff's attitude toward new ideas	.06	−.06	.03	(.20)
Director's education	(.36)	.11	.00	.15
Director's age	.04	−.07	−.10	−.15
Utility (internal) planning	—	(.30)	(.41)	.08
Coordination with comprehensive plan	—	—	—	(.29)
Coordination with land use control	—	—	—	−.04
Florida (vs. other states)	.14	−.16	−(.29)	.19
Centralization of decision making	.08	.14	.06	−.03
Size of w/s service area population	−.32	−.58	.20	.34
R^2 (adjusted)	.19	.28	.28	.32
F-ratio	2.57	3.23	3.31	3.24
Statistical signif. level	0.001	0.001	0.001	0.000

* Circled standardized coefficients are statistically significant at .05 level or better.

Thus planning—both the utility's internal planning and its coordination with the community's comprehensive plan—is positively correlated with the adoption of impact fees. We will have more to say on the tie to planning later.

Path coefficients for a number of the other utility characteristics that we expected to influence impact fee adoption are in the direction hypothesized, but they are not statistically sig-nificant. Those include the type of utility (i.e., whether the utility is a special district), the number of employees,[8] the age of the director, the coordination with land use controls, centralization of decision making, and being in the state of Florida.

Being in the state of Florida, which obviously is strongly related unilaterally to the use of impact fees (see Figure 2-1), drops out of the model once we control for growth rate, stress, the rate of increase in water or sewage treated, and the level of coordination with the comprehensive plan, all of which tend to be higher in Florida than in the other southeastern states. Our conclusion is that it is not the state of Florida per se, but its rapid growth and its mandated local planning that make impact fees more common in Florida than in other states.

PLANNING AND IMPACT FEES

Planning internal to a utility and coordination of water and sewer extensions with the comprehensive land use plan are positively related to the adoption of impact fees. Thus it is useful to explore what utilities in the Southeast are doing in those two arenas.

We measured the degree of internal planning with the three indicators listed in Table 2-7. A majority of the utilities are using each of the three indicator components. Internal planning proved to be a significant influence on coordination with land use plans and on adoption of impact fees.[9] That finding suggests that if policymakers would like to see increased coordination with land use planning take place, capacity building for internal planning as well as external coordination would be a fruitful approach. That is, improvement in the utilities' internal planning is a way to improve coordination of water and sewer extension with comprehensive land use planning and the rational basis for impact fees. Programs to provide increased educational opportunities for utility directors and utility personnel should lead not only to improved internal planning but should also pay dividends in terms of increased coordination with land use planning.

We used four indicators to gauge the current

Table 2-7. Internal Planning Among Southeastern Water and Sewer Utilities

Planning Indicator	Type of Utility (%)		
	Municipal	County	Special District
1. Use of population, land use, or buildout projections in planning for or thinking about future service areas	73%	85%	74%
2. Use of capital improvements program document that specifies needed capital improvement projects	73%	62%	54%
3. Use of formal written out objectives, policies, or rating factors to guide decisions about water and sewer extensions	63%	62%	54%
UPLAN Scale (Sum of 1–3 above) (mean)	2.1	2.1	1.9
Number of planning elements used			
None	7%	8%	15%
One	20%	23%	23%
Two	31%	19%	15%
Three	42%	50%	46%

level of coordination of water and sewer extensions with land use plans:

1. Use of comprehensive land use plans as a source of goals or policies for water and sewer extension decisions.

2. Support of the development pattern specified in the land use plan as a goal of extension policies.

3. Designation of future water and sewer service areas in land use plans.

4. Refusal to approve requested extension of water and sewer service because it would have been inconsistent with the land use plan.

In general, utilities do less coordination with the land use plan than they do internal planning. On average, municipal utilities in the sample were pursuing 1.0 of those four avenues of coordination; county utilities, 1.4; but special districts only 0.4. See Table 2–8. A majority of the municipal and county utilities (but not the special districts) were trying to support local land use goals through extension policy. Also a majority of the county utilities and 41 percent of the municipalities had used land use plans as a source of goals or policies for water and sewer extension decisions, but only 14 percent of the special districts did so. It appears that the use of special districts stifles coordination of water and sewer extension decisions with zoning and subdivision controls, and that policymakers interested in coordination between utility extensions and land use controls should work for state legislation that makes it difficult to incorporate new districts or that makes it easier for cities and counties to undertake utility extensions, so that there is less temptation in the first place to use special districts simply to solve the fiscal aspects of water and sewer infrastructure.

Improved planning capability and practice for utilities, together with improved coordination with utilities by community land use planners, should lead to improved overall growth management. Such improved plannng and coordination can be used to benefit communities in three ways. First, land use planning can provide an improved rationale for impact fees. Land use plans establish community goals and evidence of legislative intent to justify impact fees. Planners can also provide improved analyses and projections of employment and housing that address not only the amounts of land-using activities and resulting demands on

Table 2–8. Coordination of Water and Sewer Extensions with Comprehensive Land Use Plans

	Type of Utility (%)		
Indicator	Municipal	County	Special District
1. Comprehensive land use plan is used as a source of goals or policies to guide water and sewer extension decisions	41%	76%	14%
2. One goal of extension policy is to support the development pattern specified in comprehensive land use plan	61%	69%	43%
3. Future water and sewer service areas are designated in comprehensive land use plan	27%	38%	22%
4. Since 1980, service extension requested has been refused because it was inconsistent with comprehensive land use plan	20%	5%	6%
COMPLAN Scale (Sum of 1–4 above) (mean)	1.0	1.4	0.5
Number of COMPLAN elements:			
None	44%	33%	68%
One	24%	29%	16%
Two	22%	8%	12%
Three or four	11%	29%	4%

utilities but also their locational distribution and infrastructure utilization patterns. Second, land use controls provide excellent vehicles for implementing impact fees. Third, utility extension policy in general, and impact fee policies in particular, can improve the implementation of land plans, *if* utility policy and land use policy are coordinated. If not coordinated they can frustrate land use planning.

SUMMARY AND CONCLUSIONS

The survey findings and interpretations in this chapter suggest that the use of water and sewer impact fees is higher, at least in the southeastern United States, than the evidence in the literature has suggested. It is not just in Florida that impact fees and similar policies are becoming relatively common, although they are much more common there, but also in the remainder of the region. That is especially so in areas that are growing at a rapid rate and that are experiencing stress on existing water and sewer systems and areas where utility directors and staffs have the capability to innovate.

Our attempt to identify factors that explain variation in use of impact fees was moderately successful. The statistical findings suggest that both the need for alternative water and sewer extension financing mechanisms and the capacity of the utility agency contribute to the likelihood of adoption. Where there is more rapid growth, a higher rate of increase in water and sewage being treated, and more stress due to demand that exceeds the capacity of the existing system, then there is increased likelihood that impact fees will be adopted. Our findings also suggest that when a utility has a better educated director, a staff more receptive to new ideas, more internal planning, and better coordination of water and sewer extensions with land use plans, it is in a better position to formulate and implement impact fees. Table 2–9 contains the sum of direct and indirect effects of the variables we originally hypothesized would influence the adoption of impact fees. The variables are listed in order of their total direct and indirect effects on adoption of impact fees.

We have argued for increased collaboration

Table 2–9. Total Effects (Direct and Indirect) of Variables on Adoption of Impact Fees

Variable	Sum of Direct and Indirect Effects
Rate of increase in water/sewage treated	.31
Coordination with comprehensive/land use plan	.29
Stress on water/sewer system	.28
Staff attitude toward innovation	.20
Rate of growth in population and housing	.15
Internal planning in utility agency	.09
Special district (vs. city or county agency)	− .07
Director's education	.03
System expansion	none
Number of employees	none
Coordination with land use controls	none
Florida	none
Size of population in service area	none
Centralization of decision making	none

between utility planning and land use planning in order to improve the overall benefits of each to the community. Such coordination can improve the equity, efficiency, legality, and effectiveness of impact fees with respect to a broader range of goals, beyond the fiscal objectives that predominate now. At the same time, coordination can establish impact fees as an effective component of an overall growth management system that accommodates growth in an efficient and equitable manner.

Authors' Note

The research reported in this paper was supported, in part, by funds provided by the U.S. Geological Survey through Grant No. 14-08-0001-G1134. We would like to acknowledge that support and also the assistance of the University of North Carolina Water Resources Institute.

Notes

1. The survey methods carefully followed the procedures prescribed by Dillman (1978) for maximizing response rates in mail surveys.

2. It also is clear that the use of impact fees and similar policies is higher for water and sewer infrastructure than for other public facilities (Amborski et al. 1987; Frank and Downing 1987). There are two reasons for that. First, water and sewer are typically enterprise functions of local government, and governments can easily limit service to those who pay user fees. Second, because of public health restrictions, land development cannot proceed without connection to water and sewerage systems. Thus local governments have a longer history of requiring developers to install water and sewer infrastructure or pay fees in lieu thereof than is the case for parks, roads, and other public facilities.

3. That is the proportion of utilities reporting that, within their service area, local government used "land development ordinances that require developers to pay an 'impact fee' based, in part, on the costs of water or sewerage service required by their projects."

4. Frank, Lines, and Downing used an unusual two-stage procedure in their 1984 survey. They asked the 1,718 public works directors in municipalities of 15,000 people or more to report whatever agency they knew was charging a sewer impact fee, their own included. In the second stage, a questionnaire was sent to all 277 agencies nominated. There was an 81 percent response rate and 190 communities across the country were found to be using sewer impact fees. Using that procedure, the authors "feel confident that the impact fees located in this survey constitute a substantial proportion of the unknown universe of sewer impact fees (otherwise numerous exceptions would be known by us) and that the procedure gave each element of that universe an equal probability of being nominated and surveyed." In any case, their methodology was different from the more orthodox sampling and survey procedure used in our study, and therefore those findings are not strictly comparable to ours.

5. There seems to be no relationship between the use of impact fees and the use of other one-time charges. That is, the use of impact fees is just as likely for utilities that use other one-time charges as for utilities that do not use those other charges.

6. While these findings reinforce the argument that water and sewer extension and system expansion are very much dependent on private financing through fees and exactions, they should not be too surprising. Exactions, as noted in our introduction, have long been a part of water and sewer extension policy. The 1961 *Municipal Yearbook*, for example, reported that 79 percent of 673 cities in a survey required developers to pay full cost on laterals to new subdivisions. A 1969 survey by the International City Managers Association (Howe and Pigeon 1970) reported that it was not uncommon for cities to place the entire burden for sewer laterals on the individual user, either by requiring private sector provision or by charging special benefit assessments or connection fees. That same survey reported that the use of connection fees was highest in the South (87 percent).

7. For a discussion of the role of stress in producing changes in behavior of organizations, see Williams 1980.

8. Actually, when looked at in isolation of the other variables in the model, the number of employees in the agency is strongly associated with the adoption of impact fees. Where the number of employees is 20 or fewer, only 23 percent of the agencies use impact fees. Where the number of employees is greater than 40, almost half (49 percent) use impact fees.

9. Our data in that regard are not conclusive, however, because of the static nature of the indicators of utility planning and coordination with comprehensive land use planning. That is, we do not know for a fact that the internal planning preceded coordination with land use planning or adoption of impact fees, but only that they vary with one another. Thus it is plausible that the adoption of impact fees, for example, demonstrated the need for better internal planning and coordination with the community's land use plan.

References

Amborski, David P., Jane H. Lillydahl, Arthur C. Nelson, Timothy V. Ramis, Antero Rivasplata, and Steven R. Schell. 1987. State and Provincial Approaches to Development Impact Fees: California, Florida, Oregon, Colorado, and Ontario. Paper presented at the *Journal of the American Planning Association* Symposium on Impact Fees, National Planning Conference of APA, New York City (April).

Bingham, Richard D. 1976. *The Adoption of Innovation by Local Government*. Lexington, Mass.: D. C. Heath, Lexington Books.

Dillman, Don A. 1987. *Mail and Telephone Surveys: The Total Design Method*. New York: John Wiley.

Downing, Paul B. and James E. Frank. 1983. Recreation Impact Fees: Characteristics and Current Usage. *National Tax Journal* 37: 447–90.

Dye, Thomas R. and John S. Robey. 1980. Politics versus

Economics: Development of the Literature on Policy Determination. In *The Determinants of Public Policy,* edited by Thomas R. Dye and Virginia Gray. Lexington, Mass.: D. C. Heath, Lexington Books.

Florida Advisory Committee on Intergovernmental Relations. 1986. *Impact Fees in Florida.* Tallahassee, Fla.: Florida ACIR.

Frank, James E., Elizabeth R. Lines, and Paul B. Downing. 1985a. *Community Experience with Sewer Impact Fees: A National Study.* Tallahassee, Fla.: Policy Sciences Program, Florida State University.

Frank, James E., Paul B. Downing, and Elizabeth R. Lines. 1985b. A National Survey of Sewer Impact Fees. *Journal of the Water Pollution Control Federation* 57: November, 1055–1061.

Frank, James E. and Paul B. Downing. 1987. Patterns of Impact Fee Usage. Paper presented at *Journal of the American Planning Association* Symposium on Impact Fees, National Planning Conference of APA, New York City (April).

Howe, George F. and Carol A. Pigeon. 1970. Sewer Services and Charges. *Urban Data Services Report.* Washington, D.C.: International City Management Association.

Jenne, Kurt. 1984. Rational Capital Budgeting in Local Government Settings: The Effect of Situational Factors in Capital Investment Decision Making. Ph.D. dissertation, University of North Carolina at Chapel Hill, Department of City and Regional Planning.

Sabatier, Paul A. 1977. Regulatory Policymaking: Toward a Framework of Analysis. *Natural Resources Journal* 17: July, 415–60.

Snyder, Thomas P. and Michael A. Stegman, with contributions by David H. Moreau. 1986. *Paying for Growth: Using Development Fees to Finance Infrastructure.* Washington, D.C.: Urban Land Institute.

Tabors, Richard D., Michael H. Shapiro, and Peter P. Rogers. 1976. *Land Use and the Pipe.* Lexington, Mass.: D. C. Heath, Lexington Books.

Van Meter, Donald S. and Charles E. Van Horn. 1975. The Policy Implementation Process: A Conceptual Framework. *Administration and Society* 6, 4: 445–88.

Williams, Bruce A. 1980. Organizational Determinants of Policy Change. In *The Determinants of Public Policy,* edited by Thomas R. Dye and Virginia Gray. Lexington, Mass.: D. C. Heath, Lexington Books.

3

Paying for Growth: Community Approaches to Development Impact Fees

MARK P. BARNEBEY
TOM MACROSTIE
ARTHUR C. NELSON
GARY J. SCHOENNAUER
GEORGE T. SIMPSON
JAN WINTERS

The supply of federal, state, and local revenues available to pay for growth is dwindling. Faced with that fact and the need to pay for growth nonetheless, communities have had to come up with new ways to do so, often by assessing fees on new development. They usually have had little clear legislative guidance in the process, and—with few exceptions—only vague court precedents (Lillydahl 1987; Schell and Ramis 1987; Simpson 1987; Winters 1987; Kreger, Orlin, and Riesett 1987; Heath 1987). This contribution to the impact fee discussion reviews how four communities—San Jose and San Diego, California, Loveland, Colorado, and Manatee County, Florida—came to embrace development impact fees, and how the communities administer those fees. We selected those communities for review because of their diversity and their aggressiveness in finding ways to pay for growth. They are similar in two major

respects. First, prior to adopting impact fees, all the communities already exacted land dedications for parks or in-lieu fees from developers and they required developers to install all on-site facilities. Second, virtually all the communities view their brand of impact fees as ways to pay for growth and intend no hindrance to growth. But there the commonalities end. Each community approaches the problem of paying for growth differently, no doubt because of legal differences, but also because of different growth patterns, community attitudes, and staff perspectives (Barnebey 1987; MacRostie and Schoennauer 1987; Simpson 1987; Winters 1987). Since Lillydahl et al. (1988) discuss the statutory differences among the states, we concentrate here on how the different growth patterns, community attitudes, and staff directions affected the formulation of impact fee systems in the communities.

We caution, however, that other communities should not tailor their impact fee ordinances after those we review here since, as Stewart (1988) warns, the circumstances of each community dictate the form and content of any impact fee program. While the problem of paying for growth may be substantially the same among communities, and while impact fees may be an important way to pay for growth, the manner in which communities design, administer, and refine fee programs will be different. Thus, a program used in one community cannot be applied to the next, at least not without risking political dissatisfaction with the cloned system. We conclude this chapter with some words of advice to those who are considering impact fees for their communities.

EVOLUTION OF IMPACT CHARGES IN SAN JOSE

San Jose, California, may have more experience with impact fees than any other North American city. It is a low-density, suburban city occupying 170 square miles on the level Santa Clara Valley floor. Until the 1970s, it was largely a bedroom community for the Silicon Valley. Citing the 1980 population census, community leaders declared San Jose to be the "fastest-growing large city in America" (MacRostie and Schoennauer 1987). During the 1970s, San Jose's population grew by 37 percent, from 460,000 to 630,000. The city's population was a mere 95,000 in 1950. In response to growth pressures and changing political attitudes toward paying for growth, San Jose has evolved a system of impact fees, taxes, and other charges over the past two decades. The progress of that evolution is illuminating.

During the 1950s and 1960s, city residents readily embraced a growth ethic. Voters approved citywide bonds to finance new parks, libraries, sewer systems, streets, and bridges. The city limited developer exactions to on-site sewer lines, streets, street lights, fire hydrants, and street trees. San Jose did assess impact fees, however, for sewer and drainage facilities, beginning in the late 1950s, to finance leap-frog development.

The political environment began to change in the late 1960s, however. Overcrowded schools, congested roads, dwindling open spaces, and inadequate parks and libraries reduced San Jose's livability. The electorate became less willing to pay for new facilities they perceived as primarily benefiting new development. Bond issues began to fail. In 1970, the city drew an urban service line around an "urban area" beyond which the city would not annex or provide municipal services.

The first true impact charges came in 1972 when the city imposed property conveyance and construction taxes. The taxes, authorized under California statute, help finance parks, libraries, fire stations, public works storage yards, and emergency communications facilities. To relate the taxes collected to the area assessed, the city spends at least 48 percent of the revenues for parks within the city council district where contributing development is located. The conveyance tax is $3.30 on each $1,000 of valuation when real property is sold or transferred. The construction tax now levies $150 for each single-family dwelling, $75 for each unit in a multiple-family building, and 8 cents per square foot of nonresidential building constructed.

During the mid-1970s, San Jose residents voted for city-imposed school impact fees to finance new capital facilities at overcrowded schools in the 19 separate school districts serving the community. The fees pay for portable classrooms and, sometimes, for school buses to transport children to less crowded schools. School facility impact fees range from $250 to $2,500 and average about $1,000. Beginning in 1987, however, California statutes allow all school districts to assess up to $1.50 per square foot of new residential space and 25 cents per square foot of new nonresidential space.

Also during the 1970s, roads became heavily congested. In response, the city adopted a policy in its General Plan 1975–1990 that prohibited approval of any development that would cause unacceptable congestion at nearby intersections. Development could proceed, however, if the developer mitigated the congestion. Mitigation fees are really a form of negotiated exaction since they depend on project location and current traffic conditions.

A building and structures tax, adopted in 1976, partially addresses the larger problem of improving citywide streets. The tax is 1.75 percent of the valuation of new residential, 1.5 percent of new commercial, and 1.0 percent of new industrial developments. Since the tax pays only about half the cost of increasing arterial and collector capacity to acceptable levels, the city had to turn to other revenue sources. In a display of masterful timing only a few days before the effective date of Proposition 13, city officials adopted a commercial-residential-mobile home park (CRIMP) tax to fund the remaining portion of the street improvement program. The CRIMP tax is an additional 2.75 percent on new residential valuation and 3.0 percent on new commercial valuation, making total road impact taxes on those kinds of new development equal to 4.5 percent of valuation. (San Jose does not apply CRIMP to new industrial development valuation in an effort to en-

courage economic development and thereby broaden the city's tax base.)

Proposition 13, which rolled property tax assessments back and reduced city revenues, forced the city to change a number of impact charging policies. Since Proposition 13 reduced funds for maintenance and staffing of community facilities, the city decided to shift up to 10 percent of the construction and conveyance taxes to pay for those purposes as well as to pay for remodeling, renovating, and upgrading existing parks, libraries, and fire stations. Since Proposition 13 allowed for cost-recovery user fees and since the state legislature later defined connection fees as user fees, the city increased its sewer treatment plant connection fee in the early 1980s from $23 per single-family dwelling to $780 (with similar increases for other kinds of development).

Table 3–1 illustrates the variety of impact charges, and Table 3–2 indicates the total those charges cost a typical single-family dwelling. The local government applies the assessments uniformly throughout the city, although they vary by school district. San Jose's impact charges apparently have not slowed development, as the city probably will grow by the estimated 135,000 new residents projected for between 1980 and 1990. City planners observe that while individual developers sometimes complain about the high charges, they also recognize that the city needs those revenues to help pay for growth. More to the point, planners and developers alike recognize that the political climate in San Jose no longer tolerates a situation where the community at large bears the burden of paying for growth. Calls by candidates for city council for "paying as you grow" and "managed growth" reflect grassroots support for the impact charges.

Table 3–1. Projected Development Impact Fee and Tax Revenues for San Jose, FY 1986–1987[a]

Title	Rate	Projected 1986–1987 revenues	Use of funds
Commercial, residential, mobile home park construction tax	Commercial: 3% of building permit valuation Residential: 2¾% of building permit valuation Mobile home park: $950/lot	$9,460,000	Arterial and major collector streets
Building and structures tax	Commercial: 1½% of building permit valuation Industrial: 1% of building permit valuation Residential: 1¾% of building valuation	8,110,000	Arterials and major collector streets
Construction tax	Nonresidential: $.08/sq. ft. Residential: $75–150/DU	1,010,000	Library, fire, parks, public works, and parks maintenance facilities, communications facilities
Conveyance tax	$1.65 for each $500 valuation	10,300,000	Same as construction tax
Sewage treatment plant connection fee	Nonresidential: $3.07 per gallon per day of sewage flow capacity required plus additional fees for specific treatment demands Residential: $780/unit for single family, $438/unit for all other residential	3,000,000	Sewage treatment plant revenue bond debt service
Sanitary sewer connection fee	Nonresidential: $1,380/first 10 acres, $640/area in excess of ten acres Residential: $1,480/acre plus $146/unit for multiple family over seven units	1,380,000	Capital improvements to sanitary sewer system
Storm drain connection fee	Nonresidential: $1,815/first 10 acres, $865/area in excess of ten acres Residential: $1,215/acre for single family, $1,815/acre for multiple family	1,280,000	Capital improvements to storm drain system
Total		$34,540,000	

a. This table does not include school impact fees and water connection fees. School impact fees accrue directly to independent school districts and private utility companies provide water service.

SAN DIEGO'S COMMUNITY FACILITIES BENEFIT ASSESSMENT PROGRAM

In 1979 San Diego adopted a "Progress Guide and General Plan" that divided the city into urbanized, planned urbanizing, and future urbanizing areas. The urbanized area included the already built-up urban area. The planned urbanizing area included those lands that were partially developed or where developers and planners envisioned new communities. The city did not recommend developing the future urbanizing area for at least 20 years. The most significant element of that plan, however, was limiting the use of the city's fully financed capital improvement program to the urbanized area. The plan shifted responsibility for financing infrastructure in the planned urbanizing area to new development.

The city council in 1980 adopted a policy for developing the planned urbanizing area. In part, that policy requires preparation of a plan for installing and financing public facilities in proposed new communities. The city planning

Figure 3–1. San Diego's North University City Facilities Benefit Assessment Area (FBA)

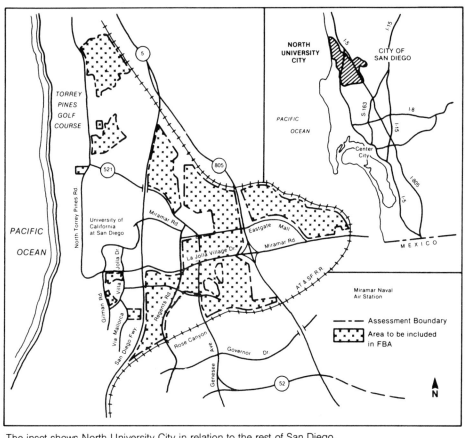

The inset shows North University City in relation to the rest of San Diego.

staff and their consultants prepare "community financing plans," comprising five principal elements. First, they estimate the future population, the number of dwelling units by type, and the number of acres of nonresidential land to be developed in the new community. Second, they prepare an inventory of the facilities needed to build the community out. The inventory includes estimates of the land acquisition and construction costs of those facilities. Third, they develop a schedule of the year or years in which each facility must be built. Fourth, they prepare an analysis recommend-

ing the best, most reasonable, available, and fiscally viable method of financing each facility. Last, the policy requires a cost–revenue analysis to show that the overall facilities installation and financing program has fiscal integrity.

To finance infrastructure in new communities, the city adopted the facilities benefit assessment (FBA) ordinance in 1980. The FBA ordinance allows city installation of streets, water, sewer, drainage, fire, school, police, traffic signaling, and other public improvements. The city does not pay for these facilities from gen-

Table 3–2. Development Impact Fees for a Typical Single-Family Detached Home[a]

Title	Per-unit cost
Commercial, residential, mobile home park construction tax	$1,284
Building and structures tax	816
Construction tax	150
Conveyance tax	330
School impact fee	250–2,500
Sewage treatment plant	780
Sanitary sewer connection fee	400
Storm drain connection fee	270
Total	$4,280–$6,530

a Based upon a typical 50-lot subdivision with 40 foot × 90 foot minimum lot size and 1,100 square foot single-family detached/zero lot line dwelling unit, which costs $100,000. Not included in this table are cost-recovery processing fees (zoning, environmental review, building permit/inspection, public works permit/inspection and on sites), which would total $1,344.00 for this typical single-family home.

eral obligation bonds but from lump sum payments collected from developments. The fees are based on the percentage of the overall planned community development for which the city issues building permits; and the funds pay for facilities as scheduled in the community plan—or sooner, if needed. Since many facilities are not scheduled for construction until five, ten, or more years in the future, the city comingles funds collected for parks, libraries, fire stations, storm drains, and freeway interchanges and uses them to pay for facilities that need construction earlier. Facilities built later are financed from funds collected for facilities that already have been built. While funds are not explicitly earmarked in separate accounts, the city does have a schedule of the projects for which it theoretically collects the funds and when specific facilities would have to be built.

The fee formula is based on "equivalent dwelling unit" (EDU) factors assigned for each land use activity that receives benefits from the facility. The formula bases transportation EDU factors on trip generation for single- and multiple-family projects, and for commercial and industrial acres; it bases park EDUs on population density for different types of residential projects. It is more difficult to assign EDUs for facilities such as fire stations and libraries. The formula assigns EDUs for those types of facilities to proposed development and multiplies by the cost per EDU. A minicomputer program determines the cost per EDU considering the year of construction, inflation, interest earnings (on accumulated funds), facility costs, and cash flow requirements. The program generates revenue–expenditure information so that officials can protect against negative cash flow.

In 1982, the city council approved North University City, the first five FBAs now operating (Figure 3–1). That community consists of more than 5,500 acres and had about 6,000 dwelling units at the time of FBA approval. The community plan projected development of an additional 16,000 dwelling units, 100 acres of commercial uses, and 600 acres of industrial uses by the end of the century. More than $54 million in public facilities was needed to support community buildout (Table 3–3). Since subdivision exactions would cover about half of the cost, the balance had to be financed from the FBA schedule. Facilities benefit assessments are $2,649 per single-family unit, $1,854 per multiple-family unit, $66,986 per commercial acre, and $16,078 per industrial acre in 1988 (Table 3–4), with increases scheduled to reflect annual inflation. The city successfully defended the arrangement through a two-year court battle.

The FBA approach has considerable political support, as the electorate supports politicians who shift the burden of paying for growth from existing to new development. In fact, the

Table 3–3. North University City—FBA Projects

Project		*Year of need	Cost (FY1985)
Number	Description		
Transportation improvements			
3.	Genesee Avenue (from Interstate 5 to Regents Road): Widen to 6-lane major with median	1992	$ 350,000
4.	Nobel Drive (from Towne Centre Road to "New Street"): Construct 4-lane primary arterial	1988	900,000
5.	Nobel Drive (from "New Street" to Interstate 805): 6-lane major street with transition	1988	860,000
10.	Regents Road from Novel Drive to Berino Court): 4-lane primary arterial	1988	260,000
18.	Regents Road (bridge over AT&SF railroad and portion of the floodplain): 4-lane	1990	7,336,000
20.	Nobel Drive @ I-5: Widen overcrossing; provide left-turn lanes, bike lanes, and sidewalk; construct new on/off ramps; construct ramp traffic signals. Acquire new right-of-way	1986, 1987	3,414,000
21.	Nobel Drive @ I-805: Construct new interchange; construct overcrossing plus left-turn lane, bike lane, and sidewalk; construct ramp traffic signals. Acquire new right-of-way	1988	4,946,000
22.	Nobel Drive (from Interstate 805 to Miramar Road): 4-lane major street	2000	1,000,000
23.	Miramar Road (from Interstate 805 to Eastgate Mall): Widen existing to 6-lane primary arterial	1985	500,000
24.	Genesee Ave. @ I-5; Widen overcrossing to 4 lanes, plus left-turn lanes, bike lane, etc.	1992	1,769,000
25.	Now Project #47		
26.	Various traffic signals (31):	1985–95	900,548
30.	Genesee Avenue (from North Torrey Pines Road to I-5 bridge): Widen to 6-lane primary arterial with median	1993	350,000
31.	Now Project #48		
33.	Miramar Street (Cooks Road from new unnamed street to Eastgate Mall): 4-lane major street and undercrossing of La Jolla Village Drive	1999	3,490,000
34.	Eastgate Mall (from Towne Centre Drive to Miramar Road): Widen existing to 4-lane collector	1993	400,000
38.	This project concerns La Jolla Colony Drive, I-5/Gilman interchange to Bren Loop Road; construct 4-lane major street to 4-lane primary arterial	1985	262,952
40.	La Jolla Village Drive (and Villa La Jolla Drive): Free right-turn lanes, 6 through lanes, pedestrian bridge	1998	701,000
41.	La Jolla Village Drive and Regents Road: Separate right-turn lanes	1990	140,000
43.	Lebon Drive and Nobel Drive: Separate right-turn lanes	1996	40,000
45.	Genesee Avenue and Nobel Drive: Separate right-turn lanes	1997	120,000
46.	I-5 and La Jolla Village Drive: Reduce width of curbed median; widen overcrossing to 6 through lanes plus sidewalk, widen off-ramps	1986	1,284,000
47.	La Jolla Village Drive: Widen to 6-lane major from North Torrey Pines to I-805 (Was Project #25)	1985	1,400,000
48.	Genesee Avenue: Construct raised median between Nobel Drive and AT&SF railroad crossing (Was Project #31)	1985	160,000
49.	Support personnel to up-date University City Community Plan	1986	45,000
	Total transportation FBA improvements		$30,729,500
Park and recreation FBA projects			
27.	Regents Road: Site acquisition, design, and development for Doyle Community Park	1988–89	$ 2,175,000
28.	Regents Road: Recreation building	1992	1,200,000
29.	Nobel Park: Site acquisition and development	1993–95	7,500,000
	Total park and recreation FBA projects		$10,875,000
	Total North University FBA projects		$41,604,500

Table 3–4. North University City Facilities Benefit Assessment Cash Flow

FY	SFDU	MFDU	CAC	IAC	$/SFDU	$/MFDU	$/CAC	$/IAC	FBA income plus interest	FBA expenditures	Net balance
											$3,350,000
1985	100	1000	30.0	40.0	$2,084	$1,458	$52,692	$12,647	$4,166,065	$2,368,500	5,147,565
1986	100	1500	30.0	100.0	2,229	1,561	56,380	13,532	6,332,173	1,685,250	9,794,488
1987	68	1200	10.0	100.0	2,430	1,701	61,455	14,750	5,313,308	4,028,400	11,079,396
1988	0	1200	10.0	100.0	2,649	1,854	66,986	16,078	5,411,286	9,039,980	7,450,703
1989	0	1200	10.0	70.0	2,887	2,021	73,014	17,525	5,302,903	1,238,106	11,515,500
1990	0	1000	7.2	50.0	3,147	2,203	79,586	19,102	4,478,006	12,396,545	3,596,961
1991	0	1000	0.0	40.0	3,430	2,401	86,748	20,821	3,670,069	1,885,045	5,381,984
1992	0	1000	0.0	30.0	3,739	2,617	94,556	22,695	3,703,790	6,216,138	2,869,636
1993	0	1000	0.0	18.8	4,075	2,853	103,066	24,737	3,729,424	968,221	5,630,840
1994	0	900	0.0	0.0	4,442	3,109	112,341	26,964	3,468,726	938,098	8,161,467
1995	0	900	0.0	0.0	4,842	3,389	122,452	29,390	4,034,834	92,957	12,103,344
1996	0	900	0.0	0.0	5,278	3,694	133,473	32,036	4,521,656	4,202,646	12,422,354
1997	0	700	0.0	0.0	5,753	4,027	145,485	34,919	4,072,908	3,202,825	13,292,436
1988	0	700	0.0	0.0	6,270	4,389	158,579	38,062	4,176,152	8,249,180	9,219,408
1999	0	700	0.0	0.0	6,835	4,784	172,851	41,487	3,882,485	11,579,851	1,522,043
2000	0	604	0.0	0.0	7,450	5,215	188,408	45,221	3,277,384	3,718,674	1,080,753
Total	268	15504	97.2	548.8	—	—	—	—	$72,891,169	$71,810,417	$1,080,752

city sees the FBA approach as both a growth management and a financing strategy, although it does not appear to have hampered San Diego's growth rate. Developers accept the program as necessary for growth. They also benefit from having some say in both the quality and the timing of the facilities for which their contributions are paying.

The program also encourages greater in-fill of the urbanized area. The city assesses no impact fees in the urbanized area, since it presumes that adequate facilities or means by which to improve facilities already exist. Still, development proposals for in-fill sites that require plan and zone changes remain subject to a variety of impact mitigation fees and negotiated exactions.

A CITYWIDE CAPITAL FACILITY COST RECOVERY SYSTEM

Unlike San Jose's impact charge program, which evolved over nearly two decades, or San Diego's FBA program, which the city applies only to planned communities in the planned urbanizing area, the capital facility cost recovery system that Loveland, Colorado, uses is a comprehensive impact fee system it adopted as one piece and applied citywide.

In 1981, the Loveland City Council asked voters to approve $40 million in bonds to pay for existing facility deficiencies and to create excess capacity for future growth. Voters rejected the proposal by an eight-to-one margin. In 1982, the council appointed an 18-member citizen advisory board, composed equally of citizens and development representatives, to consider a cost recovery approach to paying for growth. In giving the board direction, the council made what in retrospect were three very wise decisions. First, it required that service levels for new development be the same as those in the existing community. Second, it specified that all impact fees collected from such a system could benefit only new development. Third, it demanded that the fee system be clear and easily administered. The board met biweekly for 18 months.

The board also made an important policy choice early in its deliberations. It decided to mesh land use planning with facilities planning, which would maximize use of existing and projected facilities and prevent inefficient urban sprawl. The board estimated that such a move would save $200 million in future facility needs compared to the cost of serving existing development patterns. The board devoted most of its work to analyzing each community facility for its existing excess capacity, future capacity demands, timing of facility installation or expansion, and costs.

In concept, the cost recovery system requires new development to buy into the equity of existing or scheduled new community facilities. At the heart of the buy-in concept are the capital expansion fees (CEFs), which are one-time charges assessed at the building permit stage. The CEF is based on "vintage pricing," defined as the current replacement cost of the facility being financed from fees, plus "betterments" (which are improvements to the facility since its initial construction), less depreciation (if the facility is already in place). That formula assures the community that facilities will be maintained at constant levels of quality. The CEF also is based on the long-run marginal cost approach. That is, those who receive the services pay the true cost of providing them. Economists argue that marginal cost pricing induces maximum discipline and efficiency in the market for goods like public facilities and services. Long-run marginal cost pricing ensures that new residents will contribute toward long-term expansion and will pay a fee proportionate to the total number of new users the facility is expected to serve.

Figure 3–2. Steps in Estimating Capital Expansion Fees for a Facility

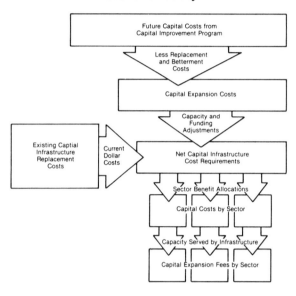

For each facility, the CEF calculation process follows five steps (Figure 3–2). First, estimate the capital costs of a major facility, then subtract the cost of replacing or modernizing the facility to maintain its usefulness to existing residents. The "adjusted" total capital cost become capital expansion cost. If the facility can serve more people than planners project will use it, the value of that "excess" capacity is subtracted from the capital expansion cost and the community as a whole pays for it. If the facility will serve fewer people than planners expect to use it at the end of the financing period, then the value of that "undercapacity" is added to the capital expansion cost. Any external funds that may be used for the facility are subtracted from the costs. The last step reveals the growth-related costs of the facility that the fees need to cover. The city then allocates growth-related costs by percent to the four major land use sectors: residential, commercial, industrial. The

Table 3–5. CEF Calculation Process: Library Example

Total capital costs from CIP	$3,354,000
Less: Replacement and betterment costs	
$\frac{32,700}{69,800} \times 3,354,000 =$	1,571,300
Capital expansion costs	$1,782,700
plus/minus: value of excess/under capacity	0
Expansion-related costs	$1,782,700
less: external funding sources	0
Net expansion-related costs	$1,782,700
times: portion of sector benefits (100% residential)	
Residential sector costs	$1,782,700
divided by: capacity in units	14,700
CEF fee per unit	$ 121

Source: City of Loveland 1983

proportion of the net growth-related costs of a facility attributable to each sector is divided by the total number of sector units (dwelling units or square feet) projected for addition to the community during the planning period. The city then establishes a fee.

An example of this procedure is the CEF calculated for the new library (see Table 3–5). The 1983 cost of a new 30,000-square-foot library designed to serve 69,800 residents is $3,354,000. The new library replaces an obsolete one that has served the 32,700 existing residents. Thus, the city considers 43 percent of the cost, or $1,571,300, as replacement or betterment costs that primarily benefit existing residents. The cost of expanding the capital facility over and above what is needed to serve existing residents is $1,782,700. Since the community plan assumes that about 37,000 people will move into the community within the planning period, and since the library is designed to serve only the current residents and the 37,000 new residents, the city does not adjust capital expansion costs by the value of remaining excess capacity or undercapacity at the end of the

planning period. Furthermore, the project probably will not receive external funds, so the plan calls for no additional adjustment. The net growth-related costs of the library are therefore $1,782,700. Since only occupants of residences are expected to use the library, the plan allocates 100 percent of the cost to the residential sector. The CEF per dwelling unit is $121. Using this approach, Table 3–6 shows the CEF schedule for all sectors and all facilities.

Some adjustments are made to the fees that particular developments might pay. For example, the city pays half the fees for low-income housing developments. In addition, the city reduces fees that it would otherwise assess on industrial projects by a factor for each new employee the firm adds to the city's payroll base after one year. The firm initially pays the fee, but the city partially or wholly reimburses it a year later.

Loveland's cost recovery system won the American Planning Association's innovative planning program award for 1986. Many communities across the nation are considering the approach today.

A NEW COUNTYWIDE COMPREHENSIVE IMPACT FEE PROGRAM

One of the newest comprehensive impact fee programs is the one that Manatee County, Florida, adopted in June 1986 for road, recreation, solid waste, and emergency medical facilities. Manatee County, between Tampa and Sarasota, grew in population from 97,000 to 171,000 between 1970 and 1985. It will approach 200,000 by 1990. Florida laws severely limit the ability of local governments to raise revenue to pay all the costs of growth (Lillydahl et al. 1988). To respond to growth, Florida has become a

Table 3–6. Capital Expansion Fees by Sector, Loveland, Colorado

Service	Residential (per unit)	Commercial (per sq. ft.)	Institutional (per sq. ft.)	Industrial (per acre)
Parks & recreation	$ 736	—	—	—
Fire protection	98	$0.07	$0.07	$ 746
Law enforcement	24	0.02	0.02	179
Library	121	—	—	—
Museum	58	—	—	—
General government	271	0.19	0.20	2,024
Streets	229	0.65	0.59	1,601
Total	$1,537	$0.93	$0.88	$4,550

Source: City of Loveland 1983

leading state in local government's use of innovative methods to finance new facilities. More than a decade of court struggle has resulted in a brand of development impact fees that is unique to that state but conceptually applicable to almost every other state and locality (Lillydahl et al. 1988; Stroud 1988; Nicholas and Nelson 1988).

The program assesses road impact fees on new development based on four factors: average trip length (ATL), daily trip generation rate (TG), roadway capacity per lane mile (Cap), and average cost of new roadway construction per lane mile (Cost). The maximum fee any development may have to pay is based on the formula:

$$\text{Maximum Fee} = \frac{\text{ATL} \times \text{TG}}{\text{Cap} \times 2} \times \text{Cost}.$$

The fee also is based on the Institute of Traffic Engineer's level of service C during the day and D during peak hours. Since average travel length ranges from 14.28 minutes in the built-up urban area to 49.08 minutes in the rural parts of the county, the program divides the county into four subareas for calculation purposes: urban, suburban, rural fringe, and rural (Figure 3–3). Cost is based on providing road facilities

Figure 3–3. Impact Fee Collection Districts in Manatee County, Florida

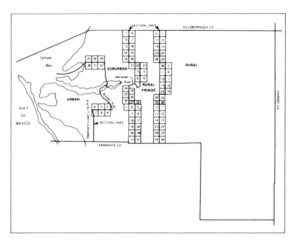

at service level C, which was set at 6,600 vehicles per day per lane mile; but that cost ranges from about $500,000 in the urban area to about $380,000 in the rural fringe and rural areas, due primarily to higher right-of-way costs in urban areas. The county applies a fee schedule based on the formula to 48 residential, commercial, industrial, and institutional uses.

The program adjusts the maximum fee downward according to three factors: a credit for funds received from state gasoline taxes used for new road construction, a capture and diversion multiplier, and a competitive factor multiplier. The credit attempts to account for double payments. About 8.5 cents per gallon of gasoline purchased in the county ultimately goes to build new roads. Thus, developments that increase traffic in the county also increase gasoline purchases and thereby increase revenues available for new road construction. Since the county receives revenues annually for a very long period, it calculates the present value of the stream of additional gasoline taxes over 25 years, using a discount rate of 9 percent, then reduces the maximum fee by that amount.

Capture and diversion factors lead to further fee adjustments. The program may double-count some trips to nonresidential destinations if it treats each stop along the way as a destination. Thus, one person's morning of shopping could be counted as multiple trips. For example, the county cited a study that showed that office development actually generates only 50 percent of the trips normally assigned to it. The figure falls to 20 percent for drive-in bank tellers. The maximum fee, then, is adjusted to that percentage.

The competitive factor adjustment was intended to keep Manatee County's road impact fees comparable to those of the neighboring and competing counties of Hillsborough (Tampa) to the north and Sarasota to the south. Still, locally vocal environmental and conservation groups argued that Manatee County should assess the full fees. As a compromise, the county commission kept the residential road impact fees at 100 percent, but reduced those for commercial, industrial, and institutional developments. For example, of the 16 commercial use categories, the county reduced 12 by at least 40 percent and the rest by about 75 percent.

Figure 3–4. The Six Public Facility Construction Districts in Manatee County, Florida

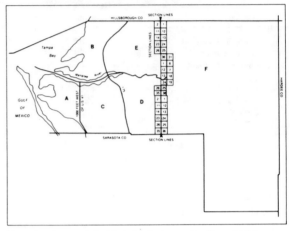

New development that locates in a construction district pays fees that are spent exclusively in that area.

To ensure that road impact fees benefit contributing development, the county earmarks fees for expenditure in one of six areas within which contributing development is located (Figure 3–4).

Other fees, collected on a countywide basis for solid waste, emergency medical services, and parks and recreation, are not expended on a district basis, however. For solid waste facilities, the county bases the impact fee on a capital facility recovery cost per daily pound of solid waste that various types of development generate. The generation rates are based on data that county consultants and the Florida Department of Environmental Regulation provide.

The county bases impact fees for emergency medical service facilities on the estimated per capita replacement costs of the existing system (including vehicles and equipment). It applies the fees only to residential developments, based on number of bedrooms; it bases assessments for hotel and motel rooms, and recreational vehicle park spaces on the occupancy rates for a two-bedroom single-family home.

The county also calculates park and recreation impact fees based on a cost recovery approach. It determines the replacement costs for 20 types of recreational facilities. Since both residents and tourists use many facilities, however, the county conducted a survey to determine the percent of those facilities that existing residents use. Residents accounted for only 18 percent of the use of beach facilities, for example. In contrast, the survey attributed more than 90 percent of the use of swimming pools and baseball fields to residents. After adjusting replacement costs for resident use, the county determined per capita replacement costs; it established an impact fee for new residential units by type. The county divided remaining costs by hotel/motel rooms and recreational vehicle spaces to determine the impact fee per new room or space. It collects no such impact fees for commercial, industrial, or institutional developments.

To take into consideration developments having nonaverage impacts, Manatee County accepts independent analysis of impacts in some situations.

WORDS OF ADVICE

For planners and public officials interested in designing development impact fee programs to pay for new facilities, we offer some words of advice: Use fairness, flexibility, innovation, and opportunism.

First, as the articles by Stroud (1988) and Nicholas and Nelson (1988) attest, there must be a strong sense that contributing development directly benefits from the fees it pays, even though the community as a whole may also benefit. Jurisdictions may accomplish that

goal by being sure that fees pay for specific facilities at specific locations or areas that the development would obviously use. San Jose accomplishes it by targeting many fees for expenditure within council districts where contributing development is located. San Diego expends fees collected within a planned community exclusively in that community. Manatee County expends road impact fees in six districts where contributing development is located. Loveland uses fees citywide, but that city is much smaller in both population and area than San Jose, San Diego, or Manatee County.

Second, fees must be grounded on some rational basis. Stroud (1988) and Nicholas and Nelson (1988) attest to that necessity. San Diego identifies the projected costs of all facilities for a planned community and derives unit costs from the analysis. Loveland's buy-in fee approach can essentially reimburse the community for excess capacity built previously but that new development is absorbing. The city also can use a capital facility cost recovery approach to estimate the per-unit value of existing facilities and thereby ascertain the funds necessary to expand those facilities or build new ones. In all cases, the community must assure contributing development that it will not use fees primarily to raise the quality of life for existing residents; that concern underlies Loveland's capital expansion fee formula (see the library CEF example). Perhaps the least rationally based program is San Jose's, where impact fees and other charges are not always clearly tied to specific facilities.

In most situations, several factors should affect the maximum impact fee that a governing body can charge. Such factors include the portion of the facility that existing residents will use most frequently, and the portion that nonresidents, such as tourists, will use. Factors may also include capture and diversion; Manatee County determined that only 50 percent of the trips generated by offices were actually uniquely attributable to the presence of the office. Fees must also be adjusted by the value of state, federal, and other nonlocal government funds available to help finance the facilities supported by fees. Finally, fees should be adjusted to reflect the taxes and other nonimpact fee payments that the contributing development may make over time and that would pay for the same facilities financed from fees. Nicholas and Nelson (1988) illuminate those concerns.

Flexibility in assessment, expenditure, and fulfilling other community policies also is necessary. Assessment flexibility can mean varying the payment amount to match the fee more precisely with the actual impact, or it can mean changing the timing of the fee. For example, Manatee County may accept a lower fee from a development if the development can submit evidence that the impact of the project will be less than that suggested in a standard formula. That allows for appropriate consideration of unique developments. Timing of payment also is important. Fee payment, whether at the development approval stage, building permit stage, occupancy permit stage, or on a phased development basis should assure local government of maximum revenues, but not at the risk of pricing development out of the market solely because of payment timing. Huffman et al. (1988) echo that concern.

Flexibility of expenditure is also important. Florida communities place impact fees in separate accounts earmarked for specific projects. Funds for various types of projects, such as roads, however, are comingled so that small amounts of fees can be pooled to pay for roads

needed earlier than other roads. San Diego's arrangement is even more flexible; that city comingles all impact fees and uses them to pay for different types of facilities as scheduled in the capital improvement program or otherwise needed.

Governments also must use flexibility in assessment to avoid contradicting other community policies. If a community wishes to encourage low-cost housing, it may reduce or waive impact fees for those projects, as Loveland does. If the community wishes to broaden its economic base by not discouraging industrial development, it may assess lower impact fees, as San Jose does, or reduce the fee in proportion to jobs added to the local economic base, as in Loveland.

Experience dictates that planners and other public officials must seize opportunities to assess impact fees. In San Jose, every time local revenues did not meet capital facility needs—whether because of Proposition 13 or electoral pressure—city officials invented an impact fee, tax, or other assessment to meet the need. In San Diego, capital financing limitations forced the city to divert all available public funds to the built-up area. But the city agreed to let outlying areas develop if developers paid the entire cost of new facilities. In Loveland, community opposition to bonds that would finance facilities primarily benefiting new development stimulated careful investigation of ways to equitably shift the burden to new development. When the city installed its capital facility cost recovery system, those same voters were so satisfied that new development would pay its appropriate share that they approved larger bond issues than those they earlier had rejected.

As a final word, however, impact fees are but

one tool available to local government to pay for growth. As the case studies suggest, most impact fees do not come close to paying for all the true costs of serving new development. Communities must continue to support many kinds of capital expansion through communitywide bond issues, maximum use of state and federal sources, and perhaps more liberal use of special assessment/benefit districts or user fees. But impact fees are here to stay, so long as communities do not abuse them.

References

Barnebey, Mark P. 1987. Impact Fees for Manatee County (Florida): The Long, Hard Road Taken. Paper presented to the Development Impact Fee Symposium, 1987 conference of the American Planning Association (April).

City of Loveland. 1983. Service Cost Recovery System: System Documentation. Loveland, Colo.: City of Loveland.

City of San Diego. 1979. Progress Guide and General Plan. San Diego, Calif.: City of San Diego.

———. 1980. Facilities Benefit Assessment Procedural Ordinance. San Diego, Calif.: City of San Diego.

———. 1982. North University City Facilities Benefit Assessment Area. San Diego, Calif.: City of San Diego.

County of Manatee. 1986. Ordinance 86-09. Bradenton, Fla.: Manatee County (Florida).

Heath, David C. 1987. Financing Growth in the Sunshine: The Impact Fee Experience in Orange County, Florida. Paper presented to the Development Impact Fee Symposium, 1987 conference of the American Planning Association (April).

Huffman, Forrest et al. 1988. Who Bears the Burden of Development Impact Fees? *Journal of the American Planning Association* 54, 1: 49–55.

Kreger, Glenn, Glenn S. Orlin, and Meg Riesett. 1987. The Impact Fee Ordinance of Montgomery County, Maryland. Paper presented to the Development Impact Fee Symposium, 1987 conference of the American Planning Association (April).

Lillydahl, Jane H. 1987. Impact Fees in Colorado: Economic, Political, and Legal Overview. Paper presented to the Development Impact Fee Symposium, 1987 conference of the American Planning Association (April).

——— et al. 1988. The Need for a Standard State Impact Fee Enabling Act. *Journal of the American Planning Association* 54, 1: 7–17.

MacRostie, Tom and Gary J. Schoennauer. 1987. Impact Fees in the Nation's Fastest Growing City. Paper presented to the Development Impact Fee Symposium, 1987 conference of the American Planning Association (April).

Manatee County Planning Department, 1983. Impact Assessments. Bradenton, Fla.: Manatee County (Florida).

Nicholas, James C. and Arthur C. Nelson. 1988. Determining the Appropriate Development Impact Fee Using the Rational Nexus Test. *Journal of the American Planning Association* 54, 1: 56–66.

San Jose Planning Department. 1976. The General Plan 1975–1990. San Jose, Calif.: City of San Jose.

———. 1984. Horizon 2000 General Plan. San Jose, Calif.: City of San Jose.

——— and Office of Management and Budget. 1981. Urban Service Program Working Paper No. 1: Service and Facility Inventory. San Jose, Calif.: City of San Jose.

———. 1982. Urban Service Program Working Paper No. 2: Analysis of Service Levels. San Jose, Calif.: City of San Jose.

Schell, Steven R. and Timothy V. Ramis. 1987. Systems Development Charges in Oregon. Paper presented to the Development Impact Fee Symposium, 1987 conference of the American Planning Association (April).

Simpson, George T. 1987. The Facilities Benefit Assessment in San Diego, California. Paper presented to the Development Impact Fee Symposium, 1987 conference of the American Planning Association (April).

Stewart, Harry. 1988. So You Want to Prepare a Development Impact Fee Ordinance? *Journal of the American Planning Association* 54, 1: 71–72.

Stroud, Nancy E. 1988. Legal Considerations of Development Impact Fees. *Journal of the American Planning Association* 54, 1: 29–37.

Winters, Jan. 1987. Development Impact Fees in Loveland, Colorado. Paper presented to the Development Impact Fee Symposium, 1987 conference of the American Planning Association (April).

4

Impact Fees Canadian Style: The Use of Development Charges in Ontario

DAVID P. AMBORSKI

In Canada, and more specifically in Ontario, requiring developers to provide or contribute to the financing of capital costs of services related to new development has been a prevalent practice for a relatively long time. It can be traced back to at least the 1950s for both the provision of services within new subdivisions and for contributions to the cost of off-site capital facilities.

This chapter provides the history, background, and application of the province of Ontario's version of what have come to be known widely as impact fees in the United States. Although the focus is on Ontario's development charges (sometimes referred to as development fees or lot levies) some comparisons are made to the legislation enabling these charges in other Canadian provinces.

In the United States, the topic of impact fees has appeared only recently in the literature and in papers presented at academic and professional conferences (Downing 1983; Snyder and Stegman 1986).[1] In Ontario, the topic of development charges was addressed earlier than in the United States in professional consulting reports (Price Waterhouse 1977), government

reports (Clayton 1973), and academic research (Amborski 1980; Hudic 1980).

The importance of this topic stems from the fiscal pressures that municipalities today endure. With revenue shortages and pressure for infrastructure renewal, local municipalities constantly are seeking additional revenue sources, particularly of the user-fee variety, to ameliorate fiscal pressures. One potential way in which funds may be freed for infrastructure renewal is to make developers financially responsible for the provision of new infrastructure. This may be considered an objective of impact fees and development charges.

The crucial question to be addressed here is how development charges came to exist in Ontario at an early time and in their particular form. To address this properly, it is necessary to outline the legal basis of the charges and the outcomes of a number of judicial appeals of municipal development charge policy.

THE ADVENT OF DEVELOPMENT CHARGES IN ONTARIO

The beginning of development charges must

be considered in the broader context of a growing trend toward making developers financially responsible for providing the services required for new residential development. After World War II, Ontario experienced increased urbanization and an associated increased demand for housing. To satisfy this increased demand, new housing was constructed and along with it, required capital infrastructure. As was the general practice of most local governments across North America at this time, local government provided and financed the required infrastructure. Local governments tended to meet increased demands for infrastructure through increased expenditure and debt financing.

Municipalities sought ways to respond to these fiscal pressures. One result, specific to Ontario, was the formation in 1953 of a metropolitan form of government in Toronto. This was a significant political decision, since it was the first metropolitan government formed in North America. A major reason for this reorganization was to enable the more rapidly growing municipalities at the fringe to take advantage of the central city assessment base when issuing debt to provide new infrastructure.[2]

Additionally, municipalities began to require developers to provide the services that were within the boundaries of the newly created subdivisions. In order to impose this condition, the municipality entered into agreements with the developers as a condition for obtaining the municipality's permission to develop and build on the land. Initially, the developer was required to install all services that were internal to the subdivision. This included the basic hard services such as roads, sewer, and water facilities.

The agreement in which these developer responsibilities were stipulated became known as a subdivision agreement. The legality of subdivision agreements as a municipal instrument was questioned in the early 1950s and it was 1959 before the legality of subdivision agreements was clarified in the provincial legislation known as the Planning Act. At this point, not only were the existence of subdivision agreements and the right of the municipality to enter into these agreements recognized, but the act also stipulated that the municipality could require for park facilities 5 percent of the land area of the subdivision or a cash payment equal to that amount of the land. This pattern reflects an increase over time in developer responsibilities in Ontario.

It was now clearly established that municipalities could make the developer financially responsible for the provision of services internal to subdivisions. In addition, the agreement required that the developer install all internal services at municipally set standards. The next step was to require financial contributions for off-site capital facilities. This practice also had its beginnings in Ontario municipalities in the 1950s. At that time, some municipalities began to request cash payments or developer charges from the firms developing or building new residential units. The basis under which these charges are made today is found in section 50(5) of the *Planning Act, 1983*. The phrase in this section, "that the owner of the land may enter into one or more agreements with a municipality," has been interpreted to include agreements in which developers are required to pay certain designated charges.

In the 1950s, the *Municipal Act* also provided some support for the application of development charges in section 309, now section 166 in the revised act. This section of the Municipal Act stipulated that when municipalities received contributions in relation to expenses anticipated due to the subdivision of lands, those funds should be used for expenditures that benefit the occupants of the land within the subdivision. It further stated that contributions received in this manner should be placed in a reserve account that is subject to the regulations placed in the act on those accounts. Basically, these regulations attempt to ensure accountability by having the funds earmarked so that they will be spent in the manner specified above.

With the enabling legislation in place, or at least the interpretation of the legislation accepted, the developer's financial responsibility for capital facilities related to new residential growth had been clearly extended by 1960 to facilities outside the subdivision.

HISTORY OF DEVELOPMENT CHARGES IN ONTARIO

The historical application of development charges is not clearly documented in Ontario. However, there are a number of reports and studies that allow trends in the use of these charges to be examined at various points in time since the 1950s. It is necessary to note that the studies cited are not directly comparable because they did not ask exactly the same questions, nor did they survey the same jurisdictions. What is provided, however, are snapshots of the use of development charges for single-family dwelling units at various points in time over the past 30 years (see Table 4–1).

The two earliest reports on development charges in Ontario were prepared in 1959 by the Citizen Research Institute, and in 1964 by the City Engineers Association. Both of these reports examined the extent of development charge use by the municipalities and the mag-

nitude of current development charges. The 1959 study found that 25 percent of the municipalities responding to its survey required the payment of development charges. In 1964, however, the City Engineers Association found that approximately 55 percent of the responding municipalities required these payments. With respect to the magnitude of the charge, the earlier survey found the highest payment to be $400 per single-family unit, while the later survey reported the largest amount to be $600 (Ontario Committee on Taxation 1967, 311–312).

Chronologically, the next major report on the issue was provided by the Ontario Committee on Taxation in 1967. The committee also carried out a survey of developer responsibility for service provision and specifically development charges in 272 municipalities in Ontario. The report did not publish specific results from the respondent municipalities but rather indicated a number of trends that had been identified over the period from 1953 to 1963. Two significant trends identified were:

1. "Over the period the use of subdivision agreements to transfer municipal service costs to developers came into much more general use."

2. "Between 1953 and 1963, the responsibilities placed upon the developer for municipal services were appreciably broadened, and an increasing number of developers were expected to make cash payments in addition to providing or paying for specific municipal services" (Ontario Committee on Taxation 1967, 311).

In 1973, the Ontario Housing Advisory Committee released a report in which the results of survey data from 56 municipalities were presented. These results indicated that approximately 75 percent of the responding munici-

Table 4–1. Trends in the Use of Development Charges

	% of Respondents Using Charges	Highest Reported Charge	Development Charge Index	Housing Price Index[1]
Citizen Research Institute–1959	25%	$ 400	100	100
City Engineers Association–1964	54%	$ 600	150	104
Housing Advisory Committee–1973	75%	$1,500	325	265
Amborski–1979	86%	$4,780	1,200	426
C. N. Watson and Associates–1985	79%[2]	$7,496	1,874	657

1. Data regarding the average price of new housing are not available. The data used to calculate the index are the Toronto Real Estate Board data for the average price of resale homes in metropolitan Toronto sold through the multiple listing service. These data provide a guide to general price trends in the housing market.

2. This decrease in the percentage of responding jurisdictions that use charges can be explained by the fact that the 1985 survey included more jurisdictions (111) than the previous survey. Therefore, it includes more small jurisdictions that do not have growth pressures and have not found it necessary to impose development charges.

palities collected development charges and the highest reported charge was $1,500 per single-family unit. The results of these early surveys, although not directly comparable, did indicate trends in increasing developer financial responsibility for the provision of services, increasing use of development charges by municipalities, and an increase in the amount of the development charge for single-family units.

Studies in 1979 and 1980 found these trends were continuing. In the first of these studies, the emphasis was on metropolitan Toronto and the regional municipalities adjacent to it.[3] It found that the development charges were collected in four of the five regional governments and in 26 of the 30 local municipalities. The largest combined local municipal and regional development charge was found to be $4,780 per single-family unit (Amborski 1980, p. 32). The 1980 survey examined the use of development charges in 129 Ontario jurisdictions and found the highest combined charge to be in excess of $5,000 (Giffels Associates Ltd. 1980, p. iii).

An update of the last survey was undertaken in 1985 and it was reported that the highest development charge was imposed in the town of Vaughan in York Region immediately north of metropolitan Toronto. The combined development charge in this jurisdiction was found to be as high as $7,496 per single-family unit.[4] The price of new single-family houses where this charge applied ranged from $104,000 to $240,000. Throughout the discussion of these reports, the focus was on the largest charge. To provide a little more perspective to this description, the last report indicated that 10 jurisdictions had charges larger than $5,000, 17 had charges larger than $4,000, and 23 had charges larger than $3,000 per single-family unit (C. N. Watson and Associates Ltd. 1985).

THE LEGAL BASIS FOR CHARGES AND MAJOR JUDICIAL DECISIONS

The somewhat tenuous legal basis for development charges in Ontario has previously been identified as being found in section 50(5) of the

Planning Act and section 166 of the Municipal Act. It is section 50(5) of the Planning Act, first enacted in 1959, that is considered the prime basis for the application of development charges. In this section of the act, the minister is authorized to impose conditions to the granting of subdivision approval that "in his opinion are advisable." Also, landowners may "enter into one or more agreements with a municipality" that may include "the provision of municipal services." In 1961, this section of the act was given liberal interpretation to allow the imposition of development charges in the landmark Supreme Court of Canada decision, *Beaver Valley Developments* v. *North York*. This decision is significant because it interpreted the above noted section of the act to allow municipalities to collect development charges.

This finding governed the setting of charges from the early 1960s until 1983 when the new Ontario Planning Act came into effect. Under the new act, the only change to the section was that the conditions imposed by the minister must now be "reasonable, having regard to the nature of the development proposed."

Although the legislation in Ontario does not specifically refer to the application of development levies or charges, a number of other provinces in Canada do have legislation that specifically enables municipalities to impose these charges. In Alberta, the Planning Act clearly stipulates that a charge for off-site services may be imposed for a specific set of hard services. The services that may be included in the charge are water supply and treatment, sewage drainage and treatment, and land related to these facilities. The Planning and Development Act in Saskatchewan not only specifies the services that may be included in subdivision agreements but also that councils may establish charges for a number of off-site facilities. The practice in major cities in Saskatchewan, however, has been to levy a charge for hard services. British Columbia, through its Municipal Act, has Canada's most detailed legislation regarding the application of development charges. It not only clearly states the rules under which the charges will be collected but guidelines also have been established regarding acceptable methods for collecting them.

Of all the provinces that allow development charges, Ontario's legislation appears to be the least clear regarding how municipalities may determine their charge policy. Both municipalities and developers in Ontario could benefit from clearer enabling legislation. This would reduce the number of current charges that are judicially challenged. In 1980, to deal with the high number of appeals, the Association of Municipalities of Ontario (AMO), prepared draft legislation that was designed to strengthen the municipal authority to impose development charges (Association of Municipalities of Ontario 1980). The development industry vehemently opposed the proposed legislation. The province requested that AMO meet with the development industry represented by the Urban Development Institute (UDI) and the Ontario Homebuilders Association to see if they could agree on draft legislation that could be presented to the province.

To date, the two interest groups have not been able to agree on draft legislation. The reasons for their disagreeing generally have been the same reasons the charges have been challenged judicially. There are two issues on which agreement cannot easily be reached. The first issue concerns which services should be included in the charge. Should the charge be limited to "hard" services that include only property-related services as advocated by the development industry, or should the charge include the capital cost of "soft" or people-related services as advocated by the AMO? Municipalities argue that all growth-related services should be part of the calculation including such people-related services as recreational facilities and libraries.

The second issue is the method by which the charge should be calculated. The basic choice is between uniform or average cost pricing, which tends to be supported by the municipalities, and site-specific pricing, a variant of marginal cost pricing which developers often advocate. The site-specific approach bases the cost on those services that are required of a subdivision in a particular geographic location. Average cost pricing averages the costs of services required for new development across the jurisdiction.

To this point, reference has been made simply to development charges being challenged judicially. It is necessary to differentiate between the two ways challenges initially may occur. In the Ontario system, development charges either may be challenged before the Divisional Court regarding matters of law or appeals may be made to the Ontario Municipal Board (OMB) regarding questions of planning under the Planning Act.

The OMB is a quasi-judicial tribunal that has jurisdiction over appeals regarding a broad range of planning and municipal finance matters. Although this type of tribunal does not have a counterpart in any planning system in the United States, it is not unique among Canadian provinces.[5] In many ways, OMB hearings are similar to court proceedings in that they hear evidence and make decisions in a judicial manner. However, the OMB is unlike the courts in that it does not have to follow the same rules of evidence and that its decisions often are not based on precedents as is typical in courts of law.

A number of judicial decisions may be examined that demonstrate both the nature of the challenges to development charges and the approach taken by both the OMB and the courts in responding to appeals. There are several decisions that tend to show a narrowing application of development charges in the mid 1970s. Prior to this narrowing of decisions, the 1976 *Mills* v. *the Land Division Committee of the Region of York* court decision provided a fairly broad interpretation of the application of development charges. This decision allowed for the imposition of fees for services that are fairly and reasonably related to subdivisions. In 1977, a decision of the OMB regarding the *Steel Company of Canada* v. *the City of Nanticoke* narrowed the application of development charges by not allowing charges to be imposed for soft services, specifically for libraries, recreation centres, or a fire hall, as the city had requested. One other decision that may be considered significant in terns of narrowing the application is the OMB decision with respect to the 1977 *Frey* v. *the Regional Municipality of Peel Land Division Committee* case. That decision indicated that the onus was on the municipality to show that the charge is necessary for the purpose stated, and is equitable and reasonable. One 1976 Divisional Court decision, *Eastcan Holdings* v. *the Town of Whitby*, limited the charges to hard services but suggested that in some cases charges for soft services may be permissible. It can be seen that these recent decisions demonstrate a trend toward narrowing the range of services that may be included in the development charge and demanding more municipal justification for each charge.

There are other decisions that shed some light on the application of development charges in terms of using uniform or site-specific pricing approaches to determine the charge. In 1982, an OMB decision accepted the application of uniform or average cost pricing in the town of Bradford. Two years later, during a different appeal in the same jurisdiction, the board rejected it in favor of the site-specific approach. Despite having accepted the average cost approach in the past, the OMB recently has tended to reduce the amount of the charge for no apparent reason. This is evident in the 1980 case of *Emmitt Developments* v. *Brampton*, which concerned a condominium development in which the charges were reduced from $4,600 to $1,500 per unit.[6] Also, in the *Wimpey* v. *Durham Region* case, which both the development industry and the municipalities had anticipated to result in an extremely significant decision, actually had a somewhat confusing outcome. The major issue was the choice between uniform and site-specific charges. In this 1982 decision, the OMB upheld the application of uniform charges across the region but reduced the amount of the levy.

There is an additional level of judicial review that may be pursued after an OMB decision. Either party may appeal the decision to the Provincial (Government) Cabinet. This in fact did occur in the Emmitt Developments case; Brampton appealed the OMB decision, but Cabinet upheld it. A December 1985 Cabinet decision regarding *Mod-Aire Homes* v. *Bradford* could be considered an indicator or guidance to development charge practice in Ontario. In this decision, it was stated that uniform charges may be set provided that they bear a reasonable relationship to the overall costs of growth. However, charges may also include additional amounts for services directly attributable to a specific subdivision.

What is seen in this brief review of judicial decisions is that clear and consistent policy direction and guidelines are not given to municipalities through the interpretations of the enabling legislation. This tends to underscore the need to clarify the legislative basis of development charges in Ontario. Since there is no clear policy direction given by the province, municipalities have tended to apply development charges in a variety of ways. This in turn has tended to lead to appeals by the development industry.

DEVELOPMENT CHARGE PRACTICE IN ONTARIO

The discussion of development charge practice in Ontario could include many facets of the issue, including the application of charges to industrial and commercial development, to rezoning and severances, and to subdivision approval.[7] However, the focus of this section is the method by which development charges are calculated for residential development. It is thus necessary to identify the services that are included in the calculation and the method or pricing rule by which the charge is determined. As previously noted, these two issues have been the basis of most judicial appeals.

Prior to discussing pricing methods, it is important to point out that the practice of setting development charges may not always be consistent with recent judicial decisions. Municipalities will not always alter their policy to be consistent with these rulings, since they may expect that developers will not appeal in response to recent decisions. This is the case because many developers have a fairly long-term stake in a particular municipality and they therefore have developed a good working relationship with the municipality.[8] It is only when municipal demands become excessive or when the housing market is weak that developers tend to appeal development charges.

With regard to the issue of which services are included in the development charge calculation, the major distinction is between what have previously been defined as hard and soft services. All municipalities that impose development charges based on some rational calculation include the capital cost of hard services in their charge. Questions arise regarding which soft or other growth-related services should be included. The most recent survey of Ontario municipalities indicates that of the 88 jurisdictions identified that impose development charges, 40 have a soft service component, 32 do not, and it is unclear in the case of the 16 remaining jurisdictions. Of the 10 jurisdictions with the highest combined charge, 9 of them have a component for soft services (C. N. Watson and Associates Ltd. 1985).

An interesting example is provided by the development charge policy in the town of Vaughan. The combined regional charge ($1,216) and local municipal charge for Vaughan ($6,289) is the highest per single-family unit in the province ($7,496). The local component of the charge includes in its calculation the capital cost of soft services that includes general government, libraries, and fire protection, as well as recreation and community services. What makes this charge policy interesting, and in fact unique in the province, is that it was developed in negotiation with a developers' group, all of whom owned undeveloped land in the Thornhill-Vaughan community. They did in fact agree to

a charge policy that included soft services, a position that is not consistent with the development industry in general.

Before explaining the pricing rules used by municipalities for their development charges, it must be established that most charges are based on some calculation. This has not always been the case in all municipalities. In the 1979 survey examining the jurisdictions closest to metropolitan Toronto, only 8 of the 28 jurisdictions imposing charges had publicly available studies showing the method of calculation for their policy. Seven jurisdictions clearly had no study while the remaining 13 claimed to have some form of internal study or calculations (Amborski 1980, p. 45). Of those that did not document their methods, charges were set arbitrarily, based on what the politicians believed was appropriate or what neighboring jurisdictions used. These practices declined due to the number of appeals that have occurred in the past six years. Municipalities are aware that today they must have well-documented studies to justify their charges.

Both the early and the more recent municipal studies tend to base their calculations on the average cost pricing approach. This, however, may be calculated in a number of ways. Some municipalities have determined the historical average costs for a typical subdivision. They then use those costs as the basis of the charge for future development. A more common approach is to estimate the capital costs for some expected increase in population over some time period and then relate these anticipated expenditures to an average cost per capita or per unit. Where services lend themselves to estimating the costs on a per capita basis, costs are converted to a unit basis by multiplying by the average number of persons expected to occupy each type of dwelling unit. Due to differences in the capital cost of servicing various development densities, expected household sizes, and types of units, a number of jurisdictions differentiate their charge by type of residential unit.[9]

Two other aspects are important in undertaking the development charge calculation. The first, which is only relevant when projecting costs, is the service standard used when estimating costs. Some municipalities have had their charges criticized when based on service standards that are significantly higher than currently exist. The second concern is with items that should be subtracted from the capital cost estimates in determining the charge. Any anticipated revenues from provincial or federal capital grants or subsidies that are related to growth in general or the specific capital facilities should be considered in the calculation. Also, some jurisdictions give consideration to existing debenture debt and/or the capitalized value of the property tax revenue from each unit that will be used to finance capital facilities from the operating budget.[10]

Site-specific or marginal cost pricing tends not to be applied by municipalities except in a very crude form. In some jurisdictions the development charge will vary geographically but only due to the complete absence of some particular service. For example, charges may be lower in rural areas where urban services such as sewer and water are not available. There tends not to be geographic differentiation of costs for a service within a jurisdiction based on the variation of the cost of providing a particular service. A cost variation reflected in development charges has been sought by developers in a number of appeals. Their lack of success in winning appeals of this nature for

the upper-tier (regional) charge is somewhat understandable. When the provincial government created regional government in Ontario, part of the rationale was to equalize service provision across each region. Presumably this would also mean equalizing or averaging costs as well.

As an example of a municipality where charges are differentiated as described above, Vaughan again can be cited. Not only are the charges varied by district or community throughout the town depending on service availability, but there is variation within neighborhoods in the Thornhill-Vaughan community. This variation occurs due to the prior existence of sewage and drainage facilities in the area.

Finally, two administrative aspects of development charge practice should be mentioned. First is the issue of when municipalities require the charges to be paid. Payment is required either at the time the subdivision agreement is signed or on issuance of building permits. The second administrative concern is accountability of development charge funds. As previously stated, the Municipal Act requires that the revenues be placed in special reserve funds and used for the benefit of the lands or residents for which they were collected.

THE FUTURE OF DEVELOPMENT CHARGES

Conclusions about the future of development charge practice in Ontario must be made within the context of relatively vague legislation regarding the application of the charges and the relatively inconsistent judicial decisions that have been delivered when charges have been appealed.

It is fair to conclude that both the magnitude of the charge and the number of jurisdictions using them will increase. With municipal financial pressures persisting, development charges provide an indirect charge which has low political cost. Municipalities will increase their charges by at least the rate of inflation and in some cases increase the range of services included in the charge.[11] Other municipalities that currently do not have charges may very well adopt development charge policies. In both cases, it can be expected that the trend of improving documentation of the formula used to establish the charge will continue in response to the specter of appeals.

The growth in the number of appeals over the next few years will depend on the housing market conditions and any changes that occur in the enabling legislation. If the market for new housing softens, developers likely will turn their attention from expansion of output to cost savings. This could entail more appeals of development charges in the absence of clearer legislation. The probability of new and clearer legislation depends on the ability of the municipalities and the developer interests to come to agreement on the legislation.

Since it is these two interest groups that have the greatest stake in the new legislation, the previous provincial government indicated that it would only revise the legislation when there was agreement between the two groups. It would appear that the current government, elected in 1984, is following the same approach. First, this requires consensus of a municipal view to be put forth by AMO and, second, consensus of a development industry position. This must, in turn, be followed by negotiation between the two interest groups to arrive at the draft legislation.

Up to this point, the municipal position in Ontario appears to have been solidified. However, obtaining an industry position acceptable to both UDI and the homebuilder organizations appears somewhat more difficult as it requires agreement first within each organization and then among the organizations.

There recently has been some indication that a development industry position has been firmly established. With this progress, the task will now be for the two interests to sit down and negotiate a compromise draft of the legislation. At this point it is difficult to speculate on the outcome of the negotiations. However, it can be anticipated that more specific legislation will be forthcoming. It would appear that after more than five years, both parties now have the resolve to develop a compromise draft legislation.

Author's Note

I wish to thank my colleagues, Jim Mars and Ron Pushchak, for the helpful comments that they made to earlier drafts of this chapter.

Notes

1. The significance of this issue is evident from the sessions that are devoted to the topic in both the academic conferences, the 1986 Association of the Collegiate Schools of Planning Conference, and the 1987 and 1988 American Planning Association conferences.

2. This was not the only reason for the formation of metropolitan Toronto but it was an important one. It is also useful to note that two of the then suburban municipalities of the metro Government, Etobicoke and North York, were among the first municipalities to impose development charges.

3. It is necessary to point out that much of the province of Ontario, and in fact most major urban areas, have two-tiered local government. Upper-tier or regional municipalities generally have responsibility for water supply, sewage treatment, garbage disposal, and borrowing as well as some social and health services. Local or lower-tier municipalities have responsibility for garbage collection, fire protection, and parks and recreation. There is

joint responsibility for planning, police, roads, water distribution, and sewer systems.

Currently there are 11 regional municipalities that encompass more than 60 percent of the province's population.

4. The reason why it is stated that the charge "may be as high as $7,496" is because the development charge for Vaughan is set at different levels for different areas of the town.

5. Other examples of this type of quasi-judicial board include the Alberta Planning Board, the Nova Scotia Municipal Board, and the Manitoba Municipal Board. However, the state of Oregon has a land use board of appeals that is close to the OMB model.

6. Although this case is somewhat different because it is a condominium development, the principle of reducing the charge is established. Charges may be imposed for condominium development in as much as they are essentially part of the subdivision approval process. The large reduction occurred in this case because Brampton could not adequately justify its charges and the development was in close proximity to the center of downtown Brampton. This area already has most basic municipal services.

7. Industrial and commercial charges are not required by all municipalities that impose residential charges. The rationale for not charging is that the property taxes paid by these uses exceed the cost of the services that they require.

Development charges may be applied to severances (land partitioning). They may also be applied to redevelopment but only for water and sewers where the need for upgraded facilities can be clearly established. For details, see the Municipal Act, section 215.

8. The structure of the development and housing construction industry in Canada is one that is dominated by large firms relative to the United States. There are few small firms in the industry. A result of larger firms is that they own larger or more land and that they often are geographically concentrated. This leads to a need to work cooperatively with a municipality since the working relationship may be for a relatively long period of time (Markusen and Scheffman 1977, Chapter 5).

9. The two ways that municipalities tend to differentiate their residential charge is by number of bedrooms or by type of unit. Where they are differentiated by type of unit, the higher density forms of development have lower per-unit charges than lower density forms of development.

10. This approach is typical of the way in which some consulting reports undertake the calculation for munici-

palities. C. N. Watson and Associates Ltd., which has undertaken a number of municipal studies, uses this approach. For example, this can be seen in their *Lot Levy Policy Study for The Town of Oakville*, August 1986.

11. A number of the municipal development charge policies require an annual or semiannual review of the policy. Others have a clause whereby the charge is increased periodically according to a published construction price index.

References

Amborski, David P. 1980. Lot Levies: Service Pricing to Finance Urban Growth. Prepared for the Lincoln Institute of Land Policy, Cambridge, Mass.

Association of Municipalities of Ontario. 1981. *AMO Reports 52: Municipal Lot Levies.* Toronto: AMO.

Bird, Richard M. 1976. *Charging for Public Services: A New Look at an Old Idea.* Toronto: Canadian Tax Foundation.

Citizens Research Institute of Canada. 1960. Subdivisions Study. *Bulletin,* June.

City Engineer Association. 1964. Control of Subdivision Development. Fifth Annual Workshop, Toronto.

Clayton Research Associates. 1973. Municipal Cash Impacts in Ontario, An Exploratory Study. Prepared for the Ontario Housing Advisory Committee, Toronto.

Derkowski, Andrzej. 1975. *Costs in the Land Development Process.* Prepared for the Housing and Urban Development Association of Canada, Toronto.

Dougherty, Laurence et al. 1975. *Municipal Service Pricing: Impact on Financial Position.* Santa Monica, Calif.: The Rand Corp.

Downing, Paul B. 1973. User Charges and the Development of Urban Land, *National Tax Journal* 26, 4: 631–37.

———, ed. 1977. *Local Service Pricing Policies and Their Effect on Urban Spatial Structure.* Vancouver: University of British Columbia Press.

——— and James Frank. 1983. Recreational Impact Fees: Characteristics and Current Usage. *National Tax Journal.*

Giffels Associates Ltd. 1981. *Giffels Survey of Lot Levy Practice in Ontario.* Toronto.

Hudic, Albert. 1980. Municipal Exactions and the Subdivision Approval Process: A Legal and Economic Analysis. *University of Toronto Faculty Law Review,* no. 38: Toronto.

Makuch, Stanley M. 1983. *Canadian Municipal and Planning Law.* Toronto: The Carswell Company Limited.

Markusen, J. R. and D. T. Scheffman. 1977. *Speculation and Monopoly in Urban Development: Analytical Foun-*

dations with Evidence for Toronto. Toronto: University of Toronto Press.

Ontario. 1980. *The Municipal Act*. Statutes of Ontario. Chapter 302. Toronto: Queens Printer.

———. 1983. *The Planning Act*. Statutes of Ontario. Chapter 1. Toronto: Queens Printer.

Ontario Committee on Taxation. 1967. *Report of the Ontario Committee on Taxation*. Toronto: Queens Printer.

Price Waterhouse Associates. 1977. *Lot Levy Study of Ontario: An Analysis of the Current Situation*. Prepared for the Urban Development Institute, Toronto.

Snyder, Thomas and Michael Stegman. 1986. *Paying for Growth: Using Development Fees to Finance Infrastructure*. Washington, D.C.: Urban Land Institute.

Town of Vaughan. 1981. *Development Charge Policy: Thornhill-Vaughan Community*.

Urban Development Institute. 1984. Position on Lot Levies. Prepared by the Land Interest Group, Toronto.

Watson, C. N. and Associates Ltd. 1985. *Municipal Lot Levies—An Update*. Toronto.

———. 1986. *Lot Levy Policy Conducted for: The Town of Oakville*.

Public and Private Sector Attitudes Toward Development Impact Fees

5

Impact Fees: The Mettle Public Officials Need to Meddle with the Market

HARRY A. STEWART

THE POLITICS

How do elected officials get the mettle to meddle in the market by imposing impact fees? Perhaps it's the fact that developed property has a constituency while unbuilt homes do not.

It is clear that continued approval of development in any jurisdiction will deteriorate the levels of service for the existing infrastructure. And that is unacceptable policy according to existing residents.

The problem to be solved is how to maintain an adopted level of service and at the same time allow new development to go forward. One alternative is to tax both already-developed property and undeveloped property in order to finance the new infrastructure. Another is to impose a fee that would require new development to help finance infrastructures that have traditionally been publicly financed.

If your solution includes taxing already-developed property, you can expect any public hearing on the issue to be dominated by a *large* number of residents (taxpayers and voters) vehemently opposed to the idea. You can ex-

pect to hear sometimes eloquent but always lengthy discussion on such issues as cost of living, standard of living, fixed incomes, what's fair, what's not fair, and who wants those people moving here anyway. It is rare to find anyone in this vocal majority who objects to development fees.

On the other hand, if your solution is to adopt a development fee that is designed to eliminate the inequity of requiring one generation of residents to provide the infrastructure for another (i.e., eliminate the inequities of a tax), you can expect opposition from the development community. The most vocal and most organized of the opposition will in almost every case be the local, regional, and perhaps state home builders association. Again, you can expect to hear sometimes eloquent but always lengthy discussions on such subjects as the cost of housing, affordability for first-time buyers, and the cost of compliance with government regulations in general.

So, on the one hand, because it is money taken directly from their pockets, you are faced with an angry, waving crowd of residents strongly opposed to taxation as a solution to maintaining levels of service for the infrastructure. On the other hand, a comparatively small number of representatives of the development community bemoan the rising costs that they will have to pass through to unknown purchasers of their product.

The question facing elected officials is, "Should we tax existing residents to pay for the cost of providing the infrastructure for newcomers or shall we require newcomers to pay their fair share of those costs?" To have asked the question is to have answered it. The mettle to meddle has been found.

THE FEE: AN INTRODUCTION

Now you have decided to meddle and want to adopt an impact fee package. Just like any other project, trying to put an impact fee package together is not an easy task. And, just like any other project, when all else fails, read the directions. The real question is, "Where in the legions of literature available on the subject do you find directions?"

The answer actually is quite simple. For local government in Florida, all of the directions needed to develop any number of impact fee ordinances are conveniently laid out by the Florida Courts in three cases: *Contractors and Builders Association of Pinellas County v. City of Dunedin*, 329 So.2d 314 (Fla. 1976); *Hollywood, Inc. v. Broward County*, 431 So.2d 606 (Fla. 4th DCA 1983); *Home Builders and Contractors Association of Palm Beach County, Inc. v. Board of County Commissioners of Palm Beach County*, 446 So.2d 140 (Fla. 4th DCA 1983). And, if that is not enough, the Florida legislature finally got into the act with its somewhat tardy recognition of impact fees in the Local Governmental Comprehensive Planning Act, Chapter 85-55,

Laws of Florida, and provided even more information on what impact fees should be.

This chapter is a practical approach to developing impact fees and so you will find a dearth of citations. The lessons learned in Florida probably apply to most if not all other states in the nation.

THE MENU

Providing the infrastructure to support growth places a financial burden on any local government. The problem becomes which facilities should be expanded with the help of impact fees. This is a problem for each unit of local government to resolve based on its unique social and economic growth patterns. You simply review the services that are deteriorating because of growth and select the impact exaction required to best fit your needs. That seems simple enough.

The following chart, created from information provided by the Florida Advisory Council on Intergovernmental Relations, shows impact fee usage in Florida counties and cities as of March 31, 1986. The numbers in each column represent the numbers of counties and cities that have enacted, have drafted, or are studying each of the listed impact fees.

Type of Impact Fee	Enacted	In Draft	Being Studied
Water	54	0	3
Sewers	55	0	3
Parks	19	4	7
Road	20	11	8
Fire	17	3	7
Drainage	4	1	1
School	2	1	3
Beach	1	0	0
Police	8	4	2
Library	1	0	0
Trash	6	2	2

As is obvious from the above chart, the menu from which local government can select an impact fee to resolve its most burning growth issue is quite varied and can get quite expensive depending on the number of burning issues. Circuit Judge Lewis Kapner, in a footnote in *Home Builders,* cautioned:

> ... If this form of public finance (impact fees) flourishes, and if the government continues to expand its functions and services as it has in the past, society will soon reach a point where "impact fee" for roads, parks, sewerage and other forms of government services will make it financially impossible to build any new homes at all, regardless of the fact that the fees will be reasonably related to the cost of the expansion.

SOME RULES NOT FOUND IN THE CASE LAW

The very first rule requires you to do what any local government worth its salt does when faced with a problem; i.e., appoint a committee. The committee undoubtedly will be permeated with development interests and its progress will be in three phases. The phases are not learned and cannot be taught. They appear to be governed solely by instinct and do not seem to vary from one jurisdiction to another.

Phase I. This phase should be called "Hell No, We Won't Pay." To everyone's surprise, the developers on the committee are diametrically opposed to impact fees of any sort. According to the committee, the appropriate governmental response to providing for growth is to raise taxes. This response is almost universally rejected by elected officials wishing to serve more than one term. Phase I generally lasts from three to six months, depending on the tenacity of the staff and the intestinal fortitude of the governing body.

Phase II. This phase should be called "Let's Study This Problem." This phase is characterized by long meetings and dissemination of extremely detailed information that is to be crunched into very oblique scientific formulas that calculate the bottom line; i.e., how much is this thing going to cost? This phase can last forever. There is no end to the universe of available formulas that could be used in calculating an impact fee. However, with some determination this phase can be limited to between six months and a year.

Phase III. This phase should be called "Love It To Death." This phase begins with the recognition by the development community that impact fees are imminent. They begrudgingly agree that this may be a partial solution to the problem; however, with just a few "friendly amendments" they can make it better. The imagination exhibited in formulating the "transition rules" or exemptions or even the application of the proposed impact fee during this phase will be directly proportionate to the legal fees paid by the development community to oppose impact fees. This phase can be expected to be the shortest. All parties are pretty well worn down by this time and are more than willing to compromise.

If you are extremely lucky, the ordinance that "the committee" has helped draft will contain some, if not most, of the elements set out in *Contractors, Hollywood, Inc.,* and *Home Builders* as essential to the proper exercise of local government's police power. One rule in this drama is absolutely critical: You cannot, under any circumstances, lose your sense of humor. If that is lost, your sanity will follow it shortly.

THE CASE LAW

So! What do the courts say? At the end of the

meat-grinder-like process of imposing an impact fee, what should the finished product look like in order to pass judicial muster? It is not the intent of this chapter to discuss the case law in detail; however, to recap ever so briefly:

1. *It must be fair.* In order to be fair, the expansion of the capital facilities must be required to accommodate the new users, and the fee cannot exceed the proportionate share of the expansion prorated to the new users.

2. *The funds must be earmarked.* To satisfy this requirement you need to show a reasonable connection between the expenditures of the funds collected and the benefit accruing to new users.

WHAT TO LOOK FOR

Whether you are representing local government in trying to defend the imposition of an impact fee or representing a developer trying to invalidate it, this section should be of some benefit. The following are examples of impact fees and the elements required to be present in each in order to pass judicial muster. This listing is intended to be a broadbrush approach and not intended as a detailed guide.

Water and Sewer

Water and sewer impact fees are the simplest of all to develop and defend. Each is a capital system that can be utilized and consumed only by those persons who actually connect to the system. It is a fairly simple task to develop empirical data to show expansion needs caused by growth. The fee may take into account an amount to pay for excess capacity carried by the existing users, as well as any future expansion required to serve new users. If bonds are outstanding on the existing facilities, a credit provision must be included to ensure that new

users get credit for amounts they will be paying to retire the debt on those bonds.

The simplicity in developing the fee, as well as the need for water and sewer systems to accommodate growth, probably account for the fact that this is the most popular impact fee in Florida today.

Parks

Park impact fees are almost tied in popularity with roads as a frequently adopted impact fee. However, park impact fees are much simpler to develop than those for roads. You need an inventory of parks available, along with an adopted standard or level of service, and a capital improvements program for expansion to accommodate new users. In Broward County, the standard adopted was three acres per 1,000 population for local parks and the same acreage requirement for regional parks. Since the existing inventory did not meet the standard, Broward approved $77,000,000 in general obligation bonds to purchase additional parkland to meet the standard it had set. Socioeconomic data from various sources were used to calculate the number of people per household, and data from the tax roles were used to calculate the average cost of land. This information was used to produce a schedule of fees and a capital improvements program was developed to accommodate new users. The developer could dedicate three acres for every 1,000 residents, pay an amount equal to the value of the land that would be dedicated, or pay the amount shown on the schedule developed.

Since bonds were issued to bring the existing inventory of parkland up to the new standard of three acres per 1,000 residents, a credit mechanism was devised to ensure that new users were only paying for the expansion necessary to accommodate them. This fee, of course, was upheld in the *Hollywood, Inc.* case.

The inventory, the average number of people per household, land value, and new lands required to meet the standard for each development were all elements necessary to support the fee and could be shown and supported by empirical data.

Roads

The level of difficulty in proving the rational nexus between a particular development and its impact on the road system is much greater than that for water, sewer, or parks. The road system is a capital system that can be characterized by nonexclusive use and joint consumption by the public generally. Calculating the specific prorated shares of expansion costs, which are attributable to new growth for water and sewer, is fairly simple. In contrast, the same calculation in the case of roads is difficult if not impossible to accomplish in a manner that accurately and consistently reflects the actual cost and benefit of the capital system to individual households.

Fortunately for those 20 Florida communities that have enacted some form of road impact fee (and the other 19 under study), the *Contractor's* court noted that "perfection" is not the standard of municipal duty. However, it would appear that an impact fee becomes less appropriate as a means of financing capital expansion as the relationship between the impact fee formula and the fee payers' actual impact on the capital system becomes more tenuous.

For roads, it is clear there will be some impact on the system by any development, whether it generates traffic or only attracts it.

Without going into a detailed analysis of Broward County's computer system (which dis-

tributes trips generated by a particular development on the roadway system based on a gravity model with designated attractors) or Palm Beach County's formula (based on some 40 zones with estimated road construction cost per land mile) suffice to say that the formulas for calculating this impact fee are becoming more numerous and less precise as each decision that expands local government's authority to impose impact fees is rendered.

However, the elements necessary to support the imposition must still be met. They just become more complex. Those elements include:

1. Adopted level of service.
2. Configuration of existing road network.
3. Trip generation rates to determine impact on the traffic system.
4. Socioeconomic data along with adopted land use plan to predict growth patterns by various types of land use and by geographical location.
5. Capital improvements plan to accommodate new users.
6. Identification of roads in the capital improvements plan that do not currently meet the adopted standard (existing deficiencies).
7. Identification of some source of revenue, other than impact fees, to improve existing deficiencies.
8. Construction cost data by various road types.
9. Land value information to calculate right-of-way costs.
10. Gas tax credit mechanism to ensure that new users get credit for future gas taxes they will pay.

Law Enforcement

The level of difficulty here is getting so great that it places this impact fee very close to the outer fringe of possibility. Orange County, Florida, and several other jurisdictions have enacted such a fee. To calculate a fee that accurately and consistently reflects the actual cost and benefit of the capital system to individual households is close to impossible. However, as had been noted previously, perfection is not the standard. Following are the elements contained in the Orange County fee:

1. A service standard index, which for Orange County is the ratio for annual service calls per field officer.

2. An estimate of the number of field personnel required in future years. A simulation model was developed to forecast the need.

3. An estimate of support personnel required (a ratio of support personnel to field personnel was used).

4. Historical data developed to show the number of calls per field officer by various land use types.

5. Estimate of capital costs to support the increase in personnel required to support new users.

6. And finally, because the level of difficulty is so great, you should throw in a complex formula to calculate the forecasted value for calls for service along with a multivariate regression analysis—Yes=a+b1X1+b2X2+b3X3+b4X4+b5X5 will do nicely.

Jails

This impact fee is added only as an example of the other end of the spectrum. Based on current case law, this impact fee is far beyond the level of difficulty that can be accomplished by mortal beings. I am unaware of any formula, including the one just mentioned, that could calculate costs and benefits to individual developments for this one. If ever there were a candidate for the courts to find that the fee imposed is actually a tax, this is the one.

ADVICE

Any jurisdiction that wants to impose an impact fee is often tempted to get a copy of one from another jurisdiction and copy it. It is not only possible, but highly likely, that a fee that has been tested in court and found to be constitutional for one unit of local government could be found unconstitutional for another that simply copies that ordinance without the proper studies and data to back up the required elements. Take your time and do it right.

6

Will Developers Pay to Play?

DOUGLAS R. PORTER

Developers may cavil at development fees in principle but accept them in practice, provided that local public officials formulate, administer, and expend fees in a reasonable manner. Most developers view fees as more desirable than case-by-case exactions and certainly preferable to halting development to await public funding for infrastructure. However, in return for contributions to pay for public infrastructure, developers want more assurance that projects will be allowed to proceed as planned and that fees will be spent wisely for necessary improvements.

OVERVIEW

Attempts at defining how developers feel about development fees should be greeted with hoots of derision: Developers are, if anything, more diverse in their opinions than are planners, a notably difficult lot to pin down. This is by way of an explanation for the unscientific nature of research for this chapter. The perspectives of developers and builders represented here have been sensed, rather than collected, from dozens of conversations, comments at meetings and conferences, and a few articles. Perhaps the most significant sources of opinion were discussions on impact fees and, more generally, exactions, that have taken place at a number of national conferences and at an Urban Land Institute policy forum during which develop-

ers and builders evaluated the rationale for and effects of development fees on their projects. In addition, Snyder and Stegman (1986) relay comments of developers made during their case studies of development fees and exactions.

Ask developers how they like development fees and they will ask in turn: In principle or in practice? In principle, they will tell you, most development fees represent a shirking of public responsibility for financing the infrastructure necessary to support new development. In practice, developers also will say, their attitude toward fees depends on a great many factors having to do with the market, their particular type of development, and the place of fees in the total scheme of public policies and regulations affecting development.

Since developers, like most other people, have learned to work in an imperfect world, they are perfectly willing to put practice before principle in order to launch a potentially profitable project. In this respect, they view development fees as the least of three evils, the other two being a halt to any development to await public financing, and the exaction of developer contributions through case-by-case negotiation. The imposition of development fees at least allows development to continue upon the payment of a fee prescribed in advance. (In holding this view, developers differ from builders, on whom fall many fees. In most states in which fees have been considered, builders have presented the most vigorous opposition, while developers typically have been more supportive.) Both developers and builders, however, will continue to press public officials to put their house in order—to provide a more reasonable context of public infrastructure planning and investment within which to develop.

The following pages present developers' concerns with the idea and practice of development fees, and will suggest how communities might best respond to those concerns in an even-handed way.

CONCERNS: IN PRINCIPLE

Developers make two points about the rightness of enacting development fees. First, they suspect that their fee payments will be used to fund facilities that benefit the entire community or special groups other than the residents and tenants of their projects. This might be called the benefit issue. Second, developers believe that fees generally are passed along to the residents and tenants of their projects, and, when fees are added to other taxes and fees paid by all community residents, new residents will pay more than their fair share of infrastructure costs. This concern—who should pay for infrastructure to serve new development—might be termed the equity issue.

The Benefit Issue

For years, developers have watched public officials play games with capital funding programs: postponing needed investments, shifting construction priorities to favor special constituencies, and scattering available funds ineffectively among too many projects. It is not surprising, then, that developers expect that not all revenues from development fees will find their way into improvements that substantially benefit new development. Fees may be used to make up for infrastructure deficiencies caused by inadequate funding in the past, or to pay for system improvements that benefit all users, not just new residents. Or, worst of all, fees will just pile up in the bank while politicians argue about where to spend them.

Such concerns are not merely academic. A Maryland county some years ago drastically raised sewer connection fees to allow major treatment plant expansion but also to make up for several years of serious undercharging for debt service expenses. In effect, new residents were being required to subsidize the water and sewer charges of previous residents. Development fees for road improvements in one Florida county are 10 times as high as those in an adjoining county, principally due to long-term underinvestment by past county administrations. And every developer has his story about a road or water line promised but not delivered in time to support his development. As one developer commented:

> Impact fees are more palatable when they are tied to specific improvements that actually get made...but when I pay a $200-a-house transportation impact fee to improve an intersection that never gets built, I get angry. My $200-a-house fee must have gone into the General Fund [Snyder and Stegman 1986].

Developers also point to downtown housing linkage programs, notably in San Francisco and Boston, as examples of errant fees. Supposedly, linkage fees are required to mitigate the impacts of commercial development on low- and moderate-income housing. The "linkage" between such development and housing, however, is strained indeed, and it is difficult to see why a circumscribed class of developers should be charged with the responsibility for dealing with what is plainly a larger community problem. Furthermore, the San Francisco and Boston programs vividly illustrate the foot-in-the-door syndrome feared by many developers: Both cities have escalated and broadened their original linkage fees to cover other public interests. Although developers may play along with linkage requirements to earn the right to build in a seller's market, housing linkage requirements in particular strike them as unfair (Porter 1985).

The Equity Issue

The question of the beneficiaries of development fees has for years boggled (and sometimes addled) the minds of analysts, public officials, developers, and others concerned with development fees. One reason for confusion on this issue is that it involves two interrelated factors: who should pay, and who actually pays. Neither of these questions has an easy answer.

In terms of who should pay, many public officials are eager to require development to "pay its own way"—that is, to make sure that new projects, and not the general public, pay for the capital facilities needed to support development. In many communities, this notion has become a test for allowing any new development to proceed. Development fees have been enacted to make sure that capital costs stemming from new projects are recovered early in the development process.

On the face of it, this idea sounds rational and reasonable but for a significant fact: Most development in the past, particularly most residential development, has not paid its own way. Traditionally, new development has depended upon investments in public facilities made over generations, in keeping with the discontinuous nature of investments in large infrastructure systems. Each increment of development has contributed to the expansion of such systems through the regular taxes and charges imposed on all residents and properties in the community. Thus, debt incurred to pay for new infrastructure is spread over an ever-increasing population, and residents can expect to pay a decreasing share of the cost of facilities provided for their use. Although high growth rates will counterbalance this effect to some extent, in many cases existing residents will not be seriously impacted by the costs of expanding capital facilities to serve new residents. Snyder and Stegman demonstrate, in fact, that only when the community growth rate exceeds the rate of inflation are existing residents financially affected. They suggest that existing residents stand to reap windfall gains from development fees that pay most or all of the costs of new infrastructure (Snyder and Stegman 1986).

It does not appear fair, then, for existing residents to gain at the expense of new residents. But this raises the incidence question—who actually bears the cost of development fees? Developers, of course, will try to pass along the cost of fees either backward to the landowner or forward to the consumer; most developers believe that the consumer ultimately pays the fee. But economists traditionally have claimed that higher costs of development in a free market ultimately will be absorbed in land prices—that a developer faced with increased costs will compensate by offering a lower price for the site. And, since all developers within a particular geographic area are presumed to be affected in a similar way, it is assumed that landowners will accept a lower price. (For a review of economists' analyses, see Downing and McCaleb in Frank 1986.)

Yet we all know that the first law of economics is that no economic system works perfectly, least of all the land market. And so we see that in a heated market, where pricing decisions are being made rapidly with relatively little opportunity for information feedback, and where landowners' price expectations are inflating daily, land prices may not be influenced by higher development costs for months or years. This also holds generally true for land in highly desirable communities, for which developers are eager to pay higher land prices. In both cases, developers and builders will usually be able to pass along the higher costs imposed by development fees to new home buyers and business tenants. Furthermore, in such relatively inelastic markets, higher costs may be accommodated in the cost equation by reducing other cost factors such as lot sizes, floor space, and amenities. Alternatively, Snyder and Stegman cite several developers who upgraded their product because fees were too significant a cost for lower priced homes (Snyder and Stegman 1986).

So, depending on local circumstances, development fees may affect the land price, the developers' profits, the quality of the finished product, or its price or rent. Public officials, of course, normally prefer that landowners and developers pay the fee. Most public policymakers would be quite satisfied if fees had the effect of reducing land prices, since they believe that those prices are windfall gains by virtue of public investments in the area. Developers' profits also appear to be popular candidates for reduction—most policymakers have little sympathy for developers' profits, forgetting that the local development process will not function long without them. If development fees are passed along to consumers in the form of higher priced or lower quality products, however, new residents in effect become the fee payers. And those new residents may not be paying only for their own infrastructure but for some of the capital facilites serving existing residents as well.

Development fees, in other words, contain the capacity for inequitable allocations of costs among community residents. On the one hand, fees paid by developers may work to subsidize facilities used by existing residents. On the other hand, as fees increase the price of new development, the values of existing properties are raised as well. Existing residents stand to gain doubly in the process.

CONCERNS: IN PRACTICE

Standing on principle, then, most developers believe that development fees probably are unnecessary if local governments accept their true responsibilities and possibly are unfair in taxing one group of people to benefit, at least in part, another group. Their reactions to proposals for development fees, however, will stem more from their understanding of the current political climate for development than from a reliance on principles.

Development fees, after all, represent a means of accommodating growth and development—you pay, you play. If developers have experienced active citizen resistance to growth or have seen the adoption of moratoria due to inadequate facilities of one kind or another, they are likely to embrace development fees as a workable alternative to stopping all development. Furthermore, if developers have encountered mounting requirements for exactions painfully negotiated with planning boards and city councils, they may yearn for the relative certainty of prestated fees. A North Carolina builder put it this way:

The exaction fees aren't laid out in advance, and they're inconsistent. They come after the fact of negotiating for the land so you can't make decisions based on total cost. Impact fees are a fact of life we can deal with [Lemov 1986].

In practice, therefore, developers may be disposed toward the employment of fees as a better way of doing business. In fact, the group gathered at a 1986 Urban Land Institute policy forum on development fees concluded just that: Development fees promise a more predictable means of accommodating growth and exacting developers' contributions than is found in many jurisdictions (Porter 1986).

Once developers are convinced that development fees will become a reality, a different set of concerns arises. First, they want some advance warning that new costs may be placed on their developments and some understanding about why those costs are appropriate. Second, developers want fees to be woven into a well-structured planning and programming process that projects infrastructure needs and taps a variety of potential revenue sources to pay for improvements. Third, developers desire some assurance that fees will be collected, administered, and expended in a responsible way, with a definite system in place to track fee payments to an ultimate expenditure for infrastructure that benefits the fee payer. Fourth, developers will insist that fees be calculated on a reasonable basis, at least taking into account other revenue sources and existing deficiencies in the infrastructure systems. Finally, if developers are expected to contribute substantial funds for public infrastructure, they will ask in return for a firmer commitment that their developments will proceed free of new regulations, and for a reexamination of the standards and requirements for infrastructure.

Surprise Avoidance

Development fees, which usually amount to a small percentage of total development costs, generally represent an irritant rather than a fatal blow to a project. Nevertheless, the first reaction of many builders and developers to an impending fee requirement is resistance. Resistance may stem from a suspicion that fees, once adopted, will be calculated and administered to favor one group or even one developer over another, or may derive from long-standing aggravation over inadequate public planning for infrastructure investment. More to the point, developers and builders may be concerned about the effects that new or increased fees may have upon their project pro formas, especially those for projects in the approval pipeline. New costs may mean that projects no longer "pencil out" or will generate smaller profits. Extended political wrangling over fees often reflects these concerns.

The antidiote to the surprise factor is quite simple and usually rewarding for all involved: Development fees should be hatched and incubated through a public–private discussion process that includes representatives of all the players in local development. Such a process provides opportunities for educating all parties on everyone's needs and objectives and allows the reconciliation of differences before entering the public arena. Above all, such discussions eliminate the surprise factor that so often stirs controversy.

The fee adoption process of Loveland, Colorado, makes the point (see Chapter 3). In Loveland, a committee of 18 members, half from the development community, spent 15 months meeting twice a week, thinking through infrastructure plans and the proper structure of a fee, before arriving at final recommendations. This discussion procedure is credited for the cooperation and support the fee program has since enjoyed.

A Planning Framework

Developers will be more willing to contribute to improving public infrastructure systems if they believe that local governments have done a reasonable job of planning for system expansions and programming available revenues to pay for them. In general, developers are more comfortable developing within a context of comprehensive plans and public improvement programs that promise some protection from the vagaries of other developers and from ad hoc decisions of public officials. They want to see their money, in other words, well spent: for facilities of proven need, efficiently planned, and fairly financed.

Perhaps this comes as a surprise to planners, but developers in many areas complain about the inadequacy of local planning—the lack of both comprehensive and detailed plans for land use and infrastructure systems, caused in large part by insufficient funding for planning. Although developers may argue about specifics, they respect the need for planning. In the absense of adequate public planning programs, it is not uncommon these days to find developers, especially of large projects, commissioning major planning efforts to establish areawide patterns of land use and infrastructure systems as the basis for their own developments. The cost of this private planning for public systems amounts to another type of exaction. Furthermore, the relegation of public responsibilities to private firms stirs questions of equity and appropriateness.

More appropriately, public planning agencies should provide a framework of public plans and programs that demonstrate the needs for capital improvements and for developement fees as a source of capital financing. This fixes one more point of certainty for developers operating in a risky field and keeps public development strategists ahead of the game.

Responsible Administration

When developers pay fees, they like to think that those funds will find their way, speedily and efficiently, into financing specific capital improvements that directly benefit the payer's project. This calls for the establishment of an accounting system that earmarks fee payments as special funds, separate from general revenues, and that tracks expenditures from those funds for capital improvements related to development in the project area.

Earmarked funds are by no means a new device in captial funding, but the cause-and-effect relationship between payments and expenditures linked to specific projects is a more ticklish administrative problem. The courts have given somewhat confusing guidance on the necessity to show the direct benefit of such expenditures to individual projects (as discussed by Nancy Stroud in Chapter 7) and local governments have tried a variety of mechanisms, some more successful than others. Regardless of the chosen procedure, the principle stands: Local governments should structure an administrative means of ensuring a reasonable relationship between payments and improvements.

In addition, developers want assurance that capital expenditures will be made in time to benefit their development during construction and marketing. Again, the courts have suggested that payments not used within a reasonable amount of time—say five to ten years—should be returned to developers. This provision encourages the construction of improvements in time to help support the development paying the fee.

Reasonable Formulation

All the arguments at the heart of the benefit issue come into play here. Development fees too often are calculated in a simplistic way that equates future infrastructure costs with the amount of new development expected, the notion being that existing system deficiencies, other tax revenue, and depreciation schedules introduce unwanted complexities into the fee formula. There is no substitute, however, for as fair as a formulation method as can be devised within the capacities of staff and data. Developers are loath to make up for inadequate past funding of infrastructure and want to pay only for a fair share of required improvements. The calculation method should employ reasonable standards for determining provision of infrastructure and logical allocations of costs among users. The fee should reflect marginal increases in needs rather than total needs and should take account of debt service on existing infrastructure and other payments made through property and other taxes. Fee formulation, in other words, will require an analytical approach that accounts for a number of financial factors.

Quid Pro Quos

If local governments require sizable commitments of funds from private developers to pay for infrastructure improvements, developers will want greater assurance that they will be able to carry out subsequent development unimpeded by regulatory changes and that the infrastructure for which they are paying is truly necessary. Perhaps the best means of vesting rights to development is through some form of written development agreement, as is allowed in California, Hawaii, Florida, and a few other states. Lacking that mechanism, local governments can structure incremental payments as projects proceed to reduce the risk that fee payments will not be realized in completed infrastructure.

Local governments should also examine their standards and requirements for infrastructure systems to reduce excessive demands, especially related to the type of development. Widths of street pavements, requirements for sidewalks, and even open space standards are examples of infrastructure that could well be tempered to avoid unnecessary costs for new construction.

CONCLUSION

For developers, development fees present an attractive alternative to no-growth ordinances and negotiated exactions. The chief advantage of fees, however, is their predictability. Therefore, local governments should take every step to provide certainty in the formulation and administration of fees. These steps should include adequate advance warning that fees are being considered, provision of a detailed planning and programming context, a thorough analysis of cost and revenue factors providing the basis for fees, sound administration practices, and timely production of the infrastructure funded by fees. All this will allow developers to plan their own market and production moves with greater assurance and less risk, thereby allowing the possibility of higher-quality and less-expensive development.

References

Frank, James E. 1986. *Development Exactions*. Chicago: Planners Press.

Lemov, Penelope, 1986. Passing the Buck. *Builder* June: 72–77.

Porter, Douglas R., ed. 1985. *Downtown Linkages*. Washington, D.C.: Urban Land Institute.

Porter, Douglas R. 1986. The Rights and Wrongs of Impact Fees. *Urban Land* July: 16–19.

Synder, Thomas P. and Michael A. Stegman. 1986. *Paying for Growth. Using Development Fees to Finance Infrastructure*. Washington, D.C.: Urban Land Institute.

Legal Defense, Issues, and Trends

7

Legal Considerations of Development Impact Fees

NANCY STROUD

Laws regarding development impact fees have changed significantly in the past decade. Previously, the courts either tended to look on such fees with suspicion — as invalid taxation against new development — or to uphold them under a loose "hands-off" approach, considering them necessary corollaries to local land use regulations. Today, however, the courts increasingly apply a stricter cost accounting approach to development impact fees, as well as to other types of development exactions. They try to determine validity by closely examining the means by which the fees accomplish their purposes.

For the most part, state courts have been the primary forum for reviewing development and other land use fees, and court cases show remarkable similarities. But the recent United States Supreme Court decision, *Nollan* v. *California Coastal Commission* (June 1987)[1] clearly indicates that the federal courts as well will require a strict accounting from local governments of how they use land development exactions.

The judicial activity with regard to development impact fees comes at a critical time in local government finance. Local governments increasingly use development impact fees to supplement funds previously, but no longer, available through taxes or intergovernmental transfers and to shift more of the burden for financing public facilities to the private developer or the newcomer (Frank and Rhodes 1987). Combined with the increasing attention the courts give to the fair allocation of those costs, the legal issues involved in the use of development impact fees have taken on greater significance than they had in the past.

There are several forms of exactions. They include water and sewer connection or "capacity" charges; subdivision land dedications or fees in lieu of land for school or park use; and a variety of other exactions, such as road improvements, fire stations, and the like, which may be required or given voluntarily and which generally are associated with large development proposals. The development impact fee is a more current form of development exaction. It consists of a cash payment, which the developer typically makes when he receives a building permit. The cash payment is usually calculated on the basis of the development's impact on specific public facilities such as roads, parks, or drainage. The community earmarks the payments to be used for expanding the capacity of the specific facility.

83

This chapter is designed to explain for planners and educators the legal rationale for development impact fees. Articles that deal with such fees from a legal viewpoint generally have not been prepared for a planning audience. Heyman and Gilhool (1964) wrote a seminal work on the subject two decades ago, and their article has been very influential in state courts. However, that article and most of the others that followed appeared in legal journals and have not made their way into planning journals. Thus, many planners have remained unaware of the legal issues and approaches to impact fees. Nonetheless, local governments now commonly use various forms of development exactions, and those exactions apply with increasing frequency to a broad range of public facilities and services.

This chapter helps fill the gap in planning-oriented literature on legal issues related to impact fees. The emergence of the "rational nexus test," the test that now represents the mainstream judicial review for development impact fees, is described. Special emphasis is put on states that have developed more specific criteria for determining the legality of the fees and decisions that can be expected to influence the further evolution of the test. The implications of *Nollan* v. *California Coastal Commission*, the first U.S. Supreme Court case to address land dedication requirements, also are analyzed. Finally, ways planners might apply the rational nexus test to prepare and defend the use of development impact fees for financing various public facilities is discussed. If planners and other public officials are aware of the rational nexus approach and modern case law, they can exert more care in designing those increasingly popular fees.

ANTECEDENTS TO THE COST ACCOUNTING APPROACH

We usually can justify development impact fees only when they meet the rational nexus test. That test requires that a new development pay only its proportionate share of the costs of new facilities needed to serve the development. For example, if a new shopping center places 20,000 new trips on the roads in the vicinity, the developer must pay only the cost necessary to provide road capacity for the additional trips. At heart, the rational nexus test is a cost accounting approach that requires local governments to vigorously analyze the impact of new development on public facilities, and then to balance the government's revenue needs against the cost concerns of the development industry. Heyman and Gilhool (1964) suggested a basic approach in an article dealing with subdivision exactions. At that time, although mandatory subdivision dedications were becoming widespread, local governments often imposed them without discernible connection to public needs or consideration of equal treatment between residents of different subdivisions (Yearwood 1966). Heyman and Gilhool argued that uniformly applicable fees, backed by careful cost accounting, were a fairer and more flexible way to handle the impact of subdivisions than were subdivision dedications. The argument received almost immediate attention when the Wisconsin Supreme Court (1965) and the New York Appellate Court (1966) wrote influential opinions adopting the proposed approach.[2] By the 1970s, cost accounting was the predominant approach for judicial review of subdivision exactions and their regulatory cousin, the development impact fee.

Historically, the courts have upheld subdivision exactions on the basis of two theories. The first held that mandatory dedications were justified in return for the valuable "privilege" of having a subdivision plat recorded (Johnston 1967). The theory recognized that the developer and the local government received mutual benefits from the establishment of planned subdivisions; it failed, however, to attach any criteria for assessing those benefits. Thus, the subdivision might dedicate land or pay fees for facilities that were never built or that were greater than those required from similar development. Similarly, the local government might receive land of little value for constructing needed facilities.

The theory of government permits and grants as benefits rather than rights fell into disfavor in the 1960s. As Charles Reich (1964) argued in a widely quoted article, entitlement to government benefits was a new and important form of property. The U.S. Supreme Court over the next 20 years gradually broadened the concept of property to include the reasonable expectation of certain government permits and grants (Van Alstyne 1977). Landau (1972) similarly criticized the concept of subdivision as a privilege, and the theory lost its persuasive effect. State cases continue to refer to the privilege theory, but more as a footnote than as a thesis. The Supreme Court, in *Nollan*, more recently rejected the description of "the right to build on one's property" as a government benefit, but the court nonetheless recognized the legitimacy of government to regulate that right.

The second theory under which courts have upheld subdivision exactions historically considered the use of such exactions under an analysis traditionally associated with special assessments or the power of eminent domain. The approach is known as the Illinois "specifically and uniquely attributable" rule. Local governments typically may collect taxes, known as "special assessments," from within special districts and use them to finance improvements for land within those districts. The Illinois rule justifies subdivision exactions only if they effectively substitute for special assessments, so that the subdivision creates the entire need for the new facilities and the fees benefit the subdivision residents exclusively. Facilities that fall under the rule typically include neighborhood parks, connector sewer lines, local streets, and the like (Reps and Smith 1963). Subdivision exactions for facilities that benefit property beyond the subdivision—arterial roads, schools, regional parks, or central sewage treatment facilities—are not justified under that approach, even if they provide significant benefits to the subdivision residents. State courts have referred to the rule frequently, but over the years the Heyman and Gilhool cost accounting approach has gradually replaced it, even in Illinois (Braithwaite and Bateman 1984).

Heyman and Gilhool argued that cost accounting could specifically relate the cost of new facilities to the exaction to avoid questions of constitutional discrimination or the unconstitutional taking of land without just compensation. As Justice Holmes explained in the landmark case of *Pennsylvania Coal Company* v. *Mahon*,[3] "if the regulation goes too far, it will be recognized as a taking," which requires just compensation under the U.S. Constitution. Heyman and Gilhool explained that conventional exactions, which governments imposed for internal facilities within the subdivision, almost automatically ensured equal treatment among subdivisions because the internal facilities related to the specific needs of each subdivision. Courts could also uphold an exaction of land or fees that provided facilities for residents outside the subdivision, however. Modern cost accounting techniques could permit a precise calculation of cost for such facilities and allow planners to allocate the costs to the subdivision according to a relevant standard of need, thereby establishing a fair fee. For example, in the case of public schools, officials could estimate the cost of providing school facilities and then allocate that cost to the subdivision on the basis of the number of students the subdivision was expected to generate. The fees would be determined according to a formula applicable to all subdivisions, and so would ensure equal treatment among all new subdivision residents. Because the subdivision paid only costs it generated, and because it benefited from the facility, the courts could consider the fees reasonable, not a taking.

By the mid-1970s, many state courts began to use Heyman and Gilhool's approach to review subdivision exactions (whether in-lieu fees or land dedications) for facilities such as streets, schools, and parks. At the same time, some courts began to use a parallel approach in cases challenging the reasonableness of fees charged for the expansion of water and sewer facilities. The courts reviewed water and sewer fees in a different legal context than subdivision exactions for a number of reasons. Governments applied the fees broadly, not only to subdivisions but to all development that needed connections to a water or sewer system; state utility statutes generally provided the first line of authority in those cases, and often specifically authorized user fees to recoup capital costs. The proprietary tradition in utilities management made cost accounting a familiar concept. However, within a short time, subdivision exaction and utilities cases began to borrow concepts

and criteria from one another. Today, the courts apply the rational nexus test applied to many types of development impact fees (Bosselman and Stroud 1985).

RATIONAL NEXUS TEST

The rational nexus analysis evolved over several years, through a number of state courts, and in a variety of applications. Until *Nollan*, few federal courts had reviewed subdivision dedication or impact fee cases, so the case law relies largely on state precedent. A typical pattern for analyzing the validity of development impact fees, however, emerged in the state courts. First, the court reviews the statutory authority for the particular exaction. Many courts read that authority broadly, and in the context of a legislative intent to manage community development effectively. Once the court resolves the authority question, it addresses the relationship between the development to be charged and the purpose and amount of the required payment. Finally, the court considers the planned use of the collected fees, including whether they are specially earmarked for specific facilities and the timing and location of their expenditure.

The first legal obstacle to acceptance of development impact fees is the question of whether a local government has sufficient authority to impose the fee. Typically, state statutes do not explicitly authorize such fees, although at least one state, Arizona, does have general enabling legislation for development fees, and the legislation applies broadly to many types of facilities.[4] State legislatures may also authorize specific local governments to enact development fees; Maryland and Tennessee have such laws. More often, however, the courts need to give a broad interpretation to local government police powers established in home rule author- ity, subdivision regulation authority, zoning enabling legislation, and utility statutes to per- mit development impact fees. The question of authority seems to be becoming less of an ob- stacle than it has been to a valid fee (Juergens- meyer and Blake 1981), but it remains a critical consideration.

Virginia and a few other states have deter- mined impact fees to be invalid per se; in those states the voluntary *proffer* must substitute for predetermined and standardized fees. The proffer is a contribution in cash, land, or con- struction that a developer makes in conjunc- tion with application for permission to develop. Although ostensibly voluntary, the proffer is in fact a negotiated exaction.[5] In a few states, courts have interpreted statutes that specifically authorize certain exactions to constitute a limi- tation on the power to levy other exactions. For example, New Jersey courts ruled that subdi- vision enabling legislation that specifically authorizes school land reservations precludes a school fee.[6] At least one state legislature (Washington's) has responded to court interpre- tations by attempting to limit the use of impact fees (Lester 1984).

If the court determines that *imposition* of the impact fee is legitimate, the next question is the amount of the fee in relation to the need for it and the use the developer will make of the property. The court typically will examine at least three issues. First, the court will determine if the development will create a need for new capital facilities. State courts vary in their re- quirement for evidence of need. Some courts, such as those in Montana and California, find it apparent that new development increases the need for new facilities, and look no further (Bosselman and Stroud 1985). Generally, courts

place the burden on the developer who chal- lenges the fee to show that there is no relation- ship between a particular new development and increased need for public facilities.

The second and more critical issue is the ex- tent to which the government requires the new development to pay its proportionate share for new facilities, but not more than its share. That is the crux of the rational nexus test. For exam- ple, in 1977 the New Hampshire Supreme Court rejected the town of Plainfield's attempt to require a subdivider to pay the total cost of upgrading highways that provided access to the project. The town argued that "but for" the new subdivision, the town would not need certain off-site road improvements.[7] The court ruled that the town could not require the subdivider to pay the total cost of upgrading highways, but only that portion of the cost that bore a rational nexus to the needs the subdivision created. The court suggested that the calculation of that proportionate share should consider both the potential traffic increase from the subdivision and the standard to which the town maintained roads. The courts have become increasingly more sophisticated in reviewing the propor- tionality of the fee and, as in New Hampshire, have begun to develop cost accounting criteria to address that issue.

The third issue in the rational nexus test is the extent to which the fee collected benefits the development that pays it. The cases on this question generally agree that capital facilities need not exclusively benefit the persons who pay for them, but that the general public also may use them (Juergensmeyer and Blake 1981). Other factors may provide evidence of suffi- cient benefit to the fee payers. The courts ap- pear more inclined to uphold development im- pact fees if the community has a definite plan as to how it will spend the money. Many courts (including those in Wyoming, Florida, and Oregon) suggest or require that the funds collected be placed in a special account to ensure that they are spent for the public facilities for which the community collected them. Courts also may require that impact fees be refunded if they are not spent within a given time. Finally, at least one state court (Florida's) has approved the practice of establishing districts or zones within which fees are to be collected and spent, ensuring a geographic relationship between the fee payers and benefits.

Emerging State Trends for the Rational Nexus Test

Exactions are becoming more commonplace, and courts have developed more explicit criteria than existed previously for precise cost apportionment. The Utah Supreme Court, in particular, has pioneered a sophisticated use of the rational nexus test. According to the Utah court, cost apportionment is more than a matter of dividing the cost of the new facility by a measure of use by each new development. At least two other circumstances need attention (Bosselman and Stroud 1985). The first occurs when a previously constructed capital facility has excess capacity that new development wishes to use. The design of a fee to reimburse or recoup a portion of the previously expended capital outlay has been termed a recoupment problem. The second circumstance occurs when several revenue sources finance capital facilities, which is fairly typical. A double charging problem develops if the development paying the impact fee does not receive proper credit for other revenues it contributes toward building the same facility, such as user fees or property taxes.

The Utah Supreme Court in the early 1980s provided some detailed guidance for those circumstances. In *Banberry Development Corporation* v. *South Jordan City*[8] the court listed several factors for considering the validity of water and park impact fees. The court indicated that developments may pay their fair share of new facilities by buying into the equity value of the existing capital system. That recoupment analysis also must consider the cost of existing capital facilities and the depreciated value of the facilities at the time of buy in. In addition, the court mandates that in calculating the recoupment costs the local government has to consider any extraordinary costs necessary to serve the new development. As for the overcharging problem, the Utah Supreme Court requires that where different revenues fund the same capital facility, the value of any comparable facilities that the development contributes and the present value of past and future revenue payments otherwise contributed by the development for the facility must be credited against the fee.

The Utah approach is the most notable example of the modern application of the rational nexus test; it provides specific guidance for cost calculations that are applied across a variety of capital facilities.

Other state courts have also examined the question of cost allocation. In *White Birch Realty Corp.* v. *Gloucester Township Municipal Utilities Authority*[9] the New Jersey Supreme Court discussed several methods of determining a fair cost allocation for a sewage connection fee. The court mandated that new connectors must pay a fair contribution to debt charges that existing users previously met, and required a detailed examination of past bond term requirements and yearly connections to determine the new users' equity share. It also required that calcu-

Exhibit 7–1

IMPORTANT IMPACT FEE CASES

Pioneer Trust and Savings Bank v. Village of Mount Prospect, 176 N.E.2d 799 (Ill. 1961). The Illinois supreme court established the "specifically and uniquely attributable" test for the review of subdivision exactions. The case involved the validity of an ordinance requiring the dedication of one acre per 60 residential lots in a subdivision for schools, parks and other public purposes. The test is most restrictive and generally requires that facilities be to the exclusive benefit of the subdivision. Generally not used in most states, and Illinois has since modified this standard to comply with the cost-accounting approach.

Jordan v. Village of Menomonee Falls, 28 Wis.2d 608, 137 N.W.2d 442 (1965), appeal dismissed 385 U.S. 4 (1966). The Wisconsin supreme court held that land dedication and in-lieu fees for educational and recreational purposes were valid subdivision regulations if there were a "reasonable connection" between the need for additional facilities and the growth created by the subdivision. The case represents the more modern trend of state review.

Banberry Development Corporation v. South Jordan City, 631 P.2d 899 (Utah 1981). The supreme court of Utah, reviewing water connection and park improvement fees, required that such fees be set so that newly developed properties bear no more than their equitable share of the capital costs in relation to benefits conferred. A number of criteria for determining the reasonableness of the fee were specifically developed including criteria regarding double charging, the depreciated value of the

existing system, and extraordinary costs in serving new development. The case sets a standard for a demanding cost-accounting approach.

Home Builders and Contractors Association of Palm Beach v. Palm Beach County, 446 So.2d 140 (Fla. App. 1983) cert. denied 451 So.2d 848 (Fla. 1984), appeal dismissed 105 S. Ct. 376 (1984). Road impact fees were upheld as valid police power regulations under county home rule powers. The county ordinance established a formula to calculate a fair share of the cost of expanding new roads; fees collected are to be spent within particular geographic zones. The court applied a "rational nexus test," under which it evaluates impact fees in light of whether new development creates a need for new road construction, the fee charged is proportionate to the needs created, and the fees are used to reasonably benefit the feepayer.

Nollan v. California Coastal Commission, 107 S.Ct. 3141 (1987). A state requirement to provide lateral beach access as a condition to a coastal permit was found to be a taking in violation of the U.S. Constitution. The required easement for passage along the coast adjacent to the residential property did not "substantially advance" legitimate state interests, a test to be applied when land use regulations are evaluated in light of the takings clause. The case results in a federal constitutional requirement for a close nexus between the fee and the purpose it serves.

---

lations of the fee include other contributions, such as *ad valorem* taxes, which the fee payer had already contributed to the sewer system.

The Ohio court, in *Amherst Builders Assoc. v. City of Amherst,*[10] approved two methods of recoupment from new users of a sewer system. The first estimates the replacement cost of the system and deducts depreciation and remaining debt for an investment basis calculation. A final fee results from dividing that cost by the number of present users of the system. The second acceptable method is based on estimated

sewage flows from particular uses, divided into the total cost of the system. Both methods assume that unimproved property benefits from the availability of the existing system, and that developers of that property should reimburse the community when it is connected with the system.

The intense interest that local governments show in the use of impact fees, and the experimentation that courts throughout the country are undertaking regarding such fees, promise that the matter of a fair cost apportionment will continue to be a critical legal issue. Many of the cases will require the court to review economic or planning methodologies based on substantial data support and expert testimony. Other issues of fairness will arise from local government decisions that require policy choices as well as technical data. For example, while most development impact fees traditionally have applied throughout the local jurisdiction adopting them, some communities have considered adopting fees in only certain areas within the jurisdiction. Montgomery County, Maryland, in 1986 adopted highway impact fees for two planning districts experiencing particularly acute growth problems. The remainder of the county is not affected by the legislation (County Council 1986). Other localities are considering exempting certain areas, such as redevelopment districts, or certain uses, such as churches, single-family homes, or high technology industries from the fees. Such an ability to pick and choose among uses and areas has obvious political attractiveness, but in the end must also have a rational basis in community circumstances to be defensible in court. To date, the case law has not addressed the question of exemptions.

A consistent criticism of development fees has been that they unfairly shift the burden of capital facility costs that the public generally bore in the past (Snyder and Stegman 1986). Usually, however, when government charges the fees in reasonable proportionality and when the fees obviously benefit the fee payer, courts have not held them to be invalid simply because they are a new method of raising revenue. Indeed, in response to criticism, some courts point to the reciprocal enhancement in value the newly developed property receives because of the community's past investment in existing infrastructure.[11]

IMPACT OF *NOLLAN* V. *CALIFORNIA COASTAL COMMISSION*

In June 1987, the United States Supreme Court decided the case of *Nollan* v. *California Coastal Commission.* It was the first exactions case the Court heard, and it was one of only a few federal decisions concerning the legality of an exaction. The Nollans had applied to the state coastal commission for a permit to demolish and rebuild a beachfront house in a residential area along California's Pacific coast. The coastal commission conditioned the permit on the Nollans' dedication of an easement for public passage along their property between edge of their seawall and the ocean. The Court found this lateral access requirement to be an unconstitutional taking of property. The Court focused primarily on the closeness of the relationship between the nature of the required easement and the purpose for which it was required.

The Court analyzed the land dedication requirement under the approach historically used in California to uphold land dedication requirements such as subdivision exactions. California has required that an exaction be "reasonably related" to the public need or burden that the new development creates or to which it contributes. California had argued that lateral access was needed to increase visual access to the beach, prevent congestion of public beaches, and overcome the psychological barrier to beach use created by a developed shorefront. Stating that it is "impossible to understand" how lateral access increases visual access to the beach or promotes the other police power purposes claimed, the Court found that there was no reasonable relationship between the exaction and the state's purposes.

The Court distinguished California's undemanding approach from land dedication cases in all other state courts. Nevertheless, we cannot consider the holding in *Nollan* to be limited to California. In one of its most important findings, the Court held that the takings clause of the Constitution requires a closer relationship between a land use regulation and the police power purposes of the regulation than it has required of other constitutional challenges. As Justice William Brennan said in his dissenting opinion, the U.S. Supreme Court has historically required that the state *means* be "reasonably related" to the state's *purpose,* or that the court find that the state "could rationally have decided" that the regulation achieves its public purpose. *Nollan* requires that the regulation "substantially advance" the state's interest. Like the state courts, then, it appears that the federal court will scrutinize a land use exaction more closely to ensure that it achieves its intended purpose. However, the *Nollan* case now gives federal constitutional stature to the relationship required.

The *Nollan* decision may encourage local governments to adopt development fees as an alternative to land dedication exactions. In the *Nollan* case, the court indicated that land dedications require the court's special attention because of a heightened risk that a land dedication requirement is a means to avoid the state's use of eminent domain to purchase property. Indeed, the court warns that although a dedication can be made a condition to a permit, a land dedication requirement standing alone would be a per se taking. Rather than requiring the dedication of land as a condition of a permit, local governments would do better to require a fee, and then use the fee to purchase land and develop facilities. As a land use exac-

tion, a fee also needs to withstand close scrutiny, but it can arguably reflect more accurately the proportionate share of the need created. The local government can probably combine such fees with other revenues to acquire and develop sufficient facilities to benefit the fee payer.

DEVELOPMENT IMPACT FEES FOR A VARIETY OF FACILITIES

Beginning in the 1980s, governments across the nation expanded the variety of development impact fees to finance capital facilities. The trend toward broadening the use of impact fees to many types of facilities is growing rapidly at the same time that careful cost apportionment is becoming increasingly important. A brief survey of impact fees illustrates the manner in which the courts to date have applied the rational nexus test to specific facility needs.

Water and Sewer System Expansion

Perhaps the most common use of development impact fees is the water or sewer system expansion fee. State utility statutes generally include authority for water and sewer fees, although community planning legislation has also been cited as broad statutory authority, as in Utah and Florida. Few will dispute the need that new development creates for water and sewer facilities. The decreasing availability of federal subsidies for treatment facilities, in fact, creates greater need for alternative revenue sources. Furthermore, even before the federal cutback, federal policy was to privatize the costs of waste treatment by requiring private users, rather than the public as a whole, to pay their proportionate share of system costs.[12] The factors for determining proportionality are most fully developed in the cases of water and sewer fees, as illustrated in the cases discussed from Utah, New Jersey, and Ohio. Local governments typically require developments to construct or pay the costs of extending water or sewer lines from the new site to the available off-site lines. To the extent that impact fees are intended to finance such off-site system expansion, their use in addition to such extension requirements may create a double charging problem, necessitating that the developer receive credit against the impact fee for such extension payments. Finally, the requirement for earmarking fees by establishing special funds has been particularly important in the water and sewer cases.

Park and Recreation Facilities

Park and recreation impact fees are also popular types of development impact fees, and a rich body of case law in almost every state supports such exactions. The perceived need for parks and recreation has changed considerably in the past few decades; a 1984 case from Texas, *City of College Station* v. *Turtle Rock Corporation*,[13] illustrates a current approach to park fees. In 1980, an intermediate Texas court of appeals attracted national attention when it held that "parks are not necessarily beneficial to a community or neighborhood" and struck down an ordinance imposing a park exaction. When, four years later, the court of appeals issued a similar opinion, the Texas Supreme Court reversed the decision, holding that a parks exaction is a legitimate exercise of the police power if it meets the rational nexus test. The more recent cases tend to be concerned, not with questions of enabling authority or the general need for parks, but with factual questions relating to allocating an appropriate cost to the developer. Decisions have both struck down and upheld park fees based on the percentage of land

developed or the number of acres of parkland required per thousand residents. Even parks professionals disagree about appropriate community standards for parks (Gold 1973), and we can expect to hear a fair amount of dispute on the topic. In addition, although courts usually defer to the local government plans to use the park impact fees, they are reviewing increasingly such factors as the actual spending program, the proposed location and use of the parks, and earmarking of funds to ensure that a benefit will indeed occur.

Road Improvements

Impact fees for off-site road improvements currently generate considerable interest across the country and may become the typical impact fee case of the future. The first use of the term rational nexus for a development exaction, in fact, was used by the New Jersey Supreme Court in its review of an off-site road improvement requirement.[14] Many courts find sufficient authority for off-site road impact fees in subdivision, zoning, or home rule powers and then focus attention on the share of the traffic demand that the proposed development will contribute to determine if the required fee or improvement is appropriate. For example, the court in Palm Beach County, Florida, explicitly applied the rational nexus test to uphold a "fair share transportation impact fee."[15] Palm Beach County charges the fee to any development that generates new traffic and applies it to development at the earliest stage in the permitting process. To avoid double charging, the county credits development for the stream of revenue it will pay that also will be used to construct transportation facilities. For example, the county calculates how much gas tax the county and the state will assess for each type of use and then credits the appropriate amount against the impact fee. The county collects the fees according to the particular traffic zone in which the development is located, and the fees are spent within that zone.

Exactions for Schools

Cases regarding school exactions have a relatively long history, very similar to those regarding subdivision parks. Heyman and Gilhool (1964) suggest that cost accounting for schools would be among the simplest calculations on the basis, for example, of the average number of students per household. Early cases in Washington and New York applied a rational nexus test that upheld school and park dedication requirements. Even states like Illinois, which apply the "specifically and uniquely attributable" test, have validated school site dedication ordinances. Because most state constitutions contain provisions for the uniform system of public free schools, as well as extensive legislation and budgeting for the financing of schools, one may argue that school impact fees are inappropriate candidates for exactions. That argument, however, has not been tested in court.

Other Public Services

Courts traditionally have considered certain other services such as fire, emergency medical, or police services as a duty the government owes the general public. Therefore, one might also argue that it is inappropriate to fund those services through impact fees. For that reason, even the undemanding California cases express concern about police and fire exactions for subdivisions. Perhaps because of social policy concerns, few court cases involve public safety impact fees, and those are generally negative. In 1984, the Massachusetts Supreme Court ruled that a Boston fire protection fee intended to finance services and facilities was an unauthorized tax because the city lacked sufficient legislative authority to enact it.[16] The court expressed concern that the essential nature of police and fire services, especially in an urban environment, requires a uniform commitment to protection from which impact fees may detract. In theory, however, planners can develop and analyze the capital cost component of such services under the rational nexus test. Given adequate legislative authority, those fees would withstand a court challenge.

A number of states have used exactions for unique public facility requirements. For example, linkage programs have received some notoriety by using development impact fees to finance housing. A few areas, including San Francisco, Boston, and some New Jersey communities, have instituted linkage programs to fund low- and moderate-income housing (Keating 1986). The San Francisco and Boston linkage programs assume that new employment resulting from the creation of new office buildings stimulates the need for housing. The proportionate share of housing attributed to the proposed development assumes a specified number of employees per square foot of office space, a certain proportion of employees who will live in the city, a certain number of working adults occupying a residential unit, and a cost for a residential unit.

In 1985, the state appellate court invalidated Boston's linkage program as unauthorized under state law, but the Massachusetts Supreme Judicial Court reversed the decision on grounds that the challenging parties did not have standing to raise the issue.[17] To date, appellate courts have not reviewed linkage programs under the rational nexus test. Like other impact fees, however, the success of a linkage program under a rational nexus challenge should depend on the authority that a state's statutes or constitution grants, on the local government's ability to show that the new development causes a need for housing, that the exaction is proportionate to the need caused, and that the exaction will be used to meet the needs of and to benefit the occupants of the new development.

CONCLUSION

In the complex legal environment of statutory and judge-made case law, it is remarkable that a standard such as the rational nexus test can become widespread. Much of the rational nexus test's acceptability comes from its common sense approach, in which the community and the developer can view the transaction from a businesslike, cost-accounting standpoint and apply it across a variety of fees and exactions. Acceptance of development impact fees in future court cases may very well depend on the degree to which legal, economic, engineering, and planning analysts can demonstrate adequately the balance of burdens and benefits the court now expects under more sophisticated versions of the test. It makes good sense for communities considering the use of development impact fees to adhere closely to the basic components of the test under which they must establish sufficient legal authority for the fee, determine that the development creates an additional need for capital facilities, establish the proportionate share attributable to each new development, and ensure that the new development benefits from the expenditure of the fee. Those four components have important planning implications. A solid methodological basis for the fee will be persuasive in distinguishing a valid fee from an unauthorized tax.

To establish legal authority, planning lawyers must review comprehensively the applicable state statutes and case law to determine what existing direction the legislature and courts provide for such exactions. That analysis may involve review not only of planning statutes related to zoning and subdivision authority, but also of public utility and financing laws, city and county power acts, and legislation that regulates substantive areas such as transportation, parks and recreation, and the like.

The determination of need that the rational nexus test requires is an area where planning expertise traditionally associated with capital improvement programming and land use planning is particularly applicable. Need determinations should result from planning studies that evaluate the existing capacity of facilities, and whether—and to what extent—occupants of new development will use those and new capital facilities. The proportionate share attribution to new development will require capital planning expertise and may require the expertise of transportation engineers, wastewater facility engineers, park planners, and others who can help estimate the use of individual facilities by particular types of development. Proportionality considerations also require that economists and planners review the anticipated and existing public financing sources that contribute to construction of the facility.

Finally, the means to ensure that development will benefit from the fee may involve restrictions on the use of the fee to particular geographic areas and its expenditure within reasonable time frames. In most cases, an earmarked account that ensures that the fee will be expended on the facility for which it is collected is advisable. In this component, as with the others, planners will probably become involved in financial, legal, administrative, engineering, and other technical matters that necessitate a comprehensive and interdisciplinary approach. In light of the rational nexus analysis, planners should study those matters carefully before adopting the development fee.

Notes

1. *Nollan v. California Coastal Commission,* 107 S.Ct. 3141 (1987).

2. *Jenad, Inc. v. Village of Scarsdale,* 18 N.Y.2d 78, 21 N.E.2d 673, 271 N.Y.S.2d 955 (1966); *Jordan v. Village of Menomonee Falls,* 28 Wisc.2d 608, 137 N.W.2d 442 (1965), app. dis. 385 U.S. 4 (1966).

3. *Pennsylvania Coal Co. v. Mahon,* 260 U.S. 393 (1922).

4. Ariz. Rev. Stat. Ann. §9-463-05. (Supp. 1986).

5. *Board of County Supervisors of Prince William County v. Sie-Gray Developers, Inc.,* 334 S.E.2d 542 (Va. 1985).

6. *W. Park Avenue, Inc. v. Township of Ocean,* 48 N.J. 122, 224 A.2d 1 (1966).

7. *Land/Vest Properties, Inc. v. Town of Plainfield,* 379 A.2d 200 (N.H. 1977).

8. *Banberry Development Corporation v. South Jordan City,* 631 P.2d 899 (Utah 1981).

9. *White Birch Realty Corp. v. Gloucester Township Municipal Utilities Authority,* 80 N.J. 165, 402 P.2d 927 (1979).

10. *Amherst Builders Association v. City of Amherst,* 402 N.E.2d 1181 (Ohio 1980).

11. *J. W. Jones Company v. City of San Diego,* 157 Cal. App.3d 745, 203 Cal. Rptr. 580 (1984); *Lafferty v. City of Payson City,* 692 P.2d 376 (Utah 1982).

12. The Clean Water Act of 1977, §201(h) (2), 33 U.S.C. 1281(h) (2) (1985).

13. *City of College Station v. Turtle Rock Corp.,* 680 S.W.2d 802 (Tex. 1984).

14. *Longridge Builders, Inc. v. Planning Board of the Town of Princeton,* 52 N.J. 348, 245 A.2d 366 (1968). The most recent New Jersey Supreme Court decision struck down the use of road impact fees as applied to an entire municipality. *New Jersey Builders Association v. Bernards Township.* No. A-55, Slip. op. 108 N.J. 237, 528 A.2d 562 (1987).

15. *Hollywood, Inc. v. Broward County,* 431 So.2d 606 (Fla. App. 1983).

16. *Emerson College v. City of Boston,* 462 N.E.2d 1098 (Mass. 1984).

17. *Bonan v. City of Boston,* 398 Mass. 315, 496 N.E.2d 640 (1986).

References

Bosselman, Fred P. and Nancy E. Stroud. 1985. Pariah to Paragon: Developer Exactions in Florida. 1975-1985. *Stetson Law Review* 14: 527-63.

Braithwaite, J. William and James P. Bateman. 1984. *Subdivisions.* Illinois Land Use Law §4.24.

County Council for Montgomery County, Maryland. Bill No. 17-86, Development Impact Fees for Major Highways. Enacted July 29, 1986.

Frank, James E. and Robert M. Rhodes, eds. 1987. *Development Exactions.* Chicago: Planners Press.

Gold, Seymour. 1973. *Urban Recreational Planning.* Philadelphia: Lea and Febiger.

Heyman, Ira Michael and Thomas Gilhool. 1964. The Constitutionality of Imposing Increased Community Costs on New Suburban Residents through Subdivision Exactions. *Yale Law Journal* 73: 1119-57.

Johnston, John D., Jr. 1967. The Constitutionality of Subdivision Control Exactions: The Quest for a Rationale. *Cornell Law Quarterly* 52: 871-923.

Juergensmeyer, Julian C. and Robert Mason Blake. 1981. Impact Fees: An Answer to Local Governments' Capital Funding Dilemma. *Florida State University Law Review* 9, 3: 415-45.

Keating, W. Dennis. 1986. Linking Downtown Development to Broader Community Goals. *Journal of the American Planning Association* 52, 2: 133-41.

Landau, Eliot A. 1972. Urban Concentration and Land Exactions for Recreational Use: Some Constitutional Problems in Mandatory Dedication Ordinances in Iowa. *Drake Law Review* 22: 71-101.

Lester, Martha. 1984. Subdivision Exactions in Washington: The Controversy over Imposing Fees on Developers. *Washington Law Review* 59: 289-303.

Reich, Charles. 1964. The New Property. *Yale Law Journal* 73: 733-87.

Reps, John W. and Jerry L. Smith. 1963. Control of Urban Land Subdivisions. *Syracuse Law Review* 14: 405-525.

Snyder, Thomas P. and Michael A. Stegman. 1986. *Paying for Growth: Using Development Fees to Finance Infrastructure.* Washington, D.C.: Urban Land Institute.

Van Alstyne, William. 1977. Cracks in the "New Property." Adjudicative Due Process in The Administrative State. *Cornell Law Review* 62: 445-93.

Yearwood, R. M. 1966. *Land Subdivision Regulation: Policy and Legal Considerations for Urban Development.* New York: Praeger.

The Development of Regulatory Impact Fees: The Legal Issues

JULIAN CONRAD JUERGENSMEYER

Local governments today are concerned with the financing and availability of public facilities. As new growth mandates expansion of existing infrastructure, local governments face the dilemma of providing new and expanded schools, parks, roads, police and fire protection facilities, and sewer and water treatment installations. Increasingly, these communities are shifting the cost of new capital improvements from existing to new development through the use of land use regulatory fees—commonly called impact fees.[1]

INTRODUCTION

The required dedication was the earliest significant land use regulation developed to shift a portion of the capital expense burden to developers. The practice of local governments conditioning their approval of a subdivision plat upon the developer's agreement to provide and dedicate certain improvements now is a well-accepted part of subdivision regulation and generally is approved by the courts.[2]

The in-lieu fee developed as a refinement of required dedications. For example, requiring each subdivision to dedicate land for educational purposes would not solve the problem of providing school facilities for developing suburban areas because the sites often would be inadequate in size and imperfectly located. The in-lieu fee sought to solve this problem by substituting a money payment for dedication of land when the local government determined that the latter was not feasible.

Although similar to the in-lieu fee, the impact fee is a more flexible approach to private funding of off-site public infrastructure. Impact fees are charges imposed by local governments against new development to fund capital improvements required by the new development. Impact fees are designed to apportion the cost of new infrastructure among the new residents who create the need for these improvements. The fees—at least in theory—represent the pro rata share of the cost of providing a public service to an individual residential, commercial, or industrial unit.

The distinction between in-lieu and impact fees results in several decided advantages for impact fees. First, impact fees can be used to fund types of facilities and capital expenses that are not normally the subject of dedication requirements and more easily can be applied to facilities to be constructed outside the development (extradevelopmental) as well as those inside the development (intradevelopmental). For example, since in-lieu fees are predicated on dedication requirements, they can be used only where required dedications can be appropriately used. In the case of sewer and water facilities, public safety facilities, and similar capital outlays, required dedications frequently are not an appropriate device for shifting a portion of the capital costs to the development because one facility (and parcel of land) can service a very wide area and there is little need for additional land to extend these services. Second, impact fees can be applied to developments platted before the advent of required dedications or in-lieu fees and thus impose on new development its fair share of those capital costs. This advantage is particularly important in a state such as Florida, where hundreds of thousands of vacant lots were platted prior to the use of required dedications by local governments.[3] A third advantage is that impact fees can be applied to condominium, apartment, and commercial developments that create the need for extradevelopmental capital expenditures but which generally escape dedication or in-lieu fee requirements because of the small land area involved or the inapplicability of subdivision regulations. Finally, impact fees can be collected when building permits are issued—when the growth creating a need for new capital facilities occurs—rather than at the time of platting.

CONSTITUTIONAL CHALLENGES TO IMPACT FEES

Developer funding of public capital facilities, whether in-lieu fees, required dedications, or impact fees, have been justified on several theories. Shifting the burden of the cost of providing new facilities from the general public to the persons who create the need for the facilities has been viewed as a logical and fair method of accommodating growth.[4] Commentators have argued that, absent developer exactions, the developer may reap a windfall at the expense of the general public, which must bear the costs generated by the new development.[5] Others have extolled the privilege theory, which holds that in exchange for the privilege of developing, the developer must be responsible for the costs of public facilities necessary to service his project.[6]

In spite of these conceptual supports, impact fees are generally subjected to a two-tiered constitutional attack. The preliminary objection is that they are not authorized by state statute or constitution and therefore are void as ultra vires. If statutory authority is found, the local impact fee ordinance is alternatively challenged as an unreasonable regulation exceeding the police power or as a disguised tax that violates various state constitutional strictures. Additionally, impact fees have been challenged as discriminatory and a violation of equal protection since different types of developers may pay varying amounts and those who developed prior to the enactment of the impact fee may have made no contribution toward infrastructure.

Impact Fees: Land Use Regulation or Taxes?

Because impact fees are conceptually and functionally similar to dedications and other land use regulations, they can be considered regulations that generally are considered valid exercises of the police power. Theoretically, however, impact fees also could be classified as taxes, particularly if a court considers hornbook distinctions between taxes and regulations.

The choice a court makes between these two classifications is important, since this issue will often determine the validity of the exaction at issue. If the tax label is adopted, the impact fee will be invalidated unless express and specific statutory authorization for the tax exists. Even if statutory authorization is present, constitutional limitations on taxation may still invalidate the statute. Alternatively, if the impact fee is construed as a police power regulation, very broad legislative delegation will suffice. The clear trend among state courts is to validate such extradevelopment capital funding payment requirements as a valid exercise of the police power. Not surprisingly, most state courts have summarily labeled impact fees either a tax or regulation in a result-oriented fashion that avoids an adequate theoretical or policy-directed explanation.[7]

Those courts applying the tax label to impact fees either implicitly or expressly rely on two rationales. The first is a simplistic observation that impact fees are a positive exaction of funds and are therefore a tax. This criterion is an untenable basis for distinction because it exalts form over function. It ignores similar police power regulations that mandate that the developer expend considerable funds for streets, sewers, and other capital improvements within the development. Also, distinction between impact fees and similar police power regulations made on the basis that impact fees are imposed before building permits are issued rather than as part of the plat approval process is a distinction without a difference. In either case, funds must be expended by the developer prior to development.

The second rationale used to label extrade- velopment impact fees as taxes is the theory that funds for education, recreation, and public safety purposes cannot be raised under the police power. This assertion is based on the conviction that such facilities should be financed solely from general revenues provided by the community as a whole. There is no constitutional mandate, however, that educational, recreational, and other facilities be underwritten by the general population rather than by the new development that creates the need for additional improvements. Furthermore, this rationale employs an unduly restrictive and inflexible conception of local regulatory power.

Some courts avoid this classification issue by viewing some impact fees as charges for services rendered, rather than as either police power regulations or invalid taxes. Impact fees under this analysis are generally upheld as authorized under general user fee statutory authority. Recent Utah decisions, for example, have upheld sewer connection fees and similar charges as neither "taxes nor assessment but payments for services rendered."[8]

Judicial Criteria for Determining the Constitutionality of Impact Fees

Two early landmark decisions placed an almost insurmountable burden on local governments seeking money payments for extradevelopment capital spending from developers whose activities necessitated such expenditures. In *Pioneer Trust & Savings Bank* v. *Village of Mount Prospect*,[9] a developer challenged the validity of an ordinance requiring subdividers to dedicate one acre per 60 residential lots for schools, parks, and other public purposes. In determining whether required dedications or money payments for recreational or educational purposes represented a valid exercise of the police power, the Illinois Supreme Court propounded the "specifically and uniquely attributable test." The court focused on the origin of the need for the new facilities and held that unless the village could prove that the demand for additional facilities was "specifically and uniquely attributable" to the particular subdivision such requirements were an unreasonable regulation not authorized by the police power. Thus, where schools had become overcrowded because of the "total development of the community," the subdivider could not be compelled to help fund new facilities that his activity would necessitate.

A related and equally restrictive test was delineated by the New York court in *Gulest Associates, Inc.* v. *Town of Newburgh*.[10] In that case, developers attacked an ordinance that charged in-lieu fees for recreational purposes. The amounts collected were to be used by the town for "neighborhood park, playground or recreation purposes including the acquisition of property." The court held that the money payment requirement was an unreasonable regulation tantamount to an unconstitutional taking because the funds collected were not used solely for the benefit of the residents of the particular subdivision charged but rather could be used in any section of town for any recreational purpose. In essence, the *Gulest* direct benefit test required that funds collected from required payments for capital expenditures be tied specifically to a benefit directly conferred on the home owners in the subdivision that was charged. If recreational fees were used to purchase a park outside the subdivision, the direct benefit test was not met, and the ordinance was invalid.

Perhaps the reason behind this initial restrictive approach was an underlying judicial suspicion that payment requirements for extradevelopmental capital expenditures were in reality a tax. Unlike zoning, payment requirements did not fit neatly into traditional conceptions of police power regulations. By applying the restrictive *Pioneer Trust* and *Gulest* tests, courts imposed the restrictive requirements of a special assessment on such payment requirements. This was consistent with perceiving them as a tax. Unfortunately, it effectively precluded their use for most extradevelopmental capital funding purposes. The *Pioneer Trust* and *Gulest* tests therefore quickly became difficult to reconcile with the planning and funding problems imposed on local governments by the constant acceleration of suburban growth. This restrictiveness also became difficult to rationalize with the judicial view of zoning ordinances as presumptively valid.

As public policy concerns about the burden of economic growth became more evident, the state courts turned away from the stringent *Gulest* and *Pioneer Trust* standards. Although the results of these decisions are progressive, the measure of police power criteria developed by the courts is far from enlightening. Some courts nominally retained the *Pioneer Trust* test but reached patently contrary results without any explanation of the discrepancy. Other courts adopted a privilege theory, under which granting the privilege to subdivide entitles local governments to require payments for extradevelopmental capital spending in return. The imposition of these payment requirements is viewed more as a part of a transaction than as an exercise of the police power. Still other courts have deferred to legislative judgments and eschewed constitutional analysis of such payment requirements.

In contrast to these result-oriented techniques, a more rational constitutional approach was suggested by the Wisconsin Supreme Court in *Jordan* v. *Village of Menomonee Falls*.[11] A two-part rational nexus test of reasonableness for judging the validity of extradevelopmental impact and in-lieu fees can be discerned in the decision. In response to a developer's attack upon the ordinance as unauthorized by state statute and as an unconstitutional taking without just compensation, the *Jordan* court addressed the constitutionality of in-lieu fees for education and recreational purposes. After concluding that the fee payments were statutorily authorized, the court focused first on the *Pioneer Trust* specifically and uniquely attributable test.

The Wisconsin Supreme Court expressed concern that it was virtually impossible for a municipality to prove that money payment or land dedication requirements were assessed to meet a need generated solely by a particular subdivision. Suggesting a substitute test, the court held that money payment and dedication requirements for educational and recreational purposes were a valid exercise of the police power if there were a "reasonable connection" between the need for additional facilities and the growth generated by the subdivision. This first rational nexus was sufficiently established if the local government had generated the need to provide educational and recreational facilities for the benefit of this stream of new residents. In the absence of contrary evidence, such proof showed that the need for the facilities was sufficiently attributable to the activity of the particular developer to permit the collection of fees for financing required improvements.

The *Jordan* court also rejected the *Gulest* direct benefit requirement, declining to treat the fees as a special assessment. It imposed no requirement that the ordinance restrict the funds to the purchase of school and park facilities that would directly benefit the assessed subdivision. Instead, the court concluded that the relationship between the expenditure of funds and the benefits accruing to the subdivision providing funds was a fact issue pertinent to the reasonableness of the payment requirement under the police power.

The *Jordan* court did not expressly define the "reasonableness" required in the expenditure of extradevelopmental capital funds; however, a second rational nexus was by implication required between the expenditure of the funds and benefits accruing to the subdivision. The court concluded that this second rational nexus was met if the fees were to be used exclusively for site acquisition and the amount spent by the village in constructing additional school facilities was greater than the amounts collected from the developments creating the need for additional facilities.

This second rational nexus requirement inferred from *Jordan*, therefore, is met if a local government can demonstrate that its actual or projected extradevelopmental capital expenditures earmarked for the substantial benefit of a series of developments are greater than the capital payments required of those developments. Such proof establishes a sufficient benefit to a particular subdivision in the stream of residential growth so that the extradevelopmental payment requirements may be deemed to be reasonable under the police power. The concept of benefits received is clearly distinct from the concept of needs attributable. As the *Jordan* court recognized, the benefit accruing to the subdivision, although it need not be direct, is a necessary factor in analyzing the reasonableness of payment requirements for extradevelopmental capital funding.

Another court addressing the difficult issue of reasonableness of an impact fee has identified seven factors to evaluate the validity of an impact fee. The Utah Supreme Court, in *Banbury Development Corp. v. South Jordan City*,[12] suggested the following as the most important factors for a local government to consider when determining the burden borne and to be borne by new development:

1. The cost of existing infrastructure.

2. The method of financing existing facilities (such as user charges, bonds, special assessments, general taxes and federal grants).

3. The extent to which new developments and existing projects have already contributed to the cost of existing facilities, such as through property taxes and special assessments.

4. The extent of future contributions, such as user charges.

5. The extent to which developers may be entitled to credit because of required common facilities.

6. The extraordinary costs, if any, in providing service to new development.

7. The time–price differential inherent in comparison of amounts paid at different times.

The *Banberry* criteria were promulgated in an attempt to deal with two problems of the proper cost apportionment in an impact fee rate determination. The first problem, recoupment, occurs because impact fees are sometimes required in situations in which a local government seeks to recoup a portion of money spent previously on capital facilities with excess capacity. The second problem, double charging, occurs when infrastructure is financed by more than one revenue source. These criteria are designed to ensure that developers pay their fair share and are not overcharged by local governments.

Another challenge to the validity of impact fees is the equal protection constitutional attack. A fee levied only on new development, it is argued, denies the equal protection of the law guaranteed by the U.S. Constitution. In an opinion letter addressing a proposed beach restoration impact fee, for example, the Maryland attorney general noted that developers of new beachfront projects (and therefore the ultimate buyers or lessees) would pay all of the cost of restoring the beachfront despite the fact that all residents would benefit by the restoration.[13] The attorney general concluded, however, that since the plan was supported by a rational basis, an equal protection attack probably would not be successful.

If a court accepts the principle of impact fees, it is likely to reject equal protection attacks. For example, in California, a city's impact fee plan was upheld as reasonable despite its varying rates for residential developers and builders.[14] Another California court rejected the argument by a home builder's association that the city's plan, which charged substantially higher fees for residential construction than for commercial development, violated equal protection. The court found the distinction between residential and commercial development to be a reasonable classification.[15]

In *Ivy Steel and Wire Co. v. City of Jacksonville*,[16] the Jacksonville, Florida, ordinance at issue imposed a water pollution control charge on those persons connecting to the city sewer system after a specified date. Plaintiff challenged the ordinance on the theory that the equal protection clause of the U.S. Constitution was violated by the fact that those persons connected before the specified date would be exempt while those who connected afterward would have to pay the fee. The federal district court found no denial of equal protection.

The Florida Supreme Court also considered but rejected an equal protection challenge in its landmark decision in the *Contractors & Builders Association* v. *City of Dunedin* case (discussed later). The Supreme Court of Colorado also recently rejected an equal-protection-based challenge in *City of Arvada* v. *City and County of Denver.*[17]

IMPACT FEES IN FLORIDA: A CASE-BY-CASE STUDY OF LOCAL GOVERNMENTS' STRUGGLE FOR CAPITAL FUNDING SOURCES

The rapid population growth that Florida has experienced in recent years has made it a prime jurisdiction for the use of impact fees to generate capital funds for growth-burdened local governments. Florida also has an especially severe problem posed by the tremendous amount of platted but undeveloped land.[18]

In many jurisdictions around the country, land has been platted only after the demands for immediate or near-term development have encompassed it. Consequently, most lots are built on soon after platting occurs. This has not been the case in much of Florida. One of the most important and infrequently discussed aspects of nearly a century of land booms and busts in Florida is that hundreds of thousands of lots have been platted but never developed. Most of the platting that occurred before the 1970s did not involve required dedications of any sort, with the possible exception of road and drainage easements. When the lots in these old subdivisions are finally built on, no contribution toward public services will have been made on their behalf. In the case of land that

was not platted prior to current requirements (perhaps even contiguous land), owners must make contributions in the form of required dedications or in lieu of payments toward public services as a condition for platting and development.

Thus, whether land currently being built on has contributed toward the capital costs of new public services depends on when the land was platted. The most recently platted land is discriminated against because economically significant exactions in Florida are a recent phenomenon. It would seem that the best, and perhaps the only, way to equalize this discrimination is via impact fees. Through the collection of impact fees at the building permit issue stage of development, the required contribution to public services, recognized by the courts as proper in connection with platting, is imposed against land that has not made such a contribution at the time of platting.[19]

Statutory Authorization for Impact Fees in Florida

Florida does not have a statute that specifically authorizes impact fees for the funding of educational, road, recreational, and other capital funding purposes. Authority to impose impact fees was found by the courts in several broad grants of power to local governments including the home rule power of Florida counties and municipalities, and the Local Government Comprehensive Planning Act of 1975 (LGCPA).[20]

The home rule powers of municipalities and counties are derived from different sources. Municipalities receive home rule powers from the Florida constitution and the Municipal Home Rule Powers Act.[21] Under these provisions, municipalities are granted the "governmental, corporate, and proprietary powers to enable them to conduct municipal government, perform municipal functions, and render municipal services," including the authority to adopt land use planning measures. This home rule power is limited in that municipalities may not enact legislation that is expressly prohibited by the state constitution or that concerns any subject expressly preempted by the state constitution or general law. Florida courts have held that the Florida Constitution grants the requisite power and authority to enact valid impact fees.[22] The LGCPA provides broad but nonspecific subdivision regulation power to local governments. The Fourth District Court of Appeal found that Palm Beach County had authority to enact a road impact fee by virtue of the LGCPA, in conjunction with the constitutional grant of home rule power.[23]

Florida's Growth Management Act of 1985 recognizes the general validity of impact fees as land use regulations and virtually mandates their use by requiring local governments to maintain adequate service levels and to adopt land use plans that are consistent with state requirements. Local governments must maintain the service levels they choose and cannot approve development that would reduce those levels. Furthermore, a community's land use plan must be consistent with local land development regulations, must be based on availability of public services, and must specifically plan for future infrastructure needs and construction. Local governments therefore must plan for assurance of adequate and available capital facilities and have been encouraged by the Growth Management Act to impose impact fees to fund those infrastructure needs.[24]

This encouragement for the use of impact fees by the Growth Management Act is stated in the statute:

> This section shall be construed to encourage the use of innovative land development regulations which include provisions such as transfer of development rights, incentive and inclusionary zoning, planned unit development, impact fees, and performance zoning. [Fla. Stat. Section 163.3203(3)]

The Growth Management Act also seems to recognize the rational nexus standard as the proper test for impact fees to meet since it further provides that

> any funds or lands contributed must be expressly designated and used to mitigate impacts reasonably attributable to the proposed development. [Fla. Stat. Section. 380.06(15)(d)(3)]

The Tax Versus Regulation Problem in Florida

If an impact fee is construed as a tax, the broad regulatory authority conferred by home rule provisions and land use planning and control statutes will be insufficient to sustain its validity because in Florida a tax must be specifically authorized by statute and authorization will not be inferred from broad delegations of authority. Several early Florida court decisions addressing the validity of impact fees for extra development facilities held that such fees were taxes and therefore unauthorized and invalid.

In *Venditti Sivaro, Inc.* v. *City of Hollywood*[25] the circuit court for the seventeenth judicial circuit labeled as invalid a tax charge added by the city of Hollywood to every building permit fee. The charge was to be paid into a special fund to be used for the acquisition, beautification, and development of parks and open space areas.

In *Broward County* v. *Janis Development Corp.*,[26] the Fourth District Court of Appeals reviewed an impact fee of $200 per dwelling unit to fund road and bridge construction. An increased fee was imposed on higher density developments because they impose a greater traffic burden on the community. The *Janis* court found the impact fee to be a tax because the ordinance failed to specify where and when the monies collected were to be used. The court so held even though the particular ordinance specified that the funds were to be expended solely for roads and bridges in or near the municipality from which they were collected. In essence, the court held that the fee was a tax rather than a regulation because it failed the direct benefit test of *Gulest*.

Also in 1975, the Third District Court of Appeals struck down an ordinance assessing a monthly charge on all property owners hooking up to fire lines over a specified size in *City of Miami Beach* v. *Jacobs*.[27] The court held the ordinance unconstitutional on its face because no earmarking of funds collected was specified.

In spite of the restrictive decisions by lower Florida courts, the Florida Supreme Court in *Contractors & Builders Association of Pinellas County* v. *City of Dunedin*,[28] held that a properly restricted impact fee that shifts the burden of extradevelopmental capital expenditures to new residents need not be considered a tax. The Builders Association attacked the validity of an impact fee for sewer and water capital funding, claiming that the money collected for capital improvements to the system was an invalid tax. Expressly distinguishing *Janis*, the court stated that, "[i]n contrast, evidence was adduced here that the connection fees were less than costs *Dunedin* was destined to incur in accommodating new users of its water and sewer system." Because the appropriate nexus had been established between the fee charged and the capital costs of expansion necessitated by the new users, the impact fee was held not to be a tax.

Florida Impact Fees in the Post-*Dunedin* Era

As discussed above, early Florida decisions adopted a restrictive approach in assessing the police power validity of land use regulations designed to shift the burden of capital expenditures for extradevelopmental facilities and improvements to new development. Both the *Gulest* direct benefit and the *Pioneer Trust* specifically and uniquely attributable tests were used by courts to invalidate ordinances requiring mandatory dedications or fees for capital funding purposes.[29] This restrictive approach was rejected by the Supreme Court of Florida in *Dunedin*.

Since the Supreme Court of Florida handed down its decision in *Dunedin*, the pressures that created the interest of local governments in enacting such fees have greatly increased, and more local governments have pursued and embraced the concept. Fortunately for local governments, a subsequent opinion in the *Dunedin* controversy and three district court opinions handed down in 1983 extend the permissible uses of local government impact fees and clarify the standards to be applied in determining the validity of impact fees.

The litigants in *Dunedin* revisited the Second District Court of Appeals shortly following the Supreme Court's decision. The trial court on remand had found that the city had corrected the defects in earmarking but ordered a refund of the fees already paid. The Second District Court of Appeals reversed, thereby preventing developers from obtaining refunds.[30] Although the holding of the court applies to a unique situation, the decision is quite significant because of the pro-impact fee position taken by the court.

Three 1983 decisions are of much greater significance. In *Hollywood, Inc.* v. *Broward County*[31] and *Town of Longboat Key* v. *Lands End*,[32] the court upheld the use of impact fees for the expansion of local government park systems; and in *Home Builders Association* v. *Board of County Commissioners of Palm Beach County*,[33] an impact fee for road improvements was upheld. In deciding these three cases, the courts in two major urbanizing appellate districts have also clarified the authority of local governments to enact such fees under their police power authority, and have adopted the reasonable nexus tests first established in the Florida Supreme Court case *Contractors & Builders Association of Pinellas County* v. *City of Dunedin*. Owing to the significance of these cases, each will be analyzed.

Hollywood, Inc. v. Broward County. This case involved a fee required to be paid to the county as a condition of plat approval to be used for the capital costs of expanding the countywide park system. Under the challenged ordinance, a subdivider had the option (with the agreement of the county) of dedicating land, paying a fee in lieu of dedicating land, or paying a fee determined by a schedule based on the number and size of dwelling units to be built.

The court first addressed the authority by which Broward County adopted the ordinance, which Hollywood, Inc. asserted was ultra vires, or beyond the constitutional or statutory powers of the county. The court noted that Broward County is a charter county which, under the Florida Constitution, maintains broad home rule powers, and which powers are to be broadly construed by the terms of the

charter itself. The court found nothing in the county charter that would prohibit the enacted ordinance. Because of the holding based on the charter powers of the county, the court explicitly found it unnecessary to address the county's argument that it was empowered to enact the ordinance under the Local Government Comprehensive Planning Act.

The court then turned to the allegation that the ordinance was unconstitutional because it established an invalid tax. Under the standards established by *Dunedin*, and with favorable reference to the Third District case of *Wald Corporation* v. *Metropolitan Dade County*,[34] and authority from other states, the court found the ordinance to be a valid exercise of the police power. Impact fees or dedication requirements are permissible, the court found, if they show a reasonable connection, or rational nexus in two ways:

1. If the fees offset needs sufficiently attributable to the growth in population generated by the subdivision, and

2. If the funds collected are sufficiently earmarked for the substantial benefit of the subdivision residents.

By adhering to these two tests, the court found that "local governments can shift to new residents the reasonable capital costs incurred on their account."

Broward County met the two tests for a valid impact fee by showing:

1. The growth generated by the new subdivisions would require new parks in order for the county to maintain its standard of three acres per 1,000 residents. The county had provided parks for existing residents through various methods such as a bond issues. The fees collected from the new residents would not exceed the costs of providing capital park

facilities for the new residents after those residents were credited for their future property tax payments for the bond retirement, and

2. The funds, by the terms of the ordinance, were earmarked to be expended "within a reasonable period of time" and for acquiring and developing parks within a reasonable distance of the subdivision (15 miles).

As a final note, the court declared, "Open space, green parks and adequate recreational areas are vital to a community's mental and physical well being," and as such the ordinance ensuring parks and recreational facilities "falls squarely within the state's police powers."[35]

Town of Longboat Key v. *Lands End, Inc.* This case concerned an ordinance requiring developers to deed land or pay a fee before final approval of development plans for the purpose of acquiring open space and parkland. The ordinance originally provided that developers would dedicate two and one-half acres for "other specified town purposes." Before the end of the trial, the town amended its ordinance to require five acres of land per 1,000 residents or a fee in lieu, and deleted the reference to "other specified town purposes." The trial court invalidated the first ordinance, finding it to establish an invalid tax on the basis that reference to "other specified town purposes" indicated that the fees were not properly restricted to park development.

The Second District Court of Appeals reversed and remanded the case to the trial court to apply the later enacted ordinance. In so doing, the district court adopted the tests established in the *Hollywood, Inc.* case, and thus provided guidance in regard to the evaluation of the later enacted ordinance. The court specifically referred to the two rational nexus tests and

stated that the fees must be shown to offset but not exceed reasonable needs attributable to the new subdivision resident, and must be adequately earmarked for capital assets that would sufficiently benefit the new residents.

Home Builders and Contractors Association v. *Palm Beach County.* In this case, decided seven months after *Hollywood, Inc.*, the Fourth District Court again upheld the use of impact fees that met the dual rational nexus test—in this case for a noncharter county and for the use of road improvements. The Palm Beach County ordinance required new land development activity generating road traffic (including residential, commercial, and industrial uses) to pay a fair share of the cost of expanding new roads attributable to the new development. The developer paid according to a formula in the ordinance that was based on the costs of road construction and the number of motor vehicle trips generated by different types of land use. Alternatively, a developer could submit his own study of his fair share of the road costs. Funds collected were placed in a trust fund for expenditure in one of 40 zones established throughout the county in which the developer was located.

Following the same line of reasoning as *Hollywood, Inc.*, the court first addressed the county's authority to enact the ordinance. The court looked to the Florida Constitution, Article VIII, Section 1(f), which grants noncharter counties "such power of self-government as provided by special or general law." The court found that Chapter 125, the county government statute, provides sufficient statutory authority for impact fees in light of the Florida Supreme Court decision *Speer* v. *Olsen*,[36] which interpreted the statute to be a grant of broad home rule power to noncharter counties in the absence of inconsistent general or special laws. The court also found, for the first time, statutory authority for impact fees in the Local Government Comprehensive Planning Act. The court rejected the Home Builders' argument that the ordinance violated constitutional equal protection provisions because in a noncharter county municipalities may "opt out" of the ordinance. Noting that the Florida Constitution itself provides that municipalities in noncharter counties may opt out, the court decided that unequal or different charges are not improper where the legislation is otherwise a valid exercise of governmental power.

Finally, the court found that the ordinance met the requirements for a valid fee rather than a tax because of the restrictions built into the assessment and use of the fee. The dichotomy between a fee and a tax, the court conceded, is "the most difficult point raised in this appeal," because "the distinction is very amorphous." The court referred to the public policy factors that should be used to characterize impact fees as regulatory rather than taxing devices—including the legislative mandate in Florida Statutes Chapter 163 that local governments must plan comprehensively for future growth—by quoting the following from Juergensmeyer and Blake, "Impact Fees: An Answer to Local Governments' Capital Funding Dilemma" (9 Fla. St. U.L.Rev. 415 [1981]):

> The appropriate framework for determining whether an impact fee is a regulation or a tax is one of public policy in which a number of factors should be weighted. The home rule powers granted local governments in Florida, the legislative mandate that local governments must plan comprehensively for future growth, and the additional broad powers given them to make those plans work effectively, indicate that

properly limited impact fees for educational or recreational purposes should be construed as regulations. Characterization as regulation is particularly appropriate where an impact fee is used to complement other land use measures such as an in-lieu fee or dedications. If an impact fee is characterized as a regulation, its validity should then be determined by reference to the dual rational nexi police power standard.[37]

The Palm Beach ordinance specifically meets the *Dunedin* tests for a valid regulatory fee, first because the ordinance recognizes costs that will far exceed the fees imposed by the ordinance. Significantly, the court held that the improvements paid for by the ordinance need not be used exclusively or overwhelmingly for those who pay; rather, improvements need only adequately benefit the development that provides the fee. The rejection of an exclusive benefit criterion explicitly puts the court with a growing number of states that accept a more flexible use of such fees so long as they bear a reasonable relationship to the needs created by the subdivision.

The validity of the fees, as recognized by these cases, is now more properly judged by how they are assessed and how they are spent. The cases adopt the dual rational nexus tests as originally set forward in the *Dunedin* case. These tests require that a local government demonstrate that the need for the fee is created by the new growth assessed (and the fee does not exceed the cost of serving the new growth), and that the funds collected are earmarked for the sufficient benefit of the new residents who pay.

DRAFTING IMPACT FEES TO PASS JUDICIAL SCRUTINY

The recent victories of impact fee proponents

in Florida and many other jurisdictions have resulted in more numerous and more varied impact fee ordinances and comprehensive plan provisions. See *Coulter* v. *City of Rawlins, Englewood Water District* v. *Halstead, City of Arvada* v. *City and County of Denver.*[38] The attention of planners, judges, attorneys, and local government officials has shifted in many states from the issues of statutory authorization, constitutional validity, tax versus land regulatory change, and rational nexus to how to draft impact fee ordinances in order to bring them within the parameters established by the courts for validity. Drafting requirements vary according to the jurisdiction in question, but some generally applicable standards can be formulated. The following basic list has been suggested for Florida but should have considerable applicability to other states as well.

1. An impact fee ordinance should expressly cite statutory authority for local government regulation of the substantive area selected.

2. A need for service or improvements resulting from new development should be demonstrated.

3. The fee charged must not exceed the cost of improvements required by the new developments.

4. The improvements funded must benefit adequately the development which is the source of the fee (even if nonresidents of the development also benefit).

5. In place of a rigid and inflexible formula for calculating the amount of the fee to be imposed on a particular development, a variance procedure should be included so that the local government may consider studies and data submitted by the developer to decrease his assessment.

6. The expenditure of funds should be local-ized to the areas from which they were collected. (Connelly, "Road Impact Fees Upheld in Non-Charter County.")[39]

Recent cases from various jurisdictions give further indications of judicial requirements that likely will be imposed on impact-fee-related ordinances. A decision by the supreme court of Arkansas[40] should prove to be a leading case in point. The city required a cash contribution from the plaintiff land developer of $85 per lot, which was to be invested by the city and eventually used for the acquisition and development of parks. The court held for the plaintiff on the basis that the city did not have a sufficiently definite plan for parks and park facilities to justify the contribution, and further noted that no provision was made for refund of the contributions should the area not be developed as expected.

Both of these points would seem to translate into principles that should be followed in formulating and drafting impact fee ordinances. The easiest to comply with is the provision that refunds should be included in the ordinance; fees can be returned if they are not properly spent for the purposes for which they were collected within a reasonable period of time after their collection. The reasonableness of the time period should probably be tied to the capital funding planning period for the infrastructure in question. If, for example, the jurisdiction works with a five-year capital improvement plan, that five-year period plus an extra year for flexibility should be stated as the refund period. The following ordinance provision should fulfill the court's concern:

Any funds not expended or encumbered by the end of the calendar quarter immediately following six (6) years from the date the impact fee was paid, shall, upon application of the fee payer, be returned to him with interest at the rate of ____ percent (%) per annum.

The more important requirement established by the Arkansas court is that money can be collected for capital expenditures only if there is a reasonably definite plan for its expenditure.[41] What the court seems to be – and should be – requiring is that impact fees and related ordinances must implement comprehensive plans. Impact fees, it should be remembered, are land use regulations, and thus their validity should be dependent upon their being an implementation of the local government's plan for capital facilities. If a fee is to be collected from new development for park acquisition and/or park facilities construction, then the jurisdiction should have a plan for parks and should have a standard for park facilities against which the validity and fairness of the parks impact fee can be judged.

Careful earmarking and restriction of funds for expenditure for the benefit of the geographic areas from which they are collected also merits careful attention. For example, in a recent Maryland case, the court invalidated a special connection charge to developers known as the System Sanitary Commission Offset Charge, or SEOC.[42] In addition to finding no valid statutory authority for the imposition of the fees, the Maryland court found that the local government had failed to properly restrict the use and handling of the monies collected. As in *Dunedin*, the Maryland court held that this lack of adequate restrictive guidelines undercut the legal justification for imposing the fees.

Lee County, Florida, has addressed this concern in its Parks Impact Fee Ordinance by requiring that all impact fees be deposited into "special trusts funds" to be used "exclusively for capital improvements within or for the benefit of the regional parks impact fee districts from which the funds were created." [Lee County, Florida, Parks Impact Fee Ordinance No. 85-24 (July 31, 1985)]. Lee County's Roads Impact Fee Ordinance No. 85-23 (July 31, 1985) similarly creates specific trust funds for the revenues collected from road impact fees. Montgomery County, Maryland, likewise has separated the revenues for its new road impact fees. The ordinance directs the County Department of Finance "to establish separate accounts for each impact fee area and...maintain records for each such account so that development impact fee funds collected can be segregated by the impact fee area of origin." (Montgomery County Council Bill No. 17-86, Section 49A-8(c), July 29, 1986).

The necessity of a tie-in between the plan and the impact fee should be stressed in formulating the impact fee and the ordinance enacting it. The following language is offered as such a possible provision in an impact fee ordinance:

WHEREAS, the Kumquat County Comprehensive Plan has determined that land development shall not be permitted unless adequate capital facilities exist or are assured; and

WHEREAS, the Kumquat County Comprehensive Plan has determined the policy that land development shall bear a proportionate cost of the provision of the new or expanded capital facilities required by such development; and

WHEREAS, the Kumquat County Comprehensive Plan determines that the imposition of impact fees and dedication requirements is the preferred method of regulating land development in order to ensure that it bears a proportionate share of the cost of capital facilities necessary to accommodate that development and to promote and protect the public health, safety, and welfare; and

WHEREAS, the Board of County Commissioners of Kumquat County has determined that Kumquat County must expand its park system in order to maintain current park standards if new development is to be accommodated without decreasing current standards, now, therefore, the following parks impact fee is hereby adopted.

The *City of Fayetteville* decision emphasizes the necessity of wedding planning and law in the formulation, adoption, and implementation of impact fees designed to fund capital expenditures for infrastructure to service new development. A recent decision by the supreme court of Utah revisits the absolute necessity for careful and highly competent economic analysis in the impact fee formulation and implementation process. Ostensibly *Lafferty* v. *Payson City*[43] simply reiterates the requirement discussed earlier in connection with the decision of the supreme court of Florida in *Contractors & Builders Association of Pinellas County* v. *City of Dunedin*[44] that impact fee monies must be earmarked so that they can be spent only for the purpose for which they were collected. More important, however, the supreme court of Utah takes the opportunity in *Lafferty* to reemphasize the economic analysis it formulated in *Banberry Development Corp.* v. *South Jordan City*[45] to guarantee that impact fees do not treat new residents unfairly "in determining the relative burden already borne and yet to be borne by newly developed properties."[46]

Complex and sophisticated economic analysis is required to assess the considerations deemed crucial by the Utah court. Nonetheless, courts in other jurisdictions will doubtless turn them into standards that impact fee calculation formulas must meet to be held valid. Even in jurisdictions in which the courts are less demanding, local developers, new residents, taxpayers, and others will doubtless require of their elected officials sound economic analysis to support impact fee programs.[47]

CONCLUSION

As far as local governments are concerned, there seems to be no doubt that the impact-analysis-oriented land regulatory measures referred to as impact fees, dedication requirements, and in-lieu payments provide at least a partial answer to local governments' capital funding dilemma by providing a means whereby local governments can require new land development to bear a proportionate cost of providing the new or expanded capital facilities required by new development. The judicial acceptance of impact fees and their characterization as land regulation charges have not come easily in many high-growth jurisdictions. Recent court decisions indicate an increasing judicial acceptance of impact fees and their role in land development regulations in general and growth management in particular.

In spite of increased judicial acceptance of impact fees, their formulation, drafting, and implementation are becoming more complicated as the courts are becoming more sophisticated and demanding in their scrutiny of such measures. Nonetheless, assiduous melding of legal, planning, and economic analysis offers hope to local governments pushed to the verge of bankruptcy by the infrastructure demands that considerable and sometimes rampant growth places on them.

The important role that impact fees now can fill for local governments should, however, not obscure their limitations. Impact fees are largely unresponsive and even insensitive to the issue of the quantity and type of growth that should be allowed to occur, and are responsive only to the issue of location of new development in terms of the availability and provision of capital infrastructure. Impact fees also are inadequate to solve such socioeconomic issues as housing and employment needs that are so closely related to growth. These limitations are indicated by the phenomenon that even though impact fees are quite new in their political and judicial acceptance they already have been somewhat relegated to second place in the eyes of many planners and planning attorneys by linkage programs that seek to broaden the responsibility of the private sector for the ramifications of new development. Perhaps the most exciting developments in regard to impact fees in the near future will relate to their interrelationship with linkage programs.

Notes

1. Many of the ideas contained herein are also contained in other publications on impact fees which include: Juergensmeyer and Blake, "Impact Fees: An Answer to Local Governments' Capital Funding Dilemma," 9 *Fla. St. U. L. Rev.* 415 (1981); Juergensmeyer, "Drafting Impact Fees to Alleviate Florida's Pre-platted Lands Dilemma," 7 *Fla. Envt'l & Urban Issues* 7 (April 1980); "Infrastructure: Paying the Costs of Growth Through Impact Fees and Other Land Regulation Changes," Chpt. 2 of *The Changing Structure of Infrastructure Finance* (J. Nicholas, ed., 1985); Juergensmeyer and Wadley, *Florida Land Use Restrictions,* Chpt. 17 (Looseleaf); Juergensmeyer, "Impact Fees After the Growth Management Act of 1985," Chpt. 13 of *Perspectives on Florida's Growth Management Act of 1985* (DeGrove and Juergensmeyer, eds.); Hagman and Juergensmeyer, *Urban Planning and Land Development Control Law,* Chpt. 9 (2nd ed. 1986).

2. See Note, "Mandatory Dedication of Land by Land Developers," 26 *U. Fla. L. Rev.* 41 (1973); Heyman and Gilhool, "The Constitutionality of Imposing In-

creased Community Costs on New Suburban Residents Through Subdivision Extractions," 73 *Yale L. J.* 1119 (1964); Jacobsen and Redding, "Impact Taxes: Making Development Pay Its Way," 55 *N.C. L. Rev.* 407 (1977); Hagman and Juergensmeyer, *Urban Planning and Land Development Control Law* Chpt. 9 (2nd ed. 1986).

3. *See* Juergensmeyer, "Drafting Impact Fees to Alleviate Florida's Pre-platted Lands Dilemma," 7 *Fla. Envt'l & Urban Issues* 7 (April 1980).

4. *See* Juergensmeyer and Blake, "Impact Fees: An Answer to Local Governments' Capital Funding Dilemma," 9 *Fla. St. U. L. Rev.* 414, 415 (1981).

5. *See* Jacobsen and Redding, "Impact Taxes: Making Development Pay Its Way," 55 *N.C. L. Rev.* 407 (1977).

6. *See* Hagman, "Landowner Developer Provision of Commercial Goods Through Benefit-Based and Harm Avoidance 'Payments' (BHAPS)," 52 *Zoning & Planning L. Rev.* (1982).

7. See *Jenad, Inc.* v. *Village of Scarsdale,* 271 N.Y.S.2d 955, 958 [1966] [court bluntly stated "(t)his is not a tax at all but a reasonable form of village planning"]; *Call* v. *City of West Jordan,* 606 P.2d 217, 220-21 [Utah 1979] [labeling the distinction an exercise in semantics, in-lieu fee held not a tax but a form of planning].

8. *See Homebuilders Ass'n* v. *South Jordan City,* 631 P.2d 899 (Utah 1981).

9. 176 N.E.2d 799 (Ill. 1961).

10. *Gulest Associates, Inc.* v. *Town of Newburgh,* 209 N.Y.S.2d 729 (Sup. Ct. 1960), aff'd, 225 N.Y.S.2d 538 (App. Div. 1962).

11. *Jordan* v. *Village of Menomonee Falls* (137 N.W.2d 442 [1965], appeal dismissed 385 U.S. 4 [1966]).

12. *Banberry Development Corp.* v. *South Jordan City.*

13. *See* Opinion No. 86-018, 71 *Opin. of Atty. Gen'l.* 87 (March 24, 1986).

14. *Westfield-Palos Verdes Co.* v. *City of Rancho Palos Verdes,* 141 Cal.Rptr. 36, 73 Cal. App. 3d 486 (2d Ct. App. 1977).

15. *Assoc. Home Bldrs.* v. *City of Newark,* 95 Cal. Rptr. 648, 18 Cal. App. 3d 107 (1st Dist. 1971).

16. *Ivy Steel and Wire Co.* v. *City of Jacksonville,* 401 F. Supp. 701 (M.D. Fla. 1975).

17. *City of Arvada* v. *City and County of Denver,* 663 P.2d 611 [Colo. 1983].

18. *See,* Schnidman and Baker, "Planning for Platted Lands: Land Use Remedies for Lot Sales Subdivisions," 11 *Fla. State Univ. L. Rev.* 505 (1983).

19. See Juergensmeyer, "Drafting Impact Fees to Alleviate the Pre-platted Lands Problem," *Environmental and Urban Issues* 7 (April 1980).

20. Florida Statutes Chapter 163, Pt. II. In 1985, the act was amended and renamed the Local Government Comprehensive Planning and Land Development Regulation Act.

21. Florida Statutes, Chapt. 166.

22. *See, e.g., Home Builders v. Board of Palm Beach,* 466 So. 2d 140 Fla. 4th DCA 1983, cert. denied, 451 So. 2d 848 (Fla. 1983).

23. Id. at 142.

24. Juergensmeyer, "Impact Fees After the Growth Management Act of 1985." DeGrove and Juergensmeyer, "Perspectives on Florida's Growth Management Act of 1985," Chpt. 13 (1986).

25. *Venditti Sivaro, Inc. v. City of Hollywood* (39 Fla. Supp. 121 [1973]).

26. *Broward County v. Janis Development Corp.,* 311 So. 2d (Fla. 4th DCA 1975).

27. *City of Miami Beach v. Jacobs,* 315 So. 2d 227 (Fla. 3d DCA 1975).

28. *Contractors & Builders Association of Pinellas County v. City of Dunedin,* 329 So. 2d 314 (Fla. 1976), *cert. denied* 444 U.S. 867 (1979).

29. See *Admiral Dev. Corp. v. City of Maitland,* 267 So. 2d 860 [Fla. 4th DCA 1972] [dictum] [applied *Pioneer Trust* test to in-lieu fees for recreational funding]; *Carlann Shores, Inc. v. City of Gulf Breeze,* 26 Fla. Supp. 95 Santa Rosa County Cir. Ct. 1966] [applied *Pioneer Trust* and *Gulest* tests to in-lieu fee for park purposes].

30. *City of Dunedin v. Contractors & Builders Association of Pinellas County,* 358 So.2d 846 [Fla. 2d DCA 1978].)

31. *Hollywood, Inc. v. Broward County,* 431 So.2d 606 (Fla. 4th DCA 1983) cert. denied, 440 So.2d 352 (Fla. 1983).

32. *Town of Longboat Key v. Lands End,* 433 So.2d 574 (Fla. 2d DCA 1983).

33. *Home Builders Association v. Board of County Commissioners of Palm Beach County,* 446 So. 2d 140 (Fla. 4th DCA 1983), cert. denied, 451 So. 2d 848 (Fla. 1983).

34. *Wald Corporation v. Metropolitan Dade County,* 338 So. 863 (Fla. 3d DCA 1976).

35. 431 So. 2d at 614.

36. 367 So.2d 207 (Fla. 1979).

37. 446 So.2d 140, 145 (3rd DCA 1983).

38. See, *Coulter v. City of Rawlins,* 662 P.2d 888 [Wyo. 1983]; *Englewood Water District v. Halstead,* 432 So.2d 172 [Fla. 2nd DCA 1983]; and *City of Arvada v. City and County of Denver,* 663 P.2d 611 [Colo. 1983].

39. *Florida Bar Journal* 54 [January 1984].

40. *City of Fayetteville v. FBI, Inc.,* 659 S.W.2d 505 [Ark. 1983].

41. 659 S.W.2d 505, 507 (Ark. 1983).

42. WSSC v. C. Mitchell & Best Co. 303 Md. 544 (1985).

43. *Lafferty v. Payson City,* 642 P.2d 376 [Utah 1982].

44. *Contractors & Builders Association of Pinellas County v. City of Dunedin,* 329 So.2d 314 [Fla. 1976].

45. *Banberry Development Corp. v. South Jordan City,* 631 P.2d 899 [Utah 1981].

46. 631 P.2d 903-4.

47. See Weitz, "Impact Fees: There Is No Free Lunch," *Planning* 12 [July 1984].

Shortcomings of Impact Fee Law and Future Trends

TERRY D. MORGAN

This chapter looks at some of the legal concerns surrounding impact fees and trends in the development of impact fee law. It consists of two parts. In the first part, note is made of the vague treatment in the law of the incidence of impact fees. Impact fees may fall inequitably on certain classes of people. It is unlikely that this concern will be addressed through the law. Similar concerns are raised with the effect of impact fees on affordable housing objectives. In the second part, trends in the evolution of impact fee law are posited. The legitimacy of assessing development for off-site improvements will be explored by courts, mostly focusing on the proportion of off-site improvement costs appropriately assessed against new development. Much of the legal evolution to come, however, will focus on the design of impact fee ordinances and their implementation. It is also conceivable that future legislation will address the affordable housing impacts of impact fees.

PLANNING CONCERNS NOT ADDRESSED BY CURRENT IMPACT FEE LAW
Equity Considerations: Incidence of Fees on Housing Consumers

Opponents of impact fees have argued that fees imposed on new residential development are inherently unfair because new housing consumers bear a disproportionate share of infrastructure costs in relation to the benefits they receive. The purchaser of new residential construction, it is said, bears the dual burden of financing new facilities and paying municipal debt on existing facilities. Further, when the new housing consumer also is an established resident of the community, the financial burden may be greater (Snyder and Stegman 1986).

Generally speaking, such concerns have played a relatively minor role in the adjudication of development exactions. The theory of double taxation has not found favor with the courts. As a constitutional restraint, double taxation occurs only when "two taxes of the same character are imposed for the same purpose, by the same taxing authority within the same jurisdiction during the same taxing period."[1] A related contention that certain kinds of facilities must be funded from general revenues, such as schools and parks, has no constitutional foundation (Juergensmeyer and Blake 1981).

Some commentators have criticized the rational nexus standard of judicial review, suggesting that the test is premised on questionable assumptions of "intergenerational equity" and undervalues the benefits of having infrastructure publicly financed (Snyder and Stegman 1986). A few courts have expressed concern about the potential for disparate treatment of new housing consumers occasioned by impact fees.[2] While some commentators view these decisions as evidence that a new judicial sophistication is at hand (Bosselman and Stroud 1985), the decisions do not suggest alternative equal protection standards under which fees might be more closely scrutinized.

It appears unlikely that standards will evolve to redress inequities associated with impact fees. The reason lies partly in the principle of separation of powers in both the federal and state constitutions. In matters of economics and social welfare, the judiciary properly is reluctant to interfere with the efforts of states and their political subdivisions to devise novel solutions to problems arising from growth. By the same token, the courts have refused to adjust the balance of competing values that is reflected in local government decision making under the aegis of equal protection. Deferential review of municipal legislation applies to exercises of the police power and the taxation power alike.

Judicial intervention also may be thwarted by the complexity of determining the incidence of impact fees. Impact fees fall disproportionately on the new housing consumer only when the developer or builder is able to incorporate the fees into the price of the new unit (Snyder and Stegman 1986). In other situations, the impact fees may ultimately be borne by the landowner rather than by the homeowner. Courts will be doubly reluctant to overturn fee ordinances under equal protection review when the facts turn on disputed expert testimony.

Interference with Affordable Housing Objectives

Another objection to impact fees is that their use defeats affordable housing objectives because of the number of households that are priced out of the market as the fees are passed along by the builders. Because fees usually are assessed on the number of bedrooms rather than on the value of the dwelling, the heaviest burden may fall on lower priced housing built for larger families. It also has been suggested that dislocations in regional housing markets may result when the adoption of impact fees in some jurisdictions forces lower income households to search in other communities for housing (Nelson 1986).

Some courts have been willing to apply more exacting scrutiny to land use regulations that result in the exclusion of low- and moderate-income households. New Jersey appellate courts have been especially vigilant in examining the scheme of municipal regulation for exclusionary impacts following the landmark decision in *Southern Burlington County NAACP* v. *Township of Mount Laurel*.[3] In that case, the New Jersey Supreme Court found that a developing municipality must provide housing opportunities for a regional fair share of low- and moderate-income households. In a subsequent decision, the court outlined substantive measures that must be considered and used in redressing exclusionary practices.[4]

The success of exclusionary challenges to impact fees depends on the willingness of state courts to elevate housing to a status deserving of special protection under state constitutional provisions. In those jurisdictions that have, the focus of judicial inquiry more often than not has been on the effects of the *total* regulatory scheme on housing availability rather than on a particular technique or program. As the New Jersey Supreme Court instructed in the second *Mount Laurel* opinion, once regional fair share obligations had been met a municipality was free to use its land use regulations to implement other important municipal objectives even if the result were to raise housing costs. In the one decision that has directly considered an exclusionary attack on impact fees, the court concluded that the "systems development charges" as a fiscal measure were exempt from scrutiny under the state's affordable housing policies.[5]

TRENDS

The future of impact fees as a means of financing new facilities and services depends not only on judicial acceptance but also on legislative initiative. Many disputed issues of equity may be resolved not by the courts but by state and local lawmakers. A discussion of some of the factors that will play a part in that future follows.

Legitimacy of Off-Site Exactions

Adequate facilities requirements involving off-site improvements increasingly have gained both legislative and judicial acceptance. As previously noted, the police power permits municipalities to define adequacy standards broadly. Courts have sustained fee systems to support parkland and recreational facilities, off-site roads and highways and school facilities (Morgan, Duncan, and McClendon 1986). State legislatures also have expressly authorized exactions to implement off-site adequacy standards. When imposed as an implementation mechanism for comprehensive plan policies, fee systems have been sustained for an even broader range of facilities, such as libraries, police protection, and fire protection.

Courts on occasion may continue to view off-site exactions as an infringement of constitutional guarantees. Undoubtedly, the majority of cases will turn on the proportionality between the fee and the needs generated by the new development for the type of facility. Statutes that authorize particular kinds of exactions may contain rigorous standards governing the exercise of the authority. In the absence of such standards, courts will continue to exhibit varying degrees of deference to determine the rationality of the fee system.

Importance of Design

The structure and design of an impact fee ordinance will continue to be of prime importance in the determination of its validity. Factors that are important in devising an ordinance include its relationship to a comprehensive plan and capital improvements program, techniques for discounting other forms of development contributions from impact fees, a method for defining development impacts and service standards, designation of service areas, and a system for collecting and administering revenues (Duncan, Standerfer, and McClendon 1986).

Plan-based fee systems should become more common, particularly in communities that have incorporated a growth management strategy into the plan. The plan provides both a data base and a set of policies that link regulatory objectives with specific implementing mechanisms. The plan thus becomes important in establishing the rational nexus between fee, impacts of development, and capital improvements. The plan itself may serve as authority for assessments on new development aimed at funding a full range of urban services in fringe areas (Morgan, Duncan, and McClendon 1986).

The problem of double charging developers to finance infrastructure is certainly one that can be expected to receive legislative attention. Many communities have long exacted sewers and roads as a condition of subdivision approval. When impact fees are imposed on top of traditional exactions, credits against fees may not be given for the value of such improvements. Another problem arises when fees are charged to new development to recoup the costs of previously constructed facilities that still have unused capacity. State legislatures may well condition the adoption of impact fee ordinances on inclusion of an accounting system that addresses such inequities. Similarly, equity problems facing housing consumers after the adoption of impact fees may be remedied by laws that require a system of credits for the value of taxes and other payments to be made by new development against outstanding debt on existing facilities and their replacement costs (Snyder and Stegman 1986; Nelson 1986).

A number of recent statutes authorizing exactions contain specific directives on fund administration. Thus, subdivision fees exacted under voluntary agreements in the state of Washington must be placed in a reserve account to fund the particular capital improvement. The funds must be expended within five years or be refunded with interest.[6] There arises a need to address how such accounts are to be established in circumstances where several governmental entities may be jointly responsible for construction of needed facilities. Statutes may authorize several agencies to collect funds independently. Lack of coordination of capital improvement programs may pose obstacles to efficient fund administration. In some instances, municipalities may be unable to expend funds for certain improvements without an intergovernmental agreement with adjacent jurisdictions.

Affordable Housing Counterweights

The effect of impact fees on the provision of affordable housing opportunities will continue as a potential restraint on widespread use of fees despite developers' attempts to prevail in court on the issue. Concerns for affordable housing already have resulted in legislation in at least one state limiting the use of fees to voluntary agreements. More legislation can be expected.

Of particular interest is whether fees can be designed to avoid disproportionate increases in moderately priced housing. The usual impact fee is based on a factor such as the number of bedrooms per residential unit rather than on the value of the dwelling. Consequently, the percentage increase in the cost of a moderately priced home from passed through fees is greater than that for an expensive home. If the fee system is designed on value, however, it risks classification as a proscribed *ad valorem* tax.

In jurisdictions that permit local governments to assess taxes and do not have property tax limitations in place, impact fees may be graduated for different types of housing. In Oregon, a graduated fee structure that was intended to promote reasonably priced housing was sustained against an equal protection challenge.[7] Fees based on the police power may not fare so well, however, in states that require a strong nexus between amount of the fee and need for additional facilities. On the other hand, some states permit cities to regulate for inclusionary zoning. Statutes also might expressly authorize a graduated fee system to serve affordable housing objectives.

CONCLUSIONS

The use of impact fees to ensure the adequacy of essential public facilities and services has met with initial legislative and judicial acceptance. Many developers also have come to realize the necessity for some means of cost shifting to finance facilities requirements. The alternative to such programs may be denial or lengthy delay of development proposals. Impact fees may also be more equitable than subdivision dedication requirements or contractual arrangements for facilities construction.

The utility of impact fees as a financing mechanism is counterbalanced by their potential for escalating housing prices and by problems in equalizing the burden of financing municipal services. Courts are unlikely to resolve such issues without substantial legislative intervention. Legislation can be expected to address both the design of impact fees and their effect on the attainment of affordable housing objectives. The tension between provision of adequate facilities and housing opportunities could be eased if fee structures validly can be graduated according to ability to pay.

Notes

1. *Associated Home Builders Ass'n* v. *City of Walnut Creek*, 4 Cal.3d 633, 642, 94 Cal. Rptr. 630, 484 P.2d 606 (1971).

2. In *Lafferty* v. *Payson City*, 642 P.2d 376 (Utah 1982), the court warned that the entire cost of new facilities should not be charged to new development, but expressed its confidence that the rational nexus test articulated in an earlier decision, *Banberry Development Corp.* v. *South Jordan City*, 631 P.2d 899 (Utah 1981) sufficiently protected the new home buyer's interests.

3. 67 N.J. 151, 336 A.2d 713 (1975).

4. *Southern Burlington County NAACP* v. *Township of Mount Laurel* (Mount Laurel II), 92 N.J. 158, 456 A.2d 390 (1983); see generally Morgan, Exclusionary Zoning: Remedies Under Oregon's Land Use Planning Program, 14 Env. L. Rev. 799 (1984).

5. *State Housing Council* v. *City of Lake Oswego*, 43 Or. App. 525, 617 P.2d 655 (1980).

6. Rev. Wash. Code Ann. sec. 82.02.020.

7. *Oregon State Home Builders Ass'n* v. *City of Tigard*, 43 Or. App. 791, 604 P.2d 886 (1979).

References

Bosselman, Fred P. and Nancy Stroud. 1985. Pariah to Paragon: Developer Exactions in Florida 1975–85. 14 *Stetson Law Review* 527.

Duncan, James, Norman Standerfer, and Bruce McClendon. 1986. Drafting Impact Free Ordinances: Implementation and Administration. 9 *Zoning & Planning L. Rep.* 57.

Juergensmeyer, Julian and Bruce McClendon. 1986. Impact Fees: An Answer to Local Governments' Capital Funding Dilemma. 9 *Florida State Law Review.* 415.

Morgan, Terry D., James Duncan, and Bruce McClendon. 1986. Drafting Impact Fee Ordinances: Legal Foundation for Exactions. 9 *Zoning & Planning L. Rep.* 49.

Nelson, Arthur C. 1986. Affordable Housing and Equity Considerations of Development Impact Fees. Unpublished paper presented at Growth Forum, Program in Community and Regional Planning, School of Architecture, University of Texas at Austin, December 12.

Snyder, Thomas P. and Michael A. Stegman. 1986. *Paying for Growth: Using Development Fees to Finance Infrastructure.* Washington, D.C.: Urban Land Institute.

Model Enabling Acts
and Model Ordinances

The Need for a Standard State Impact Fee Enabling Act

Jane H. Lillydahl
Arthur C. Nelson
Timothy V. Ramis
Antero Rivasplata
Steven R. Schell

Nearly all communities in the Unites States owe their planning and zoning powers to state enabling legislation. In turn, most states owe the impetus for adopting such legislation to the standard planning and zoning enabling acts that the U.S. Department of Commerce drafted in the 1920s. The standard acts came about in response to pleas from communities for guidance in planning and zoning in the face of mounting court challenges and vague judicial support (Kent 1964). Today, while state planning and zoning laws differ considerably, most are built on a foundation comprised of the principles in the standard planning and zoning enabling acts.

The states need a standard enabling act for development impact fees in the tradition of the standard planning and zoning enabling acts. Communities across the nation face the common problem of having to find new revenues to pay for community facilities necessitated by growth. Many communities have sought to shift the burden of paying for growth from the community at large to new development

through impact fees. Those attempts are often challenged in court, usually by developers. Although some state courts sympathize with the plight of communities and have found ways to justify impact fees, no one can predict the outcome of court involvement. Sometimes the courts uphold the enactment of fees; other times they do not. When courts reject fee ordinances, further erosion in communities' ability to meet facility needs may result.

The time has come for state legislatures to consider adopting impact fee enabling legislation. Such legislation can give needed guidance to communities when they consider implementing impact fee ordinances. It can also give courts clear criteria by which to review challenges to those ordinances. We therefore call for the preparation of a standard state impact fee enabling act in the tradition of the standard state planning and zoning enabling acts. Such a model act would set forth general impact fee principles that state legislatures can use as a guide to crafting impact fee enabling legislation. The individudal communities could then tailor specifics to local situations.

We come to this conclusion after reviewing the nature of impact fee authorization that many states give their communities. In this chapter, we report our review of four states: California, Florida, Oregon, and Colorado. Those states offer some of the nation's most diverse approaches to enabling community use of impact fees. California's legislation and judicial interpretation offer its communities a large menu of ways to assess new development for facility improvement costs, including impact taxes, mitigation fees, and impact fees. Yet statutory flexibility in the use of impact taxes and mitigation fees has eroded in recent years because of statewide initiatives such as Proposition 13 in 1978, Proposition 62 in 1986, and recent legislation.

In Florida, courts have reviewed trial-and-error attempts by communities to impose impact fees for more than a decade; the result is a unique, though rigid, set of impact fee principles by which communities throughout that state must abide. Oregon obliquely defends systems development charges under the rubric of that state's nationally acclaimed statewide land use planning legislation, even though state courts do not require that the systems development charges be consistent with that legislation. Since some Oregon communities used those charges to pay for repairs to existing facilities and not for new facilities, the 1987 Legislative Assembly adopted legislation restricting the use of the funds. The governor vetoed that legislation, however, after the legislature adjourned. Impact fees in Colorado are ad hoc in practice in the absence of specific legislative guidelines; and the state courts do not review them for consistency with the standard prin-

ciples that are applied in California, Florida, and Oregon.

Communities within the four states we discuss and elsewhere face common growth pressures and financial constraints in paying for growth. Yet, lacking the guidance of explicit state enabling legislation, communities deal with that common problem in very different ways, using their own resources. Unclear legislative authorization and vague judicial guidance force communities into trail-and-error ordinance writing that is nothing more than legal experimentation. That is not wise. We believe that a standard impact fee enabling act in the tradition of the standard planning and zoning enabling acts of the 1920s would create a common foundation on which all impact fee ordinances could rest. We now review the nature of impact fee authority and general practice in the four states, offer the reasons why a standard impact fee enabling act is needed, and discuss the major features of that act.

IMPACT TAXES, MITIGATION FEES, AND IMPACT FEES IN CALIFORNIA

Between 1970 and 1980, California's population rose from 20 million to nearly 24 million, and its population will approach 30 million by 1990. California has led the nation in the innovative, complex, and flexible use of impact assessments including impact fees, mitigation fees, and impact taxes. That, however, is changing.

Since voters passed Proposition 13 in 1978, California communities especially have sought to shift the cost of new infrastructure from exisiting to new development. Proposition 13 rolled back property tax assessments, capped property tax rates, and prevented special taxes (income, liquor, sales, use, vehicles, and property transfer) from being levied without a two-thirds majority vote of the local electorate (Chapman 1981). In the face of Proposition 13, California communities increasingly have used impact taxes, impact fees, and mitigation fees to pay for new facilities and services. More recent legislation has restricted the use of impact taxes and mitigation fees, however, and California communities are relying more on impact fees. Yet, because of legislation passed in 1987, impact fee flexibility has also been restricted. We review each of those major forms of impact charges and comment on the state of those charges in California.

In the 1960s, home rule communities in California became the first in the nation to assess impact taxes. Since 1972, the California Environmental Quality Act and its amendments have allowed mitigation fees. In addition, since the 1960s, the state has viewed impact fees as a valid exercise of both the police power and subdivision exaction authority. The differences between those revenue-generating devices are important and show both the flexibility and aggressiveness with which the California legislature has addressed the communities' needs to finance facilities. Local government may levy impact *taxes* on new construction. Technically, the community can add those funds to the general fund and expend them in a discretionary fashion; in practice the funds are earmarked for community facilities (see Barnebey et al. 1988). Impact *fees*, on the other hand, must reasonably relate to the impacts that contributing development generates (see also Stroud 1988). Mitigation fees may be assessed on development whenever it appears that new development may adversely affect the community at large. Those fees may go toward improving the infrastructure of the community at large

and not necessarily to benefiting the contributing development.

While California has used impact taxes for many years, Proposition 13 caused many people to wonder whether their use could continue without the two-thirds majority local electorate approval required of general taxes. The California Supreme Court answered that concern by interpreting impact taxes to be a tax levied for a special purpose "rather than a levy placed in the general fund to be utilized for general governmental purposes" that would need such electoral approval.[1] Proposition 62, however, which California voters approved in 1986, required two-thirds electoral approval of general taxes; the implicit purpose was to limit impact taxes as well. As a consequence, communities do not view new impact taxes as a promising way to finance new facilities.

Until recently, the California Environmental Quality Act allowed communities considerable flexibility to assess mitigation fees on new development. The fees could be, and often were, assessed on any development requiring a discretionary decision by local government, such as plan amendments, zone changes, conditional use permits, and special development permits. The original act and amendments to it since 1972 allowed communities to require mitigation of a development's significant environmental impacts (which could include socioeconomic and fiscal impacts). The legislature amended the act in 1981, however, to eliminate many of the alleged abuses of the earlier statute. Now mitigation fees come under the rubric of the state Subdivision Map Act and local impact fee ordinances. The act, in combination with the other authorizations, allows California communities the authority to require impact mitigation as a condition of development approval. Communities assessing mitigation fees must prepare a schedule of those fees, based on projections of future facilities needs, determination of the costs of installing facilities to serve development, and the fair distribution of those costs on development. While, in general, contributing development must benefit from the fees it pays, development is often assessed more than its directly attributable burden on community facilities. Nonetheless, mitigation fees are no longer as flexible a revenue raising device as they were before 1981.

Impact fees are emerging as the model form of development exaction, in our opinion. California courts require that impact fees need only be "reasonably related" to the contributing development's impact on community facilities. Legal scholars consider that standard the most liberal defense of impact fees (see Stroud 1988). The California Supreme Court has held that there need not be a direct relationship between the proposed development and the exaction if the exaction is necessary to maintain the general welfare.[2] Provided that they finance specific activities, facilities, or services, impact fees are not considered taxes and therefore do not require the two-thirds local electorate approval.[3]

Cities and counties derive authority to assess impact fees implicity from the local police power and explicitly from state statute. The state Subdivision Map Act, for example, allows local governments to impose fees for bridges and major thoroughfares, planned drainage and sewer facilities, parks, and, in Orange County, freeways. Assembly Bill 2926, which went into effect in 1987, allows local school districts to assess fees of $1.25 per residential square foot and 25 cents per commercial or industrial square foot for the provision of interim or permanent school facilities. Even impact fees, however, are coming under increasing judicial and legislative scrutiny.

California uses all three forms of development charges extensively. All San Francisco Bay area communities, for example, charge impact taxes, impact fees, and mitigation fees. In 1985 the average combined impact charges on new single-family dwellings in that region was $3,527, and as high as $8,568 in Tiburon. Assessments are generally higher in southern California. In San Diego, impact fees run to $9,500 per dwelling unit. But the California legislature has reacted to the development industry's concerns about paying for an increasingly larger share of new community infrastructure. Since 1978, the legislature has liberalized special district formation, assessment, and facility financing through tax exempt and other bonds (Barnebey et al. 1988). In 1986 the legislature enacted bills that prevent local governments from collecting most fees before final inspection, require a 60-day waiting period before new fees take effect, and require that fees assessed not exceed the estimated reasonable cost of providing the service or facility being financed.

California legislators continued to hear considerable testimony in 1987 that some cities were charging impact fees before they knew what they planned to use the money for, using fees to pay city debts, using fees presumably earmarked for one project to pay for all or part of another project across town, or collecting fees for up to ten years without spending them (George 1987). Thus, the legislature in 1987 pased AB 1600. Chief among that statute's features are provisions for specifying the improvements for which impact fees can be charged within a capital improvement plan (the statute generally limits local governments to collecting impact fees for water and sewer facilities, roads, storm and flood water control, energy generation, and parks and recreation), segregation of impact fees into special accounts, and expenditure of fees within five years of receipt or return of those fees after five years with interest (to the then-current owners of property that was charged) unless certain findings are made showing the need to use those fees as orginally intended. The bill becomes operative January 1, 1989.

Stroud (1988) registers the concern that a recent U.S. Supreme Court case, *Nollan v. California Coastal Commission*,[4] could dramatically alter the manner in which California commmunities and state agencies make exactions from developers. The case involved a beach access easement across the Nollan property in exchange for a building permit. The court ruled the exaction an improper taking because it could not be directly related to the public purpose it was alleged to further. The implication is that impact fees, since they are assessed in exchange for building permits, under some circumstances could also be considered a taking because of California's broad reasonably related standard.

While the California legislature has given its communities great flexibility in paying for growth in the past, Propositions 13 and 62 have eliminated the flexible use of impact taxes. The flexible use of mitigation fees also has been reduced since 1981 by amendments to the California Environmental Quality Act. Communities now must schedule and assess mitigation fees within the rubric of subdivision review or as an element of impact fee ordinances. By 1987, impact fees were about the only way communities could shift the burden of paying for new

facilities to new development. Yet, recent California legislation and the *Nollan* case indicate the need for a more mainstream rationale for assessing impact fees — perhaps moving away from the reasonably related standard to the rational nexus standard. In light of evolving, restrictive attitudes toward impact taxes and mitigation fees, and considering recent legislative changes that make less flexible the application of impact fees, as well as the *Nollan* case, we wonder whether California planners might want to deflect possible future challenges to impact fees by suggesting consideration of the benefit, equity, and administrative priciples embodied in the rational nexus test, which Stroud (1988) and Nicholas and Nelson (1988) discuss.

IMPACT FEES IN FLORIDA

Between 1970 and 1980, Florida's population grew by 43.5 percent and between 1980 and 1985, it grew an additional 15.7 percent. By 1990 the state's population of 12 million will make it the fourth most populous state in the nation. State officials estimate that providing infrastructure to new development will cost $60 billion between 1982 and 2000. Because of declining federal and state aid, inflation, and taxpayer resistance to increasing property taxes, known revenue sources will be able to pay for only 59 percent to 66 percent of that amount (Executive Office of the Governor 1985). Florida communities thus must find politically acceptable and legally defensible means by which to pay for growth. Many communities have turned to development impact fees, but only after considerable wrangling in courts. Until recently, the legislature has shown little interest in the topic.

Prior to 1975, a number of Florida communities applied different types of development exactions in an attempt to shift costs of new facilities to developers and away from existing residents (Bosselman and Stroud 1985). Florida courts deemed early forms of impact fees unauthorized forms of taxation, primarily because such fees did not bear a specific relation to their ultimate use.[5] In *Contractors and Builders Association of Pinellas County v. City of Dunedin* (1976),[6] for example, the Florida Supreme Court upheld the validity of water and sewer impact fees in principle, while it struck down the city's impact fee ordinance because the fees collected were not earmarked for the facilities they supposedly were financing. *Dunedin* established for Florida the dual rational nexus test, which requires that the level of impact fees must be related to the new facilities needed to serve contributing development, and that the fees must be earmarked specifically for those facilities.

In a later case, *Home Builders and Contractors Association v. Board of County Commissions of Palm Beach County* (1983),[7] the court did not question features of the county impact fee ordinance that addressed double payment and timely expenditure of impact fees. Double payment can occur when occupants of the development pay property, sales, and other taxes that also pay for the facilities financed by the impact fees that the development pays. To eliminate the double payment, the local government can either credit developments for taxes that help pay for the facilities otherwise financed by impact fees, or it can set fees at less than the actual impact costs. The latter case avoids the double payment problem when the sum of the fees and other tax payments does not exceed full cost of the facilities. The timely expenditure criterion requires local government to expend the fees on the facilities for which they were intended,

and within a reasonable time after the contributions and development take place. (There is no hard and fast rule or court standard defining "reasonable time." In time the courts may define it, but a legislative enabling act may do so more expeditiously.)

Florida courts have been unusually sympathetic to the financial needs of communities. It is as though the courts have reluctantly supplanted the legislature in telling communities how to write acceptable ordinances (Bosselman and Stroud 1985; Juergensmeyer and Blake 1981).

The Florida Advisory Council on Intergovernmental Relations (Florida ACIR) reports (1986) that since 1977, the number of communities in Florida that have levied impact fees has risen nearly ten-fold, from slightly over 20 to nearly 200. The most common impact fees are for water and sewers: Nearly 100 communities across the state have enacted them. The rapidly growing southern Florida coastal cities and counties, along with larger (although not the largest) cities and counties, use impact fees most frequently. For example, no counties under 50,000 assessed impact fees in 1986. The Florida ACIR (1986) also reports that, by the end of 1986, more than 70 percent of all cities with more than 20,000 population, and 40 percent of all counties, imposed impact fees or were considering doing so.

The Florida ACIR also reports that while the cost of providing infrastructure appears to average more than $20,000 per new home, impact fees average less than $3,000. Even in communities that assess impact fees, the community at large remains substantially obligated to shoulder the balance of the burden through taxes, user fees, and other assessments.

The Florida legislature has only recently

addressed impact fees, under the Local Government Comprehensive Planning and Land Development Regulation Act. Adopted in 1985 and amended in 1986, this act requires communities to include capital improvements in their state-mandated comprehensive planning efforts. The legislation does not codify Florida impact fee case law, however.

Case law and not legislation requires clear distinction between financing *new* facilities to support growth and improving *exisiting facility deficiencies*, which the community must finance from revenues other than impact fees. Case law implies that facility standards for new and existing residents be the same; for example, new residents should not pay for parks on the basis of five acres per thousand when the existing community standard is less. Case law also requires that the local government credit development for other taxes and fees used to finance the same facilities supported by impact fees. That avoids imposing double payments that would arise from impact fees and other exactions (but not necessarily limited to those that result from the combination of impact fees and property taxes, gasoline taxes, and other general tax revenues). Other provisions of case law seek to ensure allocation of the costs of new facilities on the basis of benefits that current and future residents will receive. Communities may allocate costs by subareas or on a community-wide basis, depending on the service area of the facility (Florida ACIR 1986).

Some Florida commentators are concerned that legislative tinkering with impact fee case law may disrupt the progress the courts and communities have made in finding ways to pay for growth.[8] Those commentators observe that a decade of wrangling through the courts has created a reasonably acceptable understanding between courts and communities on the parameters of impact fee applications. Significant legislative changes to existing law can force the courts and the communities to spend more time redefining the currently accepted parameters. If that process takes anything like the time required to reach the current level of acceptance, we believe the delay can do considerable damage to Florida communities' ability to pay for growth. On the other hand, the legislature can play a productive role in formalizing through statute much of what the courts have put into place, and then clarifying issues that courts have left unsettled. Those issues include, but are certainly not limited to, clarifying the basis on which to make community facility standards, specifying the criteria dictating when fees must be expended, making more certain that the facilities are in the geographic areas for which the fees are intended, offering a variance procedure so that idiosyncratic developments can justifiably pay different levels of fees, identifying the conditions under which fees should be refunded to contributing development (and to whom—the ultimate tenant or the original developer?), and establishing the elements of impact fee formulas to ensure that fees are calculated on an equitable basis (Juergensmeyer 1987).

SYSTEMS DEVELOPMENT CHARGES IN OREGON

According to Schell and Ramis (1987), Oregon communities have levied systems development charges since the middle 1970s. Those charges are, in part, a product of Oregon's nationally acclaimed statewide land use planning program. That program requires all communities in the state to prepare comprehensive land use plans consistent with up to 19 statewide planning goals. One of those goals, Goal 11, requires that communities provide public facilities and services commensurate with the needs of growth and find ways to pay for those facilities. Systems development charges are one way to pay for them. Some communities prefer systems development charges to communitywide financing because, they argue, without the charges an unfair burden falls on existing development in the form of higher taxes and fees. Systems development charges, therefore, are an outcome of statewide land use planning.

In practice, since the Portland metropolitan area is the only area of the state that has seen substantial growth since 1980, most of Oregon's systems development charges are assessed there. The charges average about $2,500 for single-family dwellings (Leonard 1986), roughly comparable to impact fees in Florida but less than those in the San Francisco Bay area or in Colorado. Systems development charges typically support water, sewer, street, and park facilities.

Judicial support for systems development charges depends on whether the community has a rational basis for imposing the charge only on new development and, if so, whether it has a rational basis for the schedule of charges.[9] A key court case also determined that such charges were valid where the charges were "uniform with respect to that class of property owners who, as owners of that property, had not contributed to the general water fund or to the cost of the installation of the water system.[10]

Though many charges are products of Goal 11, courts have decided that the charges are not reviewable for consistency with that or any of the other 18 statewide planning goals.[11] For example, the Oregon Housing Council argued, in part, that systems development charges assessed in Lake Oswego, an affluent Portland suburb, would raise the price of housing beyond the reach of 52,000 Portland-area households that otherwise would be able to afford homes there. They then argued that the charges violated the statewide housing goal, Goal 10, which encourages the availability of affordable homes. The court decided, however, that the charges were benefit assessments consistent with other statutes and refused to review them for consistency with statewide planning goals. The otherwise pathbreaking Oregon courts missed the opportunity to decide whether Oregon's brand of impact fees make affluent communities like Lake Oswego even more exclusionary.

Until recently, communities had little judicial and no legislative guidance in preparing and administering systems development charges. In many communities, charges were earmarked for major facility funds, such as water, sewer, park, and street funds, but not for specific projects within those funds. The locale often did not spend the funds collected within a short time after receiving them, nor did they always spend the money within the area where they collected it. Some communities spent revenues from systems development charges to correct existing deficiencies in the capacity of community facilities. Not surprisingly, the home building industry complained bitterly about the misuses of systems development charges (Hales 1986).

In 1987, the Oregon Home Builders Association threatened suit against the city of West Linn, arguing that the community enacted charges that were too high and that the money collected was being used for maintenance of existing capital facilities. The threat was dropped when the city agreed to use charges only for new facilities.

The Oregon legislature became convinced that communities needed legislative guidance to draft and implement systems development charge programs. It passed the Oregon Systems Development Act of 1987. Many communities supported the act, in part because local political pressure to use the levies for inappropriate purposes is often irresistible. The key provisions included basing charges on a rational connection between the charge and the need for increased or new facility capacity; delaying payment of the charge until the home is sold or not later than one year after the home is occupied, whichever occurs first (so that builders need not mark up housing costs to reflect those charges during construction); limiting the use of charges to pay for capital facilities that benefit contributing development, though not necessarily exclusively; and earmarking the charges to funds for specific projects. The act also would require an annual reporting of the collection and disposition of charges during the year. The act explicitly stated that the charges need not be spent within a specific geographical area; the caveat is that contributing development must benefit from the expenditure of the collected charges. The act did not give a time frame for expending the revenue collected through the charges.

But Governor Neil Goldschmidt vetoed the System Development Charge Act, in part to satisfy Portland officials' objections to the act. Officials of that city, where Goldschmidt had served as mayor in the 1970s, were concerned that many of their current exaction practices, which dated from the 1970s, would become illegal if the act became law. Nonetheless, the act was a notable legislative achievement in that it is one of the few attempts by any legislature to give communities guidance in drafting im-

pact fee programs. Supporters of the act say that it will probably be reconsidered in revised form in the next legislative assembly.

IMPACT FEES IN COLORADO

Although Colorado is one of the nation's leading states in the use of impact fees (Frank and Downing 1987), the state possesses no explicit statutory provision or statewide planning mandate that clearly enables their use. Nor have the state's courts produced any clear guidance.

In Colorado, the problem of financing new facilities to support growth was precipitated by the anticipation of the oil shale boom in the 1970s, when small Western Slope communities were experiencing rapid, though speculatively driven, growth.[12] The town of Rangley, for example, worked out an agreement with an oil shale corporation that had the company paying substantial sums for capital improvements. The town of Meeker planned to enact a systems development charge that would make developers financially responsible for the costs of extending services to their projects (Lillydahl and Moen 1983). The oil shale bust shelved Meeker's plans.

The example that those small communities set was followed by many communities in the burgeoning metropolitan complex along the Front Range (of the Rocky Mountains), from Colorado Springs to Fort Collins and including the Denver area. Many communities in that region continued to grow after the oil shale bust, and today the area has most of the impact fee ordinances in Colorado. Communities most commonly assess fees for water, sewer, park or recreation, drainage, and street facilities, and less frequently for library, police and fire, museum, administrative, and other community facilities (Lillydahl 1987). In general, impact fees that Front Range cities assess are larger than those in the San Francisco Bay area, Florida, or the Portland metropolitan area. Most of those communities subscribe to the philosophy that growth should pay a large percentage, if not all, of its own way (Lillydahl 1987).

Within the Western Slope (the western side of the Front Range), Aspen is notable among Colorado communities because it assesses not only city and county park impact fees, but employee housing fees. The employee housing fee provides low- or middle-income housing especially for workers in resort facilities. Developers have the option of paying the fees or buying existing units and converting them from free market to subsidized employee housing. Employee housing can be on- or off-site. The recently sluggish economy throughout the Western Slope, however, has induced a number of other communities in that region to reduce or eliminate some of their impact fees. Some of the ski resort towns raise revenues from real estate transfer taxes instead.

Colorado courts have not justified impact fees using the specifically and uniquely attributable,[13] rational nexus,[14] or reasonable relationship[15] tests that other states employ. That makes planners nervous about the legal justification of impact fees. Colorado state courts, however, tend to uphold impact fees that are reasonably related to the services and facilities needed for new development (Rundus 1983). For example, the Colorado Supreme Court held an impact fee to be "rationally related to the purpose...of making new development pay its own way," despite the lack of explicit enabling statutes to assess the fee.[16] In another case, the court ruled that there was rational connection between an impact fee assessed for sewer connections and new sewer facilities financed by the fee since new connections are directly related to the need for increasing capacity.[17] Colorado courts thus accept impact fees as a valid expression of police power.[18]

The Colorado Supreme Court also ruled that a service expansion fee was a valid excise tax and that it did not need voter approval in home rule communities.[19] The court did hold that the magnitude of the fee must be in relation to the induced costs being relieved. That precedent gives home rule communities considerable latitude in collecting fees without having to earmark them for special projects. One of the consequences of that case is that more communities may apply for home rule status.

Impact fee ordinances that many Front Range cities have adoped are laudable for their precision, clarity, and efficient procedures. Notable among them is the cost recovery system Loveland employs, which won an American Planning Association award in 1986 (see Barnebey et al. 1988). The Colorado Springs ordinance is based on many rational nexus principles (Snyder and Stegman 1986). Despite those exemplary examples, other communities could implement impact fee ordinances with less rigor. Lacking clear statutory guidance, judicial review of the less superior ordinances could jeopardize the future of even the laudable ones. Thus, in our view, the Colorado legislature would be well advised to consider impact fee enabling legislation patterned after the best examples of impact fee ordinances in their state and case law provisions of other states.

A CALL FOR A STANDARD IMPACT FEE ENABLING ACT

Lacking clear state legislative and judicial guidance, many communities have been forced to pioneer the use of impact fees through long, costly, trial-and-error experiments that ultimately end up in the courts. In the absence of statutory guidance, the courts must decide whether impact fees are legitimate exercises of police power. In our view, the courts should have clear legislative guidance when they review impact fee ordinances. But most state legislatures have not adopted clear or detailed impact fee enabling statutes (Stroud 1988).

The incremental and sporadic nature with which most state legislatures and courts have considered impact fees does a disservice to planners and other public officials caught between dwindling resources and growing demands. Planners and public officials need guidance to draft and administer impact fees and should demand it from their legislatures. Without guidance, communities may unwittingly embark on impact fee programs that will fail judicial review. The risks are great. Misguided impact fee ordinances may do less than intended or expected, result in the inadvertent misuse of revenue, or cause the courts to hold communities financially responsible to contributing development for unauthorized charges. Planners and public officials, especially in rapidly growing communities, should not have to be subjected to court-tested trial-and-error ordinance gymnastics like those Florida communities have faced over the past two decades. The Florida legislature has only recently begun to address the problem of paying for growth. In the meantime, communities in that state have fallen behind in meeting their facility needs while the courts have worked laboriously through the legalities of vaguely written statutes. The same scenario could evolve in other states, and the net result could be that communities ultimately may need to stop issuing building permits until the financing mess is straightened out.

We therefore advise that state legislatures (and governors) promptly consider legislation explicitly enabling communities to use impact fees and that they give clear statutory guidance in the preparation and administration of implementing ordinances. We call for preparation of a standard impact fee enabling act, probably spearheaded by the American Planning Association, in the tradition of the standard planning and zoning enabling acts that have guided the states since the 1920s. Such a standard impact fee enabling act should include the principles we outline below. These principles are based on Florida's rational nexus justification of impact fees, supplemented by considerations offered in *Lafferty* v. *Payton City* (Utah 1982)[20] (see also Stroud 1988; Nicholas and Nelson 1988). The principles are:

1. Communities must receive guidance in the type of facilities for which impact fees can be assessed, and the conditions under which communities may find that impact fees are necessary supplemental revenues to user charges, general taxes, and special assessment districts.

2. Communities must show a need for impact fees by showing where they will expend impact fees within the context of a capital improvement plan, which itself must be directly related to a comprehensive communitywide development plan.

3. Communities must show how impact fees relate to other forms of exactions, such as required subdivision or development improvements.

4. Communities must establish a rational connection between new development and the need for additional (new or expanded) facilities to serve that growth.

5. When attributing facility costs to new

development, communities must demonstrate that the need for additional facilities is occasioned by new development and not by existing deficiencies. That requires using a general planning process to determine appropriate facility standards, and formulating a capital improvement plan to schedule improvements that will correct existing deficiencies, upgrade service levels, and accommodate new developments. The costs of additional facilities must then be apportioned to existing and new development.

Communities also must determine the proportionate share of the costs that new development will bear. Several factors are involved: the cost of existing facilities, the means by which existing facilities have been financed, the extent to which contributing development has already contributed to the cost of existing excess capacity, the extent to which new development will contribute in the future to the cost of retiring debt incurred for the construction of existing facilities, the extent to which new development should receive credit for providing common facilities that communities have provided without charge to other development, extraordinary costs of serving new development, and the time–price differential inherent in fair comparisons of amounts paid by contributing development at different times. Nicholas and Nelson (1988) elaborate on those factors.

6. Communities must establish a connection between the expenditure of the fees collected from contributing development and the benefits that development derives. That must be demonstrated in two ways. First, occupants of contributing development must have some reasonable expectation that they will use the facilities. Second, such facilities must be lo-

cated where residents can use them, and they must become available within a reasonable time after occupants move into contributing development.

7. The fees should be collected in a way that reduces or eliminates the adverse effect of impact fees on housing affordability. It is likely that the consumers ultimately will pay the impact fees, and thus such fees may ultimately make housing less affordable. That is especially true where the locale assesses the fee at the building permit stage, thus requiring developers to recover the cost of paying the fee and its carrying costs by higher prices (Snyder and Stegman 1986; Huffman et al. 1988). The local government must consider delaying payment of the fee until the project is occupied, and allowing payment of that fee over five to ten years at subsidized interest rates. The purpose of those considerations is to keep the fee from having as substantial an effect on housing affordability as traditional impact fee practice (see Huffman et al. 1988; Connerly 1988).

8. Communities must assess fees on every development similarly. For example, until recently some communities in Florida exempted small-volume home builders from the fees.

9. Communities, however, should consider the effects of impact fees on the achievement of other, higher priority community policies. For example, Loveland, Colorado, uses its general fund to pay the impact fees of qualifying lower income housing and new job-generating industrial developments. There is no exemption to the payment of the fees by those developments, only a shift from the developments to the community at large to balance potentially conflicting community policies.

The principles are based on presentations made during an APA symposium on impact fees as well as our own studies. The legal principles come from current or emerging case law (Stroud 1988). Stewart (1988) identifies some of the practical, ordinance preparation considerations. Huffman et al. (1988) and Peiser (1988) discuss the economic principles. Auerhahn (1988) and Porter (1988) review the administrative implications of the principles. Connerly (1988) elucidates the social implications. Barnebey et al. (1988) review applications of many of the principles in individual communities. Nicholas and Nelson (1988) analyze the standards in the context of developing impact fee formulas. These studies and insights should help provide a foundation that the planning and legal professions can use to prepare a standard impact fee enabling act. We call upon the planning and legal professions to do so.

Notes

1. *San Francisco v. Farrell,* 32 Cal. 3d 47
2. *Associated Homebuilders, Inc. v. City of Walnut Creek,* 4 Cal. 3d 633.
3. *Trent Meredith, Inc. v. City of Oxnard,* 114 Cal. App. 3d 325.
4. *Nollan v. California Coastal Commission,* 55 U.S.
5. *Broward County v. Janis Development Corporation,* 311 So. 2d 371.
6. *Contractors and Builders Association of Pinellas County v. City of Dunedin,* 329 So. 2d 314.
7. *Home Builders and Contractors Association v. Palm Beach County,* 446 So. 2d 140.
8. Comments by Julian Conrad Juergensmeyer, Terry D. Morgan, and Nancy E. Stroud before the *Journal of the American Planning Association* symposium on development impact fees, annual conference of the American Planning Association, New York City, April 26, 1987.
9. *Oregon State Homebuilders v. City of Tigard,* 604 P. 2d 886.
10. *Montgomery Bros. v. City of Corvallis,* 580 P. 2d 190.

11. *State Housing Council v. City of Lake Oswego,* 617 P. 2d 655.
12. Knapp, D., E. Gawf, and P. Pollock. 1986. Study session on the creation of a cost recovery system. Memorandum to City Manager. Boulder, Colo.: Planning Department.
13. *Pioneer Trust and Savings Bank v. Village of Mount Prospect,* 176 NE 2d 799.
14. *Jordan v. Village of Menomomee Falls,* 137 NW 2d 442.
15. *Ayers v. City of Los Angeles,* 207 P. 2d 1.
16. *City of Arvada v. City and County of Denver,* 663 P. 2d 611.
17. *Loup Miller Construction and Zwal Paints, Inc. v. City and County of Denver,* 676 P. 2d 1170.
18. *Beaver Meadows v. Board of County Commissioners of the County of Larimer,* 709 P. 2d 928.
19. *Cherry Hills Farms, Inc. v. City of Cherry Hills Village,* 670 P. 2d 889.
20. *Lafferty v. Payton City,* 642 P. 2d 376.

References

Auerhahn, Elliot. 1988. Implementing an Impact Fee System. See Chapter 29.

Barnebey, Mark P., Tom MacRostie, Gary J. Schoennauer, George T. Simpson, and Jan Winters. 1988. Paying for Growth: Community Approaches to Development Impact Fees. See Chapter 3.

Bosselman, Fred P. and Nancy E. Stroud. 1985. Pariah to Paragon: Exactions in Florida 1975–1985. *Stetson Law Review* 14, 3: 73–109.

Chapman, J. I. 1981. *Proposition 13 and Land Use.* Lexington, Mass.: Lexington Books.

Connerly, Charles E. 1988. Impact Fees as Social Policy. See Chapter 28.

Executive Office of the Governor. 1985. Trends and Conditions for Florida. Tallahassee: Governor's Office.

Florida Advisory Council on Intergovernmental Relations. 1986. Impact Fees in Florida. Tallahassee: Florida ACIR.

Frank, James E. and Paul B. Downing. 1987. Patterns of Impact Fee Usage. See Chapter 1.

George, Sande. 1987. CCAPA Legislative Review Teams Analyze 153 Planning Bills. *California Planner* (May): 4–5.

Hales, Charles. 1986. Hunting the Cash Flow. *Building Industry Journal* (September).

Huffman, Forrest E., Arthur C. Nelson, Marc T. Smith, and Michael A. Stegman. 1988. Who Bears the Burden of Development Impact Fees? See Chapter 25.

Juergensmeyer, Julian C. 1987. The Development of Regulatory Impact: The Legal Issues. See Chapter 8.

—— and R. M. Blake. 1981. Impact Fees: An Answer to Local Governments' Capital Funding Dilemma. *Florida State University Law Review* 9: 415–45.

Kent, T. J. 1964. *The Urban General Plan.* San Francisco: Chandler.

Leonard, Richard. 1986. Systems Development Fees: City of West Linn. West Linn, Ore.: Planning Department.

Lillydahl, Jane H. 1987. Impact fees in Colorado. Paper presented to the 1987 conference of the American Planning Association (April).

—— and Elizabeth Moen. 1983. Planning, Managing, and Financing Growth and Decline in Energy Resource Communities. *The Journal of Energy and Development* 7, 2: 211–29.

Nicholas, James C. and Arthur C. Nelson. 1988. The Rational Nexus Test and Appropriate Development Impact Fees. See Chapter 15.

Peiser, Richard. 1988. Calculating Equity-Neutral Water and Sewer Impact Fees. See Chapter 26.

Porter, Douglas R. 1988. Will Developers Pay to Play? See Chapter 6.

Rundus, Jan. 1983. The Permissible Scope of Compulsory Requirements for Land Development in Colorado. *University of Colorado Law Review:* 54: 447-68.

Schell, Steven R. and Timothy V. Ramis. 1987. Systems Development Charges in Oregon. Paper presented to the 1987 conference of the American Planning Association (April).

Snyder, Thomas P. and Michael A. Stegman. 1986. *Paying for Growth: Using Development Fees to Finance Infrastructure.* Washington, D.C.: Urban Land Institute.

Stewart, Harry. 1988. So You Want to Prepare a Development Impact Fee Ordinance? *Journal of the American Planning Association* 54, 1: 71-72.

Strauss, Eric J. and Martin L. Leitner. Municipal Impact Fee Ordinance with Commentary. See Chapter 12.

Stroud, Nancy E. 1988. Legal Considerations of Development Impact Fees. See Chaper 7.

11

A Standard Development Impact Fee Enabling Statute

JEFF BACHRACH
JULIAN C. JUERGENSMEYER
ARTHUR C. NELSON
JAMES C. NICHOLAS
TIMOTHY V. RAMIS
ERIC J. STRAUSS

This chapter presents one version of a model impact fee enabling act. This model restricts the use of impact fees more than some state courts have to date, but incorporates public finance considerations, including fee calculation, collection, reporting, spending, and refund aspects. Provisions for local governments paying fees for projects that meet other policy objectives also are included. A less restrictive impact fee enabling act is offered in Chapter 13.

SECTION 1. AUTHORIZATION OF DEVELOPMENT IMPACT FEES

(A) Local governments are hereby empowered and authorized to require the payment of impact fees by new development provided that needs for capital improvements are reasonably attributable to new development, that impact fees do not exceed a proportionate share of the local government's capital improvement costs to accommodate new development, and that new development will receive a reasonable benefit from capital improvements to be financed by impact fees. This statute represents a matter of statewide concern and applies to local governments that do or that do not exercise any home rule powers.

(B) This statute codifies the principle that new development should pay a proportionate share of the cost of those capital improvements required to serve new development. The statute additionally seeks to prevent local governments from requiring new development to pay more than a proportionate share of capital improvements costs or to cure existing deficiencies in capital improvements currently provided by local governments.

SECTION 2. DEFINITIONS

(A) (1) *Capital improvement* means only the following public facilities or assets that are owned and/or operated by a local government:

(a) Water treatment and distribution facilities;

(b) Wastewater treatment and disposal facilities;

(c) Sanitary sewers;

(d) Storm water, drainage, and flood control facilities;

(e) Public road systems and rights of ways;

(f) Public parks, public open space, and recreation facilities;

(g) Police, emergency medical, rescue, and fire protection facilities;

(h) Solid waste collection, transfer, processing, and disposal facilities;

(i) Other public facilities owned or operated by a local government, the need for which may be substantially attributed to new development.

(2) *Capital improvement,* as described in paragraph (A) of this subsection, is further limited to those improvements that are treated as capitalized expenses according to generally accepted governmental accounting principles and that have an expected useful life of no less than three (3) years. Capital improvement does not include costs associated with the operation, repair, maintenance, or replacement of capital improvements. *Capital improvement* does include reasonable costs for planning, design, engineering, land acquisition, and other costs directly associated with the capital improvements described in paragraph (1) of this subsection.

(B) *Impact fee* means any charge, fee, or assessment levied as a condition of issuance of subdivision or site plan approval, issuance of a building permit, approval of a certificate of occupancy, or other development or construction approval when any portion of the revenues collected is intended to fund any portion of the costs of capital improvements for any public facilities not otherwise permitted by law. An impact fee shall not be levied for remodeling, rehabilitation, or other improvements to an existing structure or rebuilding a damaged structure, provided there is no increase in gross floor area or number of dwelling units resulting therefrom.

(C) *Proportionate share* means the cost of capital improvements that are reasonably attributable to new development less any credits or offsets for construction and/or dedication of land or capital improvements, past or future payments made or reasonably anticipated to be made by new development in the form of user fees, debt service payments, taxes, or other payments toward capital improvement costs. Credits or offsets for past or future payments toward capital improvement costs shall be adjusted for time–price differentials inherent in fair comparisons of monetary amounts paid or received at different times.

(D) As used in this statute, *reasonable benefit* means a benefit received from the provision of a capital improvement that is greater than that to be received by the general public within the jurisdiction of the local government imposing impact fees. The receipt of an incidental benefit by other developments shall not be construed as denying a reasonable benefit to new development.

(E) *Local government* means any municipality, township, county, or other governmental entity empowered to regulate the use and/or development of land.

(F) *Plan* means the local government comprehensive, general, master, or other land use plan as described in Section 3.

(G) *Program* means the capital improvements program described in Section 3.

SECTION 3. LOCAL GOVERNMENT PLANNING REQUIRED

(A) As a prerequisite to requiring the payment of impact fees, the local government shall prepare a comprehensive land use (or master or general) plan. This plan shall include a capital improvement program. This capital improvement program shall include:

(1) Areas or subareas within the jurisdiction having an aggregation of sites with development potential that could create the need for new, expanded, enlarged, or otherwise enhanced capital improvements;

(2) Standards for levels of service for the capital improvements to be fully or partially funded with impact fees;

(3) Proposed area or subarea capital improvement lists containing descriptions of the proposed capital improvements, cost estimates, timing of the projects, and proposed or anticipated funding sources.

(B) Capital improvements programs may include provisions to spend impact fees to their best advantage alone, or if those fees will be used as a part of the financing for a particular capital improvement and where expenditure of the funds may be out of control of the local government, or in combination with other funds available to the local governing body provided there is no abrogation of the reasonable benefit to be received by developments paying impact fees.

(C) Additional development areas may be added to the plan and capital improvements program if the local government so desires. Standards for such additional subareas shall be the same as in the original ones.

(D) The local government shall modify annually the capital improvements plan and make modifications to the plan and impact fee based on:

(1) Development in the past year,

(2) Public facilities constructed,

(3) Changing needs and costs, and

(4) Other factors, including availability of other funding sources.

SECTION 4. ESTABLISHMENT OF IMPACT FEES

(A) Impact fees shall not exceed a proportionate share of the cost of providing capital improvements for which the need is reasonably attributable to those developments that pay the fees. Notwithstanding other provisions of this statute, impact fees may include a proportionate share of the cost of existing capital improvements where it is shown that all or a portion of existing capital improvements were provided in anticipation of the needs of new development.

(B) In determining a proportionate share of capital improvements costs, the following factors shall be considered:

(1) The need for new capital improvements required to serve new development based on a capital improvements plan that shows (a) any current deficiencies that may exist in existing capital improvements that serve existing development and the means by which any existing deficiencies will be eliminated within a reasonable period of time by means other than impact fees to be paid by new developments and (b) any additional demands that are anticipated to be placed on specified capital improvements by new development.

(2) The availability of other means or sources of revenue to fund capital improvements including, but not limited to, user charges, taxes, intergovernmental transfers and other revenue, and special taxation or assessment districts;

(3) The cost of existing capital improvements;

(4) The method by which the existing capital improvements were financed;

(5) The extent to which new developments required to pay impact fees have already contributed to the cost of the existing capital improvements for which there was no reasonable benefit to that new development and any credits or offsets that may be due new development because of such past contributions;

(6) The extent to which new developments required to pay impact fees will contribute to the cost of the existing capital improvements in the future (through user fees, debt service payments, or other payments toward the cost of existing capital improvements) that may be reasonably anticipated and any credits or offsets that may be due new development because of such future contributions.

(7) The extent to which new developments are required as conditions of development or construction approval to construct and/or dedicate capital improvements and any credits or offsets that may be due new development because of such construction and/or dedication; and

(8) The time–price differentials inherent in fair comparisons of amounts paid and benefits received at different times and any credits or offsets that may be due new development because of such past payments paid or benefits received or because of anticipated future payments or benefits to be received.

(C) Impact fees that are assessed against new development shall be assessed in such a manner that new developments having the same approximate need for capital improvements shall be assessed the same approximate impact fee. This provision notwithstanding, the local governing body may contribute from the general or other nonimpact fee funds all or part of the impact fee assessed against certain new development that achieves other public purposes including but not limited to the provision of affordable housing and the retention of existing employment or the generation of new employment.

SECTION 5. USE AND ADMINISTRATION OF IMPACT FEES

(A) (1) Impact fees shall be spent on new, enlarged, or otherwise enhanced capital improvements that reasonably benefit those developments that pay the fees. Except as provided in subsection (c) of Section 4, to ensure that those developments paying impact fees receive reasonable benefits, the expenditure of funds shall be reasonably localized according to subareas or some other geographical limitation that provides a nexus between those paying the fees and benefits received or to be received. Local governments shall have the discretion not to utilize subareas or other geographic limitations when the size or geographic configuration of the jurisdiction would render such subareas or other geographic limitations to be impractical, unreasonable, or otherwise infeasible.

(2) Impact fees shall only be spent on those projects specified in the capital improvement plan described in Section 3.

(3) When impact fees are collected for capital improvements to be undertaken by a different local government than the one collecting the fee, the collecting entity shall enter into agreements with that local government that will make the capital improvements to ensure compliance with the provisions of this statute.

(B) Impact fee receipts shall be specifically

earmarked and retained in special funds. All receipts shall be placed in interest-earning accounts with all interest earnings accruing to such special funds and interest shall be credited at least once each fiscal period. The local government shall provide an annual accounting for each impact fee account or fund showing the source and amount of all funds collected, earned, or received and the capital improvements that were funded in whole or in part by impact fees.

(C) Impact fees shall be expended only in conformance with the plan. Fees received shall be expended within six (6) years of receipt unless there exists an extraordinary and compelling reason for fees to be held longer than six (6) years. Such extraordinary or compelling reasons shall be identified and the local government governing body shall find that such exists on the record.

SECTION 6. REFUND OF UNEXPENDED IMPACT FEES

(A) The current owner or contract purchaser of property on which an impact fee has been paid may apply for a refund of such fees. The refund shall be owed when the local government has failed within six (6) years of when the fees were paid or other such period of time established pursuant to subsection (C) of Section 5 to expend or encumber impact fees on capital improvements intended to benefit the development that paid the fees. The local government shall notify potential claimants by first class mail deposited with the United States Postal Service at the last known address of claimants. Only the current owner or contract purchaser of the property may apply for the refund. Application for the refund must be submitted to the local government within one year of the

date the right to claim the refund arises. All refunds due and not claimed shall be retained in the special fund and expended as required in subsection (A) of Section 5, except as provided in subsection (B) of this section. This right to claim a refund may be limited by the provisions of subsections (B) and (C) of Section 4.

(B) When a local government seeks to terminate any or all impact fee requirements, all unexpended or unencumbered funds shall be refunded pursuant to subsection (A) of this section. Upon the finding that any or all fee requirements are to be terminated, the local government shall place notice of such termination and the availability of refunds in a newspaper of general circulation at least two (2) times and shall notify all potential claimants by first class mail deposited with the United States Postal Service at the last known address of claimants. All funds available for refund shall be retained for a period of one (1) year. At the end of one (1) year, any remaining funds may be transferred to the general fund and used for any public purpose. A local government is released from this notice requirement if there are no unexpended or unencumbered balances within a fund or funds being terminated.

SECTION 7. CONSISTENCY OF IMPACT FEES WITH OTHER DEVELOPMENT REGULATIONS

Local governments requiring the payment of impact fees shall incorporate such fee requirements within their broader system of development and land use regulations in such a manner that new developments, either collectively or individually, are not required to pay or otherwise contribute more than a proportionate share of the cost of providing capital improvements.

COMMENTARY

Section 1. This section clearly authorizes impact fees. It authorizes impact fees inclusively to all municipalities, counties, and special service districts regardless of whether they are subject to home rule powers. It also states the principle of equity in the form of proportionate share. Additionally, this section invokes the principles of the dual rational nexus test in that needs and costs must be attributable to new development and new development must benefit from improvements funded with impact fees.

Section 2(A)(1). The definition of capital improvement is the key statutory mechanism for identifying and limiting the types of public facilities that may be charged to new development in the form of impact fees. Within each state, important policy decisions will be made in the course of determining which public facilities to include on the definition list. The list provided in the sample statute includes the facilities frequently subject to impact fees at present, excluding school facilities. At present, in addition to the list, impact fees are being assessed for public libraries, public buildings (such as court houses and public works buildings), neighborhod civic centers, and even public cemeteries. Perhaps the most controversial facility for which impact fees are assessed are school sites and facilities. School sites have long been required to be dedicated or financed in part by new subdivisions. Additionally, public school impact fees that are assessed to construct new school facilities and acquire sites exist in California, Wisconsin, and Florida. Whether schools and sites should be funded in this way is a matter that each state would have to consider based upon individual situations.

Subsection (i) is included as a catchall that the legislature may decide to include in order to allow local flexibility in adding types of facilities to the definition. The drawbacks of including subsection (i) are lack of certainty as to just which capital improvements may be included and increased risk of litigation over whether a specific facility meets the test established by this statute. However, the local government is required to plan for any facility that is to be included as a candidate for impact fees. Thus, there is a check on local governments in that any facility for which an impact fee is to be required must be included within the comprehensive, general, or master plan and capital improvement program.

Section 2(A)(2). The purpose of this subsection is to further clarify and narrow the types of improvements for which impact fees may be charged. It restricts fees to capital improvements (a term used throughout that also means facilities and projects). It further refines the meaning of capital improvement to exclude any form of operations and maintenance but to include associated costs such as planning and engineering.

Section 2(B). The definition of impact fee is intended to be inclusive enough so that local governments cannot avoid the statute's limitations by devising charges that are akin to impact fees but fall outside the definition. The net effect of this provision is to prohibit any forms of developer provision of capital improvements that are not specifically authorized in Section 2(A)(1). If the catchall is included, local governments would have the authority to impose other fees, but such inclusions would still fall under this statute. Sections 2(C) through 2(G) are standard definitions.

Section 3. The section establishes the requirement that local governments must plan for new development and for the capital improvement needs of new development. In order to impose an impact fee, the local government will have to plan for the provision of that capital improvement and distribute the cost of that provision between existing and new development in a proportionate manner. Failure to have a comprehensive, general, or master plan would mean that the local government could not impose any impact fees. Failure to have a capital improvement program would also mean that local government could not impose any impact fees. The local government would have to make specific provisions in both its plan and program for the capital improvements that are to be the subject of impact fees. Thus, if a local government wants to impose a park and recreation impact fee, it would have to have a park and recreation element within its plan. Additionally, it would have to provide for parks and recreational capital improvements in its program. If those conditions are met, the local government would be authorized to impose a proportionate share of attributable costs to new development in the form of impact fees.

Section 4. This section provides the basis for establishing an equitable impact fee system, both for determining the amount that may be charged and how and where the monies should be spent. This section invokes the dual rational nexus criteria for fee determination that have been applied by courts in several states. The result of applying those criteria is a fee that assesses those costs to new development that are attributable to new development. Moreover, fees are limited to only those costs that can be attributed. The manner in which a proportionate share of capital improvements costs is established depends on factors addressed in subsection (B).

Section 5. This section restricts the use of impact fees to capital improvements that reasonably benefit those paying the fees. The reasonableness standard invoked implies that the benefit to new development need not be exclusive. Rather, benefit would be sufficient if the development paying the fee received a benefit from the expenditure of such fees that was greater than that received by the general public. Typically, this would mean that capital improvements would be so located that new developments would make use of the facilities improved. Further, this section requires a separate accounting of impact fees.

Section 6. This section requires that unexpended or unencumbered fees be refunded to the current owner of the property. This refund provision provides the assurance of receipt of benefit with the benefit being the provision of capital improvements or a refund of the payment.

Section 7. This section requires consistency of all development regulations with the proportionate share restrictions imposed by this statute. The purpose of this section is to cause local governments to give credit or other offsets against impact fees for such things as conditions of development approval.

12

A Municipal Impact Fee Ordinance, Based on the Standard Development Impact Fee Enabling Statute, with Commentary

Martin L. Leitner
Eric J. Strauss

This chapter sets forth an impact fee ordinance based on the Standard Impact Enabling Statute provided in Chapter 11. This ordinance is designed for communities with a mayor-council or commission-manager form of government. With some modifications, counties also may be able to use it. Use of the model language in this ordinance may vary considerably due to the particular laws of the jurisdiction in which the municipality is located and due to the type and level of projected development and public facility needs attributable to that development. Not all provisions will be applicable to each jurisdiction. Some governments may not want to impose certain types of fees because of a lack of authority to solve those problems while other jurisdictions may lack certain financial powers (e.g., the ability to sell bonds based on impact

fee revenues). Further, some courts may interpret general planning and zoning statutes or home rule statutes to provide authority for impact fees; others require specific statutes to impose impact fees. This ordinance assumes that the sample standard development impact fee enabling statute has been enacted.

In our experience, the typical impact fee is designed to solve road, sewer, water supply, and drainage problems due to new development. However, this ordinance is designed to meet the needs for many other public facilities made necessary by additional city growth. This could, for example, include police, fire, and library services. The choice of public services financed through this method will be a combination of local governmental legal authority, economic conditions, and political will.

Fees usually are assessed on the basis of dwelling units for residential land uses and square footage for commercial and industrial uses. The need for impact fees also is differentiated by measurements particular to the purpose of the fee (e.g., trip generation rates for transportation impact fees). The particular public service must benefit the property. For that reason, some communities exempt industrial land uses from the payment of park impact fees. This is despite the belief of others that industry creates the need for housing and related services, such as recreation. Resolution of this issue as well as others depends as much on politics as on enabling statutes.

This ordinance is based on the experiences of fast-growing communities in California, Florida and Texas and in the Kansas City, Missouri, suburbs in both Missouri and Kansas. In some cases, a basic level of public services to new areas was provided through general revenues and in those instances impact fees were imposed to build improvements made necessary by larger and more intensive development than the land uses originally contemplated by the city's adopted comprehensive plan and/or zoning ordinance. In other cases, impact fees were used to finance all public services in an area that had experienced new growth. The language in this ordinance is designed to meet the latter situation in which both basic and extra public services are provided through impact fees. However, the provisions of the ordinance easily could be redrafted to finance only those public projects that are made necessary by a density or square footage exceeding a certain threshold level.

This ordinance assumes that the municipality has an adopted and current comprehensive plan, an official capital improvements plan, and a zoning ordinance consistent with any adopted plans. These documents provide the minimum basis for a jurisdiction to consider the imposition of an impact fee. What follows is the model ordinance organization and language. Our legal commentary on the need for the individual provision follows the ordinance.

ELEMENTS OF A MUNICIPAL IMPACT FEE ORDINANCE

Ordinance No. _____

SECTION 1. IMPACT FEE ORDINANCE

Article _____ of the City Code is hereby amended by adding thereto a new section _____ to read as: "Section _____: IMPACT FEE ORDINANCE".

A. Short Title

This Ordinance shall be known and cited as the _____ Impact Fee Ordinance. (Specify which public facilities.)

B. Findings

The city commission (council) (hereinafter "commission" or "council") hereby finds and declares that:

1. The City is responsible for and committed to the provision of public facilities and services at levels necessary to cure any existing public service deficiencies in already developed areas;

2. Such facilities and services levels shall be provided by the City utilizing funds allocated via the capital budget and capital improvements programming processes and relying upon the funding sources indicated therein;

3. However, new residential and nonresidential development is aggregated in certain development subareas. Such develop-

ment causes and imposes increased and excessive demands on city public facilities and services including, without limitation, sanitary sewers, storm sewers, water lines, roads, and parks that would not otherwise be necessary;

4. Planning and zoning projections indicate that such development will continue and will place ever increasing demands on the City to provide necessary public facilities;

5. The development potential and property values of properties in the designated development areas are strongly influenced and encouraged by City policy as expressed in the comprehensive plan and as implemented via the City zoning ordinance and map;

6. To the extent that such developments in such designated development subareas place demands on the public facility infrastructure those demands should be satisfied by shifting the responsibility for financing the provision of such facilities from the public at large to the developments actually creating the demands;

7. The amount of the impact fee to be imposed shall be determined by the cost of the additional public facilities needed to support such development, which public facilities shall be identified in a capital improvements program; and

8. The city commission (council), after careful consideration of the matter, hereby finds and declares that an impact fee imposed upon residential and nonresidential development in order to finance specified major public facilities in designated development areas the demand for which is created by such development is in the best interest of the general welfare of the City and its residents, is equitable, does not impose an un-

fair burden on such development by forcing developers and builders to pay more than their fair or proportionate share of the cost, and deems it advisable to adopt this Ordinance as hereinafter set forth.

C. Intent

This Ordinance is intended to impose an impact fee at the time of building permit issuance, in an amount based upon the gross square footage of nonresidential development or number of residential dwelling units in order to finance public facilities, the demand for which is generated by new development in designated development subareas. The City is responsible for and will meet, through the use of general City revenues, all capital improvement needs associated with existing development. Only needs created by new development in the designated development areas will be met by impact fees. Impact fees shall not exceed the cost of providing capital improvements for which the need is substantially attributable to those developments that pay the fees. The fees shall be spent on new or enlarged capital facilities improvements that substantially benefit those developments that pay the fees.

D. Authority

(Insert state constitution and citation to the sample standard development impact fee enabling statute here.) The provisions of this ordinance shall not be construed to limit the power of the City to adopt such ordinance pursuant to any other source of local authority or to utilize any other methods or powers otherwise available for accomplishing the purposes set forth herein, either in substitution of or in conjunction with this ordinance.

Definitions

As used in this ordinance, the following words and terms shall have the following meanings, unless another meaning is plainly intended: (Definitions are to be tailored to individual communities.)

1. *Building permit* shall mean the permit required for new construction and additions pursuant to section _____ of the City code. The term building permit, as used herein, shall not be deemed to include permits required for remodeling, rehabilitation, or other improvements to an existing structure or rebuilding a damaged or destroyed structure, provided there is no increase in gross floor area or number of dwelling units resulting therefrom.

2. *Capital budget* means a separate budget dedicated to financing capital improvements.

3. *Capital improvements* means public facilities that are treated as capitalized expenses according to generally accepted accounting principles and does not include costs associated with the operation, administration, maintenance, or replacement of capital improvements, nor does it include administrative facilities.

4. *Capital improvement plan* shall be a part of the comprehensive plan, which contains:

   (a) An aggregation of sites into development subareas with development potential that would create the need for new captial improvements;

   (b) Standards for level of service for the capital facilities and infrastructure to be fully or partially funded with impact fees;

   (c) Proposed subarea project lists, cost estimates, and funding sources; and

   (d) May include provisions to spend impact fees to their best advantage if those fees will be used as part of the financing for a particular capital improvement and where expenditure of the funds may be out of control of the local governing body.

5. *Capital improvements program* means the official adopted schedule of capital improvements to be undertaken, the year or month in which they will be undertaken, the time and cost of construction, and other necessary features.

6. *(City) (County)* means the (city, county) of _____, a duly constituted political subdivision of the state of _____.

7. *(Commission) (Council)* means the duly constituted governing body of the (city, county) of _____, state of _____.

8. *Comprehensive plans* means the official land use plan of the (city, county) of _____, state of _____.

9. *Costs.*

10. *Development* shall mean any man-made change to improved or unimproved real property, the use of any principal structure or land, or any other activity that requires issuance of a building permit.

11. *Development subareas* shall mean geographically defined areas of the City that have been designated in the comprehensive plan as areas in which development potential may create the need for capital improvements program to be funded by impact fees.

12. *Development subarea map* shall mean a map of development subareas in which impact fees are imposed. This map is attached to this ordinance and incorporated by reference herein as if fully set out.

13. *Gross floor area* means the total square feet of enclosed space on the floor or floors comprising the structure.

14. *Impact fee* shall mean any charge, fee, or assessment levied as a condition of issuance of a building permit or development approval when any portion of the revenues collected is intended to fund any portion of the costs of capital improvements or any public facilities.

15. *Impact fee coefficient* shall mean the charge per square foot of nonresidential development or per dwelling unit as calculated for each designated development subarea by dividing total public facility costs by the gross square footage and/or number of dwelling units.

16. *Capital improvements* shall mean any and/or all of the following, and including acquisition of land, construction, improvements, equipping, and installing of same and which facilities are identified in the capital improvements plan to be financed by the imposition of an impact fee:

(a) Parks and recreational facilities

(b) Road systems

(c) Sanitary sewers and wastewater treatment facilities

(d) Water treatment and distribution facilities

(e) Storm and flood control facilities

(f) Police and fire facilities

(g) Solid waste facilities

(h) Other facilities the costs of which may be substantially attributed to new development.

17. *Residential development* means any development approved by the local government for residential use.

18. *Site* means the land on which development takes place.

19. *Zoning districts* are those areas designated in the zoning ordinance as being reserved for specific land uses, subject to development and use regulations specified in the ordinance.

20. *Zoning ordinance* means the official adopted zoning map and text regulating all development and land use in the (city, county) of _____, state of _____.

F. Applicability of Impact Fee

This ordinance shall be uniformly applicable to development that occurs within a designated development subarea.

G. Imposition of Impact Fee

1. No building permit shall be issued for a development in a designated development subarea as herein defined unless the impact fee is imposed and calculated pursuant to this ordinance. Imposition of an impact fee is dependent on the adoption of a capital improvement plan.

2. Impact fees shall not exceed the cost of providing capital improvements for which the need is reasonably attributable to those developments that pay the fees. The fees shall be spent on new or enlarged capital improvements that reasonably benefit those developments that pay the fees.

3. Notwithstanding other provisions of this statute, impact fees also may include a proportionate assessment for the cost of existing capital improvements serving new development. To determine an equitable assessment for such existing capital facilities and infrastructure, the following factors shall be considered:

(a) The need for new facilities to serve new development based on a capital improvements plan that shows (1) any deficiencies in exisiting facilities that serve existing development and the means by which existing development will be assessed and assessments used to make up such deficiencies, and (2) any capital improvements that are attributable to the demands placed on specified facilities by new development;

(b) The need for impact fees considering the availability of other means to fund capital improvements including, but not limited to, user charges, taxes, intergovernmental transfers and other revenue, and special taxation or assessment districts;

(c) The cost of existing capital improvements;

(d) The method by which the existing capital improvements were financed;

(e) The extent to which developments paying the impact fee already have contributed to the cost of the existing facility and the credit against impact fees that may be due therefrom;

(f) The extent to which new development will contribute to the cost of the existing facility in the future (i.e., user fees, debt payments, or proportion of future taxes reasonably expected to be used for future capital costs) and the credit against impact fees that may be due therefrom;

(g) The extent to which new development is required as a condition of approval to construct facilities that substantially benefit other development and the credit against impact fees that may be due therefrom; and

(h) The time–price differential inherent in comparisons of amounts paid and benefits received at different times and the credit against or reduction in impact fees that may be due therefrom.

4. That portion of impact fee revenues reasonably attributable to the equitable assessment described in subsection (2) of this section may be spent on new or enlarged capital improvements that will reasonably benefit anticipated future development rather than those developments that have paid the fee.

5. Impact fees that are assessed against new development shall be assessed in such a manner that any new development having the same impacts on capital facilities shall be assessed the same impact fee. This provision notwithstanding, the local governing body may contribute from the general fund any part or all of the impact fee assessed against certain new development that achieves other policies including but not limited to the provision of affordable housing and the retention of existing employment or the generation of new employment.

6. In order to minimize the effect of impact fees on the cost of new development, the following mechanism or one achieving the same effect shall be used to delay payment of impact fees for construction of buildings against which fees are to be assessed.

(a) The fee shall be assessed against the parcel of real property on which the building is to be sited. A notice of the fee, including the amount owed, shall be recorded in the appropriate real property title records.

(b) The impact fee assessment shall become due and payable on the date in which title to the real property is transferred or on the date the building on which the fee is assessed is first occupied. In any event, the charge becomes due and payable two years after the assessment notice is recorded.

H. Establishment of Development Subareas

Development subareas are established as shown on the Development Subareas Map.

1. Such development subareas will be established consistent with any facility service areas established in the capital improvements plan for each capital improvement. Such areas will provide a nexus between those paying the fees and benefits received to ensure that those developments paying impact fees receive substantial benefits.

2. Additional development areas or combinations of development areas may be designated by the city commission (council) as development areas consistent with the procedure set forth in this ordinance. The city commission (council) must consider the following factors in determining when and whether to add development areas:

(a) The comprehensive plan.

(b) Any standards for adequate public facilites incorporated in the capital improvements plan.

(c) The projected full development as permitted by land use ordinances and timing of development areas.

(d) The need for and cost of unprogrammed capital improvements necessary to support projected development.

(e) Such other factors as the city commission (council) may deem relevant.

The principal reason for identifying a development area or combination of development areas is to ensure that development areas projected to experience significant development in the future will be served adequately by necessary capital improvements.

I. Development Potential (by Subarea)

(Insert plan projections.)

J. Capital Improvements Program (by Subarea)

To service the projected development, capital improvements as shown on the capital improvements program, attached hereto and incorporated herein by reference, will be required to be provided and financed via impact fees. (Specific list is required.)

K. Impact Fee Coefficients (by Subarea)

(Specific numbers are required.)

L. Calculation of Impact Fee

1. The city shall calculate the amount of the applicable impact fee due for each building permit by:

(a) Determining the applicable designated development area;

(b) Verifying the number and type of residential dwelling units and the gross floor area and type of nonresidential development for which each building permit is sought;

(c) Determining the applicable per unit impact fee; and

(d) Multiplying the applicable per unit impact fee by

(i) the appropriate number of residential dwelling units, or

(ii) the gross floor area of nonresidential development.

2. If the development for which a building permit is sought contains a mix of uses, the City must separately calculate the impact fee due for each type of development.

3. Prior to making an application for building permit, an applicant may request a nonbinding impact fee estimate from the City, which shall base such estimate on the development potential of the particular site in gross square footage of floor area or number of dwelling units given the maximum

intensity permitted by existing zoning and the applicable impact fee coeffient.

M. Administration of Impact Fee

1. *Transfer of funds to finance department:* Upon receipt of impact fees, the City finance department shall be responsible for placement of such funds into separate accounts as hereinafter specified. All such funds shall be deposited in interest-bearing accounts in a bank authorized to receive deposits of City funds. Interest earned by each account shall be credited to that account and shall be used solely for the purposes specified for funds of such account.

2. *Establishment and maintenance of accounts:* The City finance department shall establish separate accounts and maintain records for each such account whereby impact fees collected can be segregated by subarea development (specific areas must be named).

3. *Maintenance of records:* The City finance department shall maintain and keep accurate financial records for each such account that shall show the source and disbursement of all revenues; that shall account for all monies received; that shall ensure that the disbursement of funds from each account shall be used solely and exclusively for the provision of projects specified in the capital improvements program for the particular development subarea; and that shall provide an annual accounting for each impact fee account showing the source and amount of all funds collected and the projects that were funded.

4. *Annual review and modification:* The City shall annually, in conjunction with the annual capital budget and capital improvements plan adoption processes, review the development potential of the subarea and the capital improvements plan and make such modifications as are deemed necessary as a result of (a) development occurring in the prior year; (b) capital improvements actually constructed; (c) changing facility needs; (d) inflation; (e) revised cost estimates for capital improvements; (f) changes in the availability of other funding sources applicable to public facility projects; and (g) such other factors as may be relevant. Modifications to the development potential, the capital improvements program, and the impact fee coefficients shall be recommended for adoption prior to _____ of each year and shall be effective on _____.

N. Bonding of Excess Facility Projects

The City may issue bonds, revenue certificates, and other obligations of indebtedness in such manner and subject to such limitations as may be provided by law in furtherance of the provision of capital improvement projects. Funds pledged toward retirement of bonds, revenue certificates, or other obligations of indebtedness for such projects may include impact fees and other City revenues as may be allocated by the city commission (council). Impact fees paid pursuant to this ordinance, however, shall be restricted to use solely and exclusively for financing directly, or as a pledge against bonds, revenue certificates, and other obligations of indebtedness for the cost of capital improvements as specified herein.

O. Refunds

1. The current owner or contract purchaser of property on which an impact fee has been paid may apply for a refund of such fee if: (a) the City has failed to provide a capital improvement serving such property within six (6) years of the date of payment of the impact fee, or (b) the building permit for which the impact fee has been paid has lapsed for noncommencement of construction, or (c) the project for which a building permit has been issued has been altered resulting in a decrease in the amount of the impact fee due.

2. A petition for refund must be filed within one year of the event giving rise to the right to claim a refund. This right to claim a refund may be limited by subsections (3) and (4) of Section G.

3. The petition for refund must be submitted to the (mayor) (city manager) or his or her duly designated agent on a form provided by the City for such purpose.

4. Within one month of the date of receipt of a petition for refund, the (mayor) (city manager) or his or her duly designated agent must provide the petitioner, in writing, with a decision on the refund request including the reasons for the decision. If a refund is due petitioner, the (mayor) (city manager) or his or her duly designated agent shall notify the city treasurer and request that a refund payment be made to petitioner.

5. Petitioner may appeal the determination of the (mayor) (city manager) to the city commission (council).

6. The right to a refund may be limited by the provisions of subsections (3) and (4) of Section G.

P. Appeals

After determination of the applicability of the impact fee, an applicant for a building permit or a property owner may appeal the amount of the impact fee or refund due to the city commission (council). The applicant must file a no-

tice of appeal with the city commission (council) within thirty (30) days following the determination of the applicability of the impact fee ordinance, the impact fee, or refund due. If the notice of appeal is accompanied by a bond or other sufficient surety satisfactory to the municipal counsel in an amount equal to the impact fee due, as calculated by the chief building official, the chief building official shall issue the building permit. The filing of an appeal shall not stay the collection of the impact fee due unless a bond or other sufficient surety has been filed.

Q. Effect of Impact Fee on Zoning and Subdivision Regulations

This ordinance shall not affect, in any manner, the permissible use of property, density of development, design and improvement standards and requirements, or any other aspect of the development of land or provision of capital improvements subject to the zoning and subdivision regulations or other regulations of the City, which shall be operative and remain in full force and effect without limitation with respect to all such development.

R. Impact Fee as Additional and Supplemental Requirement

The impact fee is additional and supplemental to, and not in substitution of, any other requirements imposed by the City on the development of land or the issuance of building permits. It is intended to be consistent with and to further the objectives and policies of the comprehensive plan, the capital improvements plan, and other City policies, ordinances, and resolutions by which the City seeks to ensure the provision of public facilities in conjuction with the development of land. In no event shall a property owner be obligated to pay for capital improvements in an amount in excess of the amount calculated pursuant to this ordinance; but, provided that a property owner may be required to pay, pursuant to City ordinances, regulations, or policies, for other capital improvements in addition to the impact fee for capital improvements as specified herein.

S. Variances and Exceptions

Petitions for variances and exceptions to the application of this ordinance shall be made to the (mayor) (city manager) in accordance with procedures to be established by resolution of the city commission (council).

T. Credits

1. A property owner may elect to construct a capital improvement listed in the capital improvements plan. If the property owner elects to make such improvement, the property owner must enter into an agreement with the City prior to issuance of any building permit. The agreement must establish the estimated cost of the improvement, the schedule for initiation and completion of the improvement, a requirement that the improvement be completed to City standards, and such other terms and conditions as deemed necessary by the City. The City must review the improvement plan, verify costs and time schedules, determine if the improvement is an eligible improvement, and determine the amount of the applicable credit for such improvement to be applied to the otherwise applicable impact fee prior to issuance of any building permit. In no event may the City provide a refund for a credit that is greater than the applicable impact fee. If, however, the amount of the credit is calculated to be greater than the amount of the impact fee due, the property owner may utilize such excess credit toward the impact fees imposed on other building permits for development on the same site and in the same ownership.

2. The City must reasonably provide for credits for other past and future monetary and nonmonetary contributions by the developer to the construction of the same public facility, as follows:

(a) Present value of amounts contributed within the past _____ years for any land dedications, physical improvements, financial contributions, or property taxes;

(b) Present land dedications and physical improvements;

(c) Future land dedications, physical improvements, taxes, and user fees for a period of _____ years.

3. No credits shall be given for the construction of local on-site facilities required by zoning, subdivision, or other city regulations.

SECTION 2. LIBERAL CONSTRUCTION

The provisions of this ordinance are hereby found and declared to be in furtherance of the public health, safety, welfare, and convenience, and it shall be liberally construed to effectively carry out its purposes.

SECTION 3. REPEALER

All ordinances, code sections, or parts thereof in conflict herewith be and the same are hereby repealed to the extent of such conflict.

SECTION 4. SEVERABILITY

Should any sentence, section, clause, part, or provision of this ordinance be declared by a court of competent jurisdiction to be invalid, the same shall not affect the validity of the ordinance as a whole, or any part thereof, other than the part declared to be invalid.

SECTION 5. EFFECTIVE DATE

This ordinace shall take effect immediatedly on its passage.

COMMENTARY

Findings

The stated findings establish the rationale for use of impact fees. In this ordinance, the community may impose those fees against new development as opposed to general tax and assessment measures that are imposed uniformly against all properties. The findings establish the basic level of city commitment to cure existing public service deficiencies in developed areas and the relationship between such commitment and the needs created by new development. (See *Banberry Development Corp.* v. *South Jordan City* 631 P. 2d 899 [Utah, 1981].) Impact fees may finance various capital improvements including roads, sanitary and storm sewers, water supplies, libraries, fire and police facilities, and other public improvements. The findings help to establish the regulatory (police power) basis for imposition of impact fees by tying their use directly to city comprehensive planning and zoning by which such use of property is permitted. (See *J. W. Jones Companies* v. *City of San Diego*, 203 Ca. Rptr. 580 [Cal., 1984].)

C. Intent

This section states the city's intention based on findings. The impact fee is imposed at building permit issuance since that is the point at which gross square footage or the actual number of dwelling units can be accurately determined.

Fees are to be used for new or enlarged capital improvements in the manner provided throughout this ordinance.

D. Authority

The express statutory authority contained in the sample standard development impact fee enabling statute is based on the applicable state constitution and enabling statutes, including home rule provisions. A lack of basis (home rule or statute) for authority to adopt impact fees may place an insurmountable barrier in the path of communities wanting to use this financing mechanism. We designed the ordinance to be applicable within municipal boundaries unless other statutes expressly grant such regulatory (or impact fee) authority over extraterritorial land use.

E. Definitions

The definitions are to be tailored to individual communities and exceptions or special cases noted.

F. Applicability of Impact Fee

Specific subareas should be defined for purposes of more accurately and specifically calculating the impact fee coefficients and for purposes of meeting the applicable reasonable relationship legal standard. (See, e.g., *City of College Station* v. *Turtle Rock Corp.* 680 S.W. 2d 802 [Tex. 1984] and *Homebuilders Assoc. of Kansas City* v. *City of Kansas City* 555 SW 832 [Mo. 1977].)

G. Imposition of Impact Fee

The impact fee is imposed at building permit issuance. The impact fee is not related to the issuance of the building permit in the sense that the fee is chargeable to defray building permit administration or building or enforcement expenses (See *Janis Development Corp. v. City of Sunrise*, 40 Fla. Supp. 41 [Cir. Ct. 1973], affirmed, 311 So. 2d 371 [Fla. 4th D.C.A. 1975]), and *Venditti-Siravo, Inc. v. City of Hollywood*, 39 Fla. Supp. 121 [1973].) Rather, the fee is related to construction of capital improvements necessary to service the proposed development and without which the development will not be permitted; the fee must be attached at some reasonable time prior to construction. This also reflects the fact that, while the zoning creates the potential for development, it is the issuance of the building permit that brings that development to fruition thereby triggering the need for capital improvements and the fees to finance such improvements.

H. Establishment of Development Subareas

The subareas allow for the establishment of a close geographical nexus between a particular development and the capital improvements necessary to service that development. In addition, development subareas must be consistent with any facility service subareas established in the capital improvements plan. This section states the criteria for establishment of additional areas in which impact fees may be levied in the future. As a general rule, the larger the area affected, the more latitude the city has in programming necessary public facilities. However, the area cannot be so large that is does not satisfy the reasonable relationship test. Of course, in-fill development in built-up areas may not have to pay impact fees if adequate public facilities already exist. Therefore, development subareas usually will be necessary only in new or outlying areas.

I. Development Potential (by Subarea)

The city would calculate potential development in the designated development areas through a measurement of the total square footage or dwelling units permitted in the development subarea by current land use regulations. Depending on whether the city wants to provide any subsidy for new development, some or all of this potential growth will be used in the calculation of the impact fee.

J. Capital Improvements Program (by Subarea)

The capital improvement program is more than estimates of need. The capital improvement program also reflects the estimated costs, funding sources, and schedule of construction made by the city. This section calls for a list of specific projects, since identification of the projects for which funds collected will be expended is essential to the validity of an impact fee ordinance.

K. Impact Fee Coefficients

Coefficients are calculated by dividing the total cost of public facility needs per subarea by the gross square footage of dwelling units to be built in the development subarea.

The coefficient may assume that all square footage (e.g., whether office, retail, warehouse, or industrial) and dwelling units have similar impacts on facility needs and, therefore, on the costs thereof. However, it is more common to establish more accurate ratios between, for example, the relative rate at which traffic is generated for commercial versus office square footage or for single-family detached homes versus multifamily attached townhouses. Similarly, sanitary sewer use could be determined by land use and converted into gallons per day per 1,000 square feet, etc.

L. Calculation of Impact Fee

The impact fee is calculated by multiplying total development (either in square footage or number of dwelling units) by the appropriate impact fee coefficient. Total development in gross square footage or number of dwelling units is as shown on the application for building permit. In some cases, certain types of development are exempted from impact fees because of a lack of demand on public facilities (e.g., no parks impact fee for industrial property).

The impact fee estimate is authorized to allow a prospective developer to reasonably anticipate specific public facility costs that can be precisely calculated before spending large sums of money or otherwise making irrevocable commitments toward development.

M. Administration of Impact Fee

The impact fee should be collected by the city department that is responsible for issuing building permits. However, the funds collected should be transferred to the city finance department for placement into specific accounts for each designated development subarea. One of the problems of multiple development subareas is that administration of many small accounts may become difficult. Nonetheless, segregating funds, ensuring that funds collected are used exclusively for the purposes set forth in the ordinance, and no commingling with other city funds is essential to the validity of the ordinance. (*Hayes* v. *City of Albany,* 490 P. 2d 1018 [Or. Ct. App. 1971]; *Contractor & Builders Association of Pinellas County* v. *City of Dunedin,* 329 So. 2d 314 [Fla. 1976]; and *Village of Royal Palm Beach* v. *Home Builders & Contractor's Assn.,* 386 So. 2d 1304 [Fla. Dist. Ct. App.

1986].) If projects need to be built and the earmarked account is deficient, the city should lend general funds to the account.

The annual review requires the city to update the capital improvements plan and the development potential (projections of gross square footage and number of dwelling units) on a regular basis in conjunction with the overall city budgeting and capital improvements planning process. This ensures that the impact fee coefficients are reasonably related to the most current estimates and projections available.

N. Bonding of Excess Facility Projects

Projects specified in the capital improvements plan may be bonded by the city with impact fees (and other funds, if appropriated by the city) pledged to the retirement of such bonds — provided that impact fees can be pledged to retire bonds issued solely for relevant projects from the capital improvements plan. The use of bonding enables the city to provide capital improvements in a timely fashion consistent with needs created by development, but without necessarily waiting until all development is initiated before proceeding with high priority projects. In most cases, the provisions for bonding will be covered by state law. This language in this ordinance must be used consistent with applicable statutes.

O. Refunds

A mechanism is provided by which an owner of property can request a refund under three conditions: (1) the failure of a city to construct the relevant capital improvement within five years of fee payment, (2) lapse of the building permit, or (3) decrease in the appropriate fee amount. The current owner of property must petition for a refund, and the city must act on the request within a specified time period. An alternative provision not included in the ordinance is to provide for an automatic extension of time for the city to pay refunds. Another option might require agreement between municipalities and developers to accomplish the same purpose.

Q. Effect of Impact Fee on Zoning and Subdivision Regulations

The impact fee is not intended to nor does it change in any way the permissible intensity of development on any parcel of property, which is governed solely by the zoning ordinance or subdivision regulations.

R. Impact Fee As Additional and Supplemental Requirement

The impact fee is an additional requirement that is imposed by the city. It is intended to be consistent with other land development ordinances, including requirements for the collection of fees for on-site improvements in subdivisions, particularly local streets. The impact fee is not intended to substitute for or replace existing requirements for upgrading presently inadequate facilities.

T. Credits

The model ordinance permits an applicant to construct a capital improvement listed in the capital improvement plan and to obtain a credit against otherwise applicable impact fees. Further, the developer may be entitled to a credit for past, present, and future contributions (other than impact fees) toward capital improvements listed in the impact fee CIP; however, no credit is available for internal, on-site, and local facilities required by other land use regulations; e.g., the subdivision ordinance.

13

A Model Impact Fee Authorization Statute

Julian C. Juergensmeyer
James C. Nicholas

This chapter presents a model impact fee enabling statute that is more flexible than the one presented in Chapter 11. This statute allows impact fees to be used for almost any facility included in a capital improvements program, as long as dual rational nexus criteria are met. Additional detail on fee calculation, collection, expenditure, and refund also is provided.

AN IMPACT FEE AUTHORIZATION STATUTE

A bill to be entitled "State of _____ Impact Fee Authorization Act," providing a short title, providing definitions, providing authority to impose impact fees, providing for the calculation of impact fees, providing for the collection and expenditure of impact fees, providing for refund of impact fees, providing for public hearings, providing for time of assessment and collection, providing a compliance period, providing for severability, providing an effective date.

Be It Enacted by the Legislature of the State of
_____:

SECTION 1. SHORT TITLE

This act shall be known as "The _____ Impact Fee Authorization Act."

SECTION 2. DEFINITIONS

As used in this act:

1. A *capital improvement component, element, or program* is that component of a comprehensive plan that sets out the need for public facility capital improvements, the cost of such improvements, and proposed funding sources. A capital improvement component, element, or program must cover at least a five-year period.

2. A *comprehensive plan* is a coordinated general plan for the development of the area of jurisdiction of a local government, based on existing and anticipated needs, showing existing and proposed improvements in the area of jurisdiction of the local government; stating the principles to which future development should conform and the manner in which such development should be controlled; and including a capital improvement component, element, or program.

3. *Credits* are the present value of past or future payments made by new developments toward the cost of existing or future public facilities capital improvements.

4. A *developer* is a person, corporation, or-

156

ganization, or other legal entity constructing or creating new development.

5. The *discount rate* is that interest rate, expressed in terms of percentage per annum, which is used to adjust past or future financial or monetary payments to present value.

6. *Impact fees* are charges imposed upon new development by local government to fund all or a portion of the public facilities capital improvements required by the new development from which it is collected or to recoup the cost of existing public facilities capital improvements made in anticipation of the needs of new development.

7. *Local government* is any county, municipality, or any special governmental district having land use control power.

8. *New development* is any building activity or mining operation, any material alteration of the use or appearance of any structure or land, or any division of land into three or more parcels.

9. *Non-site-related improvements* are land dedications or provisions of public facilities capital improvements that are not for the exclusive use or benefit of a new development and that are not site-related improvements.

10. An *offset* is a reduction in impact fees designed to fairly reflect the value of non-site-related public facilities capital improvements provided by a developer pursuant to any local government land use regulations or requirements.

11. *Present value* is the value of past or future payments after they have been adjusted to a base period by a discount rate.

12. *Proportionate share* is that portion of total public facility capital improvement costs that is reasonably attributable to new develop-

ment less (a) any credits for past or future payments, adjusted to present value, for public facilities capital improvement costs made or reasonably anticipated to be made by new development toward public facilities capital improvement costs in the form of user fees, debt service payments, taxes, or other payments, or (b) offsets for non-site-related public facilities capital improvements provided by a developer pursuant to any local government land use regulations or requirements.

13. *Public facilities capital improvement costs* include but are not limited to capital improvement costs associated with the construction of new, expanded, or otherwise enhanced publicly owned facilities and the costs of equipment, land acquisition, land improvement, design, and engineering related thereto. Public facilities capital improvement costs do not include routine and periodic maintenance expenditures or personnel, training, or other operating costs.

14. *Reasonable benefit* is a benefit received from the provision of a public facility capital improvement that is greater than that afforded the general public in the jurisdiction imposing impact fees. Incidental benefit to other developments shall not negate a reasonable benefit to a new development.

15. *Recoupment* means the proportionate share of the public facilities capital improvement costs of excess capacity in existing capital facilities where such excess capacity has been provided in anticipation of the needs of new development.

16. *Site-related improvements* are land dedications or provisions of public facilities capital improvements that are for the exclusive use or benefit of the new development and/or that are for the exclusive purpose of safe and adequate provision of public facilities to the particular new development.

SECTION 3. AUTHORITY TO IMPOSE IMPACT FEES

(A) The local governments of this state are authorized to assess, impose, levy, and collect fees defined herein as impact fees for all new development within their jurisdictional limits. After the effective date of this act, impact fees may only be imposed by local governments pursuant to the requirements and limitations set forth in this act.

(B) Impact fees may be imposed only for those types of public facility capital improvements specifically identified in or covered by a local government comprehensive plan. These plans shall specify level of service standards for each type of facility that is to be the subject of an impact fee, and such standards shall apply equally to existing and new development.

SECTION 4. IMPACT FEE CALCULATION

(A) Local governments considering the adoption of impact fees shall conduct a needs assessment for the type of public facility or public facilities for which impact fees are to be levied. The needs assessment shall identify level of service standards, project public facilities capital improvements needs, and distinguish existing needs from future needs.

(B) The data sources and methodology upon which needs assessments and impact fees are based shall be made available to the public upon request.

(C) The amount of each impact fee imposed shall be based upon actual capital cost of public facilities expansion, or reasonable estimates thereof, to be incurred by the local government as a result of new development.

(D) An impact fee shall meet the following two tests:

1. The provision of new, expanded, or otherwise enhanced public facilities, for which an impact fee is charged, must be reasonably related to the needs created by new development;

2. The impact fees imposed must not exceed a proportionate share of the costs incurred or to be incurred by the local government in accommodating the development. The following seven factors shall be considered in determining a proportionate share of public facilities capital improvement costs.

a. The need for public facilities capital improvements required to serve new development, based on a capital improvement component, element, or program that shows deficiencies in capital facilities serving existing development, and the means, other than impact fees, by which any existing deficiencies will be eliminated within a reasonable period of time, and that shows additional demands anticipated to be placed on specified capital facilities by new development.

b. The availability of other means of funding public facilities capital improvements, including but not limited to, user charges, taxes, intergovernmental transfers and other revenue, and special taxation or assessments.

c. The cost of existing public facilities capital improvements.

d. The methods by which the existing public facilities capital improvements were financed.

e. The extent to which new development required to pay impact fees has, during at least the past five (5) years, contributed to the cost of existing public facilities capital improvements, and received no reasonable benefit therefrom, and any credits that may be due new development because of such past payments.

f. The extent to which new development required to pay impact fees may reasonably be anticipated, for not longer than the next twenty (20) years, to contribute to the cost of existing public facilities capital improvements through user fees, debt service payments, or other payments and any credits due new development because of such future payments.

g. The extent to which new development required to pay impact fees is required as a condition of development or construction approval to provide non-site-related public facilities capital improvements and any offsets due new development because of such provision.

SECTION 5. COLLECTION AND EXPENDITURE OF IMPACT FEES

The collection and expenditure of impact fees must be reasonably related to the benefits accruing to the development paying the fees. In order to satisfy this test, the ordinance must specifically consider the following requirements:

1. Upon collection, impact fees must be deposited in a special trust fund, which shall be invested with all interest accruing to the trust fund. That portion of impact fees that is recoupment may be transferred to any appropriate fund.

2. The collection and expenditure of impact fees shall be localized to provide a reasonable benefit to the development paying the fees. Local governments should consider establishing geographically limited benefit

zones for this purpose, but zones are not required if a reasonable benefit can be provided in the absence of such zones. Any benefit zones established must be appropriate to the nature of the particular public facility and of the local government of jurisdiction. Local governments shall explain in writing and disclose at a public hearing their reasons for establishing or not establishing benefit zones.

3. Except for recoupment, impact fees shall not be collected from a development until adoption of a capital improvement component, element, or program that sets out planned expenditures bearing a reasonable relationship to the needs created by the development.

4. Impact fees shall be spent for the type of facility for which they are collected and spent for public facilities capital improvements that are of reasonable benefit to the development paying the fees.

5. Within six (6) years of the date of collection, impact fees shall be expended or encumbered for the construction of public facilities capital improvements of reasonable benefit to developments paying the fees and that are consistent with the capital improvement component, element, or program.

6. Where the expenditure or encumbrance of fees is not feasible within six (6) years, the local government may retain impact fees for a longer period of time if there are compelling reasons for such longer period. In no case shall impact fees be retained longer than ten (10) years.

SECTION 6. REFUND OF IMPACT FEES

(A) If impact fees are not expended or encumbered within the period established in Section 5 of this act, local governments shall refund to the fee payer or successor in title the amount of the fee paid and accrued interest. Application for a refund must be submitted to the local government within one year of the date on which the right to claim a refund arises. All refunds due and not claimed within one year shall be retained in the special trust funds and expended as provided in Section 5 of this act.

(B) When a local government seeks to terminate any or all impact fee requirements, all unexpended or unencumbered funds shall be refunded as provided above. Upon the finding that any or all fee requirements are to be terminated, the local government shall place a notice of termination and availability of refunds in a newspaper of general circulation at least two (2) times. All funds available for refund shall be retained for a period of one (1) year. At the end of one (1) year, any remaining funds may be transferred to the general fund and used for any public purpose. A local government is released from this notice requirement if there are no unexpended or unencumbered balances within a fund or funds being terminated.

(C) Any portion of an impact fee that represents recoupment is exempted from the provisions of (A) and (B) of this section.

SECTION 7. PUBLIC HEARINGS

Impact fees shall be adopted by ordinance and the adoption of an impact fee ordinance or amendment thereto shall be by affirmative vote of not less than a majority of the total membership of the governing body, in the manner prescribed by law.

SECTION 8. TIME OF ASSESSMENT AND COLLECTION OF IMPACT FEES

All impact fees imposed pursuant to the au-thority granted herein shall be assessed prior to or as a condition for the issuance of a building permit or other appropriate permission to proceed with development and collected in full no later than the issuance of a certificate of occupancy or other final action authorizing the intended use of a structure. The local government shall have the option to select the time of assessment and collection within the guidelines set herein.

SECTION 9. COMPLIANCE

(A) No later than two (2) years after the effective date of this act, local governments shall conform all impact fee ordinances existing on the effective date of this act to the provisions of this act. Prior to such conformation, the failure of impact fees adopted prior to the effective date of this act to have met the requirements of a valid impact fee set forth in the act shall not constitute grounds for challenging their validity.

(B) Local governments requiring impact fees shall incorporate such fee requirements into their broader system of development and land use regulations in such a manner that new developments, either collectively or individually, are not required to pay or otherwise contribute more than a proportionate share of public facilities capital improvement costs.

(C) Beginning two (2) years after the effective date of this act, a local government shall not require a developer, as a condition of development approval, to contribute or pay for land acquisition or for construction or expansion of public facilities or portions thereof (except site-related improvements) unless the local government has enacted an ordinance requiring all new developments similar in land use category or nature of impact to contribute a proportionate share of the funds, land, or public facilities necessary to accommodate any impacts through the payment of impact fees as described in this section or through other appropriate means.

SECTION 10. SEVERABILITY

In the event that any provision of application of this act is held to be invalid, it is the legislative intent that the other provisions and applications hereof shall not be thereby affected.

SECTION 11. EFFECTIVE DATE

This act shall take effect on _____.

Authors' Note

The authors want to acknowledge the work of Keith Hetrick, esquire, of the Committee on Economic, Consumer, and Community Affairs of the Florida Senate.

14

Excise Taxes: Impact Fee Alternative

Eric J. Strauss
Martin L. Leitner

There is a wide variety of ways in which a city or a county can raise funds to build the new public facilities, such as roads, parks, sewers, and water lines, required by increased development. For certain facilities inside the boundaries of a subdivision, exactions such as dedication or reservation of land may be suffcient. One focus has been on impact fees as a preferred mechanism to raise money for off-site public improvements in a subdivision. However, impact fees may not be the only mechanism to raise revenue for public facilities that are located outside the boundaries of a particular residential area.

There are several reasons why a community may not want to use the mechanism of impact fees. For example, the city or county might not want to limit the geographic focus for the funds raised from impact fees to one particular subdivision. This decision might be due to political, economic, or locational concerns reflected in the adopted capital improvement plan (CIP). There may be no suitable site for a facility. In particular, since most impact fee ordinances require that collected revenues be spent within a certain time period, a city may be reluctant to build a facility within an arbitrary time frame

that is unrelated to the CIP. Impact fees are police power regulations. In some states, if funds collected from the impact fees were earmarked to a special fund but were not limited in their use to a particular geographic area (e.g., a subdivision), that proposed mechanism would fail a reasonable relationship test required of police power regulations such as impact fees.[1] Finally, impact fees, like all regulations, may not raise an excessive amount of money in terms of the regulated activity. For these or other reasons, a court may not be willing to approve an impact fee that may be neccessary to meet the public facility needs.

A potential solution to this problem is the imposition of an excise tax by a city or county. An excise tax imposes no restriction on the geographic area in which revenues are collected or spent. The purpose of such a tax is principally to raise revenue. An impact fee, on the other hand, is characterized as primarily regulatory, even though it may have an incidental revenue-raising component.[2] A local government may raise and spend money virtually at will for public facilities using the proceeds of such a tax.

The United States Supreme Court has defined an excise tax as "a tax imposed upon a particular use of property or the exercise of a single power over property incidental to ownership."[3] When a tax is levied on only one of the many incidents of ownership and all other incidents may be fully enjoyed free of the tax, the tax will be characterized not as a property tax, but as an excise tax. For example, the federal government has levied excise taxes on items such as tires, telephones, and firearms. In this context, it is important to remember that an excise tax is not upon a subdivider but upon the business of subdividing land.

Many states reserve the right to levy excise taxes to the state government. However, at least four states – California, Colorado, Arizona, and Maryland – appear to allow the imposition of an excise tax on the business of new construction by a city or a county. Other states, including Tennessee, may already have delegated this power to cities or counties. Of course, the statutory authority necessary to levy the tax in any state must be found in the laws of that state.

To help ensure the legality of this tax, a local government's objective in enacting such a tax must be:

1. To ensure that the excise tax is characterized as a tax and not a regulatory measure authorized under the police power.

2. If characterized as a tax, to ensure that the measure is classified as an excise tax and not a property tax. If the local government fails on either ground, the use of the excise tax to fund needed public facilities will be held invalid.

3. Even if the city or county enacts a measure that meets these standards, the excise tax must be legitimate according to standard constitutional and statutory analysis (i.e., rational purpose, equal protection, taking, etc.).

The principal purpose of this chapter is to demonstrate, by using case law analysis, that the public facility objectives of local government can and have been successfully achieved through use of an excise tax. Further, the chapter identifies the critical factors that the courts will use to make these characterizations. With this knowledge, a local government can structure the excise tax ordinance to conform as closely as possible with the identified objectives to ensure approval in the face of a legal review, assuming that the city or county has the initial enabling authority to levy such a tax.

CHARACTERIZATION AS A TAX

Local governments must be granted authority by their state legislatures to enact a local excise tax. Such a power, unlike a police power regulation, cannot be indirectly implied from general grants of power (such as home rule) from a legislature to a local unit of government. A reviewing court will examine carefully the purposes behind an excise tax, assuming a specific power to levy such a tax has been given to a city.

A tax must not be a direct substitute for land use regulation or growth managment. As a court stated, a tax cannot be:

> . . . a facade masking a pernicious regulatory scheme designed to halt housing projects. . . .[4]

In that case the ordinance expressly declared its purpose as strictly one for raising revenue. The court held that the manner in which the money should be generated and the purpose for which it is used is strictly a legislative judgment. A legislative matter usually is not subject to strict judicial review. Other courts might not be as liberal.[5]

Another case, from California, discusses the differences between a regulation and a tax when dealing with the subject of excise taxes.[6] On the facts of this case, the court held such excise taxes invalid when they were imposed as a condition of subdivision map approval. A detailed examination of the court's opinion provides a guide for other cities to avoid legal roadblocks to enacting a valid excise tax.

The issue in this case concerned a license tax on the business of subdividing land. The measure of the tax was determined by the number of lots being subdivided. The purpose of the tax was to pay for municipal services, including capital outlays for parks and recreation and fire protection, whose need was created by new subdivisions in the city. The tax was imposed as a condition of final subdivision map approval. An analysis of the decision shows that the conjunction of several factors contributed to the finding that the ordinance was, in part, regulatory in nature. Among the reasons for invalidity were:

1. The purpose of the tax was to mitigate the financial burden placed on the city by such subdivisions.
2. The tax was imposed on the subdivision itself rather than on the subdivider.
3. The tax was imposed as a condition of subdivision approval.
4. The state has preempted the field of subdivision control by virtue of the Subdivision Map Act in California.

Once the measure was characterized as being partially regulatory, the court held that the tax must fail because it did not meet the reasonable relationship test applicable to police power regulations such as impact fees. In this ordinance, the revenues collected from the tax were earmarked to a special fund but were not limited in their use to a particular geographic area (i.e., to the subdivision paying the tax) nor specifically limited to providing facilities made necessary by that particular subdivision.

A recent Colorado case reviewed a challenge by property owners to a service expansion fee (SEF) adopted by a local government.[7] The SEF was imposed on persons who obtained building permits from the city for new construction, additions to existing structures, and substantial alterations and reconstruction of existing buildings. Churches, schools, and government institutions were exempt. The SEF was calculated on the square footage and type of development for which the building permit was sought. The ordinance declared that its purpose was to establish an additional source of revenue to fund the expansion of city services made necessary by new growth and development. In its analysis of the excise tax, the Colorado Supreme Court first addressed the fundamental issue of how the SEP should be characterized. The opinion held that (1) the sole purpose of the measure was to raise revenue, (2) there was no mention of any regulatory function in the ordinance, and (3) therefore, regardless of its label, it was a tax.

An analysis of the decisions reveals that the guidelines for the distinction of a measure as either a tax or a regulation remain murky. It is clear, however, that an excise tax on new construction must be imposed on the person undertaking such new construction rather than on the land itself or on the process of subdivision or issuance of a building permit. An excise tax is a tax on an individual's economic activity. The tax may be collected at building permit issuance if that is simply a convenient point to ascertain the amount of the tax to be imposed and is not construed as a tax on the building permit itself.

The stated purposes for the tax may be important as well in making this distinction of a regulation versus a tax. The purposes of the ordinance should be solely for revenue-raising objectives and should not have any regulatory intent or objective. If the tax is regulatory, it will be invalidated because it cannot withstand the test for a regulatory impact fee (reasonable relationship) or for a special assessment (special benefit) because the revenues may be used throughout the city. The fact that revenues are earmarked to a particular fund (i.e., the funds collected are placed in a trust fund for use solely for the purposes specified in the ordinance and not for general governmental purposes) is a characteristic—indeed, a requirement—of a valid regulatory measure. However, identification of the intended use of the fund collected from an excise tax does not appear to be fatal to an excise tax. So long as the principal purpose of the excise tax is to raise revenue, this does not create a legal problem.

In summation, stating the purposes for which the tax is imposed in a preamble and designating a particular governmental fund for receipt of tax revenues collected may, in fact, be helpful in determining the legality of an excise tax because (a) the ordinance does not earmark, thereby distinguishing the excise tax from an impact fee regulatory measure, (b) it demonstrates that the principal objective is to raise revenues, and (c) it helps to distinguish the excise tax from a general property tax.

EXCISE TAX VS. PROPERTY TAX

In determining the constitutional or statutory validity of a tax, the courts first classify and characterize the tax as either a property, a sales, an income, or an excise tax. This characterization is significant because of varying federal and state constitutional requirements relating to uniformity, valuation assessment, and rational classifications. A property tax must be uniform for all property of the jurisdiction and cannot be different for commercial or residential classifications of property if a state constitutional uniformity of taxation clause is applicable. Other states may require uniformity within classes of property but permit variation among different types of land use. Similarly, problems of preemption by existing state or federal authority may be present for an excise tax, depending on the characterization of the tax. In other words, a local government may not be able to levy an excise tax because other governments have already reserved that power to themselves. Such characterization or labeling of a tax often determines the ultimate issue of validity.

The courts have made it clear that they will look beyond the legislative label attached to a tax measure. Time and again, courts have emphatically stated that "[t]he nature of a tax must be determined by its operation, rather than by any particular descriptive language which may have been applied to it."[8] The U.S. Supreme Court went so far as to say, "The name by which the tax is described in the statute is, of course, immaterial."[9] The legislative title and preamble language for a taxing measure may play a role in the judicial characterization of the tax. The extent of this role, however, has not been crystallized and to rely exclusively on legislative labels would be unwise. Thus, the nature of the tax continues to be a major consideration in the judiciary's "labeling" process.

Traditionally, the courts have recognized several principal criteria that determine a property tax. These include:

1. The tax is imposed on the only or one of a limited number of uses of the property.

2. The measure of the tax is based on the valuation of the property.

3. Unpaid taxes are secured by a lien on the property.

4. The tax is levied by reason of ownership.[10]

The combination of one or any of the above characteristics may be fatal to a legislatively designated excise tax. The logical approach, therefore, is to avoid the incorporation of these characteristics in the structuring of any excise tax measure.

In terms of characterization of the tax, an important question that must be answered is the definition of an excise tax. As mentioned previously, the U.S. Supreme Court has defined the excise tax as "a tax imposed upon a particular use of property or the exercise of a single power over property incidental to ownership."[11] Thus, where taxes have been imposed on one of the *only* uses of the property, such taxes have been found to be property taxes.[12] This often was a critical factor in early tax characterization cases. More recently, however, courts seem to be narrowing the boundaries of what uses constitute the *only* use of property—thereby making it easier for excise taxes to withstand property tax challenges on this basis.[13] Where a tax is levied on only the business of new construction, arguably there are still many incidents of ownership left unencumbered.[14]

The second indication of a property tax to be avoided is the measurement of the tax based on the value of the property, particularly assessed valuation of the property. Where the tax has been based on some other factor, however, the courts have been willing to avoid a property tax characterization.[15] A tax on new construction based on square footage or type of development has generally withstood property tax challenges based on valuation.

The third major characteristic of property tax to be avoided is that of securing unpaid taxes with a property lien. One way to ensure payment of an excise tax on the business of new construction is to require payment before the issuance of a building or occupancy permit or other issuance of a government license or franchise. This action avoids the necessity for a lien on the property.

The final major characteristic of a property tax is that it is levied by reason of ownership and on the owner of the property.[16] Designating the tax as a tax on the privilege of engaging in the business of new construction would help to avoid these property tax characterizations. This is especially true if the tax is coupled with the levy of such a tax against the *contractor* or *developer*, who may not necessarily be the owner of property.

Some courts have adopted a liberal reading favoring excise tax characterization, but the predictability of such decisions still is not precisely determinable. Perhaps the safest conclusion one can draw from the decisions is that they seem to indicate that the boundaries of property tax characterizations are receding while the boundaries of characterization as an excise tax are expanding.[17]

An issue that does not appear to have been discussed in any case is whether the total amount of revenue generated by the tax characterizes a measure as a property rather than an excise tax. In most cases, an excise tax, while clearly revenue raising, generates only a small portion of the taxing jurisdictions' revenues. If a proposed excise tax on subdividing land or constructing new structures will generate a very substantial amount of revenue, that fact alone may distinguish it from other excise taxes. The situation may suggest to a reviewing court that, despite the nomenclature, it is intended to substitute, in part, for the property tax or allow the property tax to be reduced. Once this linkage is made, it may be a short step for the court to conclude that the tax is, in fact, a property tax or that there is double taxation. Therefore the amount of revenue might need to be controlled.

CONSTITUTIONAL/STATUTORY ANALYSIS

Once a measure is characterized as a valid excise tax, the final analysis must be a review according to constitutional and statutory principles. These general standards of review have been applied to excise taxes in a number of cases.

Rational Purpose. Court decisions usually find that an excise tax is enacted to legitimately solve problems in high-growth areas. Rationales for approval center on the ability of the local government to receive revenues to meet and deal with serious ecological problems caused by new developments.[18] Since it is necessary to extend public services into these areas, new sources of revenue are necessary. There is a significant delay between issue of a building permit and receipt of property tax revenues. Therefore, to meet the public facilities needs, the local government has a rational purpose in enacting this regulation, i.e., to meet the needs for additional public facilities created by new growth.

Equal Protection. An excise tax cannot unreasonably discriminate between two different classes of individuals, e.g., between developers and contractors or between residential and nonresidential developers.[19] It is within the discretion of the legislative body to exact different license taxes from different classes of businesses so long as the classification rests on some rational basis.[20] When an ordinance is attacked because it allegedly violates equal protection, a court will presume the existence of reasonably conceived facts that will uphold the regulation. The burden of showing arbitrary action rests on the individual who has attacked the ordinance. In addition, ordinances that have been invalidated on equal protection grounds have been largely regulatory in nature. Taxes may legitimately discriminate between types of businesses if the classifications are reasonable.

Confiscation. Excise taxes cannot reach the point where all value of the property is overcome by high taxes. When a tax amounts to 1 or 2 percent of the sales price, it is not confiscation. Therefore an excise tax should not seek to raise an excessive amount of money. (In San Jose, California, it has reached 4.5 percent.)

Vested Rights. Excise taxes may be challenged if they are imposed on projects for which financing has already been secured and construction already begun. Proponents of this concept, from the zoning context, assume that the imposition of a tax is related to past transactions. However, cases have suggested that the imposition of new taxes or rate increases for old ones is part of the hazards of business. The fact that a tax relies on past events for its operation does not make it illegally retroactive. The excise tax is not imposed on completed transactions, but only on the ongoing business of the developer. Therefore, an excise tax does not violate vested rights. Only where a measuring formula draws on events far in the past so as to have little relation to current business will a tax be invalidated.

Notes

1. *Newport Building Corp.* v. *City of Santa Ana,* 210 Cal. App. 2d 771, 26 Cal. Rptr. 797 (1962).

2. *Westfield-Palos Verdes Co. v. City of Rancho Palos Verdes*, 73 Cal. App. 3d, 141 Cal. Rptr. 36 (1977).

3. *Bromley v. McCaugh*, 280 U.S. 124 (1929).

4. *Westfield-Palos Verdes Co.*, note 2.

5. *Id.*

6. *Newport Building Corp. v. City of Santa Ana*, 210 Cal. App. 2d 771, 26 Cal. Rptr. 797 (1962).

7. *Cherry Hill Farm v. City of Cherry Hills*, 670 P. 2d 779 (Colo. 1983).

8. *Weaver v. Prince George's County*, 366 A.2d 1048, 1055 (Md. Ct. Spec. App. 1977).

9. *Dawson v. Kentucky Distilleries & Warehouse Co.*, 255 U.S. 288, 292 (1921).

10. *County Commissioners of Anne Arundel County v. English*, 35 A.2d 135 (Md. Ct. App. 1943); *Flynn v. City and County of San Francisco*, 115 P.2d 3 (Cal. 1941).

11. *Bromley*, note 3.

12. *County Commissioners of Anne Arundel County v. English*, 35 A.2d 135 (Md. CT. App. 1943); *Flynn v. City and County of San Francisco*, 115 P.2d 3 (Cal. 1941).

13. *Weaver v. Prince George's County*, note 8.

14. *Bromley*, note 3.

15. *AMPCO Printing-Advertiser's Offset Corp. v. City of Newark*, 197 N.E.2d 285 (N.Y. Ct. App. 1964).

16. *Flynn v. City and County of San Francisco*, 115 P.2d 3 (Cal. 1941).

17. *American National Building & Loan Assoc. v. City of Baltimore*, 224 A.2d 883 (Md. Ct. App. 1966).

18. *Westfield-Palos Verdes Co.*, note 2.

19. *City of Mesa v. Homebuilder's Assn. of Central Arizona, Inc.*, 523 P.2d 57 (Aug. 1974).

20. *Westfield-Palos Verdes Co.*, note 2.

Calculating Development Impact Fees

15

The Rational Nexus Test and Appropriate Development Impact Fees

JAMES C. NICHOLAS
ARTHUR C. NELSON

Stroud (1988) observes that state courts increasingly base the validity of impact fee systems on the rational nexus test. Many planners, attorneys, and developers now view the rational nexus as the mainstream approach to setting impact fees (see Bosselman and Stroud 1985; National Association of Home Builders 1984). In the discussion that follows, we will base a set of principles for determining impact fees on case law and practice in several communities, most of them in Florida. Planners must exercise great care in applying these general principles to individual situations, however, since laws and court interpretations vary considerably among the states.

The rational nexus test chiefly involves two principles.[1] First, there must be a reasonable connection between community growth that new development generates and the need for additional facilities to serve that growth. Second, there must be a connection between the expenditure of the fees collected from contributing development and the benefits that development enjoys. In other words, the rational nexus test calls upon local government to show that growth will result in a need for the new or expanded facilities that impact fees assessed against new development will finance. Moreover, local government must show that the funds collected not only will provide the needed facilities but also will benefit the contributing development.[2]

We divide our discussion of the principles for calculating development impact fees into three parts. The first part shows how local governments attribute capital costs to new development. The second reviews considerations for determining the benefits that accrue to contributing development. The third part introduces the appropriate approaches for calculating impact fees for water and sewer, road, park, and police facilities. Appendix 15A reviews the mathematics of selected impact fee formulas.

ATTRIBUTING IMPROVEMENT COSTS

The primary factors involved in attributing improvement costs to new development are selection of facility standards and determination of the proportionate share of the cost of constructing those facilities.

Facility Standards

Communities must demonstrate that the need for additional facilities results from new development, not from existing deficiencies. To make that judgment, communities need to determine appropriate facility standards in the general planning process, and must formulate a capital improvement plan under which they will schedule improvements to correct existing deficiencies, upgrade service levels, and anticipate improvements that new development will make necessary. They then can apportion facility costs between current and new development.[3]

Sound community planning begins with projections of future population, dwelling units, employment, and business activity (Chapin and Kaiser 1979). The projections lead to determinations of future developable land and supporting facility needs. They also lead to development of standards to project the need for, and the size and quality, of community facilities. Those standards become the basis on which planners can satisfy the first part of the rational nexus test, that new development requires additional facilities.

Local governments must set or use established planning standards to justify impact fees. In a situation where a community has no explicit standard for improved parkland, for example, the community must establish such a standard. The community may have an average of three acres per 1,000 residents. That might become the official parkland standard. The local planners then would project future parkland needs in a proportion similar to a population projection. An increase of 30,000 people over 10 years would mean that the community would have to provide an additional 100 acres of improved parks within 10 years. The local government might opt to assess new development for the cost.

Suppose a community decides that its existing park standard is not adequate and establishes a standard of five acres of improved parkland per 1,000 population. If the community has 100,000 residents but only 300 acres of improved parkland, it falls 200 acres short of meeting its adopted planning standards. If the community projects that it will have 30,000 more residents within 10 years, its plan must provide for a total of 750 acres of improved parkland. Can new development make up the existing shortage? Not directly. The plan and its capital improvements component must first show how the community will eliminate the current deficiency without assessments on new development, perhaps through taxes that only current development will pay. Such taxation, which would affect new development as well, would equalize the burden of paying for existing deficiencies: All current development would be assessed the same rates for the same purpose (Callies and Freilich 1986). In such a situation, however, new development could be held responsible only for the cost of providing the additional 150 acres of parkland—the amount attributable to it. That is the approach of determining impact fees using the rational nexus test. The approach has many complications, some of which the reader may immediately see, but which we shall consider later.

Once the plan has established community facility standards and determined the existing deficiencies and future needs, the capital improvements plan can schedule necessary improvements. The courts will probably (but not always nor everywhere) require that deficiencies be cleared up as quickly as possible. In our park example, the community should make up its 200-acre deficiency within a reasonable time (usually above five years but there is no court-determined time frame—yet). As for new development, the capital improvements plan might show that community park needs will increase by 150 acres within 10 years, even if current deficiencies are resolved. The comprehensive plan and the capital improvements plan might also recommend approximate locations for those parks, locating them in reasonable proximity to planned new development.

Apportioning Cost

Determining the proportionate share of costs requires understanding the complexities of community financing and usually involves determining the following:

1. The cost of existing facilities;
2. The means by which existing facilities have been financed;
3. The extent to which new development has already contributed, through tax assessments, to the cost of providing existing excess capacity;
4. The extent to which new development will, in the future, contribute to the cost of constructing currently existing facilities used by everyone in the community or by people who do not occupy the new development (by paying taxes in the future to pay off bonds used to build those facilities in the past);
5. The extent to which new development should receive credit for providing common facilities that communities have provided in the past without charge to other developments in the service area;

6. Extraordinary costs incurred in serving new development;
7. The time–price differential inherent in fair comparisons of amounts paid at different times.[4]

1. Determining the Cost of Existing Facilities

Consider again the park example where the community has established five acres per 1,000 residents as the park standard. Suppose planners have determined that the present value of the community's expenditures for improved parkland over the past 10 years is $30,000 per acre. At five acres per 1,000 population, the cost per capita of new parks is $150, which would be the per capita impact fee charged to new residential development for new parks. Assessing fees as new residents are added to the community would be cumbersome; it is more reasonable to assess them on a per-unit-of-housing basis. If the average household size is 2.5 persons, then the impact fee would be $375 for each new home. Cost adjustments have to be made for homes built for different sizes of families, however, and many impact fee schedules base the fee on number of bedrooms and on unit type.

Most impact fee schedules do not take inflation into consideration, nor should they, because no one knows what the rate of inflation—or the actual cost of building facilities—will be over a planning period. The cost per acre of improving parkland should be recalculated and updated every year or two. Such updating should incorporate changes in other costs. The same logic can apply to the preparation of impact fee schedules for roads, schools, fire and police, library, water, sewer and drainage, and other facilities.

2. Determining How Existing Facilities Were Financed

A principal requirement of impact fee programs is to shelter existing residents from paying for new facilities required to serve new development. Conversely, new development should not have to pay for facilities being built to serve occupants of existing development. For now, we only need to determine how existing facilities were financed. For example, if property taxes have financed most existing facilities, then the land on which new development occurs has already paid for part of those parks. We will suggest how to account for earlier payments attributable to the land on which new development is constructed. On the other hand, if payments for parks or other facilities came primarily from state sales and excise tax rebates, state and federal revenue sharing or block grants, and other user fees and charges, they probably cannot be attributed to vacant land prior to development.

3. Determining How Much New Development Already Has Paid

Owners of undeveloped land do not pay user charges, sales and excise taxes, or fuels taxes on that land. However, they do pay property taxes. If property taxes have financed facilities, even in part, local government should determine the value of those payments. In Palm Beach County, Florida, for example, property taxes pay about 15 percent of the cost of new roads. Since about 18 percent of the taxable property is undeveloped, undeveloped property contributes about 2.7 percent of the capital road expenditures of the county.

Determining the appropriate fees when externally derived financial support exists for capital facilities raises a different problem. For example, the Charlotte County, Florida, library capital costs are $100.35 per dwelling unit. State of Florida library grants offset 9.7 percent of the cost annually. In such a situation, some courts will require that the fee be no more than the local government's actual cost of accommodating new development, and therefore will rule that the library impact fee should be reduced to $90.61. Otherwise, the nearly $10 per unit difference is considered an unauthorized tax. Charlotte County set the impact fee for libraries to reflect that rationale. The county applies the same logic to setting impact fees for roads, water, sewer, drainage, school, and other facilities that receive capital financing support outside local government.

4. Determining How Much New Development Will Pay in the Future

Issuing bonds is a common method of financing facilities. If bonds are outstanding when new development occurs, the development will help retire them, thus lowering debt service charges to all existing property by broadening the taxable base. Broward County, Florida, resolved the issue of crediting new development for future bond payments attributed to it in the following manner: The average cost of financing new parks necessitated by development was about $390 per new three-bedroom single-family home; but, in reality, each new home in the future would pay the equivalent of about $103 in discounted, present-value payments to retire park bonds issued to pay for existing parks. Therefore, the maximum charge against new development to pay for new parks could be reduced to $287. Since the actual fee assessed was set at $125, a court determined that the fee was less than actual cost, even after allowing for future debt service on the bond. The impact fee passed court muster.

5. Determining Credits for Facilities Installed by New Development

In addition to impact fees, many local governments require developers to install both on-site and off-site facilities that the community at large or a specific service area may use. For example, occupants of current development near new development may use facilities—such as a traffic signal—that contributing development installs. The local government should grant credit against fees for any on-site facilities or other dedications that occupants of current development in the service area use. That credit would be the value of the facility not otherwise attributed to contributing development. Types of facilities that some communities consider in offsetting impact fees that way include roads, rights-of-way, traffic signs and signals, and turn lanes. Palm Beach County, for example, deducts from impact fees the cost of any off-site roads a developer has to install. If the credit is higher than the fee, however, there is no counterpayment. Furthermore, the credit applies only to impact fees of the same kind. For example, credit for installing a traffic signal does not reduce a park impact fee.

In practice, determining appropriate credits against impact fees is a complicated and controversial exercise. Several local governments in Florida are experimenting with less controversial methods. Charlotte County credits right-of-way dedications—which are frequently mandatory—against road impact fees at 115 percent of the taxable value of the property. That approach is an attempt to simplify the determination of appropriate credit and avoid litigation.

6. Determining Extraordinary Costs

The most common way costs may change is through cost increases from inflation or other factors. Impact fee programs may accommodate inflation by providing for periodic review of fee schedules. When costs increase through other factors—for example, increasing the cost of purchasing parkland because of rising property values, irrespective of inflation—they may be passed on to new development as an extraordinary cost. Passing on those costs requires careful documentation, perhaps through appraisals.

One can attribute a second way costs may change to idiosyncracies of individual developments. St. Lucie County, Florida, for example, assesses impact fees that are nine times higher for developments on a barrier island than those for developments on the mainland. The differential occurs because of the greater cost of building roads and bridges to the island.

7. Time-Price Differential

Perhaps the most difficult consideration is the time–value of money. Situations in which that is important occur when other payments, not related to impact fees, finance new facilities over time, and when developers have to pay impact fees the benefits of which will not appear until future improvements are made.

In the first situation, local government often must install facilities to accommodate future development and must establish some equitable way to calculate the impact fee. Anne Arundel County, Maryland, calculates a road impact fee by considering the difference between the current value of motor fuel taxes that new households will pay in the future and the present value, per new dwelling unit, of new roads. New roads cost an average of $2,785 per new single-family home. That home pays $242 a year in road use taxes, about 32 percent ($77) of which is available to the county for road capital costs. What is the discounted, present value of the stream of annual fuel tax cash flow; is it higher or lower than the cost of building the roads? The answers depend greatly on the discount rate a government uses and on the period over which it calculates that rate. Anne Arundel County applied a 6 percent discount rate over 25 years and determined that the average household occupying a single-family residence will contribute $990 in motor fuels tax cash flow over 25 years in current dollars. The balance, $1,795, becomes the road impact fee. If the time were increased, the tax contribution would be higher and the impact fee lower. If the discount rate were raised, the tax contribution would be lower (more heavily discounted) and the impact fee would be higher.

But appropriate discount rates vary over time as the cost (interest rate) of borrowing money this year may be higher or lower than last year or next. Twelve percent was considered an adequate discount rate in 1981 as that was the cost to many local governments of borrowing money. Today we find that local government can borrow money at about 6 percent. Anne Arundel County, therefore, appropriately uses a flexible discount rate that reflects the yield rate of local governments' long-term municipal bonds. The county would have to pay that rate to borrow the same amount it otherwise raises through impact fees. Every few years (or better, annually), the local government should recalculate impact fee credit schedules influenced by discounted future tax receipts to reflect the existing interest rate on long-term municipal debt.

A second problem about the time–value of money involves determining the benefit to fee payers when fees are to be spent on improvements in the future. A substantial amount of time may elapse before communities can productively spend the fees. Since they accrue in small amounts, it may take some time for the fees to accumulate enough to be useful. How long contributing development waits to receive the benefit affects the present value of the benefit it receives. We offer the following adjustment.

Assume that the long-term municipal bond yield rate is 6 percent and that impact fees are put into 8 percent trust deposits when collected. The difference in rates is 2 percent. The 8 percent rate can be considered the private cost of holding funds and the 6 percent rate, the private benefit. There is, then, a net private cost of 2 percent per year for withholding expenditure of those fees that would otherwise benefit development immediately. Discounting future benefits by 2 percent per year yields a present value of future benefits over time, as Table 15-1 shows. Thus, if the facility is not built until five years after fees are paid, the present value of the benefit of the facility paid from the fees made by contributing development falls about 10 percent. If the facility is not built until 10 years after, the present value of the benefit of the facility paid by contributing development decreases by about 18 percent (to 81.71 percent of the original fee).

Lee County, Florida, uses that logic. The county determined that roads accessing a particular development would not be improved until 10 years after road impact fees were paid. It therefore discounted the road impact fees by almost 18 percent. By using that approach, the county takes benefit delays into consideration. The fee actually paid thus reflects the difference between the private and public cost of borrowing money, which is to the developers' advantage since the cost of borrowing money is higher for them than for local governments. Local governments can construct their own versions of Table 15-1, or simply use a standard discounted, present value formula (examples of which every financial text contains), to discount to their present value the impact fees used for financing certain facilities in the future.

Table 15–1. Present (Discounted) Value of Future Benefits (where the difference between the private cost and private benefit is 2 percent per annum*)

Year facility is to be built	Percent of fee to be paid
0 (Today)	100.00
1 (One year from today)	98.00
2	96.04
3	94.12
4	92.24
5	90.39
6	88.58
7	86.81
8	85.51
9	83.37
10	81.71
11	80.07
12	78.47
13	76.90
14	75.36
15	73.87

* See text for discussion.

BENEFITS TO THE FEE PAYER

We now consider how to determine whether contributing development receives adequate benefits. The rational nexus test and, indeed, the minimum standards of most states where impact fees are used, require that contributing development benefit from the fees it pays. Must the benefit be exclusively enjoyed by contributing development? How are benefits determined?

Exclusivity of Benefit

The rational nexus test does not require that contributing development *exclusively* benefit from facilities financed from the fees it pays. The relevant issue is whether contributing development *substantially* benefits. Under the substantial benefit rule, the relevant criterion is whether tenants of contributing development can be expected to use a facility. Locating the improvements where one may reasonably expect that occupants of that development would use the improvements meets the substantial benefit rule. No technical standard defines substantial benefit, however. Rather, it appears that expected use indicates substantial benefit, and use will vary from service to service and area to area.[5]

Certainty of Benefits

Going beyond the substantial benefit rule, the local government must be certain that the facility will be *accessible* so that occupants of new development can indeed use it. At issue, primarily, is the location of the improvements that contributing development finances. For example, local government could spend impact fees collected from new development on a road so far from the development that a court will fail to agree that certainty exists that the development's occupants will use it. Local planners might argue that all people are expected to use the road regardless of where it is located (at least sometimes); but a court might disagree, ruling that the road is simply too far away to be accessible to all people occupying the contributing development.

Palm Beach County resolves the problem by spending road impact fees not more than six miles from contributing development. Montgomery County, Maryland, expends road impact fees within service areas or districts within which contributing development is located.

Timing is also an issue, since courts look for impact fees to be expended within a reasonable time.[6] Communities can prepare plans that show which facilities are financed by impact fees, where they will be located, and when they will be built. Where fees do not come in as projected, or where the fees alone cannot finance the facilities, the community must show how and when it will use communitywide resources to construct them. Most impact fee ordinances in Florida also contain a refund provision, under which the fees are refunded (with interest) if the community fails to construct the planned facilities within a specified time. The most common period over which Florida communities hold impact fees is six years—one full capital improvements planning cycle of five years, plus one year.

MATHEMATICS OF IMPACT FEE CALCULATIONS

We turn now to the mathematics of impact fees. We discuss representative examples, mostly from Florida, that we feel can apply to communities around the nation. Appendix 15A shows the formulas and examples of impact fees for water, sewer, road, park, and police facilities.

Impact fees for any given community must be tailored to the financial, political, and legal constraints of that community (Nicholas 1987). Perhaps a community cannot raise revenues from current development to improve the volume of parkland from three to five acres per 1,000 residents. It cannot then expect new development to pay impact fees intended to build new parks at a rate of five acres per 1,000 residents, even if the fees are limited to providing new development with better parks than current development. The community's financial inability to overcome its deficiency therefore sets, perhaps by default, the parameter for park impact fees assessed to new development. The community probably is restricted financially, therefore, to a future of three acres of park per 1,000 residents no matter what higher standard it prefers.

The ease with which governments can implement impact fees depends on the local political climate. Proposals for impact fees in progrowth communities may fall on deaf ears. But even progrowth communities can see impact fees as a way to both accommodate growth and shelter current development from the rising costs of constructing new facilities. Alternatively, slow-growth communities may find that impact fees discriminate among classes; they may rather contain growth through non-impact fee policies.

The legal environment does much to prescribe the manner of impact fee design and implementation. We focus here on how to prepare and implement impact fees using the rational nexus test as we interpret it, and as it currently applies to communities in states where that test is more or less accepted judicial review practice. Our approach may not apply entirely to all communities in all states because of differences in judicial review standards.

Water and Sewer Impact Fees

Fees for water and sewer service, which are common, are rarely called impact fees. Rather, they are commonly known as connection fees, hook-up charges, and so forth. Those one-time fees usually recoup for the community a portion of the capital cost of providing the service. The community may also recoup portions of the capital cost through the periodic, usually monthly, water and sewer statements; a portion of that revenue usually helps to retire water and sewer facility bonds.

Table 15A-1 in the appendix presents a sample water service impact fee. We calculated that fee first on the basis of the capital cost to provide potable water for each dwelling unit of a new development (average capital cost per unit of a class of new development), and second on the basis of what that unit of new development will pay toward its capital costs out of monthly charges (credits). Calculating the credit involves determining the share of the monthly charge devoted to retiring capital costs.

Communities usually recoup sewer facility costs through sewer fees and connection fees. Like water facility costs, sewer facility costs are usually calculated on a gallons-per-day basis. We prefer another measure, however, equivalent residential units (ERUs), where the average single-family residential unit equals 1.0, which we further specify as 300 gallons per day of wastewater treatment. We base all other activities, except industrial wastewater, on ERUs. We calculate the sewer facility impact fee as the product of the ERU(s) or portions thereof that the facility will treat and the cost per ERU of the facility, minus the present (discounted) value of the portion of the monthly sewer fee allocated to capital costs. Appendix Table 15A-2 presents the formula and includes a sample schedule of ERU adjustments that Grand Junction, Colorado, uses (Frank, Lines, and Downing 1985).

Road Impact Fees

Perhaps the most important factor one should consider in determining the road impact fee is the level of service standard. The Institute of Traffic Engineers has developed six classes of highway capacity, or level of service (LOS). The highest LOS—A—is the capacity of a roadway where traffic flows at design speed without interruptions. LOS E indicates maximum capac-

ity before congestion. Communities will typically, but not always, plan for roadway capacities of LOS D, which indicates slowing and interruptions and average travel speeds at well under design speed, but represents a situation better than congestion. Depending on a large variety of geometric design considerations, a highway functioning at LOS D handles about 8,000 vehicles per lane every working day. Factors to include when calculating the fee are average trip lengths generated by different classes of land use; average daily trip ends (origin or destination) for each class of land use as the Institute of Traffic Engineers estimates; average cost of acquiring right-of-way and constructing a lane-mile of roadway; and credits to be made by each class of land use. Appendix Table 15A-3 shows a sample road impact fee formula, with an example.

Parks

Park impact fees usually are calculated on the basis of number of people expected to use them. A park impact fee formula should consider the community standards for different types of parks (typically neighborhood, community, and regional parks), the additional parks needed to serve new development, and the per capita or dwelling unit cost of acquiring and improving parkland. Appendix Table 15A-4 illustrates a formula and an example of how the cost is adjusted by a series of credits, including those for past and future property tax payments to retire local government bonds used to construct current parks; the table also indicates the contribution the local jurisdiction can reasonably expect from state and federal sources.

Police

More problematic is the use of impact fees to

pay for capital facilities to accommodate the needs of service agencies such as police, fire, human services, and emergency medical services. Such services are not delivered in fixed places or in the same manner as parks or roads; individuals and firms both require and benefit from them. Appendix Table 15A–5 illustrates one way to calculate a police facility impact fee. The community first determines the active population of a community, which consists of the number of people within the community at any given time and includes residents, commuters, and tourists on a 24-hour-per-day basis. Next, the community estimates the capital cost (building space, equipment, and vehicles) of supporting two sworn officers per 1,000 active residents (this number is merely a sample of a community police facility standard). The active residents that new development adds becomes the basis on which to assess the police facility impact fee. One can adapt the approach we suggest to allow for determination of impact fees for fire and emergency medical service facilities, as well. Considerably more research is needed to learn how we can determine and allocate impact fees for those kinds of facilities.

SUMMARY

Local goverments assess development impact fees for water, sewer, solid waste disposal, road, park and recreation, library, school, museum, administrative, fire, police, medical and health, human services, child care, and other facilities. The majority of such fees in many places outside Florida probably do not meet the design criteria we describe here because the fee methodologies are less well developed in those places. We have attempted to establish what might constitute defensible impact fees according to the rational nexus test. Indeed, many communities do employ some of those formulas or variations of them. We also suggest some improvements to existing methodology in the hope that communities will refine their own formulas before courts enforce what may be less well-informed refinements.

Our methodology has many advantages, foremost among them is that it makes use of data that usually already exist. Administrative costs should not be excessive, based on our observations. Our formulas also remove, or at least reduce, the possibility that courts would knock out impact fees as arbitrary or otherwise without adequate foundation. Yet, we believe that our formulas are not so rigid that communites cannot modify, improve, and update them as times and circumstances dictate.

Notes

1. The rational nexus test was first articulated in *Jordan* v. *Village of Menomonee Falls*, 137 N.W.2d 442 (Wis. 1965), and later clarified in *Contractors and Builders Association of Pinellas Couty* v. *City of Dunedin*, 329 So.2d 314 (Fla. 1976), *Contractors and Builders Association of Pinelllas County* v. *City of Dunedin*, 358 So.2d 846 (Fla. 1978 DCA 1978), and *Lafferty* v. *Payson City*, 642 P.2d 376 (Utah 1982).

2. There are similar approaches to forcing new development to pay for the new facilities it requires. The "specifically and uniquely attributable" test, established by *Pioneer Trust and Savings Bank* v. *Village of Mount Prospect*, 176 N.E.2d 799 (Ill. 1961), is considered rather strict compared to the rational nexus test. The reasonable relationship test, established by *Ayes* v. *City of Los Angeles*, 207 P.2d 1, is rather liberal. As Stroud reports, the rational nexus test has emerged as the mainstream approach to justifying development impact fees (see also Bosselman and Stroud 1985; Hagman and Juergensmeyer 1986; Callies and Freilich 1986).

3. See, for example, *Hollywood Inc.* v. *Broward County*, 431 So.2d 606 (Fla. 4th DCA 1983), and *Home Builders and Contractors Association of Palm Beach County* v. *Board of County Commissioners of Palm Beach County*, 446 So.2d 140 (Fla. 4th DCA 1983).

4. See Lafferty, note 2.

5. See *City of College Station* v. *Turtle Rock Corp.*, 680 S.W.2d 802 (Texas 1984), and *Hollywood*, note 3.

6. See *City of Fayetteville* v. *IBI Inc.*, 659 S.W.2d 505 (Ark. 1983).

References

Bosselman, Fred P. and Nancy E. Stroud. 1985. Pariah to Paragon; Developer Exactions in Florida 1975–85. *Stetson Law Review*, 14, 3; 527–63.

Callies, David L. and Robert H. Freilich. 1986. *Cases and Materials on Land Use Law*. St. Paul, Minn.: West.

Chapin, F. Stuart and Edward Kaiser. 1979. *Urban Land Use Planning*. Urbana, Ill.: University of Illinois.

Frank, James E., Elizabeth R. Lines, and Paul B. Downing. 1985. *Community Experience with Sewer Impact Fees: A National Survey*. Tallahassee: Florida State University.

Hagman, Donald and Julian C. Juergensmeyer. 1986. *Urban Planning and Land Development Control Law*, 2d ed. St. Paul, Minn.: West.

National Association of Home Builders. 1984. *Impact Fees: A Developer's Manual*. Washington, D.C.: NAHB.

Nicholas, James C. 1987. The Incidence and Burden of Impact Exactions. *Law and Contemporary Problems*, 50, 1: 85–100.

Stroud, Nancy. 1988. Legal Considerations of Developmental Impact Fees. *Journal of the American Planning Association* 54, 1: 29–37.

APPENDIX 15A
SAMPLE DEVELOPMENT IMPACT FEE FORMULAS

Here we present sample development impact fee formulas and examples for water, sewer, park, road, and police facilities. We can apply elements of certain formulas to others when the situation warrants. For example, our approach to calculating the credit for past and future property tax payments used to retire municipal bonds that pay for current parks can be applied to other facilities for which bonds also pay. The calculations for nonlocal government contributions to the construction of new parks also can apply in similar situations. Calcula-

Table 15A–1. Sample Water Impact Fee Formula

Water Impact Fee$_i$ = GPD$_i$ × C – Credits$_i$

Where:

GPD$_i$ = Gallons per day consumed for each use, i, estimated from city records.

C = Cost of constructing one gallon of potable water capacity.

Credits$_i$ = Present (discounted) value of that portion of the stream of future annual water service payments allocated by use, i.

tions for property taxes that new development contributes to build new roads in other parts of the community can apply to other facilities that impact fees might also help finance; such facilities may include libraries, public safety, and emergency facilities. In addition, our credit approach can extend to future sales taxes that contributing development pays, if one can show a consistent pattern of local goverment expenditures of sales tax receipts for specific kinds of facilities.

Water Facilities

Let us begin with water facility impact fees. Appendix Table 15A–1 shows our sample water treatment impact fee formula. Assume that the community determines it must expand its water collection, treatment, storage, and delivery facilities by 10 million gallons per day to serve projected growth, and the projected cost of the expansion is $20 million. Average daily consumption is 150 gallons per person, or 450 gallons per day per three-person household. Since the cost of constructing one gallon of additional flow capacity is $2.00, the straightforward water facility impact fee is $900 for a three-person dwelling. Now determine the credit. Assume the monthly water charge is $1.25 per thousand gallons with $1.00 for operation and mainte-

Table 15A–2. Sample Sewer Impact Fee Formula

Sewer Impact Fee$_i$ = ERU × C − Credits$_i$

Where:

ERU = Equivalent residential units, or units of 300 gallons per day of wastewater treatment for use, i (schedule of ERUs below).

C = Cost of constructing treatment facilities per ERU.

Credits$_i$ = Present (discounted) value of that portion of the stream of future sewer payments allocated to capital costs by use, i.

Sample ERUs for some major land use activities:

Use	ERU
Any single family home	1.00
Multifamily project, per unit	0.72
Shopping centers and stores, per 1000 square feet	0.35
Hotels/motels without kitchens, per room	0.36
Restaurants, 12 hours or less per day, per seat	0.14
Travel trailer park, per space	0.45
Churches, assembly halls, theaters, per seat	0.01
Offices and warehouses, per 1000 square feet	0.05
Nursing home, per resident	0.36
Hospital, per bed	0.89
Fast food, per employee	0.06

Table 15A–3. Sample Road Impact Fee Formula

$$\text{Road Impact Fee} = \frac{\text{ADT}_i \times \text{TL}_i}{2^a(\text{Cap})} \times C - \text{Credits}_i$$

Where:

ADT$_i$ = Average daily trip ends for each uses, i, estimated by the Institute of Traffic Engineers.

TL$_i$ = Average trip lengths for each use, i, estimated by local or state transportation agencies.

Cap = Capacity of lane at Level of Service D.

C = Cost of construction and right-of-way acquisition per lane mile.

Credits$_i$ = Discounted, present value of the stream of motor fuel and property tax revenue used to finance road capital costs for each use, i.

a. Trip ends include trips from the home or other place to a destination, and from that place back to the original place. Thus, for every time a trip begins at home or other place and then returns, the trip is counted as two trip ends. To estimate the costs per lane of road attributed to any land use, therefore, we must divide the trip ends by two.

nance and $0.25 for capital costs. At 450 gallons per day, the average household would consume about 13,500 gallons per month, for which it would pay $16.88; $13.50 of that goes to operations and maintenance, and $3.38 ($40.56 per year) goes toward capital costs. The present (discounted) value of that stream of annual revenues over 25 years, discounted at 6 percent, is $518.50, which would be the credit.[1] The impact fee thus becomes $381.50 ($900 minus $518.50). Monthly discounting would yield a slightly higher credit.

Sewerage Facilities

We calculate the sewer facility impact fee in much the same way as the water facility impact fee. We need no example here as the formula is substantially the same. Note that the fee is based on an Equivalent Residential Unit (ERU), which we further define as a three-person household generating 100 gallons of wastewater per day each, or 300 gallons per day per ERU. In Appendix Table 15A–2, the sewerage facility impact fee formula includes examples of ERU equivalents for some nonindustrial uses. The ERU calculation for industrial uses must be determined on a case-by-case basis since industry varies widely in its production of wastewater.

Roads

Appendix Table 15A–3 presents a sample road impact fee formula. We can apply the formula to a single-family home in a residential subdivision. If we assume an average of 10 trips per day per single-family residential unit, an average trip length of six miles, road capacity of 8,000 vehicles per day per lane at Level of Service (LOS) D, construction costs of $300,000 per lane mile (one lane extending one mile), and a right-of-way acquisition cost of $100,000 per lane mile, the formula would estimate an impact fee of $1,500 minus credits.

We calculate credits as the discounted, present value of the stream of motor fuel and property tax payments the local government collects from contributing development over future years to pay for new roads. Calculating those credits is important, since ignoring them results in forcing contributing development to pay twice for its impact on the community road system: once by paying the $1,500 impact fee and again, in part, by paying motor fuel and property taxes that the community uses to build new roads. We set the revenue stream at 25 years, because that is the assumed average life span of roads built today (after which the roads need major reconstruction). Assume that the motor fuel tax is 10 cents per gallon of which local government gets 20 percent, or $0.02 per gallon, for road capital costs. At an average automobile gas mileage rate of 15 miles per gallon, average of 10 trips per day every year (365.25 days per year), average trip length of six miles per trip, and discount rate of 6 percent over 25 years (or a discounted, present value revenue stream factor of 12.78), we estimated the occupants of this new home will pay $373.43 in the credit for future motor fuel taxes.

Now we determine the residential property tax credit. Assume a value of $100,000 for single-family units, a property tax rate of 20 mils against full market valuation—1 percent ($0.20 per $1,000 valuation) of which local government uses annually for building new roads (based on historical records), and a discount rate of 6 percent over 25 years (or a discounted, present value revenue stream factor of 12.78). The estimated credit for future property taxes the occupants of this new home would pay is $255.60.

Total credits thus would be $629 (rounded) and the impact fee would be $871.

Parks

For the park formula we show in Appendix

Table 15A–4. Sample Park Impact Fee Formula

Park Impact Fee$_i$ = $[P(p_i)(CP)(1 - SG)]$
$$\times [1 - (UD/BY)(PCF)] - [(DS \times ATV_i)(FCF)]$$

Where:

P = Additional park acres needed per capita of new population generated by use i.

p_i = Average number of persons per dwelling unit in use i.

CP = Cost of acquiring and constructing an acre of park.

SG = Proportion of new park acquisition and construction costs historically provided by state government or other non-local government sources.

UD = The percent of the present tax base represented by undeveloped land.

BYF = Bond year factor, which is the number of years in which debt service has been paid to retire park bonds divided by the total number of years of debt service.

PCF = The present value factor of the stream of past property tax revenues paid to provide debt service on the bonds.

DS = Property tax rate used for debt service.

ATV_i = Average taxable value of class of use, or the taxable value of specific use, i.

FCF = Present value factor of stream of future property tax payments available to provide debt service.

Table 15A–4, we include the additional credit consideration of bonds that might have been issued in the past to pay for current parks but which are retired, in part, by past and future property tax assessments on new development.

Assume that a community wants to assess park impact fees on new residential development to build new parks. However, it must give credit to new development that pays property taxes to retire 25-year general obligation bonds sold five years ago to build the current parks. Using the formula, one can calculate the past and future portions of park costs that subject development (i) will bear. Past payments relate to undeveloped land value; future payments relate to developed land value. Also consider the need to credit nonlocal government revenues that also help pay for parks.

To calculate the fee, assume the following additional factors: the cost of acquiring and improving an acre of park (including neighborhood, community, and regional) is $20,000; the adopted standards of the community call for five acres of parkland per 1,000 population; dwelling unit occupancy is three persons in this case; state and other noncommunity grants have historically paid for 20 percent of the capital costs; 15 percent of the assessed valuation of the community's property is undeveloped (this includes nonresidential property even though the fee only applies to residential property); the 25-year bond to build current parks has 20 more years of servicing; the yield (interest) on the bond is 6 percent; debt service on the bond is paid from property tax assessments of one-tenth of one mil ($0.10 per $1,000 of valuation) this year (the figure will change each year as the value of the community's property rises); and the average taxable value of dwellings to be constructed is $100,000 in this project.

The impact fee without credits is $300 per dwelling unit in this project. We anticipate continuation of state and other nonlocal government contributions to parks, which have historically accounted for 20 percent of new park acquisition and development. The fee is then $240 (or $300 × 1 − 0.25), before other credits are considered.

The credit for past property tax payment used to retire bonds consists of three parts. First, 15 percent of the taxable valuation of the community comprises undeveloped land in the current year (the year of impact fee calculation). Then, if the community has already paid five years of debt service, 20 percent of the total bond sale has already been retired by the current year. To consider the time–value of debt service between the first and the current year of the bond, we determine the present value factor of the stream of past debt service based

on the yield (interest) of the bond (6 percent), which is 5.975. Those considerations multiplied together mean that new development occurring this year must be credited 17.925 percent of the impact fee. To this point, therefore, the $240 impact fee is reduced to $196.98, or $197 rounded (82.075 percent of $240).

Now consider the credit attributable to future property tax payments made by contributing development to retire the bond. For a given single-family residence in the subject subdivision, the assessed valuation for property taxation purposes is $100,000. The assessment for debt service purposes this year is one-tenth of a mil, or $10. But this payment is made every year until the bond is retired. The discounted, present value factor of the stream of these payments over 20 years, based on the 6 percent yield of the bond, is 11.47 which, when multiplied by $10, indicates a credit for future property tax payments used for debt service of $114.70. We therefore adjust the impact fee to $82, rounded ($197 minus $114.70).

However, the debt service tax rate will probably fall in future years while taxable property values will rise for both residential and nonresidential property each year. Therefore, we cannot accurately specify what the credit will be at any given year in the future. Our formula gives greater credit than the local government should expect from contributing development over future years, so it should be defensible. The parameters of the formula should be adjusted periodically to reflect changes in past and future bond debt service payments, the probable fall in debt service tax rate as taxable property values rise, the ratio of undeveloped land value to total property value, and the cost of acquiring and building new parks.

There is also the interesting situation that the credit for the discounted, present value of the stream of future property tax payments used to retire park bonds for a house with a value in excess of $200,000 will exceed the adjusted park impact fee according to our example. Does that mean developers are due a refund of some amount? Theoretically, it should. As a practical matter, local governments keep the difference and merely waive the impact fee.

Under our formulation, it is possible that credits against impact fees can leave the community short of funds to build new parks to serve new development. That is fair, however, as new development has been and will continue to be taxed to retire bonds used to build the current parks, which we presume the community at large will enjoy. The local government must make up the shortage out of the general fund or some other source. Of course, using money from the general fund to build new parks to serve new development means that some sales and property tax that new development pays to the general fund in addition to impact fees will help to build those parks. Credit might again be considered. At some point, the proportion of the credit to be considered can become so small as to be ignored.

Police Facilities

Development impact fees can help pay for many other public purposes, including libraries, museums, government offices, emergency medical facilities, fire protection facilities, and police facilities. In Appendix Table 15A-5 we suggest a relatively simple approach to calculating police facility impact fees. The approach can be extended to the other facilities.

To determine the police facility impact fee, the community first estimates its active popu-

Table 15A–5. Sample Police Facility Impact Fee Formula

Police Impact Fee$_i$ = ($p_i \times$ C) $-$ R

Where:

i = Unit of measure on which the fee is assessed, which is either the dwelling unit or 1000 square feet of each use, i.

p_i = Number of active residents per use, i.

C = Capital cost per active resident for new police facilities including building space, equipment, and vehicles.

R = Revenues available per active resident for capital expenditures.

lation. This is the 24-hour per day, seven-day per week equivalent population of the community. Residents who commute to work, shop, or travel outside the community reduce the active population; nonresidents who commute to work, shop, or visit inside the community increase it. The active population is calculated for each major land use and then summed for a community total. That may require extensive surveying, but judgment based on spot checks and literature could suffice.

For residential land uses, for example, the active population is the average number of occupants for each dwelling unit type, times 24 hours per day, times seven days per week, times the number of occupied dwelling units. As residents do not spend every hour of every day in their residence, one must estimate the time residents spend on the premises and divide that by the total time considered. Members of a three-person household, for example, may spend two-thirds of their time on the premises over an average week. Their contribution to the active population is thus two-thirds of what it could be according to the calculation.

Nonresidential activities involve workers and visitors. Vehicle trip rates to destinations can help determine the active population of nonresidential land uses. We assign workers a period of eight hours per day, five days per week; the amount of time visitors are assigned depends on the land use. We estimate those factors for each major land use and then sum them with the residential active population. For example, if a warehouse averages 4.88 trips per 1,000 square feet per workday, dividing by two gives total round trips the warehouse generates. Of the 2.44 round trips per 1,000 square feet, say survey or published references determine that 1.25 are employees and the balance, 1.19, are visitors. We can assume that workers spend eight hours per day, five days per week, in the warehouse. Through survey research, we determine that visitors spend one hour per day, five days per week. A total of 55.95 person-hours per week is spent inside the warehouse per 1,000 square feet. As the active resident population is 168 hours per week, the warehouse's active population is 55.95/168 or 0.33 active residents per 1,000 square feet of space.

For our example, assume that the city's estimated active population is 30,000 during an average week. We can estimate the cost of providing new police facilities to each new active resident—calculated as one person present in the community 24 hours per day, seven days per week. Assume that the community's current service level is two police officers and proportional support personnel per 1,000 active residents. We also know from pricing of current police facilities (including equipment and cars) that the value of capital facilities to support two officers is $40,000. Thus, for each person added to the active population, the police facility impact fee before credits may be $40.

The fee is reduced by the value of other payments that new development makes. Assume that there is no state or federal support for financing new police facilities. The local govern-

ment must credit new development for the contributions it has made and will continue to make through sales and property taxes. New development annexed to the city has made no prior tax payments that helped finance current police facilities, but it will make such payments in the future. We can estimate the present (discounted) value of those future payments by first estimating the annual dollar expenditures for new police capital facilities per active resident. Suppose the city spends $30,000 a year on new police facilities (probably new cars and equipment). Revenues for those new facilities—an average $1 per active resident—come from property and sales taxes that existing development pays. We assume that new development will result in proportional increases in tax contributions to the local government. As in previous examples, we calculate the present (discounted) value of the stream of payments at 6 percent over 25 years, which results in a present value factor of 12.78. The credit is therefore $12.78 per active resident. The impact fee is $27 (rounded) per active resident, added to the city by new development ($40 minus a credit of $13). Thus, a new three-person household generating two active residents would pay a police facility impact fee of $54. A new warehouse like the one used in our example would pay an impact fee of $27 × 0.33, or $9 per 1,000 square feet.

Certain problems are endemic to that approach. The first is the possibility that the occupants of a new home will do all their shopping and working in the city. Yet, new shopping and employment space is not necessarily expanded. Thus the impact fee falls only on the new residences being constructed but not on the full incremental demand for police services that the residences will generate. As the number of residences grows, and as the occupants increasingly work and shop in the city, however, nonresidential space will have to be expanded to meet demands. The additional space will be assessed impact fees at the time of expansion.

Another problem is the widely variable useful life of police facilities. While the police station may last for decades, police cars may last for only three or four years. The credit for future tax contributions to the city will have the effect of overestimating the present (discounted) value of payments that would purchase new police cars, but it may underestimate the value of payments that would help finance police station expansion. The differences can be accommodated in vastly more complicated formulations than we suggest here. On the other hand, courts are more likely to accept simple formulations that account for average impacts, especially if the possibility remains that the actual impact fee charged will still fall short of the estimated cost of serving new development (with the community at large making up the difference).

The practice of assessing impact fees for police, fire, library, and other public facilities is new, and alternative formulations abound. While planners need to do more work to determine the most appropriate impact fee for-

mulation for park, road, water, sewer, drainage, and similar facilities, we believe that vastly greater work must be done to determine the appropriate fees for generically social and public safety related facilities. Even determining the accurate active resident coefficient for any given land use can be a monumental task.

Note

1. The discounted present value of money received at a given time in the future is determined by the following formula:

$$PV_0 = \frac{S}{(1 + i)^n}$$

Where

PV_0 = Discounted, present value (today) of money received in the future.

S = Amount of money to be received.

i = Interest rate expected over the period, which is also known as the discount rate. If the discount rate is to be applied monthly, then use $i/12$ to get a monthly discount rate.

n = Number of periods (years or months) between today and when the money will be received.

The same formula can be extended to determine the discounted, present value of a stream of payments to be received in future years, such as property taxes. That formula is:

$$PV_0 = \left[\frac{S_1}{(1+i)^1} + \frac{S_2}{(1+i)^2} + \frac{S_3}{(1+i)^3} + \cdots + \frac{S_n}{(1+i)^n} \right].$$

16

Traffic Impact Fees

DAVID C. HEATH
GLENN KREGER
GLENN ORLIN
MEG RIESETT

An increasing number of communities are assessing impact fees on new developement to help pay for the construction of new or expanded streets and other traffic facilities. In many communitites, the traffic impact fee is the single largest revenue generator among a variety of exactions that are also assessed. We review the application of traffic impact fees in three communities: Montgomery County, Maryland; the City of Loveland, Colorado; and Orange County, Florida. Those communities were selected for the cross section of communities they represent.

TRAFFIC IMPACT FEES: MONTGOMERY COUNTY, MARYLAND

Montgomery County, Maryland, is a suburban jurisdiction of approximately 500 square miles, northwest of Washington D.C., with an estimated population of 620,000 and an employment base of 375,000 in 1985. Much of its household growth occurred concomitantly with the rise of the federal sector between the 1930s and 1960s. Since the late 1970s, however, there has been a resurgence in housing demand in the up-county suburban fringe, paralleling the settlement of high technology and government service firms in the Interstate 270 (I-270) and the

U.S. Route 29 (U.S. 29) radial corridors. This recent housing boom has been characterized by moderate density development: in up-county Germantown, which has grown from 2,800 to 23,500 people during the past 15 years (more than half of this in the past five), four of every five homes are townhouses or garden apartments. This spurt of development has severely overloaded the public facilities in the fringe, particularly schools and roads.

As the demand on the up-county road network increased during the late 1970s, the Maryland State Highway Administration's road-building program shrank. Road projects scheduled for construction were delayed and, perhaps more significantly for the up-county, no new projects were identifed for planning and design, the very projects that just then should have been coming on line. By the time the state legislature increased the gasoline tax by four cents per gallon in 1982, the state had already dropped at least five years behind highway needs in the up-county, particularly on non-interstate roads.

Although the state's road program had declined, the pipeline of approved development continued to build out, causing rapidly increasing traffic congestion. Recognizing the need to assume some of the state's responsibility in this area, Montgomery County began to program the improvement of some state roads with local funds, a commitment that grew to $50 million by 1985. Even with this heavy investment of state and county funds, there was not enough to provide road capacity to meet the demand, especially in the outlying areas of Germantown on the I-270 corridor and eastern Montgomery County along the U.S. 29 corridor. Government began to look in earnest toward the private sector, in particular the building industry, to fill the shortfall.

Developers in Montgomery County had for some time participated in road building on a piecemeal basis so that their projects could pass the county's Adequate Public Facilities Ordinance (APFO). Enacted in 1973, the APFO holds that a subdivision can be approved only if the facilities required to serve the subdivision are guaranteed to be present at the time of occupancy. If the facilities (usually roads) were not programmed by the county, the developer could usually work out an agreement with the county to build the roads on some cost-sharing basis. These participation agreements were often quite complex, as illustrated by the Germantown "road clubs" where several developers joined contractually with the county to widen a state highway from two to six lanes and to improve another major county road.

The APF test itself was also complex. In 1982, the APF test was refined into two tests: (1) the threshold test and (2) local area review. For the threshold test, the county is split into 21 policy areas with varying levels of acceptable congestion (see Figure 16-1). In the lower part of the county, where residential and commercial density is high and transit service is frequent and extensive, an average level of service (LOS) of D/E is tolerated before the area's road network is deemed inadequate. In Germantown and eastern Montgomery County, where transit exists but is not significant, LOS C must be maintained in each policy area. If the travel from all existing and approved development, once assigned to the existing and programmed transportation network, produces a congestion level worse than the standard, then generally no more subdivisions can be approved. If the pipeline of approved development can be built without exceeding the standard, then thresholds are calculated that represent the additional residential and nonresidential development that can be approved without exceeding the standard.

If a subdivision passes the threshold test— which has been tightened over the years by restricting the definition of a programmed road— it must also pass a second screening: the local area review test. To pass local area review, the developer must demonstrate that no intersection near his development will deteriorate to below LOS E in the peak hour. This second test is critical in preventing localized congestion problems. However, in the up-county, where a large backlog of approved subdivisions had absorbed the threshold capacity, it was the threshold test that represented the major obstacle.

The events described above—a recent sustained building boom, the restriction of state spending on highways, and incremental tightenings of the APF test—converged to effect a de facto moratorium on development approvals in the very corridors targeted for growth in the county's general development plan. Impact fees were seen as a constructive way of addressing the moratorium.

Figure 16–1. Policy Areas Grouped by Transportation Service Standards (Germantown and eastern Montgomery impact fee areas superimposed)

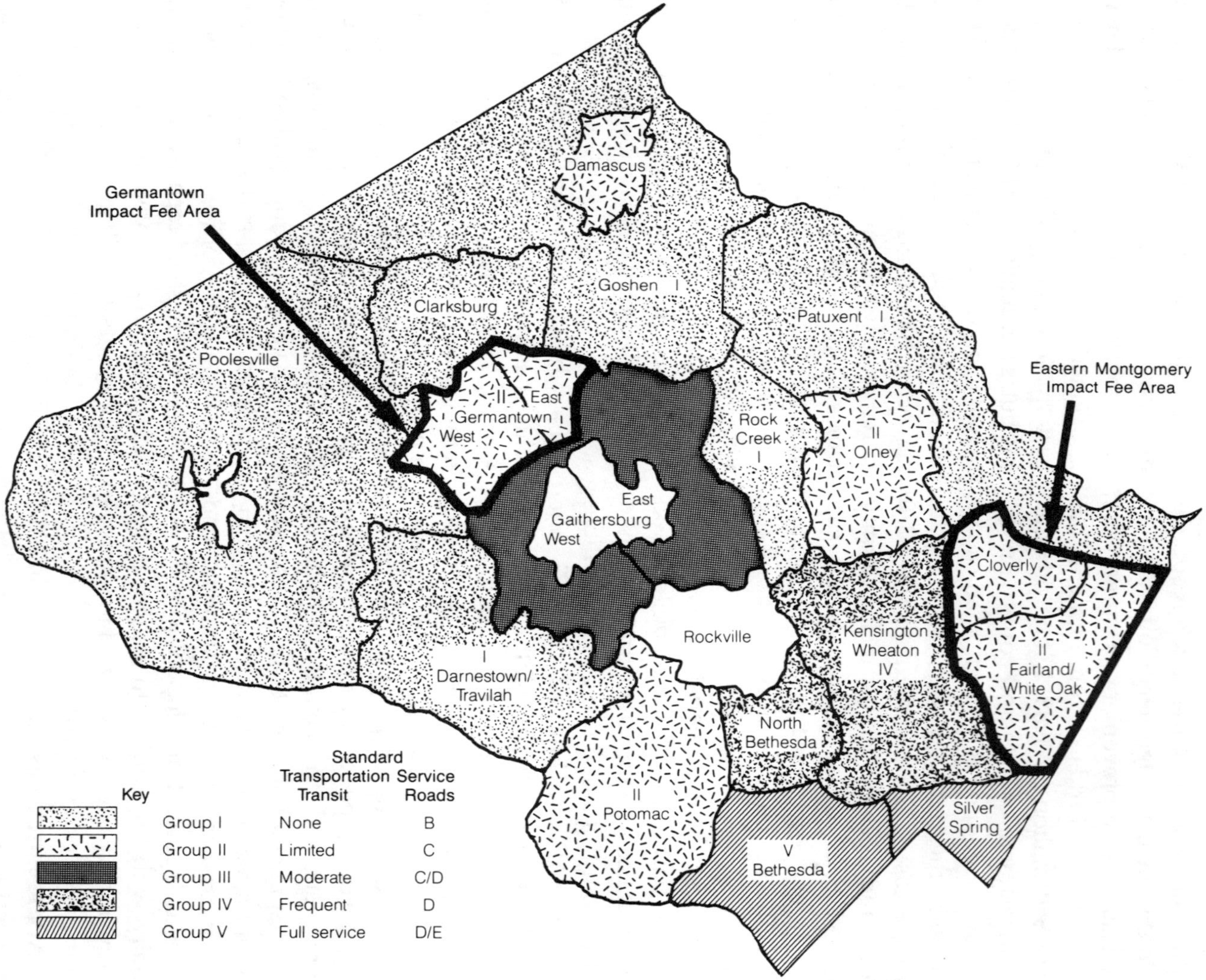

Key	Standard Transportation Service		
		Transit	Roads
	Group I	None	B
	Group II	Limited	C
	Group III	Moderate	C/D
	Group IV	Frequent	D
	Group V	Full service	D/E

Source: Montgomery County Planning Board, *1985 Comprehensive Planning Policies Report*

Provisions of the Impact Fee Ordinance

Purpose and Authority. The primary purpose of impact fees as applied to up-county is to provide for the construction of master planned highways in a manner that will allow new development to proceed. The authority for the ordinance is found in the police powers of the county's charter; the imposition of impact fees would "ensure and coordinate the provisions of adequate transportation facilities with new development so that the public health, safety, and welfare are enhanced, traffic congestion is lessened, accessibility is improved, and economic development is promoted." One advantage of the impact fee mechanism in counties like Montgomery that have home rule powers is that separate enabling legislation from state government is usually unnecessary.

Timing of Fee Collection. According to the Montgomery ordinance, impact fees are to be collected at the issuance of building permits. The framers of the impact fee law considered several different points at which to apply the fee: at subdivision approval, at building permit, and at occupancy. Several objectives had to be balanced. Applying fees at subdivision would have brought revenue to government sooner, reducing its bond interest, but also would have increased the developer's carrying cost. Since subdivisions are often cut back during buildout, developers also might have been charged more than their fair share if the impact fee were based on the size of their development at the time of the subdivision approval.

Collecting the impact fee at occupancy would have reduced the developer cost to a minimum. Occupancy also would be the point at which there would be maximum certainty about the type and size of development being charged.

However, levying the fee at occupancy would have violated the vested rights of many developers. Under Maryland law, a developer has a vested right to the use of a building once footings are in the ground. Requiring a payment from builders who, at the initiation of impact fees, had begun to build probably would have been overturned in court. The building permit was thus selected as the point of collection.

Rational Nexus. An impact fee is a special benefit assessment that must demonstrate a direct linkage between those who are charged the fee and those who benefit from it. This connection is the rational nexus that the law uses as a test to distinguish a fee from a tax. The distinction is important, as the taxing authority is usually reserved by state governments unless it is purposely delegated. Most state governments, including Maryland's, are wary of granting additional local taxing authority since this removes a potential revenue source from the state itself. A new revenue source frequently proposed for Montomery County – a piggy-back gasoline tax – is unpopular in the state legislature for this very reason.

The rational nexus test has two major components. First, there must be a clear *geographical* connection between where the fees are collected and where the funds are applied. Montgomery County keeps separate accounts for each impact fee area, ensuring that the fees from Germantown, for example, are spent only on designated road improvements in Germantown.

Second, there must be a *temporal* connection between when one pays and when one receives the benefit. In many jurisdictions this is addressed by requiring that the fee revenues be spent on facilities in a limited-year capital improvements program. Montgomery's ordinance, however, ties the revenue to *master planned* highways, which in some cases will not be provided until near the buildout of impact fee areas in 20 to 30 years. How Montgomery County's impact fee law achieves the temporal nexus is explained by its relation to the county's APFO. The impact fee ordinance states that a necessary condition for impact fees to be initially imposed in an area is that there be a threshold deficiency as defined in the APFO. In these areas, no new development approvals can be granted under the county's APFO unless further capacity is programmed.

With an impact fee ordinance in place, the county has begun to program the massive improvements that will soon eliminate the APFO threshold deficiences in the impact fee areas. By programming these improvements in anticipation of impact fee revenues to be received later, the county relieves threshold problems, enabling new development to be approved. Impact fees will reimburse the county for up to 50 percent of the county's expenditures on these improvements. However, the new developer paying these fees will receive the benefit of advancing his development through the subdivision approval stage even before he pays the fee.

Thus, the temporal rational nexus is made because roads are programmed before the fee-paying development is approved. The county must refund impact fees if it "has failed to provide impact highways in the applicable impact fee area in accordance with the applicable current Impact Fee Area Transportation Program." However, this means only that the county must make some steady progress in building out master plan roads.

Credits and Refunds. In some circumstances, a developer may not want to wait for the state or county to program and build a road necessary for his subdivision to pass the threshold test. A provision thus is made for the developer to build the road and credit the cost of the facility against the impact fee he normally would pay at building permit. This credit can be conveyed to future owners, but it cannot be transferred to another site. Furthermore, the total credit cannot exceed the amount of impact fees the developer would pay on his full development; in other words, the developer cannot receive a rebate if his road costs exceed his impact fee requirement. Regarding road participation agreements formulated before the enactment of impact fees, developers can receive a credit against their fees equal to what they owe under these outstanding contracts. Germantown road club members, for example, have a remaining obligation of $300 for each of their remaining units; they are entitled to a $300-per-unit credit against their impact fees.

Montgomery County may refund fees if it does not fulfill its commitment to build impact fee roads, if the developer's building permit lapses for noncommencement of construction, or if the project has been altered, resulting in a decrease in the amount of impact fee due. Only the current property owner may ask for a refund, and the petition must be filed within a year of the event causing the claim.

Selection of Impact Fee Areas. As described above, a mandatory prerequisite for designation of an impact fee area is that the area must have a deficiency in areawide traffic capacity. Once an impact fee area is designated, it always will remain one even if the deficiency is eliminated. Logic also suggests that an impact fee area have both a substantial amount of unprogrammed road construction and a significant amount of zoned but unbuilt development over which to spread the financial burden. In Montgomery County, two impact fee areas were identified: the Germantown impact fee area comprising the Germantown East and Germantown West Policy Areas and the Eastern Montgomery County Impact Fee Area consisting of the Cloverly and Fairland/White Oak Policy Areas (see Figure 16–1).

Calculation of Fees. The Germantown and eastern Montgomery County impact fee schedules are determined using a share method, apportioning the road costs in each area between the public and private sector, and subsequently within the private sector according to the relative traffic impact of remaining development. The calculation of the Germantown schedule is exhibited in Table 16–1. Each step is described below.

Road costs. In each area, the first task was to determine which road improvements were appropriately funded by impact fees. Mainline freeway improvements, such as the widening of I-270 through Germantown and the construction of the intercounty connector freeway through eastern Montgomery County, are needed primarily to serve through traffic and therefore should not be financed by a local benefit assessment. These projects will continue to be the responsibility of government.

On the other end of the functional scale, neighborhood and business streets are traditionally the responsibility of the private sector to provide as a requirement of subdivision. The class of roads falling between these two extremes, the arterials, were considered to be the facilities appropriate for funding by impact fees.

A complete inventory of unbuilt, master planned arterials was assembled for each planning area, including new arterial interchanges with freeways. Some minor arterials that were

Table 16–1. Fee Schedules

Land Use	Germantown	East Montgomery
Single-family residential	$1,489/unit	$1,591/unit
Multifamily residential	$ 992/unit	$1,161/unit
Office	3.36/sq. ft.	3.59/sq. ft.
Retail	3.04/sq. ft.	3.24/sq. ft.
Industrial	1.46/sq. ft.	1.56/sq. ft.
Places of worship	.18/sq. ft.	.19/sq. ft.
Private elementary and secondary schools	.29/sq. ft.	.31/sq. ft.
Other nonresidential	3.36/sq. ft.	3.59/sq. ft.

judged to be needed only as on-site improvements, and thus also likely to be a requirement of subdivision, were culled from each list. Finally, the cost of constructing each project was estimated, including design, land acquisition, and construction management costs. In Germantown, the cost of completing the impact fee roads was estimated to be about $132 million.

Private sector share. While the primary need for (or benefit from) new roads accrues to new development, some benefit is gained to the general public. Furthermore, the residents of new development ultimately will be paying property and gasoline taxes that will be used to fund arterial roads in areas not covered by impact fees, raising a difficult potential double taxation problem. Such considerations demanded that some portion of the impact fee roads should be financed with general revenues.

The percentage of remaining development in a policy area of the total amount of development at buildout is the share to be paid by the private sector by impact fees. In eastern Montgomery County, where an estimated 44.75 percent of the zoning ceiling remains to be built, 44.75 percent of the $96 millon road cost—about

$43 millon—will be raised by impact fees. Considering the double taxation issue, a policy decision was made to limit the private sector share to no more than 50 percent; in Germantown, where more than half the development remains, 50 percent of the $132 millon will come from fees.

Relative traffic impact. The private sector share of road costs are apportioned to each development according to its proportionate contribution to traffic impact. Traffic impact here is measured as peak-hour vehicle-miles of travel, and is the product of peak-hour trips generated per dwelling unit (or per 1,000 square feet of gross floor area for nonresidential), the percentage of these trips that are not stopping as part of a longer trip somewhere else (i.e., non-pass-by trips), and a relative index of trip length within the area.

Different land uses produce different travel behavior. For example, although retail uses generate more trips per 1,000 square feet than office uses, retail produces a much higher proportion of pass-by trips, and retail trip lengths are shorter. As a result, retail's travel impact index of 15.60 is less than office's index of 17.25. The fee schedules recognize eight different categories of land use because of these differing trip generation and trip length characteristics.

The next step was to determine the amount of remaining development in each land use category, multiplying each by its respective travel impact index to find the trip impact value for each category. The eight individual trip impact values are summed to a total trip impact value. The share of each category's value to the total value, mutiplied by the private sector road costs, yields the impact fee revenues to be generated by that land use catagory. When the retail revenue (in Germantown, $3.6 million) is divided by the remaining retail development there (just under 1.2 millon square feet), the retail fee is $3.04 per square foot. The two fee schedules, classified by land use, are shown in Table 16-1.

Biennial Updating. The impact fee law calls for the fee schedule to be updated every two years. Several changes can occur that would affect the fees. Road costs can change as a result of inflation, a better cost estimate, or a master plan amendment that alters the scope of projects or that adds and deletes projects. The estimate of remaining development can change, either by approved subdivisions not building to the extent expected or by rezonings. The travel impact indexes can even change if more precise travel behavior data are collected and accepted. Only the private sector shares are not subject to change.

Montgomery County presently is determining if the impact fee revenues match the county's projections in the short term. The impacts of the new fee on land prices and the cost and supply of housing also are under scrutiny. These factors will help determine whether Montgomery County seeks to expand the impact fee program to other parts of the county and/or other facilities besides roads.

TRAFFIC IMPACT FEES: LOVELAND, COLORADO

In the face of community facilities needs estimated at $40 million in the late 1970s, the Loveland City Council asked voters for approval of bonds to pay for facilities necessary to overcome existing facility deficiencies and create excess capacity for future growth. The proposal was not popular: it was rejected 88 percent to 12 percent. In 1982, the council appointed an 18-member citizen advisory board, comprised equally of citizens and representatives of the development community, to consider a cost-recovery approach to paying for growth.

In concept, the cost-recovery system requires new development to buy into the equity of existing or scheduled new community facilities. The heart of these are the capital expansion fees (CEF), which are one-time charges assessed at the building permit stage. The CEF is based on vintage pricing, which is defined as the current replacement cost of the facility being financed from fees, plus betterments (or improvements to the facility since its initial construction), less depreciation (if the facility is already in place). This assures the community that facilities will be maintained at constant levels of quality. The CEF is also based on a long-run marginal-cost approach. Economists argue that marginal cost price induces maximum discipline and efficiency in the market for goods such as public facilities and services. Long-run marginal cost pricing ensures that new residents are required to contribute toward long-term expansion and pay a fee proportionate to the total number of new users the facility is expected to serve.

For each facility, including streets, the CEF calculation process follows five steps (see Figure 16–2). To begin, total projected capital costs of the facility are estimated. If some or all of the facility must be replaced or modernized to maintain its usefulness to existing residents, these costs are subtracted. The adjusted total capital costs become capital expansion costs. If the facility can serve more people than are projected to use it, then the value of such excess capacity is subtracted from capital expansion costs, and instead is paid for by the community as a whole. If the facility will serve fewer people than are expected to use it at the end of the financing period, then the value of such undercapacity is added to capital expansion costs and thereby generates revenue for facility expansion at a future date. This step results in a figure for only growth-related costs, which are reduced by any external funds that may be used for that facility (such as state or federal funds). The resulting net growth-related costs then are allocated by percent to the four major land use sectors of residential, commercial, industrial, and institutional. The proportion of the net growth-related costs of a facility attributable to each sector is then divided by the total number of sector units (dwelling units or square feet) projected to be added to the community during the planning period.

An example of this procedure is the CEF calculated for streets. Loveland has 145 miles of streets with an average width of 38 feet. Many of the streets are in immediate need of reconstruction. The estimated expense of this reconstruction is $7 million, to be incurred over five years, as shown in Table 16–2. These costs are appropriately the responsibility of existing residents and would bring the street system back to an adequate level of service. As noted in the methodological discussion, those costs are not equitably included in the CEF cost basis.

This accumulated backlog of requirements results from insufficient maintenance expenditures. The 1982 expenditures for maintenance of streets, bridges, and alleys and several other activities is budgeted at $457,312. By comparision, the annual cost (in 1982) estimated to overlay all existing streets within the next 20 years is estimated at $509,124.

Other routine operating and maintenance expenses associated with roads include snow and ice removal, street cleaning, and street lighting. These totaled $288,023 in 1982. See Table 16–3.

Figure 16–2. Steps in Estimating Capital Expansion Fees for Streets and Other Facilities

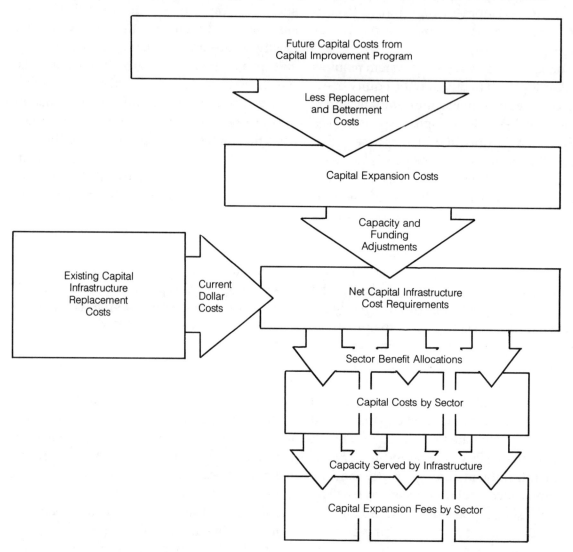

Funding for street, alley, and bridge upkeep has declined significantly in recent years. This is despite the rapid increase in the price of such petroleum-based commodities as tar and asphalt. See Table 16–4.

Traffic signs and signals have, along with streets, deteriorated somewhat in recent years. Currently, seven traffic signals at $60,000 each, for a total of $420,000, are needed to solve existing capacity bottlenecks and safety problems.

Except for those on major arterials, street lights do not exist in Loveland. Given the "current level of service" policy, the costs of adding such lights are not considered in the CEF cost basis.

The budget for traffic signs and signals has been stagnant in recent years, as shown in Table 16-5. However, the street lighting budget has grown rapidly, reflecting the major increase in the price of electricity.

Future Needs and Cost Recovery. Current needs of $7 million for street reconstruction were previously described, as were annual overlay expenses of $509,124. In addition, bridge renovation or expansion expenses to be incurred over the next 20 years total $1,200,000. Based on the location of these bridge projects, this expense can be considered an operating expense to be shared by all residents irrespective of whether they are new or existing. Similarly, $430,000 in railroad grade crossing requirements, which is the city's 50 percent share of the total cost, is attributable to existing residents.

Requirements for added capacity to existing arterials and collectors can be attributed directly to existing residents if they are needed to solve existing capacity bottlenecks and safety problems. These costs, which are the responsibility of existing residents, total $2,239,000. Other capacity additions to existing streets, totaling $4,947,000, are attributable to new residents. Once these expansions are completed, new and existing residents will share the maintenance of the entire road system.

Standards. Developers presently are required to build all roads within their developments, to build or expand all abutting roads to the full width required, and to build the full width required to connect to the nearest arterial. Limited reimbursment of costs for noninterior streets by subsequent developers sharing the same facilities is made in some instances.

Table 16–2. Expenses for Reconstruction

Year	Capital Needs
1	$3,653,000
2	2,369,000
3	599,000
4	316,000
5	62,000
Total	$6,999,000

Table 16–3. Maintenance Expenses

	1982 Budget
Snow and ice removal	$ 79,414
Street cleaning	67,589
Street lighting	141,020
Total	$288,023

Table 16–4. Prices of Materials

	Expenditure
1970	$ 229,112
1975	284,414
1976	666,083
1977	871,253
1978	912,967
1979	1,135,311
1980	1,003,805
1981	518,604
1982	457,312

Table 16–5. Budget for Traffic Signs and Signals

	Budget
1980	$71,419
1981	50,488
1982	58,775

As part of this project, an extensive review of the existing street standards was conducted to develop an equitable allocation of developer responsibility. The intent of the new street improvement policy is to ensure that new development pays the full capital cost of street improvements resulting from new growth. Major provisions of the new street policy include:

• The current service level on the street system is at capacity and any widening of existing streets should be paid for by new development.

• New development should not be charged for pricing or upgrading the existing street system.

• Funds collected from new development shall be used only for the benefit of new development.

• Any credit granted to a developer toward a street capital expansion fee will not be linked to any reduction in other general fund capital expansion fees.

Specific street standards under the new street policy developed in connection with this project. Local streets remain the responsibility of developers, with costs for collectors and arterials shared between the developer and the community in general. Other traffic improvements are funded through a systemwide capital expansion fee.

Capital Expansion Fee. The capital expansion fee (CEF) for street improvements was calculated according to specific estimates of systemwide improvement needs. The current transportation plan for the city requires a total requirement of $38.7 million in capital needs, as shown in Table 16–6.

To allocate the appropriate share of systemwide improvement costs to alternative land uses, trip generation characteristics were considered in order to reflect system usage attributable to development types. The results of those calculations are shown in Table 16-7. Weighted averages were estimated for each of

Table 16–6. Costs of Capital Needs

Systemwide Improvements	CEF Cost Basis
Streets*	$28,217,975
Bridges	6,115,500
Signals	2,100,000
Rail Crossings	2,235,000
Total	$38,668,475

*Street cost excludes middle 34-foot section that is direct developer responsibility.

Table 16–7. Shares of Systemwide Costs

Development Type	CEF per Unit, Acre, or Sq. Ft.
Residential	$ 229.00/unit
Commercial	0.65/sq. ft.
Industrial	$1,601.00/acre
Institutional	0.59/sq. ft.

the major land use catagories based on the detailed calculations.

Some adjustments are made to the fees that might be paid by particular developments, however. For example, half the fees for low-income housing developments are paid by the city. In addition, to broaden the economic base of the community, the fees that otherwise would be assessed on industrial projects are reduced by a factor for each new employee the firm adds to the city's payroll base after one year. The fee is initially paid by the firm, but is partially or wholly reimbursed from the city a year later.

Loveland's cost recovery system, which won the APA's innovative planning program award for 1986, is an approach many communities across the nation are considering today.

TRAFFIC IMPACT FEES: ORANGE COUNTY, FLORIDA

Development of the Orange County transportation impact fee came after more than a decade of unprecedented growth. Although much attention has focused on the proliferation of tourist attractions in Orange County, such as Walt Disney's Magic Kingdom and the Experimental Prototype Community of Tomorrow (EPCOT), Orange County has experienced growth in terms of employment expansion and residential construction.

In terms of employment, Orange County has become a site of corporate expansion. Harcourt Brace Jovanovich, Inc., moved its national headquarters to Orange County. Westinghouse moved its Steam Turbine Generator Division to Orange County, and also has obtained approval for the construction of the Quadrangle, a 465-acre high technology corporate business center. The Martin Marietta Corporation, which already has major facilities in Orlando, constructed a plant that specializes in microelectronics and ultimately will contain 1.835 million square feet.

Other major employment expansions that have been approved in unincorporated Orange County over the past several years include the International Corporate Park (ICP), Central Florida Research Park, and the Airport Industrial Park-Orlando (AIPO). Each of these projects approaches or exceeds 1,000 acres and will employ thousands of employees.

The housing market in Orange County also has been extremely healthy. In 1985, building permits for 17,669 dwelling units were issued, an increase of more than 5,000 units from 1984. Large residential developments in excess of 5,000 units are not uncommon. Examples of these projects include Granada (5,130 units), Huckleberry (6,877 units), Hunter's Creek (9,354 units), and Meadow Woods (5,806).

As this growth occurred, the various infrastructures became increasingly stressed. Rural two-lane roads typically carry urban traffic volumes in excess of their already limited capacity. This problem has been compounded by insufficient funds to make the appropriate system improvements. Revenue sources available to local governments in Florida traditionally have been extremely limited. Under the Truth in Millage (TRIM) legislation, property tax increases are limited.

In terms of transportation funding, counties in Florida received until 1983 revenues only from a two-cent-per-gallon gasoline tax for roadway construction and a one-cent-per-gallon gasoline tax for roadway maintenance. In 1983, in conjunction with federal and state motor fuel tax increases, the Florida legislature gave counties the authority to enact local option gas taxes of up to four cents per gallon. Orange County promptly passed the full four-cent tax in 1983.

Transportation impact fees were the last of four impact fees implemented in Orange County. Work on the transportation impact fee began in 1983. To ensure that the transportation impact fee and other impact fees were accepted by the development community, the Impact Fee Advisory Board (formerly the Select Committee on Transportation Assessment Systems) was formed. The committee comprised developers, builders, and consultants. Prior to authorizing staff to proceed with the development of impact fees, this committee requested staff to evaluate 10 alternative funding mechanisms including a gas tax increase, *ad valorem* tax increase, municipal service taxing units (MSTU), resort tax, toll facilities, modifications to homestead exemption, immediate placement of structures on tax roll, sales tax revenue, revenue sharing fund increase, and motor license tag fees.

Without state enabling legislation, the majority of these alternatives were quickly eliminated. Although there was support for the use of MTSUs, this funding mechanism was dismissed for several reasons. First, when a MSTU is established, all properties within the district are taxed or assessed equally. Therefore, existing residents and property owners would be required to subsidize new growth. Second, MSTUs typically are used to fund localized improvements such as street lights, road pavings, and retention ponds. MSTUs could not address the issue of through traffic on arterial roadways. Finally, MSTU assessments usually are placed on a property owner's tax bill and collected over a number of years. This process would not provide Orange County with sufficient funds in a timely manner, unless bonding was used. However, Orange County has had a pay-as-you-go philosophy in terms of road construction. On the analysis of the various alternative funding sources, the advisory board reluctantly agreed to pursue the development of a transportation impact fee.

County staff initiated in 1983 a 15-month modeling effort to determine the roadway needs over a five-year period. A five-year planning period was used to ensure that the resulting impact fee was consistent with the capital improvements program. The transportation planning package, MicroTRIPS, was used in the Needs Network modeling effort. To the extent possible, the modeling effort attempted to replicate the Orlando Urban Area Transportation Study (OUATS). The results of the modeling effort showed that approximately $150 million would be needed over the five-year period to substantially improve the county road system. These costs included both state and county roads. However, virtually all of the needed road projects consisted of improving two-lane roads. Limited access and/or freeways were not addressed in the impact fee system.

The roadway projects in the Needs Network were divided into three subareas based on maintaining a rational and uniform relationship between the total roadway costs within each subarea and the growth increment projected within each benefit area. Upon the establishment of the benefit areas, projects were prioritized based on the following criteria:

1. Volume/capacity (v/c) ratio.
2. Realistic construction schedule in five-year period.
3. Preexisting developer agreements/voluntary impact fees.
4. County versus state roads.
5. Developments not reflected in socioeconomic data used in modeling process.

Because some of the roadways in the Needs Network had existing traffic deficiencies, costs were divided between growth-induced costs and existing deficiencies. LOS D was chosen as a service standard for the transportation impact fee system. The LOS D capacity for a two-lane road was calculated to be 12,600 vehicles per day (vpd). If a two-lane roadway carried more than 12,600 vehicles per day, it was considered to have an existing deficiency. The existing volume was then divided by the improved capacity to arrive at a percentage that was applied to the total cost of the roadway. The resulting dollar amount was considered to be the responsibility of the county, while the remaining costs were to be covered by impact fees. Although the entire Needs Network was estimated to cost $150 million, only $132 million could be attributed to new growth, while the remaining $18 million was needed due to existing deficiencies.

Once the roadway needs were established, the methodology for the transportation impact fee was developed. Staff recommended an improvements-driven system in which the impact fee was based on a list of roadways to be improved or built. The recommended methodology consisted of the following components:

1. The total number of new trips in unincorporated Orange County between 1985–1990 was calculated. This number was derived by applying generally accepted trip generation rates promulgated by the Institute of Transportation Engineers (ITE) to the projected growth increment. (The trip generation rates were divided by two in order to equally assign costs between the origin and destination of a trip.)

2. The total roadway costs were divided by the projected number of trips to determine the cost per trip.

3. The cost per trip then was applied to trip generation rates to derive the gross impact fee.

4. To ensure that developers were not required to pay an impact fee as well as gas taxes, a motor fuel tax credit was formulated. This credit was subtracted from the gross impact fee to arrive at the net impact fee.

Given the costs of the Needs Network, the resulting impact fees were enormous. The potential impact fee for a single-family house would have been $3,064.75, while 1,000 square feet of a bank was calculated at $58,843.20. Because these fees were not economically or politically feasible, a series of alternatives was

Table 16–8. Transportation Impact Fee Calculation for Recommended System

$$\text{Impact Fee} = \frac{ADT \times TL \times DF}{2\,(Cap)} \times C - C^+\,PD$$

Where:

ADT = Average daily trip ends promulgated by Institute of Transportation Engineers (ITE).

TL = Trip length derived from Orlando Urban Area Transportation Study (OUATS).
1. 6.64 miles—Residential.
2. 6.16 miles—Retail.
3. 7.05 miles—Nonretail.
4. 6.73 miles—Hotel/motel.

DF = Percent new trips derived from diversion study.

Cap = Capacity of lane mile at level of service D (7,500 vehicles per day).

C = Cost of right-of-way acquisition and construction for one lane mile ($600,600).

C^+ = Motor fuel and license revenue credit.

PD = Police decision made by Orange County Board of County Commissioners to fund 52 percent of the growth-induced needs, given the availability of local option gas tax revenues and state matching funds.

developed. Each alternative funded a different portion of the Needs Network ranging from 17 percent to 61 percent. To the extent possible, those alternatives were pegged closely to impact fees for single-family units such as $500, $1,000, and $1,500 per unit.

Support formed around an alternative that would fund 52 percent of the Network at LOS D, after a credit for other revenues the county would receive because of the new development (gasoline taxes, for example). Under this scenario, a single-family house would have been assessed $1,570.50 per unit, while a small commercial center would have been charged $18,516.13 per 1,000 square feet.

Table 16–9. Recommended Fee Schedule of Typical Land Uses

Trip Generation	Trip Length	Percent New Trips	Land Use	Total Impact Fee	− Credit	= Net Impact Fee	52% of Net Impact Fee
10.00	6.64	100	Single-family residential unit	2,658.66 −	618.31 =	2,040.35	1,060.98
6.10	6.64	100	Multifamily unit	1,621.78	377.17	1,244.61	647.20
4.80	6.64	100	Mobile home unit	1,276.16	296.79	979.37	509.27
10.50	6.73	100	Hotel/motel room	2,829.42	658.02	2,171.40	1,129.13
17.70	7.05	100	1,000 sq. ft. office (<100,000 sq. ft.)	4,996.39	1,161.98	3,834.41	1,993.89
14.30	7.05	100	1,000 sq. ft. office (100,000–200,000 sq. ft.)	4,036.64	938.78	3,097.86	1,610.89
10.90	7.05	100	1,000 sq. ft. office (>200,000 sq. ft.)	3,076.87	715.57	2,361.30	1,227.88
117.90	6.16	49	1,000 sq. ft. retail (<50,000 sq. ft.)	14,249.01	3,313.81	10,935.20	5,686.30
82.00	6.16	48	1,000 sq. ft. retail (50,000–99,999 sq. ft.)	9,708.01	2,257.74	7,450.27	3,874.14
66.70	6.16	61	1,000 sq. ft. retail (100,000–199,999 sq. ft.)	10,035.31	2,333.86	7,701.45	4,004.75
50.60	6.16	74	1,000 sq. ft. retail (200,000–299,999 sq. ft.)	9,235.42	2,147.83	7,087.59	3,685.55
41.90	6.16	74	1,000 sq. ft. retail (300,000–399,999 sq. ft.)	7,647.52	1,778.54	5,868.98	3,051.87
49.70	6.16	74	1,000 sq. ft. retail (400,000–499,999 sq. ft.)	9,071.16	2,109.63	6,961.53	3,620.00
37.20	6.16	81	1,000 sq. ft. retail (500,000–999,999 sq. ft.)	7,431.95	1,728.41	5,703.54	2,965.84
37.10	6.16	81	1,000 sq. ft. retail (1,000,000–1,250,000 sq. ft.)	7,411.97	1,723.76	5,688.21	2,957.87
34.10	6.16	81	1,000 sq. ft. retail (>1,250,000 sq. ft.)	6,872.62	1,584.37	5,228.25	2,718.69
16.70	7.05	100	1,000 sq. ft. hospital	4,714.10	1,096.33	3,617.77	1,881.24
5.43	7.05	100	1,000 sq. ft. industrial	1,532.79	356.47	1,176.32	611.69
3.86	7.05	100	1,000 sq. ft. manufacturing	1,089.60	253.40	836.20	434.82
4.88	7.05	100	1,000 sq. ft. warehousing	1,377.54	320.37	1,057.17	549.73
164.40	6.16	52	1,000 sq. ft. restaurant	21,085.30	4,903.69	16,181.61	8,414.44
192.00	6.16	30	1,000 sq. ft. bank	14,206.84	3,304.01	10,902.83	5,669.47

Note: Table uses < (less than), > (more than), − (minus), and = (equal) signs.

More than $41 million would be collected in a five-year period. This was in addition to $4.8 million in state funds, $20.5 million in local-option gas taxes, and $6.6 million in county general funds to alleviate current deficiencies that should not be the responsibility of new development to pay. Total road improvement funds during this period will be about $73 million.

SUMMARY

In the face of dwindling federal and state resources for new road construction and opposition from existing residents to financing new streets out of local taxes, growing communities have been forced to look for new revenue sources to pay for the construction of new or expanded streets needed to serve new development. The traffic impact fee systems developed and applied by the three communities reviewed here are among the many that have been adopted by communities across the nation. The approaches used by those communities are relatively similar: average impacts are estimated, street improvement costs estimated, and fee schedules prepared and applied to development based on square feet or bedrooms. Other traffic improvement fees are assessed that are not reviewed here. Whatever method is used, local governments across the nation, whether fast- or slow-growing, are finding ways to shift the burden of paying for transportation improvements to new development and away from state and federal sources (which have been dwindling in real terms since the 1960s) and from the community at-large (which cannot or will not make up the difference).

References

City of Loveland. 1983. *Service Recovery System: System Documentation*. Loveland, Colo.: City Hall.

Heath, David C. 1987. Financing Growth in the Sunshine: The Impact Fee Experience in Orange County, Florida. Paper presented to the Development Impact Fee Symposium, 1987 American Planning Association conference (April).

Kreger, Glenn, Glenn S. Orlin, Meg Riesett. 1987. The Impact Fee Ordinance of Mongomery County, Maryland. Paper presented to the Development Impact Fee Symposium, 1987 American Planning Association conference (April).

17

Site-Specific, Nonrecoupment vs. General Formula, Recoupment Impact Fees

JAMES E. FRANK

In 1981, Broward County, Florida, adopted an impact fee for roads that has two unique dimensions. First, it is a nonrecoupment fee, charging development only for those roadway links that are currently operating above capacity and therefore are in need of improvement, making no attempt at cost recovery for roads that have sufficient capacity to accommodate the development's traffic. Recoupment refers to the common practice of setting the magnitude of the impact fee to include the recovery of the cost of previously installed capacity now made available to the development being charged the fee. That is, the dollar amount of the impact fee paid by a development is related both to the cost of newly installed capacity necessitated by the development as well as the cost of facilities for which expenditures were made at some earlier date and which now are correctly regarded as sunk costs. Recoupment fees are also known as buy-in charges and cost recovery schemes. The Broward County road impact fee is the opposite, a nonrecoupment fee, charging only if the development places traffic on roads already experiencing traffic vol-

umes in excess of their capacities. It is the only impact fee known to this author to use a nonrecoupment approach.

Second, the fee's methodology is unique because it performs a customized, site-specific computation of the amount of the impact fee for each development subject to the levy. This means that no two developments pay the same fee and that the exact amount of the fee cannot be known precisely without executing the methodology. In designing impact fees, one is always presented with the question of how much specificity is appropriately incorporated in the computational methodology for calculating the impact fee. A generalized procedure uses average conditions to compute an impact fee for all locations and, potentially, for all development types. Thus, impact fees of equal magnitude may be levied on a dwelling unit no matter where in the system's geographic space it is to be located and possibly for all dwelling unit types and sizes. In contrast, the site-specific analysis employs estimation procedures selected because they reflect the values of variables known to have systematic effect

204

on the distribution of impacts as they cluster around the mean. In this case, what is allowed to vary can be both the characteristics of the development being charged a fee and the infrastructure system for which the fee is being levied. The purpose of this exposition is to describe the Broward County impact fee and to explore some of the implications of these two unique dimensions.

THE GENERAL DIMENSIONS OF IMPACT FEES UNDER PREVAILING JUDICIAL CRITERIA: THE RATIONAL NEXUS TEST

Whereas 20 years ago there existed several competing judicial rationales for impact fees, with each enjoying almost equal popularity in state courts, today the leader is the rational nexus test. The emergence of the rational nexus test reflects the search for an approach to the funding of community facilities that establishes an equitable balancing of interests in that difficult middle ground between general revenue funding and exclusive beneficiary financing. It is easy to establish the principle that facilities benefiting the entire community should be paid for by everyone through general taxation. It is also easy to agree on the principle that facilities benefiting a few people should be paid for by them through special assessment or mandatory construction and dedication requirements. The difficult area lies in the middle between these two extremes and it is here that the rational nexus test, as applied to impact fees, has been honing a set of standards to balance the individual and community interests.

The rational nexus test has three parts that limit the imposition of impact fees to situations in which:

- New facilities are necessitated by the new development,

- The amount of the fee bears a reasonable relationship to the cost of providing facilities to serve the new development, and
- The collected fees are spent to construct facilities benefiting the development paying the fee.

The second and third dimensions of the test are typically interpreted to mean that impact fees can be charged for no more than a pro rata share of providing facilities to serve new development and that the fees, once collected, must be earmarked and expended to construct facilities benefiting (serving) the developments paying the fee. Notice that facilities necessitated by and benefiting *several* developments are not precluded so long as the relative financial participation of each development is in proportion to its attributed need, and providing that the facilities constructed are those that will serve the developments having paid the fee (e.g., fees collected to construct neighborhood parks must be used to build parks in the vicinity of the development, not on the other side of town).

It is the first dimension of the rational nexus test that is one of the two concerns of this chapter because that is the aspect bearing on the question of recoupment. The central question is whether or not the rational nexus test, by requiring that impact fees be limited to those circumstances in which new facilities are necessitated by new development, restricts the use of impact fees to the financing of facility capacity yet to be constructed, or whether fees can be levied to reimburse local government for the cost of previously constructed facilities, the capacity of which is now being made available to the new development. The answer obviously turns on the interpretation of the phrase "necessitated by new development" and whether local government can anticipate that necessity by installing facility capacity ahead of time and later recovering the cost thereof by charging recoupment impact fees or whether impact fees can be assessed only when capacity is insufficient at the time of development approval.

IMPACT FEES DISTINGUISHED FROM IMPACT TAXES

Impact fees are not to be confused with impact taxes. The distinction is critical for what this chapter discusses. Impact taxes are permissible in California and Arizona, but nowhere else. They take the form of occupational license taxes levied on home builders in proportion to the number of dwelling units constructed in the previous year by the builder seeking license renewal. As taxes, they can be set at any level needed to balance the budget (short of being confiscatory) and may be placed in the general fund and expended for any legitimate municipal purpose. They are a much more flexible source of revenue than regulatory fees levied under the police power, being unencumbered by the standards of reasonableness dictated by the rational nexus test.

BROWARD COUNTY'S ROAD IMPACT FEE

Prior to 1976, Florida communities that adopted impact fees were probing the murky water of unenunciated judicial standards. Several earlier attempts by local governments to construct judicially acceptable impact fee ordinances had been rebuffed by the courts, including an attempt by Broward County in 1973 to levy a land use fee for roads and bridges. After a decade of trial and error, localities had only piecemeal impressions of what was judicially impermissible, but little in the way of a comprehensive rationale to point to what would constitute a permissible approach. That all changed in 1976

with the Florida Supreme Court's decision in *Contractors and Builders Association of Pinellas County* v. *City of Dunedin* in which the court went beyond what would have been minimally dispositive (striking down Dunedin's ordinance because of insufficient earmarking of the impact fee funds) and enunciating a comprehensive rationale for impact fees to illuminate the path of judicial approval for subsequent ordinances. Since then, impact fee adoptions have proceeded at a rapid pace in Florida.

In 1975, Broward County engaged IBM Corporation to write the first-generation version of what was to become the TRIPS Model. Calling it BIZTAM (Broward Impact Zoning and Transportation Assessment Model) and operating as a custom software developer, IBM produced a model for assessing not only the traffic impacts of new development, but the estimation of air quality and fiscal impacts as well. From 1975 to 1980, BIZTAM was used in the county's development review process to estimate the traffic impacts of projects seeking development approval. In 1981, in anticipation of formalizing the impact assessment procedure in an impact fee ordinance and requiring all developments to pay the fee, the county undertook a comprehensive appraisal of the model, together with its required data structures, data updating procedures, and administrative environment within which the model operated. The result was a completely rewritten program that integrated several aspects previously not internalized and allowed the trip generation and distribution components to be done on separate trip purposes. Data updating procedures were systematized and given appropriate budget support, a minicomputer was purchased to run the model, and the entire operation was situated in the Planning Department.

BROWARD COUNTY'S NONRECOUPMENT FEE

The TRIPS model performs a site specific analysis of the amount of traffic expected to be generated by the development proposed for the site. It distributes these trips to destination zones in Broward, Dade, and Palm Beach counties and assigns the trips to specific paths through the street network. The capacity of each road segment to which traffic is assigned is evaluated and those that will be performing below the county's adopted level of service are noted for improvement evaluation, costing, and cost apportionment. The improvement cost of each deficient roadway receiving traffic from the development site is assigned to the development in proportion to its contribution to traffic volume. When summed across all roadway segments to which development traffic is assigned, this constitutes the development's impact fee.

Because the development paying the fee is charged only for those roadway segments on which its traffic is expected to be placed and, within that set, only for those segments that have insufficient current capacity to accommodate that traffic, the resulting fee does not charge for previously installed capacity, even for those road segments that will carry significant volumes of the development's traffic. Hence the characterization of this approach as a nonrecoupment impact fee. Further, the analysis is specific to the site and the development proposed, reflecting trip frequencies unique to the uses proposed for the site and trip lengths consistent with the spatial location of trip destinations in the three-county area. Hence the characterization as a customized treatment.

Generation and Distribution Done by Trip Purpose. Details of the model's operation include the fact that the trip generation analysis and trip distribution procedure are done using four separate trip purposes: home-based work, home-based shopping, home-based other, and non-home-based, before aggregating to determine interzonal average daily traffic. Trip generation rates are the standard ones from the Institute of Transportation Engineers, with modifications to reflect trip purpose based on data from Broward County Urban Area Transportation Study (BATS). The gravity model distribution procedure employs a standard gravity model formulation with travel time exponents (impedance factors) derived from the areawide study as well. Because the model estimates traffic for specific development sites and the total number of trips involved is never expected to constitute a significant proportion of total network traffic, the assignment algorithm employs an all-or-nothing procedure.

Dependence on UTPS Modeling. The TRIPS model is able to operate on a minicomputer with reasonable throughput speed because it does not perform a comprehensive simulation of the traffic system as is the case with mainframe modeling chains such as the Urban Mass Transportation Administration's Urban Transportation Planning System (UTPS). Rather, it takes observed network volumes as given and simulates only the incremental effect of the new development on the traffic system. The modeling procedure operates on a link-node network of approximately 1,100 road segments superimposed on 350 analysis zones, called Centers of Influence by the initial authors of the program. The ADT capacity and observed volume for each road segment are supplied to the program's data base as are the BATS productions and attractions for each of the analysis zones. The result is the bypassing of the standard

UTPS zonal trip generation analysis based on socioeconomic data, other than that applicable to the development site. Also bypassed is the trip distribution analysis required to compute interzonal trips for all zone pairs, as well as the entire procedure for balancing productions and attractions and the necessity to calibrate impedance factors to minimize the difference between synthetic and observed volumes. A final saving in computational time and memory requirements results from not having to undertake minimum path network assignments for interzonal traffic other than the incremental volumes resulting from the site's proposed development.

Maintenance and Updating of the Data Environment. Of great importance to the accurate operation of the TRIPS algorithm is the maintenance of the data environment within which the model resides and upon which it depends. Periodic reevaluation of trip rates, impedance coefficients, and road capacities occur more or less automatically during BATS five-year updates, since those values are derived from the larger study's modeling. But a five-year update interval is insufficient for road capacities in those instances where substantial road improvements are being installed. The difficulty arises, of course, when improvements are made that improve the capacity of a road segment so much that impact fees no longer should be assessed for that road. In those circumstances, the new capacity of the roadway is hand computed and entered into the data base upon completion of the construction project. Zonal productions and attractions, also derived from BATS modeling, need to be updated more often than every five years, requiring special procedures. The need for data updating occurs when one or more of the 350 analysis zones experi-

ences new development of sufficient magnitude to substantially alter the spatial distribution of productions and attractions, and hence, the outcome of the gravity model distribution procedure. In this situation, data describing the magnitude of the new development must be obtained from building officials, possibly in one of the two adjacent counties, to facilitate modification of the productions and attractions for that analysis zone. (The data will not automatically appear in the impact fee levying process because, in Broward County's case, the impact fee is levied when subdivision approval is granted, not when a building permit is issued. Hence, even within the county, a substantial proportion of the development orders being approved will not be subject to the impact fee procedures because of previously platted land. It has been the county's experience that discovery of this phenomenon is more of a problem than the measurement of it.) The way that this is implemented is to update zonal productions and attractions on a yearly basis, working from changes in socioeconomic data and permit records.

Updating Link Volumes and Tracking Prior Approvals. ADT volumes in all instances necessitate ground counts. Further, the need for periodic updating in order to reflect traffic growth and the need for the coverage of the network to be reasonably comprehensive require a well-organized and explicitly funded traffic count program. The Florida Department of Transportation traffic count program is a start, but it is not sufficient in either coverage or frequency. A further difficulty arises because Broward County levies its impact fee at the time of subdivision approval, much earlier in the development process than impact fees levied at the time of building permit issuance. Because considerable time may elapse between payment of the fee and arrival of the traffic that necessitated the fee, special procedures are required. The situation arises when one considers the question of how to treat traffic expected to result from a development site that has been given subdivision approval and paid its impact fee, but has not yet been built and occupied. Take the hypothetical situation in which a road segment currently has available capacity to accommodate 1,000 vehicles per day. Today a development is reviewed for subdivision approval that will place 900 trips on the roadway, so no impact fee is computed for this road segment. Tomorrow another development seeks approval for a subdivision that will also place 900 vehicles per day on the road. Technically, it should be charged an impact fee because most of the available capacity in the roadway has been spoken for even though the traffic count will not reflect the presence of the traffic for some time. This is handled by creating an "accumulated approved traffic" data file for the elements of the network. Contained in this file, which is incremented each time a subdivision is approved, is the yet-to-arrive traffic for all approved-but-unbuilt developments. This file is decremented each time a project is completed, thereby avoiding double counting of the development's traffic in the updated ground count and the accumulated approved traffic file.

Link-by-Link Cost of Expansion. The cost of road improvements is apportioned to the development on the basis of the proportion of the road improvement's capacity attributable to the development's traffic. The improvement costs that drive this computation are derived from the capital improvements program, and in turn from public works estimates. Because the county has a right-of-way dedication ordinance,

the cost estimated for right-of-way aquisition is modest and represents the amount estimated to be unattainable from the operation of the dedication ordinance.

Link-Specific Trust Funds. Earmarking of impact fees has been a sensitive issue on judicial review and frequently has been the deciding factor in whether the levy being reviewed is classified by the courts as a tax and thereby guaranteeing its speedy death. In order to avoid even a hint of insufficient earmarking, Broward County's road impact fee system employs a set of trust funds organized on a link-by-link basis. This set of accounts accumulates and tracks impact fee contributions to each of the 1,100 or so road segments in the network as development after development is reviewed and assessed an impact fee for those road segments with insufficient capacity to which the estimated traffic is assigned. The amount of impact fee contributed to each trust fund is distinguishable by contributing development so that the benefit accruing to the development when the facility is constructed can be substantiated.

Pooling Funds to Construct Improvements. One of the most difficult problems to solve arises from the fact that, even though the total amount of impact fees collected in a system is substantial, the amount available for construction of a specific improvement may only amount to a fraction of the construction cost, thereby necessitating the utilization of monies from elsewhere to make up the deficit. This will occur when a facility-by-facility accounting system is employed because it takes contributions from numerous developments that place traffic on a roadway before a particular capacity improvement is paid up. Further, if preexisting deficiencies exist, the financial responsibility for them is rightly assignable to other than new development being assessed an impact fee, requiring that nonimpact fee monies be employed to fund that portion of the project. Deferring discussion of the funding of preexisting deficiencies for the moment, the problem of fractional funding is partially solved in Broward's case by the use of an explicit pooling policy whereby the available monies in several trust funds can be aggregated and used to construct a single facility. But this cannot be done indiscriminately. An explicit set of criteria and procedures must be followed in order to guarantee that expenditure of monies from the trust funds benefits the paying developments, even when pooling is accomplished. The way this is done is as follows: At the time of initial impact analysis and fee determination, the average dollar contribution made by the development to each of the roadways on which the development's traffic is assigned is computed. Based on that average and the distribution of contributions taken across all road segments, a minimum contribution is defined, above which a roadway improvement is considered to be of *substantial benefit* to the development. All road segments on which a development has paid a contributing impact fee then are eligible for pooling of that developer's impact fee contributions to a substantial benefit link. In other words, any link defined to be of substantial benefit to a development can receive pooling contributions from all links on which that development paid a fee, up to the dollar amount paid by the development. That way the beneficiation aspect of the rational nexus test is maintained.

The Role of the Capital Improvements Program. There are two ways in which the capital improvements program has an impact on the operation of the impact fee system. First, since the Broward fee is a nonrecoupment one, once a road improvement is constructed, no longer will the county be able to collect impact fees for that road until its capacity is again used up by the incremental growth in traffic over a period of years. The result is that the definition of what constitutes a completed project, from the standpoint of showing its new capacity in the link network of the model, becomes important. This is tied to the question of what constitutes an already committed and funded road improvement for purposes of the model and here is where the capital improvements program plays an important role. When a road improvement has worked its way from the sixth year of the program to the first year, the capital budget year, it is considered to be a fully funded fait accompli and the TRIPS network file is modified to show the augmented capacity as if it were completely installed. The rationale for this is that the underlying purpose of the impact fee is to provide funds for new capacity that must be built in order to accommodate growth, but that once the board of county commissioners votes to allocate funds in the capital budget, then the funds are considered to be available and the impact fee is no longer needed to provide them.

Funding Prior Deficiencies with Nonimpact Fee Money. Prevailing judicial standards for judging the reasonableness of impact fees as an exercise of the police power point to the necessity to compute the magnitude of the impact fee at a level not exceeding the development's fair share of the cost of constructing the facilities needed to serve the development. This effectively precludes the use of impact fee monies to remediate preexisting deficiencies and requires special procedures to compute the proportion of a road improvement that is rightly allocated to new growth taking place after commencement of the fee system versus the proportion assignable to previous development and correctly financed out of general tax sources. In order to respond to these criteria, a data file was created at the start of the impact fee system that recorded each road segment considered to be over capacity and noted the magnitude of the ADT volume in excess of capacity. Each time a roadway improvement is planned, the volume of traffic constituting preexisting deficiency is noted and the proportion of improvement cost attributable is assigned to general revenue (i.e., not impact fee) responsibility.

IMPLICATIONS OF NONRECOUPMENT IMPACT FEES

There are several implications of using nonrecoupment impact fees such as those used in Broward County. Chief among these is the possibility of increased judicial defensibility resulting from what has come to be viewed as a very conservative approach to the computation of impact fees in Florida. Having had an earlier impact fee for roads invalidated by the courts, Broward County hoped to avoid a repetition of that outcome by intentionally choosing an approach that took no chances. The system that was eventually designed reflects standard traffic estimating practice applied to each development according to its location within the road network and reflecting its proposed development program. It also uses an elaborate system of trust funds to keep track of collected fees and to make certain they are expended to benefit the paying development. The procedures implemented to ensure that network descriptions, traffic counts, and approved developments are kept up to date are sufficiently thorough to

cause many planning offices to envy them. In fact, while judicial defensibility was the primary motivation behind the choice of both a nonrecoupment approach and a methodology capable of performing site-specific analysis, a synergistic result was the installation of far more planning capability than otherwise would have been possible.

Another advantage of Broward's approach is the possibility of creating incentives for in-fill development. Developments locating at points in the road network where ample capacity exists are charged (potentially) no impact fee, whereas developments locating where congestion is already substantial are charged high fees. Because of this, the spatial pattern of impact fees should provide incentives that bias development decisions in the direction of sites where road capacity is currently available. Whether or not this effect actually occurs is dependent on:

1. The forward shifting of the economic incidence of the impact fee in the form of higher prices for the development product rather than backward shifting in the form of lower land values, and

2. The locational differential in impact fees being sufficiently large to overcome other economic factors that also vary by location, such as market area, accessibility, and so forth.

While hard data are unavailable on these questions, anecdotal evidence and some theoretical viewpoints support the idea that in-fill development is stimulated by such a system.

But the advantages of such a system of impact fees are not without countervailing costs. The most obvious drawback of a nonrecoupment approach is that the total amount of money collected to build new roads is only a fraction of what it would be if cost recovery of installed capacity were practiced. This would allow the county to collect an allocated share of the cost of roadways currently operating at better than adopted level of service when that capacity is made available to the new development seeking development approval. Notice that this is not the unacceptable practice of charging new development the cost of buying into roadways already operating below level of service where no improvement will be made. Although data are not available to systematically compare the magnitude of the impact fee across numerous developments on a recoupment versus nonrecoupment basis, a rough estimate of the cost of available capacity of all road segments at the time of impact fee adoption came to $300 million. This is the amount that was potentially "recoupable" over time, had the decision been made to levy a recoupment fee.

Another serious drawback to nonrecoupment fees is the set of perverse incentives displayed to road system managers and investment decision makers. It is not farfetched to conclude that the most rational course of action for the county to employ in order to maximize its income from impact fees is to keep the road system chronically congested. Because the expenditure of funds to improve the capacity of a roadway automatically halts the further collection of impact fees for that roadway (assuming that the improvement is sufficient in magnitude to create unused capacity) the disincentives to undertake that expansion are considerable. This is complicated by the fact that the county usually has to put up general revenues to fund either the remediation of deficiencies that preexisted the establishment of the impact fee system or to make up any shortfall in impact fee trust fund balances because not all

of the developments that eventually will use the road improvement have shown up and paid into the trust fund.

IMPLICATIONS OF CUSTOM-CALCULATED FEES

Mention has been made of the fact that a major factor in Broward's choice of an impact fee strategy was defensibility in the face of judicial scrutiny. The substantial emphasis that the courts place on the idea of charging impact fees only for those facilities needed to serve the development argues for a procedure that gets quite explicit about where in the network the development's traffic is apt to show up and then for computing the fee to reflect that assignment. The further judicial interest in making sure that impact fees, once collected, are not treated as general revenue but are set aside to be spent only to construct the facilities found necessary and beneficial to the development makes a detailed system of trust funds and expenditure safeguards attractive. There is no doubt that the customized computational procedure and detailed system of trust funds will greatly assist judicial defensibility of the impact fee system, should Broward County's impact fee ever be taken to court.

On the other hand, it can be argued that Broward's approach is considerably more detailed than is now necessary, given the way that history has unfolded since the county adopted its impact fee. At the time of adoption, no road impact fee had successfully negotiated the hurdles of the Florida courts, although impact fees for water and sewer had done so. Two years later, Palm Beach County's road impact fee was upheld and since then most Florida communities adopting an impact fee for roads have emulated that approach. The Palm Beach

County fee is based on a very simple methodology that estimates the average number of lane miles of roadway needed to serve a land use type. The number of lane miles does not vary by location and no account is made for the availability of existing capacity, since it is a recoupment fee. A cost per lane mile is applied to derive the allocated cost per unit of development. The result is a schedule of fees by land use type that is applied to all developments in the county. Of course, there was no way that Broward County could have anticipated the court's action on the Palm Beach County impact fee and therefore the customized analysis methodology was an appropriate and conservative strategy.

A major advantage of the Broward procedure is the assignment of locationally fluctuating fees that reflect the actual variation in the cost of providing facilities. Developments locating in remote areas will have longer trip lengths than those locating closer to concentrations of trip destinations and will pay higher fees as the result. This is desirable in order that the fees reflect as fully as possible the actual cost of providing facilities, thereby acting as cost-based prices that display to those making development decisions the true cost implications of those decisions. Of course, this depends on forward shifting of the incidence of the fee rather than backward shifting, in a manner similar to that mentioned earlier in the discussion of the implications of nonrecoupment. If the customized impact fees do behave as cost-based prices, then all the efficiency effects resulting from the market discipline associated with prices are derivable as well.

A further implication of custom-calculated fees derives from the lack of certainty of not having a schedule of fee amounts adopted in

the ordinance and published for all to see. This has two effects. At first, the uncertainty causes anxiety in the development community because the magnitude of the fee for a particular site is unknown and therefore cannot be included in the pro forma computations. As time passes, a general understanding of the level of fees becomes known throughout the community and builders and developers can make reasonably accurate estimates based on experience. This process is aided by the county's willingness to run the TRIPS model for any site and development configuration, charging a modest processing fee and giving overnight turnaround if the batch queue is not stacked and three days' turnaround at the extreme. The result is that not only is anxiety reduced, but some elements of the development community now use the model as a planning tool when evaluating several competing sites.

The uncertainty of not having a posted fee schedule also operates to change the dynamics of the political process of adoption. Although numerous test runs of the model were produced before adoption so that all interested parties could examine an array of typical fees, the process of intergroup bargaining and coalition building was different than that observed in communities adopting general formula fees. In the latter, the relative treatment of single-family homes versus apartments versus retail stores versus other uses is starkly apparent by scanning across the schedule of impact fees per unit. An interest group's perception of the equity of the treatment accorded it by the impact fee schedule then determines its stance in further efforts to influence the outcome of the adoption process. This tends to make very apparent the self-interests of subgroups within the development community, such as home builders, shopping center developers, and industrial developers. In the case of an impact fee methodology such as Broward's, the self-interest of these groups is not as readily discernible and coalitions are more likely to remain intact.

The final implications of a custom-calculated approach to impact fees is its cost. Several years of development and testing of the TRIPS model preceded its legal adoption as the methodology for impact fee assessment. Even after adoption, its administration requires much more than simply looking up the fee per dwelling unit on a fee schedule and multiplying by the proposed number of units to get the fee. Traffic counts must be refreshed at least annually. Zonal productions and attractions require periodic updating. Improvements made to roadway segments must be accounted. Assigned traffic from prior development approvals must be specially handled. Link-specific trust funds must be maintained. Pooling of funds among trust funds must be done carefully and the result recorded to ensure integrity of expenditure beneficiation. All of these things do cost money and there is no doubt that a model that performs in this way is more expensive than a general formula computation. Then again, these are all desirable operations of a good planning office, so it may be that the cost is offset by the improved quality of road planning the methodology makes possible.

APPENDIX 17A
TRAFFIC REVIEW AND IMPACT PLANNING SYSTEM: SUMMARY DESCRIPTION

The Traffic Review and Impact Planning System (TRIPS) model used by Broward County performs four essential tasks: (1) It estimates the traffic impact of each development; (2) It evaluates the capacity of road segments that are likely to be impacted; (3) It estimates the cost of improvements; and (4) It calculates the development's fair share of the cost of the planned improvements.

Traffic impact is estimated by first calculating the number of trips a proposed development is likely to generate. Then a gravity model—an algorithm common in long-range transportation planning—is used to distribute trip ends (purposes) among destination zones throughout the county. Finally, development-induced trips are assigned to those paths that constitute the minimum travel-time routes to the destination zones.

The gravity model is based on the principle that the number of trips between the development site and the destination zones is a function of the strength of trip attraction of both places and the distance between them, expressed as time. The distribution procedure is executed four times, once for each of four standard trip purposes: Home-based shopping, home-based work, home-based other (school, recreation, miscellaneous) and non-home-based. A "tuning factor" is built into the model to ensure that its predictions of travel behavior correspond as closely as possible to the predictions made by the county's transportation planners.

After the development-induced trips are assigned to the network, the TRIPS algorithm evaluates the capacity of each road segment. It does this by comparing average daily traffic capacity (ADT) at the level of service required by the Broward County Land Development Code to the sum of these items: (1) existing

Figure 17A–1. The TRIPS Algorithm and Road Network

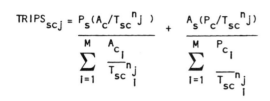

Where:

TRIPS_{scj} = number of trips of trip purpose (j) between the site (s) and the COI (c)

P_s = number of trips produced at the site

A_s = number of trips attracted to the site

P_c = number of trips produced at the COI

A_c = number of trips attracted by the COI

T_{sc} = travel time between the site and the COI

n_j = the tuning factor for trip purpose j

M = number of COIs

The impact fees cannot be used to correct past sins. Roads that are already over capacity, indicated by bold lines, are not improved to higher capacity by impact fees but, rather, by general funds. The map shows the built-up portion of Broward County.

volume, (2) assigned volume for previously evaluated developments that have not yet been constructed, and (3) assigned volume for the development currently being evaluated. No impact fee is computed for those road segments where the level of service is not impaired or for roads that need improvement but for which no improvement is shown in the county's cost-feasible transportation plan for the year 2000.

For congested road segments that are scheduled for improvement, the model estimates the cost of the improvements plus the ADT capacity anticipated to be gained thereby. County planners then compute the development's impact fee on the basis of the proportion of the improved road's capacity that can be assigned to the development's traffic.

Once a plat has been approved and an impact fee levied, the TRIPS model functions something like a trust fund accounting device. It keeps track of the fees paid by each plat, monitors the accumulation of contributions to each road improvement, and notes the status of each improvement on the capital improvements program schedule.

The TRIPS algorithm is dependent upon the availability of two sets of data, both of which must be maintained in reasonably current form. The first is a road network file containing a link-node description of both the existing network of arterials and collectors and the network committed in the capital budget. Associated with each of the links in this file are several standard parameters describing each road's physical attributes and traffic performance characteristics. These parameters include type of area, type of facility, ADT capacity, current ADT, approved ADT, and cost of planned improvements.

ADT capacity reflects current road charac-teristics and must be updated as improvements are made. Current ADT is based upon ground counts, which are updated quarterly. Approved ADT refers to the number of trips assigned to the road segment during previous TRIPS runs but for which the development is not yet built. Once a previously approved development is occupied, its approved trips are deleted from the data base, since they will now show up in the current ADT.

The road network used in TRIPS is a skeleton version of the full network normally run for urban area transportation studies, with most of the purely local service roads deleted. In order to account for off-network trips and to adjust for the resulting overestimation of assigned trips, the total of trips assigned by the TRIPS model is reduced by 14 percent—the proportion of trips assigned by the commonly used Urban Transportation Planning System program package (UTPS) to local roads not specified in a skeleton network.

A second data file contains information associated with existing land uses within some 350 zones, or "centers of influence" (COI). A COI is defined as an area with relatively homogeneous traffic attraction and production characteristics. Each COI is attached to one or more connecting nodes, or loading links; all trips originating or terminating in the COI are assumed to load onto the road network through these links. The number of trips originating from and terminating at each COI (productions and attractions) is computed from the most recent UTPS run and updated twice a year. It is the COI file that supplies production and attraction figures for input into the gravity model distribution procedure described earlier.

18

Responding to the Impact of Downtown Development: Linkage Programs and Comprehensive Planning

W. DENNIS KEATING

In contrast to the long-standing decline of the American central city, many cities recently have experienced a resurgence of commercial development, primarily in the central business district (CBD). A development boom producing new office buildings, hotels, and mixed-use projects has been welcomed by cities anxious to attract new business and employment and increase their tax base. In the past, in the face of the continuing business exodus to suburbia, central cities used a variety of competitive economic incentives to retain existing business and attract new development. These included local tax abatement and development subsidies through the HUD's Urban Development Action Grant (UDAG) program, industrial revenue bonds (IRBs), and tax increment financing. While these incentives have been somewhat effective, a major impetus for recent CBD commercial development has been lucrative tax shelter provisions in the 1981 Economic Recovery Act (now limited by the 1986 tax reform legislation).

When this private CBD development has not been publicly assisted, cities have not aggressively pursued concessions from developers. In competition with each other, as well as with their own suburbs, cities typically have attached few or no strings to their development approval. Where they have imposed regulatory controls (e.g., minority hiring), this usually has resulted from federal policies where federal economic programs have been used to subsidize private developers.

This prevailing pattern of downtown growth promotion began to change in those cities where the cumulative impact of a CBD development boom resulted in negative, rather than postive, impacts. Increased commuting by suburban employees created burdens on public transit systems. Since new CBD projects often provide new jobs primarily for suburban commuters, concern has been expressed for the plight of unemployed city residents who were largely bypassed. In tight housing markets, new development attracted workers interested in living in the central city, creating additional pressure on the housing market and leading to displacement caused by gentrification. And in some cities, environmental and preservationist groups deplored the impact of new high-rise development on the urban environment, including the destruction of historic buildings.

These problems became more important issues as federal general aid to cities and urban programs for employment training, subsidized housing, infrastructure (e.g., sewers), and mass transit declined under the conservative administration of Ronald Reagan beginning in 1981 (Peterson 1986). Cities with CBD development booms increasingly were unable to obtain the federal funding necessary for these impacted areas. Unable to finance much needed infrastructure and services, or successfully obtain substitute state funding, cities were forced to look elsewhere.

THE EMERGENCE OF LINKAGE POLICIES

A few cities began to emulate their suburban counterparts. Many suburbs long have required developers of residential subdivisions to provide at their own expense necessary infrastructure (parks, roads, sewers, schools) and services (fire and police). The home builders then have tried to add these costs to the price of new homes or charged the new owners special assessments to pay for those required improvements. In some suburbs facing a severe shortage of below-market housing, inclusionary zoning policies have been adopted. These required large-scale residential developers to provide a certain percentage of their new units at a below-market price. This can be achieved either through public subsidies or differential pricing in which the buyers of a majority of the units subsidize the lower income buyers of the inclusionary units (Mallach 1984). Suburban fiscal impact development policies now generally are accepted.

The urban version of this approach has been dubbed downtown neighborhood linkage. Five cities—Berkeley, Boston, Jersey City, San Francisco, and Santa Monica—have adopted linkage policies since 1981. They are designed to ameliorate the negative impact of large-scale commercial development on day care, employment, housing, open space, and transit. Commercial developers have the option of either paying impact fees or providing the required facilities or services. These are determined either by formula or through negotiated development agreements. Developers must agree to these requirements in order to obtain development approval. The origin, implementation, and significance of linkage policies in Boston, San Francisco, and Santa Monica have already been extensively described and analyzed (Fulton 1985; Gruen 1985; Hartman 1984; Keating 1986; Muzzio and Bailey 1986; Silvern 1985). In Boston and San Francisco, they are part of the process of planning the post-industrial city (Perloff 1980).

Linkage is a limited response to the negative impacts of large-scale downtown development. Linkage impact fees have been modest, in part due to the fear of driving developers away. The benefits of linkage exactions may not be realized until well after negative development impacts occur. For example, Boston's linkage program allows developers to pay impact fees over a seven-year period, reduced from the original twelve-year period following the completion of their project.

The legality of linkage programs has been

challenged. Developers have claimed that cities lack necessary statutory authority to impose these exactions, the impact fees are arbitrarily calculated, and constitutional guarantees of due process and equal protection are violated (Diamond 1983, Bosselman and Stroud 1985). Boston and San Francisco have successfully defended their linkage policies in the courts.

ALTERNATIVES TO LINKAGE

Several cities have adopted a variation of linkage. Some cities, including Boston, Denver, Hartford, Miami, New York, San Francisco, Seattle, and Washington, D.C., have also instituted incentive zoning (Shirvani 1981). If developers want to exceed height and density ceilings (expressed in floor area ratios—FARs), they can voluntarily agree to provide public amenities in return for a density bonus. Incentive zoning does not mandate payment of impact fees by developers. Instead, those who choose to provide the amenities receive a valuable *quid pro quo,* additional rentable space, which is not the case in linkage programs.

Incentive zoning may not provide the benefits obtained through linkage requirements because it is not mandatory. It has also been criticized as zoning for sale in which developers' financial gains may exceed the public benefits derived (Kayden 1978). Planners often oppose its use as circumvention of urban design guidelines and zoning.

A second alternative to linkage is downtown assessment districts. They generate tax revenue from all businesses, not just from new projects, to mitigate the negative impacts of rapid growth. However, because of the combined opposition of established businesses and public agencies dependent on this source of revenue,

the creation of such districts is unlikely in most cities (Keating 1986).

COMPREHENSIVE PLANNING

Linkage and its alternatives suffer from a common fault. They represent an admission that unabated, unplanned growth is the only way to promote the economic revitalization of America's declining central cities. Given the history of competitive municipal boosterism in the United States, the cyclical nature of real estate development, and the weakness of municipal planning, it is understandable that American cities do not have long-range comprehensive plans that guide economic development. Instead, they mostly rely on the private market and private investment for economic growth and revitalization. In view of the continuing fiscal stress of most central cities and the decline of federal urban aid (Gottdiener 1986), localities find it difficult to provide increased or improved infrastructure and services to meet the needs of new development.

Development impact fees through both linkage and incentive zoning programs have provided some needed revenue to offset the negative impact of urban growth. However, it is not likely that many cities will adopt linkage policies. They typically have been implemented only after progressive political coalitions supportive of regulating CBD growth have attained control of municipal government (Muzzio and Bailey 1986). This has occurred in only a few cities (Clavel 1985). It is likely that more cities may adopt incentive zoning for large-scale projects in the CBD because it is voluntary and provides developer incentives, thereby creating little developer opposition.

However, as previously noted, both linkage and incentive zoning policies have inherent limitations. In addition, they have been criticized both by developers and planners for their ad hoc nature. If there is no formula for developer contributions, then critics object to project-by-project negotiations. The results of such negotiations can vary widely. For example, community housing activists criticized San Francisco's housing linkage program for its flexible interpretability and inadequate exactions (Keating 1986). Even where a developer exaction or voluntary contribution formula exists (usually expressed on a dollar-per-square-foot basis), the impact fee policy may not be effectively related to the city's downtown plan, if one exists. The impact fee policy also may not relate to the city's planning for economic development and capital improvement programs. Furthermore, housing policies and programs may be vague as to the actual use of linkage impact fees.

A better approach is to incorporate impact fee policies into a comprehensive growth-management planning process. Cities like San Francisco, facing continued CBD growth and its attendant problems, must engage in comprehensive and strategic planning. As part of that growth-management planning, cities should coordinate levels of growth and the timely provision of predicted levels of facilities and services necessary to accommodate the development. This is the essence of growth-management planning. Included in these calculations would be any impact required or expected. These are typically identified in an environmental impact statement. Then, if the city or a developer were unable to provide necessary infrastructure and services even with exaction fees, the city could limit or phase in growth.

This type of planned phased development is the same as that popularized by suburban and rural communites like Ramapo, New York, and Petaluma, California. Only a few major cities (e.g., San Diego) have emulated their example by adopting a comprehensive growth-management plan. Of course, most cities do attempt to coordinate development planning and project approval with infrastructure and capital improvements planning and budgeting and service delivery but this has rarely resulted in consistent long-range comprehensive planning.

SAN FRANCISCO'S DOWNTOWN PLAN

San Francisco is one of the few American cities that has recently attempted to develop such a comprehensive downtown plan. After several years of research and debate, San Francisco adopted in August 1985 a much-heralded Downtown Plan (Adams 1984). This plan was narrowly approved by a 6–5 vote of the city supervisors. Preceding this was a protracted political struggle over the future of San Francisco's CBD. San Francisco's CBD growth since the 1960s has been phenomenal. In response, citizen and neighborhood groups have fought to restrict high-rise development in order to limit its negative architectural, economic, environmental, housing, and transit impacts. Four citizen initiatives to limit CBD growth were defeated in San Francisco between 1971 and 1985. Hartman argues that the 1979 and 1983 initiatives again forcing the issue to a popular vote prompted the city to develop and propose the plan that it unveiled in August 1983 in an effort to undercut the appeal of anti-high-rise opposition (Hartman 1984). Neighborhood-based pressure led San Francisco to adopt the first municipal linkage program in 1981 (Gruen 1985; Keating 1986). San Francisco had previously instituted a downtown density bonus system (Svirsky 1970) and developed comprehensive urban design guidelines (Jacobs 1978).

The most significant aspect of the Downtown Plan is that it imposed annual average growth ceilings of 950,000 square feet in the CBD for the next three years. This temporary ceiling was imposed in recognition of excessive office development that had negatively affected housing, transportation, and parking capacities within San Francisco. A temporary building moratorium preceded adoption of the plan. The imposition of even temporary growth ceilings is unusual in the history of American urban planning.

The Downtown Plan reduced CBD FARs, promoted historic preservation through a transferable development rights system, and instituted new height, bulk, and design regulations to further implement the city's urban design plan and to promote solar access.

The anti-high-rise movement criticized it as a thoroughly inadequate response to the problems created by overdevelopment. The criticisms of San Francisco's Downtown Plan have been detailed by Chester Hartman (Hartman 1984, pp. 272–79). Hartman also criticizes San Francisco's transit and housing impact fee policies as inadequate (Hartman 1984, pp. 282–92).

Hartman's view is that the plan does not really limit high-rise development. Instead, it simply shifts development to other areas of the city, in particular South-of-Market and Mission Bay, which are the sites of massive development projects which he discusses. The plan only covers the CBD; therefore, impact fees for projects outside the CBD are being negotiated on an individual project basis. In view of what he regards as inadequate impact fee policies for housing and transit, he concludes:

By allowing more office growth without first insuring the housing and transportation to accompany it, the Plan puts the cart before the horse. Major transit improvements take 10–25 years from concept to completion and their public funding sources are uncertain, as are housing subsidization funds; privately financed office buildings take 3–4 years. What the Planning Commission approves are buildings to be soon built, whose impacts are soon felt; mitigation measures are more in the nature of a wish list. The Downtown Plan ignores the rest of the city and its relation to downtown, issues of quality of life, neighborhood preservation and class relations. [Hartman 1984, p. 275]

The positive aspect of San Francisco's Downtown Plan is that the city's impact fee policies are no longer isolated from its comprehensive planning. The negative aspects are the limitations of the coverage and scope of the plan and the impact fee policies themselves.

However, the latter changed dramatically in November 1986 when a citizen initiative to strengthen the Downtown Plan passed by a narrow margin (*Planning* 1986). This culminated the 15-year campaign to control high-rise development that Hartman describes. The initiative halved allowable large-scale CBD development and called for revision of the Plan by January 1988 to better protect neighborhoods, strengthen linkage policies, and alleviate the negative impacts of this development on a citywide basis.

Santa Monica also followed San Francisco's lead. Initially, its impact fee policy was implemented through individual development agreements regulating large-scale development. The city found this process to be overly cumbersome and costly. So, in October 1984, Santa Monica incorporated its impact fee policies into the new land use element of its master plan.

Since the adoption of its original housing linkage policy in December 1983, Boston has begun the process of revising its downtown zoning. While Seattle rejected a housing linkage policy, its housing density bonus policy is part of the downtown land use and transportation plan that it adopted in 1984 (Keating 1986). In contrast, New York City's incentive zoning policies are negotiated ad hoc project-by-project. While they are tied to the preservation of special districts in mid-town Manhattan, open space, mass transit, and affordable housing, they cannot be said to be integrated effectively into a comprehensive citywide planning process (Ponte 1982).

Linkage policies that are not linked to comprehensive long-range planning may fail for a number of reasons. Growth impact problems may outpace the benefits of linkage programs, whose implementation should precede rather than follow project development. There may be inadequate information on the cumulative impact of all CBD growth. If linkage impact fees are based only on the direct impact of individual projects, then they may prove to be inadequate to mitigate the larger problems caused by cumulative CBD growth (Adams 1985). If the use of impact fees is not coordinated carefully with ongoing planning and programming, then their effectiveness may be lost because these limited funds are not best used to serve their intended purpose. Instead, they may simply be used for short-term stopgap funding or as a substitute for lost federal funding without being targeted to mitigate the impact of large-scale development.

METROPOLITAN PLANNING

Beyond the recommended connection between municipal linkage programs and local comprehensive planning, what makes even more sense is to shift development away from over-developed core areas of central cities to less developed areas within a metropolis. This would, of course, require effective regional planning. Metropolitan planning that effectively regulates land use planning and development is a rarity in the United States (Levin 1967).

To deal effectively with overdevelopment of the central city or its CBD, metropolitan planners could seek to shift certain types of development to suburban areas where, for example, sufficient housing is available and less commuting is required for office workers. In fact, many corporate offices, including so-called back offices, have moved to the suburbs, where office rents are usually less than those in the central city CBD (Dowell 1986). This is one reason why central cities in competition with their suburban counterparts for new commercial development fear losing office and retail complexes and hotels. In the absence of very strong state-mandated regional planning, it is most unlikely that any central city would go beyond San Francisco's temporary ceiling on development and encourage the regional decentralization of large-scale commercial development, thus shifting some new development to its competitors.

CONCLUSION

In view of the lack of metropolitan planning, it is to be expected that the present pattern of development will continue, with market decisions largely determining the location of large-scale commercial development. While it is not likely that many major cities will be faced with overwhelming growth problems, many, like Boston and San Francisco, will have to deal with the serious problems caused by rapid overdevelopment of the CBD. Ad hoc linkage and incentive zoning programs will not provide answers to all of these problems.

Linkage and incentive zoning programs can best be used to deal with the impact of growth when they are incorporated into a local comprehensive planning process—both citywide and downtown—that takes into account not only land use, physical development, budgetary concerns, infrastructure, urban design, and economic development, but also social equity and the relationship of downtown growth to neighborhood preservation and development. Two of the best models are Cleveland's 1975 Policy Planning Report (Krumholz 1975) and Chicago's 1984 Development Plan (City of Chicago 1984; Judd and Ready 1986). Both highlight the need to address social as well as economic and physical development issues, important because CBD growth does not necessarily benefit the population of central cities. Scarce resources may be diverted to downtown development to the detriment of moderate- and low-income neighborhoods whose residents will not enjoys its benefits. Equity planning, together with linkage policies, and, it is hoped, a reversal of recent federal policies reducing urban aid, is the best hope for a more equitable revitalization of our central cities.

References

Adams, Andriette. 1985. The Cumulative Impact Assessment in CEQA. *Western State University Law Review* 12: 801–17.

Adams, Gerald. 1984. A Last Ditch Effort to Save Downtown San Francisco. *Planning* 47, 9 (February): 4–11.

Bosselman, Fred and Nancy Stroud. 1985. Mandatory Tithes: The Legality of Land Development Linkage. *Nova Law Journal* 9: 381–412.

City of Chicago. 1984. *Chicago Development Plan*.

Clavel, Pierre. 1985. *The Progressive City: Planning and Participation 1969–1984*. New Brunswick, N.J.: Rutgers University Press.

Diamond, Susan. 1983. The San Francisco Office/Housing Program: Social Policy Underwritten by Private Enterprise. *Harvard Environmental Law Review* 7: 449–86.

Dowall, David E. 1986. Endangered Species: San Francisco's Back-Office Employees. *Urban Land* 45, 8 (August): 9–13.

Fulton, William. 1985. On the Beach with the Progressives. *Planning* 51, 1 (January): 4–9.

Gottdiener, M., ed. 1986. *Cities in Distress: A New Look at the Urban Crisis*. Beverly Hills, Calif.: Sage Publications.

Gruen, Nina. 1985. A Case History of the San Francisco Office/Housing Linkage Program. In *Downton Linkages*, edited by Douglas Porter. Washington. D.C.: Urban Land Institute.

Hartman, Chester. 1984. *The Transformation of San Francisco*. Totowa, N.J.: Rowman and Allanheld.

Judd, Dennis and Randy Ready. 1986. Chicago, Illinois: A Reform Agenda in a Hostile Environment. In *Reagan and the Cities*, edited by George Peterson and Carol Lewis. Washington, D.C.: The Urban Land Institute Press.

Jacobs, Allan. 1978. *Making City Planning Work*. Chicago: American Society of Planning Officials.

Kayden, Jerome S. 1978. *Incentive Zoning in New York City: A Cost-Benefit Analysis*. Cambridge, Mass.: Lincoln Institute of Land Policy.

Keating, W. Dennis. 1986. Linking Downtown Development to Broader Community Goals: An Analysis of Linkage Policies in Three Cities. *Journal of the American Planning Association* 52, 1 (Spring): 133–41.

Krumholz, Norman. 1975. The Cleveland Policy Planning Report. *Journal of the American Institute of Planners* 41 (Spring): 298–304.

Levin, Melvin R. 1967. Planners and Metropolitan Planning. *Journal of the American Institute of Planners* 33 (March): 78–90.

Mallach, Alan. 1984. *Inclusionary Housing Programs: Policies and Practices*. New Brunswick, N.J.: Center for Urban Policy Research, Rutgers University.

Muzzio, Douglas and Robert Bailey. 1986. Economic Development, Housing, Zoning: A Tale of Two Cities. *Journal of Urban Affairs* 8, 1 (Winter): 1–17.

Perloff, Harvey S. 1980. *Planning the Post-Industrial City*. Chicago: APA Planners Press.

Peterson, George, ed. 1986. *Reagan and the Cities*. Washington, D.C.: The Urban Institute.

Planning. 1986. California Voters Speak up on Growth. 52, 12 (December): 29.

Ponte, Robert. 1982. New York's Zoning Solution. *Planning* 48, 12 (December): 10–14.

Scott, Randall, W., ed. 1975. *Management and Control of Growth*. Washington, D.C.: Urban Land Institute.

Shirvani, Hamid. 1981. *Urban Design Review: A Guide for Planners*. Chicago: APA Planners Press.

Silvern, Paul. 1985. Negotiating the Public Interest: California's Development Agreement Statute. *Land Use Law* 37, 1 (October): 3–9.

Synder, Thomas P. and Michael Stegman. 1986. *Paying for Growth: Using Development Fees to Finance New Infrastructure*. Washington, D.C.: Urban Land Institute.

Svirsky, Peter S. 1970. San Francisco: The Downtown Development Bonus System. In *The New Zoning: Legal, Administrative and Economic Concepts and Techniques*, edited by Norman Marcus and Marilyn W. Groves. New York: Praeger Publishers.

19

Defensible Linkage

CHRISTINE I. ANDREW
DWIGHT H. MERRIAM

The American city has developed a Jekyll-and-Hyde personality with two faces. While economic prosperity has brought rejuvenated urban areas replete with gleaming skyscrapers, rehabilitated neighborhoods, and sophisticated shopping centers, poorer areas have become shabbier, with increasing crime rates, uprooting of longtime residents as neighborhoods become gentrified, and growing numbers of homeless. The problems today's cities face are not new. Since World War II, federal, state, and local programs and policies have sought to solve them. Supporters herald each attempt—including the New Society, the New Frontier, the Model City, Urban Development Action Grants—as "the solution" to urban problems. Despite some successes, a miracle cure remains elusive; as the flow of federal and state funds diminishes, cities must begin to solve the problems on their own. Although no single strategy is likely to be the long-sought cure-all, planners and politicians hope that linkage programs will help provide affordable housing and expanded municipal services.

Supporters praise linkage as a solution to urban needs. Opponents, on the other hand, allege that this planning tool illegally attempts to shift responsibility for correcting social ills to the urban commercial developer and that it will ultimately force commercial development away from downtown and thus will exacerbate existing problems. In light of those objections and recent Supreme Court decisions involving challenges to land use regulations, any planner seeking to produce a legally defensible linkage program must identify and analyze areas of potential liability, narrowly focus the necessary regulatory requirements, and minimize the economic harm to affected property owners.

This chapter addresses those issues and the underlying legal concerns and will demonstrate that the introduction of a well-designed linkage program into a suitable economic environment can be both a successful and a legally defensible means to alleviate a variety of municipal problems.

WHAT IS LINKAGE?

The term *linkage* has been defined in terms of the manner or style in which atoms, radicals, molecules, chromosomes, magnetic flux, and the like are united. For planners and politicians, however, linkage refers to a variety of programs that require developers to contribute toward new affordable housing, employment opportunities, child care facilities, transit systems, and the like, in return for the city's permission to build new commercial developments.

Following adoption of a widely publicized linkage program in San Francisco in 1981, planners and politicians began to look toward linkage to help them address a variety of social needs. Cities scattered across the country have since adopted linkage ordinances or programs or have considered them[1] (Steinbach 1986; *Zoning News* 1986a, pp. 2–3; 1986b, p. 4).

Underlying every linkage program is the fundamental concept that new downtown commercial development is directly "linked" to a specific social need. The rationale is fairly simple: Not only does the actual construction of the commercial buildings create new construction jobs, but the increased office space attracts new businesses and workers to fill new jobs. The new workers need places to live, transit systems, day care facilities, and the like. From the perspective of linkage proponents, the new commercial development is directly linked both to new employment opportunities and to increased demands for improved municipal facilities and services. Supporters believe that the developer who profits from constructing a new commercial development logically should help pay for increases in municipal services and facilities. Thus, linkage constitutes an attempt by the city to ensure that the prospering developers share their profits and help satisfy the needs that result from new commercial growth.

Linkage is also, in part, a response to a decrease in federal funding, to new limitations on tax-exempt bonds for nonpublic purposes, and to the natural reluctance of political incumbents to raise taxes. It offers distinct benefits in the form of new and improved services or facilities that neighborhood groups—the traditional opponents of new commercial development—can understand and endorse. In addition, linkage programs place the cost of those improvements on major commercial developers who may come from outside the city and thus do not have a political power base or constituency within the city.[2]

Despite supporters' contentions that linkage is not a throwback to the antibusiness sentiment of the 1960s, developers are skeptical, if not openly hostile, and have begun to challenge the validity and legality of linkage in the courts. As a result, if a municipality wishes to enact a linkage program that developers will accept, it must ensure that the developer—like the city—will benefit.

Linkage programs can vary greatly depending primarily on the creativity of program promoters and the economic and political environment of the city. Most linkage programs combine requirements imposed on downtown developers with a juicy carrot or two in the form of benefits, special treatment, or other inducements. Some linkage programs demand concessions only from developers who want to benefit from particular tax, financing, planning, or land use incentives; others affect those who want to build in certain areas of the city or to construct a building in excess of a specified square footage. Linkage is likely to be successful and to avoid legal challenge if the city makes incentives so appealing that the developer truly desires to participate. In short, the more attractive a project is from the developer's point of view, the more likely it is that the developer will be willing to satisfy the city's requirements and the more likely it is that the city will actually obtain a significant municipal benefit.

A successful linkage program first must work economically; that is, it must benefit both the developer and the municipality without imposing unacceptable burdens on either. Second—and the prime focus of this chapter—the program must have sufficient legal foundation to enable it to withstand any legal challenge from opponents. In short, linkage must be both workable and defensible.

IS LINKAGE WORKABLE?

If a linkage program is to succeed politically, legally, and economically, it must be equitable and make sound economic sense. Regardless how well conceived or how laudable a program's objectives are, linkage will not succeed if the market cannot support increased commercial developments.[3] If the market is weak, if the city is not in a desirable location, if existing fees, taxes, and the like have already eroded the incentive to build or rehabilitate commercial space in the inner city, developers will simply move their projects elsewhere. Thus, the planner's first step when designing a linkage program must be to analyze the existing market to ensure that linkage will provide incentives, rather than disincentives, to commercial developers. Program planners must also consider the nature of the linked "payment." If the program does not provide the city with sufficient funds to achieve and maintain program objectives, or if it renders the commercial project economically infeasible from the developer's point of view, it will not work politically and probably will not pass judicial muster.

Planners must weigh carefully a program's burdens and benefits to ensure that the program is fair to all affected parties. Any program that is not equitable, or that developers or neighborhood groups perceive as inequitable, probably will fail politically and certainly will face legal challenge. Equity in putting the so-called touch on developers requires that the program goals be reasonable when balanced against the concessions the city will grant to the developer. Similarly, planners must ensure

that the program addresses real needs and that the ultimate recipients are those in need rather than members of special interest groups.

IS LINKAGE DEFENSIBLE?

To be legally defensible, a linkage program must pass two tests.[4] First, it must be a valid exercise of an authorized municipal power; second, it must be able to withstand constitutional challenges.

Is the Municipality Authorized to Enact a Linkage Ordinance?

Courts have had relatively few opportunities to review existing linkage programs. The objectives and philosophical underpinnings of linkage, however, are related to those of exactions and impact fees.[5] Consequently, when ruling on the legal validity of linkage ordinances, courts probably will perform a legal analysis similar to the two-step analysis they employ when ruling on the legality of development exactions.

As a first step—and regardless of whatever label the legislative body may have attached to the program—the court will determine whether the ordinance is a tax or a regulation. To help it make that threshold determination, the court must look both to the municipal intent in enacting the legislation and to the actual operative effect of the program. If the court determines that the city adopted the ordinance to generate general revenues or to pay for nonspecific facilities or improvements, it will probably hold that the fee constitutes a tax. Since most jurisdictions severely restrict a municipality's authority to tax, the court probably will rule that the ordinance is not a valid exercise of an authorized power. On the other hand, if the municipality segregates the funds that the ordinance generates and designates them for specific improvements clearly linked to the new development, a court could declare that the fee is legitimate. The ordinance, thus, would be a regulation enacted pursuant to the police power, that is, the implied power to control and regulate land use for the benefit of the public health, safety, and general welfare.[6]

Court decisions have greatly expanded the scope of the police power. Originally, the police power allowed the municipality to regulate land use for the benefit of public safety, health, and morals through building codes, setback requirements, and the like. Eventually, it came to include regulation of land use for the benefit of the general welfare. By the 1950s, a municipality could exercise its police power to regulate the spiritual as well as the physical, aesthetics as well as morals. In short, a legislative body exercising its police power today has the authority to determine that "a community should be beautiful as well as healthy, spacious as well as clean, well-balanced as well as carefully controlled" (*Berman* 1954). Broadened by judicial interpretation, the police power remains a dynamic concept. As a result, an ordinance that the courts at one time considered an invalid exercise of the police power may gain validity (*Miller* 1925). Linkage proponents, when arguing that a given ordinance constitutes a clear exercise of the police power, should attempt to capitalize on the evolving nature of that power.[7]

Demonstrating that a linkage ordinance involves an appropriate exercise of the police power in general, however, does not necessarily mean that the municipality has authority to enact it. Although each state holds the inherent authority to regulate land use through exercise of the police power, municipalities do not. Municipalities possess only the authority their charters grant or state statutes delegate to them. Thus, to uphold a linkage ordinance as duly authorized, the court also must investigate the source of the city's authority to enact it.

Linkage opponents in Boston have challenged that city's authority to adopt a linkage program[8] and other municipalities will undoubtedly face similar challenges. Clearly, the resolution of the issue depends largely on the jurisdiction's statutory framework, that is, zoning enabling acts and other relevant statutory provisions. If the city does not have such authority, legal challenges are likely to prevail. Therefore, linkage proponents should encourage adoption of specific enabling legislation that authorizes municipalities to regulate for a clearly stated public purpose.[9] In the case of housing linkage programs, for example, the enabling legislation should authorize the municipality to adopt regulations to ensure the existence of adequate housing for workers near their places of employment.

Is the Ordinance Constitutional?

The constitutionality of a linkage ordinance is conceptually distinct from issues raised regarding the program's authorization under state law. Since courts prefer not to decide constitutional issues, they will dispose of matters on procedural or statutory grounds whenever possible.[10] Nevertheless, challenges to land use controls can be, and are, brought under a variety of state and federal constitutional provisions.

An attack on linkage on constitutional grounds may challenge the particular ordinance *on its face;* that is, the opponent will ask the court to declare that the ordinance or statute violates certain constitutional protections regardless of how it may be applied in a given case. Alternately, opponents may allege that the ordinance is unconstitutional *as applied* to them; that is, the statute itself may be valid but is not constitutional as applied in the particular case before the court.

Linkage opponents may raise several constitutional arguments against an ordinance or program. They may challenge land use controls in general, and linkage in particular, as violating procedural due process, substantive due process, or equal protection requirements, or as a taking of property without just compensation.[11]

Regulation as Taking. The taking clause of the Fifth Amendment of the U.S. Constitution made applicable to the states by the Due Process Clause of the Fourteenth Amendment (*Chicago Burlington & Quincy R.R. Co.* 1887), provides that "private property shall [not] be taken for public use, without just compensation." Initially, courts ruled that the taking clause applied only when a government actually took possession of property for a public use. Thus, when a government appropriated property from a private landowner for a road or a school or a park, the government had to pay just compensation. By the early twentieth century, however, the Supreme Court had begun to invalidate regulations it considered confiscatory. In a landmark decision, Justice Holmes stated that "the general rule at least is that while property may be regulated to a certain extent, if regulation goes too far, it will be considered as a taking" (*Pennsylvania Coal Co.* 1922). Unfortunately, Justice Holmes did not provide an easy test of when the regulation went too far. Although the Supreme Court has stated that "the mere assertion of regulatory jurisdiction by a governmental body does not constitute a regulatory taking" (*United States* v. *Riverside Bayrew Homes,*

Inc. 1985), the point at which government action crosses the line between regulation and taking is still debated.

Costonis (1984) has concluded that the Court's cumulative taking precedents have addressed four types of land use regulations: those that restrict the uses to which an owner may devote his land, those that require an owner to do certain things on his land, those that obligate an owner to suffer "temporary physical invasions" of his land by the government or its agents, and those that obligate an owner to suffer permanent physical occupations" by either the government or its agents. The Court has adopted a per se rule whenever there is an actual permanent, physical invasion; that is, when such an invasion occurs, no matter how large or how small, and "without regard to whether the action achieves an important public benefit or has a minimal economic impact on the owner," a taking has occurred for which the government must pay compensation (*Loretto* 1982).

To determine whether an action triggers the Fifth Amendment's just compensation requirement when there is no permanent physical invasion, courts consider the economic impact of the regulation on the property owner, the police power objective the regulation promotes, and the character of the government action involved. In so doing, the Supreme Court has "long recognized that land use regulation does not effect a taking if it 'substantially advance[s] legitimate state interests' and does not 'den[y] an owner economically viable use of his land'. . . ." (*Nollan* 1987). Thus, "[t]he determination that governmental action constitutes a taking is, in essence, a determination that the public at large, rather than a single owner, must bear the burden of an exercise of state power in the public interest" (*Agins* 1980). In short, the Fifth Amendment preserves government power to regulate, but subjects that power to the dictate of "justice and fairness" (*Deltona Corp.* 1981). Thus, assuming that a linkage ordinance does not constitute a physical invasion—for example, by requiring the developer to dedicate a portion of its building for a public purpose—courts probably will use a similar balancing test when asked to determine whether or not a linkage ordinance constitutes a taking.

Until the spring of 1987, the Supreme Court had tended in recent years to dispose of the cases that raised various taking issues on procedural grounds without reaching the substantive legal issues.[12] On March 9, 1987, however, the Court ruled that provisions of a Pennsylvania mine subsidence statute did not constitute a taking (*Keystone Bituminous Coal Assn.* 1987). Although the facts of that case may appear to many—including the four justices who filed a dissenting opinion—to be very similar to those of *Pennsylvania Coal Co.* v. *Mahon*,[13] the Court characterized the statute in the latter case as one advancing a "private benefit" statute, and the former as one advancing a "public benefit." Having made that distinction, the Court proceeded to weigh the public interest in preventing activities that are "tantamount to public nuisances" against the private interest burdened by the legislation.[14]

On June 26, 1987, the Supreme Court rendered its decision in a takings case that raised issues similar to those a linkage opponent may raise (*Nollan* 1987). The Nollans had applied to the California Coastal Commission for a permit to demolish an existing beach house and construct a permanent home on the site. The commission approved the application on the condition that the Nollans record a deed restriction acknowledging the right of the public to pass and repass along their 10-foot beach. The Nollans sued and won, but the appellate court overturned the trial court's ruling; the appellate court relied on two recent California state court decisions that held that an exaction that reduces the value of property but does not deprive the owner of reasonable use of the property does not constitute a taking (*Grupe* 1985; *Remmenga* 1985). The appellate court also ruled that a dedication requirement is justified if the burdened project contributes to the need the dedication seeks to address, even if the project standing alone did not create that need (*Nollan* 1986). The Nollans then appealed the appellate ruling to the Supreme Court and won. The Court held that the easement was a "permanent physical occupation" of the Nollans' property but apparently did not decide the case on physical invasion grounds. Instead the Court analyzed the condition as a regulatory decision and reiterated its standard that land use regulations must "substantially advance" the "legitimate state interest" sought.

The *Nollan* decision clearly has the potential for affecting many kinds of development exaction programs, including linkage programs. While the majority opinion takes issue with the dissenters' claim that it was articulating a new standard in land use law, the Court seems to have expressly rejected the requirement that there be a rational relationship between the condition and the government objective in favor of a new "substantially advances a legitimate state interest" standard. The Court indicated that it would be more sensitive to exactions and conditions that allowed physical invasions or involved the actual conveyance of property. It also suggested that a condition would be permissible and would not constitute a taking if the condition serves the same government purpose as that justifying the prohibition of the activity or use in question. In short, a permit condition serving the same legitimate police power purpose as a refusal to permit the development would not constitute a taking if the refusal to allow the development would not itself constitute a taking. Thus the lesson of the *Nollan* case for linkage supporters and for planners attempting to draft and implement linkage ordinances is that there must be sufficient evidence in the record of the required nexus between the need advanced and the proposed prohibitions, exactions, and conditions.[15]

Due Process. The due process clause of the Fifth Amendment provides that no person may be deprived of life, liberty, or property without due process of law. Once again made applicable to state and local action by the Fourteenth Amendment, the due process clause covers two types of due process: procedural and substantive.

Procedural due process requires that the procedures used in government decision making be fair. Since legislative action generally is not limited by procedural due process, challenges to land use regulation on those grounds generally involve allegations that administrative decision making, rather than legislative actions, did not satisfy the requirements.[16] Thus, a procedural due process challenge to a linkage ordinance or program probably would not occur at the enactment level, but rather would be triggered by the application of the particular ordinance or program. Such a challenge typically would include allegations that the administering body did not follow statutory requirements, including those dealing with publication of notice and right of appeal.

Substantive due process, on the other hand, is a more amorphous concept, which ultimately requires that a municipal body act in a manner that is not arbitrary and capricious when it enacts laws and regulations and renders decisions. When reviewing a substantive due process challenge to land use regulations, courts generally consider whether that regulation or decision bears the required relationship to a legitimate government goal, that is, to the promotion of public health, safety, and general welfare. Thus, *Nollan* was also, in large measure, a substantive due process case.

Courts have applied varying standards when ruling on an allegation that an exaction program violates substantive due process. By far the strictest standard from the perspective of the city is what has come to be known as the *specifically and uniquely attributable test.* Under that test, a municipality may require only that a developer assume costs or other obligations that are specifically and uniquely attributable to the subdivision activity (*Pioneer Trust & Sav. Bank* 1961). Thus, to prevail over a constitutional challenge, the city must establish that the developer's activities generated a need and that the benefits from the exaction accrue directly to the developer and to the subdivision. There is little likelihood that a municipality will prevail if the court applies the specifically and uniquely attributable test. As one commentator has noted (Karp 1979, p. 284), it "is virtually impossible to prove that the need for any public facility is specifically and uniquely attributable to the people in a given subdivision."

Other courts, however, taking a broader approach, apply a *reasonably related test* (*Ayres* 1949). That criterion considers an exaction valid if it bears a reasonable relationship to use of the facilities by present or future inhabitants of the subdivision. Thus, to avoid having to satisfy exaction requirements under the reasonably related test, a developer would have to prove that there is no reasonable connection between the proposed project and the exaction. The city, provided that it exercised an authorized power when enacting the program, would simply need to prove that the exaction was not wholly unrelated or completely unnecessary to the project either at present or in the near future.

The third test that courts typically employ when ruling on exaction programs falls in the middle ground between the stringent specifically related and uniquely attributable test and the lenient reasonably related test. The *rational nexus test* requires only that there be a rational connection between the exaction and the project (*Longridge Builders* 1968). Thus, the midlevel test is similar to the specifically and uniquely attributable test in that it examines both needs and benefits; the midlevel test differs by requiring less evidence to demonstrate the validity of the requirement.

Although courts generally uphold exaction programs (even those that extract less traditional public services and amenities such as open space) under either the rational nexus or the reasonably related test, linkage may not fare as well. Traditional exaction programs can generally demonstrate a clear connection between the proposed development and the need for the particular service or facility. Given the more tenuous relationship between the benefits and burdens of a linkage program, if the *Nollan* case does indeed create a new substantially advances standard that is closer to the specifically and uniquely attributable end of the continuum, municipalities will have a harder time defending linkage programs, especially where

the program is designed to resolve broad public problems for which the specific project bears no real blame in a cost-accounting sense (Bosselman 1985).

Linkage opponents will argue that the connection between the program goal and the proposed development is irrational, unreasonable, and nonexistent. For example, in response to arguments by linkage proponents that new office space creates new employment opportunities and thereby increases the demand for affordable urban housing, the developer will argue that prior local population growth and economic expansion created the demand for new office space. In addition, developers may argue that office employees provide services for the resident urban population and thus the need for expanded office and commercial space increases only as that resident population grows and requires increased services. Another possible argument involves establishing regional boundaries: developers may argue that not only do downtown offices serve an area that extends well beyond the city limits, but also that, typically, only a modest percentage of downtown office employees live within the city.[17] Therefore, according to the developer the problem is a regional one whose solution also must be regional.[18] If linkage fees are to survive such challenges, the city cannot simply make generalized conclusions but must demonstrate the correlation between, for example, jobs and housing, and must quantify both the overall extent of that need and the proportion attributable to a particular development.

Equal Protection. The Fourteenth Amendment of the Constitution requires that the law treat similarly situated persons equally. Under that requirement, an opponent might challenge the constitutionality of a linkage ordinance either on its face or as applied. For example, the developer most likely would challenge a linkage program because it applies only to commercial development. An as-applied attack would occur when the opponent contests not the constitutionality of the ordinance or program but the specific manner in which the government applies it to his property. For example, an 1880 San Francisco ordinance eliminated the use of wooden buildings for hand laundries. The Supreme Court held that even though the law was constitutional on its face, it violated the equal protection clause, as applied, because the municipality routinely granted exemptions to Caucasians who owned wooden laundries while it forced all Chinese who owned such laundries to give up their businesses (*Yick Wo* 1886).

Courts employ different tests when reviewing equal protection challenges, depending on the nature of the regulation, the rights involved, the individuals affected, and the interest that is burdened. If an ordinance creates what is called a suspect class (race, national origin, and, to a certain extent, sex) or involves a fundamental interest (right to privacy, right to travel, right to vote, or any explicit constitutional guarantee such as freedom of speech) the court will apply a strict scrutiny standard. To withstand attack when a court applies strict scrutiny, the ordinance must serve a compelling government interest. Except where a suspect classification or the infringement of a fundamental right exists, the equal protection clause is violated only if the treatment given bears no rational relationship to a legitimate government purpose.[19] For example, the village of Belle Terre, New York, enacted a zoning ordinance that restricted land use to one-family dwellings and defined the term family to exclude households of more than

---

Exhibit 19–1. Court Decisions Relevant to Linkage Exactions

Agins v. City of Tiburon, 447 U.S. 255 (1980).

Allied Structural Steel Co. v. Spannaus, 438 U.S. 234, (1978).

Ashwander v. Tennessee Valley Authority, 297 U.S. 288, (1936).

Atlantic Coast Line R.R. Co. v. City of Goldsboro, 232 U.S. 548 (1914).

Ayres v. City Council, 34 Cal. 2d 31, 207 P.2d 1 (1949).

Barton v. Atkinson, 228 Ga. 733, 187 S.E. 2d 835, (1972).

Beckman v. Teaneck Township, 6 N.J. 530, 79 A.2d 301 (1951).

Berman v. Parker, 348 U.S. 26 (1954).

Bonan v. City of Boston, 398 Mass. 315, 496 N.E. 2d 640 (1986).

Candid Enterprises, Inc. v. Grossmont Union High School District, 39 Cal. 3d 878, 218 Cal. Rptr. 303 (1985).

Chicago Burlington & Quincy R.R. v. City of Chicago, 166 U.S. 226 (1897).

Deltona Corp. v. United States, 657 F.2d 1184 (Ct. Cl. 1981), cert. denied, 455 U.S. 1017 (1981).

First English Evangelical Lutheran Church of Glendale v. County of Los Angeles, —— U.S. ——, 107 S. Ct. 2378 (1987).

Grupe v. California Coastal Commission, 177 Cal. App. 3d 719, 223 Cal. Rptr. 28 (1986).

Kaiser Development Co. v. City and County of Honolulu (Civil No. 84-0389) (D.C. Ha.)

Keystone Bituminous Coal Assn. v. De Benedictis, —— U.S. ——, 107 S. Ct. 1232 (1987).

Longridge Builders v. Planning Board 52 N.J. 348, 245 A.2d 336 (1968).

Loretto v. Teleprompter Manhattan CATV Corp., 458 U.S. 419 (1982).

Louisville v. Fiscal Court, 623 S.W. 2d 219, (Ky. 1981).

McDonald, Sommer, and Frates v. Yolo County, —— U.S. ——, 106 S. Ct. 2561 (1986).

Metropolitan St. Louis Sewer District v. Ruckelshaus, 590 F. Supp. 385 (E.D. Mo. 1984).

Midland Co. v. Kansas City Power & Light Co., 300 U.S. 109 (1937).

Miller v. Board of Public Works, 195 Cal. 477, 234 p. 381 (1925).

New Orleans Waterworks Co. v. Louisiana Sugar Refining Co., 125 U.S. 18, 30 (1888).

Nollan v. California Coastal Commission, 177 Cal. App. 3d 719, 223 Cal. Rptr. 28 (1986).

Nollan v. California Coastal Commission, —— U.S. ——, 107 S. Ct. 3141 (1987).

Parks v. Watson, 716 F.2d 646 (9th Cir. 1983).

Pennsylvania Coal Co. v. Mahon, 260 U.S. 393 (1922).

Pioneer Trust & Sav. Bank v. Village of Mount Prospect, 22 Ill. 2d 375, 176 N.E. 2d 299 (1961).

Remmenga v. California Coastal Comm'n, 163 Cal. App. 3d 623, 209 Cal. Rptr. 628 (1985).

San Telmo Associates v. City of Seattle, 108 Wash. 2d 20, —— P.2d —— (1987).

Thorpe v. Housing Authority, 393 U.S. 268 (1969).

United States v. Riverside Bayview Homes, Inc., —— U.S. ——, 106 S. Ct. 455 (1985).

United States Trust Co. v. New Jersey, 431 U.S. 1 (1977).

Village of Belle Terre v. Borras, 416 U.S. 1 (1974).

Williamson County Regional Planning Commission v. Hamilton Bank, —— U.S. ——, 105 S. Ct. 3108 (1985).

Yick Wo v. Hopkins, 118 U.S. 356 (1886).

two persons unrelated by blood, adoption, or marriage. The Supreme Court upheld the constitutionality of the ordinance, noting that it did not involve any fundamental right but rather involved a type of legislative line-drawing that the court will accept if the law is not arbitrary and if it bears a rational relationship to a permissible state objective (*Village of Belle Terre* 1974).

The right to develop property is not a fundamental right and commercial developers are not a suspect classification (*Candid Enterprises, Inc.* 1985). Thus a linkage ordinance probably will survive an equal protection challenge on its face if the legislation bears a rational relationship to a legitimate government purpose. A developer could, however, challenge a linkage program as applied if program requirements are not extracted in a consistent manner from all developments that fall within the ordinance's parameters. The developer probably would win such a challenge if the linkage program were not uniformly administered.[20]

CONCLUSION

Assuming that linkage can be defended on legal grounds, the only task remaining is for the municipality to develop a program that will work politically and economically. Accomplishing that objective requires careful study and decision making and necessitates the successful completion of a series of tasks. The planner must do the following:

1. Understand the market. Carefully study the local commercial real estate market to determine whether it is strong enough to support a linkage program. Review the alternative methods for extracting "payments" to determine which will provide adequate funds over time. For example, should payments be on the basis of a fixed, up-front payment for each square foot of new space or should there be a lease tax or a combination of both? What are the special or locational advantages and disadvantages of downtown development? What types of tenants are attracted to downtown? What gap, if any, exists between downtown and suburban rent levels? Consider the types of exactions to be extracted and the incentives to be granted to the developer with an eye toward ensuring that both the public and the developer benefit. Consider whether the various payment options should be in kind or in cash, or if they should be public–private joint ventures. The objective is to provide developers with flexibility that may encourage participation in the program. Can the municipality tap other revenue sources (for example, special assessments or benefit districts, sales taxes, or employment taxes) to achieve the same objective or to provide a more stable long-term source of funds from a wider tax base?

2. Identify and analyze the downside risks of a linkage program. Carefully consider whether adoption of a linkage ordinance will create a fluctuation or temporary halt in downtown development. Do the gains from linkage contributions outweigh possible reductions in future direct and indirect tax revenues from proposed commercial projects that developers might elect not to build?

3. Development strategy. Develop a strategy designed to maximize the municipality's ability to defend linkage. Obtain a consensus regarding the best approach to solve the problems. Establish a task force that involves all of the affected interest groups but do not start building coalitions until all the facts about target populations are in hand and you have determined the best economical way of addressing the problem.

4. Provide a solid legal foundation. Determine whether new enabling legislation is absolutely necessary. If it is, decide if there is a reasonable probability of getting it passed. Be prepared to demonstrate that there is an actual linkage between the need being addressed and commercial development. Quantify the need, calculate the proportionate need attributable to the development, and evaluate the impact of the development on revenue sources. Earmark all funds collected through linkage to ensure that they actually are spent to achieve the stated objective. Establish the basis on which the municipal authority should enact a linkage ordinance.

5. Prepare a back-up program. Recognize that a linkage ordinance may not withstand political or legal challenges. Do not assume that you are going to be successful in defending your program, despite the hard work and careful thought that preceded it. Develop alternative solutions (for example, a system of voluntary contributions by developers or joint ventures involving the private and the public sector) to achieve program needs. Remember the golden rule of good planning: You are operating within a dynamic system and therefore must constantly monitor, review, and modify the program.

Notes

1. Shreveport, Philadelphia, Detroit, Atlanta, Boston, and Washington, D.C., for example, have linked project approval and/or financing assistance with the creation of employment opportunities for city residents and minorities. Los Angeles allowed a developer to construct a $1.9 billion office-commercial complex in return for construct-ing a new art museum and subsequently established a Downtown Cultural Trust Fund, using contributions from developers, that is to be used to develop and refurbish cultural facilities and to sponsor cultural events, including live performances in the downtown area and a biennial arts festival. Addressing yet another need, the cities of Concord and San Francisco, California—after first determining that the growth in their employment bases created, and thus was linked to, an increased demand for child day care—enacted ordinances that extract space and/or fees from developers to support child care services and facilities. (See Achtenberg 1984 for a comparative summary of housing impact mitigation and linkage programs in effect or under consideration in several cities.)

2. As evidence of the political significance of linkage, every candidate for the office of mayor of Boston endorsed some form of linkage program during the 1984 election campaign.

3. See Porter (1985) and Keating (1986) for a general discussion of the potential fiscal impact of a linkage program and the economic factors that a planner must consider when designing a linkage program.

4. For additional discussions of the legal issues that linkage programs raise, see Bosselman and Stroud (1985); Major 1987.

5. Extracting certain "payments" from subdividers in the form of an exaction is a land use technique that has evolved, both in terms of the objectives being addressed and the form of the "payment" extracted. The first land use regulations designed to shift the burden of financing the cost of capital improvements to the developer required that the developer dedicate land for municipal improvements such as streets. As the pace of development increased, so too did the use of development exactions. Thus, rather than simply obtaining the land needed for subdivision improvements, cities began to require that the developers actually construct basic infrastructure facilities or pay a fee in lieu thereof. Finally, although initially limited to infrastructure requirements, as courts began to broaden the concept of the public welfare, cities began to extract design requirements, and other amenities in return for necessary building permits, variances, and zoning approvals. Thus exactions now address many needs and occur in many forms, including land dedications and in-lieu and impact fees. (See Curtin 1986; Morgan, et al. 1986 for more extensive discussion of legal issues raised by exactions, dedications, in-lieu, and impact fees.)

6. For a general discussion, see Connors and McNamara (1987). Judicial recognition that such a program constitutes a regulation rather than a tax, however,

is far from guaranteed. On April 16, 1987, for example, the Supreme Court of the state of Washington ruled that the Housing Preservation Ordinance of the city of Seattle imposed an unconstitutional tax on a limited number of property owners. The ordinance in question required that any property owner who wanted to demolish low-income housing units and convert the property to a non-residential use obtain a housing demolition license. In order to obtain the license, the property owner not only had to give current tenants relocation notice and assistance but also had to replace a specified percentage of the lost low-income housing with other suitable housing or, in lieu thereof, contribute to the city's low-income housing replacement fund. The court rejected the city's argument that the ordinance was a regulation and not a tax. Noting that state statutes precluded cities from levying "any tax, fee or charge, either direct or indirect. . .on the development, subdivision, classification, or reclassification of land," Wash. Rev. Code §82.02.020, the court concluded that shifting the social costs of development to the developer is a tax and absent specific legislative pronouncement authorizing it". . .[the tax] is impermissible and invalid." *San Telmo Associates* v. *City of Seattle*, 108 Wash. 2d 20, _____ P. 2d _____ (1987).

7. There is, for example, legal precedent supporting the enactment of a linkage ordinance. As Mr. Justice Douglas once stated, "[t]he misery of housing may despoil a community as an open sewer may ruin a river." *Berman*, 348 U.S. at 32.

8. Abutting landowners recently asked the Massachusetts courts to rule that city approvals of an amendment to Massachusetts General Hospital's Development Plan was invalid and to declare the Boston linkage statute null and void. Historically, Massachusetts courts have long recognized the supremacy of the Commonwealth's General Laws over local legislation. As a result, when asked to defend a zoning ordinance, a Massachusetts municipality must point to an express delegation of authority from the commonwealth that allows it to exercise its police power in the manner being challenged. The general laws of the commonwealth grant to cities and towns the power to grant special permits increasing the permissible density of population or intensity of use within a proposed development if the petitioner or applicant, as a condition of the permit, provides housing to persons of low and moderate income. Mass. Gen. L. §9-40A. The city of Boston, however, received its power to adopt a zoning code pursuant to its own enabling statute that does not include specific authorization for the type of linkage exaction imposed by the Boston ordinance. The Supreme

Judicial Court, the commonwealth's highest court, overturned the lower court decision in favor of the abutting owners and dismissed the claim as one that was not yet ripe for adjudication because the plaintiffs had not demonstrated that enactment of the ordinance injured them or threatened them with injury. Thus, the higher court did not reach the issue of whether or not Boston lacked statutory authority to adopt an ordinance imposing developmental impact project exactions upon developers. *Bonan* v. *City of Boston*, 398 Mass. 315, 496 N.E. 2d 640 (1986). Recognizing that lack of authority to enact the program could be a fatal defect, the city of Boston has sought the enactment of special legislation granting to the city the authority to enact a linkage ordinance.

9. In Connecticut, for example, during the 1987 legislative session, the chairpersons of the Joint Planning and Development Committee introduced legislation specifically enabling cities and towns exercising zoning powers—whether pursuant to the Zoning Enabling Statute or pursuant to the power to regulate land use authorized by the provisions of a special act—to enact linkage ordinances. *An Act Concerning the Municipal Response to Certain Problems Relative to Proposed Development, Committee Bill No. 258.* The bill, although reported favorably out of committee, was recommitted to the committee where it effectively died on the conclusion of the legislative session.

10. As Justice Brandeis once noted, "[t]he Court will not pass upon a constitutional question although properly presented by the record, if there is also present some other ground upon which the case may be disposed of. . . . Thus, if a case can be decided on either of two grounds, one involving a constitutional question, the other a question of statutory construction or general law, the Court will decide only the latter." *Ashwander* v. *Tennessee Valley Authority* 297 U.S. 288, 347 (1936).

11. In addition, a challenge to a linkage ordinance may allege that the ordinance violates the contract clause of the United States Constitution. *See, e.g., Kaiser Development Co.* v. *City and County of Honolulu* (Civil No. 84-0389) (D.C. Ha.); *Keystone Bituminous Coal Assn.* v. *De Benedictis*, _____ U.S. _____, 107 S. Ct. Constitution provides that "[n]o State shall. . .pass any law impairing the obligation of contracts. . ." Thus, the contract clause prohibits the use of legislative authority to impair contractual obligations. *Allied Structural Steel Co.* v. *Spannaus*, 438 U.S. 234, 244 (1978); *Thorpe* v. *Housing Authority*, 393 U.S. 268, 278 (1969). It applies to government contracts, *United States Trust Co.* v. *New Jersey*, 431 U.S. 1 (1977), as well as private contracts. *Allied Structural Steel*, 438 U.S. at 234. Although the contract impairment prohibition does not cover the actions of

administrative or executive officials, *New Orleans Waterworks Co. v. Louisiana Sugar Refining Co.*, 125 U.S. 18, 30 (1888), it does apply to state laws and to legislative-type actions, such as municipal ordinances, *Atlantic Coast Line R.R. Co. v. City of Goldsboro*, 232 U.S. 548, 555 (1914), or administrative rulings enacted under delegated state powers *Midland Co. v. Kansas City Power & Light Co.*, 300 U.S. 109 (1937).

In a recent case, the developer and landowner plaintiffs argued that 1982 amendments to the city of Honolulu's general plan, the enactment of the Honolulu development plan, withdrawal of the right to build a resort, and other acts of the city violated their constitutional rights under the contract clause. In granting the city's motion for summary judgment with respect to the contract clause issues, the court recognized the distinction between the impairment of contract and action that may result in one party breaching an existing contract. *Kaiser Development Co. v. City and County of Honolulu* (Civil No. 84-0389) (D.C. Ha.). Thus the contract clause does not bar governmental action that affects the profitability of contracts, even where the effect reduces the likelihood that one or more of the parties will perform their obligations under the contract. *Metropolitan St. Louis Sewer District v. Ruckelshaus*, 590 F. Supp. 385, 389 (E.D. Mo. 1984).

The Supreme Court has set out a three-part test for determining whether or not regulations constitute an impairment of contract. The court must first determine whether the law or regulation in question operates as a substantial impairment of a contractual relationship. Thus, adoption of a linkage ordinance may make a particular development less profitable, but, as long as it does not impair the obligations between contracting parties, the ordinance does not violate the contract clause. If a court should determine that the ordinance does substantially impair a contractual obligation, it must then consider whether or not there is a significant and legitimate public purpose behind the regulation and whether the effect of the ordinance on the rights and responsibilities of the parties to the contract is appropriate to the public purpose justifying the regulation. *Keystone Bituminous Coal Assn.*, 107 S. Ct. at 1252-53.

A developer also may base a contract clause claim upon reasoning similar to that presented by the plaintiffs in the Honolulu case and argue that a prior approval from, or agreement with, the city precludes adoption of a linkage ordinance. The Supreme Court, however, has established clearly that the contract clause does not require that a state adhere to a contract through which it assigned an essential attribute of its sovereignty. *United States Trust Co.*, 431 U.S. at 23. As the Court noted, "[i]t is often stated that

'the legislature cannot bargain away the police power of a State.'" *Id.*, citing, *Stone v. Mississippi*, 101 U.S. 814, 817 (1880). Thus, a municipality generally cannot bind itself with regard to future zoning or other legislative decisions. *See, e.g., Beckmann v. Teaneck Township*, 6.N.J. 530, 79 A.2d 301 (1951); *Louisville v. Fiscal Court*, 623 S.W. 2d 219, 224 (Ky. 1981); *Barton v. Atkinson*, 228 Ga. 733, 187 S.E. 2d 835, 843 (1972). *See* also Callies (1987) for a discussion of the factors that a court may consider when asked to rule upon the validity of a development agreement pursuant to which a municipality appears to have contracted away its police power.

12. In both 1985 and 1986, the Supreme Court accepted cases that raised issues involving temporary takings and the payment of money damages in lieu of invalidation of the legislative enactment only to sidestep the issues raised by deciding the cases on procedural grounds. *Williamson County Regional Planning Commission v. Hamilton Bank*, _____ U.S. _____, 105 S. Ct. 3108 (1985); *McDonald, Sommer, and Frates v. Yolo County*, _____ U.S. _____, 106 S. Ct. 2561 (1986). Unfortunately, the Williamson and McDonald decisions clearly indicate that the Court will not listen to any taking argument until the "injured party" has exhausted all state procedures available for obtaining compensation. Thus, obtaining ultimate judicial resolution of taking issues is a tedious, costly, and time-consuming process.

13. One commentator, after noting the similarities between *Keystone Bituminous Assn.* and *Pennsylvania Coal*, suggested that the difference in outcome was due not to differences in the facts or statutes but to a shift in societal values and to the fact that the Subsidence Act was "established with a better administrative record citing the public health, safety, and welfare concerns involved" (Curtin 1987, p. 17).

14. On June 9, 1987, the Court rendered the decision in yet another takings case. (*First English Evangelical Lutheran Church of Glendale v. County of Los Angeles* 1987.) The plaintiff church had developed 12 of 21 acres of land that it owned in a canyon located on the banks of Mill Creek in the Angeles National Forest as a camp, "Lutherglen," for handicapped children. In 1978, a flood destroyed the camp's buildings and in 1979, the county of Los Angeles adopted an interim ordinance prohibiting the construction or reconstruction of any building or structure in an interim flood protection area that included the land on which Lutherglen had stood. The church promptly sued the county alleging, among other counts, that the ordinance constituted a taking by overregulation. The California court of appeals, relying on a decision of the

California supreme court, held that money damages were not available for a temporary taking. Thus, the procedural posture of the case before the U.S. Supreme Court was such that the Court was not asked to decide whether or not a taking had actually occurred but rather to rule on the issue of the appropriate remedy when property is taken through land use regulation. The Supreme Court overruled the California court of appeals and held that damages, in the form of just compensation, should be paid to landowners whose property is taken, even only temporarily, by overregulation and remanded the decision for trial to decide whether or not there was a taking. Although the decision resolved a long-standing question regarding the availability of damages for temporary takings, it also raised new questions. The Court, itself, recognized that its holding would "undoubtedly lessen to some extent" the flexibility of land use planners and governing bodies when enacting land use regulations but noted that "[w]e limit our holding to the facts presented, and of course do not deal with the quite different questions that would arise in the case of normal delays in obtaining building permits, changes in zoning ordinances, variances and the like which are not before us" (*Id.* at 2389).

15. In *Nollan*, the commission argued that the public purposes advanced by the lateral access condition included protecting the public's ability to see the beach, overcoming the "psychological barrier" to using the beach created by shorefront development, and preventing congestion on public beaches. The Court, for the purpose of rendering its decision, assumed that the commission could deny the Nollans their permit if their house (either alone or by reason of the cumulative impact of area shoreline construction) would substantially impede those purposes, unless the denial would interfere so drastically with the Nollan's use of their property as to constitute a taking. Although the Court specifically stated that, given those assumptions, the commission could have attached some conditions (for example, height limitations) to the permit or even require that the Nollans provide a viewing spot on their property for the public in order to protect the public's ability to see the beach, it rejected the argument that providing lateral access across the Nollan's beach to members of the public who were already on public beaches advanced those interests.

16. Although Fifth Amendment procedural due process protections do not apply to legislative decision making, there are indications that the traditional approach to legislative action may be weakening at the state level. For example, some states have passed "sunshine" laws designed to prevent certain procedural abuses that may occur during the legislative decision-making process. *See, e.g., Fla. Stat. Ann.* §286.011. However, as one commentator has noted, the trend is unclear at best (Hagman 1986, p. 299).

17. For example, Boston residents hold only 30 percent of the jobs in the city. "One More Blow for America's Cities" (Powell, Walsh, and Healy 1986, p. 31).

18. Kopelman and Merriam (1985) discuss the development of the regional general welfare concept and the tests employed by states to measure consistency with regional general welfare programs.

19. In recent years, the Supreme Court has occasionally used a middle ground standard, most typically in cases involving gender-based classifications. Under this medium-level standard, the court determines whether or not the purpose being advanced is substantially related to an important governmental interest.

20. Both the San Francisco and Boston linkage programs, for example, provide some opportunity for negotiation, and thus potentially are opening the door to equal protection challenges. There is legal precedent that suggests that distinctions drawn between parties negotiating with municipalities must satisfy the equal protection standard. One court, for example, has held that a city's denial of a request to vacate a street constituted a denial of equal protection. The city charter provided that when the city vacated a street, the party to whom the property reverted must pay the city just compensation. Following negotiations, the developer agreed to pay $1.00 for each square foot of street that was vacated—even though that was more than twice the amount previously charged per square foot—and to convey to the city an easement over a 20-foot strip of property owned by the developer. The city, however, wanted to acquire the rights to subsurface geothermal wells and therefore wanted the strip dedicated to the city. In response to the developer's equal protection challenge, the city argued, among other things, that its desire to acquire the geothermal wells was rationally related to the vacation of its streets. The courts, however, concluded that there was no rational basis "for distinguishing between those seeking vacations of streets who own geothermal wells and those who do not...The distinction drawn...[between the developer] and others who secured vacations was not rationally related to any cognizable governmental interest in vacation and is precisely the sort of arbitrary discrimination proscribed by the equal protection clause." *Parks v. Watson*, 716 F.2d 646, 654-55 (9th Cir. 1983). In addition, although the Nollans did not challenge the actions of the California Coastal Commission on equal protection grounds when the Court rendered its decision in *Nollan*, it noted that:

If the Nollans were being singled out to bear the burden of California's attempt to remedy these problems, although they had not contributed to it more than other coastal landowners, the State's action, even if otherwise valid, might violate either the incorporated Takings Clause or the Equal Protection Clause. [*Nollan*, 107 S. Ct. at 3147 n. 4]

References

Achtenberg, Emily P. 1984. Housing Mitigation and Linkage Programs. Unpublished comparative summary prepared for Hartford Linkage Task Force. Jamaica Plain, Mass.

Bosselman, Fred P. 1985. Downtown Linkage. In *Downtown Linkages*, edited by Douglas Porter. Washington, D.C.: Urban Land Institute.

———— and Nancy E. Stroud. 1985. Mandatory Tithes: The Legality of Land Development Linkage. *Nova Law Journal* 9, 3: 381–412.

Callies, David L. 1987. Background Paper for Fees and Development Agreements. Paper prepared for the American Planning Association Conference on Land Use Law for Planners and Lawyers.

Connors, Donald L. and Catherine W. McNamara. 1987. Development Exactions: Attack and Defense. Paper prepared for 1987 American Planning Association Conference on Land Use Law for Planners and Lawyers.

Costonis, John J. 1984. Making Sense of the Taking Issue. In *1984 Zoning and Planning Law Handbook*, edited by J. Benjamin Gailey. New York: Clark Boardman Company.

Curtin, Daniel J., Jr. 1986. Dedications, Exactions, and in-Lieu Fees as a Land Use Planning Tool: The Inverse Condemnation-Taking Issue. Paper prepared for the 1986 Annual Conference of the National Institute of Municipal Law Officers.

————. 1987. Status of Exactions After *First Lutheran Church* and *Nollan* cases. Paper prepared for 1987 Annual Conference of Municipal Law Officers.

Hagman, Donald G. and Julian C. Juergensmeyer. 1986. *Urban Planning and Land Development Control Law*, 2d ed. Lawyer's edition. St. Paul, Minn.: West.

Karp, James P. 1979. Subdivision Exactions for Park and Open Space. *American Business Law Journal* 16, Winter: 227–94.

Keating, W. Dennis. 1986. Linking Downtown Development to Broader Community Goals. *Journal of the American Planning Association* 52, 2: 133–41.

Kopelman, Steven G. and Dwight H. Merriam. 1985. Regional General Welfare: The End of a Trend? *Fifteenth Annual Proceedings of the Southwestern Legal Foundation Institute on Planning, Zoning, and Eminent Domain*. Albany, N.Y.: Matthew Bender.

L.A. Exactions for Culture. 1986a. *Zoning News* February: 2–3.

Linkage Fees for Day Care. 1986b. *Zoning News* August: 4.

Major, Linda Dodd. 1987. Linkage of Housing and Commercial Development: The Legal Issues. *Real Estate Law Journal* 15: 328–52.

Morgan, Terry D., James B. Duncan, and Bruce McClendon. 1986. Drafting Impact Fees. Part 1: A Legal Foundation; Part 2: Technical Planning and Administrative Guidelines. *Zoning and Planning Law Report* 9, 7/8: 50–62.

National Institute of Municipal Law Officers. Committee on Consumer and Tenant Protection. 1986. *Annual Report:* 10–12. Washington, D.C.: NIMLO.

Porter, Douglas R., ed. 1985. *Downtown Linkages*. Washington, D.C.: Urban Land Institute.

Powell, Stewart, Maureen Walsh, and Melissa Healy. 1986. One More Blow for America's Cities. *U.S. News and World Report* 101, 5 (September 29): 31.

Rohan, Patrick J. 1987. *Zoning and Land Use Controls*. New York: Matthew Bender.

Steinbach, Carol. 1986. Tapping Private Resources. *National Journal* 18, 17: 993.

20

Flexible Linkage in Berkeley: Development Mitigation Fees

Neil S. Mayer
Bill Lambert

Mitigation fees are a form of linkage fee used in California. Berkeley's mitigation fees are negotiated for all nonresidential downtown projects, but these fees also must show a legally defensible relationship to the projects' impacts.

The city of Berkeley has been at work putting in place an extensive menu of such fees, based on careful analysis of project impacts and the possibilities for offsetting them without making responsible development economically infeasible. The effort concentrated first on case-by-case analysis and negotiations for projects already in the city's review pipeline and then on establishing permanent standards for future projects.

An array of conceptual and practical issues arises in actually applying the broad concept of mitigation fees to specific types of project impacts and then to local circumstances. The authors of this chapter have had responsibility, within Berkeley's Office of Economic Development (OED), for establishing mitigation fees as a part of the city's project review process. The chapter draws on that experience and on assessment of related efforts elsewhere to:

• Identify the local economic and political

factors that affect the ability of a city to establish mitigation fees.

• Describe a menu of items to be mitigated by fees and other actions and the ways such a menu may be assembled.

• Discuss the critical analytic tools that must be used to establish fees in a credible way and to negotiate with individual developers or set permanent standards.

• Show how to compute project impacts and corresponding appropriate impact fees for major components of the mitigation menu.

• Examine the central role of targeting project opportunities to local residents in establishing a satisfactory mitigation package.

• Assess the process and product of negotiating mitigation fees in two pioneering individual cases.

• Analyze the issues involved in moving from ad hoc negotiations to systematic fee systems.

A PROPER SETTING

The city of Berkeley has several key dimensions that make it particularly well suited for the development of a program of systematic mitigations of the impacts of new large-scale projects.

These conditions appear to be important in determining potential for successful mitigation efforts in other locations as well.

Berkeley has a strong market for research and development and office space. We concentrate throughout on the downtown office market—and mitigations for developments in that area—in order to simplify discussion. Berkeley's downtown has experienced a modest boom in office construction over the past five years, adding space at an annual rate exceeding 5 percent of the existing office stock. A generally strong economy driven by the university's presence, Berkeley's outstanding location and transportation system within the Bay Area, high resident incomes, and other postive factors have contributed to the rapid absorption of new space. Even with tax-benefit-induced development producing office space surpluses throughout the region, Berkeley's office vacancy rate has remained in the 5 to 9 percent range, less than half of that of major surrounding areas such as San Francisco, Oakland, and burgeoning suburban centers. The strong market for space of course means that developers are eager to build and have some willingness to accommodate city government concerns in order to gain approval for their projects. It means also that the city perceives itself as able to obtain concessions, rather than needing to offer them.

A second key condition in Berkeley is the high value community members place on environmental protection. Many residents have been concerned about the traffic and other impacts of recent new development on surrounding neighborhoods and on the downtown itself. These specific concerns build on a strong continuing interest in ecologically sound, human-scaled patterns of land use. Many citizens are eager to limit total development, to make sure that its negative environmental impacts are mitigated, and to support those elected political leaders who pursue such policies. The importance of environmental issues provides for a willingness to reject development projects unless they offer good benefits and offset their environmental costs—a willingness of which developers are aware.

A third condition in support of a mitigation program is the readily demonstrable need to offset growing problems that new development is seen to exacerbate. Berkeley has a very tight and expensive housing market, and as a result, has experienced in recent years sharp losses in the economic and ethnic diversity that its citizens want to retain. Gentrification has changed many neighborhoods. Workers in new buildings clearly add to the current competition for housing and new workers with lower incomes would have great difficulty affording Berkeley housing without assistance. It is easy then for citizens and policymakers to identify a need for new office development to pay to support affordable housing, by far the most expensive mitigation item. The shortage of child care services—affordable or otherwise—similarly is apparent and has a parallel mitigation implication. Recent losses of blue collar and some other entry-level jobs also heighten concerns about loss of opportunity for people in Berkeley of limited means, making the targeting of jobs in new projects to local residents in need of work another social mitigation concern. (Although it is unclear how much of other job loss results from office development, the concern that any development provide good new opportunities is high).

Tight municipal fiscal conditions, generated particularly by California's Proposition 13 spending limits and by Reagan-era federal cutbacks, make it clear that new development projects must pay their full marginal costs, and not leave impacts on ordinary public infrastructure and services or on social needs for housing and child care to be paid out of other general revenues. The readily apparent social needs, coupled with limited governmental fiscal capacity, create substantial pressure to establish a broad range of mitigations beyond those corresponding to environmental concerns.

A condition supporting a mitigation program is the process and policies of development review and approval in Berkeley. Any project of significant scale requires discretionary approval by the the city's Board of Adjustments. Projects may be disapproved on broad grounds of negative impact even if they fall within existing zoning standards for scale, height, setback, and so forth. This offers an opportunity to impose mitigations on an ad hoc basis as a condition for project approval. The active participation of neighboring residents in public review processes by the board, and by the city council on appeal, encourages setting of mitigation conditions regarding environmental concerns such as traffic and parking.

The present city council majority was elected on a platform notably including limitations on development and making sure that any buildings deliver major benefits and offset their costs. The council has keen interests in both the social and environmental areas where mitigations are being sought. It came to power partly in reaction to its opponents' approval of a large office building that in the view of many negatively impacted adjacent neighborhoods without delivering sufficient benefits. The current council established the city's new Office of Economic Development and assigned it the task of preparing mitigation standards and negotiating with individual developers. The council is committed to a policy of limiting new development and gaining major net benefits for each square foot approved.

In sum, there is a strong market for Berkeley office space, tight control over its development, and a limited political willingness to allow its construction. As a result, obtaining approval to build has a high economic value to potential developers making them more willing to provide mitigations. The city has readily identifiable needs—both socioeconomic and environmental—that are exacerbated by new development and call out for offsetting mitigation. And it has added the technical capability to assess project impacts and the funds and actions needed to compensate for them and to negotiate for those corresponding mitigations. Based on our experience in Berkeley and observation of other localities, these conditions are critical to the establishment of a strong system of mitigations for major development both in our city and elsewhere.

THE MENU

Berkeley's mitigation program includes a long list of components that have been addressed several at a time but not all at once in other localities. Interest in and impetus for these items have come from a variety of sources.

Housing and Child Care. Current city planning commissioners have a high degree of policy interest in the mitigation field. This interest arises in significant part out of the commission's responsibility for setting zoning standards, which currently are under major revision for the downtown and other parts of the city and may well in the future contain mitigation provisions in ordinance form. Commissioners are aware of a few other cities' actions to mandate that new projects offset their impacts on already unmet demands for affordable housing and child care. They also have taken substantial responsibility as a commission for developing other programs to protect and expand the affordable housing supply. The planning commission directed the Office of Economic Development to include housing and child care provisions in the mitigation package. It is important to note that some other housing activists prefer little or no office development with potential sites reserved instead for housing.

Transportation and Public Art. Each of these areas has a substantial constituency of its own, represented in part by the city's transportation commission and the civic arts commission. A major push for funding for alternatives to the single-passenger auto resulted in city council adoption of a transportation services fee to be paid by new office developments, prior to consideration of a full mitigation package. The current broader mitigation effort will expand on that fee. The civic arts commission developed its own draft 1-percent-for-art ordinance (percent of construction costs) and asked for its inclusion in a future mitigation package.

Employment Targeting. Impetus for programs to ensure that project jobs go to residents in need of work comes from several sources. The city council, the board of adjustments, and the planning commission have indicated informally their interest in reviewing the Office of Economic Development's work program and in mandating job targeting in specific projects that have come before them since OED began creating the targeting programs. Members of the city's low-income, particularly minority, communities have taken interest in the potential to target job opportunities in new projects.

OED has set targeted job generation as its prime goal. Job generation and employment targeting overlap closely, because OED recognizes— as do others—that the job needs of lower-income residents will be met principally outside their immediate neighborhoods in places such as the downtown.

Public Works and Public Safety. The city manager's office, with its responsibility for assembling a workable municipal budget, is concerned that new buildings pay their own way in at least meeting their marginal costs for standard services. Mitigation payments, added to general taxes, are a way of ensuring that result.

Payments in Lieu of Taxes. A special factor in Berkeley is that offices leased to the university by private developers are exempt from property taxes. Such leasing is a common occurrence given the immediate proximity of Berkeley's downtown to both the university campus and the offices of the statewide university system. The city council, often at odds with the university regarding the latter's special powers, seeks a policy to require that offsetting payments from developers of such leasing occurs.

Of importance to other cities is not so much the specifics of these sources of impetus— though they are no doubt illustrative—but that each component of the mitigation package does arise from a constituency. Given competing demands on projects and limits on the total willingness and ability to contribute to public goals, components with no voice are likely to receive little mitigation attention. This is somewhat less true in Berkeley where there is the goal of developing and maintaining a complete overall package. But, as is discussed later, without participation by spokespeople for these component interests, even a project with a strong mitigation package may be disapproved in response to other legitimate concerns.

TOOLS FOR ANALYSIS AND NEGOTIATION

Berkeley currently is negotiating mitigations on an ad hoc basis for individual projects and is in the process of developing standards that it can apply on a more systematic basis to buildings of specified size, use, and location. For both ad hoc and systematic approaches, two types of analyses have proved critical. Our experience, and external conditions, make it clear that these same analyses ultimately will be critical in other localities as well.

Project Impact

Detailed analysis of expected project impacts and the dollars and/or other direct actions necessary to mitigate them is first. It is not immediately apparent what the appropriate fee is to mitigate the pressures a new office building will place on the availability of affordable housing or on the maintenance of existing infrastructure. But, as the next section will show, it is possible to make reasonable approximations of first the impetus and then the costs of offsetting them.

At least for each major mitigation component, we estimate the number of "impacters" generated by a specific development (workers, car trips, etc.), the effects they would produce that will require mitigation (housing demand, requirements for city services, etc.), necessary actions to compensate for those effects, and dollar costs to city or developer to carry out the actions. The models that represent this process of approximation are set up as computer programs to allow efficient analysis of further projects and to make adjustments to key parameters as desired.

A credible means of estimating impacts and corresponding mitigations is necessary for several reasons. Legal challenges where mitigations have become substantial in amount are growing. A primary element of successful legal defense has been the ability to show a reasonable relationship between fees charged and costs incurred by a municipality and its citizenry. In California, numerous bills have been introduced in the legislature to require that any development fees established demonstrate this relationship to costs; eventually some verson is likely to pass.

In case-by-case negotiations, it is important to be able to show the developer a rationale for the mitigations being sought. The developer then is forced to recognize that there are real impacts that local decision makers will likely want to see offset—that negotiation is not simply on a city-wants-large-payments, developer-wants-small, basis. If, when a project eventually goes to the board of adjustments for consideration, the developer has not agreed to a mitigation package that OED considers acceptable, it is important to have an understandable rationale to present to decision makers in the face of potential developer protests. Similarly, in setting systematic standards for future projects, it is significant in gaining public approval for their adoption to show that mitigations approximate the costs of offsetting actual impacts. Mitigations may otherwise be successfully attacked as excessive or insufficient by prodevelopment and antidevelopment constituencies.

Project Financial Feasibility

The second critical form of analysis in setting up a mitigations program is assessment of project financial feasibility, with mitigations included in project cost. In Berkeley, OED set up conventional project pro formas both for individual project negotiations and for analyzing potential systematic standards. To give our models credibility and accuracy, we met with members of the development community to help establish key parameters such as construction costs and leasing rates.

In case-by-case negotiations, we need to know from our own independent analysis what levels of mitigations are consistent with reasonable project rates of return. We request developers' pro formas, check parameters, and perform our own analyses. We then have the accurate information about the developer's true feasibility cutoff line; such information is necessary to negotiate the best possible mitigation package without driving off a potentially desirable project. Since it is impossible to know each key parameter with certainty, we find it valuable to carry out analyses of the sensitivity of rates of return to variation in the parameters. Even more useful are sensitivity analyses for varying levels of mitigation payment. These let us assess the developer's change in return rate, given a change—addition or reduction—in the mitigation package. Having a standard pro forma in place on computer is key to such analysis. Note that a city's staff must have a reasonable level of sophistication about project economics to use pro forma analysis successfully. For example, developers will want to draw attention to their first-year return in the form of cash earned over cash invested. More meaningful analysis is of course a multiyear internal (or similar) rate of return, reflecting both net cash flows over time and expected capital gains.

In setting permanent mitigation standards, it is equally important to perform feasibility analysis. Berkeley, at least, wants to offset its costs as fully as possible in the mitigation package. If a city seeks only a small payment for one or two mitigation components, as many have done, it need not concern itself with detailed assessments of project finance. But our estimates show that full-cost mitigations are sufficiently high to have major feasibility impacts. We necessarily use the pro forma tool to balance the level of mitigation that is needed with what is possible. We ultimately will tell the decision makers who will act on permanent standards that the proposals before them represent some percentage (100 percent for some types of projects, less for others) of full mitigation cost, lowered from 100 percent as necessary in order to retain project feasibility. They will have to decide whether projects' job and general tax and business activity benefits warrant any shortfall from full mitigation.

FORMULATING THE MITIGATION PACKAGE

Several cities that currently use mitigation measures as a means to offset development impacts rely on a rather arbitrary dollars-per-square-foot calculation to determine the ultimate fee. In our efforts to rationalize the fee derivation process, to strengthen both our legal basis and our negotiating position with developers, we saw straight per-square-foot calculation as inappropriate in most cases. Although some of the components—public art, payments in lieu of taxes, and transportation—are based on direct calculations from physical parameters of a project, the remainder of the mitigation categories use as a starting basis the number of added employees that the project will generate. Those employees are seen to produce impacts on demand for various services that must be met in

Figure 20–1. Steps in Estimating Housing and Child Care Fees

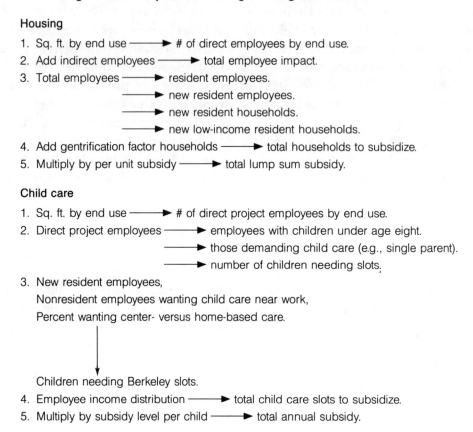

Housing

1. Sq. ft. by end use ⟶ # of direct employees by end use.
2. Add indirect employees ⟶ total employee impact.
3. Total employees ⟶ resident employees.
   ⟶ new resident employees.
   ⟶ new resident households.
   ⟶ new low-income resident households.
4. Add gentrification factor households ⟶ total households to subsidize.
5. Multiply by per unit subsidy ⟶ total lump sum subsidy.

Child care

1. Sq. ft. by end use ⟶ # of direct project employees by end use.
2. Direct project employees ⟶ employees with children under age eight.
   ⟶ those demanding child care (e.g., single parent).
   ⟶ number of children needing slots.
3. New resident employees,
   Nonresident employees wanting child care near work,
   Percent wanting center- versus home-based care.

   Children needing Berkeley slots.
4. Employee income distribution ⟶ total child care slots to subsidize.
5. Multiply by subsidy level per child ⟶ total annual subsidy.

part by public action. The focus of the discussion immediately is translated to human terms, then to human needs, and finally to the cost of meeting them. Figure 20–1 summarizes the steps of that calculation.

To determine the number of employees in any project, we divide the amount of leasable space in various end uses by the average number of square feet per employee in that end-use category. An office building, a retail development, and a manufacturing plant all of equal size would produce considerably different levels of impacts due to their differences in employees per square feet.

We then calculate the actual demand or use that might result from each of these end-user employee groups for the specific mitigation component at issue. This is best illustrated by examples. We look here at housing and child care mitigations for an office-retail mixed-use development. After we estimate the numbers of office workers and retail employees based on project size, we add a specific number of spin-off jobs, or indirect employees—those additional workers, hired in other local businesses as a result of project businesses and project employees spending their earnings in Berkeley. Some of both the project and indirect employees will live in Berkeley, and a deduction is made for them. For housing mitigation, our concern is only with impacts of new workers who choose to reside in Berkeley. Thus, a further reduction is made in the estimated housing demand to reflect only the percentage of local workers residing locally (census as source). For child care, we are concerned about demands generated both by resident workers and by nonresident workers who seek child care near their workplace. We use national and local statistics to determine for each employee group the percentage who will seek child care, based on key parameters such as number of single parents and number of children at ages needing child care. We then apply data on proportions of parents seeking home-based and center-based care, and care in proximity to work versus proximity to home, to the total seeking child care, to determine new demand for center-based care within Berkeley. Depending on the age mix of the children, the demand can be broken down further into infant/toddler care, preschool care, and latch-key programs.

The data and the formulas thus far concern themselves with numbers of employees needing housing or child care services. A conversion must be made at this point to *households* to allow consideration of households' ability to pay for services without aid. Local census data can provide the average number of workers per household, children per household, and ages of children to produce this conversion.

No city can or should assist and subsidize all project employees' households who might need child care services or housing (or other services). For each isolated service need, our focus in Berkeley is on only those low- or very low-income households that need special assistance. Within each of the end-use employ-

ment categories (office, retail, manufacturing) different household income structures exist. We apply appropriate income distributions for each employment category to the total number of the category's households seeking housing or child care in Berkeley as the result of a new project, to establish households in need of aid—isolating the number of households that are at or below certain household low-income levels (using 80 percent of the county's median income). It is these households' needs that mitigation fees should, ideally, be sufficient to meet.

In the housing area, we made one further refinement. Because of Berkeley's tight and competitive housing market, there is a great deal of community concern over loss of racial and economic diversity due to rising housing prices. Our housing demand formula also compensates for this gentrification factor by assuming that a set proportion of employees from all income levels will buy down and hence compete with current residents of lower income levels, adding to the demand in need of mitigation. The actual mitigation demands created by this gentrification effect are small given our assumptions about the amount of buydown, but the political concern by community constituencies is not. And the actual effects in the housing market may in fact exceed the rough guesses we have used to date. Further analysis is needed.

Once we compute the number of households in need of assistance, the final step in establishing mitigation needs is to estimate the cost of assisting each one. For a housing mitigation, we estimate the cost of constructing a new apartment unit of modest size in Berkeley and then the annual cost of amortizing its mortgage and paying for its operation. We assume a lower income household could pay 30 percent of its income for rent. Using these figures, we obtain the amount of a one-time lump sum capital subsidy that would be sufficient to make the remaining annual apartment cost match the household's contribution toward rent. That lump sum is the per-household subsidy that we multiply by the number of impacted lower income households to determine a project's housing mitigation fee.

For child care, we estimate the cost per child to construct a child care facility and multiply it by the total number of children needing care to establish a lump sum mitigation. We also analyze the difference between what lower income households could pay annually for child care (using state of California program guidelines) and the Berkeley market rate. We multiply this difference by the number of child-care-impacted lower income households for a given project to determine a permanent annual child care subsidy.

An important aspect of a number of our mitigation measures is the developer's option to carry out mitigating actions instead of paying fees, either on-site or at an approved off-site location. The direct action and on-site options often are preferable for both the city and the developer. From the public viewpoint, it is considerably more cost effective for the developer to construct, say, residential units on-site than to pay the city, which must in turn locate land and carry out a separate project. From the developer's viewpoint, a more valuable and marketable property results if at least certain mitigation components, such as public art or child care, are included as part of the overall site amenities. As the architect for a project currently in negotiations states, "We'd much rather invest the money in an enhanced project than turn it over to the city." The city therefore sets

alternative standards, specifying the number of housing units, child care slots, and so forth and adding the pattern of prices at which they should be provided. Developers then can choose the direct delivery alternative.

After determining a project's mitigation fees and on-site developer actions, the OED gives careful consideration to the pay-in schedule. The fees are either start-up or construction fees to produce a specific tangible structure (artwork, housing, child care center, infrastructure), or ongoing annual fees to subsidize or support continuing operations of a program such as subsidized child care slots, alternative transportation programs, or additional fire department services.

Too many payments up front pose the greatest threat to project feasibility. We allow even some of the lump sum fees to be paid over several years as a project is completed, fills up, obtains permanent financing, etc. Too many delayed payments could pose collection problems for the municipality. Our legal staff now is developing a contract format that will bind the developer to ongoing payments through the city's ability to place a lien against the subject property in the event of payment default.

The complexity of this entire mitigation-setting process actually offers an important advantage. It makes the balancing of mitigation needs and project feasibility easier. To some extent, it is possible to maintain the desired level of mitigation fee and accommodate project feasibility by manipulating the payment or action schedule for the multiple mitigations.

THE CRITICAL ROLE OF EMPLOYMENT TRAINING

One of the most important elements of mitigation agreements now being sought from developers in Berkeley is a strong provision for the hiring of target population groups. Specifically, developers are asked to commit to participation in a first-source hiring program. Under first source, when a job opening occurs in an approved project, the employer notifies the employment coordinator in the OED before seeking a worker from elsewhere. The city is allowed a very short period to provide the names of qualified candidates for the position, according to qualifications established by the employer. The employer is required to interview the city-provided candidates first, but retains complete control over whether to hire any of them or to seek workers elsewhere.

In Berkeley, first source applies to job openings in construction of new buildings, in operating them, and in permanent positions in the firms that locate within the new structures. The developer agrees to first source, requires construction contractors to participate, and includes participation as a provision in the lease of incoming tenants. The inclusion of permanent positions in tenant firms is critical to the long-term value of the program, providing job opportunities as expansion and turnover occur. A first-source program that applied only to construction jobs would be dependent on a continuing stream of new development to generate targeted job potential. Neither Berkeley's already built character nor its environmental sensitivity to new building would allow such an employment strategy to be of much continuing value.

When OED is notified of a job opening, it screens and refers candidates made known to it principally by city-funded job-training agencies. The great majority of candidates are economically disadvantaged and are, as a result, Berkeley residents in need of work. High per-

centages are minorities, women, and disabled people. Concentration is on entry-level and limited-skill positions, and certain very high skill jobs may be exempted for the first-source program entirely.

The developer of a large project already in the pipeline when OED was created was the first to be approached about first source and the first to agree. He initially was concerned that lenders might be wary of the provision covering tenant leases, but found that this was not an obstacle. Since then, first-source agreements have been obtained covering about 1,300 potential positions (construction and permanent) in projects requiring city approval or using city resources—not only in new private developments but with contractors hired to do city work, such as repairing city streets. While there is at times some initial resistance, particularly with respect to the tenant provision, city firmness and now the ability to refer to numerous existing agreements have been persuasive. It is equally important that what is ultimately asked of any employer is very little, namely, to take a first look at prescreened city-provided candidates and hire them only if the employer is satisfied with them. In the long run, the success of the program depends heavily on generating a service rather than a burden by supplying properly trained workers through the city's and other job training and placement programs. First source mandates only first notification and interviewing; actual placements depend on its positive employment service character.

The first-source requirement is not a mitigation in the now at least somewhat conventional sense of a payment to offset a cost generated by a new project. How does it tie in to other standards set for new development? In fact, in several ways its role is pivotal. First, new buildings are inherently of somewhat limited value if they do not do a good job of generating local employment for those in need. Given California's Proposition 13 in particular, their net fiscal contribution is limited. Local job provision is a critical part of a rationale to approve development at all, before any other mitigations are considered. In a relatively small city like Berkeley, 90 percent of job opportunities in new development may go to commuters from outside in the absence of any deliberate intervention. If few jobs go to meet local social concerns for employment opportunity, it is difficult to justify the local environmental costs of traffic, pollution, and so forth that can be reduced by other actions but hardly eliminated. Second, if few jobs in each project serve local needs, then many large projects are needed to have a substantial effect on unemployment problems. The cumulative environmental and social impacts become much more difficult to mitigate.

Third, the higher the proportion of new project employees coming from outside, the more expensive it is per square foot of new development to offset newly generated demands for affordable housing, child care, etc., sought in Berkeley by some of the new workers. Our financial feasibility analysis shows that, without an effective program to target jobs to people already living in the city, many projects may be unable to afford to mitigate their full impacts. The city (and developer) could then be faced with choosing no project or building one that imposes major net costs on local citizens and government. First source, or a similar job-targeting program, is thus central to making new development—any particular project—attractive and feasible fiscally, socially, and en-

vironmentally, even with other mitigation standards in place.

One further aspect of Berkeley's first source "mitigation" is worth noting. For any given project, the city estimates the cost of carrying out a first-source referral program, based on number of probable job openings, and asks the developer to help pay for staffing it. Proper first-source operation is a staff-intensive activity that could otherwise become a fiscal burden as it expands in coverage.

EXAMPLES OF NEGOTIATIONS

The first project in which the city of Berkeley and OED sought to obtain a full package of mitigations was a proposed six-story, 100,000-square-foot structure with ground floor retail uses and offices above. Call it Project A. Our experience with this project provided many important lessons for future work in Berkeley and should be illustrative of key issues and problems elsewhere.

Our dealings with this project were on an especially ad hoc basis; no systematic standards for mitigations had as yet been analytically developed, much less proposed or adopted publicly. In this context, detailed analysis of the project's impacts and the costs of offsetting them was extremely useful, providing a substantial basis for discussion with the developer and clear reference point for OED. We spent considerable time explaining to the developer the rationale for each mitigation component. We were fortunate that Project A's developer was very understanding of our intent and clearly wanted to find ways to meet community needs consistent with project feasibility. Our feasibility analysis, building from the developer's own costs statement and pro forma, did in fact prove accurate in assessing how large a total package we ultimately could obtain and allowed us to hold firmly to that package. A simple chart, relating expected rate of return to variations in initial lump sum payments or annual contributions of varying sizes, also proved highly valuable in making instant decisions in face-to-face negotiating sessions. Overall, extensive analytic effort, though time-consuming, more than proved its worth.

The negotiating took place in the context of OED confidence that the ultimate city decision makers would seek approximately the level of mitigations for which we as staff were pressing—that they would trust our judgment in making demands and expect the developer to respond. The developer too came to believe that the mitigations were crucial to approval of his project. Our experience with Project A and others makes clear that establishing that base of political support is crucial in obtaining a good package for the city. Another important aspect of expectation about policy decision making was the developer's belief about the potential for approval for projects other than his. The developer and his sources of financing have made clear that the fact that Berkeley is very unlikely to approve significant numbers of competing office projects in the future—and certainly none very quickly—is a key contributor to the economics of their project and to their willingness to pay mitigations to gain its approval. Concern for the environment here clearly is also good business for the city and for the developer.

Negotiations on Project A produced an array of mitigations and other actions that are likely unique in their scale relative to project size (with dollar outlays alone amounting to about $1.25 million in lump sum payments and more than $35,000 per year indefinitely into the future) and in the diversity of the menu. They demonstrate both the high level of costs that a project imposes on a community and the extent of the mitigations that can be obtained in a strong market for a project whose development costs total only $15.2 million.

Project A's mitigation menu included the following:

• Housing mitigation payments, totaling $888,000, for affordable housing provision off-site.

• Child care subsidies of $18,000 per year for the life of the building.

• One percent of construction cost ($99,600) to be dedicated to art in publicly accessible spaces in and around the building.

• A transportation services fee of $194,000 (one-time), or $19,400 per year for 30 years, to be used to encourage transportation alternatives; $20,000 to set up residential preferential parking near the building; and transit subsidies for all employees.

• Commitment to first-source hiring for construction, building management, and tenant enterprises, with placement services paid for in part by a $10,000 annual fee for the life of the building.

• A public works impact fee of $44,000.

• Agreement to reimburse the city for any tax losses due to leases of the building to the university.

The outcome of negotiations established strong precedents for both our case-by-case and later systematic mitigation requests and requirements. The developer agreed to the payments and actions and his financing sources concurred, making the strongest possible counterargument to contentions from other developers that our standards were unrealistic and infeasible, and strengthening our confidence in the quality of OED's analysis.

Other Elements

There is a sharply dissonant note in the process of Project A, however, which has its own important lessons. When the project went to the board of adjustments, with its hefty mitigation package, it was nonetheless rejected on grounds of negative impact on neighboring residents who turned out to oppose it. The city council, recognizing the precedent-setting value of its mitigation package, has since directed that Project A be reconsidered after some reduction in scale; but approval at this stage is unlikely.

The outcome to date reflects the critical importance of other factors besides a mitigation package. Especially in Berkeley's case, these are environmental concerns. But the broader issue is that mitigations must fit into a context of some consensus about land use choices. Mitigations are, after all, efforts to offset, always imperfectly, the costs imposed by new development and—particularly in the case of job targeting—heighten project benefits. If the proposed office or other use is viewed unfavorably in a particular location, then we can end up negotiating mitigations for the wrong project (too large, undesired use, etc.). Project A is proposed for a downtown site zoned for office uses and allowing much larger scale than its developer planned. But the site is near the border of downtown with a residential area. Much of Berkeley's zoning is considered out of date, and a planning committee is in the process of proposing revisions. OED asked members of the board of adjustments and planning commission at the outset whether to base negotiation on the project as proposed or to press immediately for a smaller structure. Absent new policy, their best answer was to act on the developer's proposal. Mitigations will work more successfully as part of a new consensus about development policy, once it is reached and formally established in the zoning ordinance—defining both what development is to be allowed and what is to be required of it, based on the community's current thinking and values.

Another major lesson of the Project A process is that groups with an interest in mitigation components will have to speak up in the context of specific land use decisons to further that interest. Some members of the community may have believed that the project had sufficient value as setting precedent for targeted job opportunities to warrent its immediate approval but, unlike concerned neighbors, those parties did not speak at the board of adjustments' public hearing and may well have been unaware of it. How to involve this diversity of interests in balanced public discussion is an important question for Berkeley and other planners. Both neighbors and other groups need to be involved early on in project planning to achieve good outcomes. As often happens elsewhere, neighbors did not concern themselves with Project A, despite invitation to do so, until the point of decision making; many other groups never became involved.

Experience with a second project involving mitigation negotiation, Project B, illustrates the importance of dealing with projects whose basic content is at least acceptable to the community. Project B provides for the reuse of a largely unutilized former manufacturing facility as a mixed-use development totalling about 155,000 square feet. The project as finally negotiated meets many community objectives. It fits comfortably in what is already a largely nonresidential area and provides for housing (in improved living–working space at subsidized rents) for current artist-tenants and new ones. Surrounding neighbors—residential and business—have no quarrel with the principal uses and scale. The development also includes preservation of two existing structures along with compatible new construction. Within that context, it was possible to shape a mitigation package that met specific project-associated concerns and—not without controversy, largely over preserving a large smokestack—to obtain project approval. The mitigation package, again taking advantage of Berkeley's strong market, amounts to about $1.5 million in present value or about $12.50 per square foot of commercial space.

Project B's mitigation menu included:

• Eighteen subsidized living–working housing units on site, rent protections for current tenants, and $47,000 in cash to subsidize two further housing units off site.

• A commitment to first-source hiring by both developer and tenants, and $22,000 over several years to help pay for city operation of the program.

• A 5,000-square-foot child care center on site, providing 132 slots, including 16 slots subsidized for low-income parents.

• A $118,000 payment for street improvements, a transit subsidy for employees, and other carpooling and bicycling provisions.

• An 8,000-square-foot theater provided at a deeply subsidized rent to a community theater.

• A $100,000 fund set aside to help small businesses in the area purchase their own buildings (to help minimize any displacement effects).

• Agreement to reimburse the city for any tax losses due to leases to the university.

In the case of Project B, a development that was basically acceptable to begin with was transformed through negotiated mitigation fees and direct actions into a showcase for the meeting of social goals. At the same time, the project remained profitable to the developer, who agreed to the mitigation package, allowed for the retention of a major local employer who will expand into it, and provides prospects for local employment and tax revenue generation.

LOOKING AHEAD TO MORE SYSTEMATIC IMPLEMENTATION

OED and the city are continuing along dual tracks in putting mitigations into place: negotiating on specific projects already in the pipeline and readying a set of proposals for systematic, consistent mitigation standards for future projects.

A principal question for the long run is the extent to which standards should be tightly fixed rather than flexible and negotiable. Should each mitigation be set by formula, so that if one knows a project's size, mix of uses, and perhaps location, only a computer is involved in assessing a series of cash payments? Or should there be more room left for special considerations?

Fixed standards have some highly attractive characteristics. They offer certainty to the developer about the amount of fees to add into total development costs. Developers can then take mitigations into account from the start in considering the feasibility of undertaking specific projects and the price to bid for developable sites. The community and its representatives can set standards as a matter of policy in public forums, and then they too have certainty about the benefits they will receive from development. Indeed, a community may be able to obtain more in mitigations with fixed standards, because their costs are more likely to be fully capitalized into site prices than if the mitigations are of uncertain amount and appear dependent on financial feasibility, given land prices among other costs. City staff is relieved of a burdensome negotiating task— one that may arouse suspicion and, at least, raises questions of how it should be conducted as a result of the generally less than fully public nature of such negotiations. Projects may be processed more quickly without this task. Developers who do not want to cooperate with the city's mitigation system can eliminate themselves from the start.

On the other hand, flexibility can have advantages as well. Projects may have desirable special characteristics that affect their financial capability but cannot easily be laid out and assessed in advance (e.g., a costly effort at historic preservation). Or they may involve job opportunities of particular kinds that make the city eager to ease their path by foregoing some payments. Economic conditions may change in ways that are difficult to build into formulas. The best mitigations may be diverse direct actions rather than cash payments, particularly in such areas as handling traffic impacts. Attempts to put all these issues in formula form are especially risky in situations where full mitigations bring development projects fairly close to the margin of feasibility, as our analysis shows they might in Berkeley and suggests they may well do in other localities.

We anticipate setting up clearly stated standards for each type of mitigation. Those standards will provide for a range of fees (or actions) in each case. The top of the range will represent the full cost of mitigating each item, and negotiations will allow for payments as low as 50 percent of that level. If a project provides especially desirable benefits or more than mitigates its impacts in one area, then negotiations within the established ranges will provide for potential reductions in other mitigations.

We are still assessing how the process of negotiating the flexible elements should be integrated into the city's existing development review processes. Issues include whether to pursue full agreement with developers or to propose conditions for the board of adjustments to set, and how and when to judge what the board will do in setting project scale and use. Again, community consensus on desired land uses is a precondition to successful mitigation. We also are assessing how to ensure that mitigation fees are collected over time without incurring high administrative costs. And we are examining how to ensure that mitigation fees are used to offset the identified impacts. Establishing mitigation standards is a complex process in itself, requiring the extensive analysis we have described earlier; but it is inherently dependent as well on careful integration with more traditional issues of policymaking and effective program operation.

Economic Basis for Linking Jobs and Housing in San Francisco

LINDA L. HAUSRATH

This chapter summarizes the basis for and an approach to the derivation of housing mitigation requirements for future office building projects. The specific purpose of this analysis was to provide the basis for the office-housing production program that San Francisco adopted.

The chapter has four sections: a summary description of the relationship between employment growth and housing markets, a summary of the implications of office employment growth for San Francisco's housing market, the basic strategy for mitigating housing market impacts, and the derivation of housing mitigation requirements for office development in San Francisco's downtown area. The chapter concludes with some observations about other issues that arise in considering the implementation of a housing mitigation program.

RELATIONSHIP BETWEEN EMPLOYMENT GROWTH AND HOUSING MARKETS

There is a relationship between employment growth and housing markets, the basis for which lies in economic and housing market theory. We can see that relationship between

office employment growth in San Francisco and the city's housing market. The following points summarize the general relationship and describe the market dynamics involved.[1]

Building development and changes in use of space accommodate employment growth. The growth of business activity and employment creates demand for additional space. That demand, in turn, leads to the construction of new buildings and to changes in the use of space in existing buildings.

Employment growth means growth of employed labor. In general, the number of workers newly employed equals the number of additional jobs. But since existing workers may take the new jobs, we cannot assume that the newly employed individuals necessarily work at the new jobs.

Increases in employed labor means population growth in the area. However, the amount of population growth could be less than needed to accommodate the growth of employment because of either increased labor force participation or reduced unemployment.

Population growth translates into increased

demand for housing. The amount of increase depends on how the increment of employment and population growth divides into households (workers per household and persons per household). The type, purchase price or rent, and location of that housing depend on the demographic and income characteristics of the new households, as well as other factors that affect housing preferences and financial resources available for housing.

Housing market adaptations to accommodate greater demand result in expansion of the housing supply and in changes in the use of the existing housing stock. The adaptation process involves five steps.

1. Additional worker households seeking housing will add to the demand for the existing stock, increasing competition for it and eventually raising housing prices and rents.

2. The supply of housing will expand to the extent that increased purchase prices and rents cover the costs of producing new housing. That will occur when prices and rents rise enough to justify in-fill housing that replaces lower density development, in-fill housing on vacant sites previously passed over as less desirable for residential development, upgrading or conversion to housing of structures previously used for other purposes, and development of housing beyond the urban periphery.

3. Higher income households will be able to secure their preferred housing by moving either into the new units or into housing vacated by residents who move into the new housing.

4. The amount of money the majority of households can afford is inadequate to pay for new housing. The squeeze that develops as those households compete for the now inadequate supply of low- and moderate-priced units will continue until a number of households choose new units, even at a greater cost, thus relieving some of the pressure for units at lower purchase prices and rents. That resolution will limit the price escalation but it will leave prices and rents higher than they were before the accommodation to growth.

5. Higher prices also will create pressures to increase occupancy of existing housing by increasing the number of persons per household or the number of households per unit. That will reduce demand for additional units. While adaptations can occur in many market segments, the greatest pressures to make changes will fall on subgroups that can least afford the increased purchase prices or rents needed to justify new construction.

Market adaptations pose the most problems for those who have limited resources for housing. Those households usually have little potential for increasing their housing expenditures. Typically, they also have limited flexibility as to where they can live. As a result, lower income households are more likely than others to have to choose between accepting lower quality housing and increasing occupancy as the only feasible adaptations to the market sqeeze.

OFFICE EMPLOYMENT GROWTH AND SAN FRANCISCO'S HOUSING MARKET

Even without office employment growth in San Francisco, demand for housing in the city will continue to be strong. Many households currently living elsewhere in the Bay area would prefer to live in San Francisco. Future inmigrants into the region also will include many who want to live in the city.

San Fancisco will expand its supply of housing, but the private market will be unable to supply new housing for a large segment of the population. Although the difficulties in producing affordable housing arise from many factors and exist throughout the region, it is relatively more difficult to produce housing in the central city. High land costs and the lack of vacant land result in the need to build at higher density and with higher construction costs; those factors help account for the relatively high threshold level of purchase prices and rents needed to attract residental development to the city.

Analysts expect the prices and rents for housing throughout the region to remain higher relative to incomes and to other goods and services than they were in the 1960s and 1970s. In San Francisco, purchase prices and rents will remain relatively higher than in many other parts of the region, even without increases in office employment. The prices and rents will be higher with office employment growth than they would be without it. Although not all the additional office workers will live in the city, some will. Many of those workers will be willing to pay higher prices for housing in the city to save the time and cost of commuting from outlying areas. Many of them will be able to pay more for housing than some current and potential future residents.

Office workers who live in the city will compete for the existing supply of housing. Those with greater financial resources will support production of housing by the private market. Those with lesser financial resources will add to the competition for the stock of housing available at prices and rents below those needed for new construction. To the extent that prices and rents remain below that threshold,

the supply of those types of units will not expand. Instead, prices and rents of existing units will move higher, occupancies will increase, and pressures to upgrade the existing stock will grow.

The higher purchase prices and rents, particularly for relatively lower cost housing in older neighborhoods, will have a number of implications over time. Some people will decide not to move into the city, and some existing residents will move out in search of more acceptable housing elsewhere, given the price. Many individuals who continue to live in San Francisco will pay higher prices and rents for the same city housing. Still others, unable or unwilling to pay more, will accept city housing that does not fully meet their preferences or needs. And finally, owners of existing units will benefit to the extent that the value of their housing appreciates.

Generally, households with fewest financial resources will make the most sacrifices to adapt to more competitive market conditions. San Francisco has and will continue to attract a large number of people who will have difficulties in securing housing. Those people include renters, younger persons, those holding entry-level jobs, the elderly and others on fixed incomes, immigrants, and poor and unemployed persons.

MITIGATION

Basic strategy

Mitigation is aimed at producing housing for the additional office-worker households (or for households with similar characteristics) that need or want to reside in the city. Private developers will supply some units, at purchase prices and rents that cover the costs of new construction. Therefore, mitigation strategy should focus on producing housing that developers will not otherwise build—housing at purchase prices and rents below those needed to cover the costs of new construction. Expanding the housing supply in the lower price and rent ranges should accommodate the influx of new office workers who otherwise would compete with existing residents for the limited stock of such housing. That expansion will limit the escalation of housing prices and rents and will be of most help to those with limited financial resources and housing options.

The following section discusses the derivation of housing mitigation requirements using that strategy, highlighting the approach, and providing a step-by-step summary of the methodology for quantifying the required number of units and the cost of providing those units.

Derivation of Housing Mitigation Requirements

The approach used here to derive housing mitigation requirements for future office building projects in San Francisco views office growth within the context of overall *future* growth, both in San Francisco and in the rest of the Bay area. The approach relies on forecasts through the year 2000 that provide consistent scenarios of employment, labor force, and housing and focus on where people work and live.[2] The mitigation requirements derived below reflect those scenarios and are calculated using estimates from them.

This approach focuses on overall office growth rather than on the occupants of individual buildings. Although I apply housing mitigation requirements to individual office building projects, the specifics of each project or the businesses that will occupy it are not relevant

Figure 21–1. Derivation of Housing Mitigation Requirements for Office Building Development

Steps for calculating housing mitigation requirements

TASK 1: Determine additional San Francisco households with office workers

    Step 1: Estimate net addition of office space
    Step 2: Estimate net addition of office employment
    Step 3: Estimate net increase in office workers residing in San Francisco
    Step 4: Estimate additional San Francisco households with office workers

TASK 2: Determine additional San Francisco housing to mitigate impact of additional households and determine cost of producing that housing

    Step 5: Estimate additional housing needed to accommodate additional households within the city
    Step 6: Estimate subsidy required to produce housing affordable to additional households

Source: Recht Hausrath & Associates

for deriving mitigation requirements. Instead, the net addition of office space that a project contributes is treated as an incremental part of total office growth over an extended period. The additional economic activity that the growth of office space accommodates is not necessarily located in the new building, since a firm already located in the city may move into the new building, leaving its old space to be occupied by a new firm.

Step-by-Step Derivation of Housing Mitigation Requirements.

The derivation of housing mitigation requirements for San Francisco office development involves two major tasks. The first is to anticipate how many additional San Francisco households with office workers the office development will generate. The second task is to determine the price and rent characteristics of the additional housing the city will require to mitigate the impact of additional households, and to estimate the cost of producing that housing. Figure 21–1 identifies the steps I considered in deriving estimates under each of the tasks. The process and variables apply to all office space throughout the city. The specific numerical values used are those established for future office space and office activities in San Francisco's downtown C-3 district, an area including the largest concentration of commercial activity and employment in the city.

The steps described below were used to develop requirements that apply per unit of building space. To simplify the calculations, I derived the housing mitigation requirements for the net addition of one million gross square feet feet of office space. The resultant requirements, expressed per unit of building space (per one million square feet or per one square foot), apply to all office building development during the 1981–2000 forecast period.

TASK 1: *Determining the number of additional San Francisco households with office workers*

Step 1: Determine net addition of office space

Office space in new building	–	Office space demolished in older building(s)	=	Net addition of office space

The following steps assume the net addition of one million gross square feet of C-3 district office space.

The net addition of office space represents the difference between the amount of office space in the new building and the amount demolished in an older building to allow for new construction. It excludes space in retail use (stores, shops, bars, and restaurants).

Step 2: Estimate net addition of office employment

Net addition of office space	÷	Employment density factor	=	Net addition of office employment
1,000,000 gross square feet of additional C-3 district office space	÷	268 gross square feet per C-3 district office employee	=	3,731 additional office workers in C-3 district

The employment density factor in step 2 applies to future C-3 district office activities and reflects the mix of office activities analysts expect by 2000. Its application to an individual project assumes that the density of employment in the building will reflect the average future density for all similar office buildings in the district. The density of 268 gross square feet per office employee incorporates an average vacancy factor of 5 percent. By accounting for vacancy, I assumed that a small amount of space is always unoccupied to allow for mobility of tenants. The density factor was based on analysis of future C-3 district employment and space under San Francisco's downtown plan and on data from C-3 district employer surveys and the land use inventory.

Step 3: Estimate net increase in office workers residing in San Francisco

Net addition of office employment		Ratio of net addition of office workers residing in San Francisco to net addition of office employment		Net increase in office workers residing in San Francisco
	×		=	
3,731 additional C-3 district office workers	×	31 percent	=	1,157 additional C-3 district office workers residing in San Francisco

The ratio to which step 3 refers identifies the increase in number of office workers residing in San Francisco as a function of the increase in office employment. The ratio was derived from the forecasts of C-3 district office growth from 1981 to 2000 prepared for the Downtown Plan Environmental Impact Report (EIR).

The report predicts that, over time, the *number* of C-3 district office workers who live in San Francisco will increase, but that the *percentage* will decline, from an average of 51.6 percent in 1981 to 45 percent in 2000. That prediction is based on a combination of two factors. First, future labor force and housing growth in San Francisco are not expected to increase in proportion to growth in office employment. Second, the labor force and housing elsewhere in the Bay area will increase by larger amounts than in San Francisco. Thus, persons who live outside the city will hold an increasing proportion of office jobs. The net addition of office workers residing in San Francisco compared to the net addition of C-3 district office jobs indictates that about 31 percent of additional workers 1981 to 2000 will live in the city.

Step 4: Estimate additional San Francisco households with office workers

A. Estimate additional office workers in additional households

Net increase in office workers residing in San Francisco	×	Percentage of additional workers in additional households in San Francisco	=	Additional office workers in additional households in San Francisco
1,157 additional C-3 district office workers residing in San Francisco	×	45 percent	=	521 additional C-3 district office workers in additional San Francisco households

B. Estimate number of additional households

Additional office workers in additional households in San Francisco	÷	Average number of San Francisco workers in San Francisco households with office workers	=	Additional San Francisco households with additional office workers
521 additional C-3 district office workers in additional San Francisco households	÷	1.35 San Francisco workers per C-3 district office worker household residing in San Francisco	=	386 additional San Francisco households

The net increase in office workers residing in San Francisco does not necessarily lead to equal net increases in households and housing units, since an increase is forecast in the average number of workers per household across the city. That includes both households already in existing housing stock and those who move into the city because additional housing units become available. Many of the additional office workers living in San Francisco will come from households that have more members in the work force, because of changes in the employment status of ongoing residents (more residents working and more workers holding office jobs), and from households new to the city (with more members in the work force) replacing those who move out of the existing housing stock. The impact on the housing market, however, arises primarily from additional households competing for housing units. Thus, mitigation demands that we identify the additional office workers in additional households.

From the forecasts for the Downtown Plan EIR, we can estimate that about 55 percent of the increase in employed residents citywide from 1980 to 2000 could occur because of an increase in the number of workers per household in San Francisco, assuming the existing number of households and the existing housing stock. The remaining 45 percent of the increase could occur because of housing growth and the net addition of households in the city. If the same percentages applied to the increase in number of office workers residing in San Francisco, 45 percent of that increase would represent additional households in the city. That assumption was used in the step 4A calculation.

The future average number of workers per household with C-3 district office workers was used to predict the additional number of households that would need housing mitigation. The 1.35 figure in step 4B reflects expected conditions in 2000, which was derived from a survey of employees in the C-3 district; U.S. census data; and analyses of employment, population, and demographic trends for San Francisco.

Result of Task 1. Task 1 determined that 386 additional San Francisco households will be associated with the addition of one million square feet of C-3 district office space from 1981 to 2000. That represents 0.000386 additional San Francisco households for each additional square foot of C-3 district office space.

TASK 2: Determining additional San Francisco housing to mitigate impact of additional households, and determining cost of producing that housing

Step 5: Estimate additional housing needed to accommodate additional households within the city

A. Estimate additional housing units

Additional San Francisco households with office workers	=	Additional housing units needed to mitigate housing market impacts that will otherwise occur in San Francisco
386 additional San Francisco households	=	386 additional housing units needed in San Francisco

B. Estimate affordability

Additional housing units		Percentages needed in various HUD income categories to be affordable to the additional office worker households in San Francisco		Additional housing units needed in San Francisco by HUD income categories so as to be affordable to additional households
	×	× 20%	=	77 units affordable to households with incomes averaging 50% of HUD median income
		× 21%	=	81 units affordable to households with incomes averaging 80% of HUD median income
386 additional housing units needed	×	× 8%	=	31 units affordable to households with incomes averaging 120% of HUD median income
		× 7%	=	27 units affordable to households with incomes averaging 150% of HUD median income
		× 44%	=	170 units affordable to households with incomes above 165% of HUD median income

To derive the percentages in step 5, I first developed forecasts of increases in C-3 district office worker households in various household income categories from 1981 to 2000. The 1981 household income distribution for C-3 district office workers residing in San Francisco came from the survey of employees in that district. The Downtown Plan EIR employment analyses and forecasts yielded the change in distribution from 1981 to 2000. The increases in households in various income catagories reflect the growth of office business activities and changes over time in the mix of office activities, each

with somewhat different household income distributions for their workers. The change in household income distribution does not assume any change in the relationship between household incomes and housing costs.

The second substep was to compare the increases in the C-3 district office worker households in the various income categories with data used by the U.S. Department of Housing and Urban Development (HUD) to identify median incomes for households in the San Francisco region. The comparisons assumed an average household size of 2.1 persons, which the C-3 district employee survey indicated was the average for C-3 district office worker households residing in San Francisco. The result was a translation of the household incomes into a distribution according to the income catagories that HUD often uses to evaluate housing affordability.

Step 6: Estimate the extent to which subsidies would be required to produce housing affordable to additional San Francisco households

Additional housing units to accommodate additional San Francisco households in various HUD income categories		Subsidy (if any) required because the prices/rents that households can afford are not high enough to cover the costs of housing production		Cost of producing housing in San Francisco that is affordable to the additional San Francisco households
	×		=	

For-sale housing:
(77 units × $69,440 subsidy per unit) +
(81 units × $45,600 subsidy per unit) +
(31 units × $13,800 subsidy per unit) +
(197 units × 0 subsidy per unit)

= $9,468,280*

Rental housing:
(77 units × $69,240 subsidy per unit) +
(81 units × $50,790 subsidy per unit) +
(31 units × $26,180 subsidy per unit) +
(27 units × $7,730 subsidy per unit) +
(170 units × 0 subsidy per unit)

= $10,465,760*

* In 1984 dollars.

Three substeps were used to calculate the cost of producing housing affordable to the additional households. The first was to identify the prices and rents that households in the various HUD income catagories could afford to pay. I assumed that households could pay 30 percent of gross income for rental housing and used a gross rent multiplier of 7.5 to identify the unit value that those rents could support. The multiplier came from data on 1983 and 1984 sales of apartment buildings in San Francisco. For ownership housing, I assumed that households could allocate 38 percent of gross income for mortgage principal and interest, property taxes, fire insurance, and homeowner association dues. The calculation of house price that share of income could support involved the following assumptions: 30-year mortgage at 13 percent interest, 10 percent down payment, property taxes at 1.25 percent of price, and fire insurance and homeowner association dues at $1,200 per year.

Next, I compared the affordable rental housing values and the affordable purchase prices to the cost of producing housing, assuming standard wood frame construction for units and household incomes averaging 50, 80, 120, and 150 percent of the HUD median income. According to the experience of the Mayor's Office of Housing and Economic Development, constructing such units in San Francisco costs an average of $100,000 each (in 1984 dollars) including land and all other costs of construction. (Costs per square foot range from $100 to $125 for units of 800 to 1,000 square feet.) The differences between the affordable rental values and purchase prices and the $100,000 per unit cost provided an estimate of the subsidy (if any) required to produce affordable housing.

Rental housing for households whose incomes average 50, 80, 120, and 150 percent of median income needs some subsidy. Those are the groups HUD usually categorized as very

low, low/moderate, moderate, and middle income. Ownership housing for the very low, low/moderate, and moderate income groups also needs some subsidy.

Third, multiplication of the amount of subsidy per unit by the number of units in each group identified the total cost of supplying the housing. If no subsidy is required, there is no net cost since the price/value of the unit fully covers development cost.

Result of Task 2. Task 2 determined that it would cost $9.5 million to $10.5 million (in 1984 dollars) to supply affordable housing in San Francisco for the additional households associated with the addition of one million square feet of office space in the C-3 district from 1981 to 2000. That amount translates into $9.47 to $10.47 per square foot of additional office space in the C-3 district.

Summary of Mitigation Requirements

Applying the strategy to provide housing for the additional San Francisco households with office workers and the approach of the cumulative perspective of growth over time results in a formulation we can use as the basis for requiring developers to provide housing or to pay the city to produce housing. The analysis summarized here supports either of two requirements. One is that San Francisco require office project developers to build 0.000386 housing units for each square foot of additional office space in the C-3 district[3] and that the new units be affordable to additional office worker households according to the distribution listed in step 5. The other requirement is that the city charge office project developers a fee of $9.47 to $10.47 per square foot of additional office space in the C-3 district and that the funds collected be used to produce housing.

THE OFFICE-AFFORDABLE HOUSING PRODUCTION PROGRAM

The city and county of San Francisco adopted the Office-Affordable Housing Production Program (OAHPP) through a board of supervisors' ordinance in August 1985. The ordinance, based on the analysis and requirements summarized here, requires that an office project developer construct housing or pay an in-lieu fee. The ordinance requires that, if the developer elects to construct housing units, construction must be 0.000386 units per net additional gross square foot of office space; a certain percentage of those units must be affordable to low- or moderate-income households for 20 years. If a developer elects to pay the in-lieu fee, the ordinance currently requires $5.34 per net additional gross square foot of office space, to be used for the development of housing affordable to low- or moderate-income households. In recognition of the numerous assumptions in the analysis, the city selected that smaller in-lieu fee rather than the amounts identified in this analysis—$9.47 to $10.47.

COMMENTS

An approach to determining an office–housing linkage exaction is shown in this chapter. But planners and decision makers considering implementation of a similar housing mitigation program should remain cautious and evaluate the approach and calculations within the context of their local economies and housing markets. Different jurisdictions may require different assumptions and, perhaps, different steps in the calculations.

Before implementing a housing mitigation program, communities also should address other issues regarding the implications of such a program. For example, I do not discuss who would bear the cost of the exactions—land owners, developers, or office tenants—although San Francisco did consider the issue in the process of adopting an ordinance; other communities should consider it before they implement housing mitigation programs. Similarly, this chapter does not discuss whether the location of development would shift if a housing assessment were imposed. Finally, this chapter does not consider the problems of a city with less demand for office space than San Francisco. With lower land values and a resistance to higher rents, such a city may well find it difficult to impose exactions without discouraging the development it needs, both for the jobs it provides and for its contribution to the tax base.

Author's Note

This chapter is an edited version of a report entitled "The Economic Basis for an Office-Housing Production Program," prepared for the San Francisco Department of City Planning in July 1984. Throughout that project, J. Richard Recht, my partner, and Wallace F. Smith of the University of California, Berkeley, provided valuable insights and critiques.

Notes

1. The following is intended as a generalized summary of the relationship between employment growth and the housing market, highlighting the factors and market dynamics involved. The purpose is to alert planners to the considerations involved in attempting to link jobs and housing. It is important to understand that the relationship is complex and not direct. Housing texts provide much more background (e.g., Smith 1970).

2. Recht Hausrath & Associates prepared detailed forecasts of office growth in downtown San Francisco and of the residence patterns of office workers as a part of a major study effort whose purpose was to analyze the implications of alternative zoning policies for the C-3 district. We undertook extensive data collection and in-depth economic and real estate market analyses. The study

also focused on downtown workers: where they live and their household and housing characteristics. The surveys and forecasts provided the basis for the housing mitigation requirements summarized in this chapter. The specific forecast scenarios used assumed the downtown plan policies that the city eventually adopted. Those forecasts appear in the environmental impact report prepared for the downtown plan (see San Francisco Department of City Planning 1984).

3. The requirement is equivalent to about one housing unit for every 2,950 square feet of additional office space. Stated another way, a typical new building that adds 350,000 square feet of office space would have to provide 135 housing units.

References

Recht Hausrath & Associates. 1984. *The Economic Basis for an Office-Housing Production Program*. Oakland: Recht Hausrath & Associates, for the San Francisco Department of City Planning.

San Francisco Department of City Planning. 1984. *Environmental Impact Report, The Downtown Plan EE81.3*, certified October 18, 1984. Volume 1, pp. IV.B.1–IV.B.90, IV.C.1–IV.C.61, and IV.D.1–IV.D.98. Volume 2, pp. C.1–C.5, F.1–F.2, G.1–G.59, H.1–H.32, and I.1–I.40.

Smith, Wallace F. 1970. *Housing, The Social and Economic Elements*, Berkeley: University of California Press.

Market Effects of Office Development Linkage Fees

FORREST E. HUFFMAN, JR.
MARC T. SMITH

In an effort to address housing affordability problems, several cities recently have applied linkage fee programs to the development of office space. San Francisco was the first to do so, when it implemented its Office Housing Production Program in 1981 (Recht Hausrath & Associates 1984). Santa Monica and Boston implemented linkage programs soon after (Muzzio and Bailey 1986); and Seattle, Miami, and Hartford have followed (Tegeler and Silverstein 1985). City officials in New York, Chicago, Washington D.C., and Cambridge, Massachusetts, have discussed linkage fee programs (for discussion of those programs see Porter 1985; Keating 1986a). Strong office sector growth, reduced federal funding for housing programs, and studies that linked development of downtown office space to the need for new housing all helped to spur the programs.

Linkage fees link development in the central business district to the provision or subsidization of low- and moderate-income housing. The rationale for linkage programs is that new office development has both direct and indirect effects that exacerbate problems of providing affordable housing. The direct effect occurs because demolition of housing units to clear a site for office development displaces households. Indirect effects include the increased value of real estate, which results from the more intense use of land, and the additional housing demand from new employees attracted to the building. Linkage programs have generally taken the form of an exaction per square foot of office space; the developer usually pays it over several years. Proceeds from the fee help reduce the cost of housing for the low- and moderate-income groups that the new building displaced.

Development impact fees have been more commonly associated with housing than with office development. In their application to housing, impact fees have given rise to concerns that they may decrease housing availability. One commonly may assume that developers will pass the fees to home buyers in the form of higher house prices. An alternative might be to pass the fees backward by paying lower prices to owners of developable land. If the developer cannot pass on the fees, he must accept lower profits or curtail development. The same three possibilities pertain to office exaction fees.

In considering the imposition of housing

impact fees, Weitz (1985) analyzed four types of submarkets in which the price elasticity (sensitivity) of housing demanders and suppliers varied from highly elastic to rather inelastic. The extent to which home buyers bear a fee depends on the supply-and-demand conditions in the local market. Snyder and Stegman (1986) argue that impact fees will fall totally on the buyer only in communities that the buyers consider more attractive than other nearby locations. In such markets, buyers will accept price increases (inelastic demand). In markets where demand is elastic and users can substitute, developers must pay less for the land or take a lower profit. Paying less for the land is a likely result in the longer run, as developers capitalize the impact fee into future bid prices for land (Ellickson 1981).

The office market differs significantly from the home ownership market in scale of development, length of construction period, type of tenant occupancy, and other factors. Thus the effects of an office exaction fee may differ from those we might expect in a housing fee. In this chapter we examine the implications of such a fee from the perspective of a developer faced with an exaction fee and discuss the resultant potential effects on the office market. First, we look at the effect of the fee on a developer's return, assuming that the developer cannot pass it on to a tenant or landowner. Second, we explore the effect of the exaction on a specific project in a price-sensitive market. Third, we consider the implications for office markets in general.

CAN THE DEVELOPER ABSORB THE FEE?

Exaction policies may be either a one-time fee or a series of payments over several years be-

ginning when the project goes into use (e.g., $5 per square foot paid over five years). Exaction fees that the developer absorbs instead of passing on to renters or predevelopment landowners have a negative effect on cash flows, and play a role in investment decisions.

In making investment decisions, developers of new office space are motivated by the profit they expect the building to generate. Expected profit derives from two sources: cash flow while the developer owns the building and the proceeds when he sells it. These benefits are balanced against the equity investment made by the developer, thus

$$\text{Profit} = f(\text{cash, sale, equity}) \quad \text{(1)}$$

where

Profit = Expected profit.
Cash = Expected annual cash flows.
Sale = Expected net proceeds from the sale of the building.
Equity = Equity downpayment by the developer.

Annual after-tax cash flows consist of the revenues (rents) earned from the project, less all expenses

$$\text{ATCF} = (\text{NSF} \times \text{R} - \text{VSF} \times \text{R}) - \text{OE} - \text{DS} - \text{TX} \quad \text{(2)}$$

where

ATCF = After-tax cash flows.
NSF = Net rentable square feet in the building.
VSF = Vacant rentable square feet.
R = Rent per square foot.
OE = Operating expenses for the building.
DS = Debt service (mortgage payments).
TX = Income taxes.

We can calculate the rate of return from the project, k, by a trial-and-error procedure that determines the present value of the future expected cash flows at different rates of return. We have the project's rate of return when the present value of the cash flows equals the equity amount contributed (or when the net present value is zero). Thus

$$0 = \left[\sum_{n=1}^{N} \frac{ATCE_n}{(1 + k)^n} + \frac{Sale_N}{(1 + k)^N} \right] - Equity \quad (3)$$

where

N = Holding period for the investment.

k = Rate of return (internal rate of return).

The developer will make the investment if the project's expected rate of return from the investment is equal to or exceeds the minimum amount acceptable, given other opportunities open to him and considering the level of risk involved. To compensate for higher risk, the developer requires a higher rate of return on the investment.

A linkage fee placed on new development has two effects on the feasibility of the project. First, if the developer cannot pass on the costs to the tenants or to the previous landowner, his cash flows are reduced by the amount of the exaction each year, so that equation 2 becomes

$$ATCF_n = (NSF \times R_n - VSF \times R_n) - OE_n - DS_n - TX_n - LE_n \quad (4)$$

where

LE_n = The linkage exaction in the nth year.

Second, the exaction increases business risk and thereby adds an element of uncertainty to the project for the developer. The risk is the result of the increased potential that the income during the early years of occupancy will not cover the cost of the exaction, so that the developer will need to either meet those expenses out of pocket or else default. It is not surprising that the developer may have difficulty in meeting the expense of the exaction, given the slow lease up of speculative office development and the necessity of offering rent concessions to attract anchor tenants (Nourse 1985). Therefore, when a local governnment levies exaction fees on office space and increases the risk of the investment, the developer will have to increase his rate of return. Developers may have some projects whose expected rate of return is sufficient even with the linkage to encourage them to proceed. However, proposed projects that barely meet the required rate of return without the fee do not fall into that category. Projects with rates of return close to the required rate are likely to occur in cities where oversupply or lack of demand results in competitive pressures that lower returns to minimally acceptable rates. Marginally acceptable rates of return are also more likely in general since the passage of the Tax Reform Act of 1986 reduced the tax advantages associated with real estate investment. The act requires that returns to the developer depend more on economic feasibility and market conditions than on tax write-offs.

To illustrate the effect of an exaction fee, we performed a discounted cash flow analysis (an application of equation 3) for a hypothetical but typical office building in the Philadelphia central business district. We made the following assumptions:[1] The building is a $40 million project, to be financed with a $30 million mortgage loan and $10 million of the investor's own equity funds; the $10 million portion is invested at the initiation of the project; construction costs are $120 per square foot; the mortgage loan is for 30 years at 11 percent interest; the investor is in a 28 percent tax bracket; and the analysis is based on the tax laws in effect as a result of the Tax Reform Act of 1986.

We also assume that leasing of the building

Table 22–1. Annual Cash Flow without Exaction*

Cash flows	Year							
	1	2	3	4	5	6	7	8
Gross potential income	$1,520.0	$11,980.8	$12,460.0	$12,958.4	$13,476.8	$14,015.8	$14,576.5	$15,159.5
Less vacancies	8,640.0	5,990.4	1,246.0	1,295.8	1,347.7	1,401.5	1,457.7	1,515.9
Effective gross income	2,880.0	5,990.4	11,214.0	11,662.6	12,129.1	12,614.3	13,118.8	13,643.6
Less operating expenses	2,790.1	2,873.8	2,960.1	3,048.9	3,140.3	3,234.5	3,331.6	3,431.5
Net operating income (NOI)	89.9	3,116.6	8,254.0	8,613.7	8,988.8	9,379.7	9,787.2	10,212.1
Less total debt service	3,870.1	3,870.1	3,870.1	3,870.1	3,870.1	3,870.1	3,870.1	3,870.1
Before-tax cash flow (BTCF)	(3,780.2)	(753.5)	4,383.9	4,743.6	5,118.7	5,509.6	5,917.2	6,342.0
Less (tax) or add savings	7.0	7.0	7.0	(93.7)	(1,148.2)	(1,266.6)	(1,390.5)	(1,520.4)
After tax cash flow (ATCF)	(3,773.2)	(746.5)	4,390.9	4,650.0	3,970.5	4,243.0	4,526.6	4,821.6
Sale price								77,319.5
ATCF at sale								29,484.5
After tax rate of return (ATIRR)								20.1%

* In thousands of dollars.

will begin immediately and that it will be 25, 50, and 90 percent occupied at the end of years 1, 2, and 3. That assumption reflects the slow lease up of office space and the possibility that a portion of the building is occupied by tenants who received substantial rent concessions during the initial occupancy period. Occupancy rates level off at 90 percent, which is the average rate in Philadelphia central business district office markets (Jackson-Cross Company 1987). The developer will hold the building for eight years before selling it. We assume rents are $32 per square foot, and 360,000 square feet are leasable. Rental levels increase at the rate of 4 percent, and operating expenses increase by 3 percent annually. The sales price in year eight is based on the capitalization of the eighth year's income at a 15 percent capitalization rate.

Table 22–1 shows the resultant annual cash flows and the rate of return (ATIRR) for the eight-year holding period.

Without the exaction, the rate of return is 20.1 percent. If we assume the developer requires a minimum return of 20 percent to make the investment, he would do so if no exaction were imposed.[2] If an exaction were imposed, it would increase the risk and therefore raise the required rate of return.

Table 22–2 presents four possible exaction fee implementation scenarios. In every case the first 100,000 square feet are exempt from the exaction, a common practice that alleviates the burden of the exaction on smaller projects. Each case is based on the imposition of a $5 per square foot fee. In the first scenario, the total impact fee of $5 per square foot is imposed in

Table 22–2. Effect of Impact Fee on Rates of Return

	Percent return
Full occupancy	
No fee	20.1%
$5/square foot first year, included in construction costs	18.6
$1/square foot per year, first five years	19.3
$1/square foot per year, first five years after 70% occupancy	19.6
Lower occupancy	
Rent = $33/square foot, 80% maximum occupancy	15.1
Rent = $33/per square foot, 70% maximum occupancy	7.5

the first year. The rate of return falls to 18.6 percent. The second scenario calls for an exaction fee of $1 per square foot per year over five years. Imposing the fee over five years increases the rate of return to 19.3 percent. The third scenario does not impose the exaction until the building reaches 70 percent occupancy. Postponing the fee increases the rate of return slightly to 19.6 percent.

The $5 fee lowers the developer's rate of return from about 0.5 to more than 1 percent, a significant loss if projects are already generating minimal returns. Given alternative investment opportunities potentially available to real estate developers, those decreases could be enough to drive development from the market.

For a shorter holding period (i.e., a sale during a period for which developer still owes the exactions) the impact of the exaction would be greater because the selling price would have to be lower to account for the exaction obligation that a new buyer would have upon purchase of the building.

CAN DEVELOPERS PASS THE FEE TO TENANTS?

The previous discussion assumed that the developer could not pass fees through to tenants. However, in certain markets, doing so may be acceptable if the central business district market is insensitive to rent increases for office space. We cannot predict exactly how tenants in specific markets will react, but clearly in some cities, over specified periods, demand is relatively inelastic. For instance, in recent years agglomeration economies in San Francisco, Boston, and Manhattan seemed to combine with a lack of developable sites to make exaction fees acceptable to office tenants. In a survey of 10 developers affected by impact fees in San Francisco and one in Santa Monica, Keating (1986b) found that the fees appeared not to be a critical factor in office developer decisions. In cities that do not have inelastic markets however, the ability to pass the fee to tenants may be more limited.

A significant portion of office space users are becoming increasingly footloose, that is, willing to locate in areas other than the central business district. The Office Network reports that traditional downtown areas contained 57 percent of all U.S. office space in 1981, but by 1986, 57 percent of construction was occurring outside central business districts (Fulton 1986). Movement to the suburbs originally affected primarily back office workers such as clerical employees; but increasingly middle management, accounting, law, and other service workers are also moving to suburban locations. Archer (1981) finds that relatively few firms today depend on a central business district location.

Office employers can be more mobile in part because transportation, communications, and other technological advances remove the necessity that they be close to complementary activities. If office space users are footloose, firms may move at least a portion of their employees to less expensive locations outside the central business district rather than pay higher rents once rent levels reach some threshold. To the extent that office tenants have alternative location opportunities, prices are determined by competitive pressures. Elasticity in rental prices is a function of mobility. Developers who earn returns that just meet required rates would be less likely to survive in areas where office user mobility makes it impossible to pass on linkage costs.

Vacancy statistics indicate the difficulty of raising rents in central business districts. The office overbuilding in many cities during the early 1980s resulted in high vacancy rates (Dowall 1986). Office vacancy levels have increased steadily in downtown areas from less than 5 percent in 1980 to more than 15 percent in 1986. For instance, in 1982 San Francisco and Boston had downtown office vacancy rates of less than 5 percent. By 1986 San Francisco's downtown office vacancy rate was approximately 15 percent and rising. The vacancy rate in Boston approached 15 percent in 1985 before leveling off at about 10 percent in 1986 (Coldwell Banker 1986b).

Furthermore, recent construction will result in even higher vacancy rates in the near future. Those vacancy rates will drive down the rate of new construction. Experts contend that additional office space construction nationwide should average about 50 percent less than levels that have occurred over the previous decade (Warren, Gorman and Lamont 1987). With such amounts of vacant space providing competitive alternative locations for potential tenants, it is difficult to impose a rent higher than market averages for a building subject to an exaction.

ANALYSIS: PHILADELPHIA OFFICE MARKET

To consider the situation in a city more typical of downtowns in the United States, we analyzed the results of a survey that the Philadelphia City Planning Commission conducted.[3] The survey provides evidence that certain office space users are willing to move outside the area.

Philadelphia, like many other large cities, has experienced a large increase in center city office space construction in the 1980s. The sixth largest downtown office market in the United States, the city has more than 35 million square feet of office space. Developers added more than 5 million square feet between 1980 and 1985; approximately 5 million square feet currently are under construction. Vacancy rates have been lower in Philadelphia's center city market than national averages. For example, for 1984 to 1986, the office vacancy rate averaged about 10 percent, while the national average was 15 percent. At the same time, the suburban Philadelphia office vacancy rate was close to 16 percent; the national average for similar locations outside large cities was 20 percent.

In 1985, Philadelphia's city planning commission surveyed a random sample of 982 likely office users in the Philadelphia central business district; 290 recipients returned usable responses, a response rate of slightly less than 30 percent. Of the 290, 40 percent were in finance, insurance, and real estate (FIRE); 16 percent in architecture, engineering, and design; 7 percent in advertising and public relations; 5 percent in administrative offices; and 4 percent in legal offices. The sample may not reflect the universe of office tenants in the city in either size or type of activity, in that architecture, engineering, and design are particularly overrepresented and legal offices are underrepresented in the sample. Nonetheless, the sample responses are indicative of the types of office users in the Philadelphia central business district.

More than half of the respondents were from small firms with only one office and another 36 percent were from regional headquarters or branch offices. Only 5 percent reported that their previous office location was outside the central business district. None of those respondents had moved downtown from outside the central business district in the previous three years. Most of the growth in office space demand thus appears to have come from movement within the central business district. However, a significant portion of firms (5 to 10 percent) do move each year; those firms may be sensitive to rent levels.

The questionnaire included a series of questions about the importance of a center city location and factors that would influence firms in their search for a new location. Thirty-five percent of the respondents ranked a central business district as "absolutely essential," while about 50 percent ranked the central business district as only somewhat important. Legal firms, accounting firms, and nonprofit organizations were most likely to indicate that a central business district was essential. Factors that seemed particularly important to firms locating in the central business district were employee access, nearness to other businesses, transit services, and meeting and entertainment facilities.

When asked about relocation plans, 26 percent of the respondents indicated that they were considering a move. Respondents believed that costs were lower in suburban areas than downtown (rents for premium space in the suburbs ranged up to $16 per square foot, compared to the $18 that more than 25 percent of the respondents were paying downtown). Suburban areas were also attractive because they offered lower parking costs and greater parking availability, less congestion, greater security, and improved accessibility for clients and employees. Many respondents also said that taxes were another factor that made the downtown area less attractive.

In summary, the survey indicates that the central business district office market derives most of its growth from firms already there. While some firms seldom change locations, more than 25 percent of the firms in the central business district would consider relocating outside it. New construction in the city may worsen the inaccessibility, traffic congestion, and parking problems to which many firms are sensitive. Thus, some firms would consider moving to the suburbs; if new office buildings in the central business district have to charge higher rents because of an exaction, the demand for that new space will drop.

Given the results of the survey of office space users in Philadelphia's central business district, some degree of sensitivity to rental increases is likely in office markets. Anticipated increases in vacancy levels because of new construction will increase the sensitivity of office tenants to the rent increases. Experts expect that once offices currently under construction are ready for occupancy the oversupply will extend through the year 1991 (Wallace 1987). The additional supply will drive rents down, making it less likely that tenants will suffer an increase in rents for some space.

We have not calculated price elasticities of office space demand in Philadelphia and similar markets and thus we do not know how much office space demand would decline with, say, a $1.00 increase in rent. To explore the situation, we examined two hypothetical cases to look at the sensitivity of prototypical building returns to a decline in occupancy expected to result from the increased rent where demand is sensitive to price. The maximum occupancy rate was changed from the 90 percent in the base case (above) to 80 percent and then to 70 percent. In the first case, with 80 percent occupancy, if we increase the initial rent from $32 to $33 per square foot to absorb the fee, the rate of return declines to 15.1 percent. With the same rent but with the maximum occupancy at 70 percent as in the second case, the rate of return falls to 7.5 percent (Table 22–2). In the nonexaction case, with a maximum occupancy rate at 90 percent and rents at $32 per square foot the rate of return was 20.1 percent.

Those assumed declines in occupancy rate are relatively large, but they do illustrate that price elasticity in demand significantly affects developer rates of return. That is true, however, of anything that affects construction costs — including exactions. It is thus problematic for a developer to pass on the fee in a market that is highly price elastic. In price-sensitive markets, office space exaction fees ultimately drive away office space tenants once the rental costs surpass the convenience of the location.

EFFECTS ON THE OFFICE MARKET

Exactions increase the cost for the developer of new space. If the developer cannot pass on those costs, he must bear them. The developer may grant concessions to new lessees, but doing so will further reduce the cash flow available, at least in the short run. If the rents reflect the exaction fee and potential tenants locate elsewhere, high vacancy levels reduce

developer returns significantly, as we have shown.

A developer could bear the additional costs of the exaction directly only if he were in a short-run "abnormal profits" situation. Abnormal profits are a result of receiving returns above those required to entice the developer into investing. Unfortunately it is difficult for officials to detect the presence of such profits in that inefficiencies inherent in real estate development markets make it difficult to ascertain "true" rates of return. Also, there may or may not be abnormal return available to all developers even if some are earning rates of return higher than required. While some developers may earn sufficient profits to continue their projects, exactions will drive those barely earning the required rate of return prior to an exaction levy from the market.

Since some developers would not build in a marginal profit market, the supply of office space would fall over time as existing facilities deteriorate or become obsolete. The time period in which the market would be undersupplied would depend on the number and financial strength of the remaining developers and the changes in demand during the period. If demand remained stable, the reduction in supply would lead to higher rents. If demand increased, rents would rise even further. Higher rents would offset the higher costs imposed upon developers, so that eventually they would build again and increase the supply of office space. But the higher rents are the result of changing market forces over time, and are only indirectly attributable to the exaction. Further, the total supply would remain lower than in the absence of exactions (Rosen 1984).

A key aspect of exactions is that they apply only to new construction, so that they do not affect existing buildings. That benefits the owners of existing facilities and penalizes developers of new buildings in two ways. First, since developers would have to charge higher rents to cover the exaction, those rents would be above market level. Second, since rents eventually would rise for existing offices as well, owners of the existing buildings would earn windfall profits by not having to pay the exaction. That being the case, one might argue that a tax should apply to existing buildings as well.

In the long run, the fee might be passed back to landowners, but only if the developer can anticipate the linkage fee and negotiate an adjustment in the purchase price of the land. Further, landowners would accept a lower price for their land only if they had no alternative uses that would result in a higher price for the site. Thus some sites would not be available for office use at a lower price. It is also likely that, given the long lead time necessary for development, developers may already own many potential office sites in a city, and therefore cannot pass the cost back to the previous owner.

CONCLUSIONS

This chapter has shown that developers can pass linkage costs to the consumers of the real estate only if those consumers are not sensitive to rent increases necessary to recover the exaction. In price-sensitive markets, the imposition of a tax in the form of a linkage fee results in the availability of fewer offices than the city would have if it did not impose them. Thus the effort to use the linkage fees to generate substantial new housing for low- and moderate-income households would backfire. The fees might in reality stifle employment growth and thus exacerbate the economic problems of the urban area.

Of critical importance is the elasticity of demand for the space being supplied. Since office and service enterprises have become more flexible in their location decisions, tenants might bear the costs to a point, but eventually they will relocate to escape the additional rental costs. The elasticity of demand will depend on the strength of the agglomeration economies inherent in the urban area and the dynamics of its real estate markets. Business conditions, financing considerations, governmental incentives, and any unique characteristics attractive to the potential space user will be important.

Given the likelihood that costs in most cities will not fall on tenants or prior landowners, and that therefore the developers will have to absorb additional costs, cities will have to find incentives that make exactions workable. Those incentives may include such things as expeditious processing and property tax abatements to developers. However, some types of inducements may not overcome the costs of linkage fees. For instance, density bonuses for additional office space may not result in marginal gains to the developer if the exaction also applies to each additional square foot of added space.

Important also are the burdens and benefits to those who carry the cost, relative to the owners of existing buildings who might receive windfall gains. Exactions imposed only on new development can result in abnormal profits to owners of existing space. Exactions are an attempt to more equitably distribute societal costs. However, to ensure equitable treatment, a comprehensive tax, perhaps a transfer or sales tax, would distribute the costs more evenly across all office building owners (Appel 1987; DeGiovanni 1986).

Further, the footloose nature of firms also

implies that the housing problem that exactions are supposed to address may be a regional problem more properly addressed at a regional level. If firms are willing to locate in suburban areas, a comprehensive approach that considers impacts of new development in outlying areas as well as the central business district is necessary. Suburban growth may, in fact, lessen housing pressures in the central business district while creating problems in outlying areas. However, a regional linkage fee may drive firms to other regions with lower rents.

Development impact fees of various sorts are becoming increasingly common as local governments seek ways to meet the public costs of development. They may be appropriate when the costs imposed relate directly to benefits received, such as with a transportation exaction. In such cases, the benefits may allow the developer to recover some of the cost through higher rents. The relationship is less clear for housing linkage policies and thus the impacts of the program on the local office market potentially are more severe.

A city may decide to impose an impact fee in the interests of equity to address perceived undesirable problems that result from office space development. In making that decision, however, the city should be aware of the potential adverse effects in office markets and should balance funds lost in the city against the funds generated for housing purposes. The city must consider carefully the ultimate results and the costs of obtaining those results before it institutes possible barriers to needed economic activity.

Notes

1. We obtained all rental data, vacancy rates, and operating expense data from surveys of the center city

market that the Jackson-Cross Company published (1986; 1987). Construction cost estimates were obtained from a discussion with a representative of a nationally known Philadelphia-based firm, Turner Construction, Inc. The financing terms are for a partially amortized (or "bullet") loan typical in the Philadelphia market. Ling and Peiser (1987, p. 40) discuss those loans and other financing alternatives.

2. Not all developers require the same rates of return for specific real estate projects. Mallach (1984, p. 85) notes,

> The level of profit which a developer considers "acceptable" varies from developer to developer and from year to year depending on a multitude of factors. As a result, it is more or less impossible to establish a specific number as a "fair" or "reasonable" profit on a development. Depending on the circumstances, it may range from 8 percent to 20 percent or more. It must be remembered that the profit calculated before construction begins is hardly assured profit, it is in essence, a backup risk and contingency factor, which, given the nature of the development industry, is often substantially eroded by the time the books are closed on a profit.

For this study, we used a procedure commonly employed to compute required rates of return (see, for example, the analysis of the effects of the new tax laws on real estate investment in Follain, Hendershott, and Ling [1987]). The calculation is a weighted average cost of capital determination, which we calculated using Philadelphia data. The result of the procedure is a 20 percent rate of return, which compares favorably to the rate of return exhibited in the cash flow model presented. Thus the rate of return of the specified project would be acceptable.

3. Philadelphia City Planning Commission, 1985, *Analysis of Center City Office Survey,* unpublished report, City of Philadelphia, July.

References

Appel, Willa. 1987. Facing the Urban Housing Crisis. *Real Estate Finance Journal* Winter: 37–43.

Archer, W. A. 1981. The Determinants of Location for General Purpose Office Firms Within Medium Size Cities. *American Real Estate and Urban Economics Association Journal* 9: 283–97.

Coldwell Banker. 1986a. *1986 United States Real Estate Forecast.* Los Angeles: Coldwell Banker.

———. 1986b. *Office Vacancy Index of the United States.* Los Angeles: Coldwell Banker.

DeGiovanni, Frank. 1986. Creating Neighborhood Funds, Conference on Balancing Downtown and Neighborhood Development. Philadelphia: Institute of Policy Studies, Temple University.

Dowall, David. 1986. Planners and Office Overbuilding. *Journal of the American Planning Association* 52, 2: 131–32.

Ellickson, R. C. 1981. The Irony of Inclusionary Zoning. *Southern California Law Review* 54: 1167–84.

Follain, James R., Patric H. Hendershott, and David C. Ling. In press. Understanding the Real Estate Provisions of Tax Reform: Motivation and Impact. *National Tax Journal*.

Fulton, William. 1986. Office in the Dell. *Planning* 52, 7: 13–17.

Gruen, Claude. 1985. The Economics of Requiring Office Space Development to Contribute to the Production and/or Rehabilitation of Housing. In *Downtown Linkages*, edited by Douglas Porter. Washington, D.C.: Urban Land Institute.

Jackson-Cross Company. 1987. *1987 Market Report*. Philadelphia, Penn.: Jackson-Cross Company.

———. 1986. *19886 Market Report*. Philadelphia, Penn.: Jackson-Cross Company.

Keating W. Dennis. 1986a. Housing/CD Linkages: A Tested Strategy. *Journal of Housing* May/June: 101–103.

———. 1986b. Linking Downtown Development to Broader Community Goals. *Journal of the American Planning Association* 52, 2: 133–41.

Ling, David C. and Richard Peiser. 1987. Choosing Among Alternative Financing Structures: The Developer's Dilemma. *Real Estate Review,* 17: 39–48.

Mallach, Alan. 1984. *Inclusionary Housing Programs: Policies and Practices*. New Brunswick, N.J.: Center for Urban Policy Research, Rutgers University.

Muzzio, Douglas and Robert W. Bailey. 1986. Economic Development, Housing and Zoning: A Tale of Two Cities. *Journal of Urban Affairs* 8, 1: 1–18.

Nourse, Hugh O. 1986. Comment on Rental Price Adjustment and Investment in the Office Market. *American Real Estate and Urban Economics Association Journal* 14: 163–64.

Porter, Douglas, ed. 1985. The Linkage Issue: Introduction and Summary of Discussion. In *Downtown Linkages*. Washington, D.C.: Urban Land Institute.

Recht Hausrath & Associates. 1984. *Summary of the Economic Basis for an Office Housing Production Program*. Oakland, Calif.: Recht Hausrath & Associates.

Rosen, Kenneth. 1984. Toward a Model of the Office Building Sector. *American Real Estate and Urban Economics Association Journal* 12: 261–89.

Smith, Halbert C. and John B. Corgel. 1987. *Real Estate Perspectives*. Homewood, Ill.: Richard D. Irwin.

Snyder, Thomas P. and Michael A. Stegman. 1986. *Financing the Public Costs of Growth*. Washington, D.C.: Urban Land Institute.

Tegeler, Philip and Rosalind Silverstein. 1985. Hartford Demands a Quid Pro Quo. *Planning* 51, 6: 18–19.

Warren, Gorman and Lamont. 1987. *WG&L Real Estate Outlook* 10, 1. Boston: Warren, Gorham and Lamont.

Wallace, Linda S. 1987. There's Office Space Galore and the Glut Is Expected to Worsen. *Philadelphia Inquirer*, August 5.

Weitz, Stevenson. 1985. Who Pays Infrastructure Benefit Changes: The Builder or the Homebuyer? In *The Changing Structure of Infrastructure Finance*, edited by J. C. Nicholas. Cambridge, Mass.: Lincoln Institute of Land Policy.

Issues Surrounding Development Impact Fees

A Public Choice and Efficiency Argument for Development Impact Fees

ROBERT A. BLEWETT
ARTHUR C. NELSON

Development impact fees can be used as a pricing instrument that guides development and allows the planning process to adjust efficiently to unforeseen changes in economic conditions. To explain the effects of impact fees on the efficiency of the development and planning process, this chapter first examines the relationship between urban spatial structure and the pricing of public services. A system of pricing that allows for efficient development and explores the political resistance to such a pricing scheme is outlined and then reasons why impact fees are an imperfect but practical alternative to the preferred pricing system are discussed. The probable effects of impact fees on growth and development are examined, and the chapter concludes by analyzing the ability of impact fees to aid in the planning process so as to improve development efficiency in the community. The orientation of the discussion is toward the application of impact fees to single-family residences. This is done only for expediency. Concepts can be applied to multifamily and nonresidential development.

RATIONALE FOR EFFICIENT PRICING OF PUBLIC SERVICES

The methods used to finance local public services affect the pattern of urban development. Residential density and distance from a sewer treatment plant, for example, influence the costs of providing sewer service. If the true costs of providing sewer services are subsidized and new development does not pay its full share of those costs, inefficient development will occur. Thus, the failure to adequately design a system of charges for public services sewers can lead to inefficient development—which may be characterized as urban sprawl. To more fully understand how this might happen, we need to look at the general nature of the costs of providing local public services. These costs can be divided into three basic components:

1. The capital costs of producing the service. Examples are a sewerage treatment plant and a school building. As a rule, these facilities are subject to economies of scale and declining average cost. Being a function of the

number of users, these costs usually are independent of their distance from the facilities or density of development.

2. The costs associated with the delivery of the service. Examples include the costs of sanitary sewer lines or school buses. Generally, these costs increase proportionately as distance increases. Increased residential density usually results in economies. For example, greater density allows for economies due to larger sewer pipe sizes. School bus routes are shorter if students are picked up in densely developed areas.

3. The short-run costs of actually producing the good. Like the first component, these are independent of density or distance. Only these costs are determined by actual use; for example, the cost of actually processing the sewerage once collected.

Average cost pricing results from a policy to charge everyone equally for the same service, regardless of the real cost to provide that service. For example, sewer fees set on an average basis would charge connections to homes on half-acre lots 10 miles from the treatment plant the same as homes on 5,000-square-foot lots one mile from the plant. As a result of average cost pricing, outlying developments are subsidized by other residents. Urban sprawl therefore occurs if the new development does not take account of the additional or marginal costs of providing service to it.

Traditional public finance economists advocate marginal cost pricing in the form of a three-part tariff as a alternative to average cost pricing. One part of the tariff would be a charge for the costs of the capital facility used to produce the good, such as the cost of construction of a sewer treatment plant or a school building. The charge would be a flat fee per connec-

tion or house since the charge does not vary by density or distance.

The second part of the tariff would be a charge for the costs of delivering the service, such as the cost of extending sewer lines to the house. It would essentially be a flat rate per house based on the average cost of extending the sewer line to that and other homes in the same subdivision. The longer the line and the less density, the higher the charge. Table 23–1 illustrates the variation in annual capital facility and service delivery costs between projects of different densities in Loudon County, Virginia.

The third part of the tariff would be a charge for actual use based on the short-run costs of producing the service. It would be a charge, for example, on the per-unit cost of processing sewerage. It could be based on the volume of sewerage passing out of the home and into the sewer line. More typically, it is based partly on the volume of water passing through a water meter into the home.[1]

Planners can argue that urban sprawl would not be subsidized if public service charges were designed with the three-part tariff in mind. More distant and less dense development would only occur if its expected benefits to both developers and purchasers exceeded its additional or marginal costs to the public. Developers would not build and purchasers would not buy homes in efficient developments since the charges would price such development out of the market. In theory, the primary task of planners simply would be to determine the long-term site of central facilities. The market would then dictate appropriate land use patterns. Though this discussion is simplistic, it does convey that the beauty of marginal cost pricing is that it forces developers to take account of all the fiscal costs and benefits of

Table 23–1. Annual Capital Facility and Service Delivery Costs for 1,000 Housing Units, Different Densities, Loudon County, Virginia[1]

	Rural Sprawl[2]	Rural Cluster[3]	Medium Density[4]	High Density[5]
Costs that vary with density:	$4,052	$3,609	$2,621	$2,555
School operating costs	3,046	3,046	2,256	2,256
School transportation costs	187	153	67	33
Road maintenance costs	110	55	38	26
Water, sewer operating costs	709	355	260	240
Costs that do not vary with density:	$ 908	$ 908	$ 908	$ 908
Public schools capital costs	243	243	243	243
Law enforcement	165	165	165	165
Fire/rescue services	58	58	58	58
Health/welfare services	295	295	295	295
General administration	147	147	147	147
Total Annual Costs	$4,960	$4,517	$3,529	$3,463

1. Prototypical communities of 1,000 units each housing 3,260 people with 1,200 students.
2. One unit per five acres.
3. One unit per one acre.
4. 2.67 units per acre.
5. 4.5 units per acre.

Source: Smyth and Laidlaw (1984).

development before they come to have their plans approved.

Political Resistance to Marginal Cost Pricing

If marginal cost pricing results in efficient development patterns and improves community welfare, why hasn't the method been used? Why were regulations imposed to control growth in hundreds of communities during the 1960s, 1970s, and into the 1980s if marginal cost pricing were available? The answers may be found by examining the costs and benefits of those implementing land use controls. Communities may care more about their own welfare than the welfare of society as a whole.

One reason communities choose not to employ marginal cost pricing is that they do not want to discriminate among members of the community, especially if the community is homogeneous in many respects. In many communities, for example, there is only one flat charge for residential water, no matter how far away a residence is from the supply source or how much water that residence would use. There is also a practical consideration at work here: It is rather difficult to employ differential charges to distinguish between 300 yards and 200 yards from a facility, for example. It is sometimes just as easy to charge everyone the same, especially in relatively compact communities.

More problematic is the provision of education. Not all households have children to send to schools. Public schools, however, are financed substantially by the community at large, and the local burden tends to fall on everyone through the property tax structure. The simple argument is that nearly every household has or will send children to schools, so everyone pays for the benefits ultimately received. Other arguments are used as well. What seems to be the underlying concern, however, is that, if the marginal cost of public schools were indeed assessed to those using the service, the service would be priced out of range of users. Marginal cost pricing is not clearly cognizant of social equities.

Another reason residents might oppose marginal cost pricing of services, at least on new residential development, is that taxes on commercial and industrial enterprises subsidize residential public services. Extension of these services may mean sharing this subsidy with new residents, thereby lowering the benefit enjoyed by existing residents.

Congestion of existing public facilities caused by growth usually implies increased charges to restrict demand so as to help alleviate the congestion. Marginal cost pricing requires that all residents, both new and existing, be charged more. After all, each resident can be viewed as the marginal resident since each contributes to the total level of congestion. Marginal cost pricing may mean that not only new residents, but existing residents pay more.

Thus, if they do not choose to impose marginal cost pricing, and therefore development discipline, communities must be prepared for and respond to the inefficient growth that follows. Initially, communities facing growth would find it in their self-interest to build capital facilities needed to provide public services for the current and some of the new residents. Facilities therefore would have excess capacity. Facility capacity would not be designed with economic efficiency in mind, however. Communities rather would design facility capacities to maintain or achieve a desired

scale of the future community. Residents may prefer a low-density suburban future to a high-density urban future, even in progrowth communities. This would occur if community leaders and developers are essentially of the same mind to deny future entry into the market by outside developers. Especially in rapidly growing areas, community facilities may be deliberately planned to limit growth.

In a sense, communities act like clubs. That is, communities can be viewed as economic clubs that provide services to their members or, in this case, residents (Buchanan 1965; Sandler and Tschirhart 1980). If the clublike behavior of communities results in facilities being built too small from an economic efficiency point of view, growth is limited too soon. When the excess capacity is filled, and exceeded, congestion of facilities like roads and schools occurs. Growth controls then are imposed to prevent the community from suffering declining welfare since current residents would not be compensated for their loss of welfare occasioned by increasing or overuse of certain facilities. With each new resident, marginal costs to existing residents increase. Thus, to prevent rising marginal costs occasioned by growth and insufficient facilities, additional growth may be opposed by the members of the community club regardless of the benefits to society as a whole (Blewett 1983). In this scenario, when marginal cost pricing is opposed because the club prefers to assess the same prices on all its members, future membership is consciously limited by undersizing facilities. Membership capacity in the community is reached and new people are discouraged from joining because their membership would reduce the welfare of existing members. Even if the welfare gained by new members upon joining a community would exceed the welfare lost by existing members, admission will be denied or delayed.

A PUBLIC CHOICE ARGUMENT FOR DEVELOPMENT IMPACT FEES

If self-interest rather than social welfare better explains admission behavior, then the losers, or current residents, will block development unless compensated by the winners, or new residents. Impact fees allow such compensation. In a sense, impact fees allow new residents to buy their way into the community club. Only beneficial growth will occur since the exisiting members will set fees for the new members. In fact, Loveland, Colorado, assesses such a buy-in fee on most development (reduced fees are assessed for low-cost housing, however).

These new member fees or impact fees, if reasonably designed can approach the efficiency of marginal cost pricing without reducing the welfare of existing members. This can be achieved if the fees include only the capital and delivery cost components of the three-part tariff discussed earlier. The capital cost component must be a flat charge assessed per housing or other unit of measure to finance the marginal or additional costs of capital facilities. The delivery cost component is based on the distance away from central facilities as well as density of development. These two charges comprise the initial impact fee as they are based on the marginal costs of the expected future use of the facilities. The variable production or operating cost component of the tariff remains assessed upon use and is not part of the impact fee. The fee is assessed prior to occupancy. If such a fee represents merely the additional costs imposed on the community by new development, then it will allow only efficient development to occur. The impact fee will approximate the effects of marginal cost pricing in that development would have to pay its way by financing the full additional cost of providing new public service facilities to development. If the net benefits of development do not exceed the public service costs, then developers will not find it in their self-interest to build. They will build only if the net benefits to them exceed the public costs represented by the impact fee.

Such an impact fee can only be efficient if properly determined and allocated. This may be impractical, if not impossible, with administrative structures currently in place. Impact fee administration will likely be somewhat inefficient, though preferred over the alternatives. Inefficiencies should result in new development paying for additional capacity that may benefit existing residents. This usually results in higher-than-efficient capital costs. Existing residents could economize on building additional capacity by restricting their use of new facilities or by building larger facilities at the start. But impact fees give them little incentive to do so. Depending on the level, therefore, impact fees may force new development to pay the community's entire marginal cost of creating and delivering service, even though the community receives at least some benefits. Some development that would occur if true marginal cost pricing were used would not happen. Still, to many developers and community leaders, the choice is not between true marginal cost pricing and impact fees but rather between impact fees and inefficient growth controls as true marginal cost pricing is politically ruled out.[2]

Impact Fees for Fiscal Enhancement

Communities employing development impact fees also may choose to use them to enhance their fiscal base beyond that needed simply to cover the capital facility and delivery costs associated with new development. This is accomplished when the impact fee is used to artificially reduce the volume of development, raise the unit value of all real estate in the community, and thereby enhance the fiscal base of the community. The analogy here is with growth control efforts that reduce the supply of buildable land and increase fiscal surplus to existing residents.

A community's ability to use impact fees for fiscal enhancement will depend in large part on its ability to significantly affect the total supply of buildable land in an urban area. In the case of a community that has little effect on the total supply, attempts to gain excessive revenues through fees would lower the net benefits of development and development would tend to move elsewhere. However, if a community's growth policies can have a significant effect on the total buildable land supply in an urban area, impact fees can be raised so as to maximize revenues. These higher fees also would overly restrict residential growth. By forcing development to pay more than all the marginal costs of new facilities, thereby reducing construction of new housing, the price of new housing would increase, as would the value of existing houses (if they are close substitutes). Thus, if public officials want to raise property values throughout the community and its fiscal base as well, they would increase the fee even higher so as to further restrict development. By analogy, recent empirical work on the price effects of growth management policies supports this assertion (Landis 1986).

While courts hold that impact fees are to be limited to actual costs (Stroud 1987), the reality is that there is much leeway in the setting of fees (Callies and Freilich 1986). For one thing, they are subject to projections and forecast costs that can be based on a variety of assumptions (Porter 1983). Planners have discretion as to the type of service paid out of fees. Impact fees are now used to compensate for the added burden development puts on police and fire facilities and equipment, storm and sanitary sewers, museums, libraries, parks, roads, solid waste refuse, and emergency medical facilities. Some communities even assess fees for increased space at city hall. Fees can be used to force new residents to help finance services that are already being provided to existing residents. Since the community merely has to indicate how new development may affect costs or increase the demand for service, the burden of proof is on the developer to show that such a fee is unreasonably based. And even if fees are unreasonable, the delays caused by litigation can be expensive and builders may figure that it just does not pay to fight city hall in court.

IMPROVING PLANNING EFFICIENCY

Planning is a dynamic process since planners must, among other things, anticipate future demands for different land uses and plan the siting of capital facilities. Planners essentially engage in economic forecasting. They must forecast future land use requirements that are subject to numerous economic forces. The task of forecasting long-range housing and related demands makes the task of forecasting next year's GNP look like child's play.[3]

What happens when these forecasts prove wrong? Here we explore how the planning process can adjust to inevitable and unanticipated changes in economic conditions over time. The argument is that the appropriate use of impact fees can greatly increase the efficiency of the development and planning process. Fees are more than a method of compensation; they can be used to generate spontaneous adjustment in the development process so as to improve the efficiency of the urban spatial structure. In this sense, and if properly used, variations in impact fees can offer the planner a safety valve when the forecasts inevitably miss.

Suppose that market conditions change after some facilities are installed. The facilities were installed under a different economic reality. While we can change forecasts, we cannot change the public investment decisions already made. How will the current system allow adjustments? Will the system adjust by developers seeking, and receiving, zoning variances and other exemptions from planning boards? How can planners distinguish between outcomes that are in response to legitimate changes in economic conditions and those that are the result of political interference? In fact, there is little that prevents the planning process from prohibiting inefficient variances and exemptions.

Impact fees change decision making in such a way that planners can distinguish between efficient and inefficient development. Planners make initial projections as to new residential growth and plan public facilities accordingly. Some installation of facilities is undertaken. Schedules of impact fees are established to ensure that development pays its way. These schedules should provide for deviations in planned land use. If the time, location, or density of development is different from that planned, then the fees are set so there is compensation for the increased fiscal burden of alternative development. This can be accomplished by establishing an impact fee formula that varies impact fees by the time, location, and density of development. In fact, many fee systems in place today are based on these factors. It must be emphasized that the fees are not designed to punish or discourage developers who want to go against the plan. Rather, the purpose of these fees merely is to allow for efficient, fiscally responsible change.

If such a system were in place when market conditions changed, developers who want to build at levels not anticipated by planners will take all the costs and benefits into account. The fee schedule, based on a formula taking into account the timing, location, and density of development, would allow developers to consider any number of development alternatives. Only efficient growth will occur. If developers calculate incorrectly or make wrong decisions, then it is they who suffer losses of possible profits. Even if they are wrong, the impact fee schedule ensures that there will be no uncompensated external costs imposed on the community.

Much bureaucratic and political red tape thus is avoided with impact fees. The planning system is more fluid and adaptable and less subject to regulatory rigidities. If planning boards exempt a certain developer from certain fees, it will be obvious that special favors, rather than a legitimate variance resulting from changing economic conditions, are being granted. Impact fees act to minimize inefficient political interference in the planning process by making such interference more visible.

This is not administratively easy, however. For example, once a sewer system is installed, impact fees could be adjusted to cover cost as the nature of demand changes over time. Those who moved into the community earlier would not be affected by the changed impact fee. If demand increases, the fee would have to rise to cover the cost. The more the fee is raised, however, the greater the downward pressure on demand. An administrative solution to this problem would be to charge existing residents their share of the cost burden, through variable user fees, property taxes, or another mechanism. This would probably be politically unpopular.

IMPACT FEES AS A CONSTRUCTIVE REFORM

Public choice theorists would not assume that there is an "invisible hand" efficiently guiding public policy decisions. Instead, planners may find that the political outcomes associated with land use regulation seem to be guided by an "invisible foot" that is as likely to make matters worse as better. To help rid us of this invisible foot, we need what recent Nobel laureate James M. Buchanan refers to as a constructive reform (1986). A constructive reform of an institution changes the way decisions are made rather than changing personnel. Past calls for reform often failed to alter radically the planning process, despite claims to the contrary (e.g., Cutler, 1979). Calls for better-educated planners, more coordination, more careful planning, and so forth may be desirable changes, but they do not constitute real institutional reform. They merely strive to use the same institution more efficiently without altering basic behavior. They do not address the incentives that contribute to decisions being less than the best.

Impact fees are an example of a constructive reform in planning. They are an institutional reform that changes the incentives faced by participants deciding issues of urban residential growth. A sort of safety valve is provided that improves the dynamic efficiency of planning

by allowing planning to adjust better to unforeseen changes in economic conditions. Impact fees force developers to take account of the fiscal costs, not just the benefits, of residential growth. There is no divergence between those who make a decision and those who bear the burdens of the decision. This is not only equitable but also allows impact fees to approach the efficiency of marginal cost user charges. All economically efficient growth is allowed, and inefficient growth is priced out of the market by the fees. Impact fees also lack the pecuniary costs that marginal cost pricing imposes on current residents. Fees protect current residents but allow new residents to buy into the community and its publc services. Only mutually beneficial development occurs. Planning is more adaptable and less subject to regulatory rigidity. Political interference is minimized because it is more visible.

Some properties may be lost if impact fees are imposed in a municipality that can significantly affect the supply of developable land in an area. In this case impact fees will tend to overly restrict residential growth. However, further study is needed before it can be concluded that impact fees are any worse than other land use controls under similar market conditions.

Notes

1. For an excellent and more thorough explanation of the costs of local public services and a practical system of marginal cost user charges see Downing (1977a).

2. Downing (1977b) maintains that a properly designed system of marginal cost user charges will overcome such political opposition. However, his analysis ignores the short-run adjustment problems addressed here.

3. Some critics of zoning and land use regulation do not seem to appreciate some of the dynamics of planning public infrastructure (e.g., Siegan, 1983; Fischel, 1985). They view regulation in a static framework and provide an analysis of how better specification of property rights

can avoid nuisances associated with conflicting land uses. However, the transactions costs become very large when dealing with public goods across time periods. While many insights of the property rights approach are significant, planners have been needlessly alienated by those critics. Planners must deal with problems the economists do not address and still operate within the basic institutional structure of zoning.

References

Blewett, Robert A. 1983. Fiscal Externalities and Residential Growth Controls: A Theory-of-Clubs' Perspective. *Public Finance Quarterly* 11: 3–20.

Buchanan, James M. 1965. An Economic Theory of Clubs. *Economica* 32: 1–15.

———. 1986. Quest for a Tempered Utopia. *Wall Street Journal*, November 14, p. 30.

Callies, David L. and Robert H. Freilich. 1986. *Cases and Materials on Land Use*. St. Paul, Minn.: West.

Cutler, Richard W. 1983. The Dilemma of Modern Zoning. In *A Planner's Guide to Land Use Law*, edited by Stuart Meck and Edith M. Netter. Washington D.C.: Planners Press.

Downing, Paul B., ed. 1977a. Policy Perspectives on User Charges and Urban Spatial Development. In *Local Service Pricing Policies and Their Effect on Urban Spatial Structure*. Vancouver, B.C.: University of British Columbia Press.

———. 1977. Suburban Nongrowth Policies. *Journal of Economic Issues* June 11: 387–400.

Fischel, William A. 1985. *The Economics of Zoning Laws: A Property Rights Approach to American Land Use Controls*. Baltimore: The Johns Hopkins University Press.

Landis, John D. 1986. Land Regulation and the Price of New Housing: Lessons from Three California Cities. *Journal of the American Planning Association* 52: 9–21.

Porter, Douglas R. 1983. Exactions—An Inexact Science. *Urban Land* 42: 34–35.

Sandler, Todd and John T. Tschirhart. 1980. The Economic Theory of Clubs: An Evaluative Survey. *Journal of Economic Literature* December 18: 1481–1521.

Siegan, Bernard H. 1983. No Zoning Is the Best Zoning. In *A Planner's Guide to Land Use Law*, edited by Stuart Meck and Edith M. Netter. Washington, D.C.: Planners Press.

Smythe, Robert B. and Charles D. Laidlaw. 1984. *Residential Growth in Loudon County: Density-Related Public Costs*. Washington D.C.: American Farmland Trust.

Stroud, Nancy. 1987. The Legality of Development Impact Fees. Paper presented to the 1987 Conference of the American Planning Association. Boca Raton, Florida: Burke, Bosselman and Weaver, Attorneys at Law.

24

Evaluation of Impact Fees Against Public Finance Criteria

DOUGLASS B. LEE

Local government imposition of impact fees on new real estate development has been debated on grounds of both efficiency and equity, although these concepts seldom are formally articulated. In regard to efficiency, the issue is whether impact fees improve, worsen, or have no effect on the total net benefits generated by a group of scarce resources. In regard to equity, the issue concerns the fairness of such fees, meaning the equal treatment of equals. Vertical equity—effects on the distribution of income—also has been mentioned, and can be considered as a possible goal of impact fees.

Historical Patterns of Local Public Finance

In the old days, general revenues were raised through the property tax to be expended for the good of the community. Politics had some effect on the types of improvements made (e.g., streets and police versus parks and civic buildings), but the idea of each property getting back a fair return on its investment was suppressed. Sometimes you had to wait your turn, until the public works program caught up with your neighborhood.

As urban areas become more fragmented—whether as separate jurisdictions or as neighborhoods within a single city—the issue of tax-service parity began to surface. Suburbs withdrew from transit and other districts that did not provide them with service equal to their tax contributions. Possibilities for revenue redistribution, or tax base sharing, became lessened whether the redistribution was progressive or regressive.

Fiscal zoning arose in the late 1960s as communities became more activist in their efforts to control growth. New development was scrutinized to assess whether it paid its own way, but the answer (given the methods used) was obvious beforehand: The greater the number of school children, the greater the deficit, and that meant high-density family residential was worst, and commercial and industry best. Hence the search for clean industry.

Exclusionary Zoning

Because it was intuitively obvious that family residential could not be zoned out, implementation of fiscal zoning was both subtle and slight. The closest thing to a head-on confrontation was the case in Mt. Laurel, New Jersey, concerning low- and moderate-income housing.

Impact fees bring this gradual transformation another step, in large part because the exclusionary effects are less apparent to the person who thinks regulations define outcomes and markets do not. It now becomes easier to demand that new development "pay its own way" without making it seem as if moderate-income families with children are being zoned out.

Comment

Thus we end up with what amounts to a contract for services between developers and localities. The conclusions of this analysis are summarized in the last section of the chapter. Not to give anything away, the prescriptions offered are substantially at odds with current thinking on the subject of impact fees.

1. Where impact fees are suitable financing instruments (water and sewer infrastructures), other already existing instruments (special assessment districts) are superior.
2. Where efficiency can be improved only by use of metered user charges (transportation), impact fees cannot perform this function, although they can maintain equity without worsening efficiency.
3. Where vertical equity considerations predominate (schools and low income housing), impact fees or linkage fees are unsatisfactory instruments and should not be used.

This does not (quite) leave impact fees without a role to play. A few specialized niches remain, which may have large revenue impacts in certain situations, but use of impact fees should be, and probably will be, severely constrained. To fuel up for the theory and analysis that lies in between, the reader may wish to skip directly to the conclusions, then return below for the logical underpinnings.

POTENTIAL PURPOSES OF IMPACT FEES

Motivation for the use of impact fees is fiscal expediency, in that public agencies can obtain revenues when bond issues or tax increases are rejected, and developers can get their projects approved at a modest price. Because of the many conflicting interests at stake, however, the rationales for this arrangement need to be reviewed carefully. In judging impact fees as a financing instrument, it will be necessary to consider what an ideal instrument would look like, how close an approximation can be achieved by impact fees, and what alternative instruments or actions are available or likely to be used if not impact fees.

Capital Investment Market Test. Three objections might be raised against development: developers make too much profit, the development is necessary but causes undesirable side effects, and the developer serves demand that is unnecessary. Developers function as intermediary decision makers, between existing landowners and other factors of production, on the one hand, and future residents, employers, and consumers on the other. Efficient allocation of resources potentially can be enhanced by confronting users, or intermediary decision makers such as developers, with the costs of their actions. If developers or future residents are not willing to pay for the capital costs they necessitate, then perhaps the demand for that particular development should be scaled back or postponed.

For this test to be valid, developers must be confronted with the full cost—no more and no less—of their actions, on behalf of their future customers. If environmental quality is to be maintained at optimal levels, for example, then developers may need to incur pollution control expenses, reduce the density of development, and raise the price of their output.

Indirect User Charges. Fees imposed on real estate development fall between general taxes, at one end, and direct user charges, at the other. In current practice, impact fees must be tied to a particular type of improvement, and the calculation of the fee rate must be based on a formula that estimates the costs created by the development. For impact fees to work as user charges, they should be designed so as to encourage consumers to make beneficial choices from the standpoint of society as a whole.

Success of an indirect user fee is usually a trade-off between the efficiency gains from more direct charges versus the costs of imposing and collecting such charges. Metered charges are more effective at encouraging consumers to economize on usage, especially peak demand. Impact fees, as lump sum charges, cannot have an effect on consumption once they are paid.

They can, however, act as prices on the undesirable side effects of development, and serve to internalize environmental costs that would otherwise be imposed on others as a result of the development. Like effluent or emission charges, they are potentially more effective than regulatory mechanisms such as design standards and land use controls.

Fairness or Equity. Most often fairness or equity means that those persons giving rise to costs should pay them, perhaps with exceptions made for those from whom payment would create a hardship. A level playing field, equal treatment of equals, each person shouldering his/her responsibility, and no free riders are some of the notions that can be seen as underlying popular ideas of fairness. Another rationale is that the increase in the value of land is created by general government, so the public as a whole should receive compensation from those who benefit. If developers make excess profits by, in effect, selling something that is not theirs, then impact fees may increase public revenues at the expense of developer profits, without increasing housing costs.

Neutral horizontal equity means that policies are not biased in favor of, or against, any particular group. Both within segments of new development and between old and new, the calculation of fair share cost allocations has received much attention. While this effort is directed at achieving equity in the political arena, so that public acceptance will result, evaluation of horizontal equity requires more explicit tests to detect bias.

Income Redistribution. While horizontal equity (fairness) emphasizes process, or good rules, vertical equity emphasizes outcomes, namely, a more egalitarian income distribution. Thus, if impact fees serve to take income from the haves and transfer it to the have-nots, vertical equity is improved.

Ideally, income redistribution is implemented through taxes, rather than user charges, so as to minimize distortions away from efficient consumption and production. Unless impact fees are primarily viewed as taxes (which does not appear to be the case), redistributional impacts are a secondary effect rather than the main object.

POTENTIAL ABUSE: SHIFTING COST BURDENS ONTO OTHERS

Ownership of land in a growing urban area is likely to appreciate in value, and the owner has the option of retaining and consuming that value or selling it and using the proceeds to buy something else. This property right, however, does not entitle the owner to continue to receive urban services at their historic prices. If the demand for sewage treatment has gone up, and also its unit cost, then existing users as well as new residents should pay the higher costs. That the previous user was there first and the newcomers created the additional costs does not matter. Where some valuable resource is at stake, all consumers should be faced with the same price structure, reflecting the value of the resource to the marginal user who is priced off.

Not only is the existing resident likely to object to paying increased costs just to stay put, the existing resident has a strong incentive to increase the cost burden on new development for at least four reasons:

1. *Less Competition.* An increase in the price of new housing (to the extent that impact fees are passed on to buyers and tenants) raises the market value of existing developed real estate for which the new housing is a competitive substitute, at no cost to the existing owner. The strategy is analogous to protectionism, in which a community attempts to preserve its current income by shutting out competition from the rest of the world. The community will not be as prosperous as it would be without barriers, but existing residents will get to enjoy what prosperity there is.

2. *Monopolize Supply.* An increase in the cost of new development reduces the amount of new housing that is supplied. Anything that constricts supply wthout affecting demand has the effect of raising the price of the existing stock.

3. *Lower Taxes.* A reduction in the taxes on existing development reduces the cost burden to the existing resident and increases the market value of the property, because both tax burdens and service benefits (which would remain unchanged) are capitalized into housing prices.

4. *Exclude Undesirables.* A higher price on new development discourages those would-be residents who are undesirable because they have lower incomes and higher service demands. Perhaps the greatest grounds for suspicion is the fact that the persons negatively impacted by development fees are not residents of the jurisdiction imposing the fees and have no political voice in local decisions, other than through local developers. Legal protection for the rights of potential future residents has been a thorny problem for many years and no clear principles have been established, but the burden of evidence lies on the community to substantiate the legitimacy of its fees or restrictions on new development.

WHAT IS EFFICIENCY?

The goal of creating the maximum net benefits possible from the resources available is called efficiency. It is the total benefits to society (and all its members), minus the total costs of providing the benefits. Efficiency is determined by both production and consumption decisions, which allocate resources to alternative (competing) purposes.

Social Efficiency Criterion. While it is possible to draw some inferences about efficiency from observing outcomes (e.g., congested transportation, inadequate sewage treatment capacity, incompatible development), efficiency pertains more to the *process* of decision making than to the outcomes. The fundamental criterion states that each category of output (each "market") should be expanded until the marginal costs of an additional unit equal the marginal benefits. This is represented graphically in Figure 24–1. From the standpoint of society, the object is to produce the right amount

Figure 24–1. Optimizing Social Efficiency

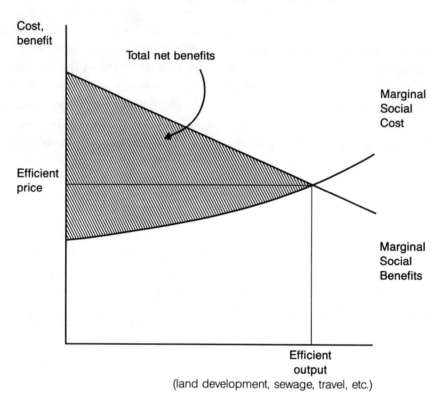

(land development, sewage, travel, etc.)

of output. If all relevant costs and benefits are internal to the producers and consumers making the decisions, then it is possible for private markets to tend toward efficiency without outside guidance. In this case, the criterion becomes price equal to marginal cost.

When the public sector is involved, the calculation of efficiency must be more explicit. Because impact fees primarily affect private decision makers (developers, service consumers, travelers), evaluation of efficiency rests on whether impact fees cause producers and consumers to internalize the right costs into their decisions. Governments participate actively in many sectors of the economy, particularly in land use development, water and sewer pro-

vision, transportation, schools, and subsidized housing. The types of government decisions that affect efficiency can be categorized into pricing, investment, and regulation (which affects private sector pricing and investment). Investment in capital facilities determines whether capacity is efficient, and pricing determines whether the capacity is efficiently used.

Efficiency Impacts on Development. Impact fees potentially may affect the efficiency of development, as well as the efficiency of the associated public services. Overcharging new development causes too little to occur, while undercharging results in too much. Underinvestment in sewage treatment capacity restricts growth inefficiently, while overcapacity may stimulate unwarranted growth. Low transportation user fees encourage sprawl development. High education fees result in underconsumption of schooling.

For infrastructure located on the land being developed, the developer is routinely required to provide the facilities as an in-kind contribution to the stock of public infrastructure. Where on-site facilities will serve a larger community (e.g., school, park, major arterial), the developer may bear only part of the full cost. Off-site facilities also may be contributed in-kind, through negotiation. Although similar principles apply to the imposition of on-site requirements as to off-site, the former are not financed through impact fees. Hence, the central question to be addressed is what kinds of off-site infrastructure should be financed through impact fees, and how much of each kind?

Capitalization of Future Cost Streams. With only minor exceptions, an impact fee is a lump sum charge, meaning that it occurs once, in this case in the lifetime of the building. Moving across to the other end of the spectrum (from fixed to variable), charges can be periodic, or they can occur on a daily use basis.

If the stream of future charges were known, exactly or probabilistically, whether annual, daily, or other, then this stream could be capitalized into a single lump sum, at the present or at some other point in time. This is simple discounting. Once the charge is capitalized, however, any incentive effects are over. An impact fee can create an incentive in regard to the particular development decisions affected by it, but that is the end of its efficiency impact.

Actual equivalence occurs only if the short-run price elasticities are zero. Imagine that all of a family's future purchases of prime beef

were charged as a single initial payment, and were free from then on: Consumption would be significantly different under the two methods of payment. Only where they would be the same either way will lump sum charges approximate the correct usage charges.

Daily or annual charges, whose magnitude is affected by use, even if use is determined only by an on-or-off decision, continue to have efficiency impacts each time a usage decision is made. Thus impact fees have inherent limitations for promoting efficiency.

Fixed versus Variable Costs. Because an impact fee is a lump sum charge, it is more likely to be applicable to fixed costs than variable costs. Not all capital costs are fixed, nor all operating costs variable. To the extent that facilities deteriorate from use, this portion of capital expenditures is a variable cost. Also, some operating costs may bear no relationship to use (they occur even if there is no use), hence they are fixed. As an overall pattern, however, impact fees are more likely to be applicable to some portion of capital costs, and not to operating costs.

MARGINAL COST PRICING

The criterion for efficient pricing is for price to equal marginal cost in all markets at all times. To the extent this criterion is followed, the amount of each good and service that is supplied and consumed will generate the maximum net benefits (benefits minus costs) for the total of all resources available. By letting price reflect the demand site of the equation, it is assumed that the (private) demand curve represents marginal (social) benefits from consumption of the associated output.

A prime virtue of marginal cost pricing is that all users are forced to confront the costs of their use and make decisions accordingly. When the output in question is a public service – i.e., one provided by government – there is no presumption that efficiency occurs automatically. If public agencies choose to produce the right amount of output and ration it optimally, this may be the result of conscious decision or blind accident, but not market incentives. For public services, then, evaluation of efficiency must be the result of explicit analysis. Whether and how efficiency can be improved depends on the nature of the relevant markets and the available alternatives.

Congestion Pricing. The specific form of marginal cost pricing that pertains to public facilities can be called congestion pricing, in that there is some limitation on the capacity of the infrastructure to produce output, and the facility becomes overloaded or congested when use approaches capacity. The suitability of marginal cost pricing for rationing scarce capacity is somewhat dependent on the ease with which marginal cost can be measured and priced, but it is more dependent on other characteristics of the services, as will be discussed below.

Although the basic theory has been presented many times,[1] it is worth reviewing here because its specific features are so important in deciding whether impact fees are suitable or not. Figure 24–2 represents the output of a service for which there is a constraining capacity, and variable costs of producing that output are constant until the capacity limitation exerts an effect. For transportation, congestion appears in the marginal cost curve as delay, increasing the travel time required per trip. For sewer and water systems, pipes may back up, availability of supply may be slowed or reduced, and effluent may be left untreated. For education, classrooms may be become crowded, and schools put on double sessions.

Short-Run Revenue Surplus. Wherever congestion is a limiting factor, the suppy can be efficiently rationed by increasing the price until demand matches the capacity. Congestion implies that the *average* cost rises as capacity is reached, which in turn implies that the *marginal* cost is rising even faster. This deviation between the marginal and average costs means that the price for efficiently rationing the scarce capacity of the facility is higher than the average variable cost of producing the output, so a revenue surplus is produced in the short run. This surplus is a return to capital, or a payback on the fixed investment, and justifies replacing or expanding capacity if the benefits exceed the costs. The investment cost does not enter into the marginal cost curve, which depends only on variable costs.

Take, for example, water supply. As more users are hooked into the system, available capacity becomes scarcer and hence more valuable. If capacity is exceeded for only some periods during the day, or some seasons, then only peak charges are needed to reduce excess demand for water and spread out use. As demand increases, per-unit charges should increase correspondingly, causing users to economize on their consumption effluent (e.g., long showers, lawn watering) when the price is greater than the value of the consumption. For the typical household, water demand is price elastic, meaning that there are ways to cut down without much suffering.

The efficiency of any given set of prices also depends on whether the investment in the capital facilities that determine capacity is itself efficient. Users should pay congestion charges wherever bottlenecks exist in the system, and

Figure 24–2. Marginal Cost Pricing

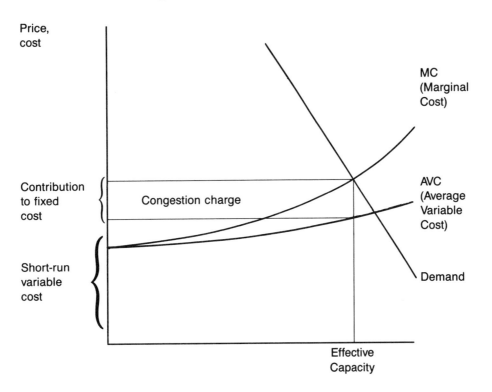

bottlenecks should be removed whenever the benefits to users justify the costs. In general, equilibrium will occur at some positive level of congestion, especially if demand as a whole is stable or growing. Thus, efficiency sized (e.g., highway) facilities will be congested at least some of the time, and efficient pricing will produce revenues (user fees minus operating costs) that will pay at least some portion of the capital costs.

Long-Run Investment. The theory of marginal cost pricing is based on short-run cost, meaning that something is fixed. When that something is capacity, efficient pricing imposes a toll or a capacity charge to ration the scarce capacity. Thus, pricing applies to consumption, not

to investment. Impact fees cannot be set at short-run marginal cost because they are inherently lump sum (long-run) charges.

It is possible to view a capital decision to build a sewer line as the point of consumption, but only because efficient short-run pricing with respect to use of the pipeline is assumed to be zero. This is the same as saying that price elasticity is zero (the demand curve is vertical), meaning that no change in price will affect the amount consumed. In such circumstances, neither variable pricing nor lump sum charges serves any purpose. If short-run price elasticities are low and collection cost savings from simpler fees are high, the approximation may be better than the theoretical ideal.

Long-run efficiency occurs as a response to short-run efficiency, along with suitable conditions (constant returns to scale, no externalities, etc.). Although sometimes alluded to, long-run marginal cost pricing is, at best, an approximation, but it is not a theory. Pragmatically, it is reasonable to believe that decisions are more likely to be efficient if the decision makers are directly confronted with the full costs and benefits of their decisions, whether short run or long run, but the theory of marginal cost pricing only asserts this for the short run. The long run takes care of itself. One can argue that each increment of development should pay the increment of costs for which it is responsible, but this is only an analog of marginal cost pricing.

Scale Economies. It can be claimed that infrastructure systems enjoy decreasing unit costs, or increasing returns to scale. If so, then efficient short-run charges will be inadequate to finance capacity, and a fixed charge may be applied, either in addition to metered usage charges (creating a multipart price), or instead of usage charges. Scale economies urge that excess capacity be built in at each step, while efficient short-run charges should be kept low so as not to discourage users who would derive benefits above marginal cost. Road strength and capacity can be increased at decreasing cost per lane or inch of thickness, bigger pipes can be buried at small incremental cost, and larger treatment facilities and reservoirs cost less per gallon than small ones. Whether the deficit between efficient prices and long-run cost should be covered by a fixed charge on *users* is a pragmatic rather than theoretical question, but such a charge is certainly acceptable in theory and desirable in practice.

To the extent that lump sum charges are more efficient than, or at least as efficient as, metered usage charges, they should be levied on all users of the system, not just new development. On-site pipe or road, of course, is constructed by the developer, and nearby off-site pipe may be shared among owners within a small geographic area, through an assessment district or its equivalent. The cost can be recovered in the form of an annual charge or a single lump sum (at, say, the time of development), but it should be the same for all properties that are served.

If, in fact, there are scale economies, then long-run unit costs should go down, rather than up. Short-run prices however, may be justifiably low if there is excess capacity for periods of years. The danger is that new development will be attracted to the low prices, which will rise as capacity is reached. Avoiding this involves calculating the long-run capital cost at the point the decision to invest is made, and allocating those "average incremental" costs to the benefiting properties.

Actual unit costs seem to rise, however, for several reasons. Investment is not planned and executed efficiently, and errors increase as the scale of the system increases. Political decision making becomes more complex, offsetting some of the potential cost savings of larger systems. Networks become more extensive to take advantage of greater treatment or supply capacity, so travel takes place over greater distances. Land, excavation, and construction become more costly as an area urbanizes and becomes more dense.

APPLICABILITY CHARACTERISTICS OF IMPACT FEES

Because the applicability of impact fees is dependent on certain characteristics of the capital infrastructure that fees are intended to pay for, the discussion below is broken into five categories. The first category—water, sewer, and drainage facilities—is the most common area of application and the one for which impact fees are most suitable. The second category is fire, police, parks, libraries, and other facilities for which a bounded geographic service area can be defined. Transportation infrastructure comprises the third category, and impact fees have a significant but limited role in this sector as indirect user charges. Schools form the fourth category and housing the fifth; the conclusion offered here is that impact fees are unsuitable for either category.

Water, Sewer, and Drainage Improvements

The most useful concept for guiding the financing of water, sewer, and some other infrastructure types is the special improvement district. Such districts also are called special assessment districts, special purpose districts, and municipal utility districts. Both the concept and the institutional mechanism of special improvement districts have been around for some time, although their popularity waxes and wanes. By and large, they could be used much more than they are, and in part this reticence is due to weak understanding of the economic principles for calculating assessments.

An Ideal Special Assessment District. Imagine a situation in which entrepreneurs sought to formulate independent service districts, within which sewerage and treatment facilities would be constructed on the basis of contracts between property owners and sewer providers. A district would consist initially of a group of properties and a sewer system optimized for those properties. Formation of the district would start with some relatively critical decision factor, such as the location for treatment and discharge. Properties would be added into the district so long as the incremental cost of the associated users was less (through scale economies) than the average cost of previous users. With each increment, the entire system would be reoptimized, including treatment capacity, and locations and sizes of pipes. To the extent that further expansion of output produced long-run scale economies, additional consumers would reduce average cost, despite the additional costs in length and size of pipe required to serve them.

At some output, scale economies would be exhausted, and additional properties could not be brought in without increasing average cost. This, then, is the interpretation of marginal cost: It is the incremental (reoptimized) cost of adding an additional consumer to the system, at the time of the *design* of the system. Hence, *all* consumers are "marginal," not just the ones last to arrive. Many different and overlapping districts could be designed, gradually weeding out those that could not provide the lowest unit costs to enough locations to achieve scale economies. If scale economies were large, districts would be large, perhaps only one for a metropolitan area; if scale economies were small, the result would be many small districts.

Fair Share Charges. Two implications now emerge. First, for those inside a district, the charge for membership would be the same for all, i.e., average cost in the sense of total cost divided by total users. Location and length of connecting pipe would be irrelevant. Because the district as a whole benefits from the inclusion of each member, through lower unit cost, then the *fairest* way to charge is equally to all, or else according to benefits. Second, some properties are bound to be left out because they add more costs than they would pay, the price being average cost. Such "interstitial" users would have to pay a surcharge above average cost in order to be included. For these users, a higher entry fee would be efficient, because it would force the developer to judge whether the demand for development at the site could support the additional charge, which other ("better" located) properties did not have to pay.

All of the above assumes that the price elasticity of sewage production is zero, negating any benefits that might occur from direct user charges. So long as toxic products are kept out at the source, and water supply is properly priced, this is approximately accurate as a function of the number of persons. Occupancy, however, is somewhat more price elastic, in that the higher the price of a dwelling unit, the higher the expected number of occupants. This is because the lower the price per square foot, the more square feet each occupant will buy or rent. Thus, the correct occupancy to assume in calculating the per-dwelling-unit charge depends on knowing housing prices and market demand in advance.

Impact Fees as Special Assessments. Whenever the infrastructure investment creates a fixed capacity (streets, sewerage, sewage treatment), the efficiency of impact fees depends on the price elasticity of demand for consumption of that capacity once it is provided. For sewage collection or water distribution, scale economies in sizing and laying of pipe make it reasonable to believe that correct investment usually will be such as to eliminate congestion (excess flow) in most of the pipes. In other words, efficient pricing of the pipe capacity will almost always be close to zero in use, so that fixed charges tied to land development will not be nondistorting in the short run and efficient

in the long run. For sewage treatment or water supply this is less true, and for streets it is much less true.

Thus the usefulness of impact fees is for operationalizing the concept of the special improvement district, sometimes where the ideal solution involves numerous separate and overlapping districts (e.g., for collectors, trunks, and interceptors), without having to formally create the districts. The analysis that would be relevant to the formulation, cost estimation, and benefit distribution of a special assessment district is the same as the analysis that should be done for impact fees. Whatever fees are determined must apply to all properties in the district, whether previously developed or not.

Density Incentives. Within these bounds, impact fee sewer financing can be efficient. How do we reward properties for developing more intensively, rather than spreading out to the hinterland? The answer is that compact development would lower unit costs to the point that more remote or low-density development would raise unit costs, and thus incur a surcharge (which would not have happened if the intensive development were omitted). Now, suppose the intensive development occurs after the district has been finished? If this exceeds existing capacity, then the question is simply one of incremental cost; if the opportunity still is available to lower unit costs, then the intensive development can receive a discount relative to others. Decisions have to be based on forecast and risk, and adaptations made when conditions change. Suppose expected development does not show up? Avoidable costs should be recovered as best as possible, and sunk costs distributed equitably but in a nondistorting manner. Such outcomes should be anticipated and provided for in the design of the district.

The appropriate intensity of development can be estimated beforehand, and it does not matter whether the current owners or residents actually consume the service provided; the value of the property is enhanced. Hence, benefiting properties can be identified and assessed, whether they become developed or not. Sewer rights can be detachable from land ownership to the extent that sewer access could be transferred from one owner to another, permitting higher density in one place for lower in another. When such a transfer occurs, the parties to the transaction must compensate the district for any increase in total costs resulting from a redistribution of service. The closer an impact fee can emulate this ideal special assessment district, the more efficient it will be.

The Timing of Development. Suppose two parcels are part of the same district, but one is building out immediately and the other later. The carrying costs of constructing infrastructure for the latter must be offset by scale economies from larger output, otherwise the two would not be in the same district. A large lag, however, between payment of the assessment and actual hookup means a reduced level of benefits, relative to properties that develop early. One way to equalize this imbalance is to apply the same assessment rate on all properties, but time the collection date to coincide with expected development, thus lowering the real cost to later development. This timing, however, should not be affected by *actual* construction, since there should be no pricing disincentive to hooking in, once the sewer capacity is on line. The actual payment can be at the time of district formation, at expected time of development, or at actual development, so long as the real (constant dollar) discounted value of the assessment remains the same.

In practice, several actions could minimize this problem. Construction of both treatment capacity and sewerage could be staged to match development, while still preserving whatever scale economies exist. Subsequent stages could be accelerated, postponed, or abandoned in response to market conditions. High levels of uncertainty could be dealt with by breaking construction into separable stages, even if some scale economies were sacrificed.

Storm Drainage. The clearest case for impact fees pertains to storm drainage facilities. Impact can be measured directly as the peak volume of runoff leaving the site, after development, with the impact fee based on the cost of absorbing that runoff elsewhere. If on-site devices can be fashioned to reduce runoff to zero, then there should be no impact fee. In contrast, paving over a hillside would result in the maximum fee.

Efficiency gains are clear. The developer compares the cost of on-site retention with the fee schedule, which in turn is based on off-site costs, and selects the optimum combination. If the fee schedule is correct, the developer's choice will be best for the community. Essential to this success, of course, is the relationship between the actual volume of runoff—after the developer has taken mitigating measures—and the fee.

Parks, Police, Fire, and Other

Wherever a service is broken into districts, the capital facilities can be financed on a special district type of arrangement. If direct user fees are not applicable (they might be for recreation facilities, for example, but not for open space), then a lump sum or annual assessment creates little or no distortion. Perhaps libraries should not be financed with impact fees, for reasons discussed later in regard to schools. The others fit within the special district concept, and can be financed with properly calculated impact fees.

Service Districts. The basis for calculating the fee bears some scrutiny. Distance may be relevant, or the value of the property served, or some other measure of the cost of providing the service to the property or the benefits to the property or its occupants from having the service.

For many of these services, not only capital costs but many operating costs are fixed in the short run, meaning that lump sum charges do not entail significant losses in efficiency. A one-time, service-forever impact fee method of collection, however, is certainly less sensible than an annual fee.

Equal Treatment. Consistency is important, although it is not necessary that each district follow the same procedures. One district could levy a lump sum assessment on benefiting properties, while another could rely more on user fees. What must be consistent is that each district—old development or new—be separately responsible for its own capital infrastructure cost, for each category so financed. If existing residents finance police stations out of current general taxes, then new development should not be charged an impact fee if it will also be subject to the same general tax levies.

Transportation Facilities

Although impact fees are most frequently used for water and sewer facilities, transportation or traffic impact fees are also major areas of application. Streets and highways are distinctly different from pipeline infrastructure. Even if short-run demand were inelastic, off-site origins and destinations are not sufficiently predetermined to be able to assign off-site segments of the network to particular development. It would be conceptually possible (with zero price elasticities) to define a large number of service areas and impose the constraint that properties within each area should pay the costs of roads within that service area, except for through traffic, but the practical ambiguities still would be enormous. Because price elasticities are not zero, there is no point in seriously considering a special assessment district analogy for streets. Instead, they should be financed with direct user fees. Only some small portion of the street system that gives direct access to property can be financed efficiently through impact fees, and the bulk of this is on-site to most development.

Ideal Transportation User Charges. Congestion indicates that the price to the user is too low. If we then ask how impact fees can reduce congestion, it must be either through increasing the price or through expanding capacity. Do impact fees cause capacity to be efficiently expanded? Not any better than any other general revenue source, which is to say, no, they don't. Do impact fees increase the price to users? Again, no. On their face, traffic impact fees cannot do anything for efficiency.

Let's look more deeply. Table 24–1 lists the possible responses of travelers to an increase in user charges at times and places where congestion currently exists, i.e., to efficient peak charges. Clearly, a flat impact fee cannot induce any of the first eight responses because it cannot differentiate between the time of day or route of the trip. If we then peruse the possible developer responses to impact fees, the answer to the question depends on how the impact fee is calculated. Reduction in units or

Table 24–1. Traveler and Developer Responses to Prices

Travel Behavior Responses:
1. Reschedule trip.
2. Forego trip.
3. Combine purposes.
4. Combine vehicles (carpool).
5. Shift to higher occupancy mode.
6. Shift to off-peak period.
7. Shift to off-peak direction.
8. Shift route.
9. Shift origin of trip (home).
10. Shift destination of trip.

Developer Responses:
1. Reduce units or square feet.
2. Reduce trip origins.
3. Reduce trip destinations.
4. Relocate trip origins or destinations.
5. Change land use.

square feet reduces trip generation at the site, but increases total vehicle miles of travel. If based on actual trip origins or destinations (not a priori averages), there is some stimulus created for the developer to reduce trip making without reducing units or square feet. If only peak trips were counted, then the best solution for developers would be peak road pricing. Finally, impact fees might lead to a different location for trip ends or a different use of land, if the fees had a differential impact by location or type of use. It is unlikely that any such revisions would have favorable efficiency impacts.

Traffic Impact Fees. Working backward from what would be efficient user charges, impact fees can be evaluated as to how well they approximate such charges in comparison to other alternatives. Efficient highway charges would be imposed almost exclusively based on direct use, although multipart prices can be (and are)

charged to vehicle owners for access to the highway network as annual use fees. On-site road improvements are charged to property buyers in the initial sale of the property, but there is no separate itemization of costs.

For such improvements – subdivision streets, office parking, shopping center circulation – the efficiency loss from a lump sum charge rather than direct use fees is negligible if the design and construction standards of the facilities are correct. This means that lane widths, gutters and storm drains, pavement strength, etc., are built to levels that would be ideal in order to maximize long-run net benefits. Design standards that require overly costly roads, or permit shoddy construction that must be rebuilt at public expense, are inefficient. By and large, however, such on-site improvements are reasonably close to being ideal in practice under present policies.

For off-site improvements, the relationship is much less clear. To the extent that direct user charges or user taxes pay for highway costs, all users pay them on a continuing basis, and it is arbitrary to single out new residents or users associated with new development. Alternatively, to the extent that general taxes pay for highways, new residents contribute through property, sales, and income taxes, the same as do existing residents, so no separate charge for new development is justifiable. From yet another perspective, a lump sum or annual membership charge as a substitute for direct use fees – which might be suitable for local or uncongested roads – should be collected from *all* users, not just from those generated by new development.

Capitalized Value of Access. When real property changes hands, the sale price includes a value for access to transportation. This market value reflects the level of transportation use that would be efficient for the particular location, whether or not the owner uses transportation at a higher or lower rate. Thus a household or firm can buy into the network, consume transportation services, and recover the remaining capitalized value on selling. The price of this access will depend on the cost of new development, the property and other taxes used to finance transportation services, and the levels of direct user fees.

The only effect of impact fees on this value is in the cost increment imposed on new development. If the impact fees substitute for what would have been property taxes, say, then new residents will pay more for access but less in property taxes. Existing residents, however, will enjoy only the latter. Therefore, it is fair (and perhaps efficient as well) to charge new development *only* if existing residents have built up a surplus of capital facilities that have been paid off faster than they are being used, and shares in this equity can be sold to developers. Because access to this already existing stock is aquired through property rights, developers will charge buyers for the access whether or not the developers are charged. Thus, in these particular circumstances, previous taxpayers will recover some of their previous investment, and the impact fee will not be shifted forward.

This result can be efficient, however, only if users are undercharged on a direct basis. Higher property prices obtained because access rights generate consumer surplus affect the distribution of income and hence equity, but their ostensible tie to transportation is ephemeral. The market, not an impact fee formula, will determine the amount of this premium. Whereas, if direct user fees are inefficiently low, an explicit charge for infrastructure will tax away some of the unpriced benefits that are capitalized into land values. The efficiency of this indirect mechanism then depends, as before, on the magnitudes of the relevant price elasticities, low elasticity implying low efficiency loss.

Equity Without Efficiency. Despite the impossibility of using impact fees as a substitute for efficient road pricing, they can maintain the existing level of inefficiency while distributing the costs more equitably. This claim is based on several premises. First, highway user taxes pay less than half the long-run costs of highways, and the bulk of the subsidy comes directly or implicitly from local taxpayers. Existing residents have inherited or paid for a stock of roads that is not earning revenues fast enough to cover full replacement costs. Second, with no changes in the inefficient utilization of roads, new residents require lane-miles of road stock in the same proportions as existing residents. Hence, new consumers can be asked to contribute a similarly unproductive stock of assets as previous property owners.

One obvious error in some current practice is the calculation of traffic impact fees based on loading the network with the new development's traffic and looking for congestion. This violates the basic principle of impact fee design, namely, that all users face the marginal cost. Removing some existing users would eliminate the congestion, so any group of users could be called the marginal consumers. Moreover, if existing users are not paying peak congestion charges, there is no reason new development should. As with other infrastructure, it only matters that the agreed-upon miles of road are provided, not which roads are paid for by which development, or whether the revenues are actually spent on roads.

Schools

Primary and secondary education primarily is a local government responsibility, but there is a great deal of ambiguity as well as controversy over who is responsible for what. States provide school aid, ostensibly to equalize tax burdens, and the federal government has recently added education to its roster of cabinet-level agencies.

Education as a Public Good. Methods of financing education, mechanisms for service delivery, and the purposes of education all are controversial and often are confused. Some people claim that market processes will produce the best system at the least cost, because it is in the interest of all citizens and parents to secure good education for themselves and their children. Others maintain that equal opportunity requires public provision of most, if not all, primary and secondary education services.

The truth almost certainly lies in between. Some share of the motivation for basic education is the self-interest of the family and student, and some share is in the shared values and common understanding that society depends on. Of the common or public share, part is subject to local discretion and part is of national concern. The difficulty, then, is in separating these so that different purposes can be accomplished without treading on others.

Public purposes typically are effected through educational standards (requirements), subsidies, and public provisions of service. Denominational and other private schools are acceptable providers, so long as they are not racially discriminatory, but they do not receive public subsidy. The content of the public share of the curriculum is difficult to specify, how-ever, and so most basic education is in public schools, rather than contracted or subsidized privately operated schools. The effectiveness of an educational voucher system, for example, would depend, in part, on how well public purposes could be accomplished while relinquishing a degree of control to private providers.

If basic education were a purely private good, then consumers (or their parents) could be charged directly for the full costs. To the degree that there is a public purpose, the costs should be borne by the community, with the share falling on each taxpayer bearing no relationship to the load placed by the taxpayer on the educational system. To the degree that the purpose is national in scope, the burden on any individual community should be unrelated to its contribution of the student load.

The boundaries between responsibilities are not clear, and the principles themselves are not explicitly recognized, but they are implicitly followed. Perhaps most illuminating is a recent Kansas City case, in which a judge ordered a doubling of the local school tax levy, plus an income tax surcharge on those working in the district, whether residents or not. The judge is quoted as stating, "A majority has no right to deny others the constitutional guarantees to which they are entitled."[2] His action implies that the minimum standards for the performance of public education are not being satisfied, and that it is primarily the local community (which consistently voted down school tax increases) that was failing its *legal* requirements. Obviously the judge has no authority to command state or federal government revenues, but this would not justify burdening local taxpayers if he believed they were already doing their part.

Equitable School Impact Fees. The implications of the foregoing for impact fees are two-fold. First, the number of school children associated—directly or indirectly—with new development is not only irrelevent, it should be illegal for impact fee purposes. Second, the bases on which a valid impact fee could be levied on new development for educational purposes are thin if not nonexistent.

To scale a tax or fee according to the number of school pupils is an indirect charge on consumers, albeit crudely communicated. It entertains the prospect that a group of prospective residents could be excluded from the community because they were unable or unwilling to pay to have their children educated to at least the minimum standards and perhaps a higher community standard. If such direct charges are acceptable as mandatory (at present they are voluntary at the individual level, through private schools, or collectively voluntary at the community level, for all residents), then the charges should be collected from the families at the time of enrollment. Thus, indirect user fees for school children cannot be justified.

A valid formula would have to be scaled to whatever local tax base was used for schools, generally the property tax, and the amount based on the value of the accumulated capital stock, net of depreciation and remaining debt. In this way a community could sell equity shares in the net worth of its school facilities whether or not they needed to be expanded to accommodate additional residents. The revenues should be used for capital replacement or expansion if such expenditures are warranted, but the funds should not be otherwise earmarked.

Housing

Programs that require developers to provide some amount of low- or moderate-income housing as a condition for permit approval are called inclusionary zoning or linkage. The required housing units may be provided on-site, off-site, or through payments made by the developer. Although these housing exactions have been in use for roughly 10 years and are popular in Boston and San Francisco, they have not been fully tested as to their legality.

Income Redistribution. The intent of linkage programs is to increase the stock of housing and reduce its price to households with below-average income, and this requires that some share of the population give up some of its income or claims on resources. Exactly who the losers are, whether they have high or low incomes, whether the developer carries the burden through reduced profits, and other empirical questions have not been fully resolved. The amount and distribution of the transfers undoubtedly vary depending on the local housing market and the ways in which developers can satisfy the requirements.

As a purpose, income redistribution is regarded as equitable if the sacrifice imposed on taxpayers is in proportion to their income (or progressive with respect to income) and the recipients of the benefits are those of inferior means. Even if the redistribution is clearly from rich to poor, it is desirable that all rich persons contribute comparably, and that the benefits be distributed among a substantial share of those who are worthy. An almost random sacrifice imposed on a minority of households, for the benefit of a selected few, is not generally considered to be a satisfactory income redistribution effort.

Aside from the narrowness of the tax base (new development) and the necessary small number of beneficiaries, linkage programs do not meet the test of equal sacrifice. Unless existing residents in a given community are taxing themselves to provide low- and moderate-income housing for others, there is little justification for taxing new residents and activities. As an income redistribution program, inclusionary zoning is a process whereby one group (current voters) tells another group (developers) to give money to a third (low- and moderate-income families). From this perspective, such programs appear inequitable.

Taxes versus User Fees. Enabling legislation, courts, and current practice all have placed a lot of emphasis on the relationship between the fees charged and the costs created by the development. The term impact fee itself implies that it is not a tax. Although public finance notions of efficiency and equity have not been readily apparent in this scrutiny, the strong implication is that fees to cover the costs of infrastructure are acceptable whereas taxes on development are not. Why this might be so is a question for which the answer must be invented.

As a tax on development, the issue of associated costs would be irrelevent, even if there were separate taxes for water, sewer, and highways. A real estate transfer tax, for example, is not constrained to cover specific costs, while a special improvement district fee is so constrained.

In addition to this apparent intent to prohibit development taxes, a tax imposed on such a narrow base (however lucrative) is inherently suspect. The ideal of a tax that is imposed on a broad base and is nondistorting of consumption and production choices clearly is not achieved. In addition, taxation imposed on new development by existing residents looks like an attempt to shift the tax burden to those who are unrepresented, i.e., foreigners living abroad.

Taxes imposed on in-commuters but not local residents, or development restrictions that require substantially different development from what already exists (e.g., much higher income levels) have been overturned by courts. No clear legal theory guides these decisions, but some concept of equal sacrifice seems to be involved. As taxes, then, impact charges cannot pass several tests of equity, so they must be justified on cost-of-infrastructure grounds, i.e., as indirect user fees.

A Tax on Development. Linkage programs clearly do not fall under the user fee rationale, and can be justified only as special taxes. What purpose the revenues are put to is largely irrelevant; general tax revenues are augmented by some amount, and municipal expenditures can by choice be augmented a like amount. If a worthy purpose is required to justify the tax, then any such purpose that the government already does or could engage in could be named. Despite the linkage terminology, the tie between the tax and the expenditure purpose is inherently a tenuous one.

Nor does the practice of in-kind contributions of particular on-site or off-site units change the essential character of the tax or the linkages. If a tax on development is valid, then the use of the revenues should not matter. Such a tax, however, is extremely suspect because of the benefits that accrue to current property owners at the expense of potential or actual future residents who have little political representation in the decision process.

PRINCIPLES OF IMPACT FEE DESIGN

The previous sector-by-sector review of impact fee considerations represents the application of general guidelines spelled out here in summary form. Although generalizations can be

Table 24–2. Types of Urban Services, Characteristics, and Financing of Capital Infrastructure Costs

Service	Key Characteristics	Ranked Financing Alternatives
Sewer	Large-scale economies Low efficient usage charges Inelastic short-run demand Fixed capital costs	Special district Metered usage charge Impact fee
Water	Scale economies Elastic demand Fixed capital costs	Metered usage charge Special district Impact fee
Drainage	Fixed long-term cost	Impact fee
Fire	Defined service district Fixed operating costs	Annual service fee Property tax Special district Impact fee
Police	Defined service district Fixed operating costs	Property tax Special district Impact fee
Park	Defined service district Fixed operating costs Unrestricted community access	Property tax Special district Impact fee
Library	Defined service district Fixed operating costs Unrestricted community access	Property tax Special district Impact fee
Highways	Short-run variations in demand High variable costs High-demand elasticity	Metered user charge Special district
Transit	Short-run variations in demand Elastic demand Restricted service range	Metered user charge Special district General tax
Schools	Unrestricted access	Government grants General tax
Subsidized Housing	Means tested access Income redistribution objective	General tax Government grants

stated succinctly, their implications for design and suitability of impact fees often are not self-evident. Thus, the particular form that a principle takes when applied to roads, for example, can be found by referring back to the section on roads. Table 24–2 lists many of the types of infrastructure that are of interest along with the important characteristics affecting the ap-

propriateness of the impact fees and a ranking of various financing methods.

As can be seen from the right-hand column, when impact fees are acceptable they are always the least preferred alternative. Desirability of impact fees for these purposes is highly dependent on circumstances and the manner in which the fees are calculated and imposed.

While the principles listed below do not uniquely prescribe impact fee formulas and calculations, they provide a checklist for testing different infrastructure types for applicability.

Which Services to Consider. Although impact fee design is separated here into three subareas, guidelines listed for one area also may have consequences for other areas. Which categories of services may be suitable for impact fees depends on existing and future financing instruments, equity, and potential efficiency goals.

1. *Equity Means Pay Your Way.* The community believes or accepts that it is equitable for direct users to bear the costs of the facilities or service, and nonusers should not have to pay (other equity interpretations are ability-to-pay and benefits received).

2. *No Metered User Charges.* Marginal cost pricing is tied to short-run variable costs, and its application requires that use be metered, as in a congestion charge that efficiently rations use of existing capacity. Direct usage fees can recover not only variable costs, but some or all of fixed costs as well, and are superior for this purpose to impact fees.

3. *Zero Price Elasticity.* Impact fees can substitute for metered user charges only when the price elasticity of demand is close to zero. When it is not, fees should be either tied to actions the developer can take to effectively meter and price use or otherwise alter consumer behavior (e.g., charging separately for parking, constructing transit access), or else not used.

4. *Scale Economies.* If substantial economies of scale exist, then the recovery of some portion of fixed capital costs through lump sum charges such as special assessments, hookup or impact fees, and annual access charges,

can be efficient. If, in addition, short-run marginal cost is close to zero (no congestion, or depreciation from usage), then the entire capital cost can be financed through lump sum charges.

5. *Pure Public Goods.* Impact fees should not be used for the provision of public goods, of the nonrival type. These are services or benefits (such as national defense and air quality) whose supply is not diminished by the presence of other consumers. Some portion of primary and secondary education falls into this category.

6. *Income Redistribution.* Impact fees should not be used for purposes of income redistribution, because this transforms the fees into taxes levied on one group for the benefit of another.

Calculating the Charges. The basic formula for the amount paid by a given property is costs minus credits, where credits consist of allowances for amounts previously paid or to be paid in the future.

1. *Everybody is Marginal.* All users should pay marginal cost, not just new ones, and not just those who appear to be the cause of the overload.

2. *Paid-Up Capital Stock.* The revenues extracted from new development through impact fees can be based on costs that existing resident/users have already paid. This condition suggests either that some capital stock has been installed by previous residents and is now being sold to new residents, or that previous residents will be exclusively responsible for their own infrastructure.

3. *Assigning Costs.* For investment (i.e., long-run) decisions, fair share cost is the long-run marginal cost of adding one more user, which is equal to average (incremental) cost at the margin. All users in the increment pay the same average incremental cost. A user whose long-run marginal cost is above the average cost for the increment should pay the higher cost.

4. *Tied to Actual Impacts.* If the impact is to be reduced (say, demand for peak capacity) without reducing the scale of development, then the impact fee should be calculated in such a way that the fee is lower if the impact itself will be lower.

5. *Property-Specific.* Impact fees should be specific to the circumstances of the property being charged. Fixed flat rate (e.g., per unit or per square foot for all locations) impact fees can have little beneficial efficiency impact.

6. *Changing Standards.* The community may raise or lower standards for parks, treatment capacity, roads, etc., so long as either there are no spillovers (costs and benefits are internal to the properties affected) or the community changes standards for everyone. The change must be documented by a public purpose rationale.

Execution of the Contract. Once the fee has been determined for a particular property, then the result is a de facto contract between the municipality and the developer.

1. *Service Must Be Delivered.* Service on which the impact fee is based must, in fact, be provided within the time period and other terms of the contract. This does *not* require that current revenues be earmarked for the particular service, or be spent on it, or spent in a timely fashion; nor is the local government absolved from providing the service if revenues are insufficient. Because the government has made itself the sole supplier of the services it provides, it incurs an obligation to meet reasonable demand at a reasonable price, subject to judicial review and penalties for nonperformance. Communities should be permitted to charge new development for excess capacity that has already been paid off by existing or previous residents.

2. *Separate District Financing.* If new development is charged for the provision of particular services, then the financing of those services for the preexisting portions of the new community must be financed separately. Each explicit or implicit district so formed can finance each of the separately financed services in whatever manner it chooses (within legal bounds), so long as the burden falls on property owners within the district. One district could use impact fees and another a property tax, but the property tax could not apply to the district within which impact fees were collected. A sales tax, for example, would not be acceptable, because its burden is not limited to district property owners.

Fundamentally, fees should be higher if the impact is higher, and lower if the impact is lower. This requirement can be met at two levels. The least demanding level is for developments with larger impacts to be charged higher impact fees than developments with lesser impacts. Thus whatever formula is used to set the fee levels, whether complex or simple, whether uniform or property-specific, the relationship should be so as to increase the fee for development having increased impacts.

The second level is attained when fee levels are set in such a way that a given development can reduce its fees by altering its design or management so as to reduce its impacts. This might be achieved through design changes, management functions, or service metering. For example, a traffic impact fee based on the number of dwelling units or square feet of floor space will meet the first level (if different types of land use are properly calibrated), but not the second. To serve the higher standard, the impact fee should be lower if a development can demonstrate that its traffic generation will be less than the rate assumed for its type of development (perhaps through tenant mix or a traffic management plan). Efficiency can only be served effectively by the second type.

Irrelevant Factors. Because existing guidelines for impact fees dwell on a number of factors that are, in fact, not relevant to the design or implementation of impact fees, some of them have been extracted from the material above and repeated here in succinct form.

1. *Peak level of service* (share of capacity already used). The first 10 percent is just as costly as the last 10 percent. If an impact fee is used to charge for capacity, it is a long-run charge, and all users should pay the same charge. While this is not marginal cost pricing, it is an equitable analog.

2. *Timing of payment.* The real (net of inflation) base-year dollar charge, to each property affected, should be determined at the time the investment decision is made. The liability then becomes fixed, in base-year dollars. The later the charge is paid, the higher it will be, as a result of inflation and interest charges. Developers may be given a choice as to when the payment must be made, but the real burden of the impact fee should be unaffected by when it is paid, i.e., there is no saving on the fee from postponing development.

3. *Actual use or earmarking of revenues.* What the impact fee revenues are spent for, and when, is immaterial. What matters is that the contract between the developer and the municipality be fulfilled, whether this involves the expenditure of revenues or whether the revenues received from fees are too much or too little.

4. *Existence of plans.* Sound plans based on realistic assumptions and astute analysis can provide strong documentation for various actions, including impact fees. Plans are not necessary, however, and plans based on incorrect assumptions are no better than obstacles.

5. *Development causes the additional infrastructure.* As with level of service, the existence of excess capacity or the lack of it is unimportant. If the development uses the infrastructure, charges can be imposed whether or not the infrastructure preexists the development.

6. *Apportionment by fair share formula.* Allocation of costs to properties should be accomplished by means of a formula that is fair, but whether it is depends on the concepts and their implementation, not on the name given to the formula. It may sound fair and not be, or vice versa.

7. *Fees used to create benefits to payer.* The property that is paying impact fees should receive the benefits created by whatever services are agreed on, but it is immaterial for what the fees are actually used.

Alternative Instruments. When compared to direct user charges for most services, impact fees would appear to be a distant second best. Many alternatives currently in use, however, are many times worse, while a few are as good or better. Development moratoria are the absolute worst, and can only be justified on emergency grounds resulting from incompetent planning on the part of the public sector. Lack of sewer capacity is the commonest trigger for moratoria, but suburban congestion may be another tempting rationalization for stopping growth. Use of general taxes and grants for infrastructure are also highly inefficient, and impact fees are likely to be a better substitute at the margin despite the inequity between old and new users. User taxes (excise taxes) are inferior to impact fees in making a correspondence between where the payments are made and where facilities are improved, but superior on price elasticity grounds in altering consumer behavior.

Mechanisms that are clearly superior to impact fees, beside direct user fees, are negotiated development exactions, if handled skillfully, and special improvement districts. The problems with exactions are the need for astute negotiators on the public side, the uncertainty in how long the process will take and what the outcome will be, and its vulnerability to political intervention, whether socially beneficial or not. The problem with special districts is the general lack of skill or experience in administering such districts so as to achieve efficiency and equity. With only modest effort, though, special districts could achieve the benefits of impact fees without the ambiguities and inequities, while metered user charges could reduce the need for facilities as well as the interjurisdictional financing problems inherent in facilities like transportation.

Notes

1. See Herbert Mohring. 1976. *Transportation Economics*, Cambrige, Mass.: Ballinger Publishing Company.
2. *Newsweek*, October 12, 1987, p.98. Courts have previously taken over managment of schools and imposed requirements that necessitated taxes, but this seems to be the first case of a specific court-imposed tax levy.

References

Dawson, Grace. 1977. *No Little Plans*. Washington, D.C.: The Urban Institute.

Fulton, William. 1987. Exactions Put to the Test. *Planning* December: 6–10.

Greenberg, Froda with Jim Hecimovich. 1984. *Traffic Impact Analysis*, PAS Report 387. Chicago: American Planning Assocation, October.

Lee, Douglass. ca 1978. *Nuisance Law Applied to Land Use Control*. North Side Neighborhood Preservation Study, Iowa City, Iowa: Department of Community Development, Iowa City.

Musgrave, Richard A. and Peggy B. Musgrave. 1984. *Public Finance in Theory and Practice*, 4th ed. New York: McGraw-Hill.

Nicholson, Walter. 1985. *Microeconomic Theory: Basic Principles and Extensions*, 3d ed. Chicago: Dryden Press.

Porter, Douglas R. and Richard B. Peiser. 1985. *Financing Infrastructure to Support Community Growth*. Washington, D.C.: Urban Land Institute.

Snyder, Thomas P. and Michael A. Stegman. 1978. *Paying for Growth: Using Development Fees to Finance Infrastructure*. Washington, D.C.: Urban Land Institute.

Transportation Research Board. 1986. Development Impact Fees for Financing Transportation Infrastructure. *Circular* 311, Washington, D.C.: TRD, December.

Who Bears the Burden of Development Impact Fees?

Forrest E. Huffman, Jr.
Arthur C. Nelson
Marc T. Smith
Michael A. Stegman

Policymakers in general and planners in particular do not want developers to pass development impact fees to purchasers or renters of housing or occupants of nonresidential buildings. Rather, they want developers to pass fees backward to landowners or absorb them through reduced profits (Duncan, Morgan, and Standerfer 1986; Sandler and Denham 1986; Weitz 1984). Developers claim that they will simply pass development impact fees forward if they cannot pass them backward (Snyder and Stegman 1986). Landowners, however, might argue that they will not sell unless they get their price (Dowall 1984). So who pays development impact fees? The answer depends on many factors. Planners should be knowledgeable about those factors. This chapter explores the incidence and effects of impact fees on residential and nonresidential real estate. We conclude that consumers—home buyers, renters, or nonresidential tenants—will pay the major share of development impact fees over time. Furthermore, we conclude that the use of high impact fees in one part of a metropolitan area can cause a shift in development pressure, socioeconomic mix, and fiscal structure throughout that area.

WHO PAYS DEVELOPMENT IMPACT FEES ON HOUSING?

Development impact fees intend to shift the burden of financing new infrastructure from the community at large to the owners of developable land, developers, or buyers of new homes. Most planners assume that buyers of new housing will pay the fees through higher prices or lower house and lot quality, or both (National Association of Home Builders 1984). On the other hand, tax incidence theory, which one may apply to impact fees (Weitz 1985), suggests that a rise in the cost of new housing construction, associated with a rise in fees or taxes, should be capitalized to some extent as lower raw land values (Ellickson 1977). Since home builders cannot sell homes if the costs of ownership are appreciably higher than for comparable new or existing homes elsewhere in the market, builders, in theory, must pay less for land, lower the housing quality, or take lower profits (Snyder and Stegman 1986). Which view

Figure 25–1. Who Bears Development Impact Fees?

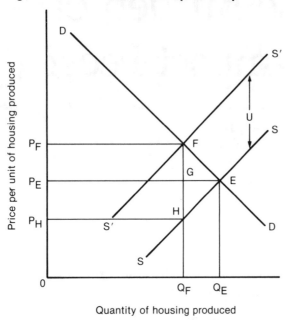

Quantity of housing produced

The incidence of development impact fees will be similar to the incidence of other kinds of taxes (see Musgrave and Musgrave 1984). Since the housing industry is competitive before the fee, the community housing demand (DD) and housing supply (SS) schedules are in equilibrium. Following Weitz (1985) and Sandler and Denham (1986), Q_E is the pre-fee output of housing and P_E is the pre-fee price of that housing. With the imposition of the fee, denoted on Figure as U, the supply schedule shifts to S'S' and housing output is reduced to Q_F. The post-fee price of housing paid by home buyers rises to P_F, but the price received by the developer falls to P_H. The community receives the fee shown in rectangle P_FFP$_H$H. The share paid by the developer, whether from profit or lower land cost, is P_EGP$_H$H, and the share paid by the home buyer, whether in higher finished price or lower quality, is P_FFPeG. The share of the development impact fee burden may shift back and forth between developers and home buyers depending on the demand and supply characteristics (elasticities) of the housing market.

is correct? We consider that question first in a general theoretical context and then under different supply and demand conditions. We will consider short- and long-term effects of impact fees on housing markets and housing prices, developer entry or exit, and landowners. We then will review how impact fee policies of a community can affect the distribution of growth and fiscal benefits throughout an entire metropolitan area.

Figure 25–1 illustrates our view of who bears development impact fees. We believe the incidence of development impact fees will be similar to the incidence of other kinds of taxes (see Musgrave and Musgrave 1984). Since the housing industry is competitive before the fee, the community housing demand and housing supply schedules are in equilibrium. When a fee is imposed, the housing output diminishes as the post-fee price buyers pay for homes rises but the price the developer receives falls. Thus, both the developer and the home buyer may share in the payment of the fee, whether in higher finished price or lower quality. The share of the development impact fee burden may shift back and forth between developers and home buyers, depending on the demand and supply characteristics (elasticities) of the housing market.

Impact Fee Incidence Under Different Supply and Demand Conditions. Changing relationships between housing demand and supply can vary the incidence of development impact fees in several ways. First, consider the demand side of housing production, or how home buyers respond to changes in housing prices. Dowall (1980) observes that a submarket of a larger metropolitan area probably will be more sensitive to price of housing than the entire metropolitan area because competition gives opportunities for substitution between submarkets. If housing prices increase in one community, people will gravitate toward other similar communities. However, highly desirable communities within the metropolitan area may not have close substitutes and the housing submarket may not be as sensitive to price in those communities. In small urban areas, the entire housing market also may be somewhat insensitive to prices because the competition is limited.

Next, consider the supply side of housing production. Developer entry into a housing market is highly sensitive to changing market conditions (Muth 1960). Barriers to developer entry, such as high land prices, land use regulation, and development impact fees, also affect housing supply (Weitz 1985). Those demand and supply considerations affect the incidence of impact fees under a number of market conditions; we shall discuss the three most common: where buyers are insensitive to housing price and there are no barriers to developer entry; where buyers are insensitive to housing price and there are barriers to developer entry; and where buyers are sensitive to housing price and there are no barriers to developer entry. Table 25–1 illustrates who bears the residential development impact fee under those conditions.

The first situation—buyers are insensitive to changes in price and there are no barriers to developer entry—exists in isolated communities where there are no close substitutes or in suburbs of large metropolitan areas that have unique environmental, socioeconomic, and other attractions. Because consumers are insensitive to small or modest changes in housing prices, developers can pass the fees along to home buyers. Snyder and Stegman (1986) report that for a large developer in Colorado Springs, Colorado, to finance and manage a $6,170 development impact fee and still earn a profit of around 10 percent, he had to mark the fee up by 28 percent to account for the associated financing and overhead burdens. While the fee accounted for 8.2 percent of

the price before marketing, it accounted for 10.5 percent of the actual sales price. Weitz (1985) concludes that buyers in such communities would probably pay more than 80 percent of the development impact fee in the form of higher prices.

In the second situation—buyers are insensi-

Table 25–1. Payment of Residential Development Impact Fees

Supply and demand condition	Result
Buyers are insensitive to price changes and there are no barriers to entry by developers (e.g., smaller, isolated, desirable urban areas like Colorado Springs).	Developers can mark up housing costs by nearly the full cost of the fee plus a factor equivalent to the cost of administering the fee. Buyers pay the largest share of the fee.
Buyers are insensitive to price changes but there are barriers to developer entry (e.g., highly desirable places within larger metropolitan areas like San Jose, California).	Developers will change their market orientation to higher income households. Lower- and middle-income households will be squeezed out of the community and into nearby communities that are close substitutes. Buyers pay the largest share of the fee.
Buyers are sensitive to price changes and there are no barriers to developer entry (the most common situation).	In the short term, both buyers and developers share the burden (see Figure 1). Unless developers offset their share of the fee by reducing lot or dwelling unit size, quality, and amenities, or by reducing the cost of land purchase, their share of the fee burden will come out of profit. Assuming capital is relatively mobile, developers will exit the market after they have sold their pre-fee inventory. They will reenter the market when demand raises prices to a level that restores profit to its pre-fee levels. Thus, in the long term, buyers will pay the largest share of the fee, unless landowners reduce their price.

tive to changes in price but there are barriers to developer entry—developers will shift their market orientation toward affluent households. In San Jose, California, for example, high developer entry costs, relatively high impact charges (in the form of both impact fees and taxes), and invariable land and production costs combined with a housing market that was insensitive to modest price increases and forced developers to change market orientation to affluent households (Landis 1986). By the end of the 1970s, construction of starter homes had virtually ceased; lower and middle-income households were squeezed out of San Jose and into nearby communities in the metropolitan area. In that situation, buyers of new homes in San Jose bore the greatest share of the fees.

But not all communities are like Colorado Springs or San Jose. A third (and perhaps the most common) situation exists where buyers are sensitive to price and there are no barriers to developer entry. That situation occurs in many suburban areas in larger metropolitan housing markets where home building is competitive and suburbs differ in the application of development impact fees. In such areas, both buyers and sellers have to share the impact fee in the manner illustrated in Figure 25–1, at least for the short term. Unless developers offset their share of the fee by reducing lot or dwelling unit size, quality, amenities, or land price, their share of the fee will come out of profit. Assuming that capital is mobile, developers will move out of the market after they sell their pre-fee inventory, and construction may grind to a halt in the community. Since capital, labor, and material prices are beyond the developers' control, only a reduction in land price by the cost of the fee may keep the developer in that submarket.

Would landowners bear a large share of the development impact fees burden? The evidence in that regard is unclear. According to property tax theory (Mieszkowski 1972; Aaron 1975), when home buyers are price sensitive and developers are competitive, developers should bid less for land that has high property taxes, because high property taxes will reduce developer (and landowner) rates of return. Paying less for the land, then, should keep the final house package competitively priced. By analogy, high impact fees should force developers and landowners to behave similarly. Thus, at least a portion of the development impact fee burden would be passed backward to landowners in the long term. Property tax incidence theory suggests, however, that the size of the shift will be small. Furthermore, impact fees are assessed against development, not on land, and may not be applied until years after the land is acquired. The size of the fee varies even among similar tracts of land, due to different scales of development, development timing, and other regulatory and market conditions. For those reasons, landowners and developers may not be able to accurately discount land value to offset the fees.

Landowner behavior also may make it difficult for developers to shift the burden of fees. Many landowners do not consider the time-value of money (Snyder and Stegman 1986). They do not realize that cash from a sale now at a lower price may be invested so that, with interest on their funds, they would realize more money in the future than sale of the property at a higher price would generate later on. Instead, landowners have a "reservation" price below which they will not sell, and they will keep their land off the market until prices rise to that level (Dowall 1984). Nevertheless, if land values are rising in a community, the eventual sale of a property at the reservation price could be equivalent to a fall in price if the price at which the property is sold is lower than it would have been in the absence of the fee.[1]

Developers generally will not willingly reduce their profit margins (Schechter 1976). If builders cannot factor development impact fees into their production costs, they will reduce production levels, reduce housing quality, or shift to more affluent markets. Thus, if market conditions do not permit the developer to pass fees on to home buyers, and if landowners are unwilling to accept lower prices, impact fees will force developers to reduce production or leave the market. As supply falls relative to demand, excess housing demand forces prices to levels that would restore post-fee profits to their pre-fee levels (Ellickson 1982). In that situation, home buyers pay impact fees in the long term.

There is yet another dimension to the question of who bears impact fees. If housing prices in a community rise because of impact fees, the price of existing homes that are close substitutes for new homes will also rise. That results in a windfall profit to owners of existing homes.

Socioeconomic and Fiscal Impacts of Housing Impact Fees. Finally, we are concerned about how high impact fees might change the socioeconomic mix of communities, and about the distribution of fiscal benefits throughout a metropolitan area where only a few communities assess the fees. In highly desirable markets, builders will respond to high impact fees by simply ignoring lower income households in favor of households that can afford more expensive housing. For example, Snyder and Stegman (1986) report that average prices of new homes in the Orlando area rose from the

$40,000 to $50,000 range into the $60,000 to $80,000 range, largely because builders could not appropriately factor sizable fixed development impact fees into production costs unless they catered to more affluent households. That kind of response to impact fees changes the socioeconomic mix of the community. Such a reorientation of residential developments is a nearly unavoidable effect of development impact fees in many areas of the nation (Dowall 1984).

Impact fees also may generate unexpected fiscal income for communities. There should be a windfall to local governments in the form of a higher property tax base as housing prices rise to higher levels. The consumption-related tax base will also rise as more affluent households who settle there will probably spend much of their incomes in the community. Expenditures for indigent services will fall as lower income households are squeezed out of the community.

WHO PAYS DEVELOPMENT IMPACT FEES ON NONRESIDENTIAL BUILDINGS?

Since development impact fees are assessed on most kinds of nonresidential development, it is only appropriate to discuss who pays those fees. Impact fees on nonresidential development help pay for roads and for water, sewer, drainage, fire, and police facilities. In recent years, San Francisco, Boston, Seattle, Santa Monica, and other highly desirable locations have assessed impact fees on office developments constructed in their downtowns to subsidize the production of low- to moderate-income housing (Keating 1986). The rationale for those linkage programs is that new office development reduces housing affordability through both direct and indirect effects. The direct effect occurs through the demolition of housing units to clear sites for office developments. The indirect effect occurs when the introduction of businesses that create more jobs and add more households to the market increases housing demand. Whether governments assess impact fees for infrastructure and housing production, the question remains of whether tenants, developers, or landowners pay nonresidential development impact and linkage fees.

We do not consider the situation where development impact fees improve nonresidential development quality, as in road impact fees that improve accessibility. Instead, we focus on the market response to impact and housing linkage fees that change land and production prices without clearly improving the quality of nonresidential development.

Builders of office, retail, industrial, or other nonresidential developments are motivated by the profit they expect the development to produce. Profit comes from two sources: cash flow during ownership and capital gains from sale. Operating expenses, debt service (mortgage payments), depreciation (wear and tear and replacement needs), and taxes on property and income all reduce cash flow (rents) and capital gains. The builder can calculate a rate of return by comparing the amount of profit generated to the down payment (initial investment). For example, a development that realizes a $61,000 profit after five years on a $100,000 initial investment gets a 10 percent rate of return, since $100,000 invested for five years at 10 percent would accrue $61,000 in interest.

Developers base their investment decisions not only on the expected profit, but on the perceived risk of the investment. Risk is reflected in the required rate of return needed to justify

the investment. For example, if a passbook savings account in a bank offers a 6 percent return, a developer is not wise to make development investments that yield 6 percent or less since the savings account is a safe investment, while investment in real estate carries significant risks. The rate of return that would justify investment rises with the amount of risk. As a rule of thumb, investors in the current market need to realize rates of return on high-quality real estate of 7 to 8 percent in regional malls, 8 to 9 percent in offices, 9 to 10 percent in strip shopping centers, 10 to 12 percent in hotels, and 12 to 13 percent in miniwarehouses (Moore 1986).

Since development or housing linkage impact fees usually come from cash flow during the first five or so years of the development, cash flow that is critically important in the short term is reduced. Given the slow rate of leasing of speculative office developments in recent years and the necessity of rent concessions to induce the major tenants needed to attract other, smaller tenants (Nourse 1986; Dowall 1986), impact fees require developers to increase the rate of return they expect from investments. Furthermore, if developers perceive that the fees reflect a political environment antagonistic to investment, the rate of return they need to justify investment may increase by another increment to reflect that increased risk. They will not make investments that yield only pre-fee rates of return.

One way a developer may attempt to recover the cost of impact fees is by passing it on to tenants in the form of higher rents. The ability to do so depends on the sensitivity of prospective tenants to higher rents. We do not know the extent of that sensitivity with certainty, but some evidence suggests that a significant and growing portion of office space tenants are footloose (Archer 1981). That is, they are willing to substitute space outside of downtowns and outside of jurisdictions that assess impact fees if such areas otherwise meet their needs for transportation, communications, and other means of accessibility. Even nonfootloose tenants may relocate their back office activities rather than pay the higher rent in close-in locations. To the extent that tenants have alternative location opportunities, competitive pressures determine rents for nonresidential space and those pressures are beyond the control of the developer. Inefficient or poorly capitalized nonresidential developers are less likely to survive in markets where they cannot pass along development and housing linkage impact fees to tenants.

Imagine that Figure 25-1 applies to nonresidential development. In a competitive pre-fee market where supply and demand are at equilibrium, rents can only increase if demand increases. If impact and linkage fees are imposed, the cost of supplying new development rises. The developer and tenant share in the payment of that fee. But if rents cannot be increased immediately to offset rising costs, developers will have to pay all fees. Furthermore, if developers are competitive and cannot afford to pay any of the fee in the first place, then they will not produce new space. As obsolesence and deterioration reduce the current supply, and if demand remains unchanged, the reduction in supply will eventually lead to higher rents. If regional demand for space increases, rents will rise even higher. Increasing rents would ultimately give developers the capability to reenter the market as post-fee rents would justify investments with acceptable rates of return. But since impact fees are assessed only on new construction and since impact fees will

constrain new construction until rents rise to a level that justifies new construction, owners of existing buildings receive windfall increases in rents. As with residential housing, owners of existing commercial buildings benefit when impact fees cause rents for all space to rise. In that situation, all tenants eventually pay the fees in the form of higher rents throughout the area where the fees are assessed. Capital is shifted in the short term to outlying communities that do not have impact or linkage fees, where rents will be reduced since the inflow of capital will result in excess supply and downward pressure on rents.

Even where developers can raise rents because of monopoly advantages of location—as in Manhattan and San Francisco—at some point demand levels off as a result of rent increases. Firms will find alternative locations once the rent level exceeds the value of agglomeration economies and advantages inherent in such locations. Only firms that are very insensitive to price would remain. And since technology is making firms increasingly footloose, firms are becoming more, and not less, price sensitive. For example, the vacancy rate in downtown San Francisco in 1986 was 19.2 percent (The Office Network 1986), higher than the national average of 18.3 percent. More than 28,000 back office jobs relocated out of that city between 1976 and 1985 (K. Nelson 1986).

The ability to pass impact and linkage fees along to tenants is limited. If they cannot pass fees along to tenants, developers have two choices. They can try to get landowners to bear all or part of the fees. But nonresidential, and especially downtown, land markets are exceedingly complex and landowners probably will refuse to pay a substantial portion of the fee in the form of lower sales prices. Landowners will not accept a lower price if current or alternative uses give them a comparable return. If landowners have information or believe that rents will rise due to constrained supplies the fees induce, they will refuse to lower their price. Also, since most kinds of major nonresidential development require several years in planning, many developers purchased or optioned their sites years ago and cannot easily gain concessions from the previous landowner. Where scarcity of land is combined with unique locational advantages, landowners will not absorb development impact and linkage fees.

The second choice developers have, if they cannot pass on fees to tenants or convince owners to sell at lower prices, is to accept lower profits. Some policymakers and planners believe that developers already receive excess or abnormal profits, and that they can simply reduce their profit margins to acceptable levels. That assumption is not reasonable on its face since, if it were true, nonresidential construction would be vastly more active than it is. In reality, the barriers to entry into nonresidential development are far greater than for most residential development. Impact and linkage fees increase the already sizable risk of nonresidential development; and, since industry standards for rates of return are not very flexible, developers are unlikely to survive with lower profits. They may accept lower profits in the short term to liquidate existing inventory, but in the long term they will not do so because they cannot earn less and still remain in business.

WHO ULTIMATELY PAYS THE FEES?

Who ultimately pays development impact and linkage fees? There has been little empirical evaluation of how the market responds to impact fees, but there is considerable information to suggest that, on the whole, tenants (homeowners, renters) pay the majority of the fees. Landowners may pay a portion, but developers are unlikely to pay any of the fees in the long term.

Developers can pass impact fees along to landowners only if the market for buildable land is highly competitive and if supply can be expanded just as quickly as demand warrants. That is not possible because expanding the supply of buildable land requires installation of the very infrastructure for which development impact fees are supposed to pay. The lag between receipt of the fee and its expenditure can be several years. Communities can expand the supply of buildable land by paying for infrastructure in advance, using general obligation bonds and other long-term financing. Impact fees could then be used as buy-in charges to reduce indebtedness communities incur in anticipation of development. The reality, however, is simply that communities probably will not expand supply unless development pays the fees first. Thus, there will nearly always be a lag as supply will always be catching up to demand. Landowners know this and expect to receive land prices that do not fully account for impact fees. About the only way landowners can be charged the cost of the fees in the market is if every jurisdiction in the nation assessed the same fees everywhere. That is not likely.

Developers cannot pay impact fees in the form of lower profits since, in a competitive economy, profits are already at levels of return that justify the cost, bother, and risk of investment compared to alternative uses of investment capital. Developers will stop production and not resume until demand exceeds supply to a point where necessary profit levels are restored. And if developers believe the presence of development impact fees reflects an antagonistic development environment, they will reflect that increased risk by demanding a higher rate of return on investment.

So, who bears the burden of development and housing linkage impact fees? We believe that residents of jurisdictions that assess impact fees will pay the fees in the long term. Where development impact fees are assessed on housing, residents of new and existing housing ultimately pay them in the form of higher purchase prices and rents, or of lower housing quality. Where development and housing linkage impact fees are assessed on nonresidential development, especially offices, the fees will push tenants who are sensitive to rising rent levels out of the community and will dissuade prospective tenants from choosing that jurisdiction. The jurisdiction is then denied a certain amount of future economic development.

Who are the beneficiaries of development impact fees? In general, the owners of existing real estate benefit by receiving windfalls in two ways. First, rising entry and production costs reduce supply until excess demand forces rents to rise. Owners of existing holdings therefore gain increased rents if their property is competitive with new, more expensive buildings that must pay the fees. They gain another windfall when the jurisdiction uses impact fees to upgrade community facilities, thereby making the community even more attractive.

Some communities will gain, but at the expense of others. Communities with real estate markets that are modestly insensitive to price and barriers to developer entry gain three windfalls. First, the property tax base rises as prices rise to pay the fee. Second, as prices rise, only more affluent occupants move into the community, thereby increasing taxable sales throughout that community. Third, as affluent occupants displace lower income occupants, community expenditures for indigent services fall. But other communities will bear the burden of displaced development and increased fiscal stress.

HOW CAN PUBLIC OFFICIALS MITIGATE THE NEGATIVE EFFECTS OF IMPACT FEES?

Public officials generally have not come to grips with the housing and equity effects of development impact fees. Although difficult to accomplish, there are at least eight tactics officials might employ to reduce the negative effects of impact fees (Weitz 1984):

1. Ensure that long-range community plans adequately foresee future demand for developable land by providing that land with infrastructure and thereby keep the land market from internalizing supply shortages attributable solely to unserviced land.

2. Give adequate notice to developers that development impact fees are being considered. This will allow them greater leverage in negotiating more favorable purchase agreements with landowners.

3. Tailor impact fees to the effects that specific developments have on communities. Fixed assessment fee schedules that account for categorical variation of impacts and variable fees should be preferred.

4. Attempt to ensure a competitive land market. In a tight land market, where demand for land exceeds supply in the short term, officials might consider increasing the supply of buildable land by allowing for greater densities or adding to the supply of vacant buildable land.

5. Ensure consistent land use practices. In communities where landowners perceive

that allowable land use intensities can be easily upgraded, developers may be forced to pay land prices that are only justified by such more intense development. This is not to say that regulations should be inflexible, just that they should be administered in a predictable way that sets reasonable limits on the manner in which the land market can operate.

6. Full property tax assessments and rates should be levied on vacant land. Assessing vacant land at its full value for property tax purposes will prevent landowners from using preferential tax programs or underassessments to subsidize their holding costs. Preferential property tax programs therefore should not be extended to urbanizable land.

7. Collect development impact fees as the home is sold, rather than at the platting or building permit stages. This saves developers from paying fees with money borrowed at commercial interest rates and having to mark up prices to reflect the costs of administering the charge.

8. Make greater use of long-term special assessment financing in lieu of development impact fees. This maintains the policy to shift the financing burden to new development, but allows that burden to be paid over time and at lower than commercial lending rates. Home prices are not as influenced by long-term special assessment encumberances as they are by impact fees.

PARTING WORDS

Many questions related to who bears the burden of paying impact fees beg for answers based on empirical analysis. Those questions involve the extent to which landowners bear the burden, the effect of different levels of impact fees on the socioeconomic mix of communities, the distribution of fiscal benefits within a region where communities assess different levels of impact fees, and the preparedness of communities to accommodate development displaced by impact fees. Broader questions also relate to how urban and regional form is affected by differential application of impact fees throughout an area and whether money gained from the fees makes regional growth more or less efficient. We implore our colleagues to undertake such empirical efforts.

Note

1. While theory suggests that landowners should bear a major share of the impact fee burden, especially in housing markets where buyers are relatively sensitive to price and there are not barriers to developer entry, the question of whether landowners really do bear a major burden has not been answered to our satisfaction. We see a need for empirical research in this area.

References

Aaron, Henry. 1975. *Who Pays the Property Tax?* Washington, D.C.: The Brookings Institute.

Archer, W. A. 1981. The Determinants of Location for General Purpose Office Firms within Medium Size Cities. *American Real Estate and Urban Economics Association Journal* 9: 283–97.

Dowall, David E. 1980. Methods for Assessing Land Price Effects of Local Public Policies and Actions. In *Urban Land Markets*, edited by J. Thomas Black and James E. Hoben. Washington, D.C.: Urban Land Institute.

———. 1984. *The Suburban Squeeze*. Berkeley, Calif.: University of California Press.

———. 1986. Planners and Office Overbuilding. *Journal of the American Planning Association* 52, 2: 132–32.

Duncan, James B., Terry D. Morgan, and Norman R. Stranderfer. 1986. *Simplifying and Understanding the Art and Science of Impact Fees*. Austin, Tex.: City of Austin Planning Department.

Ellickson, Robert C. 1977. Suburban Growth Controls: An Economic and Legal Analysis. *Yale Law Journal* 86, January: 385–512.

———. 1982. The Irony of Exclusionary Zoning. In *Resolving the Housing Crisis*, edited by M. Bruce Johnson. Cambridge, Mass.: Ballinger Publishing Co.

Keating, W. Dennis. 1986. Linking Downtown Development to Broader Community Goals. *Journal of the American Planning Association* 52, 2: 133–41.

Landis, John D. 1986. Land Regulation, Market Structure, and Housing Price Inflation: Lessons from Three California Cities. *Journal of the American Planning Association* 52, 1: 9–21.

Mieszkowski, Peter. 1972. The Property Tax: An Excise Tax or a Profit Tax? *Journal of Public Economics* 1, 2: 73–96.

Moore, Thomas. 1986. The New Rules for Investors. *Fortune* December 8: 33–36.

Musgrave, Richard A. and Peggy B. Musgrave. 1984. *Public Finance in Theory and Practice.* 4th ed. New York: McGraw-Hill.

Muth, Richard F. 1960. The Demand for Non-Farm Housing. In *The Demand for Durable Goods,* edited by Arnold C. Harberger. Chicago: University of Chicago Press.

National Association of Home Builders. 1984. *Impact Fees: A Developer's Manual.* Washington, D.C.: National Association of Home Builders.

Nelson, Kristin. 1986. Automation, Skill, and Back Office Location. Paper presented to the Association of American Geographers. Berkeley, Calif.: Department of Geography, University of California.

Nourse, Hugh O. 1986. Comment on Rental Price Adjustment and Investment in the Office Market. *AREUEA Journal* 14, 1: 163–64.

The Office Network. 1986. *International Office Market Report* October. Houston, Tex.: The Office Network.

Sandler, Ralph D. and Edward T. Denham. 1986. Transportation Impact Fees: The Florida Experience. Paper presented to the 1986 meeting of the Transportation Research Board, Washington, D.C. (January).

Schechter, Barry. 1976. Taxes on Land Development: An Economic Analysis. In *Economic Issues in Metropolitan Growth,* edited by Paul R. Portney. Baltimore: Johns Hopkins University Press.

Snyder, Thomas P. and Michael A. Stegman. 1986. *Financing the Public Costs of Growth.* Washington, D.C.: Urban Land Institute.

Weitz, Stevenson. 1984. Funding Infrastructure for Growth. Appendix B. In *Impact Fees: A Developer's Manual,* edited by National Association of Home Builders. Washington, D.C.: National Association of Home Builders.

———. 1985. Who Pays Infrastructure Benefit Charges? In *The Changing Structure of Infrastructure Finance,* edited by James C. Nicholas. Cambridge, Mass.: Lincoln Institute of Land Policy.

26

Calculating Equity-Neutral Water and Sewer Impact Fees

RICHARD PEISER

Communities use the marginal cost pricing rationale to justify impact fees on the assumption that users should pay the marginal cost of providing urban services for new growth. Marginal cost, the cost assigned to incremental growth, "represents the sum of all immediate expenditures undertaken by a jurisdiction that otherwise would not have occurred." (Burchell and Listokin 1978, p. 435). According to the marginal cost pricing rationale, if a new subdivision requires $1 million of new sewer capacity for 1,000 homes, the incremental cost per home would be $1,000. If new residents are charged the marginal cost of urban services through impact fees, a $1,000 impact fee per home would be assessed.

The difficulty with determining impact fees is that they are rarely so clear-cut. The $1,000 fee is appropriate only if all 1,000 homes are sold or pay the impact fee at day one, or alternatively, if carrying costs and inflation are zero (i.e., the providers do not care when they are repaid).

This chapter addresses the issue of how to determine equitable impact fees. While it focuses on water and sewer services, the techniques apply to impact fees for any facility. The chapter draws on data from 83 small municipal utility districts (MUDs) in Texas to illustrate how planners can calculate impact fees from available accounting data. The MUDs are special districts, averaging 100 to 1,000 acres, that provide water, sewer, and drainage services to new subdivisions throughout the Houston metropolitan area (see Peiser 1983).

To begin, one must assess the full economic cost associated with incremental growth. Full economic cost includes all capital and operating costs associated with a public facility over its lifetime. Impact fees normally are associated with the recovery of capital costs; operating costs usually are recovered from user fees or some form of tax.

The approach for setting impact fees determines whether early or later residents pay for infrastructure. Conceptually, the most equitable method for setting impact fees is one that spreads the burden among users, based on the benefits they receive. While impact fees may help finance special public goals such as stimulating growth in selected areas, the measure of equity used here is neutral with respect to geographic and income distribution. An *equity-neutral* impact fee is one in which all users pay the same fee for the same level of service, regardless of when they move into the community, adjusted for the length of time they use the service.[1]

Because impact fees are collected over time as an area develops, the amount of excess capacity that the community must carry in the early years critically affects the cost burden. Economies of scale in water and sewer facilities have an important bearing on impact fees because many communities build larger facilities than they need, anticipating that eventually the need will grow; they justify the expenditure in terms of taking advantage of the presumed economies of scale—i.e., lower cost per unit at capacity for larger capacity facilities (U.S. Environmental Protection Agency 1973a; 1973b; 1973c). However, where absorption of the excess capacity takes several years, not only must impact fees be higher, but the political pressure to transfer the burden to future residents is greater. Cities may be caught in a vicious circle where, by raising impact fees, they slow the rate of growth, which necessitates still higher impact fees.

This chapter has four objectives: to illustrate how different methods for calculating impact fees shift the burden between early and later residents; to demonstrate a method for calculating equity-neutral impact fees; to examine how the equity-neutral fee varies with changes in rates of interest, inflation, and absorption; and to discuss the relationship among excess capacity, economies of scale, and impact fees.

I conclude the following: Impact fees, if set properly, can achieve an equity-neutral result. Equity-neutral fees depend strongly on financing and absorption assumptions. Economies of scale must be significant for cost savings at capacity to outweigh the carrying costs for the period during which the excess capacity is absorbed; therefore it may be preferable to build smaller facilities with smaller excess capacity. An equitable approach must include regular adjustments to accommodate discrepancies between the initial assumptions about inflation and absorption rates used for setting the impact fees and the actual rates.

The first section of the chapter describes the application of marginal cost pricing to impact fees. Next the results of full economic cost analysis for MUDs in Texas are presented, and then the MUD results are used to explore how alternative methods for computing impact fees determine whether early or later residents bear the cost burden. After that, the results of a number of sensitivity tests on equity-neutral impact fees and how impact fees can be adjusted to maintain equity over time are shown.

APPLICATION OF MARGINAL COST PRICING TO IMPACT FEES

Each water system is unique, but generally they all consist of three components: acquisition and production facilities, treatment plants, and outfall points.

Water and wastewater service costs do not follow the traditional smooth pattern where some level of service minimizes cost. Instead, because facilities are expanded in large chunks rather than incrementally to accommodate greater capacity, costs tend to follow a stair-step pattern. Comparisons of systems must control for differences in water source and purity and for sewage effluent quality. For example, transmission costs from a single large reservoir are higher than those from ubiquitous wells.

Construction costs for water and wastewater treatment plants depend on design capacity, local labor and material supply markets, and quality and type of treatment. Factors that affect ongoing operations and maintenance costs

(O&M) include design capacity, degree of treatment required, labor, chemical and power costs, and repair and replacement costs. The size of the service area directly affects transmission costs, as demonstrated by Clark and Stevie's water supply cost model (1981).

Capital expenses for facilities normally come from impact fees, while some form of user charge typically pays for O&M costs. Where the local government can identify distribution lines with a particular subset of users, it is appropriate to charge those users directly. Communities often require land developers to install internal water and sewer lines in new subdivisions, the costs of which they pass on to home buyers. Common facilities that benefit everyone in a service area present the major funding dilemma, especially where they involve major capital expenditures in advance of development. The capital facilities include water reservoirs and wells, treatment plants, and water and sewer mains and collectors that connect a number of subdivisions to the central facilities.

Marginal cost pricing provides the economic basis for paying for the common facilities. Turvey (1976) and Clark and Stevie (1981) developed the theory of marginal cost pricing for water facilities. Hanke and Wentworth (1981) adapted Turvey's approach for wastewater facilities. Turvey's principal contribution is the notion that the marginal costs relevant to decisions should not relate just to one year but to the average marginal cost over a number of years. Efficient development of water and wastewater facilities involves phasing of the investment in such a way that it will minimize the present value of the cost per connection by spreading it to all users over time. Because communities expand facilities in irregular increments and time intervals, it is not sufficient to design and build facilities to minimize user cost at final capacity. To do so often means that users during the buildout period bear a disproportionately high share of the cost burden because they carry large amounts of excess capacity.

Appendix 26A presents the derivation of average marginal costs (AMC). To estimate AMC, planners must make an accurate estimate of full economic costs. That is easier for planned than for existing facilities. Estimating full economic cost is difficult because the primary data source is usually accounting data. Accounting data often include overhead, site conditions, maintenance contracts, and other items not related to the direct economic cost of the facility. Also, construction contracts often overlap different facilities. For example, a single contract may cover sewer plant grading and road grading, making it difficult to accurately determine full sewer plant costs, which include grading. Similarly, accounting information, collected primarily for financial reporting, may combine costs for several facilities into a single account for depreciable capital assets. Despite the difficulties of estimating full economic cost, some calculation must precede determination of impact fees. Equations A.3 to A.5 in Appendix 26A describe how to calculate marginal costs from typical accounting data.

How do we go from average marginal cost to impact fees? As Snyder and Stegman (1986) note, Turvey's AMC measure provides the economic rationale for impact fees but does not necessarily provide the best impact fee estimate.

The main problem with employing the AMC concept is that it implies charging for the capacity assigned to a dwelling unit whether or not that dwelling unit is actually built and utilizing the capacity constructed for it. Owners of unsubdivided tracts rarely are in a position to pay their shares. Also, residents presumably derive greater benefits from the facilities than owners of vacant land. While governments theoretically can charge landowners for the AMC of providing services, doing so is impractical. Impact fees provide a financing mechanism for making the AMC concept operational.

FULL ECONOMIC COST ANALYSIS OF MUNICIPAL UTILITY DISTRICTS

One of the major problems in estimating full economic costs for either existing or new systems is that of identifying incremental costs with incremental users. Municipal utility districts (MUDs), a form of special district in Texas, offer a unique opportunity to study water and sewer costs; the MUDs have complete records, which allow us to trace the entire history of capital investment and associated capacity for a district.

The data base analyzed here consists of 83 MUDs in the Houston metropolitan area. All of the MUDs included in the study were created after 1972, and service areas range from 98 to 1,133 acres. We obtained data from bond issue prospectuses, annual reports, and interviews with MUD operators.[2]

The critical variable for estimating impact fees is cost per connection or cost per connection equivalent.[3] MUD data include a statement of the ultimate size for each subdivision. The statement is included in the prospectus when MUD bonds are issued, making it easy to calculate costs per connection at capacity. On the other hand, while the prospectus includes commercial, multifamily, and industrial acreages, it does not include the density of buildout. Therefore, the estimate of connection

equivalents may differ from what is actually built, although water and sewer treatment and flow capacities limit the degree of variance.

Table 26-1 presents the average capital costs per connection for all MUDs in the sample.[4] The table illustrates the range in costs for MUDs of different sizes. Direct costs represented 70 percent of the total, with line costs representing about two-thirds of direct cost. Table 26-1 also indicates that average costs were higher for smaller districts—those of less than 200 developed acres—than for larger ones. Of course, all the MUDs in the data sample are small relative to most municipal and regional water and sewer systems. However, average total costs are lower than the $8,750 per connection for the city of Dallas Water Department.[5] The small size of the MUDs does not appear to lead to significantly higher utility costs.

The costs in Table 26-1 represent the average net present value (NPV) per connection for all MUDs in the data sample. Impact fees would be based on costs for individual systems. Nevertheless, we can use the average system costs to illustrate the computation of impact fees. Alternative methods for computing impact fees are presented in the next section.

ALTERNATIVE METHODS FOR COMPUTING IMPACT FEES

Since the MUDs have no existing residents at the time of inception, future users must bear 100 percent of the costs—$8,439 per connection, or $4,877,000 for the average system of 578 connections. While other methods, such as taxes or user fees, could recover some or all of the capital cost, let us assume that impact fees are the sole method of cost recovery.[6]

The government may collect impact fees in a variety of forms: developers may pay at the

Table 26–1. Average Costs Per Connection[a]

Acres[b]	Sewage treatment cost	Water treatment cost	Line cost	Total direct cost	Administrative cost	Total cost
<200	$959	$1144	$4173	$6276	$2782	$9058
	(705)	(1046)	(2231)	(3062)	(1280)	(4046)
>200	811	507	3635	4953	1805	6758
	(499)	(418)	(1171)	(1466)	(652)	(1786)
Total	919	973	4028	5920	2519	8439
Percent of total	10.9	11.5	47.7	70.1	29.9	100.0

a. All 83 utility systems were built between 1973 and 1983. I converted the costs to 1984 prices using a construction price inflation index for Houston. Numbers in parentheses are standard deviations.
b. Acres represent total acres developed to date in the sampled MUDs.

Table 26–2. Indexed vs. Level Payment Impact Fees (no inflation, 5 percent interest)

Year [1]	Remaining capacity in dwelling units [2]	Starts for year [3]	Alternative A: indexed fees					Alternative B: level fees		
			Beginning unamortized infrastructure investment [4]	Indexed adjustment 5%[a] [5]	Impact fee for year [6]	Total fees for year [7]	Ending unamortized infrastructure investment [8]	Level payment[b] [9]	Total fees for year [10]	Present value of impact fee per house[c] [11]
1	578	72	$4,877,742	$5,121,629	$ 8,861	$637,988	$4,483,641	$10,451	$752,504	$10,451
2	506	72	4,433,641	4,707,623	9,304	669,889	4,037,935	10,451	752,504	10,451
3	434	72	4,037,935	4,239,832	9,769	703,382	3,536,449	10,451	752,504	10,451
4	362	72	3,536,449	3,713,272	10,258	738,551	2,974,721	10,451	752,504	10,451
5	290	72	2,974,721	3,123,457	10,771	775,479	2,347,978	10,451	752,504	10,451
6	219	72	2,347,978	2,465,377	11,309	814,253	1,651,124	10,451	752,504	10,451
7	146	72	1,651,124	1,733,680	11,875	854,965	878,715	10,451	752,504	10,451
8	74	74	878,715	922,650	12,468	922,650	0	10,451	773,407	10,451
9	0		0	0	0	0	0		0	0
NPV at 5%[d]						$4,877,742			$4,877,744	

a. The 5 percent adjustment represents interest costs of 5 percent per year.
b. I calculated the level impact fee iteratively by solving for the amount that just retires the $4,877,742 investment as the last house is started.
c. Present value, discounted at the rate of inflation. Because inflation is zero, the present value is the same as the impact fee in column 9.
d. NPV = net present value, discounted at the rate of interest.

time of subdivision platting; home builders may pay when they obtain building permits; home buyers may pay at the time of home purchase or through annual charges. A popular misconception is that developers and home builders bear the major cost burden. They are merely intermediaries who bear the burden only in very soft markets or where they are caught owning a lot of land when the impact fees are passed. In soft markets, the burden is passed backward to owners of undeveloped land in the form of lower land prices, through a process similar to tax capitalization. In tight markets, the fees may be added to other costs and passed forward to future home buyers and building owners.

Tables 26–2 through 26–4 present four alternative methods for computing impact fees. They illustrate how the method of computing impact fees determines whether early or later

Table 26–3. Impact Fees with 100 percent Financing, No Inflation, 5 percent Interest[a]

| | | Alternative C | | | Alternative D | | | | | | |
| | | | | | | Accrued debt service account | | | | | Total |
Year [1]	New connections [2]	Cumulative connections [3]	Annual debt service [4]	Annual cost per user [5]	Annual fees collected at $677/user [6]	Beginning balance [7]	Interest at 5% [8]	Deficit accrued [9]	Surcharge $218.83/user [10]	Ending balance [11]	annual impact fee [12]
1	72	72	$391,403	$5436	$ 48,756	$ 0	$ 0	$342,647	$ 15,755	$ 326,891	$896
2	72	144	391,403	2718	97,512	326,891	16345	293,891	31,511	605,616	896
3	72	216	391,403	1812	145,263	605,616	30281	245,135	47,266	833,765	896
4	72	288	391,403	1359	195,024	833,765	41688	196,378	63,022	1,008,810	896
5	72	360	391,403	1087	243,780	1,008,810	50440	147,622	78,777	1,128,096	896
6	72	432	391,403	906	292,536	1,128,096	56405	98,866	94,532	1,188,834	896
7	72	504	391,403	777	341,292	1,188,834	59442	50,110	110,288	1,188,099	896
8	74	578	391,403	677	391,403	1,188,099	59405	0	126,481	1,121,023	896
9	0	578	391,403	677	391,403	1,121,023	56051	0	126,481	1,050,593	896
10	0	578	391,403	677	391,403	1,050,593	52530	0	126,481	976,642	896
11	0	578	391,403	677	391,403	976,642	48832	0	126,481	898,993	896
12	0	578	391,403	677	391,403	898,993	44950	0	126,481	817,462	896
13	0	578	391,403	677	391,403	817,462	40873	0	126,481	731,854	896
14	0	578	391,403	677	391,403	731,854	36593	0	126,481	641,966	896
15	0	578	391,403	677	391,403	641,966	32098	0	126,481	547,584	896
16	0	578	391,403	677	391,403	547,584	27379	0	126,481	448,482	896
17	0	578	391,403	677	391,403	448,432	22424	0	126,481	344,425	896
18	0	578	391,403	677	391,403	344,425	17221	0	126,481	235,166	896
19	0	578	391,403	677	391,403	235,166	11758	0	126,481	120,443	896
20	0	578	391,403	677	391,403	120,443	6022	0	126,481	−16	896

a. Base fee = $677, surcharge = $218.83; $218.83 is the solution, solved iteratively, that gives an accrued debt balance of approximately zero (−16) at the end of 20 years.

Equations:

[3] = [3]$_{t-1}$ + [2]$_t$

[4] = Annual debt service (the annuity payment on total investment of $4,877,742 at 5 percent interest for 20 years).

[5] = [4]/[3]

[6] = [3] × $677.17

[7] = [11]$_{t-1}$

[8] = [7] × 5%

[9] = [4] − [6]

[10] = [3] × $218.83

[11] = [7] + [8] + [9] − [10]

[12] = $677 from [6] + $218.83 from [10]

residents bear the burden of carrying excess capacity.

Table 26–2 shows the first two alternatives, which assume that the city will collect the fees in their entirety, without financing, when it issues building permits. The table assumes that total capacity for 578 dwelling units (or connection equivalents) will be absorbed over eight years at the rate of 72 units per year.

Column 6 shows alternative A, where impact

fees are indexed at 5 percent, based on annual carrying costs. I derived the index by adding interest for each year to the beginning unamortized balance (column 4), and dividing the indexed adjusted balance (column 5) by the remaining capacity (column 2). If all 578 homes were built in year 1, builders would all pay the same $8,861 cost per user. However, if they build only 72 homes in year 1, as the table illustrates, the carrying costs are added to the

Table 26–4. Four Alternatives for Setting Impact Fees

Year	One-time fee		Annual fees 100% financing	
	A Indexed fee	B Level fee	C Current fee	D Equity-neutral fee
	CASE 1: 0% Inflation, 5% Interest			
1	$ 8861	$10,451	$5436	$896
2	9304	10,451	2718	896
3	9769	10,451	1812	896
4	10,258	10,451	1359	896
5	10,771	10,451	1087	896
6	11,309	10,451	906	896
7	11,875	10,451	777	896
8	12,468	10,451	677	896
9–20	0	0	677	896
	CASE 2: 5% Inflation, 10% Interest			
1	$ 9283	$12,667	$7957	$ 918
2	10,211	12,667	3979	964
3	11,232	12,667	2652	1012
4	12,356	12,667	1989	1062
5	13,591	12,667	1591	1116
6	14,950	12,667	1326	1171
7	16,445	12,667	1137	1230
8	18,090	12,667	991	1291
9–20	0	0	991	1356–2319

Calculations for case 1 (I have omitted the calculations for case 2 for brevity):
  A: Later residents carry entire burden of carrying excess capacity (Table 2, column 6).
  B: Early residents carry more of the burden in terms of present value. Zero inflation represents a special case where later residents may pay more than their fair share because of the shorter remaining economic life combined with zero decline in purchasing power. Their burden increases with inflation. (Table 2, column 9).
  C: Early residents carry entire burden (Table 3, column 5).
  D: Early and later residents carry equal burdens (Table 3, base fee + surcharge).

total that later residents must pay. Alternative A thus places the entire burden of carrying excess capacity on future residents.

By comparison, alternative B (columns 9–11) shows the effects of a constant impact fee. That alternative would mean an assessment of $10,451 per home. The fee is higher than the orignal $8,439 average cost per connection because everyone shares the costs of carrying the excess capacity. For alternative B, I assumed inflation is zero and that all residents pay the same fee in present value terms discounted at

the inflation rate. That leads to an equitable solution, so long as later residents can use the facilities for the same length of time as the early residents.[7] However, as inflation increases, more of the burden falls on early residents because the value of the impact fee declines in real terms.

Table 26–3 shows alternatives C and D, which assume that the capital cost is financed over 20 years. Instead of a one-time, front-end charge as illustrated in alternatives A and B, the current users pay the impact fees each year.[8] Like Table 26–2, Table 26–3 presents the case where inflation is zero. The impact fees are financed at a rate of 5 percent (real interest of, say, 2 percent and risk premium of, say, 3 percent, with zero inflation).

Column 5 illustrates alternative C, in which *existing* users bear the full burden of carrying excess capacity. The annual debt service to finance the total capital cost would be $391,400 or $677 per connection at buildout. Alternative C simply divides the annual debt service among the current users each year. Annual fees decline from $5,436 per user in year 1 to $677 per user in year 8, assuming an eight-year buildout.[9] Consequently, current users bear the full burden of excess capacity, while future users bear none. If, in addition, new users have to pay a front-end impact fee, that would simply reduce the annual fees by the amount collected from initial fees. In reality, some of the annual burden would be charged to owners of undeveloped land in the form of taxes, but the extreme impact on early residents is clear.

Equity-Neutral Solution

An equity-neutral impact fee charges all users the same fee, as measured by present value discounted at the inflation rate, regardless of when they move into the community. Alternative D, columns 6–12, shows one possible equity-neutral solution.

Like alternative C, alternative D annuitizes the impact fee over the 20-year financing period.[10] The computation of the impact fee consists of two parts: a base payment and a surcharge. I calculated the base payment by dividing the annual debt service of $391,403 by the number of users at capacity—578 connections, or $677 per connection per year. During the buildout period, however, a shortfall occurs between the total revenue collected and total debt service because the current users must carry the excess capacity for later residents. If the annual shortfall accrues, also at 5 percent interest, a surcharge per current user of $218.83 per year just pays off the accrued debt associated with carrying the shortfall. Thus, each user would pay a total of $896 per year. Annual payments would remain the same for each user over the 20 years. That solution makes the burden of carrying the excess capacity equal for all users. Early residents must still carry a portion of the excess capacity, but the annual cost is the same for everyone. In effect, the $218 excess capacity surcharge represents the cost per year to residents who move to the subdivision before others do.[11] The computation procedure for alternative D is explained in Appendix 26B.

Alternative D is an equity-neutral solution under the assumption that the financing period equals the economic life (the number of years before the facilities need replacing or renovating). If the financing period is shorter than the economic life, residents who live in the community after the debt is repaid enjoy the facilities at no cost. We can still achieve an equity-neutral result by solving for the annual total economic cost using the economic life instead of the financing life (see Table 26–3, equation 4). As before, we calculate the debt service in equation 4 using the financing life. Since the financing period is shorter than the economic life, the annual debt service will exceed the annual economic cost during the financing period. The shortfall between the annual debt service and the annual economic cost would accrue along with the shortfall associated with the excess capacity, as illustrated in Table 26–3, column 7. To calculate the base payment, one would divide the annual economic cost by the number of users. Residents would retire the accrued deficit by paying the sum of the base payments and the surcharge, computed by solving for the amount of money that exactly retired the accrued deficit by the end of the economic life. In this way, all residents would pay the same amount, in present value terms, over the entire economic life of the facilities.

Equity-neutral impact fees can come from one-time payments or annual payments. The one-time fee is simply the present value of all future base payments and surcharges computed over the remaining economic life of the facilities. Early residents will pay more than later residents, but only by an amount equal to the present value of the difference in cumulative annual payments. Where they pay the impact fee in a lump sum, they should recover the remaining value of the utility services when they sell their homes.

To summarize, the four alternatives illustrate how the method of calculating impact fees determines who bears the major burden for carrying excess capacity. Table 26–4 presents a comparison of payments under the four alternatives. The outcomes range from placing the full burden on existing residents (alternative C) to placing the full burden on future residents (alternative A). Note that inflation exacerbates the impact of the shift in burden.

SENSITIVITY TESTS

Equity-neutral impact fees depend on a number of variables, including economic life, financing period, interest rates, inflation rates, and growth rates (see Snyder and Stegman 1986). The following tables demonstrate the sensitivity of equity-neutral impact fees to interest, inflation, and growth rates. For simplicity, assume that the economic life equals the financing period of 20 years.

Table 26-5 shows the sensitivity of alternative D impact fees to inflation and interest rates, holding absorption constant. Because inflation is a component of interest rates, assume that the two elements move in parallel with a 5 percent spread representing real return and risk. The calculation procedure follows that in Table 26-3. To achieve an equity-neutral solution, later users should pay the same annual fee as early users, in terms of present value (discounted at the rate of inflation). Thus, the annual fee per user (Table 26-3, column 5) and the surcharge (Table 26-3, column 10) increase each year at the rate of inflation.

Table 26-5 illustrates that the equity-neutral base payment and the surcharge increase only marginally for higher rates of inflation and interest. At 15 percent interest and 10 percent inflation, the base payment increases from $677 to $716 and the surcharge increases from $219 to $224. The difference is small because the annual payments increase each year by the rate of inflation (called indexing). If that were not so, the difference would be much larger. If the interest rate were 15 percent with no indexing, the base payment would be $1,348 and the surcharge would be $823, for a total payment of

$2,171, as compared to a payment of $940 with indexing. Furthermore, the lack of indexing places a much larger burden on early residents as the real cost to later residents declines because of inflation.

Table 26-6 shows the sensitivity of impact fees to slower growth rates. Slower growth means that absorption of capacity is slower and, consequently, that current residents must pay for excess capacity for longer periods. Base payments do not change with slower absorption because they depend only on use at full capacity. However, the surcharge for carrying the excess capacity increases dramatically if the number of units is less. For example, the surcharge would be $219 for 72 housing starts per year, but would jump to $588 if there were only 36 starts per year (each figure assuming a 5 percent interest rate).

Economies of Scale, Excess Capacity, and Impact Fees

The strong sensitivity of equity-neutral impact fees to absorption rates (Table 26-6) underscores the issue of economies of scale, that is, the lower cost per unit of service that results from having larger capacity facilities. Systems engineers favor larger systems for that reason. Larger systems, however, require longer to reach capacity use. To achieve not only equity-neutral but also cost-effective impact fees, the benefits associated with economies of scale must outweigh the carrying costs of excess capacity. Table 26-7 illustrates the trade-off for a system with double the capacity of the average MUD in the sample.

If system capacity is doubled to 1,156 connections while absorption remains 72 units per year, costs per connection must fall by 30 percent to $5,907 (case 8) for equity-neutral impact

Table 26–5. Sensitivity Tests on Inflation and Interest Rates, Impact Fees with 100 percent Financing

Case	Average annual absorption[a]	Interest rate (%)	Inflation rate (%)	Base payment (year 1)	Excess capacity surcharge (year 1)	Total payment (year 1)
1	72/year	5	0	$677.17	$218.82	$895.99
2	72/year	6	1	681.07	219.26	900.33
3	72/year	7	2	684.98	219.70	904.68
4	72/year	8	3	688.90	220.15	909.05
5	72/year	9	4	692.82	220.62	913.44
6	72/year	10	5	696.74	221.09	917.83
7	72/year	11	6	700.67	221.57	922.24
8	72/year	12	7	704.61	222.06	926.67
9	72/year	13	8	708.55	222.56	931.11
10	72/year	14	9	712.50	223.07	935.57
11	72/year	15	10	716.45	223.58	940.03

a. Each case presents the equity-neutral payment for the following number of connections per year: 72, 72, 72, 72, 72, 72, 72, 74, in years 1 through 8, respectively, for a total of 578 connections.

Table 26–6. Sensitivity Tests on Slower Absorption (100 percent Financing)

Case	Absorptions per year	Interest rate (%)	Inflation rate (%)	Base payment (year 1)	Excess capacity surcharge (year 1)	Total payment (year 1)
1	72	5	0	$677.17	$218.82	$895.99
2	72	10	5	696.74	221.09	917.83
3	72	15	10	716.45	223.58	940.03
4	57	5	0	677.17	300.49	977.66
5	57	10	5	696.74	303.70	1000.44
6	57	15	10	716.45	307.22	1023.67
7	36	5	0	677.17	587.89	1265.06
8	36	10	5	696.74	595.11	1291.85
9	36	15	10	716.45	602.88	1319.33

fees to be lower than the base case with 578 connections ($905 versus $918). If savings in capital costs are less than 30 percent per connection, the *smaller* system has lower equity-neutral impact fees. That occurs because the benefit from carrying lower excess capacity in the smaller system outweighs the benefit from lower costs per connection (economies of scale) in the larger system.

If absorption increases by, say, 50 percent, to 108 starts per year, the savings per connection will be less dramatic than 30 percent. Because of the faster absorption, a 10 percent savings

in capital costs per connection (case 5) results in comparable total impact fees ($923 versus $918). On the other hand, if absorption falls below 72 dwellings per year, the cost savings must be even larger than 30 percent to cover the excess capacity carrying costs.

Adjustments for Actual Absorption Rates

Tables 26–2 to 26–7 present solutions based on projected assumptions about the number of connections per year. Actual absorption and inflation rates, however, vary over a 20-year period and will differ from initial assumptions.

Table 26–7. Trade-Off between Economies of Scale and Absorption (5 percent inflation, 10 percent interest)

Case	Economies of scale ratio[a]	Total capital cost	Connection capacity	Cost per connection	Absorption starts per year	Base payment (year 1)	Surcharge (year 1)	Total payment (year 1)[b]
Base Case								
1	1.0	$4,877,742	578	$8439	72	$697	$221	$918
Double capacity								
2	1.0	9,755,484	1156	8439	72[c]	697	595	1292
3	1.0	9,755,484	1156	8439	108[d]	697	329	1026
4	0.9	8,779,936	1156	7595	72	627	536	1163
5	0.9	8,779,936	1156	7595	108	627	296	923
6	0.8	7,804,387	1156	6751	72	557	552	1109
7	0.8	7,804,387	1156	6751	108	557	263	820
8	0.7	6,828,839	1156	5907	72	488	417	905
9	0.7	6,828,839	1156	5907	108	488	230	718

a. Ratio of capital cost per connection to that of base case.
b. Payments are annual impact fees that current residents pay for 20 years.
c. 72 units per year for 15 years, 76 units in the 16th year.
d. 108 units per year for 10 years, 76 units in the 11th year.

Table 26–8. Impact Fee Adjustments for Actual Absorption Rates (5 percent inflation, 10 percent interest)

Year [1]	Units absorbed [2]	Cumulative units absorbed [3]	Base charge [4]	Base revenue [5]	Present value of base revenue [6]	Surcharge [7]	Revenue from surcharge [8]	Present value surcharge [9]	Total base payment plus surcharge [10]	Present value of total payment[a] [11]	Total payment, anticipated absorption[b] [12]
1	72	72	$696.74	$50,165	45,605	$221.09	$15,918	$14,471	$917.83	$874.13	$917.83
2	50	122	731.58	89,253	73,763	344.92	42,080	34,777	1076.50	976.42	963.72
3	60	182	768.16	139,805	105,038	308.24	56,100	42,149	1076.40	929.84	1011.91
4	60	242	806.56	195,189	133,317	323.66	78.325	53,497	1130.22	929.84	1062.51
5	45	287	846.89	243,059	150,921	395.78	113,588	70,529	1242.67	973.67	1115.63
6	45	332	889.24	295,227	166,648	415.57	137,968	77,879	1304.81	973.67	1171.41
7	45	377	933.70	352,005	180,634	436.35	164,502	84,415	1370.05	973.67	1229.98
8	45	422	980.38	413,723	193,005	458.16	193,344	90,197	1438.55	973.67	1291.48
9	45	467	1029.40	480,732	203,877	481.07	224,660	95,278	1510.48	973.67	1356.05
10	45	512	1080.87	553,408	213,363	505.13	258,623	99,710	1586.00	973.67	1423.86
11	45	557	1134.92	632,150	221,565	530.38	295,421	103,543	1665.30	973.67	1495.05
12	21	578	1191.66	688,782	219,467	556.90	321,887	102,563	1748.56	973.67	1569.80
13	0	578	1251.24	723,222	209,492	584.75	337,982	97,901	1835.99	973.67	1648.29
14	0	578	1313.81	759,383	199,969	613.98	354,881	93,451	1927.79	973.67	1730.71
15	0	578	1379.50	797,352	190,880	644.68	372,625	89,203	2024.18	973.67	1817.24
16	0	578	1448.47	837,219	182,203	676.92	391.256	85,149	2125.39	973.67	1908.10
17	0	578	1520.90	879,080	173,921	710.76	410,819	81,278	2231.66	973.67	2003.50
18	0	578	1596.94	923,034	166,016	746.30	431,360	77,584	2343.24	973.67	2103.68
19	0	578	1676.79	969,186	158,470	783.62	452,928	74,057	2460.41	973.67	2208.86
20	0	578	1760.63	1,017,645	151,266	822.80	475,574	70,691	2583.43	973.67	2319.31
NPV @ 10%					$3,339,418[c]		$1,538,324[c]				

a. The total payment is discounted at the rate of inflation (5 percent).
b. Column 12 shows the pattern of "total base payment + surcharge" for the absorption rate in year 1 under the assumption that the actual absorption rate had equaled 72 units per year.
c. Net present values of the base payment and the surcharge discounted at the interest cost of 10 percent sum to the initial capital cost of $4,877,742.

Table 26–8 shows how to adjust annual impact fees to reflect differences between actual and projected absorption rates. One could make similar adjustments for inflation which, for simplicity, are held as constant. Deviations between actual absorption and initially assumed absorption rates are important because bond holders of the underlying debt will want to be paid regardless of how many new residents move into the service area.

Planners could use several adjustment mechanisms to handle expected absorption over future years. The adjustment mechanism in Table 26–8 assumes that future absorption will equal the current year's actual absorption.[12] The surcharge is recalculated each year for the remaining years based on the number of *actual housing starts* for the year. Table 26–8 (column 10) shows that the total payment, adjusted for changes in absorption, ranges from $917.83 in year 1 to $2,583.43 in year 20. Both the base payment (column 4) and the surcharge (column 7) increase at the inflation rate of 5 percent per year, which causes all residents to pay the same amount each year in present value terms.

In year 2, actual absorption is 50 units instead of the projected 72 units. To finance the additional excess capacity that results from slower absorption, the total payment increases from $963 (column 12) to $1,076 (column 10). Similar adjustments each year are based on actual absorption. After year 4, absorption levels off at 45 units per year. Consequently, the surcharge calculated for year 5 – $1,242 – increases smoothly for years 6 through 20 at 5 percent inflation. Absorption rate needs no further adjustments because actual absorption is assumed to equal the anticipated absorption in year 5 for future years.[13]

CONCLUSION

Planners can learn several lessons from the analysis. Politically determined impact fees (based on what the traffic will bear), as well as most standard formulas for calculating impact fees, lead to an unfair distribution of the burden of paying for urban infrastructure in a community. The burden falls disproportionately on either early residents or later residents, depending on how the fees are calculated. Equity-neutral impact fees correct the inequities. They are not hard to calculate and planners who fail to try do a disservice to both current and prospective residents of their communities. Inequitable impact fees can have significant consequences on a community's growth rate and competitive position relative to other communities.

The main issue is how to carry the costs of excess capacity during the period in which the community is developing. One way of achieving equity-neutral impact fees is to divide the fees into two parts: a base payment for financing the cost per connection at capacity and a surcharge for carrying the excess capacity during the buildout period. The surcharge equalizes the carrying cost for all users regardless of when they move into the community. While the case illustration presented annual impact fees, analysts can derive one-time fees by computing the present value of future annual impact fees.

Tables 26–5 to 26–8 illustrate that equity-neutral fees depend highly on the assumptions for inflation, interest, and growth rates. Inflation exacerbates the inequities of nonequity-neutral fees. Equity-neutral impact fees increase with inflation as well as with slower absorption rates because, in such situations, earlier residents must pay for excess capacity for longer periods (Tables 26–5 and 26–6). Table 26–7 shows the trade-off between economies of scale and the cost of carrying excess capacity. If capacity is doubled with no increase in the rate of growth in the community, the savings in cost per connection must be at least 30 percent to compensate for the additional cost of excess capacity. While the results depend on the particular assumptions, they demonstrate that economies of scale must be substantial for users to realize net benefits. My results suggest that planners should temper traditional engineering approaches that favor larger systems to take advantage of economies of scale; they need to understand the costs for carrying excess capacity.

While planners, theoretically, can design equity-neutral impact fees, existing bond instruments for financing water and sewer facilities do not readily accommodate payment patterns tied to uncertain rates of future growth. Bondholders want to be paid regardless of how many people move into the community each year. Further research should address how financial markets can assist in the attainment of equity-neutral fees. Planners must develop some mechanism to smooth over the differences between bond payments and revenues generated from uncertain impact fee collections before truly equity-neutral fees can be achieved. It may not always be possible to attain perfect equity, but community leaders should understand the consequences of inequitable distribution of the financing burden if they fail.

Author's Note

I would like to thank Edward Kaiser and Arthur C. Nelson for unusually helpful comments and suggestions. They are absolved of any responsibility for errors.

Notes

1. Facilities that have finite life require the adjustment for duration of enjoyment. For example, if a sewer plant has a 20-year life, a home buyer who enjoys the benefits of the plant for 20 years should pay more than one who enjoys it for only 19 years.

2. I thank Ron Welch, who spent many hours going through financial prospectuses and cross-checking account data with system operators. Juran and Moody, Inc., provided generous access to information.

3. Connection equivalents convert nonresidential development to its equivalent in terms of residential demand. One acre of office development is equivalent to 4.396 single-family units, based on average suburban densities in Houston. One acre of apartment land is equivalent to 25 dwelling units.

4. A technical report by Peiser and Welch (1985) contains a detailed breakdown of the data in Table 26–1.

5. Costs for Dallas were adjusted by adding internal line costs and administrative costs to make them comparable to those for MUDs (Peiser and Welch 1985).

6. Impact fees include distribution costs, which home builders often pay on a lot-footage basis. In actuality, MUDs require the developer to pay 30 percent of the interior distribution costs, which they pass on to the future home buyer in the lot price.

7. Theoretically, alternative B provides an equity-neutral solution only for the strict assumptions of zero inflation and infinite economic life.

8. This method is similar to a revenue bond tax for a special district. Only the beneficiaries of the service of the district must pay.

9. Technically, since two years' interest is built into the administrative cost, the first year represents the first year of home sales, with a two-year construction lead time. Some lots would be sold in year 2 following issuance of the bonds.

10. Annuitized means that the total cost is converted into a level annuity payment that exactly covers interest on, and repayment of, the total cost over the financing period.

11. If we assume inflation, the surcharge would increase each year at the assumed inflation rate. The initial surcharge would give an ending "accrued debt service account" of zero in the twentieth year.

12. Alternatively, one could calculate a moving average. That approach would smooth out some of the effects of the real estate cycle.

13. Table 26–8 assumes that all payments are made at the end of the year based on actual absorption for the

year. In practice, builders would, presumably, pay the impact fees when they receive building permits. If they have to pay fees in the middle of the year, they would calculate the amounts based on the anticipated absorption rate. Then they would either pay the difference between actual and the expected absorption, or carry over the additional charges into calculations for subsequent years.

References

Burchell, Robert W. and David Listokin. 1978. *The Fiscal Impact Handbook.* New Brunswick, N.J.: Center for Urban Policy Research.

Clark, Robert M. and Richard G. Stevie. 1981. A Water Supply Cost Model Incorporating Spatial Variables. *Land Economics* 57, 1: 18–32.

Hanke, Steve and Roland Wentworth. 1981. On the Marginal Cost of Wastewater Services. *Land Economics* 57, 4: 558–66.

Peiser, Richard. 1983. The Economics of Municipal Utility Districts for Land Development. *Land Economics* 59, 1: 43–57.

———— and Ron Welch. 1985. *Economies of Scale in Water and Sewer Construction Costs for New Subdivisions.* Technical Report TRERC-885-1M-490. College Station, Tex.: Texas Real Estate Research Center.

Synder, Thomas P. and Michael A. Stegman. 1986. *Paying for Growth: Using Development Fees to Finance Infrastructure.* Washington, D.C.: Urban Land Institute.

Turvey, Ralph. 1976. Analyzing the Marginal Cost of Water Supply. *Land Economics* 52, 2: 158–68.

U.S. Environmental Protection Agency. 1973a. *The Economics of Clean Water.* Washington, D.C.: U.S.E.P.A.

————. 1973b. *Estimated Staffing for Municipal Wastewater Treatment Facilities.* Washington, D.C.: U.S.E.P.A.

————. 1973c. *Guidelines for Cost Estimates of Municipal Wastewater Systems.* Washington, D.C.: U.S.E.P.A. Office of Water Program Operations.

————. 1978. *Construction Costs for Municipal Wastewater Treatment Plants.* Washington, D.C.: U.S. Government Printing Office.

APPENDIX 26A
CALCULATION OF MARGINAL COSTS

Turvey illustrates that the appropriate marginal cost to use for decisions is the discounted average cost:

$$NPV = \sum_{t=1}^{T} MC_t(1 + r)^{-t} \qquad (A1)$$

where NPV is the sum of the present values of the marginal cost (MC_t) in year t, discounted at rate r. The discounted average marginal cost (AMC) is calculated by annualizing the NPV over the period of payment (T):

$$AMC = NPV \left[\frac{r}{1 - (1 + r)^{-T}} \right] \qquad (A2)$$

AMC represents an annuitized estimate of marginal cost. In other words, AMC represents the level of annuity payments that will provide interest on and amortization of the full economic cost (NPV) over the life of the facility. According to the marginal cost pricing rationale, that would be an appropriate basis for determining impact fees.

The basic problem with implementing a pricing scheme based on marginal cost is how to measure it. In a full economic cost model, we must obtain a complete accounting of all capital and operating costs over the life of the project. Thus, full economic cost (C_{FE}) is the present value of all capital and operating expenses associated with a particular facility over its lifetime.

$$C_{FE} = \sum_{t=1}^{T} (1 + r)^{-t}[C_t + O_t] \qquad (A3)$$

where C_t is capital cost and O_t is operating cost in year (t). Operating costs are annual expenses associated with operations and maintenance, and usually recovered through monthly user charges. MC_t in Equation A1 is equal to C_t divided by the incremental addition to capacity Q_t:

$$MC_t = \frac{C_t}{Q_t} \quad (A4)$$

If water and sewer facilities are administered by the same authority, we can measure C_t by summing the costs for each component:

$$C_t = L_t + W_t + S_t + A_t \quad (A5)$$

where L_t = line cost, W_t = water supply and treatment plant cost, S_t = sewerage treatment plant cost, and A_t = administration, interest and other costs in year (t).

Given accurate measurements of each capital cost item in Equation A5, and incremental design capacities associated with each expenditure in Equation A4, we obtain the information necessary for calculating average marginal cost in Equation A2.

APPENDIX 26B
COMPUTATION OF EQUITY-NEUTRAL IMPACT FEE

The equity-neutral impact fee must satisfy the condition that the present value of revenues from the base charge (BASETOT) plus the present value of total revenues from the surcharge (SURTOT) equals the total capital cost financed by impact fees (COSTOT):

$$COSTOT = BASETOT + SURTOT \quad (B1)$$

where

$$BASETOT = \sum_{t=1}^{T}[B(1 + i)^t(1 + r)^{-t}]N_t \quad (B2)$$

$$SURTOT = \sum_{t=1}^{T}[S(1 + i)^t(1 + r)^{-t}]N_t \quad (B3)$$

B = base charge, S = surcharge, i = inflation rate, t = year, T = financing period, N_t = number of users in year (t). B and S are calculated from the following equations:

$$B = \left[COSTOT\frac{g}{1-(1+g)^{-T}} \right]/N_{cap} \quad (B4)$$

where

$$g = \frac{(1 + r)}{(1 + i)} - 1 \quad (B5)$$

r = interest rate, N_{cap} = Number of users at capacity. The annual surcharge (S) is computed iteratively to solve equation (B3) so that the sum of the present values of the annual surcharges equal SURTOT. [Note: r is the nominal interest rate. It represents the sum of the real rate of interest, a risk premium, and the inflation rate for calculating the initial annuity payment to amortize COSTOT over T periods where the annuity payments are adjusted each period by the inflation rate (i).]

Ethical Issues in the Use of Impact Fees to Finance Community Growth

Timothy Beatley

Many communities and states recently have embraced the practice of imposing impact fees as a way to fund the costs associated with new growth. There is little dispute that this financing technique is increasingly popular and that many other states and localities are on the verge of adopting it. Thus, it is an opportune and appropriate time to examine a number of political, moral, and ethical implications that may stem from this trend. Much of the recent work in the impact fee area has focused either on the programmatic descriptions of such techniques or on the legal issues involved in their use. Little analysis of the broader value questions has been conducted.

This chapter will identify at least the major ethical dilemmas raised by the increasing use of impact fees. The outcome of this analysis is necessarily uncertain and necessarily mixed. Impact fee systems neither will be wholly assailed nor wholly embraced—rather, a number of precautions are identified. Where possible, suggestions are tendered for mitigating possible inappropriate and unethical outcomes. This ethical analysis leads to my own positions about the responsible use of impact fees. Yet even for

readers who do not agree with those conclusions, the chapter at least will provide a greater understanding of the ethical assumptions and issues that arise and must be considered. And while I draw from the experiences of specific impact fee programs at a number of points, the chapter is intended to address the broader *trend* of using impact fees. The problems of intertemporal fairness; factors that may influence the ethical seriousness of those problems; the more general question of what constitutes a fair allocation of the costs of new growth and development; several key questions having a bearing on that determination; the broad issues of political representation, social exclusivity, and sense of community and the implications that the use of impact fees holds for advancing or undermining those values; and several ethical issues that arise during the actual administration of an impact fee system are examined here.

ALLOCATION OF THE BENEFITS AND COSTS OF GROWTH
Problems of Intertemporal Fairness

The basic philosophical concepts behind

impact fees are not new. Subdivision exactions (either in the form of dedicated land or fees in lieu of dedication for such created needs as parklands and schools) have been imposed for many years (Juergensmeyer and Blake 1981). What is different is both the mechanisms through which this accounting for created needs occurs and the extent or proportion of the costs of growth being shouldered in many communities by new development. The linkage programs implemented in San Francisco, Boston, and other places also certainly are variations on the impact fee concept and are considered at a conceptual level in this chapter.

Despite basic similarities between contemporary impact fees and more traditional subdivision and exactions requirements, it is relatively clear that new growth and development are being required to pay an increasingly greater share of the costs associated with growth. Such a trend raises a number of questions concerning the equity with which these costs are distributed in the community. One obvious equity quandary is what I refer to as the *problem of intertemporal fairness*.[1] That is, under impact fee arrangements new growth may be required to assume a greater share of the initial costs of growth compared with existing and older development. Do new residents and developers have a legitimate claim that such a practice is inequitable?

Is it reasonable for a new resident or a developer encountering an impact fee to ask the community on *what basis* are the rules being changed? Why should new residents be treated differently than were the existing residents? A number of replies could be offered; many would not satisfy the new resident. It might be argued, for instance, that building and land development always have taken place within a politically and economically dynamic environment. The rules are, in a sense, always changing and while it is perhaps unlucky that newer residents are caught in this political period where greater contributions for growth-generated public facilities are required, it is certainly not unfair. It also might be argued by established residents that these are not coercive policies, because new residents have the freedom to locate in other communities and regions of the country where such practices may not be common. Thus, the freedom to exit reduces the seriousness of these differences in intertemporal treatment (see Hayek 1960). A related reply is that if the market can sustain these higher contributions then they must in fact be acceptable to new residents. There are undoubtedly many desirable qualities about the community that counterbalance impact fee contributions, established residents might argue. Moreover, the established residents might contend that it has been their many years of tax contributions, civic activities, and so forth that have created many of the qualities that attract new residents in the first place. It is only fair, so the argument might go, that new residents be required to provide greater up-front contributions.

Intertemporal differences also may be defended by references to broader changes in the patterns of public finance and legal decisions that support those practices, which indicate that the use of impact fees is not restricted to that particular locality. Indeed, in some places, such as Florida, localities are being strongly encouraged to use such techniques (Bosselman and Stroud 1985). New residents and developers of new projects naturally should have adjusted their expectations in accordance with these changing patterns (Beatley 1985). Such a policy also raises serious questions concerning political representation; these are addressed in a later section.

The nature of this possible intertemporal equity problem would seem to depend to some extent then on the history of growth and development in a particular community or region. It may be important to determine the extent to which preimpact fee practices assessed new development for its impacts, such as through subdivision exactions or other means. Where assessment of new development has been a predominant, historically prevalent practice, and where the demands of such practices have been consistently and stringently imposed, it may be more difficult to argue that the development rules have in fact dramatically been changed. The age and historical progression of development in a community or region also may be an important variable. In many areas, impact fees, or substantial subdivision exactions, have essentially accompanied the emergence of these areas, especially in high-growth, new areas of the country—e.g., Sunbelt jurisdictions where fairly recent community growth has doubled, tripled, or perhaps quadrupled the size of small jurisdictions (both in terms of geography and population size). In contrast, perhaps, would be changing the rules in such established urban areas as Buffalo or Boston. The distinction between new and old rules in the former case would seem, then, to be less dramatic and thus perhaps less inequitable.

While the policy significance we give the intertemporal problem will depend on answers to a number of questions addressed below, one solution would be to split the difference between the contributions made by new residents and established residents. An attractive theoretical position would be to approximate the upfront contributions that *would be made by all res-*

idents if one rule were applied throughout the growth and development of a locality. Such a hypothetical contribution then would be used to determine the share new development should pay for new facilities and the share that should be funded through general tax revenues. The accounting methodology necessary to compute such hypothetical values would, of course, be quite complex.

It can be argued that the significance of these intertemporal inequities also will depend on the size of the impact fees assessed and whether they gradually are introduced. The intertemporal inequity created by changing the ground rules of development may be substantially greater where the amount of the fees is *very* large. It is, of course, difficult in ethical analysis to separate this question from the questions of who ultimately bears the brunt of the new costs and for what purposes such fees are exacted. That is, it seems entirely reasonable that we may want to balance the intertemporal inequity of changing the rules in a dramatic way with the fact that such fees ultimately and primarily are borne by land speculators and owners of raw land who otherwise unfairly would reap socially created wealth.

The intertemporal fairness question aside, how much of the costs of growth should new development be required to pay? This I will refer to as the *fair allocation question*. To properly answer this question requires that we first consider and address several important subsidiary questions. It requires us to consider the distributive effects of impact fees in relation to the social and economic positions and circumstances of those affected. The categories of questions that follow are important in determining the ethics of using impact fees. It is important to note that some of the concerns address the use of impact fees (or other similar forms of exactions) *under any circumstances* while other questions raise issues about the use of impact fees *in a particular community context* or under particular social, political, and economic circumstances.

Who Benefits from Growth?

Implicit in much of the support for impact fees is that those who benefit directly from public services and facilities ought to bear the costs and, moreover, ought to bear them in proportion to the level of benefits received. In the public finance literature this is typically referred to as the benefit standard (Beatley and Kaiser 1983; Snyder and Stegman 1986). Yet, while intuitively appealing on one level, it can be argued that impact fees that impose most of the costs of new development directly on it ignore the many broader ways in which the beneficiaries of such growth extend to the larger community. For example, consider a case in which a new industry locates in the community. As a result of this new primary industry, a ripple of economic activity is created, and it generally can be expected that income and employment levels will increase in response. Let us assume that heavy impact fees for capital improvements are imposed both on the industry itself and on the accompanying building and new residential growth stimulated by the industry. While at a narrow level it is certainly true that the industry and its associated residential and other growth are the direct beneficiaries of the new roads, sewer and water service, and so on, the many economic ripples created by this new growth suggest that the indirect beneficiaries are much more widespread. The more extensive and widespread these ripple effects are, the less defensible high impact fees would seem to be.

As a further example, consider the impacts of a new residential development without the assumption of an accompanying industry. Does such a beneficiary argument still hold? Perhaps not. However, if the community in question were a major retail or commercial center, this new development may do much to stimulate economic ripples similar to the previous industrial case. Under different assumptions, of course, these communitywide benefits may be much more difficult to envision. Take, for instance, a proposed industrial development project in a suburban community where no major commercial or industrial uses exist and thus where no immediate economic ripple effects can be detected. In this case, indirect beneficiaries of new roads, sewers, and so forth may be located primarily in other adjoining or nearby localities. A local impact fee may make much more sense from the point of view of the benefit standard, although regional taxation devices, such as tax base sharing, ideally would seem to be required here (e.g., Plosila 1976). In any event, it can be argued that impact fees are less justifiable under the benefit standard because of these broader patterns of communitywide benefits.

A related question is the extent to which *landowners* in high-growth, high-demand areas have benefited or are benefiting from growth. Impact fees may in many situations be supported ethically because they constitute a tax on this windfall. The extent to which the costs of impact fees actually are capitalized into the value of undeveloped land will, of course, depend on many factors including the price elasticity of demand for this land (see Duncan, Morgan, and Standerfer 1986). Where an impact fee largely reduces the value of otherwise highly priced land it may be more morally defensible. Here, it can be argued, the fee is doing nothing more than simply taking away an undeserved gain. That is, it is the public and other investments of the community at large that primarily are responsible for this value increase and thus in this sense nothing truly deserved or earned is being taken away (Hagman 1975). There has, of course, been a long and controversial debate concerning the merits of this argument and the use of impact fees falls squarely within this debate (Hagman and Misczynski 1977).

Taxing away the speculative increase in land values appears consistent with intuitive notions of merit and desert. While there are many ways in which desert or merit can be defined, Americans historically have attributed a high value to work and effort and the fairness of rewarding those attributes (Feinberg 1970; Weale 1983). Windfall gains fly in the face of a notion of desert based upon labor, effort, productivity, or individual contribution. Moreover, for society to permit individuals to become millionaires simply because the public and private sectors make certain investments in certain locations (e.g., highways and shopping centers) would seem to undermine this fair return to labor ethic.

Extracting the full costs of growth and development from landowners with appreciating land values involves several ethical dilemmas, however. First is the objection of the landowners that to impose such an impact fee is to unfairly thwart legitimately formed expectations about the use of land and the expected profits to be obtained therefrom (e.g., see Beatley 1985). Here problems of differential treatment similar to those mentioned earlier are encountered. Moreover, the landowner might contend that such an imposition is unfair because property taxes for years have been paid based on the market value of such land. Many current landowners could contend, and legitimately so, that previous landowners have largely been the beneficiaries of social growth and the attendant high property values (i.e., they have already sold out) and that newer owners of such land actually have not been the major recipients of such windfalls (i.e., because they had to pay high fair market land prices).

The legitimacy of landowner claims that windfall extraction is unfair will depend on several factors. Perhaps the most obvious is the extent to which the entire windfall is extracted. In most or many situations, the impact fee imposed will not be large enough to cause the elimination of the entire windfall, but rather will only reduce its size. An additional variable is the extent to which landowners have indicated an intention to develop. Legal rulings concerning estoppel and determinations of investment-backed expectations become important. From a practical point of view, it may be difficult to determine whether intent to develop is present. It does seem intuitively fair, however, that where land has been put to a continuous, economically viable use (e.g., agriculture) that expectations about its developability would be given less weight.

An additional factor is the historical pattern of property taxation evident in the community. As noted, the imposition of impact fees can lead to substantially lower raw land values, which in turn implies that the previous property taxes paid on this land, based on preimpact fee market values, were *too high* given the changing market conditions. Landowners subject to the capitalization effects of new impact fees could argue, and legitimately so, that they are deserving of some form of tax rebate to compensate for this effect. Again, however, it can be replied that such outcomes are unavoidable risks in a dynamic political and economic environment, and that these taxes were reasonable in light of the development rules in place at the time (Beatley 1985). In many cases, these lands historically have been taxed at their use value rather than at their market or potential development value, and in these cases such a concern is not as relevant (e.g., see Keene et al 1976).

Of course, the imposition of impact fees actually may do little to correct such inequitable windfalls. The problem is that in highly desirable areas the fee will simply be passed along to home owners in the form of higher prices or lower quality (Snyder and Stegman 1986). Furthermore, if new home prices rise, so will prices of competitive existing homes. The price increase becomes a windfall to existing residents, and impact fees in some situations may not reduce but rather increase undeserved windfalls.

Thus, many individuals benefit from new growth—indeed many established residents benefit. The construction of new roads and the building of shopping centers, parks, and recreational facilities lead in important and tangible ways to economic and other benefits. Rapid increases in existing land values are a common result. Many benefits may be less quantifiable and socially broader, perhaps the benefits obtained from the amenities that can be supported through larger population bases (e.g., opera, art museums, specialty shopping areas) as well as the cultural and social diversity that urban growth may provide.

A key question is the extent to which the benefits of those creating the new growth pressures (e.g., builders, landowners, new residents) can be distinguished from the benefits experienced by the larger community. Distinguishing among those benefits, at least in any precise way, is difficult. However, where the benefits are assumed to be more widespread, a policy of imposing the *full* costs of growth seems unjustifiable. Under the benefit standard, the important task is to determine the appropriate relationship between benefits unique to new development and larger community-wide benefits.

An important question in addition to who *does* benefit from growth is who *should* benefit from growth. This ultimately depends on beliefs about the appropriate role of government and the principles and concepts of social justice it should advance or protect. These issues are addressed more specifically in a later section on the potential exclusivity effects of impact fees.

Who Can Afford to Pay for Growth?

While it appears that impact fees are intended largely to respond to the benefit standard, perhaps a more appropriate criterion is ability to pay (see Snyder and Stegman 1986). Impact fee systems usually are not designed to be responsive to this standard nor are they usually defended on those grounds.

To defend the use of impact fees on the basis of ability to pay (i.e., over general jurisdiction-wide revenue raising), is to suggest that newer residents (or builders, developers, landowners) are in some sense better situated financially to pay for the costs of growth. It may be, for instance, that the existing community is made up primarily of lower income and working class citizens, while new development is occurring in the outer, more exclusive areas and is primarily upper income. Impact fees might be supported by elected officials as a way of more equitably paying for requisite services and facilities. Elected officials might even acknowledge that the broader community does benefit from this growth and that if the city were better situated financially (i.e., if the existing community were not so poor) it would assume a larger share of these costs.

An ability-to-pay standard also implies that impact fees may be deemed appropriate in some situations and not so in others. Where the fee is applied, for instance, to homes that are valued at $200,000, the impact fee may be a highly desirable way of funding the costs associated with growth. Where the ability of new home owners to pay such a tax is substantially lower—for instance where homes are more modestly priced, say $30,000—it would appear to make more sense to fund the costs of new growth through other means, perhaps through a communitywide property tax. In those situations, impact fees are regressive in their effects. Thus the ethical defensibility of an impact fee would be greater in the former case than in the latter.

Impact fee systems that result in lower raw land prices and thus reduce the large speculative gains on such land would appear to be more responsive to ability to pay. Speculative gains are, of course, unrealized or potential gains and as such it can be argued that the impacts of that loss will never truly be felt by landowners. But this argument may not be universally true. There are numerous examples to the contrary, for instance the case of the long-term farmer who depends on the occasional sale of a lot to keep his or her agricultural operation financially afloat. I would argue that, generally speaking, owners of raw speculative land are in a better financial position to assume the costs of impact fees than are the potential consumers of most new housing (at least moderate- and low-income housing).

How might an impact fee system be more responsive to ability to pay? One approach would be to distinguish in the application of impact fees between those who can and cannot best afford to pay for the costs of growth. In the same ways that circuit breaker programs have been used to reduce the burden of property taxes, so also could such a system be developed for impact fees. For instance, impact fees might be waived for projects oriented to low- and moderate-income residents. Similarly, impact fees might be tied to a sliding scale so that the proportion of the costs of growth-related facilities (e.g., roads and sewers) assumed by new development directly is proportional to ability to pay. Those prospective residents most capable of paying might be required to assume the full costs of their growth. Projects involving low- or moderate-income housing might have the majority of these costs assumed by the general public. In some communities, such as Loveland, Colorado, impact fees have been structured so as to make them less regressive.

Who Generates the Costs of Growth?

An additional ethical vantage point is obtained by asking who *generates* or is responsible for the costs associated with growth. This might be described as the *culpability standard* and conceptually is different from asking *who benefits*. Conventional thinking suggests that new developments should be required to pay for the costs and disamenities *caused* or *created* by it (Jacobson and Redding 1977). The issue is more complicated than this, however, and a number of important questions emerge here.

One question relates to the fairness with

which different classes or types of growth are assessed for the costs. Is it equitable to impose an impact fee on new commercial or industrial development to pay for such things as new schools? As the editors of *Nova Law Journal* reported, "Certainly no factory or store ever increased the number of children in the public school system."[2] It seems, however, that in important ways this may not be true. Perhaps the direct cause of the community cost is the presence of new families with children, yet often the indirect cause is the location or presence of new commercial and industrial growth which attracts or requires families to follow close behind. Such determinations of how the costs of growth actually are generated will have implications for the fairness with which different groups and individuals in the community are treated.

It is perhaps important to note here that the ways in which the costs of growth are perceived and defined may differ substantially among individuals. For instance, while the increased traffic congestion that results from new development may be viewed with great disdain by established residents who remember the community when requisite travel times were not as great, newer residents may not view it as a problem. For those moving to the community from, say, New York or Los Angeles, such levels of congestion may not be viewed as bad at all—perhaps even a marked improvement. In this light, new residents may not view excessive exactions to provide for traffic improvements as important or legitimate. As a further example, some people believe that new park areas should be provided at a high number of acres per resident, while others may see little need for *any* such facilities (e.g., they may value regular trips to nearby state and federal recrea-

tional areas). In a sense it might be argued by those builders, developers, and home owners unhappy about being forced to pay such fees that people should be allowed to vote with their feet; that is, to make choices about combinations of amenities that are most valuable to them (e.g., see Neenan and Ethridge 1984). Developers may argue that if X acres per person of parkland is desired by new housing consumers, then there are plenty of projects and communities in which they could live where amenities at such levels *could* be found. Other things being equal, the argument goes, developers and builders should be left to do as they please.

A culpability standard, then, seems to suggest that those groups and individuals directly involved in creating growth-related impacts—that is, builders, developers, home owners—should be the ones to incur and pay for those costs. In contrast, it can be argued that the owners of raw land actually have little to do with the direct generation of those impacts and consequently should not be forced to pay for them. They are simply the fortunate beneficiaries of growth and development patterns they have done nothing to directly cause or bring about. Consequently, under a culpability standard, impact fees would appear more ethically defensible where the market conditions are such that these fees will be borne primarily by new home owners, and not capitalized in the form of lower raw land prices. The application of a strict culpability standard here, however, seems intuitively unacceptable from an ethical point of view precisely because it ignores the benefits and expects the immediate growth catalyst (e.g., the builder, developer) to shoulder the entire burden. Certainly culpability justifies imposing impact fees on those individuals, but it seems that where benefits accrue to other individuals in the community, such as owners of underdeveloped land, they should share in the costs of growth as well.

By way of clarification, consider a situation where a culpability standard alone might apply. A developer might be required to pay an impact fee to cover the costs of installing certain public drainage or flood control improvements, without which preexisting home owners would be negatively affected (i.e., by new flooding created by the development). While the new development certainly benefits in a sense from those improvements (without them the project would not have been permitted), the main justification stems from culpability—the new development is being held *responsible for* the potential damages and environmental impacts it forces onto others in the community.

Exactions as Quid Pro Qro Trading

An additional ethical perspective is to view the imposition of impact fees and other forms of exactions as the fair outcomes of a kind of quid pro quo trading. The public is willing to permit development to occur in particular ways and at particular intensities in exchange for certain contributions made by the developer. This is the theoretical basis for many of the early subdivision exactions, viewing public approval and acknowledgment of the subdivision of land as a privilege and not a right. The contemporary use of this theory supposes that the public gives up something in exchange for something—certain rights and benefits it holds—in exchange for something else of equal or greater value. While typically this exchange will have a direct relationship to costs created by development, this relationship need not in theory be *exact* or *precise*. A developer may be asked

to contribute to the conservation of a sensitive and important regional environmental resource in exchange for development approval.[3] This may be a regional need that is not directly or immediately created by the proposed development nor a resource from which the development would directly or immediately benefit. The growing interest in linkage programs reflects this public perspective (Keating 1986).

The quid pro quo theory has its greatest appeal where the public is being asked to grant rights or benefits that are in some sense extra or beyond those given under the existing planning rules or framework. Some exactions are imposed as a condition of rezoning, say from an agricultural or low-intensity use to a high-density residential or commercial use. A question arises as to whether this case presents a unique ethical situation when compared to the case where a landowner just wants to develop his or her land at the designated uses and levels of intensity. Here perhaps one could argue that the exaction is warranted regardless of the extra facility demands that may result because it in a sense serves as compensation to the community—it serves to balance the otherwise inappropriateness of this use as defined in advance by a comprehensive and long-term land use plan (see Nova Law Journal 1980). The logic here may be the same as that used to justify the provision of additional density under a bonus/incentive zoning or transferable development rights program (e.g., see Marcus 1980).

The trade or exchange may be justified from the public's point of view by reference to the costs generated by a proposed project or the benefits received from it. In this way, the concepts discussed above become relevant as well. It seems that there are other legitimate arguments that also further justify the types of exaction required, for instance, under linkage programs (i.e., improvements and expenditures for broader social needs that may extend beyond a particular new project or development). A strong argument for requiring substantial contributions rather than communitywide taxation to pay for such things as low-income housing or health care is that these exactions are tapping into a process of wealth generation to which the public is a consenting party (even where no zoning changes or regulatory concessions are given). It does not seem unreasonable for the public to lay claim to a portion of the profits generated from, for instance, a proposed office–commercial complex. An additional argument is one from political practicality. While some would argue that many of the broader social goods and services provided through exactions should be financed by the larger public (e.g., through a higher property tax rate), exactions may be the only politically feasible way to finance such needs.

The quid pro quo trade raises the ire of builders and developers who view impact fees and other forms of exactions as a kind of extortion. Yet, from the public's point of view, this is unfair because little coercion is actually involved. Developers and other actors involved in the process of land development are free to choose other localities and regional markets in which to practice their trade if the basic ground rules are unacceptable (e.g., Hayek 1960).

Quid pro quo arrangements that involve public zoning concessions raise serious ethical questions concerning how fairly the resulting public costs are distributed. Often it is the residents of particular neighborhoods who must live with the traffic congestion, air pollution, noise, crime, and other impacts of the increased density that the public permits in exchange for

exactions. While the quid pro quo bargain may be efficient from the perspective of the broader public (i.e., it produces net public benefits), particular residents and neighborhoods may believe they are unfairly bearing the brunt of the costs associated with such trades. Adding to this sense of inequity may be the unexpected nature of the density/intensity changes permitted. Landowners and neighborhood residents may legitimately point to the community's plan and land use regulations as the source of certain expectations that such more intense uses would not be permitted to occur. The ability of developers to bargain in this way for desired zoning changes may cast doubt on the stability and efficacy of a community's entire planning and land use program.

An interesting question is the extent to which a particular bargain or trade is ethical. Assuming that zoning and land use concessions are not to be given lightly, at what level of return is the public willing to endure the negative consequences of such concessions (i.e., the consequences of modifying a carefully developed community plan)? A strict utilitarian criterion would suggest that it is sufficient to determine that the benefits from the monetary and other concessions made by the developer exceed the negative consequences of diverging from the community's planned pattern of growth. These negative consequences, and the ways in which they manifest themselves (e.g., highly borne by surrounding residents), suggest perhaps that a trade should be acceptable only from the public's point of view when the benefits are *far* in excess of these costs, perhaps at least 2 to 1, or 3 to 1, or even 5 to 1. Such a trade would also be more acceptable ethically where the concessions made by the developer are used in some way to *compensate* affected residents and neighborhoods (e.g., through the financing of certain neighborhood amenities) or used to finance improvements that at least partially *mitigate* these negative effects (e.g., improvements to deal with new transportation problems).

An additional dimension to the ethics of this kind of public–private trading is the amount of profit or benefit the private developer or property owner reaps from the transaction. Even though it may be determined that the public will receive an acceptable return from a proposed trade, the transaction still could be viewed as unethical because the amount of profit reaped by the developer is obscenely high. Because these are public rights being traded away, and because negative social consequences are attached to such trades, the concessions asked for and given by the developer should bear a direct relationship to these profits. To do otherwise would amount to a sort of fire sale at the public's expense.

A parallel might be drawn between the imposition of impact fees under equal quid pro quo trading and the use of equity sharing in public–private partnerships (Fosler and Berger 1982). Equity sharing involves a similar public–private bargain—the public provides certain financial contributions or backing, typically in exchange for a percentage or share of the profits generated by the project. This suggests both that precedent exists for this normative perspective and that experience with public–private partnerships may provide some practical guidance in determining what constitutes a fair trade.

POLITICAL REPRESENTATION, SOCIAL EXCLUSIVITY, AND SENSE OF COMMUNITY

Heavy reliance on the use of impact fees and other exactions on new development raises several additionally and potentially serious ethical quandaries. One involves the concept of political representation and the extent to which such fiscal tools circumvent or undermine this prized American value. Indeed, this country initiated its struggle for independence in response to the perceived inequity of being taxed without meaningful representation. Similar criticisms can be leveled at impact fees. It is one thing for a locality and its duly elected representatives to decide to tax itself for some desired public service or facility but perhaps another thing entirely to place heavy financial burdens on future individuals who have had no opportunity to participate in the decision or to influence it in any way. Butler and Myers (1984, p. 437) echo similar concerns about the use of independent taxing districts in Texas (municipal utility districts):

> Unrepresented in the development negotiations are the interests of the future housing consumer. The development industry argues that it serves those interests by seeking to provide an adequate supply of housing. The city also claims to represent the interests of the future consumers. Nevertheless, the outcome of MUD negotiations typically burdens future consumers with financial exactions. The costs of growth are being shifted to the future residents of MUDs through surcharges that will be attached to monthly utility bills in those districts, even after the city annexes the property. Once these future consumers are in place and able to vote, one wonders, will future city councils sustain the long-term commitments to levy special surcharges set by the present city council?

Ceteris paribus, individuals who are assessed such fees, particularly when they are high fees, ought to have a hand in the political decision making through which they are imposed. Yet, proponents of impact fees can argue that this is not as significant an ethical problem as perhaps initially supposed. First, while future or prospective residents may not have had the opportunity to influence directly past decisions, the possibility of their addition to the local voting and political bloc surely would dictate that current elected officials consider their interests and views. Politicians and elected officials often act prospectively—that is, in accordance with how they believe voters and constituents will react at some point in the future. They will not run the risk of new residents helping to "throw the rascals out of office." There are, of course, problems with this argument, including the very real possibility that elected officials can ignore with impunity this prospective dissatisfaction. Current representatives may in fact be able to gain off-setting political support from existing residents by shifting tax burdens away from this group.

It is also possible that in a high-growth community the discontent of new residents will lead to a sort of chain reaction in which they become highly supportive of placing similar fees on even newer residents. They've paid theirs, they might argue, and now it's time for new residents to pay their fair share. This may or may not be a healthy attitude to promote—a sort of bash the newest resident attitude.

Another view is that the interests of future constituents already are being voiced by surrogate representatives with similar concerns and interests. Builders, developers, and landowners typically are vocal in their opposition to high impact fees and voice concerns about their inequity. They can thus be supposed to represent many of the interests of future residents. While this is undoubtedly true to some

extent, it is obvious that (a) the interests of these surrogate groups and future constituents may be substantially divergent (e.g., developers may not be as adamant in their opposition to impact fees if they know that they can pass much of the cost along in the form of higher housing prices), and (b) these surrogate groups may be considerably less effective and hold considerably less credibility in the eyes of elected officials than would members of the general population (e.g., developers are perceived by many to have a biased, one-sided view of the world).

Other arguments also can be employed in debunking the political representation concerns. One possible retort is that these impositions, particularly where the fees are not excessive, do not interfere with any fundamental liberties. Individual housing consumers, for instance, have the choice of avoiding the fees simply by locating in some other community or by purchasing a home in an already developed area of town. There are, consequently, ways of escaping these impositions, at least in theory. In many specific situations such consumers may, in fact, have considerably less freedom than proponents of impact fees may suggest because of geographical limitations (e.g., location with respect to employment), time constraints, and so on.

Current representatives may argue that it is entirely appropriate for them to set the standards by which they will permit the entrance of new development and new constituents into the community. This is almost a proprietary view of the community and its expansion, and resembles in some respects the quid pro quo bargaining concept discussed earlier. Another, more theoretical perspective that might be embraced is the idea that new residents *would* in fact *consent* to the fees if they were actually participating in the political process. The basis of the consent could involve a number of things from a sense of fairness (e.g., "Yes, because as new residents we are creating these problems we ought to pay for them.") to political expediency (e.g., "While as new residents we don't like the high fees we realize they are necessary to get the project built.").

A final reply to this concern is that in some situations many of the new homes in a developing area may be purchased by those who are already residents of the community. Snyder and Stegman (1986) report that surveys of new home buyers have found this to be partially true. Where the percentage of new constituents made up of old constituents is fairly high, it can be argued that these individuals in fact have had an opportunity to influence policy. Concerns about the lack of political representation are, in these cases, less serious.

It is difficult to resolve the problem of political representation in any ethically definitive way. Arguments for political representation are convincing enough to dictate caution and moderation on the part of elected officials when encumbering future constituents with such financial obligations. On the other hand, local officials typically make numerous decisions that affect future residents in important and fundamental ways and in which such future constituents have little say. These decisions range from the siting of public investments such as roads and hospitals to the regulation of permissible private development (e.g., the permissible height of buildings). The ways in which impact fees encumber future residents may not be very different than these more conventional encumbrances. Yet, planners and public officials must acknowledge the lack of political representation as a real and legitimate ethical con-

cern, and it may suggest that ultimately this negative dimension must be balanced against the other more positive aspects of using impact fees.

The proliferation of impact fees as an approach to financing the costs of new growth raises interesting ethical questions about the larger sense of public or community that exists in a locality. Under a conventional communitywide revenue-raising device, such as a property tax, funds are—in theory at least—collected and distributed according to the broader communitywide goals and objectives. Taxpayers contribute in taxes and elected officials distribute the funds to those communitywide demands of greatest importance or priority.

A movement toward impact fees as a public finance tool segments or separates the collection and distribution procedures of government. That is, a traffic impact fee is collected and then must be used to address traffic control problems. While the extensive use of impact fees certainly does not preclude the collection of general revenue/communitywide forms of taxation, it does reduce their political viability. Newer residents in the community are not likely to support both the imposition of extensive impact fees and substantial increases in general revenue raising (e.g., property taxes). As Stegman (1986, p. 2) notes, "Residents who must pay for their own schools may not continue to support the use of their tax dollars to finance school replacements, and as such residents become more numerous in a community, political support for general-revenue financing is likely to diminish." What may develop over time is a sort of narrow compartmentalizing attitude—i.e., where the only legitimate public expenditure pattern is one where a user is identified and taxed, and where the proceeds of this tax are used to benefit the user. What could in theory result is a movement away from a larger notion of the public interest. It is interesting that the impact fee movement comes at a time when notions of broader public civics or public interest appear on the decline (Bellah et al. 1985).

Another somewhat different dimension to this possible effect is the proprietary perspective that might be taken by those who pay high impact fees. That is, residents who have paid large fees for the construction of a new road or the expansion of a park system may become resentful when members of the broader public use those facilities. While their resentment may be legitimate, again the consequences are that it may be much more difficult to create and maintain a broader sense of community.

The increasing use of impact fees also raises serious questions about the effects of such a system in increasing the exclusivity of communities—that is if the costs associated with moving to a community are increased, is the ultimate effect that certain classes of individuals are excluded from the community? As noted earlier, the extent to which the costs of impact fees are borne by the new housing consumer (as opposed to, say, the landowner) will depend on a number of factors. In many locations, however, it is clear that serious price impacts will result and that under an impact fee system lower- and moderate-income residents will find it increasingly difficult to locate there (Dowall 1984). It has been theorized by some, using the theory of clubs, that imposing certain restrictions on the entrance of new residents into a community may be rational from the point of view of existing residents; that is, necessary to prevent the overcrowding of certain "club goods" such as streets, schools, and environmental quality (Blewett 1983).

The fundamental ethical issue here is the extent to which cities must be accessible to all income and social classes, and the extent to which they should adopt taxing, regulatory, and other policies that enhance accessibility (or at least do not lead to its reduction). The late Paul Davidoff frequently stated his belief that cities are not country clubs (e.g., Davidoff 1975). Yet an impact fee can act like a membership fee. As noted above, there is substantial evidence that impact fees in many situations will serve to increase considerably the cost of new housing. Moreover, as Snyder and Stegman (1986, p. 97) observe, these effects are particularly evident in "...highly desirable communities whose environmental features and amenities are distinct enough to make them much more attractive places to live than other nearby locations." What this perhaps foreshadows is a further exaggeration of the spatial differences between the haves and have-nots. Use of impact fees also may lead to a general communitywide escalation in housing prices, making it difficult for new residents to purchase even existing, older housing in the community (Snyder and Stegman 1986, p. 98).

Leaving aside the empirical question of whether the price of new housing is increased through the use of impact fees, to what extent are cities to be viewed differently than private clubs? I would argue that cities (and towns, counties, etc.) are significantly different from an ethical point of view for a number of important reasons. Among these:

1. Cities are political entities in which individuals have the opportunity to use the most basic of political franchises (i.e., voting, participating, voicing their opinions). Here

political equality, not economic or social position must dictate; as such, cities must strive to be as open and inclusive as possible.

2. Cities as governmental units possess powers that have the potential of affecting human lives in numerous and widespread ways; the potential effects of being deprived of "membership" are much greater.

3. Cities are a part of a broader social and governmental network (part of a region, state, nation) and as such are linked economically, socially, and constitutionally to other jurisdictional units. Cities have an obligation to acknowledge and adhere to extralocal constitutional and ethical standards (e.g., an obligation to provide for a certain regional fair share of low- and moderate-income housing).

Given that public communities are fundamentally different from private clubs, they are subject to broader principles of social justice and governmental conduct. Whether one views exclusivity effects as a problem depends in large degree on what one believes the obligations of government in fact are, and the appropriate principles of social justice it should recognize and pursue. Some of these, particularly those which relate to public finance, have been identified and discussed above. I have argued elsewhere that a primary principle of government in guiding growth and development is ensuring conditions in which the benefits and opportunities of the least advantaged are maximized *first*, before those of other social or economic groups and the public at large (specifically Rawls's difference principle; see Rawls 1971; Beatley 1984). Exclusivity as a result of local fiscal and land use decisions is a concern because it tends to reduce the range of social and economic opportunities available to indi-

viduals and tends to solidify existing economic conditions and positions. Impact fees that induce a land use pattern of clublike communities may be substantially counter to such fundamental notions of social justice.[4] Again, it will depend on the exact configuration of such programs and their actual empirical effects.

The Rawlsian difference principle suggests that social justice will not permit government policies that maximize welfare for the entire community at the expense of the least advantaged. This is a strong principle and one that is no doubt unacceptable to many planners and politicians. We need not invoke such a stringent principle, however, to raise serious questions about the ethics of impact fees and other growth-related policies. I would suggest that the concept of *equality of opportunity,* with its strong roots in American political and social history, is sufficient to question the legitimacy of impact fees that lead to exclusivity effects, or at least to ensure greater care in their use (Rae 1981).[5] Inequalities of opportunity might be said to exist where, irrespective of their natural talents and abilities of individuals, they are disadvantaged in terms of their social starting points—i.e., in terms of the instruments and means by which to advance in society. Clearly, spatial patterns of social exclusivity affect the nature and quality of these instruments and means in numerous ways (e.g., decent housing, education, health care, development of personal self-esteem, and so on).

Equality of opportunity supports the need to keep social and economic exclusivity to a minimum. It lends support for exactions programs that seek to require contributions for the provision of basic goods and services that advance fundamental equality of opportunity while questioning exactions programs that may reduce the availability of such goods, including but not limited to affordable housing.

We must also be concerned with the broader spatial implications of impact fee use. Situations may arise where some localities in a region or state are using impact fees while others are not. Again, where the fees involved are quite high, impact fees may constitute a sort of membership or admittance fee, in turn creating or exacerbating the social and economic differences between communities. One set of communities may emerge as the "best" clubs, while others emerge as the least desirable clubs, i.e., places to live. Such a system creates or reinforces a spatial pattern of social and economic inequality. While such patterns are not new, and often not primarily the result of impact fees, an impact fee system can serve to increase these intercommunity effects. At the very least such a finance system does not serve (at least on its face) to mitigate or reduce those social effects.

We must face up to the possibility that impact fees may be used to intentionally exclude certain groups, much in the way that zoning has been used in the past. We must confront the possibility that many localities will embrace the impact fee approach not primarily for its fiscal attractiveness, but rather precisely because it *does have exclusionary effects*. Intent is clearly a difficult thing to identify in practice but certainly impact fees will be supported by some precisely because of these kinds of effects. The exclusionary issue aside, some may support impact fees because they view them as additional roadblocks to any type of future growth and development, helping to slow growth and perhaps to displace it to other areas where impact fees are not in use. This raises additional ethical concerns.

In some communities it may be argued that to forego employing a fiscal revenue-raising device like an impact fee would lead to restrictions on urban growth that would in fact end up being *more* restrictive. That is, a situation may ensue where the locality refuses or is politically stifled in attempts to keep pace with the public facility demands of local growth. This was found to be an objective of impact fees used in Florida (see *Nova Law Journal* 1980, p. 143). Without impact fees or other similar forms of capital facilities financing, local growth may progress at snaillike speed, with the attendant results of exclusivity and social inaccessibility. It can be countered again, however, that where the growth being facilitated is primarily upper class or upper income, the results may be no better.

This raises the broader question of the extent to which impact fees, through their ability to get certain facilities financed more quickly and easily, are responding to other important values that often must be included in the equation. Take, for example, a situation where, because of the imposition of an impact fee, a long-needed sewer treatment plant that would not have been feasible before it is constructed (e.g., suppose that current residents refused to pass several bond referenda to fund such improvements). As a result, the town is able to move away from heavy reliance on on-site septic tank disposal that threatens to contaminate a highly productive groundwater aquifer. The aquifer, it might be further assumed, is the primary source of drinking water in the region. Even though the imposition of impact fees may raise the cost of new housing and thus make the community more exclusive, it is perhaps reasonable to argue that this is an acceptable outcome when weighed against the health risks and economic impacts of contaminating a regional aquifer. These types of side benefits to using impact fees necessarily must be balanced against the exclusionary and other negative effects that may result.

The extent to which impact fees will cause exclusionary results will, for instance, depend on how the revenues from such fees are actually used and the actual modifications to public expenditure patterns that result. A possible and interesting position is that impact fees will do much to advance social equity because they free general community funds that can then be used for such things as public day care or housing assistance. This argument seems particularly plausible in this era of fiscal constraint and declining federal assistance for social services and programs (e.g., Juergensmeyer and Blake 1981). It can be expected that in such a period the squeaky-wheel phenomenon prevails (i.e., money will go to fill the potholes, build the freeway exchange, correct the traffic congestion) and less visible social needs will get shortchanged. Impact fees may not contribute anything directly to assisting the least advantaged groups in the community, yet they may prevent a drain on the public purse that would harm the interests of such groups. Of course, to argue this position requires certain assumptions about the political leadership in a particular locality; that is, there certainly is no guarantee that once such funds are made available they will be used to address such important social needs. Rather, impact fees may simply free local funds that can now be used to finance an additional golf course.

It also might be argued that impact fees can be used as a pricing system to allocate scarce community resources such as classroom space or sewage treatment capacity—and thus will serve to increase allocative efficiency. In theory, impact fees would be assessed in areas where capacity would be exceeded but not assessed in areas where substantial excess capacity existed. The result is, again, a freeing of public revenues to advance other public objectives and goals.

The freeing up of funds argument also raises interesting questions of whether and to what extent a locality should afford priority to the needs and interests of the least advantaged who are already residents of the community, rather than focusing on efforts to alleviate the burdens imposed on the new or prospective disadvantaged (e.g., by keeping the cost of new housing as low as possible). A locality may be able to free funds that can be used for low- and moderate-income social programs by imposing high impact fees on new development. In exchange, the imposition of the fees may tend to make the community more economically and socially exclusive. Conversely, a locality might opt to finance a greater share of the costs of new growth through general revenue funds, perhaps leaving fewer funds available for social programs, yet containing the costs of new housing and in turn reducing the community's level of social exclusivity. I would argue that public officials must assess the particular circumstances at hand and undertake those mixtures of financing strategies that have the greatest impact on promoting equality of opportunity. This will, of course, depend on numerous causal and empirical assumptions. If reducing or eliminating the use of impact fees will not have a significant effect on enhancing the availability of low- and moderate-income housing, then it probably makes sense to use impact fees to free other public funds that *could* be used to provide such goods and services. On the other hand, if the funds freed through impact fees are likely to be used primarily to purchase additional luxury goods (e.g., golf courses) it may make little sense to sacrifice *any* level of increased housing prices to free funds.

Important ethical issues also arise from intercommunity differences in the use of impact fees, again raising basic questions about the uniformity with which similarly situated individuals are treated. Consider two similar, perhaps adjacent, localities. Assume that one has decided to employ an impact fee while the other has not. The second community believes it has an obligation to fund a major portion of the costs of new growth on a communitywide basis. In the first community, several classes of individuals subject to impact fees may feel that they are unfairly treated compared to the individuals in the second adjoining locality. The owner of undeveloped land in the impact fee community feels that the somewhat lower price he or she must settle for (see Chapter 25) is unfair. The new home buyer wanting to locate in that community views the somewhat higher purchase price that must be paid (again see Chapter 25) as unfair. Even certain residents in the nonimpact fee community will feel unfairly treated. For instance, established home owners, in theory, either will be required to pay higher property taxes (or other taxes) than would be the case in the impact fee locality or pay the same taxes but receive a smaller, less extensive package of community services.

It can be argued again that these types of regional spatial inequities are mitigated to some extent by the fact that (1) individuals are somewhat mobile and can exit a community if they want, and (2) such taxing and financing decisions are arrived at through a democratic-representative process (one which at least incorporates the preferences and desires of the existing population). (See Hayek 1960, pp. 340–357.) Each of these mitigating assumptions of course can be challenged. Mobility does the landowner no good whatsoever because he is not able to transport his land and place it in a locality that does not employ an impact fee. While it can be argued that prospective residents can choose to locate where impact fees are not used or are less costly, often individuals have little flexibility in where they reside, for employment, transportation, or other reasons.

ETHICAL ISSUES IN IMPLEMENTING THE FEE SYSTEM

Assuming that a jurisdiction has overcome many of the initial questions about the use of impact fees in general, there are of course many ethical questions concerning how impact fees are calculated and, more generally, how impact fee requirements are administered (Porter 1986). Several of the more important of these are identified here, but this certainly does not provide an exhaustive review. Moreover, many of these questions have been identified in the impact fee literature, although they have not been dealt with in any very thorough or systematic fashion. Many of these issues, and their potential resolution, already have been foreshadowed in previous sections. Indeed, many of the broader ethical questions raised in earlier sections must be answered before these administrative and programmatic issues can be resolved.

One dilemma identified in much of the impact fee literature is the *threshold problem.* That is, which developments should be considered large enough to be required to pay impact fees? It is a complaint of many developers of large projects that they are unfairly assessed while numerous smaller developments escape the fees. Any ethically defensible impact fee system must apply uniformly to all sizes of growth and development—operational equity requires the imposition and collection of fees for small developments, even where the administrative costs of doing so are very high. A second type of threshold problem involves when a proposed project is likely to create public demand or need for some service or facility. In Broward County, Florida, for instance, projects are assessed impact fees only if they will lead to traffic demands that exceed existing capacity. This can result in a situation where a proposed development approved on day 1 is permitted without the imposition of impact fees, while a similar development approved on day 2 is required to pay substantial traffic improvement fees. An equitable impact fee system would seem to dictate that all development be assessed for demand created—even for those projects where existing capacity is sufficient.

As noted earlier, questions also arise concerning the types of uses to which impact fees should apply. Should fees to cover such facility needs as schools and libraries be applied to commercial and industrial as well as residential projects, for instance? In most cases, in the absence of compelling arguments to the contrary, impact fees should be assessed broadly to all such uses. This will ensure a wider and more equitable distribution of the costs of growth (e.g., with costs perhaps even assessed to the ultimate consumers of commercial and industrial goods).

Numerous operational questions also arise in the calculation of the impact fees. Should they be assessed on a square footage basis, according to the number of bedrooms, and so on? Conventional wisdom, and legal decisions,

suggest that where possible this calculation process should be logically related to the impacts generated. Assessments on the basis of the number of bedrooms may be an appropriate method, for instance, because it is a reasonably good proxy for the number of new school-aged children who will be added to the community. Yet, this will depend on which ethical criteria are embraced. Calculating the fee based on number of bedrooms may be defended on the basis of the benefit principle or culpability, but may not at all be responsive to ability to pay.

As we have seen, an interesting pricing approach would be to create a graduated fee system responsive to ability to pay. While such a calculation procedure would not completely ignore costs created or benefits received, it might permit the shifting of some of the costs of this growth onto those higher income uses better able to afford them.

An additional programmatic issue is when the impact fee should be imposed. Is it fair to ask developers to make the contributions on project approval or is it more equitable to require the fees to be paid closer to the time at which the impacts actually occur, benefits are received, etc.? Shouldn't fees be paid in a phased or sequenced fashion so that contributions are not made prematurely (e.g., so that the developer or home owner is not required to pay for a road or park far in advance of their ability to use these facilities)? Again, the ethical criteria will have an influence. While it may seem appropriate to impose an impact fee at the time of project approval under the concept of quid pro quo trading (i.e., because the bargain or exchange is in a sense consummated then), under a benefit or culpability standard this may not be deemed as appropriate.

These are but a few of the ethical questions that emerge from the consideration of practical operational issues. A full discussion of these operational issues is beyond the scope of this chapter, yet the preceding analysis of the broad ethical and value dimensions to the issue should be useful to planners and program administrators in developing and implementing impact fee systems.

CONCLUSIONS

This chapter has identified several of the primary ethical issues that arise from the use of impact fees. As with most discussions of ethical issues it will raise more questions than it will answer. Indeed, answers in the usual sense are extremely elusive in this type of analysis. I have argued several primary ethical points, however. First, the initial imposition of a system of impact fees raises serious questions of intertemporal fairness and equity, both within the community and within the broader regional network of communities. The seriousness of these inequities depends on the particular historical patterns of private and public investment financing, and the goals and objectives development exactions, including impact fees, are intended to serve.

Second, the ethical defensibility of impact fees will depend both on the ethical standards embraced by communities and the actual empirical effects of such fees. A number of possible evaluative positions have been identified and examined, including the benefit principle, ability to pay, culpability, and the theory of quid pro quo trading. I have argued that, in situations where the costs are borne prmarily or in large degree through lower raw land prices, the imposition of impact fees is, certeris paribus, more justifiable. I have suggested that this outcome is responsive to the benefit standard and the ability to pay standard as well as fundamental notions of merit and desert.

I have argued strongly for the notion of equality of opportunity and the importance of protecting and advancing this concept through public finance policy. Where impact fees, either because of their magnitude or the conditions under which they are imposed, serve to raise the costs of new housing for low- and moderate-income families, and thus increase the exclusivity of these communities, they are less ethically defensible. While impact fees may often in a narrow sense respond to a benefit standard, they may serve to thrust the costs of growth on those groups least able to afford them (i.e., by essentially pricing many individuals out of the market). As we have seen, this is not always the case. For instance, where impact fees raise the cost of new homes from $200,000 to $250,000, it can be argued that such fees are very responsive to ability to pay. Impact fees are less objectionable here because the market would not provide low- or moderate-income housing even in the absence of high impact fees.

Another major conclusion is that the defensibility of impact fees will depend on their effect on the broader spending decisions and land use patterns that result in the community. For instance, while impact fees may raise the cost of new housing, they may be more acceptable from the point of view of advancing community accessibility and equality of opportunity if their use serves to free funds to be used to advance those ends (e.g., through whatever means, rehabilitation of existing homes, construction of low-income housing, provision of social services, etc.). As a further example, such fees may be justified because without them community growth and development would be stifled — growth that would provide substantial benefits (e.g., employment, transportation, shopping, etc.) to several of the most disadvantaged neighborhoods in the community. The negative effects of impact fees on the price of housing may have to be balanced against other important values advanced by their use (e.g., the protection of regional water quality).

These conclusions hold implications for *how* impact fees are used. It is usually not simply a question of whether or not to use them, but in what ways and to what degree they should be used. Impact fees are more ethically defensible where their proceeds are used to finance in part or in toto programs that serve to enhance the community's overall accessibility and equality of opportunity (e.g., by financing the construction of low- and moderate-income housing, job training programs, day care facilities, mass transit, etc.). Impact fees, as with any public finance tool, must be judged against these broader social and economic goals.

The question of political representation is difficult to resolve. On the one hand it seems unfair to impose impact fees on an element of the constituency that has no direct representation of their opinions or interests. Yet, many political decisions are made in this way, and prospective residents are not coerced in any fundamental way into paying the fees. Planners and public officials should be sensitive to this issue and ultimately may need to balance this negative aspect against the positive features of an impact fee system.

Notes

1. Snyder and Stegman (1986) refer to this as the problem of intergenerational equity.

2. The editors acknowledge in their note the inadequacies of this statement: "It can be argued that commercial and industrial properties don't directly add children to the school system but their employees do add children to the school district. Commercial and industrial properties pay school *ad valorem* taxes and presumably, impact fees would be assessed on the same theory." *Nova Law Journal* 1980, p. 180.

3. The 1987 decision by the U.S. Supreme Court in *Nollan v. California Coastal Commission* (55 U.S.L.W. 5145, June 23) casts doubt on the legality and constitutionality of this type of rationale. Specifically, this case involved efforts by the state of California to condition the issuance of a development permit to a beachfront landowner on the provision of an easement for public beach access. The court theorized that permit conditions could only be imposed that were designed to mitigate the direct impacts of the structure — if the outright prohibition of the structure involved would not eliminate the problem, then the imposition of permit conditions designed to address the problem would also not appear legitimate and thus not a constitutional exercise of police power. In the words of Justice Scalia, writing for the majority, "Unless the permit condition serves the same governmental purpose as the development ban, the building restriction is not a valid regulation of land use but an 'out-and-out plan of extortion.'"

4. There is, of course, considerably more to Rawls's theory of justice than the difference principle. Rawls derives his Two Principles of Justice, of which the difference principle is the essence of the second, through hypothesizing about which standards would be agreed upon under certain idealized social decision-making conditions. Rawls refers to this hypothetical construct as the Original Position, and specifies a number of important conditions that would prevail there, including the Veil of Ignorance that would prevent individuals from knowing, among other things, information about their own personal life circumstances. See Daniels 1976; Barry 1973; and Nozick 1974.

5. A requirement similar to equality of opportunity actually is included by Rawls as a constraint on the workings of the difference principle. Specifically, Rawls requires that all social inequalities be subject to the doctrine of "fair equality of opportunity." This is a far-reaching stipulation requiring society to provide necessary minimum levels of education, job training, etc., to ensure that all individuals of similar talents and abilities will have a fair chance to secure social and economic positions. This is very close to the definition I have in mind here and is obviously quite different from the more narrow, formal

sense in which equality of opportunity is often used in this country (e.g., individuals should not be discriminated against because of race or sex). Rae (1981) distinguishes between prospect-regarding and means-regarding forms of equality of opportunity. While local exclusionary policies certainly will have an influence on both types, I am primarily arguing here for a means-regarding definition.

References

Barry, Brian. 1973. *The Liberal Theory of Justice*. Oxford: Clarendon Press.

Beatley, Timothy. 1985. Expectations and Promise-Making in Land Use Policy. Paper presented to the annual conference of the Collegiate Schools of Planning. Atlanta (November).

———. 1984. Applying Moral Principles to Growth Management. *Journal of the American Planning Association* 50, 4: 459–69.

——— and Edward Kaiser. 1983 *Financing Community Infrastructure: An Exploratory Review and Assessment of Alternative Approaches*. Raleigh, N.C.: North Carolina Board of Science and Technology.

Bellah, Robert, et al. 1985. *Habits of the Heart: Individualism and Commitment in American Life*. New York: Harper and Row.

Blewett, Robert A. 1983. Fiscal Externalities and Residential Growth Controls: A Theory-of-Clubs Perspective. *Public Finance Quarterly* 11, 1: 3–20.

Bosselman, Fred P. and Nancy E. Stroud. 1985. Pariah to Paragon: Developer Exactions in Florida, 1975–85. *Florida State Law Review* 14: 527–63.

Butler, Kent S. and Dowell Myers. 1984. Boomtime in Austin, Texas: Negotiated Growth Management. *Journal of the American Planning Association* 50, 4: 447–58.

Daniels, Norman, ed. 1977. *Reading Rawls: Critical Studies of a Theory of Justice*. New York: Basic Books.

Davidoff, Paul. 1975. Working Toward Redistributive Justice. *Journal of the American Institute of Planners* 41, 5: 317–18.

Dowall, David. 1984. *The Suburban Land Squeeze: Land Conversion and Regulation in the San Francisco Bay Area*. Berkeley, Calif.: University of California Press.

Duncan, James B., Terry D. Morgan, and Norman R. Standerfer. *Drafting Impact Fee Ordinances*. Austin, Tex.: City of Austin.

Feinberg, Joel. 1970. *Doing and Deserving*. Princeton, N.J.: Princeton University Press.

Fosler, R. Scott and Renee A. Berger, eds. 1982. *Public-Private Partnership in American Cities*. Lexington, Mass.: Heath and Co.

Hagman, Donald. 1975 A New Deal: Trading Windfalls for Wipeouts. In *No Land is an Island*. San Francisco: Institute for Contemporary Studies, 169–86.

——— and Dean Misczynski. 1978. *Windfalls for Wipeouts*. Chicago: ASPO Press.

Hayek, Friedrich A. 1960. *The Constitution of Liberty*. Chicago: University of Chicago Press.

Jacobsen, Fred and Jeff Redding. 1977. Impact Taxes: Making Development Pay Its Way. *North Carolina Law Review* 55: 407–20.

Juergensmeyer, Julian Conrad and Robert M. Blake. 1981. Impact Fees: An Answer to Local Governments' Capital Funding Dilemma. *Florida State University Law Review* 9, 3: 415.

Keating, W. Dennis. 1986. Linking Downtown Development to Broader Community Goals: An Analysis of Linkage Policy in Three Cities. *Journal of the American Planning Association* 52, 2: 133–41.

Keene, John et al. 1976. *Untaxing Open Space*. Washington, D.C.: Council on Environmental Quality.

Marcus, Norman. 1980. A Comparative Look at TDR, Subdivision Exactions, and Zoning as Environmental Preservation Panaceas: The Search for Dr. Jekyll without Mr. Hyde. *Urban Law Annual* 20: 3–73.

Musgrave, Richard and Peggy Musgrave. 1973. *Public Finance in Theory and Practice*. New York: McGraw-Hill.

Neenan, William B. and Marcus E. Ethridge. 1984. Competition and Cooperation Among Localities. In *Urban Economic Development*, edited by Richard D. Bingham and John P. Blair. Beverly Hills, Calif.: SAGE Publications.

Nova Law Journal. 1980. Note on Impact Fees: National Perspectives to Florida Practice; A Review of Mandatory Land Dedications and Impact Fees that Affect Land Developments. *Nova Law Journal* 4: 137–86.

Nozick, Robert. 1974. *Anarchy, State and Utopia*. New York: Basic Books.

Plosila, Walter H. 1976. Metropolitan Tax Base Sharing: Its Potential and Limitations. *Public Finance Quarterly* 4, 2.

Porter, Douglas. 1986. The Rights and Wrongs of Impact Fees. *Urban Land*. May.

Rae, Douglas. 1981. *Equalities*. Cambridge, Mass.: Harvard University Press.

Rawls, John. 1971. *A Theory of Justice*. Cambridge, Mass.: Harvard University Press.

Snyder, Thomas P. and Michael A. Stegman. 1986. *Paying for Growth: Using Development Fees to Finance Infrastructure*. Washington, D.C.: Urban Land Institute.

Stegman, Michael A. 1986. Development Fees for Infrastructure. *Urban Land* May: 2–5.

Weale, Albert. 1983. *Political Theory and Social Policy.* London: MacMillan Press Notes.

28

Impact Fees as Social Policy: What Should Be Done?

CHARLES E. CONNERLY

It seems that everyone is in favor of impact fees. City governments are often confronted with rapid growth and fear that they will not be able to pay for the infrastructure that growth requires. They look to impact fees as the way to avoid substantial increases in property taxes and still provide for new roads, sewers, and other capital improvements. Many developers also prefer the certainty of formula-driven impact fees over the uncertainty inherent in less structured bargaining over exactions (Snyder and Stegman 1986).

Federal and state officials regard impact fees as a positive step to help pay for rapid population growth. Federal support for local infrastructure costs has declined (Nelson 1987), and state officials in rapid growth states, expecially those such as Texas and Florida that traditionally do not have low taxes, welcome the idea of states having to pick up the tab for growth. Finally, discussions on impact fees, such as the *Journal of the American Planning Association*'s symposium at the 1987 APA national planning conference, indicate that most planners agree that such fees are desirable. Those planners see the real questions as focusing on how to implement fees in a manner that produces adequate revenue and, at the same time, keeps them defensible in court.

What can be wrong with something like impact fees that has so much support? I argue that, based on their effects on housing cost and availability,[1] impact fees are *bad social policy*, are *bad for the planning profession*, and that governments should consider alternatives.

IMPACT FEES ARE BAD SOCIAL POLICY

Although the boundaries between economic, political, and social policy overlap in substantial ways, we can define social policy as the set of policies "through which government seeks to correct inequities, to improve the condition of the disadvantaged, and to provide assistance to the less powerful" (Morris 1979, p. 1). That definition raises fundamental questions about the social policy implications of impact fees: Do they correct or exacerbate inequities or are they neutral?

Tentative answers to those questions arise from the growing literature on the imposition of impact fees and their effects on housing costs (Downing and McCaleb 1987; Snyder and Stegman 1986; Ellickson 1982; see Chapter 25). Although researchers have done few, if any, empirical studies on impact fee incidence, incidence theory suggests the following:

1. Except where they have purchased land

prior to establishment of a fee system, developers are able to pass the costs of impact fees to others. They either capitalize impact fees by paying less per unit of land or pass the fees on to consumers.

2. In regions with relatively uniform impact fees across jurisdictions, consumers will not be able to escape the imposition of those fees and thus may have to absorb their cost when they pay for developed property. That is especially probable when the county imposes the impact fees.

3. Where impact fees are not uniformly levied, developers nonetheless tend to pass on the costs to consumers where the demand is high. Most communities that have impact fees are growing rapidly, which means that they are, by definition, high-demand communities.

4. Even where developers cannot pass the cost of impact fees to consumers, they may not be able to purchase land at a discount that reflects those fees. Several studies (Dowall 1984; Snyder and Stegman 1986) indicate that landowners simply may not sell their land to developers who will not pay the asking price. In such situations, developers must either bear the cost of impact fees or postpone development until demand is high enough so that they can pass the costs on to home buyers.

5. The size and effect of impact fees can be substantial. In California, impact fees in the early 1980s averaged $4,400 to $6,100 per dwelling (Snyder and Stegman 1986, p. 75); by the mid-1980s fees were as high as $7,000 to $10,000 per dwelling (Frank and Downing 1987). Colorado communities had similar fees in 1984 (Snyder and Stegman 1986, p. 74). In Florida, individual impact fees are as high as $2,100 and the composite size of impact fees is undoubtedly higher (Florida Advisory Council on Intergovernmental Relations 1986, p. 100).

The effect of impact fees on monthly housing costs varies with the interest rate charged on the dwelling's mortgage. Snyder and Stegman (1986) calculated that, with a 10 percent interest rate on a 30-year mortgage, each $1,000 of impact fees adds $315 to the annual income a household will need to purchase a home. A $5,000 impact fee therefore increases the minimum income required to purchase the home by around $1,600.[2]

Although such an increase in required income seems small, it can prevent a substantial number of households from purchasing a new home. Also, because housing cost-to-income ratios increase as income declines (U.S. Bureau of the Census 1984), households with moderate incomes probably will have to pay a higher percentage of their income to purchase a new home than will higher income households. Consequently, moderate-income households are more likely than higher income households to be financially unable to purchase houses on which impact fees apply. Moreover, in the absence of significant federal housing subsidies, few alternative resources exist to help meet the requirements of lower income housing if impact fees raise development costs. Before the Reagan administration cuts in funding for subsidized new construction, developers could use federal housing dollars to pay the higher costs imposed by impact fees. Currently, however, the lack of such federal subsidies limits the use of major resources for new affordable housing primarily to reduction of development costs through increases in permitted density and decreases in subdivision and building code requirements, and to the use of federal tax incentives, such as tax-exempt bonds and the new low-income housing tax credit. For the former, impact fees clearly negate all or part of the savings produced by deregulation of local zoning, building, and subdivision codes. With the latter, recent changes in the 1986 Tax Reform Act tighten the income-targeting requirements of federal tax incentives to the extent that even a small increase in annual carrying charges can make the difference between a feasible and an infeasible project. Without some other form of subsidization, housing developments that depend on those federal tax incentives often barely are feasible and the addition of impact fees can prevent them from being built (Guggenheim 1986). Impact fees, therefore, can have significant negative effects on housing costs, particularly for low- and moderate-income households.

Expressed more broadly, impact fees are bad social policy because they exacerbate the problems associated with providing decent, affordable housing to all. The decline in federal housing subsidies has coincided with, if not contributed to, an increased housing crisis, as most dramatically evidenced by the increase in the homeless (U.S. Conference of Mayors 1987). The proliferation of impact fees contributes to the crisis by making decent housing even less available than it was previously to poorer households.

As with large-lot zoning and other housing consumption regulations, impact fees also are bad social policy because they can help perpetuate racial segregation. Because of the persistent differentials in black and white incomes, housing costs driven up by impact fees will serve as additional barriers to racial integration—a problem that characterizes many metropolitan areas.

More generally, impact fees are bad social policy because they are exclusionary. In the words of Paul Davidoff:

> Inclusionary policy is about sharing. It is about building a community where all members are made part of the whole, where they are integrated into the community. Inclusion is the opposite of exclusion, which prevents some members of a society from joining in a community or drives the poorer members out of a community where they already live. *Exclusion is a poor policy in a democracy* (emphasis added). [Davidoff 1985, p. 1]

Because communities can use impact fees to perpetuate economic and racial exclusion, those fees will be one of many barriers that continue to "solve" our social problems by segregating the disadvantaged so that the rest of society can pretend the poor and their problems do not exist. But only by including the disadvantaged in all communities are we ever going to be forced to deal directly with them and their problems.

IMPACT FEES ARE BAD FOR PLANNING

Impact fees also raise serious questions about the roles of planners and the clients they serve in growing communities. On one hand, impact fees permit planners to play an important role in establishing a substantial fiscal base for communities without overburdening current taxpayers. But in fulfilling their roles as important fiscal agents, "impact fee planners" essentially define the public interest to include only the needs of the community for which they currently work.[3] Such planners therefore eschew a role that seeks to address broader social issues, such as housing inequities, and thereby reduce planning to a narrow, technical role.

Instead of pursuing such historic ideals as advocacy planning or "the city beautiful," those who become impact fee planners enhance the idea of "the city selfish," and narrow the focus of the profession to helping existing community residents save money. The result is a planning profession that is reduced to a rather technical role, which, in turn, reinforces a status quo characterized by unequal access to good housing and communities. Instead, planners should call attention to the responsibilities communities have to address the housing and social problems of the regions in which they exist.

What to Do About Impact Fees

In response to the concerns outlined here, planners should look very carefully at retaining property taxes as the primary source of financing for a growing community's infrastructure (except for schools, hospitals, and the like, which should be supported by general taxation). Reliance on property taxes, in which all members of the community share in the costs of new infrastructure, reduces the financial burden that impact fees place on low-income housing. From the standpoint of making new housing more affordable to lower income households, that is a sensible move. Moreover, because property taxes are, in part, a function of a property's market value, such taxes on lower cost housing will cost less per dwelling unit than an impact fee. Governments assess impact fees on the basis of estimated demand for infrastructure; those fees do not usually distinguish between, for example, a three-bedroom, $45,000 house and a three-bedroom, $120,000 house.

But continued reliance on property taxes in rapidly growing areas will require increased taxes for current residents. Where impact fees are already substantial or growth is very rapid,

the increase may be unacceptably high to those residents (Snyder and Stegman 1986). In those circumstances, planners may have to accept the necessity of impact fees. At the same time, however, they should examine ideas for mitigating the negative effects of impact fees on low-income housing.[4]

Planners should seek to develop alternative sources of funding so that low-income housing is not stifled because of impact fees. Funding could come from local sources, and a city could even pledge a portion of its general fund for payment of impact fees for lower income housing. Unfortunately, when strapped with the high costs of paying for rapid growth few communities voluntarily will commit a portion of their general fund to pay impact fees for low-income housing.

Consequently, planners should lobby the states and the federal government for increased support to cover the costs of impact fees for low-income housing. Such support could come through increases in federal and state grants for infrastructure and could be tied to infrastructure costs associated with the development of low-income housing.

Given recent fiscal trends, increased state and federal grants for infrastructure may not be forthcoming. As an alternative, local governments can use state or federal tax incentives to help reimburse developers of low-income housing for impact fees and other development expenditures. Currently, the federal low-income housing tax credit, enacted in the 1986 Tax Reform Act, enables developers of *rental housing* to recover a sizable portion of the costs associated with impact fees in exchange for meeting fairly strict low-income targeting guidelines (Guggenheim 1986). The tax credit is equal to 9 percent per year of the development costs (new construction or rehabilitation) of low-income housing.[5] Developers take the credit on the full amount of development costs (minus the cost of land) for each of 10 years. The tax credit applies to all development costs, including such soft costs as impact fees, which allows developers to use it to shift part of the burden of impact fees to the federal government. Hence, a portion of the impact fees becomes "tax expenditures," which are simply revenues lost to the U.S. Treasury because of a tax deduction or credit. For investors in low-income housing, the tax credit results in a dollar for dollar reduction in taxes, which when coupled with tax deductions for interest, depreciation, and operating expenses, results in significant tax savings.

Tables 28–1 through 28–3 illustrate a case study of how the tax credit eases the burden of impact fees on housing costs. The case is based on development cost estimates made for development of a three-bedroom, single-family home in Sanford, Florida, a small city in the Orlando metropolitan area. (See Figures 28–1 through 28–3 for input data and assumptions for the respective tables.) These costs represent expected savings obtained through: (1) design of a small dwelling unit (960 square feet), (2) reduction in lot size to 4,300 (40 feet by 108 feet) square feet, made possible by zero-lot-line zoning, and (3) development by a nonprofit housing development corporation.

In the Orlando MSA, where the 1987 median income is $30,500, the maximum annual income for a family of four to qualify as low income under the low-income housing tax credit is 60 percent of this or $18,300. In addition, rent cannot exceed 30 percent of the maximum monthly income for this unit minus an allowance for utilities (assumed to be $75 in this

Figure 28–1. Input Data, Assumptions, and Financing Information for Table 28–1.

Low-Income Housing Tax Credit: No Impact Fees, Single-Family, Three-Bedroom Rental House

Assumptions:		
House Type		Single-Family, Three-Bedroom
Number of Units		Rental
Place		Orlando MSA
Household Size		4
MSA Median Income		$30,500
Household Size Adjustment		60%
Maximum Income for LITC		$18,300
Maximum Gross Rent to Qualify for Tax Credit		
(30% of Income)		$458
Utility Allowance		$75
Max. Net Rent to Qualify for Tax Credit		$383
Investors' Desired Rate of Return		15.00%
Investors' Marginal Tax Bracket		
(Assumes Corporate Investor(s))		34%
1st Mortgage Assumptions		
Interest Rate		10.0%
Term		30
2nd Mortgage Assumptions (Deferred Payment, Interest Accruing)		
Interest Rate		10.0%
Term		15
Total Development Costs		
Non-Profit Development Costs		$30,944
Land Value		$2,592
Development Costs Minus Land Value		$28,352
Low-Income Housing Tax Credit (9%)		$2,552
Annual Depreciation Allowance		$1,031
Total Required Equity Investment		$12,409
Percent of Development Costs		40%
Remaining Development Costs to be Paid for		
First Mortgage Amount @ 10%		$18,535
Percent of Development Costs		60%
Second Mortgage Amount @ 10%		$0
Percent of Development Costs		0%
Total Sources of Funds		$30,944
Percent of Development Costs		100%
First Mortgage Amount		$18,535
Second Mortgage Amount		$0

Debt Service, Costs, Rent	Annual	Per Month
First Mortgage	$1,952	$163
Second Mortgage	$0	$0
Total Operating Costs	$1,200	$100
Replacement Reserve	$293	$24
Gross Effective Income (Debt Service + Operating Expenses + Replacement Reserve)	$3,445	$287
Vacancy Loss (5%)	$161	$15
Gross Potential Income	$3,626	$302
Percent of Income Spent on Housing	30%	30%
Minimum Income Required for Rental	$12,087	$1,007
Required Private Investment	$12,409	

Table 28–1. Low-Income Housing Tax Credit: No Impact Fees, Single-Family, 3-Bedroom Rental House

Projected Rents	1	2	3	4	5	6	7	8
Rent	$ 3,626	$ 3,626	$ 3,626	$ 3,626	$ 3,626	$ 3,626	$ 3,626	$ 3,626
Less: vacancy loss	181	181	181	181	181	181	181	181
Effective gross income	3,445	3,445	3,445	3,445	3,445	3,445	3,445	3,445
Less: operating expenses	1,200	1,200	1,200	1,200	1,200	1,200	1,200	1,200
Net operating income	2,245	2,245	2,245	2,245	2,245	2,245	2,245	2,245
Debt service	1,952	1,952	1,952	1,952	1,952	1,952	1,952	1,952
Replacement reserve	293	293	293	293	293	293	293	293
Before tax cash flow	0	0	0	0	0	0	0	0
General partner share 1%	0	0	0	0	0	0	0	0
Limited partner share 99%	0	0	0	0	0	0	0	0
Statement of Taxable Gain or (Loss)								
Net operating income	2,245	2,245	2,245	2,245	2,245	2,245	2,245	2,245
Less: interest	1,849	1,838	1,826	1,813	1,798	1,782	1,765	1,745
Less: depreciation	1,031	1,031	1,031	1,031	1,031	1,031	1,031	1,031
Taxable gain (loss)	(635)	(624)	(612)	(599)	(585)	(569)	(551)	(531)
Tax or (saving) at 34%	(216)	(212)	(208)	(204)	(199)	(193)	(187)	(181)
Tax credit	(2,552)	(2,552)	(2,552)	(2,552)	(2,552)	(2,552)	(2,552)	(2,552)
Total tax or (saving)	(2,768)	(2,764)	(2,760)	(2,755)	(2,750)	(2,745)	(2,739)	(2,732)
General partner share 1%	(28)	(28)	(28)	(28)	(28)	(27)	(27)	(27)
Limited partner share 99%	(2,740)	(2,736)	(2,732)	(2,728)	(2,723)	(2,718)	(2,712)	(2,705)
Limited partner ATCF	2,740	2,736	2,732	2,728	2,723	2,718	2,712	2,705
Investment	(12,409)							
Net benefit	(9,669)	2,736	2,732	2,728	2,723	2,718	2,712	2,705
NPV limited partner share @ 15%	13,785							
Minus 10% syndication fees	1,378							
Net equity contribution	12,406							
NPV of tax credit @ 15%	12,806							

Projected Rents	9	10	11	12	13	14	15
Rent	$3,626	$3,626	$3,626	$3,626	$3,626	$3,626	$3,626
Less: vacancy loss	181	181	181	181	181	181	181
Effective gross income	3,445	3,445	3,445	3,445	3,445	3,445	3,445
Less: operating expenses	1,200	1,200	1,200	1,200	1,200	1,200	1,200
Net operating income	2,245	2,245	2,245	2,245	2,245	2,245	2,245
Debt service	1,952	1,952	1,952	1,952	1,952	1,952	1,952
Replacement reserve	293	293	293	293	293	293	293
Before tax cash flow	0	0	0	0	0	0	0
General partner share 1%	0	0	0	0	0	0	0
Limited partner share 99%	0	0	0	0	0	0	0
Statement of Taxable Gain or (Loss)							
Net operating income	2,245	2,245	2,245	2,245	2,245	2,245	2,245
Less: interest	1,723	1,699	1,673	1,644	1,612	1,576	1,537
Less: depreciation	1,031	1,031	1,031	1,031	1,031	1,031	1,031
Taxable gain (loss)	(510)	(486)	(459)	(430)	(398)	(362)	(323)
Tax or (saving) at 34%	(173)	(165)	(156)	(146)	(135)	(123)	(110)
Tax credit	(2,552)	(2,552)	0	0	0	0	0
Total tax or (saving)	(2,725)	(2,717)	(156)	(146)	(135)	(123)	(110)
General partner share 1%	(27)	(27)	(2)	(1)	(1)	(1)	(1)
Limited partner share 99%	(2,698)	(2,690)	(155)	(145)	(134)	(122)	(109)
Limited partner ATCF	2,698	2,690	155	145	134	122	109
Investment							
Net benefit	2,698	2,690	155	145	134	122	109

instance). Hence, monthly rent cannot exceed $383 per month.

Table 28–1 shows the case in which no impact fees are charged. Investor equity is calculated on the assumption that the project will be syndicated and that corporations will invest as limited partners. Consequently, after-tax investor returns are calculated assuming the 34 percent corporate marginal tax rate applies. The balance of development costs are assumed to be borrowed from a private lender at a 10 percent rate for 30 years. The second part of Table 28–1 shows a 15-year projection of revenues and costs and shows that investors can expect a 15 percent internal rate of return on their equity investment.

Tables 28–2 and 28–3 are the same as Table 28–1 except that impact fees of $2,500 and $5,000 are assumed, respectively. The effect of the tax credit on this increase in impact fees can be seen in Table 28–4. With no impact fees, the present value of the tax credit is $12,806. With an increase of $5,000 in impact fees, the present value of the credit increases by $2,259 or about 45 percent of the impact fee amount. Hence about $0.45 of every $1 in impact fees is recovered by the investors, assuming a 15 percent discount rate. The increased value of the tax credit, in turn, limits the amount by which debt service must be increased and therefore limits the amount by which rents would have to be raised.

Unfortunately, the low-income housing tax credit prevents developers from using it to reduce completely the negative effects of impact fees on low-income housing. First, the tax credit only partly absorbs the increased development costs associated with impact fees. Consequently, as shown in Table 28–4, monthly rents and minimum incomes must increase,

Figure 28–2. Input Data, Assumptions, and Financing Information for Table 28–2

Low-Income Housing Tax Credit: With Impact Fees of $2,500, Single-Family, Three-Bedroom Rental House

Assumptions:		
House Type		Single-Family, Three-Bedroom
Number of Units		Rental
Place		Orlando MSA
Household Size		4
MSA Median Income		$30,500
Household Size Adjustment		60%
Maximum Income for LITC		$18,300
Maximum Gross Rent to Qualify for Tax Credit (30% of Income)		$458
Utility Allowance		$75
Max. Net Rent to Qualify for Tax Credit		$383
Investors' Desired Rate of Return		15.00%
Investors' Marginal Tax Bracket (Assumes Corporate Investor(s))		34%
1st Mortgage Assumptions		
Interest Rate		10.0%
Term		30
2nd Mortgage Assumptions (Deferred Payment, Interest Accruing)		
Interest Rate		10.0%
Term		15
Total Development Costs		
Non-Profit Development Costs		$33,444
Land Value		$2,592
Development Costs Minus Land Value		$30,852
Low-Income Housing Tax Credit (9%)		$2,777
Annual Depreciation Allowance		$1,122
Total Required Equity Investment		$13,511
Percent of Development Costs		40%
Remaining Development Costs to be Paid for		
First Mortgage Amount @ 10%		$19,933
Percent of Development Costs		60%
Second Mortgage Amount @ 10%		$0
Percent of Development Costs		0%
Total Sources of Funds		$33,444
Percent of Development Costs		100%
First Mortgage Amount		$19,933
Second Mortgage Amount		$0

Debt Service, Costs, Rent	Annual	Per Month
First Mortgage	$2,099	$175
Second Mortgage	$0	$0
Total Operating Costs	$1,200	$100
Replacement Reserve	$315	$26
Gross Effective Income (Debt Service + Operating Expenses + Replacement Reserve)	$3,614	$301
Vacancy Loss (5%)	$190	$16
Gross Potential Income	$3,804	$317
Percent of Income Spent on Housing	30%	30%
Minimum Income Required for Rental	$12,680	$1,057
Required Private Investment	$13,511	

Table 28–2. Low-Income Housing Tax Credit: With Impact Fee of $2,500, Single-Family, 3-Bedroom Rental House

Projected Rents	1	2	3	4	5	6	7	8
Rent	$3,804	$3,804	$3,804	$3,804	$3,804	$3,804	$3,804	$3,804
Less: vacancy loss	190	190	190	190	190	190	190	190
Effective gross income	3,614	3,614	3,614	3,614	3,614	3,614	3,614	3,614
Less: operating expenses	1,200	1,200	1,200	1,200	1,200	1,200	1,200	1,200
Net operating income	2,414	2,414	2,414	2,414	2,414	2,414	2,414	2,414
Debt service	2,099	2,099	2,099	2,099	2,099	2,099	2,099	2,099
Replacement reserve	315	315	315	315	315	315	315	315
Before tax cash flow	0	0	0	0	0	0	0	0
General partner share 1%	0	0	0	0	0	0	0	0
Limited partner share 99%	0	0	0	0	0	0	0	0
Statement of taxable gain or (loss)								
Net operating income	2,414	2,414	2,414	2,414	2,414	2,414	2,414	2,414
Less: interest	1,988	1,977	1,964	1,950	1,934	1,917	1,898	1,877
Less: depreciation	1,122	1,122	1,122	1,122	1,122	1,122	1,122	1,122
Taxable gain (loss)	(696)	(685)	(672)	(658)	(642)	(625)	(606)	(585)
Tax or (saving) at 34%	(237)	(233)	(228)	(224)	(218)	(212)	(206)	(199)
Tax credit	(2,777)	(2,777)	(2,777)	(2,777)	(2,777)	(2,777)	(2,777)	(2,777)
Total tax or (saving)	(3,013)	(3,009)	(3,005)	(3,000)	(2,995)	(2,989)	(2,983)	(2,975)
General partner share 1%	(30)	(30)	(30)	(30)	(30)	(30)	(30)	(30)
Limited partner share 99%	(2,983)	(2,979)	(2,975)	(2,970)	(2,965)	(2,959)	(2,953)	(2,946)
Limited partner ATCF	2,983	2,979	2,975	2,970	2,965	2,959	2,953	2,946
Investment	(13,511)							
Net benefit	(10,528)	2,979	2,975	2,970	2,965	2,959	2,953	2,946
NPV limited partner share @ 15%	15,012							
Minus 10% syndication fees	1,501							
Net equity contribution	13,511							
NPV of tax credit @ 15%	13,936							

Projected Rents	9	10	11	12	13	14	15
Rent	$3,804	$3,804	$3,804	$3,804	$3,804	$3,804	$3,804
Less: vacancy loss	190	190	190	190	190	190	190
Effective gross income	3,614	3,614	3,614	3,614	3,614	3,614	3,614
Less: operating expenses	1,200	1,200	1,200	1,200	1,200	1,200	1,200
Net operating income	2,414	2,414	2,414	2,414	2,414	2,414	2,414
Debt service	2,099	2,099	2,099	2,099	2,099	2,099	2,099
Replacement reserve	315	315	315	315	315	315	315
Before tax cash flow	0	0	0	0	0	0	0
General partner share 1%	0	0	0	0	0	0	0
Limited partner share 99%	0	0	0	0	0	0	0
Statement of taxable gain or (loss)							
Net operating income	2,414	2,414	2,414	2,414	2,414	2,414	2,414
Less: interest	1,853	1,828	1,739	1,768	1,733	1,695	1,652
Less: depreciation	1,122	1,122	1,122	1,122	1,122	1,122	1,122
Taxable gain (loss)	(561)	(536)	(507)	(476)	(441)	(403)	(360)
Tax or (saving) at 34%	(191)	(182)	(172)	(162)	(150)	(137)	(123)
Tax credit	(2,777)	(2,777)	0	0	0	0	0
Total tax or (saving)	(2,968)	(2,959)	(172)	(162)	(150)	(137)	(123)
General partner share 1%	(30)	(30)	(2)	(2)	(1)	(1)	(1)
Limited partner share 99%	(2,938)	(2,929)	(171)	(160)	(148)	(136)	(121)
Limited partner ATCF	2,938	2,929	171	160	148	136	121
Investment							
Net benefit	2,938	2,929	171	160	148	136	121

although not by as much as they would if there were no tax credit. Second, the tax credit can be used only to subsidize the cost of rental housing. Third, developers cannot use it on behalf of households earning more than 60 percent of the area's median income. Although many of the excluded households cannot afford to do so, they still must pay the full amount of the impact fees passed on to them. Fourth, the tax credit is often too small, without the addition of other subsidies, to permit development of feasible low-income projects (Guggenheim 1986). Hence, planners should not feel that the tax credit does any more than partially help in shifting the costs of impact fees away from the consumer.

Because of the limits of federal assistance, planners should lobby for and advocate expansion of programs such as the low-income housing tax credit and infrastructure grants to help mitigate the negative effects impact fees have on the production of affordable, decent housing for low-income households. At the same time, planners should seriously question any use of impact fees in jurisdictions where a continued reliance on property tax funding of infrastructure will not result in politically unacceptable increases in property taxes for existing residents. Again, if governments force low-income housing projects to pay all the infrastructure costs associated with building them, it will be even harder than it is now to develop such housing.

Notes

1. Although this chapter focuses on the effects of impact fees on residential development, local governments also apply impact fees to industrial and commercial development and therefore those fees could have impact on the location of such activities.

2. This assumes the entire impact fee is added to the

Figure 28–3. Input Data, Assumptions, and Financing Information for Table 28–3

Low-Income Housing Tax Credit: with Impact Fee of $5,000, Single-Family, Three-Bedroom Rental House

Assumptions:		
House Type	Single-Family, Three-Bedroom	
Number of Units		
Place		Orlando MSA
Household Size		4
MSA Median Income		$30,500
Household Size Adjustment		60%
Maximum Income for LITC		$18,300
Maximum Gross Rent to Qualify for Tax Credit (30% of Income)		$458
Utility Allowance		$75
Max. Net Rent to Qualify for Tax Credit		$383
Investors' Desired Rate of Return		15.00%
Investors' Marginal Tax Bracket (Assumes Corporate Investor(s))		34%
1st Mortgage Assumptions		
Interest Rate		10.0%
Term		30
2nd Mortgage Assumptions (Deferred Payment, Interest Accruing)		
Interest Rate		10.0%
Term		15
Total Development Costs		
Non-Profit Development Costs		$35,944
Land Value		$2,592
Development Costs Minus Land Value		$33,352
Low-Income Housing Tax Credit (9%)		$3,002
Annual Depreciation Allowance		$1,213
Total Required Equity Investment		$14,593
Percent of Development Costs		41%
Remaining Development Costs to be Paid for		
First Mortgage Amount @ 10%		$21,351
Percent of Development Costs		59%
Second Mortgage Amount @ 10%		$0
Percent of Development Costs		0%
Total Sources of Funds		$35,944
Percent of Development Costs		100%
First Mortgage Amount		$21,351
Second Mortgage Amount		$0

Debt Service, Costs, Rent	Annual	Per Month
First Mortgage	$2,248	$187
Second Mortgage	$0	$0
Total Operating Costs	$1,200	$100
Replacement Reserve	$337	$28
Gross Effective Income (Debt Service + Operating Expenses + Replacement Reserve)	$3,736	$315
Vacancy Loss (5%)	$199	$17
Gross Potential Income	$3,985	$332
Percent of Income Spent on Housing	30%	30%
Minimum Income Required for Rental	$13,283	$1,107
Required Private Investment	$14,593	

Table 28–3. Low-Income Housing Tax Credit: With Impact Fee of $5,000, Single-Family, 3-Bedroom Rental House

Projected Rents	1	2	3	4	5	6	7	8
Rent	$3,985	$3,985	$3,985	$3,985	$3,985	$3,985	$3,985	$3,985
Less: vacancy loss	199	199	199	199	199	199	199	199
Effective gross income	3,786	3,786	3,786	3,786	3,786	3,786	3,786	3,786
Less: operating expenses	1,200	1,200	1,200	1,200	1,200	1,200	1,200	1,200
Net operating income	2,586	2,586	2,586	2,586	2,586	2,586	2,586	2,586
Debt service	2,248	2,248	2,248	2,248	2,248	2,248	2,248	2,248
Replacement reserve	337	337	337	337	337	337	337	337
Before tax cash flow	0	0	0	0	0	0	0	0
General partner share 1%	0	0	0	0	0	0	0	0
Limited partner share 99%	0	0	0	0	0	0	0	0
Statement of taxable gain or (loss)								
Net operating income	2,586	2,586	2,586	2,586	2,586	2,586	2,586	2,586
Less: interest	2,130	2,117	2,104	2,088	2,072	2,053	2,033	2,010
Less: depreciation	1,213	1,213	1,213	1,213	1,213	1,213	1,213	1,213
Taxable gain (loss)	(757)	(744)	(731)	(716)	(699)	(680)	(660)	(637)
Tax or (saving) at 34%	(257)	(253)	(248)	(243)	(238)	(231)	(224)	(217)
Tax credit	(3,002)	(3,002)	(3,002)	(3,002)	(3,002)	(3,002)	(3,002)	(3,002)
Total tax or (saving)	(3,259)	(3,255)	(3,250)	(3,245)	(3,239)	(3,233)	(3,226)	(3,218)
General partner share 1%	(33)	(33)	(33)	(32)	(32)	(32)	(32)	(32)
Limited partner share 99%	(3,226)	(3,222)	(3,218)	(3,213)	(3,207)	(3,201)	(3,194)	(3,186)
Limited partner ATCF	3,226	3,222	3,218	3,213	3,207	3,201	3,194	3,186
Investment	(14,593)							
Net benefit	(11,367)	3,222	3,218	3,213	3,207	3,201	3,194	3,186
NPV limited partner share @ 15%	16,238							
Minus 10% syndication fees	1,624							
Net equity contribution	14,614							
NPV of tax credit @ 15%	15,065							

Projected Rents	9	10	11	12	13	14	15
Rent	$3,985	$3,985	$3,985	$3,985	$3,985	$3,985	$3,985
Less: vacancy loss	199	199	199	199	199	199	199
Effective gross income	3,786	3,786	3,786	3,786	3,786	3,786	3,786
Less: operating expenses	1,200	1,200	1,200	1,200	1,200	1,200	1,200
Net operating income	2,586	2,586	2,586	2,586	2,586	2,586	2,586
Debt service	2,248	2,248	2,248	2,248	2,248	2,248	2,248
Replacement reserve	337	337	337	337	337	337	337
Before tax cash flow	0	0	0	0	0	0	0
General partner share 1%	0	0	0	0	0	0	0
Limited partner share 99%	0	0	0	0	0	0	0
Statement of taxable gain or (loss)							
Net operating income	2,586	2,586	2,586	2,586	2,586	2,586	2,586
Less: interest	1,985	1,958	1,927	1,893	1,856	1,815	1,770
Less: depreciation	1,213	1,213	1,213	1,213	1,213	1,213	1,213
Taxable gain (loss)	(612)	(585)	(554)	(521)	(483)	(442)	(397)
Tax or (saving) at 34%	(208)	(199)	(188)	(177)	(164)	(150)	(135)
Tax credit	(3,002)	(3,002)	0	0	0	0	0
Total tax or (saving)	(3,210)	(3,200)	(188)	(177)	(164)	(150)	(135)
General partner share 1%	(32)	(32)	(2)	(2)	(2)	(2)	(1)
Limited partner share 99%	(3,178)	(3,168)	(187)	(175)	(163)	(149)	(134)
Limited partner ATCF	3,178	3,168	187	175	163	149	134
Investment							
Net benefit	3,178	3,168	187	175	163	149	134

Table 28–4. Financial Impact of Impact Fees

	Monthly Gross Rent	Minimum Income Required	Present Value of Tax Credit Needed
No Impact Fee	$302	$12,087	$12,806
Impact Fee: $2,500	$317	$12,680	$13,936
Impact Fee: $5,000	$332	$13,283	$15,065

mortgage principal and that 30 percent of income goes to pay housing costs (see Snyder and Stegman 1986).

3. Actually, such planners are primarily meeting the needs of current residents who do not plan to move to a new residence in their community. Hence, for example, the burden of impact fees will be felt by the children of existing households when they grow up and look for housing in their parents' community.

4. It does not appear that impact fees can be waived for low-income housing. First, reducing or waiving moves an impact fee closer to being considered a tax rather than a fee. Communities that lack the state authority for such a tax would therefore be unable to reduce or waive the impact fee (Florida Advisory Council on Intergovernmental Relations 1986). Second, because impact fees are often pledged for payment of bonds issued by the community, waiving those fees can be interpreted as violating the city's contract with the purchasers of its bonds. However, communities can charge the fee and then pay that fee from the general fund, as is done in Loveland, Colorado, and Broward County, Florida.

5. Developers can also take a 4 percent credit for the acquisition of low-income housing. Beginning in 1988, however, these credit percentages will fluctuate as the exact percentage will be indexed to the "applicable federal rate," which is the average interest rate, compounded annually, for mid- and long-term U.S. Treasury securities. In the case of the credit for new construction or rehabilitation, its actual value is that percentage of development costs (minus the cost of land) that results in the present value of total tax credits (over 15 years) equal to 70 percent of total development costs (or 30 percent of acquisition). Consequently, the actual credit percentage will vary from month to month, but once a development is placed into service, the credit percentage is fixed.

References

Davidoff, Paul. 1985. Zoning as a Class Act. In *Inclusionary Zoning Moves Downtown*, edited by Dwight Merriam, David J. Brower, and Philip D. Tegeler. Chicago: Planners Press.

Dowall, David E. 1984. *The Suburban Squeeze: Land Conversion and Regulation in the San Francisco Bay Area.* Berkeley, Calif.: University of California Press.

Downing, Paul B. and Thomas McCaleb. 1987. The Economics of Development Exactions. In *Development Exactions*, edited by James E. Frank and Robert Rhodes. Chicago: Planners Press.

Ellickson, Robert C. 1982. The Irony of Inclusionary Zoning. In *Resolving the Housing Crisis*, edited by M. Bruce Johnson. Cambridge, Mass.: Ballinger Publishing Co.

Florida Advisory Council on Intergovernmental Relations. 1986. *Impact Fees in Florida.* Tallahassee: Florida Advisory Council on Intergovernmental Relations.

Frank, James E. and Paul B. Downing. 1987. National Experience With Impact Fees. Paper presented at 1987 American Planning Association National Planning Conference, New York. April.

Guggenheim, Joseph. 1986. *Tax Credits For Low Income Housing.* Washington, D.C.: Simon Publications.

Morris, Robert. 1979. *Social Policy of the American Welfare State: An Introduction to Policy Analysis.* New York: Harper and Row.

Nelson, Arthur C. 1987. Impact Fees as an Emerging Method of Infrastructure Finance. *Florida Policy Review.* 2, 2 (Winter): 22 and 26.

Snyder, Thomas P. and Michael A. Stegman. 1986. *Paying for Growth: Using Development Fees to Finance Infrastructure.* Washington, D.C.: Urban Land Institute.

U.S. Conference of Mayors. 1987. *Status Report on Homelessness in America.* Washington, D.C.: USCM.

U.S. Department of Commerce. Bureau of the Census. 1984. *Annual Housing Survey: Part C, Financial Characteristics of the Housing Inventory for the United States and Regions, 1983.* Washington, D.C.: U.S. Government Printing Office.

VIII

Implementing and Administering Development Impact Fee Programs

29

Implementing an Impact Fee System

ELLIOT AUERHAHN

Impact fees are a popular new source of revenues for local governments to fund capital improvements. A rapidly growing literature concerns the ordinances required to assess impact fees and the approaches to calculating approprate amounts for the assessments. The efforts needed to implement impact fees successfully have received little attention. As with most legislation, the effectiveness of an impact fee depends heavily on a well-conceived strategy for implementation. The legal and fiscal differences between impact fees and other common sources of capital funding for local governments heighten the need to think through the administrative needs of impact fee assessments.

Broward County, Florida, has assessed impact fees since 1977, making it one of the first local governments to do so. With a decade of experience, the lessons Broward County has learned should help other governments initiating or contemplating impact fee assessments. This chapter outlines some of the major administrative concerns local governments should address in designing an impact fee system. It stresses the need for a high degree of coordination that will enable various components of the local government staff to carry out effectively an impact fee assessment program. Also,

it focuses on ensuring that the system's design incorporates mechanisms to achieve the primary purpose of impact fees—producing revenue for capital improvements.

A brief introduction to Broward County offers some perspective on the evolution of its impact fees. The county is on the southeast coast of Florida, between Dade (which includes Miami) and Palm Beach counties. Among Broward's 28 municipalities, the most populous are Fort Lauderdale and Hollywood. The 1986 estimated population of 1.15 million compares with figures of roughly 334,000 for 1960, 620,000 for 1970, and 1.02 million for 1980 (Broward County 1983). The county's rapid growth during the 1970s far outstripped the pace of infrastructure development to serve that growth. The county looked to impact fees in the late 1970s and early 1980s as part of a series of measures to reduce the deficiency of capital facilities, and to prevent further growth from creating new deficiencies. The highlights of that series were the following:

• Amendment of the Broward County Charter to provide for platting requirements, giving the county commission an opportunity for review of development proposals throughout the county (1976).

- Adoption of the Broward County Land Use Plan, which established maximum densities and intensities of land uses throughout the county (1977).
- Adoption of a park impact fee ordinance (1977).
- Approval of a $250 million general obligation bond issue for roads, parks, libraries, and other capital improvements (1978).
- Adoption of a school impact fee ordinance (1979).
- Initiation of road impact fee assessments (1979).
- Adoption of the Broward County Land Development Code, which established minimum standards for infrastructure provision, which development must achieve or guarantee prior to the issuance of development permits for new construction. The code also put the school, park, and road impact fees under one ordinance.

In general, the impact fees in Broward County are a pay-as-you-go alternative to provide adequate infrastructure prior to occupancy of new buildings. The system assesses park and school impact fees on residential development only; the amount of the fee depends on the type of dwelling unit and on the number of bedrooms. The road impact fee system, named Traffic Review and Impact Planning System (TRIPS), uses a computerized simulation of the impact of each proposed development. The assessment is based on specific roadways planned for improvement. The county assesses road impact fees on all types of new development, with the amount depending on the location, type, and size of the proposal. In 1986, the three impact fees generated a total revenue of $9.54 million, excluding construction and dedication obligations accepted in lieu of impact fees.

The county developed mechanisms to administer the impact fees over several years. Continuing from the adoption of the Land Development Code in 1981, the major implementation events have been the following:

- Adoption of TRIPS.
- Adoption of formal policies for road impact fee spending and credits (1984).
- Implementation of a specialized accounting system for road impact fees (1984).
- Initiation of an enforcement mechanism for impact fee collection (1985; see below).
- Centralization of record keeping for all three impact fees (1985).
- Amendment of impact fee waiver policy (1986).

Some of the major considerations that the county has addressed in the 10 years of implementing impact fee assessments are outlined below.

ASSESSMENT

Regardless of whether an impact fee system provides for a flat rate (i.e., per dwelling unit or per square foot) or a rate that varies with type and location of land use, it needs to include policies on how much to charge in unconventional cases. Among the most common of the unconventional situations are demolishing a structure and constructing a building on the same site, adding on to an existing structure, adding buildings adjacent to an existing, related use, and constructing facilities whose cost rates are difficult to determine. Facilities whose cost is difficult to determine may include an adult congregate living facility, a combination retail outlet and warehouse, or a combination church and school. Policies may also need to address developers who change plans for the distribution of uses in mixed-use projects at various stages of the approval and development process.

The ultimate objective of assessing impact fees is to provide the local government with revenues it can spend for capital facilities. To ensure that the government assesses and collects the fees in a manner that facilitates spending requires close collaboration with budget and accounting staffs. The system should avoid accumulating separate accounts that are too small to be useful, or rigidly restricting the use of revenues in such a way that they cannot be used because a specific capital improvement is delayed.

Broward County experienced that problem initially with its road impact fees. It deposited the revenues in hundreds of accounts, each earmarked for a specific roadway improvement. Most accounts contained too little money to be useful, and the legislation failed to anticipate the need for combining the revenues. Thus, the county limited its own ability to spend funds. Eventually, the county reduced the number of accounts and changed the legislation to enable the mixing and accumulating of the revenues under specific conditions.

While attempting to avoid such problems, the assessment system also must adhere to legal constraints regarding the relationship between the use of the revenues and the impacts of the contributing development. Restrictions on Broward's park impact fees illustrates the rational nexus principle. The county may spend fees it collects for local parks only within 2.5 miles of the contributing development; it may spend fees it collects for regional parks within a 15-miles radius.

CREDITS AND WAIVERS

Two issues closely related to assessments are the granting of credits and the availability of waivers. Both of those areas need well-defined

and justified policies, or developers will besiege the agency with requests for every imaginable exception to the rules.

The government often grants credits against impact fees when the developer contributes in some fashion above and beyond the government's requirements. The government should establish a policy on what types of activities are eligible for credit (e.g., construction of facilities, dedication of land, design of facilities) and on how it will fix a value for those activities. The policy also should set a procedure for granting the credit by formal agreement, by resolution of the governing board, or by administrative function. That procedure may also specify the appropriate time to grant the credit in relationship to the development process and in relationship to the activity generating the credit. The government also needs to establish a policy to cover instances where a developer receives credit in excess of his current obligation. The policy must specify the allowable use of "excess" credit, and address whether credit accrues to the land or to the owner.

Waivers of impact fees can easily become a major distraction for the staff and the governing board. Any waivers should be defined very specifically, with justification for excluding related cases. Broward County currently may waive impact fees for only three categories of development, each with specific eligibility criteria: public facilities, low- and moderate-income housing, and facilities for higher education. The county abandoned a recent effort to extend the waiver provisions to certain private social service organizations when it realized that virtually any nonprofit organization would qualify for the waiver if the intended groups qualified.

Broward County recently amended its impact

fee legislation to require that revenues lost through fee waivers be replaced from another source. That provision has merit from two viewpoints: the attorneys may argue that it enhances the validity of the trust fund standing of the impact fee system, and the governing board will hand out waivers with much more discretion if it has to replace the waived funds.

COLLECTION AND DISBURSEMENT

The collection of impact fees may seem straightforward. However, even though an impact fee ordinance specifies the amount and timing of payments, other questions need to be answered.

First, who will collect the fees? If several types of impact fees are established, a central collection point will help avoid duplication of record keeping and will save time for the developer. Centralization requires well-defined procedures and close coordination among the various staffs involved.

Second, what records of payments are necessary, and who needs copies of the information? The collecting agency and accounting and budget staff need to coordinate closely. Broward uses a five-copy receipt, so that records can go to the person who pays, the planning office, the accounting office, the engineering staff, and (for parks fees) the parks staff.

The accounting procedures need to ensure that impact fees get spent only for facilities necessary to meet the impact of new development, not to remedy preexisting deficiencies. If the impact fee ordinance segregates the revenues geographically (e.g., by district), the accounting should be similarly segregated. The system also should make available information on where impact fees from individual developers are spent.

Since impact fees usually are among the most restrictive capital revenues a local government receives, they often require specialized accounting mechanisms. For most impact fee systems, the connection between the source (the developer) and the use of the funds (capital projects) must be part of the accounting system.

As we have seen, governments institute impact fee systems to generate new revenues and thereby enhance capital improvement programs. But in what ways will those revenues affect priorities in the capital program? For example, will the availability of impact fees for a project automatically move that project to a higher priority than it would otherwise have? Are there conditions under which the collection of impact fees for a capital project dictates that the project be immediately budgeted and constructed? The government should consider such influences at the initiation of an impact fee program.

Another budgetary concern is how the local government projects impact fee revenues for future budgets. Since those revenues are tied to development activity, the government may not be justified in assuming a stable income from year to year. In addition, since the revenues generate income from interest while they are being held, the local government needs to adopt a policy on the expenditure of that income.

ENFORCEMENT

Enforcement mechanisms probably are the least considered aspect of impact fee administration. Yet planners should not assume that an impact fee system works smoothly on its own. Factors that may need enforcement include timely payment and appropriate land use.

Timely payment of impact fees should be a concern only if the impact fee system involves multiple permitting jurisdictions. Broward County, for example, collects impact fees but municipalities issue building permits. Broward established an enforcement system that involves checking each permit for delinquent payments and informing the municipal building officials when a developer fails to meet impact fee obligations. The system has resulted in timely payment of the fees. Average monthly fee revenues now total about $800,000 compared to $409,000 prior to the monitoring system.

If the government bases the amount of the impact fee on how the developer will use the land, it may need to devise a method to enforce the land use restriction. The government could accomplish its aim through monitoring occupational licenses and changes of use at the local building department. Broward County, however, adopted an alternative method, placing a note restricting the use on the face of the plat recorded in the public records.

DATA MAINTENANCE

The local government needs to check or update on a regular basis the data on which it bases the impact fee calculations. That will keep the assessments current and may put the government in a stronger position in case a developer challenges the impact fee system in court.

First, the local government should establish the appropriate frequency at which it updates each element of the data and should designate the staff responsible for doing the job. For some elements, such as population projections, an annual update is appropriate, while changes with more drastic effects, such as the openings of new major public facilities, may need more frequent attention.

Efficient data maintenance requires the es-

tablishment of links between agencies and within staffs. That may involve interaction with line agencies that construct facilities, as well as links with planning and budgeting staffs.

Next, the government must make a policy decision on what changes staff may make to the data or the system, and what changes must remain within the governing board's jurisdiction. It is important to avoid the opportunity for, or even the appearance of, arbitrary staff decisions affecting the amount of a developer's impact fee assessment.

Third, the government needs to decide the circumstances under which external events should cause an unscheduled reevaluation of the assessment data. Such situations could include, for example, the approval of a very large development or a substantial change in programmed or planned capital facilities.

CONCLUSION

Adoption of impact fee legislation is only part of the work a local government needs to do to implement a successful fee program. Efficient implementation requires coordination and input from many groups, including legal, budget, accounting, planning, and permitting departments, and from line agencies involved in capital improvements. More important, planners must design the implementation mechanisms to facilitate spending the impact fee revenues on the capital improvements for which they were assessed. Focusing on that objective, within the appropriate legal constraints, is the key to successful administration of impact fees.

Reference

Broward County (Florida) Office of Planning. 1983. *Broward County Statistical Summary 1983*; see also update sheets for October 1986.

30

Rose Bushes Have Thorns

J. RICHARD RECHT

Impact fees are probably the hottest topic in land use planning today. The number of cities and counties that have adopted or are considering adopting impact fee ordinances is growing rapidly. Yet there are a number of problems involved in the use of impact fees that have received little attention. It is a thesis of this chapter that these problems, like thorns in a rose bush, are inherent in the nature of impact fees and the situations in which they are used. This chapter identifies and discusses a number of these problems in an effort to provide perspective to those considering or using impact fees.

The intent is not to develop a case either for or against impact fees. Rather it is to illuminate a number of the factors involved so that those who participate in the process of evaluating, implementing, or administering impact fees understand the problems involved.

As used here, the term impact fees refers to payments made to local governments by developers of projects. The payments provide funds to be used to mitigate the impacts identified as associated with new development. Impact fees are distinguished from mitigation requirements imposed on a project-by-project basis in that they are determined on the basis of a fee schedule adopted by the city that applies to a large number of projects. Examples of fees include amounts assessed: (1) per bedroom of residential development to provide funds for school facilities, (2) per auto trip generated daily for road or transit improvements, and (3) per 1,000 square feet of office space to subsidize low- and moderate-income housing. Other public service areas in which impact fees have been adopted include sewer and water systems, park and recreation facilities, and open space, libraries, and child care facilities.

BASIS FOR IMPACT FEES

The general rationale for impact fees is the perspective that the existing community should not be disadvantaged by new development: new development should not be subsidized – it should pay its own way. If, therefore, a linkage is established between new development and disadvantageous impacts (a rational nexus), the impacts should be mitigated if possible. If funds are required to pay for public infrastructure or facilities necessary to maintain the existing level of services while accommodating new development, then the new development should provide these funds. A city program that identifies the impacts of new development and assesses fees to mitigate those impacts is therefore considered appropriate.

The most general legal basis for the right of cities to adopt impact fees is their police power. This is the same legal basis underlying most planning and zoning laws. In other words, impact fees are a reasonable element of cities' activities to provide for the health, safety, and welfare of their citizens.

More specific legislation may also be involved. The use of impact fees is perhaps most prevalent in California. The California Environmental Quality Act (CEQA) specifically allows local jurisdictions to require impact mitigation as a condition of development approval. However, impact fees are not mentioned in the CEQA legislation, reflecting the fact that such fees (except for utility infrastructure) did not exist at that time. In many California cities with impact fees, the idea of a schedule of fees evolved in the context of CEQA review of specific projects and was adopted as a more systematic approach to mitigation.

Subsequent legislation by the California legislature has facilitated the use of impact fees; with regard to schools, for example, the legislature specifically authorized local government to assess residential development fees for temporary classroom modules and, recently, authorized school districts to levy fees on nonresidential development to provide a share of the funds necessary for new schools. It has also adopted legislation to curb abuse of the use of impact fees.

It is important to understand that an impact fee is not a tax. (It is particularly important in California where taxes require a two-thirds approval of the electorate.) Impact fees require a casual relationship between those assessed and the impacts mitigated with the revenues; taxes do not. Furthermore, because impact fees can be used only to mitigate identifed impacts, the fee schedule is limited, unlike a tax rate. The limit is the level at which adequate proceeds for mitigation purposes are generated.

POLITICAL SUPPORT FOR IMPACT FEES

Much of the political support for impact fees arises directly from the appeal of the rationale that the community should not be disadvantaged, at least in the area of public infrastructure and facilities, by new development. This has not always been a prevalent concern. Local government policies used to reflect a general opinion that growth more often than not was beneficial to cities. The jobs and homes provided were considered benefits to present residents and it was thought that new development would provide economies of scale in the delivery of public services and the provision of public infrastructure. The facilities and infrastructure necessary to accommodate growth therefore were funded with general obligation and revenue bonds and thus paid for by both existing and new residents and businesses.

The picture today is not characterized by the same degree of optimism about the advantages of growth; there is more concern about the disadvantages of growth. Conditions such as crowded schools, inadequate water during drought years, and traffic congestion—which is by far the most resented impact—are matters of concern. It is not surprising that impact fees are politically popular today although they were scarce a decade or two ago.

Though the rationale that new development should pay its own way is the stated reason for the adoption of impact fees, it would be naive to assume that impact fees are not supported for other reasons. One reason simply is that they provide revenues for needed/ politically popular improvements. Cities and counties see themselves without adequate resources to provide the improvements demanded and the situation has been worsening with the presence (or threatening possibility) of property tax limitation initiatives such as Proposition 13 in California and a trend of diminishing federal support to local government.

There are several reasons why fees on new development appear to city officials to be an appropriate revenue source. One of the criteria in the selection of revenue sources is ability to pay. The large increase in land values and the large profits made in real estate in the past two decades offer an indication that landowners and developers can afford to provide some of the funds needed for facilities and infrastructure. There is a long history of planning thought that supports this perspective. In *Garden Cities of Tomorrow: A Path to Peaceful Reform*, Ebenezer Howard argued that urban land values are high because the presence of residents provides customers, employees, and so forth. Yet the benefit of high land values accrues to the landowner rather than to the local population whose presence creates the value. Howard advocated the public ownership of land so that the value would accrue to the local residents rather than the landowners. He believed that land rents could then provide revenues for needed public services. Visualized as a tax on land value, impact fees are an appropriate revenue source, given Howard's logic.

Support for impact fees as a revenue source also is based on the perception that the fees are paid by developers (few in number, perceived as greedy, and often nonresidents) and/or newcomers to the community. Seeking revenues from such a source engenders less political opposition than imposing more taxes or fees on local residents and businesses.

Finally, impact fees also are supported by those who are against new development. Many people live in situations where they believe that additional development is disadvantageous even if public infrastructure and facilities are made adequate to accommodate it. The negative aspect of this position is often characterized as the drawbridge syndrome, which is a tendency to prefer a community no larger than was necessary to provide room for the person having this preference. In any case, people against new development see the fees as an added cost that may decrease the amount of development.

Not surprisingly, developers are the principal opponents of impact fees. Their primary plea is that fees increase the cost to the consumer (especially for housing). In some situations they claim that the fees are so large as to make projects infeasible. On the other hand, developers sometimes support the adoption of impact fees, either because they see them as inevitable or because they sense that the payment of an "admission fee" will encourage the acceptance of new development.

THE IMPACT MITIGATION MODEL

Having a rationale for impact fees and political support for them does not guarantee a smooth road for the city considering adopting an impact fee. Impact fees have some built-in problems. Some of those problems are identified and analyzed here.

The first area to check for difficulties with impact fees is the impact mitigation "model." This model expresses the connection between new development and the impact fee schedule. In so doing it provides a basis (i.e., justification) for the fees. The assumption inherent in the model is that a competent analysis will:

1. Forecast development and its possible impacts.

2. Identify the improvements needed to mitigate the impacts.

3. Estimate the cost of those improvements.

4. Design a fee schedule that provides revenues equal to the cost and, if necessary, allocates the cost among development in proportion to the share of responsibility for the impacts.

The traffic impact fees levied on development in Concord, California, serve as an example that can be expressed in the terms of this model:

> **Step 1**–A projection of the amount of residential and commercial development likely to occur over the next 15 years, along with calculations of the number and location of trips generated by the new development.
>
> **Step 2**–A determination by traffic engineers of the road improvements necessary to accommodate those trips.
>
> **Step 3**–An estimation that the improvements would cost from $100 million to $160 million, depending on the standards assumed and that other funding sources could contribute about $30 million.
>
> **Step 4**–A finding that based on the contribution to the impacts, it was reasonable to set the fees at about $1,900 per peak-hour trip generated ($1,900 per residential unit and about $2.00 per square foot of office space).

During the two years following the analysis, the impact fee ordinance moved slowly through the process of adoption. Pressure from the developers led to a reduction of the time horizon to five years (to be followed by subsequent five-year programs) and compromises that shifted some of the projects from the first five-year program to a later period. The ordinance adopted in 1983 contained an assessment of only $440 per peak-hour trip, about one-fourth the amount recommended by the planning study two years earlier. The relative political position of large versus small development was reflected in the requirement that large development had to mitigate traffic impacts in the vicinity (unless the fee was less), a requirement usually two to three times as expensive. In 1985, after the development community had come to accept the fee and the real estate market had improved, the fee was raised to $966 per peak-hour trip.

Another example is the housing impact fees imposed on office development in San Francisco:

> **Step 1**–A projection that on the average each 1,000 square feet of office space would be occupied by about four employees, that 40 percent of these employees would live in San Francisco, and that 1.8 working adults would occupy each residential unit.
>
> **Step 2**–A conclusion that housing subsidies were required to provide housing for employees who could not afford new market rate housing if the availability and rent levels of low- and moderate-cost housing were not to be impacted (it was assumed that developers would supply the needed market rate units without financial assistance).
>
> **Step 3**–An estimation of the cost of the subsidies required by comparing the cost of new housing with the range of incomes of the employees, with the resultant estimate being that a range of $9.47 million to $10.47 million would be required to provide the subsidies needed for one million square feet of building space.
>
> **Step 4**–The finding that a fee in the range of $9.47 to $10.47 per square foot of office space (with the recommendation that it be adjusted annually to reflect inflation) would generate the needed revenues.

The San Francisco Board of Supervisors adopted an ordinance setting the housing impact fee at $5.34 per square foot in 1985 and providing for an annual adjustment for inflation (with the alternative that the developer could directly build the housing if it chose to do so). The choice of a figure of $5.34 was "in recognition of...the potential inexactitude of the final calculation." The adopted ordinance also exempted all development except for office buildings in excess of 50,000 square feet.

The assumption of any impact fee mitigation model is that the findings/products will be an acceptable basis for the impact fee program. It would appear that for findings to be acceptable they must be objective and nonarbitrary. In other words, any qualified professional should arrive at essentially the same findings. Uncertainty regarding the future should be acknowledged, but it should not affect the findings so much that the fee would be radically different under alternative reasonable future conditions. Perhaps even more important, the findings ideally should be based on professional standards; they should not depend on arbitrary choices between alternatives, choices about which reasonable people could and do differ. However, each of the four steps in the model listed above is a source of difficulties in meeting these criteria.

IMPACTS OF ANTICIPATED DEVELOPMENT

One of the problems with the first step, the projection of development and its impacts, is that a single, accurate forecast is expected. In reality, however, every future has some degree of uncertainty; the nature and timing of local development will be affected by external economic and social forces, future decisions by the city, and landowner/developer choices. The forecast used as a basis for determining fees is likely to be much less certain than the city coun-

cil adopting the fees would like to acknowledge. In some cases the degree of uncertainty is such that the appropriate projection of the future is best expressed as a range of two or more alternative futures with a probability associated with each. Such a projection may be too complex to be acceptable as a basis for impact fees, though it is technically possible to use it. In such situations the professional technicians involved would prefer to justify a fee based on a range of possible outcomes. The consultants to San Francisco reported their findings in terms of a range of housing impact fees; the city rationalized the adoption of a significantly lower fee than justified by the findings in terms of the qualifications expressed in the report.

Another problem in the task of projecting development and its impacts is the choice of a reasonable planning horizon, an appropriate time period to be covered in the analysis. Sometimes the analysis ignores the time element and includes all remaining potential development in the analysis. This approach usually works well only if the development of vacant and underutilized land will occur in a few decades and the situation thereafter will be stable. In the majority of situations, development and/or redevelopment will continue to occur over a longer period; therefore a shorter time frame, typically 10 to 25 years, is used for planning purposes.

In some cases the choice of period makes a significant difference. If the development in the period chosen falls a little short of requirements some expensive infrastructure improvements (e.g., a new sewer treatment plant or a new freeway intersection and associated arterial), then the impact fees will be much less than if the period is a few years longer and the expensive infrastructure is required. A longer time period has the advantage of including a larger number of major cost items, thus making the results less dependent on the inclusion or omission of any one project. This is illustrated in the effect of the compromise on a five-year time period accepted by the city of Concord. The problem also can be mitigated by allocating credit for the capacity remaining at the end of the period that will be used further in the future. In other words, if a new road arterial to be built to accommodate growth will only be 50 percent utilized by the development project in the time period, then only 50 percent of the arterial's cost is considered an impact of this period's growth.

IMPROVEMENTS TO MITIGATE IMPACTS

Two problems are cited here illustrating the difficulty of identifying the improvements needed to mitigate the impacts. One is that the improvements needed are a function of the level of service. Different assumptions regarding the standard of service result in different findings as to the improvements required to provide that level of service. For example, the cost of the improvements needed in the Concord street impact fees program varied from $100 million, based on the standard the city had been using, to $160 million, based on the standards stated in the general plan.

As another example, some California residents who are frustrated by the impacts of development have pushed initiatives that would require that new development be responsible for any improvements necessary to maintain traffic flow at Level of Service (LOS) C during peak rush hour. For instance, LOS at the problem intersections in Alameda typically is B or C for the majority of the day and drops to D or E during the peak period.

The problem of an appropriate LOS is often ignored in impact analyses. Yet it is conceptually and practically a difficult problem. Planners are likely to believe that it is appropriate for cities to select a LOS and then require new development to mitigate its impacts to that standard. Those taking that position, however, must consider the difficulty illustrated in the traffic example described above. Developers will not consider it equitable if they are required to provide funds for a LOS higher than city residents are willing to pay for in the absence of new development.

It might appear that the solution is to use the existing average LOS in the city. Yet this approach has problems in many situations. For example, a city that is upgrading to a higher standard as "funds are available" will find it unacceptable. In particular, a very small city may have been making do with inferior facilities reflecting standards of decades ago because of its lack of a tax base. It does not want to perpetuate the situation with obsolete standards applied to new development. And, of course, developers would object to the cost involved in maintaining the current traffic level in a small town with very little traffic.

The treatment of opportunity costs is another problem in the identification of improvements necessary to accommodate growth. If existing facilities, a sewer plant for example, have adequate capacity to accommodate half the new development projected for the period, should the fees reflect only the new capacity needed or should they also include the opportunity cost of the existing capacity that will be utilized (offset by its share of any outstanding indebtedness)? The emotional support for the latter approach is likely to be stronger if the present residents feel they have already paid for the plant through sewer charges or taxes.

COST ESTIMATES

The third step in the model, the estimation of the costs, also has its inherent difficulties. This is illustrated by the problem that often arises when the infrastructure is currently inadequate, lacking capacity even without new development. For example, consider a road that currently has a width of two lanes, for which demand already exists for another two lanes, and for which projected new development will require another two lanes, for a total of six lanes. The costs of adding only two lanes well could be: (1) less than the cost of adding the fifth and sixth lanes because of economies of scale or (2) greater than the cost of adding the fifth and sixth lanes, if the property costs for these last two lanes are higher due to the presence of structures in the right-of-way. In either situation it will seem intuitively obvious both to the city staff and to the developers which cost should be assigned to new development; needless to say, they will not agree as to the appropriate perspective.

PROVISION OF REQUIRED REVENUE AND ALLOCATION OF FINANCIAL RESPONSIBILITY

It will not suprise the reader that the equitable allocation of the costs among projected new developments is usually the more difficult component of this step. One type of situation that presents problems is when usage is not a good indicator of the benefit. For example, a least expensive water distribution system alternative may use a new trunk line to serve areas A and B. The new line is the only feasible alternative for delivery to area A. In contrast, area B can be served at modest additional cost either through the pipeline to serve area A or through an alternative new line. The developers in area A will feel that all development should be assessed at the same rate. The developers in area B will be furious if asked to pay more than the cost of the inexpensive new line.

Another type of difficult situation exists when it is not clear which link in the causal chain should be regarded as responsible for the impacts. For example, we long have operated on the assumption that housing generates the need for schools. An alternative perspective, however, is that jobs result in employee households with children who require schools; the location of housing only determines the preferable locations for the schools. It is interesting to remember the earlier observation that the state of California, which has effectively assumed financial responsibility for funding education and a large share of the cost of new schools, recently has authorized impact fees on nonresidential development to pay for school facilities.

The four steps in the impact fee model can be compared in terms of their potential to create headaches for those involved in the process. The projection of impacts, the first step, may be a headache to the planning technician, but serious controversy is not likely. As severe conflicts of interest are not likely, the "noise" at this stage comes primarily from those fighting the process. The estimation of costs also is not likely to be a major source of controversy. The identification of improvements necessary to accommodate new development, however, often generates heated reactions, most often because the developers react in horror to the standards the city identifies as appropriate. The allocation of the costs is by far the largest source of controversy. The financial interests are apparent to those involved, complete with price tags that can exceed the cost of purchasing the land.

STRATEGIES FOR PLANNERS

The litany of problems described above is not intended to be exhaustive; it is intended to illustrate the range of problems involved. Nor have the difficulties been described in order to set the stage for some revelations that render the difficulties irrelevant. The difficulties are real, they result in real problems for cities seeking to use impact fees, and, because they are inherent in the nature of impact fees, no amount of advice can make them disappear.

As planning staff usually have primary roles in the consideration of impact fees, they have the responsibility and the incentive to mitigate potential problems. There are a number of approaches planners can use to minimize as much as possible the damage from these inherent difficulties. First, it is recommended that planners call attention to the fact that the process has its problems. A city council eager to jump on the impact fees bandwagon should be cautioned as to the hard work and difficult political choices likely to be involved. If not warned, when the council encounters difficulties, its frustration may be vented on the staff involved in the process.

Second, careful analysis and documentation of the findings are well worth the effort. In situations where controversy is anticipated, planners may be tempted to hold down planning costs, reasoning that the resolution of the issues primarily will be political rather than a matter of professional planning recommendations. This perspective is usually shortsighted.

One reason for the value of careful work is that the documentation of the analysis usually provides much of the content of the political exchange. If the record provides the information relevant to the various interests, heated irrelevant arguments tend to be discredited. On a more personal basis, planners know they are likely to be the target of much opposition by those seeking to discredit the process. A solid analysis with careful documentation tends to minimize the damage of such attacks.

Another component of a planner's strategy is to be conservative in the assumptions and findings on which the fee schedule is based. A pattern of cautious underestimating can make a substantial contribution to the credibility of the analysis. It is true that the proceeds from the fees will not meet the target, but that will also be the case in the event an attack on the credibility of the analysis leads to compromises or even a rejected fee program.

Finally, and most important, planners should recognize that the adoption of impact fees is a political decision, that it takes place in a political process, and that an efficient and realistic resolution of conflicts of interest contributes to the successful adoption of an impact fee program. Planners can facilitate the political process in several ways. The problems should be pushed to the forefront; the perspectives of all interests should be presented constructively; opportunities for personal exchanges should be provided; and a number of alternatives together with their consequences should be set forth. The problems will not disappear, but these strategies should help the process proceed as successfully as possible.

Index